TEXTUAL RESEARCH ON THE NATIONAL SPORTS IN ANCIENT NORTHERN CHINA

www.royalcollins.com

Textual Research on the National Sports in Ancient Northern China

Written by **HUANG Cong**

Translated by **GAO Fen**
Shaanxi Normal University

Books Beyond Boundaries
ROYAL COLLINS

Textual Research on the National Sports in Ancient Northern China

Written by HUANG Cong

Translated by GAO Fen
Shaanxi Normal University

First published in 2023 by Royal Collins Publishing Group Inc.
Groupe Publication Royal Collins Inc.
BKM Royalcollins Publishers Private Limited

Headquarters: 550-555 boul. René-Lévesque O Montréal (Québec) H2Z1B1 Canada
India office: 805 Hemkunt House, 8th Floor, Rajendra Place, New Delhi 110008

© HUANG Cong, 2023

All rights reserved. Without limiting the rights under copyright reserved above, no part of this publication may be reproduced, stored in or introduced into a retrieval system, or transmitted in any form or by any means (electronic, mechanical, photocopying, recording or otherwise), without the prior written permission of both the copyright owner and the above publisher of this book.

ISBN: 978-1-4878-1199-0

To find out more about our publications, please visit www.royalcollins.com.

We are grateful for the financial assistance of *Shaanxi Normal University's Fund for the Translation of the Humanities and Social Sciences in China* (陕西师范大学中华学术外译项目基金) in the publication of this book.

Contents

List of Figures / vii
Introduction / ix

CHAPTER I
Origin and Sprout of the National Sports in Ancient Northern China / 1
1.1 Origin of the National Sports in Ancient North / 1
1.2 Sprout of the National Sports in Ancient North / 5
1.3 Image of Sports in Ancient Northern National Rock Paintings / 7
1.4 Summary / 14

CHAPTER II
Initial Development of the National Sports in Ancient Northern China / 21
2.1 Sports Activities of Buyeo and Goguryeo / 21
2.2 Sports Activities of Sushen, Yilou, and Wuji Clans / 24
2.3 Sports Activities of Xiongnu / 27
2.4 Sports Activities of Wuhuan and Xianbei / 35
2.5 Sports Activities of Ethnic Groups in the Western Regions / 53
2.6 Summary / 58

CHAPTER III
All-Round Development of the National Sports in Ancient Northern China / 79
3.1 Sports Activities in Koryo, Paekje, Silla, Mohe, and Bohai / 79
3.2 Sports Activities of Turks / 83
3.3 Sports Activities of Huihu / 93
3.4 Sports Activities of Tuyuhun / 99
3.5 Sports Activities of Tangut (Dangxiang) / 109
3.6 Sports Activities of Khitan / 124
3.7 Sports Activities of Jurchen / 131
3.8 Summary / 142

CHAPTER IV

Rise and Fall of the National Sports in Ancient Northern China / 155

4.1 Sports Activities of Uyghur / 155
4.2 Sports Activities of Mongol / 158
4.3 Sports Activities of Manchu / 177
4.4 Decline of Ancient Northern National Sports / 208
4.5 Summary / 209

CHAPTER V

Origin and Evolution of Wrestling in China / 215

5.1 Germination and Formation of Wrestling in the Qin and Han Dynasties / 215
5.2 Development of Sumo from the Wei and Jin to the Tang and Song Dynasties / 229
5.3 Prevalence of Wrestling in the Liao, Jin, and Xixia Dynasties / 243
5.4 Rise and Development of Mongolian Wrestling / 251
5.5 Prosperity of Wrestling in the Qing Dynasty / 260
5.6 Summary / 271

CHAPTER VI

Origin and Evolution of Polo in China / 281

6.1 Origin of Polo / 281
6.2 Methods and Rules of the Ancient Polo Game / 294
6.3 Spread, Development, and Evolution of Polo in Ancient China / 304
6.4 Summary / 334

Acknowledgments / 343

Bibliography / 345

Index / 359

List of Figures

Fig. 1-1   Dance on the Painted Pottery Basin Unearthed in Datong County, Qinghai Province / 3
Fig. 1-2   The Arm Dance in Helankou Rock Painting / 9
Fig. 1-3   Fighting Image in Lushan Rock Painting / 10
Fig. 1-4   Horse Riding Image in Yeniugou Rock Painting / 10
Fig. 1-5   Hunting Images in the Rock Paintings of Baldakur Mountain, Yumin County, Xinjiang / 11
Fig. 1-6   Arm Dance in the Rock Painting of Kangjiashimenzi, Hutubi County, Xinjiang / 12
Fig. 2-1   Hunting Picture of Goguryeo / 23
Fig. 2-2   Three-Color Acrobatic Figurines Unearthed in the Tang Tombs / 55
Fig. 3-1   "Dancing Horse Cup" on the Silver Teapot / 104
Fig. 3-2   Tuyuhun Hunting Picture / 105
Fig. 3-3   Tuyuhun Sacrificial Picture / 107
Fig. 3-4   Riding and Shooting Picture in the Liao Dynasty / 126
Fig. 3-5   Diagram of Khitan's Weiqi / 129
Fig. 3-6   Backgammon in the Liao Dynasty / 130
Fig. 3-7   Picture of Khitan Children's Rope Skipping / 131
Fig. 3-8   Picture of Two-women Chess-playing in the Jin Tomb / 135
Fig. 3-9   Brick Sculpture of Drum-beating and Dancing Child Figurine in the Jin Dynasty / 136
Fig. 3-10 Brick Sculpture of Gong-beating Dance in the Jin Dynasty / 136
Fig. 4-1   Hunting Picture of Yuan Emperor Shizu / 160
Fig. 4-2   Picture of Xuanye in Armor / 183
Fig. 4-3   Painted Hanging Panel of the Emperor Qianlong Archery / 185
Fig. 4-4   Picture of One Shot, Two Deers / 185
Fig. 4-5   Picture of the Emperor Qianlong Archery / 185
Fig. 4-6   Picture of the Hunt in Mulan Hunting Ground / 194
Fig. 4-7   Picture of Bed Sled Game / 200
Fig. 4-8   Picture of the Partial Ice-Play / 202

Fig. 4-9   Pictures of Some Speed Skating and Figure Skating Movements in the Qing Dynasty / 203
Fig. 4-10   Picture of Skates in the Qing Dynasty / 204
Fig. 5-1   Picture of Jiao-Di in the Wooden Grate of the Chu Tomb / 217
Fig. 5-2   Part of the Mural of Jiao-Di / 223
Fig. 5-3   A Seal of Jiao-Di / 223
Fig. 5-4   Bronze Plaque of Jiao-Di of Huns in the Han Dynasty / 224
Fig. 5-5   Jiao-Di Mural Unearthed from the "Dance Tomb" / 231
Fig. 5-6   Jiao-Di Mural Unearthed from the "Jiao-Di Tomb" / 232
Fig. 5-7   Jiao-Di Mural in Goguryeo / 232
Fig. 5-8   Jiao-Di Embossment Inkstone / 233
Fig. 5-9   Image of Sumo in the Western Wei Dynasty in the Embossment of Grottoes / 233
Fig. 5-10   Sumo Figures from the Northern Zhou Period in Dunhuang Mogao Grottoes / 234
Fig. 5-11   White Clay Pot of the Liao Dynasty / 246
Fig. 5-12   A Pair of Jin Sumo Clay Figurines in Weinan, Shaanxi Province / 250
Fig. 5-13   Shanpu Camp Wrestling / 264
Fig. 5-14   Four Events of the Banquet (Partial) / 265
Fig. 5-15   Woodcut Wrestling Pictures of the Qing Dynasty / 267
Fig. 6-1   Pictures of Polo Playing in Prince Zhang Huai's Tomb in the Tang Dynasty / 287
Fig. 6-2   Polo Playing in the Liao Dynasty / 288
Fig. 6-3   Mural of Horse Riders Preparing for Polo / 288
Fig. 6-4   Pictures of Horsetail for Polo / 297
Fig. 6-5   **Polo Club in Different Dynasties** / 298
Fig. 6-6   Emperor Seeking Pleasure (From the Imperial Palace) / 302
Fig. 6-7   Hanyao (Waist Ornament) in *Tang People Playing Polo* by Li Gonglin / 303
Fig. 6-8   Song People Playing Polo / 303
Fig. 6-9   Mural of Preparing for Polo with a Club in Hand / 311
Fig. 6-10   Part of the Pabric in Which a Children Were Striking Ball / 332
Fig. 6-11   A Pottery Pillow with the Picture of a Child Playing Chuiwan / 333
Fig. 6-12   A Pottery Pillow with the Picture of a Child Playing Chuiwan for Fun / 333
Fig. 6-13   A Volume Page of *People Playing Ball Games under Musaceae Trees* / 333
Fig. 6-14   A Mural of Children Playing Chuiwan in the Yuan Dynasty / 333
Fig. 6-15   Part of the Portrait of a Lady / 333

Introduction

WITH THE FAST-GROWING ECONOMY'S IMPACT ON people's values, the lifestyles and needs of the common people have also changed dramatically. Sports have gradually become indispensable in daily life, and society has tried to meet this need in various ways. Especially under the status quo of world economic integration and cultural diversity, sports have been elevated to a very high position in society, which has become a symbol of measuring the political, economic, and cultural development level of a country or a region. Therefore, many countries and regions have started to attach greater importance to sports. In particular, some developing countries or regions take sports as a way of communication, a window, or a medium to expand their influence on the outside world and manifest their images, political systems, and economic development potential, so as to attract financial investment and accelerate economic development. In a multi-ethnic country, the sports system is also crucial to strengthening inter-ethnic exchanges and promoting unity. This situation was fully reflected in ancient Chinese society.

Five thousand years of Chinese civilization have created its splendid ancient culture, and sports culture is one aspect of it. Northern national sports culture, among other things, is an essential part of the sports culture in ancient China. In ancient times, the national sports culture in the north of China was neither an independent social phenomenon nor a human activity separated from complicated social activities. On the contrary, due to the influence of the living environment, the level of productivity development, ideology, and other factors, sports culture is closely linked with agricultural productions, people's lives, wars, and other social activities. Particularly, various sports activities are directly evolved from production practice, religious sacrifice, war disputes, and other related events. Through functional transformation, a relatively independent cultural system is formed.

The ancient northern national sports played an important role in the whole society in achieving the function transformation and after completing the functional transformation. For example, those roles are enriching people's cultural life and enhancing their physical fitness; promoting the improvement of productivity and economy; strengthening the exchanges among different nationalities to facilitate the formation of pluralistic integration of the Chinese nation, etc. This book focuses on sports as a culture, examining its development forms in ancient production practices, military activities, and social life, as well as its role in national social life and the formation of the pluralistic integration pattern of the Chinese nation.

In *Chinese National History*, edited by Wang Zhonghan, there are four universal issues in the development and change of ancient national history.[1] This thesis fully clarifies the national relations and the development of national society in ancient China. It provides the theoretical basis of national historiography for this book to demonstrate the problems of ancient northern ethnic sports. A proper understanding of the progress of ethnic sports in the north in ancient times can only be achieved through a thorough understanding of the history of ethnic development, economy, culture, ethnic relations, and other basic conditions of the society of the time. To carry out this research work in depth is not only of fundamental significance for excavating and sorting out the ancient national sports culture in China, but also has certain reference value on how to develop and utilize national sports resources, improve the physical quality of the entire people, enhance national self-confidence and cohesion, and thus promote national unity.

This research is mainly put forward under the background of "one mainstream" and "one major theme" in modern society. "One mainstream" mainly means that human society pays more attention to the excavation and collation of traditional culture. With the development of modern society, the improvement of people's quality of life, and the gradual satisfaction of material needs, there is a higher demand for spiritual fulfillment. Therefore, the excavation and collation of traditional culture have become a new focus of economic development; on the other hand, it can meet the spiritual needs of mankind. The same goes for sports culture. Especially at present, we are faced with the coincidence between traditional sports culture and foreign sports culture. The traditional sports culture is confronted with both opportunities and challenges. It not only shares the mission of national fitness with modern Western sports but also bears the mission of entering the Olympics in some projects. To objectively and accurately understand the history and face the reality, we must strengthen the research on traditional sports culture. Ancient Chinese northern ethnic sports culture had a far-reaching impact on the development of ancient Chinese sports and even greatly impacted Europe, Central and Western Asia, India, Japan, and other places. The study of history has a positive historical and practical significance for the development of traditional Chinese sports. "One major theme" mainly refers to the study of ethnic social issues. With the development of the global modern ethnic society and the influence of religion on society, some ethnic social problems have become prominent, which have become factors that cannot be ignored in affecting social stability, national stability, and the steady development of human society. The study of ethnic social problems has turned out to be an important focus of humanities and social sciences in the world. As mentioned above, the development of national sports culture in ancient northern China once played an important role in the development of ancient society. And it is well-known that history has significant reference value to today's society. As for some problems in the evolution of modern society, we can find solutions through the study of ancient society, by summing up experiences, drawing lessons, and learning from history in some aspects. Through sports activities, the enthusiasm of Chinese people of all nationalities can be mobilized to unite and participate in nation-building.

Sports is a kind of physical culture, which is formed in the long-term development of human beings to strengthen the physique, exercise will, and promote communication. It is closely connected with the daily life of the broad masses of people. In a sense, it is a comprehensive expression of the social material life, economic level, science and culture, spiritual outlook, national character, and physique of a country, nation, or region in various historical periods. According to what has been said before, the sports culture of ancient ethnic minorities in China is an organic part of ancient social culture. The splendid ancient civilization of the Chinese nation is not only created by the Han nationality, but also by people of all ethnic minorities. The research on the sports culture of ancient ethnic minorities in China can not only investigate the evolution of society and the change of population relationships, but also deepen the understanding of the history and culture of ethnic minorities, and understand their influence on the Han society as well as their contribution to the ancient Chinese civilization.

The civilization produced in the ancient north of China not only has a status unmatched by other regions in China but also possesses some critical influence on the history of world civilization. Throughout history, a dozen of Chinese dynasties were founded in the northern region, which had far-reaching impacts on politics, economy, culture, and other fields. Particularly in the thousands of years of interaction between the Central Plains and the surrounding ethnic minorities, China has formed a "you have me, I have you" ethnic integration pattern. In foreign exchanges, the northern region also occupies a leading position. Especially under the circumstance that the ancient maritime industry was not fully developed, the role of the Northern Silk Road seemed particularly important. The spread of ancient Chinese civilization was very active in the north, and cultural exchanges between ethnic groups were very frequent. The sports cultural exchange among the nationalities in the north of China must also be an integral part of this trend.

Throughout the research on the history of Chinese ethnic minorities and ancient Chinese sports, we can rarely find any systematic study on the sports culture of ancient Chinese ethnic minorities in academic circles at home and abroad. However, in the study of the ancient history of China, as an indispensable part of minority culture, the importance and necessity of minority sports research are self-evident. In addition, the author has participated in the academic activities of the Chinese Sports History Society many times in recent years, and found that few scholars pay attention to the research of ancient northern ethnic sports history; the author also learned that there were basically no domestic scholars talking about the sports culture of ancient northern nationalities during the conference of Northeast Asian Sports History Society. In such an important professional academic conference, there are no scholars involved in the discussion of ancient northern national sports culture, which implies that China has no right to speak in this respect, and there is still a large gap in its research. Therefore, the author hopes to provide readers with a window to understand the sports culture of ancient Chinese minorities through this research.

To sum up, the author believes that it is of great significance and necessity to conduct a comprehensive, systematic, and in-depth study on the history of ancient northern national sports culture, starting from either the understanding of history, or as a practical reference, or as a reference for the future.

After consulting a large number of materials, it is found that there are still some deficiencies in the study of ancient northern national sports in China: First, at present, there is no monograph that systematically, comprehensively, and deeply studies the history of ancient northern national sports. Some existing research results (especially domestic ones) mostly appear in the form of papers, so their research is either limited to a certain ethnic group or a certain sport form. Staying at a single level, its research is bound to be limited, especially based on the overall view that ancient northern ethnic sports cannot be formed and viewed. Therefore, it is difficult to construct a theory to fully reflect the connotation of this national sports culture. Second, the existing achievements are only scattered research, without constructing a complete theoretical system, which is difficult to reflect the characteristic culture of ethnic minorities and their interaction with Han culture. Third, the existing research mainly stays at the level of knowledge narration, which fails to explore deeply the reasons behind this special social phenomenon or cultural existence, as well as its impacts on social development. Of course, there are many reasons for this phenomenon, such as the lack of full awareness of the great significance of studying the history of national sports in ancient northern China, some authors' partial understanding of the development history of the ancient northern ethnic groups in China, insufficient mastery of the historical materials of the northern national sports, or limitations of the research methods and perspectives.

In general, there are still obvious deficiencies, and there is still a lot of research space in many aspects, although academic circles have produced some results on ancient Chinese minority sports, and have made some achievements. Based on the above shortcomings, the author believes that in the research field of sports history of ethnic minorities in China, we should take Marxist historical materialism as the guidance, strengthen the researchers' historical knowledge and ethnological cultivation, and employ both traditional research methods and modern scientific means, and systematically, comprehensively and deeply study the sports' of ancient ethnic minorities from the basic historical facts to the actual needs of modern society thereby contributing to the social development.

Certainly, the accumulation of early academic achievements is very valuable. This book tries every means to base on the existing research results, and accordingly makes a comprehensive study of the ancient northern national sports. For example, in the following textual research of two topics, the author sorted out the views of various schools and conducted a lot of work on the establishment of new materials and new ideas. In particular, the academic research of famous historical experts such as Xiang Da, Luo Xianglin, Wang Yao, and Jin Qicong have provided great enlightenment and reference to the study of this book. Though polo and wrestling are two old topics, the author found many new research points and obtained some new viewpoints on the basis of those references, which enriched the academic achievements of national sports in China to a certain extent, and produced a new research perspective as well as opened up a new research field.

According to the research needs, this book is divided into two parts. The first part mainly systematically investigates the development history of ancient northern national sports, and the second part includes research on wrestling and polo.

In the first part, the author divides the development of ancient northern national sports into four main stages: origin and sprout, initial development, all-around development, and rise and fall. Generally speaking, it is very difficult to stage the evolution of ancient northern ethnic sports in China, because the imbalance of the development of various nationalities makes the overall progress of national society in different periods inconsistent. Therefore, we mainly refer to the overall progress of several ethnic groups in a certain period, especially the sports development of this nation in its heyday. For example, in the Shiwei period, the Mongol's sports development level was very low; in the Heishui Jurchen period, the Manchu's sports development level also remained low, but when they entered Shanhai Pass and unified the whole country, their sports were integrated into the national sports system, reaching the peak of the whole ancient northern national sports. Therefore, we stage the development of ancient northern national sports on the whole due to the specific needs of the study.

The first part mainly overviews the sports history in the ancient northern ethnic groups, including Chapters One to Four.

Chapter One mainly discusses the origin and sprout of the national sports in ancient northern China. Based on the documents, inscriptions, and archaeological materials, this book first makes a preliminary understanding of the ecology and human activities in the early Northern region, the economic production, and lifestyle, in order to have a perceptual description of the regional sports culture described later. Secondly, it expounds on the sports image in the ancient northern ethnic rock paintings, which are the cultural remains of the early development of various nationalities. By understanding these rock paintings, we can get an early picture of the social foundation of the origin and germination of the northern national sports, and sense the remarkable characteristics of the ancient northern national sports on the whole. The results show that the ancient northern ethnic sports in China mainly originated from hunting activities, farming and animal husbandry, religious activities, war, music and dance art, etc. The early sprouting sports were mainly some activities closely related to production and life, war, and religion, such as fishing, swimming, hunting, climbing, running, throwing, martial dance, witch dance, archery, stone playing, jumping, and other activities. The main performance for sports activities in this period was that they used the body directly or used simple tools to complete a certain action or activity in order to obtain food, escape, sacrifice, express emotion, and so on.

Chapter Two mainly discusses the ancient northern national sports in the initial development period. This book describes and conducts necessary textual research on the sports-related historical facts of several dominant ethnic groups from Pre-Qin to the Southern and Northern Dynasties, such as Buyeo, Goguryeo, Sushen, Yilou, Wuji, Xiongnu, Wuhuan, Xianbei and other nationalities in the Western Regions. Through the research, we believe that with the development of society, the sports culture of the northern ethnic groups is also constantly developing, and their sports activities are becoming increasingly rich, which is in line with the progress of social productivity at that time. As a typical representative of the northern nomadic people, mounted archery had just emerged and developed in this period. It was formed through the long-term production practice, riding, and shooting training in military activities by the ancestors, which profoundly affected the relationship between the northern ethnic groups and the Central Plains as well as the ethnic pattern.

Chapter Three mainly discusses the all-around development of national sports in ancient northern China. This stage mainly refers to the periods from the Sui-Tang Dynasty to the Song, Liao, Jin, and Xixia Dynasties in China's history, mainly including the ethnic groups of Koryo, Paekje, Silla, Mohe, Bohai, Turks, Huihu, Tuyuhun, Tangut, Khitan, Jurchen, and others. It has a certain relationship with the ethnic groups of early Buyeo, Sushen, Xiongnu, Xianbei, and others. Sports culture also has its inheritance, which develops with social progress. In the long-term cultural exchange, various nationalities have produced distinctive regional sports cultures. Their productivity level has been significantly improved, and their sports activities have become rich and colorful, involving a wide range of people, who were in the stage of comprehensive development. During this period, sports activities not only retained the characteristics of production skills but also displayed military practicability more prominently. Entertainment and fitness were developed in an all-around way, and diversified sports characteristics appeared. Sports activities are reflected in people's production and life, military activities, entertainment and fitness, religious beliefs and sacrificial activities, and other occasions. Many sports activities are closely linked with other social cultures, especially the combination of sports activities and feudal etiquette, which highlights the characteristics of the integration of national customs and Chinese traditional culture. These sports activities together constitute the cultural system of ancient northern national sports, which profoundly affect the formation and development of traditional Chinese sports.

Chapter Four mainly discusses the rise and fall of the ancient northern national sports. This stage mainly refers to the Yuan, Ming, and Qing Dynasties in Chinese history. During this period, the northern minorities mainly included Mongol, Uyghur, Hui, and Manchu. Mongol and Manchu established the Yuan and Qing regimes respectively, which realized the territorial integration and ethnic integration in ancient Chinese history. The level of productivity has been further improved; plus, the economy of agriculture and animal husbandry has achieved effective complementarity. As a result, sports activities were rich and colorful, and people at all levels participated. In addition, sports organizations and management had rules and regulations, and sports projects were constantly innovating. In the context of the national unification and the rapidly developing national economy, some practical military sports activities came more into the peoples' lives, which to a large extent promoted the evolution of national sports and realized the fusion and prosperity of ancient northern national sports culture. Yet, on the other hand, because of the corruption and incompetence of the late Qing government, the national strength was weak, and the people were in dire straits. The introduction of modern Western sports led to a rapid decline of the northern national sports from its prosperity.

The second part concerns research on wrestling and polo, including Chapter Five and Chapter Six.

Chapter Five and Chapter Six respectively select the typical wrestling and polo sports of the northern nationalities in ancient China. From the aspects of the origin, development, and evolution of the events, as well as their communication among ethnic groups and their social functions, the book deeply discusses the development, evolution, exchange, and contribution to the social development of the ancient northern ethnic culture. In addition, in the process of textual research, the book further sorts the case systematically through theoretical elaboration, thereby highlighting the practicality of the theory.

Finally, there are several problems worthy to be explained: first is about the concept of sports in this book. In ancient China, there was no word for sports, which was imported from the outside world.[2] However, it cannot be said that there were no sports in ancient China. It is just the difference in cultural symbols under different cultural backgrounds. We should not mechanically apply the concept of modern sports to explain and explicate the ancient sports phenomenon. Like other cultures, such as religion, sports have gone through primitive forms and national forms, and then risen to the world culture, and created new sports in the process of historical development. Modern science, technology, and productivity are incomparable to ancient times, and so is the quality of life. Therefore, modern people's demand for sports should be different from that of ancient times, which can be seen from the creation and setting of modern sports events. Of course, many modern sports events are developed on the basis of ancient national sports, especially those that mainly reflect human function, or those closely related to the survival of ancient human beings, such as running, jumping, throwing, swimming, and then equestrian, archery, skills and so on. From modern sports, we can see the shadow of ancient sports, but we cannot use the concept of modern sports to define ancient sports. In ancient China, sports were often expressed in terms of "health preservation," "guidance," and "Jiao-Di," which were closely related to arts and other social lives. Therefore, they were sometimes collectively referred to as "Baixi (Variety Plays)," "acrobatics," "Sanyue (play)," and "Li (etiquette)," which were specifically manifested as fast race, *Chaoju* (jumping to exercise kungfu), climbing, throwing, shooting, defending, *Jirang*, Jiao-Li, swinging, riding and shooting, swimming, skiing, *Chuiwan*, *Jiju* (horseback polo), Budaqiu, polo playing, *Lüju* (ball hitting on donkeys), wrestling and other colorful events.

At present, there is not a unified understanding of the sports concept in academic circles at home and abroad. Especially in different social living environments and under different cultural backgrounds, its concept becomes different due to the different starting points and perspectives. For example, in ancient Greece, the birthplace of modern sports, the sports terms often seen in its literature are gymnastics, competitions, games, competitors, athletes, training, militarism education, etc. The concept of "Gymnastics" in ancient Greece is very similar to today's "sports," which refers to all body-building exercises or techniques. It is the umbrella term of all body-building exercises and the pronoun of broad-sense sports. After the mid-18th century, capitalist relations of production were established in some Western European countries. Modern sports developed with the rise and establishment of the education system, and the word "sports" came into being. "Physical education" was the earliest English version of "sports," and then British outdoor sports developed and flourished. At this time, sports and gymnastics were mixed. With the progress of gymnastics in Germany and Sweden and outdoor sports in Britain, "Physical Culture" came into being. The concept of health care is interpreted as "the law of physical exercise" in French. After 1917, the Soviet Union used Physical Culture as a broad concept, and Eastern European countries also accepted the concept after 1945. In the context of modern social development, the concept of sports is used very actively in foreign countries. For example, American sports theorists have defined sports as "Physical Education is the art and science of human movement."[3] From 1960 to 1963, the concept of sports in foreign countries still maintained its traditional connotation, stressing that sports are a kind of body-based education; from 1964 to 1970, some people criticized the above concept, expanded its extension, and attributed all human activities except productive activities to sports; from 1971 to 1976, people required to call the science and technology of body movement collectively as sports. Today, the United States sets the Department of Health Physical Education and Recreation to describe the traditional settings of the Department of Physical Education.

China has given different missions to sports in different periods, so the connotation and extension of sports concepts have changed.[4] Among sports concepts, the author agrees with Mr. Yang Wenxuan's definition: "Based on physical exercise, sports is an educational process to enhance physical fitness."[5] The sports discussed in this book are carried out under this concept. The research subject of the book are the sports activities created and engaged in by the ancient northern nationalities in the long-term history.

In the process of social development, human beings always follow a potential law: to develop in survival, compete in development, and survive in competition. Survival is the substantial expression of the existence of all creatures in the world. In promoting the development of productive forces, human beings cannot avoid this law. Competition is common in biological groups, let alone human beings, which is such a group with ideology. There are various ways of competition, and it is a relatively common phenomenon to realize competition through fights. In the cold-weapon era, war was a very common form of fight. War can quickly solve some problems among groups and fully reflect the relationship among survival, competition, and development. In the ancient battlefield, every war was a real embodiment of physical fitness and tactics. Therefore, the study of some issues in ancient wars can provide views and materials for sports research. Especially in the embryonic stage of sports, sports activities, and war were inseparable. Sports' characteristics were not obvious enough until they were separated from military activities. Even in this case, sports still served the military to a large extent. Generally speaking, sports activities develop step by step through human survival struggles. Absolutely, in the discussion of ancient northern national sports' origin, we will also find that some life skills and entertainment games later developed into sports.

The sports activities mentioned in this book are the cultures created by the ancient northern nationalities, which are vital in the family of the Chinese nation. Although the study may not involve all the ancient northern groups, the sports activities of the nationalities included in this book are typical and representative. In addition, some smaller ethnic groups, such as Sushen and Fuchen, are unable to be conducted an in-depth discussion on their sports activities due to the lack of historical records. However, owing to the fact that they have continuity with some later ethnic groups, or have a greater impact on other ethnic groups, they are also involved in the study as far as possible.

The second is the definition of the research area. According to the national language culture, ethnic origins, economic types, customs, and living areas, Mr. Lin Gan argues that the northern nationalities in ancient China can be roughly divided into five or three systems (ethnic groups). In a broad sense, the ancient northern nationalities can include those who once lived in the northeast, the north and south of the desert, and the northwest. In a narrow sense, the ancient northern nationalities only include the nationalities of three systems of Xiongnu, Turks, and Donghu (including Mongolia), which once lived in the north and south of the desert.[6] According to the national administrative divisions of the People's Republic of China, northern China includes 15 provinces, autonomous regions, and cities, including Heilongjiang, Jilin, Liaoning, Inner Mongolia, Beijing, Hebei, Tianjin, Shandong, Shanxi, Henan, Shaanxi, Gansu, Qinghai, Ningxia, and Xinjiang. Considering the broad sense of the concept of ancient northern ethnic groups, this book is based on the national administrative division standards to expound on the data, involving the sports culture of some major ethnic minorities living in the northeast, the north, and south of the desert and the northwest from Pre-Qin to the end of the Qing Dynasty.

There is still a long way to go in the study of ancient national sports in northern China or even of ancient national sports. There are many aspects worthy of our common attention. At present, on the basis of the existing research, the author is exploring how to transform the ancient national sports culture into productive forces in order to contribute to the development of the modern national economy and society. The author expects that more young scholars can join the research and make greater efforts for the prosperity of national culture and social development.

In the research process, due to the lack of knowledge structure and the limited level of comprehension, we cannot completely and accurately analyze the national sports culture of this period. There are still many remaining problems and analyses that need to be improved. Your criticism and correction are cordially appreciated. Of course, we also hope that more scholars can make greater contributions to the research of national sports and put forward valuable opinions and suggestions for the development of disciplines and the prosperity of national culture.

NOTES

1. Wang Zhonghan, *Chinese National History*, 2nd. ed. (China Social Sciences Press, 1994). The history of Chinese ethnicity is full of learning and complex relationships, and I have only a superficial knowledge of the subject, so I dare not presume to add to it. The authoritative *Chinese National History*, edited by Wang Zhonghan, is not to be changed at will. Therefore, the discussion of the origins of ethnic groups, ethnic relations and the development of ethnic societies in this book is mainly based on this work, and I will not refer to it in detail below.
2. In ancient Chinese literature, the term "sports" has never been used. The term "sports" was introduced from Japan, and the English term is "Physical education," which is a direct translation of education about bodies. The earliest Chinese term "sports" appeared in 1902 in a translation works *National Sport Science* published in the *Hangzhou Baihua Newspaper*, and in the *Wuxi Sports Association's Charter* and *Wuxi Sports Association's Republican Charter* published by *Political and Art News Letter* in Shanghai in 1903. This is the earliest evidence of the use of "sports" in China. Before this, China also used a similar concept based on the German military gymnastics (Gamnastics). Gymnastics was introduced to China around 1894. *Presented School Regulation*, approved by the Qing government at the time, explicitly provided for the introduction of gymnastics (i.e., physical education classes) at all levels and in all types of schools.
3. Wang Jinglian and Zhao Chongzhen, "On the Historical Evolution of Sports Concept," *Journal of Anhui University* (Philosophy and Social Sciences Edition), no. 6 (1995): 89–91.
4. The concept of sports was introduced into China in modern times, obviously with military connotations; during the period of the Republic of China and the War of Liberation, sports was also mainly used in military exercises. It was only after the liberation that Comrade Mao Zedong formally put forward the slogan of "Promote physical culture and build up the people's health," which was a sign that sports had entered into the overall fitness of all people. Sports in new China was greatly influenced by the development of sports in the Soviet Union. It not only had the mission of sports fitness, but also the ideological and political education as well as moral education. With the great political function of world competitive sports, China's sports was fulfilled with more connotation. At present, the connotation of sports in China's sports academia is still in research.
5. Yang Wenxuan and Chen Qi, "The Logical Problems of Sports Concepts," *Journal of Physical Education*, no. 1 (1995): 44–47.
6. Lin Gan, *General Theory of the Northern Nationalities in Ancient China*, 1st ed. (Inner Mongolia People's Publishing House, October 1998), 6.

CHAPTER I

Origin and Sprout of the National Sports in Ancient Northern China

As a human social activity, sports are believed by most studies to originate from social practices such as productive events, religious activities, and war. The author agrees with the above views and believes that to clarify the origin and sprout of sports activities, we must go back to the most primitive period of human beings, starting from the living environment and needs of human beings.

1.1 Origin of the National Sports in Ancient North

According to the literature: "In ancient times, there were a number of people but many beasts, and people were overwhelmed by animals, insects, and snakes … people ate the fruits of wild plants and shellfish, which had a fishy smell and hurt the intestines and stomach. So, they were more inclined to fall ill." "In ancient times, men did not have to farm, for the wild fruits were enough to eat; women did not need to weave, for the fur of animals were enough to wear."[1] This shows that in primitive society, people lived a life of gathering, fishing, or hunting. The production mode of gathering, fishing, and hunting mainly relies on people's physical ability. They obtain food through climbing trees and cliffs, swimming, jumping into the streams, throwing, and other physical activities. As far as primitive society is concerned, the economic life, culture and education, and the fight among individuals at that time had certain requirements on people's bodies, in both skills of physical strength and physical activities. The sports items of the northern nationalities in ancient China were gradually produced under the background of meeting the above social needs. Through the research, we believe that the northern national sports are rooted in the production activities and social life of ancient ethnic groups, mainly in the following aspects:

Firstly, it originated from the collection, fishing, and hunting activities of ancient northern nationalities. Collecting, fishing, and hunting were the main production activities of primitive human beings. In primitive society, due to the low productivity and hard life, "there were several people but many beasts," people suffered from the invasion of wild animals, disease, and starvation, so they had to rely on collecting, hunting, fishing, and other activities to sustain and reproduce.

In the long-term engagement, they summed up a series of experiences: they chased wild animals, crossed mountains and rivers, used sticks and threw stones, and fought barehanded with wild animals. In the process of engaging in these physical movements for a long time, the prototype of primitive sports in hunting and dancing, as a form of expressing primitive production activities, gradually evolved into some sports events. As Plekhanov once said, "When the hunter has the impulse to re-experience the joy caused by using his strength in hunting, he does the action of imitating animals again and creates his own unique hunting dance."[2] In this way, human beings began to realize the relationship between them and nature to a certain extent and consciously passed on the impulse to experience again the pleasure caused by strength in hunting to others. These were the form and symbol of the transformation from productive activity skills into sports in primitive society. And these sports activities directly reflect the needs of people's survival, life, and production at that time. They are the concrete embodiment of survival capability and the components of production and life. These activities not only make people's brains and bodies more and more sound but also develop physically some technical movements such as turning, climbing, rolling, crossing, leaping, jumping, swimming, and throwing. In primitive society, human beings used stones as weapons and caught prey by throwing, which required repeated practice of far and accurate throwing. As they got more and more prey, some weapons became the tools of the game. In 1976, thousands of stone balls were unearthed in Xujiayao, Yanggao County, Shanxi Province. According to textual research, these balls were made by human beings living 100,000 years ago. Generally speaking, stones could not be finely ground when hunting. Only when people play games or sacrifice with stones as utensils will they be made into stone balls. It can be seen that this kind of sports activity of playing stone ball derived from hunting activities. Similar hunting activities in ancient China are also reflected in the earliest written records, such as "Jiashen King's fierce tiger" in *Tieyun Canggui Collection* and "It hopes to rain for nice hunting this evening" in *Prequels to Yin Xu Shu Qi*. If we desire to capture wild animals such as tigers and elephants, we can imagine how difficult it is even nowadays. Without certain skills, courage, and strength, it is impossible to accomplish the above tasks. It can be seen that sports are formed by using, experiencing, and imparting a series of collecting, fishing, and hunting skills in long-term production activities.

Secondly, it originated from the farming and animal husbandry of the ancient northern nationalities. When the northern ethnic society developed to a certain stage, farmland work appeared in some areas. Thus, people didn't have to chase animals to satisfy their hunger all day long. And the custom of offering sacrifices to gods became increasingly enriched as a traditional event, which was later changed to the form of a performance. For example, in *Lü's Spring and Autumn Annals · Midsummer · Ancient Music*, it is recorded that in ancient times, when Ge Tian's music was played, three people held oxtails and tapped their feet to sing and dance to eight songs. The first chapter was called "Zai Min," the second called "Xuanniao," the third called "Suicaoht," the fourth called "Fenwugu," the fifth called "Jingtianchang," the sixth called "Jiandigong," the seventh called "Yidide," and the eighth called "the extreme of beasts."[3] This is the most ancient performance in China's literature, which reflects the yearning for a flourishing population, lush vegetation, good harvest, and livestock breeding at that time. The performers hold the oxtail and gain pleasure from the movements of their hands and feet. This kind of performance form of singing and dancing with oxtail is vividly and concretely confirmed in the Neolithic colored pottery basin with dancing patterns unearthed in Sunjiazhai, Datong County, Qinghai Province. The painted pottery basin with dancing patterns was excavated in a primitive society tomb of Majiayao culture type in the autumn of 1973. Its inner wall clearly depicts three groups of dancers, with five in each group, singing and dancing hand in hand in circles (see Fig. 1-1).

Fig. 1-1 Dance on the Painted Pottery Basin Unearthed in Datong County, Qinghai Province

There are four parallel banded patterns on the bottom of the basin, representing the pool water. Wearing headdresses and tail ornaments, the dancers are singing and dancing in the same direction, passionately and joyfully, just like "arm in arm, stepping on the ground for rhythm," as described in *Miscellanies of the Western Capital*.[4] Among the unearthed cultural relics of the same age as the painted pottery basin with dancing patterns, there are also pottery drums, whistles, and other musical instruments. The pottery drum unearthed in Minhe County, Qinghai Province, in the Neolithic age, is oblong. One end of the drum is smaller, the middle part is thinner, and the other is trumpet-shaped. There are two rings on the drum attached to a tether for beating the drum on the body. The pottery whistle is now in Liuwan Cultural Relic Station in Ledu County, Qinghai Province. There are holes in the pottery whistle, which can blow out four different sounds. In primitive sports activities, people used to take advantage of local materials, such as stone, wood, and leather, to hit each other, even clapping hands and feet or legs, beating rhythm, singing, and dancing, which was the performance of people's celebration and entertainment. To a certain extent, the above-mentioned documents and archaeological materials show that people in labor created agricultural and pastoral sacrificial entertainment and game activities. They are out of the expectation of the harvest of labor, or the sacrifice celebration after the harvest of labor, to encourage, wish, and harvest. These activities demonstrate that farming and animal husbandry provide material and a source for the formation of sports.

Thirdly, it originated from the religious activities of ancient northern nationalities. Due to the lack of understanding of natural science, primitive human beings were confused and feared some natural phenomena, and they believed that all things had souls. At first, they worshiped totems, and later on, clan communes worshiped their ancestors. After the emergence of slavery, worship developed into a kind of witchcraft, which was claimed to be the early religious belief. The primitive dance was often a collective activity led by a chieftain and enjoyed by everyone. Besides hunting and fighting training, it was also used for entertainment. The *Book of History · Yu Dian* once recorded: "I would like to strike the stone chime so that the dance team playing the role of beasts can dance to the melody of the music."[5] This is a form of expression in which tribes with various beasts as totems dance one after another to support Yao as the leader of the tribal alliance. Since the emergence of primitive religion, there has been a sacrifice, followed by the emergence of the original religious monks—witches. In the early days, the witch was run by the chief, which can be confirmed by the people of Oroqen or Ewenki: "The use of witch songs and dances in sacrifices has turned this artistic activity from entertaining people into entertaining gods."[6] In this way, dance, which has artistic and sports factors, is related to religious sacrifice. When religious groups developed in society, they also provided a fixed activity place, crowd, and economic basis for the sports activities, which directly or indirectly promoted the occurrence and development of many sports events. Especially in physical and mental exercise, religious groups have carried out in-depth and extensive practices and developed various martial arts with traditional cultural heritage, such as martial arts and meditation, which gradually became the dominant events of traditional Chinese sports.

Fourth, it originated from the wars of the northern nationalities in ancient times. The formation of competitive events is mostly related to military training. Attacking wild animals or other groups and self-defense are important in primitive human social activities. In the period of clan commune, the primitive war took place in order to fight for living space, sacrifice, or revenge. Along the evolution of history, the level of productivity varied greatly to the different degrees of progress of each clan. Some of the more advanced clans, in order to survive and develop, plundered the population, property, and living space of others to enrich and strengthen themselves. Therefore, to prevent outward invasion and protect the interests of the clans, other clans carried out self-defense and self-aid. As a consequence, the war broke out. After the clan commune, conflicts of interest among tribes sometimes needed to be resolved by force. Thus such historical phenomena occurred like "Hui, who made the bow and Yimu, who made the arrow, were all the emperor's ministers."[7] and "*Cuju* (ball-hitting), created by the emperor, manifested the military power."[8] It can be seen that archery, fencing, and *Cuju* were all rooted in ancient wars. Wars promoted the development of weapons and the evolution of fighting skills, so it became necessary to train tribal members in physical and military techniques in advance, which further evolved into the driving force for the occurrence and prosperity of ancient sports. Many of our ancient northern national sports were developed during the war.

Fifthly, it originated from the music and dance art of the ancient northern nationalities. Primitive dance is a vivid form of body language in early human development and is also one of the origins of human sports. Dating back to our ancestors' period, human beings lived in the grasslands or forests and had a lifestyle of farming or animal husbandry or both. In long-term production and work, they have accumulated a certain number of subsistence materials and production experiences. They have learned a lot of body movements from nature or animals to express their emotions or understanding of nature and society. Primitive music and dance reflect the difficult course of humanity's struggle against nature in the ignorant and barbarous period and demonstrate the life of early human beings as well as their activities in a unique form. With the development of society, this kind of activity not only inherits the original attributes but also differentiates into new functions as an important part of human sports.

1.2 Sprout of the National Sports in Ancient North

The sprouting of ancient northern national sports is mainly reflected in the primitive society and some production activities as well as the social life of various ethnic groups in the primitive stage, which are embodied in the following aspects:

The production and utilization of tools. The ancient ancestors not only made full use of their strength and techniques but also used tools when hunting. These tools also entered the field of sports the long historical evolution, such as knives, sticks, ropes, javelins, bows and arrows, balls (stones), boats, etc. Archaeological research shows that human beings used bows and arrows in the Paleolithic age, and then in the Neolithic age, bows and arrows were widely used in wars. For example, in 1963, archaeologists excavated a stone arrowhead about 28,700 years ago in Shuo County, Shanxi Province, indicating that the local people had begun to make and use bows and arrows at that time. The tip of a stone cluster is embedded in the 10th thoracic vertebrae of tomb II M24 in Taosi City Site, Xiangfen County, Shanxi Province. The end of the stone arrowhead is seen in the left rib of the owner, who was found to die of arrow injury.[9] In the Neolithic tomb site of Jiang County, Shanxi Province, it was discovered that a dead man was shot in the head by an arrow, and the stone arrowhead punctured his nose bone. In the Yangshao cultural cemetery in Beishouling, Baoji City, Shaanxi Province, there are bunches of bone arrowheads between the knees of the deceased in tomb No. M17.[10] Engels once pointed out that "bow and arrow are decisive weapons for the age of ignorance, just as firearms are for civilized times."[11] For ancient northern primitive people, the use and popularity of bows and arrows have their special significance. It not only greatly improved the ability to capture wild animals for some hunting tribes, expanded the species, quantity, and scope of hunting, but also required people to step up training, created conditions for the occurrence of animal husbandry, and unintentionally promoted the production of sports.

Inventing a bow and arrow was not easy, as М.Ильин and Е.Сегал pointed out, "It took thousands of years for man to make an arrow. At first, it was not arrows that were shot from the bow but the pitchfork that was already invented. Thus, the bow had to be made very large at that time—as high as a man."[12] The bow was the same height as a man, which is reflected in a large number of rock paintings in northern China. Shooting arrows with a bow can hit the target even from a long distance. It's undoubtedly a great creation in technique and one of the achievements in the history of human culture. The ancient people employed tools to carry out some hunting or purposeful training. Hunting was reflected in many rock paintings in northern China, and archery learning was also recorded in ancient Chinese literature, as cited "Before the age of 15, the ancients learned everything since childhood. He was taught by his father and elder brother to shoot and then learned philology as he grew older. He was asked to master ritual etiquette as well as martial arts."[13] In the inscriptions on bones and tortoise shells and inscriptions on bronze in the Yin and Zhou Dynasties, the characters such as hunting, shooting, netting, etc., all vividly depicted the original shapes of those hunting tools.[14] The manufacture and utilization of hunting tools of northern nationalities can also be proved in the investigation of modern ethnology. Bulu, a unique hunting tool of Mongol, was used to fight against animals. The hunters often practiced and held accurate and long-distance throwing competitions for better mastery, which gradually transformed into the present throwing sports.

Make and use of game apparatus. The most powerful evidence of ancient games was the thousands of stone balls found in Xujiayao, Yanggao County, Shanxi Province, in 1976. These balls were made by human beings 100,000 years ago. In addition, stone balls buried with children were also excavated in the late Neolithic site of Banpo, Xi'an, which were finely made with smooth surfaces, and some studies believed that they were used for games.

The emergence of music and dance. There were records of three people dancing with oxtail in *Lü's Spring and Autumn Annals · Midsummer · Ancient Music*.[15] The pottery basin with dancers' patterns excavated at the Shangsunjia Village of Datong County in Qinghai Province also displayed this performance form. Wearing headgear and tail ornaments, the dancers were moving in the same direction, singing and dancing in circles. Just like "arm in arm, stepping on the ground for rhythm" described in *Miscellanies of the Western Capital*. The pottery drums, whistles, and other musical instruments were contemporary among the unearthed cultural relics as the pottery basin. In primitive sports, people used local materials, such as stone, wood, and leather, to hit each other. They were singing and dancing, even beating their hands and feet or legs, mainly for rhythm. There are such records in *Huainanzi*, "In the era of Shun, Miao (a tribe in ancient time) who did not obey. So, Shun practiced the rule of virtue, stopped the war, and employed shields and axes in singing and dancing."[16] It is easy to see that music and dance are also a form of the germination of ancient sports manifested from the above literature records and archaeological discoveries.

The development of sports in folk customs. In ancient times, most of the northern nationalities lived in high mountains, deserts, and plains under deplorable conditions. At that time, human thinking was relatively simple, and tools were crude. And the unique national sports have gradually evolved from long-time labor and social life. The modern ethnological survey discovered that fishing was one of the main productive labors of the Hezhe nationality living in the Heilongjiang Basin. In the long-term work, Hezhe people accumulated rich fishing experience. They were so familiar with the habits of various fish that they could identify their species according to the ripple in the water and then stab them quickly with a harpoon. Naturally, they often killed them with a single shot. But different fish had different ways of spearing. To master the technique of catching fish, people learned to stab grass balls first. Throwing the straw grass ball on the ground, which rolled forward to act as if the fish were swimming, people harpooned quickly to hit the target, thus forming the traditional national sport "stab grass ball." Hitting "Bulu" in Mongolian means throwing, which has thousands of years of history. Bulu is made of a small bent stick, like a sickle, wrapped with aluminum, copper, iron, and other metals or melted with aluminum and poured into the pattern. The herdsmen often used Bulu to beat the birds and animals. Today's Bulu competition has two ways: long-distance shots and accurate shots. Another example is the Ewenki nationality's "swinging the pole to lasso a horse," which was the production labor of horse training. To lasso the unruly horse, the trainer should not only have great arm strength, waist, leg, skillful riding skills, and brave and indomitable will but also have a fast-running horse. Otherwise, the lassoed horse will pull the rider off the mount. In today's lassoing competition, dozens of strong athletes cheer on the horse, wave the lassoing pole, and chase the horse. When the horse is caught, the riders rush up quickly to wrestle the horse to the ground. From these ethnological investigations, we can see that some national sports also sprout in rich folk activities.

1.3 Image of Sports in Ancient Northern National Rock Paintings

The ancient northern nationalities recorded sports in production activities and social life in the form of rock paintings, which provided valuable information for us to study.[17] Some scholars have praised that the rock paintings are unrestrained and vigorous, always involving moving, running, shooting, and fighting. People and animals in rock paintings showed the value of life and the prestige of power in their activities.[18] The primitive stone-carved rock paintings act as a mirror of the early history of human beings, reflecting the tough struggle with nature in the period of ignorance and wilderness. These rock paintings in northern China are rich in content, including local natural resources, social customs, production situation, and cultural features at that time. They are widely distributed, including Yinshan rock paintings in Inner Mongolia, Ulanqab rock paintings, Badain Jaran Desert rock paintings, Helan Mountain rock paintings in Ningxia, Hexi Corridor rock paintings in Gansu Province, Haixi rock paintings in Qinghai Province, Altai Mountain rock paintings in Xinjiang, Tianshan rock paintings and Kunlun Mountain rock paintings.

Archaeologists found that in Yinshan of Inner Mongolia and Ulanqab areas, there were Hetao people belonging to the Paleolithic age, who were the remains of Dayao culture and Zhalai Nuoer culture. After the Neolithic age appeared the Neolithic culture which revealed the hunting economy; Fuhe Culture, which mainly showed an agriculture-dominated economy and hunting-supplemented economy; Hongshan Culture, typical of the agricultural economy; the lower-level culture of Xiajiadian; Dawenkou phase I and II culture. Some of these belong to the original culture system of the Central Plains, and others belong to the Mongolian Plateau. During the Xia and Shang Dynasties, there were clans or tribes known as "Guifang" and "Xunyu" in this area. Before and after the establishment of the Zhou Dynasty, the most active nomadic tribes in the northern grassland were Xunyu, Xianyun, and Quanrong. During the Spring and Autumn Period and the Warring States Period, there were other clans and tribes besides the above-mentioned, such as Linhu, Loufan, and Xiongnu, known as the northern barbarians, who then migrated with animal husbandry and pioneered westwards. In the late Warring States Period, with the development of society, many independent clans gradually formed into larger tribal alliances in a certain area. Among them, Xiongnu and Donghu were the two main tribal alliances with different ethnic groups. By doing so, the long primitive social history of clans and tribes in northern China ended, and the transition to a slave society began.

The rock paintings in Inner Mongolia can be traced back to the Neolithic period and extended to the Ming and Qing Dynasties. Among them, the rock paintings from the early Iron Age (equivalent to the Spring and Autumn Period to the Han Dynasty) to the middle ancient times (from the Northern Dynasties to the Tang Dynasty) revealed the economic form, customs, and beliefs, production, and life as well as some ideological concepts of the nomads in northern China. The contents of Yinshan rock paintings included hunting, grazing, animals, livestock, war, fighting, dancing, reproduction, gods of heaven, Sun God, symbols, etc., mostly in various animals and hunting scenes. Hunting paintings include single-person hunting, double hunting, hunting around, hunter or riding a horse, or riding a camel. In the dance pictures, some of the dancers are bald, with wings and tails, as if they were hunting. Hunting weapons include sticks, ropes, arcs, knives, bows, and arrows, and bows and arrows are the most popular. There are also many scenes of raising livestock where people touch and lead animals. Dogs are the closest animals to human beings, as they appear in many hunting scenes, followed by goats, sheep, camels, horses, cattle, and reindeer. The contents of Yinshan rock paintings reflected the creation of nomadic people in northern China and a long historical process starting from the stone age to the iron age, or the primitive age to the civilization age. This is obviously not the work of a specific nationality in northern China, but of many. Di, Xiongnu, Xianbei, Turks, Qiang, and Mongol in China have all been active in this area, which may be the works of some of them.[19] The content of Ulanqab rock paintings reflected the production and living of nomadic hunting groups, which were featured by the obvious local color, including herdsmen, dancing, field grazing, hunters, hunting, etc. These paintings were not of the same era, but they lasted for a long time, which can be traced back to the lower-level culture stage of Xiajiadian (about the Shang Dynasty) and extended to the Qin and Han Dynasties. Specifically, these should be the works of some ethnic groups in northern China, such as Shanrong, Donghu, Wuhuan, Xianbei, Xiongnu, and Mongol, which were active in this area.[20] According to the incomplete statistics, there are more than 30,000 pieces in these two regions, revealing mainly the history of their production and life. At the same time, they also reflect the general situation of the germination of national sports in ancient Inner Mongolia.

Since ancient times, there have been many ethnic minorities who were good at singing and dancing in Northwest China. Thus, dance had become an indispensable part of their lives. The art form advocated by the northwest ancestors was the combination of music and dance, just as Sima Qian said in the *Historical Records*, "Singing, expressing his heart; dancing, demonstrating his behavior."[21] According to some historical records, the ancient ancestors often gathered together after hunting. They knocked on the rock and danced rhythmically to imitate the movements and gestures of birds and animals. This can be called "birds dance with all kinds of wild animals," "attract the phoenix to dance," and "hit the rock, and animals dance together,"[22] which is the true reflection of the hunting dance of the ancient northwest minorities.

The rock paintings depicting the dance images of primitive ancestors in Northwest China are mainly concentrated in Heishan and Qilian Mountains in Gansu Province, Helan Mountain in Ningxia Hui Autonomous Region, Gangcha Halonggou in Qinghai Province, and Tianshan,

Altai, and the Kunlun Mountains in Xinjiang Uyghur Autonomous Region. The stone-carved rock paintings here truly recorded the local nomadic people's social life, hunting production, domesticating animals, religious beliefs, totem worship, and other historical events.

At present, more than 2,000 pieces of rock paintings have been found in Helan Mountain of Ningxia, which means that it is another treasury of rock paintings in ancient northern China. And the themes include grazing, hunting, war, animals, plants, and so on. For example, the rock paintings in Helankou are mainly composed of human faces, and more than 200 rock paintings involved hand prints, footprints, blue sheep, red deer, and group dance (see Fig. 1-2), hunters holding bows and swords, disguised hunters, and hunting. There are also vivid images of duet dance in the Heishanmao rock paintings, Xiaozaogou, Dawukou, Shizuishan City, and Ningxia. Most images are of people and animals, along with scenes of grazing and hunting. The themes of Helan rock paintings reflect the economy of animal husbandry and hunting characterized by the nomadic people in northern China. The time-honored painting can be traced back to the Pre-Qin Dynasty and extended to the Ming and Qing Dynasties.[23] Rock paintings in Helan Mountain were the product of multinational people who have been active in this area. All kinds of ancient people's face images and group dance pictures in Helan Mountain rock paintings are very artistic. Their ethnic style seems to be inherited from Yinshan rock paintings in Inner Mongolia.

Fig. 1-2 The Arm Dance in Helankou Rock Painting[24]

The rock paintings excavated in Gansu Province are mainly located at the northern foot of Qilian Mountains, which has been a place for nomadic groups since ancient times. There were 34 places of rock paintings found in the Daheigou mountainous area, in which more than 200 pieces depict deer, Megaloceros, goat, argali, yellow sheep, bison, tiger, elephant, dog, fox, etc. Hunting pictures, among other things, take up a large proportion. Most of them are collective hunting, varying from two to six people.[25] The topics include human beings, various animals, dancing, hunting (collective hunting), shooting geese, and so on. For example, in the painting S24 of Heishan rock paintings, there are two people riding horses and three shooting camels. The horse-riding picture shows that the rider holds the rein and raises his whip in a galloping manner; the camel shooting picture is about the hunters shooting at the camel with a bow and arrow; the pictures of S25, S33, S35, H10, H21, M1, M2, and M3 all have similar scenes; the pictures of S3, S6, S35, S57, and S94 have dancing images, too. Besides, the themes of Gansu rock paintings also belong to the nomadic culture of our country, which lasts for a long time. The rock paintings of Qilian Mountains, Heishan Mountain, and Sidaoguxingou were possibly completed by Yuezhi, Wusun, or Xiongnu from the Pre-Qin to Qin and Han Dynasties. The Buddhist rock paintings and Tibetan inscriptions in Hongliugou, Heishan mountain, made by Tubo, Qiang, or Mongol, could be dated back to as early as the middle Tang Dynasty and late to the Song and Yuan Dynasties.[26]

Discovered in 1972, the Heishan rock paintings in Gansu Province were the early cultural relics of the Qiang people, Da Yuezhi, or early Xiongnu, which were inferred to be the works before Zhang Qian went on a mission to the Western Regions in the Western Han Dynasty. The portraits are scattered on the shiny purple-black rocks on both sides of the long ravines and canyons, and more than 30 places have been discovered successively.[27] The main theme of the portrait is hunting, including people, wild animals, livestock, shooting geese, etc. The pictures are vivid, and the characters are powerful. For example, in a hunting scene, several huge buffaloes and longhorn deer are surrounded by hunters who hold bows and arrows. The buffaloes raise their tails and horns to make the posture as if they were ready to flee or compete with the hunters, the tension of which is vividly displayed in the painting. In addition, there are also some lively drill pictures. "The characters in the picture are mostly dancing. There is a large scene depicting nearly 30 characters who are divided into three groups with different numbers: upper, middle, and lower, which are arranged in horizontal lines. They wear ornaments on their heads made of wild bird feathers and dress in diversity, including long skirts, shorts, and no skirts, yet they are all with wide shoulders and slim waists, illustrating the bodybuilding of tribal warriors … These warriors may be practicing martial arts or be practicing dancing. At this stage, "martial art" and "dancing" are hard to distinguish.[28]

There are two representative rock paintings in Qinghai: one is the Lushan rock paintings in Tianjun County, with more than 180 paintings discovered depicting all kinds of deer, yaks, and birds, the scenes of yak and deer hunting, and the war of bow shooting (see Fig. 1-3). The other is the Yeniugou rock paintings, with more than 160 pictures excavated in total, and 90 percent of them are animal pictures. The vivid hunting pictures include the scene of hunting cattle, in which hunters kneel on the ground holding bows and arrows ready to shoot. In addition, there are also images of horse riding and mounted archery (see Fig. 1-4) and arms dance.

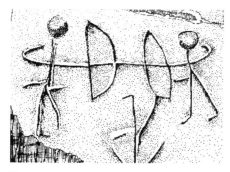

Fig. 1-3 Fighting Image in Lushan Rock Painting

Fig. 1-4 Horse Riding Image in Yeniugou Rock Painting

Many rock paintings have been preserved all over Xinjiang, which reflects the unique primitive art culture in the Paleolithic and Neolithic ages. There are many ancient rock paintings with rich themes in the Altai and Baldakur mountains in the north of Xinjiang. Like the hunting scenes (see Fig. 1-5), the tools are mainly bows and arrows. In the Du'ate cave in Habahe County, a painting shows a scene of fighting in which a man was holding a knife and a stick in his right hand and a triangular shield in his left hand. There are also paintings of grazing life, such as walking to graze, riding to graze, and social life, like fighting, war, and dancing. In Tangbaletas of Altai Mountain, there is an exquisite group dance picture with maroon stone which is artistically designed and finely framed. The picture comprises two groups, the top one plus the bottom one. The top group is composed of five people arranged in a line. The leader on the left is decorated with three fork-shaped short horns on his head, and the third one wears a double fork-shaped short horn. Their arms stretch out, and their feet move apart. On the right, a branch-like religious sacrificial object is erected. The bottom one is still a group dance of five people, yet in a circular formation. The dancers' arms are extended vertically, and the leading role wears short horns with double forks on his head, and his two feet spread out to make a tiptoe march. Good teamwork among the five active dancers with their dramatic performance and harmonious cooperation formed a strong artistic contrast with the upper group of dance movements.

Fig. 1-5 Hunting Images in the Rock Paintings of Baldakur Mountain, Yumin County, Xinjiang[29]

There are many prehistoric primitive sports scenes in the rock paintings in Tianshan, Xinjiang. For example, some rock paintings in Hutubi County displayed dancers with makeup imitating animals, wearing animal tail decorations, antlers on their heads, and feather headgear, singing and dancing hand in hand. There are also images of solo, duet, and multiplayer dance (see Fig. 1-6). Among them, the dancers all have headgear and tail ornament, wearing animal skin and holding ox tails or prey to rotate. This is completely consistent with the original musical scene in *Lü's Spring and Autumn Annals · Ancient Music*. "Once upon a time, Getianshi (an ancient tribe) danced accompanied by music while three people danced and sang eight songs with oxtail in their hands."

Fig. 1-6 Arm Dance in the Rock Painting of Kangjiashimenzi, Hutubi County, Xinjiang

From Korla in the west to the Shule River in the East, there are nearly 300 pictures of Xingdi rock paintings on the Kuluke Mountains, many of which reflect the religious sacrifice, campaign prayer, and hunting celebration of the primitive ancestors. According to Hu Bangzhu's field trip records, in one duet dance of these paintings, the dancers face forward, putting one hand on his partner's shoulder with two legs bent. The right dancer's left arm moves downward, and the left dancer's right-hand stretches, holding an object like a sheep which may be a kind of sacrificial dance. Another group of duet dances is featured by different characteristics: the dancer on the left looks like a half man and half beast with long feathers on his head. This might be a kind of simulated dance or a kind of witchcraft.[30] In addition, there is some freestyle fighting by primitive ancestors, such as handstands in the air, which fully demonstrate the sports skills of ancient Xinjiang people.

The above rock paintings can be described as the epitome of the material and spiritual life of the ancient northern nationalities, regardless of topics and forms. They vividly record the reproduction, sex, war, labor, celebration, religious sacrifice, totem worship, cultural entertainment, and many other life scenes of the primitive ancestors. Among them, the most attractive parts are various kinds of vivid body movements. In terms of functions, the rock paintings related to sports above can be divided into the following four categories.

Primitive religious dance. In primitive society, the level of productivity was extremely low in ancient northern China. People were puzzled by many natural phenomena, so they produced an animistic worldview and primitive religious concepts, i.e., the surrounding world was full of supernatural beings and magic, and each natural phenomenon was dominated by different "gods." Based on this concept, they naturally needed to use primitive sacrifice and witchcraft to realize the personification of gods and achieve their life fantasies and wishes. The religious dance in northern China's ancient rock paintings focused on animal worship, gods, and totems. As a social ideology and cultural phenomenon, religious dance has always been rooted in the interaction process between man and nature. Thus, dance was very important in religious rites, just like what Engels demonstrated: "Each tribe has its own formal festivals and forms of worship, dance, and competition. Dance is the main component of all religious ceremonies."[31] Moreover, animal worship was the most common form for the ancestors of northern nationalities. In the ancient hunting society, animals were the essential conditions for human survival. This "sense of dependence on nature and the idea of regarding nature as an arbitrary and personality entity" serve the basis of sacrifice as the essential behavior of natural religion.[32] Meanwhile, it was also an important form to worship these animals so as to obtain the help of gods. These primitive rock paintings were decorated with "all kinds of sacrificial rites and incantations are covered with religious colors, which are the products of religiousness, mystification, and idealization of real life."[33] The dance was related to the success of hunting and the multiplication of livestock, no matter whether the dancers worshiped the magical animals in fantasy or prayed for the real animals. Lastly, totem worship is an inevitable stage in the evolution of human civilization. According to the characteristics of regional culture, most of the totems of the ancient nomadic people in the north of China were birds and beasts. Later, with the development of animal husbandry, herdsmen needed a climate and environment with fair weather and abundant pasture. Sun, moon, stars, wind, rain, thunder, and lightning in celestial bodies naturally became other objects of worship for them. It can be seen from the rock paintings, there were many pictures that mimicked the images and movements of totems, such as imitating young frogs, the movements of birds and animals, or praying for some natural objects. It is concluded that some imitations are just the embryonic form of ancient northern national sports.

Hunting activities. The social advancement of the nomadic people in northern China was always closely related to the natural environment, which formed the necessary condition for the development of ancient hunting and animal husbandry. The production and life of the ancestors living hunting have been widely reflected in many hunting rock paintings. Hunting in primitive society was mostly carried out in clans with blood relationships, which determined the collective action of ethnic groups at that time. For example, there are pictures of collective hunting around the captured antelope, north goat, argali, and birds; scenes of excitement due to the acquisition of a large number of wild animals; and the happiness of 14 herdsmen characterized by the passion of nomads. From the composition and content analysis, it seemed that a clan in the transformation process from the hunting industry to animal husbandry started to have the capacity to domesticate wild animals and graze on natural grassland, and thus revel in the way of changing grassland or after harvest. In addition, the most common form of rock painting was cheering around the prey by one or more people. Hunters were familiar with the different habits of various animals, as well as their actions and experiences in hunting, which promoted the formation and evolution of the hunting economy in clan society. These rock paintings not only expressed people's happiness but also imparted hunting knowledge, which had become a major factor in the emergence and development of ancient northern national sports.

War scenes. In the competitive primitive society, wars always broke out among clans and tribes for survival or other reasons, such as plundering, invading, and blood revenge. Therefore, the records of wars in the rock paintings were essential. The war scenes displayed in the rock paintings, whether imitating war drills, training warriors, celebrating, or sacrificing, were almost all exquisite expressions of commemoration. There were such pictures in the rock paintings: the front three people were in the same posture: bending arms, drooping elbows, straddling legs, all of whom had tail decorations. The first person had a double braid, the second one opened his fingers, and the third held the oxtail where a head under his feet was placed to sacrifice gods, which was undoubtedly the head of the slain at the upper left. There were another two in the picture, both of whom wore tail decorations with arms extended: the upper one's body was short and thick, his legs wide open as if he were jumping forward. The man below wore a tail ornament, right leg upright, left leg outstretched, with a head landing on his right. The contents of the above-mentioned pictures were not only the form of people celebrating their success or offering sacrifices to the dead warriors, but also the psychological reflection which might force the enemy to fear, forgive, or thank God's help. Obviously, it can be seen that this kind of rock painting reflecting the war scenes of clans had strong practicability and utilitarian purpose as those imitating hunting.

Entertainment dance. There were many entertaining dance scenes in rock paintings. At that time, people gathered around because they got food, stocked up, or won the war when they came back. They expressed their emotions and encouraged each other to have fun through singing and dancing. The ancients said, "People adore music, and they would like to sing and dance anytime and anywhere."[34] Dance has always been an instinctive and ultimate expression of joy. There were a great number of entertaining dance scenes in the ancient northern rock paintings, with a strong flavor of hunting and animal husbandry. These simple and natural dances, manifest the interdependent, self-entertaining, and entertaining customs of ancient clans and tribes, constituting an integral part of ancient northern national sports activities.

1.4 Summary

This chapter mainly discusses the origin and sprout of ancient northern national sports. From the above-mentioned early human culture in China, as well as the information shown in rock paintings and oracle bone inscriptions, the author believes that the northern national sports mainly originated from the production activities and social life of the ancient northern people, such as collecting, fishing, hunting, farming, animal husbandry, religious activities, war, music, and dance. The sprout of sports is mainly manifested in the production and utilization of tools and game apparatus, the emergence of music and dance, and the development of some folk activities.

From the basic form of sports, it is closer to life than other art forms, such as singing, dancing, and drama, and can directly reflect human sports skills. Ancient northern national sports, especially in fore-ancient times, focused on the performance and evolution of human body potential. The original sports were not only for expressing beauty or plot but also demonstrating a kind of skill, especially related to labor and military, such as fishing, hunting, swimming, climbing trees and cliffs, jumping streams, and so on, which all breed some sports skills. In addition, it was also shown in the production and use of tools and weapons, such as sticks, ropes, knives, bows and arrows, boats, and arms.

Sports are a kind of physical culture movement gradually produced and developed by human beings according to production and social life needs. In a sense, on the day of evolution from ape to man, at the same time, when primitive human-made tools, the rudiments of sports sprouted. It is very difficult to explain the origin of national sports in the north of China correctly and comprehensively due to the different periods of their development, the geographical and social environment, and the productive forces. In ancient books, they were mixed with temple music and dances, religious rituals, folk games, hunting, wars, and martial arts, which revealed diversity in ancient ethnic sacrificial rites or hunting. For example, at that time, there were performances that imitated the movements of birds and beasts, and the shows with the theme of training animals not only reflected superstitious nature but also displayed certain sports skills. Therefore, in discussing the origin and sprout of sports, we mainly summarize their common features.

The third part of this chapter vividly reproduces part of the scenes of people's production and social life with the images of sports in rock paintings. We can vaguely see the origin and sprout of the early sports culture of the northern nationalities.

The emergence and progress of all ethnic cultures are determined by internal and external factors such as the geographical environment, the means and modes of production, and the interaction between ethnic groups. Although the subjective initiative of human beings has been improved and their dependence on the environment has weakened, they can never eliminate its constraints. To summarize, as the geographical and natural environment are the indispensable basis of human survival and development in each stage, the progress and style of national culture are also affected by these factors. Regarded as a culture, sports must also follow this rule.

The nomadic and hunting culture in ancient northern China was basically based on grassland, forest, mountain, and desert. This special geographical environment had a profound and lasting impact on the social survival and culture of the local ethnic groups. Compared with the farming economy in the Central Plains, although there were a few oasis agriculture irrigated by inland rivers and groundwater in northern China, the nomadic economy played a leading role. Human beings always carry out special cultural creations in a certain environment. The geographical environment of deserts, mountains, sandstorms, dry and cold in northern China determines the cultural characteristics of the northern ethnic groups—hunting as the main mode of production, which specifies an unstable lifestyle, low productivity, and ability to resist natural disasters, and strong dependence on the environment. Therefore, in the absence of a scientific understanding of nature, they regarded the desert, mountain, sun, and other living environments as the incarnation of God. They worshiped wolves, eagles, and other animals as totems, and thus Shamanism became a common primitive religion of northern nationalities.

According to *Historical Records · Biography of Xiongnu*, "The ancestors of Xiongnu are the descendants of the Xia clan … They migrate after water and vegetation, have no citadels or places of regular residence, and do not engage in agricultural production, yet they possess their own share of land. There is no writing or books, but people's actions are regulated by words. It is the custom of Xiongnu to be nomadic when there is no war, and shooting birds and animals is considered a profession. When the situation is urgent, everyone practices the skills of attacking and fighting by nature in order to invade and plunder. When the war situation is favorable, they attack further; on the contrary, when it is unfavorable, they retreat. They are not ashamed of running away. As long as there is profit to be made, there is no regard for propriety and shame."[35] This passage comprehensively summarized the features of nomadic production and life: without city walls and cultivated land, people moved around and made a living nomadic; the development level of social civilization remained low, and the nation had no written language. They attached importance to the individual value, and everything was in favor of the individual. At the same time, the ethnic group as a whole paid attention to the overall progress of the collective. Xiongnu upheld that "the strong and healthy people are noble, the old and weak people are humble," and "the strong people eat delicious food, the old people eat leftovers." The main purpose was to protect the survival of the strong because they were the backbone to ensure the survival and development of this nation. On the other hand, such measures were also used to explore all the nation's strengths, whether the elderly, women, or young people, as long as they could fight, they would be rewarded. Another example was that the Turk sergeants could own the goods they obtained in the war and took the prisoners of war as their slaves. All these encouraged people to participate in the war as much as possible, and constantly strengthened their training so that they could be more tenacious in the battle. As a consequence, all the people in the north were good at riding and fighting and were becoming extremely brave.

Animal husbandry, hunting, and plundering were the common lifestyles of the northern nationalities in ancient times. Turks, Khitan, Jurchen, Tangut, and later Mongol had similar lifestyles to Xiongnu. The essence of war and plunder was to survive. From the cultural point of view, it was to maintain or transmit the specific culture of a nation in a certain ecological environment, and objectively promote the development of culture. Due to the ethnic characteristics and psychological tendency of the northern nomadic people restricted by their geographical and natural environment, it was vital to highlight animal husbandry, hunting, and the training of related skills and tactics. In order to make the next generation fully occupied to adapt to the living environment of nomadic society, many ethnic minorities attached great importance to the education of military, physical, and survival skills.

For a long time, the people living on the grassland in northern China have lived a nomadic life. They had their own unique features, quite different from those in Central Plains. It's proven throughout history that "the mode of production of material life constrains the social, political, and intellectual life process in general."[36] Due to the influence of internal and external factors, and chronological and geographical conditions, the evolution of human society reveals the difference in speed of progress and the diversity of historical development; as stated in the *Capital*, "this does not prevent the same economic basis from showing infinite variations and gradations in its appearance, even though its principal conditions are everywhere the same. This is due to innumerable outside circumstances, such as natural environment, race peculiarities, and historical influences, all of which must be ascertained by the thorough analysis."[37] Since ancient times, there were many clans or tribes of different races in the northern region of China, who migrated with the seasons and lived a nomadic life. This kind of tribe was composed of several families, and a tribal leader was produced among the parents. If a leader is expected to lead all production and development of the tribe, he must be brave and resourceful. This phenomenon was particularly prominent in the ancient northern nationalities of China, which indicates the environment produced the ancient northern national sports.

The dependence of human beings on the geographical and natural environment facilitated this factor to become particularly important. Under these circumstances, the ancient northern national sports are bred and developed. As the basis of the progress of human history, the geographical and natural environment is not only the foundation of implementation and completion of human activities but also the objective factors restricting sports activities. These two factors exerted the primary impacts and placed the basic dependence on human sports activities. Plus, this interrelationship has been accompanied by the whole process of the germination, development, and prosperity of national sports. At the same time, from the emergence of some sports, we can also see the direct role of the geographical environment, such as skiing in the snow, swimming in rivers, lakes, and seas, and ice play can only be carried out in cold regions. Thus, it can be summarized that in the early stage of human society, the geographical environment strictly restricted the production and distribution of some sports events, so the national sports in the north of China also followed such a rule under this specific circumstance. Northern China is suitable for animal husbandry because it is rich in aquatic products, but has less farmland; as a result, the ancient people in this area mainly engaged in animal husbandry. In addition, the northern part of China is a cross-region from the temperate zone to the frigid zone, the winter is long, and the climate is relatively bad. As a consequence, this environment determines people's way of living, and forms of their activities, resulting in different coping experiences and feelings of life, further contributing to the major differences in thinking mode, psychological quality, cognitive ability, and concept. Most ethnic groups living and prospering here have a strong physique and no fear of hardship, attach importance to martial arts, and excel at hunting, riding, and shooting.

According to the regional features, the ancient northern nationalities created a lot of ethnic sports with significant regional characteristics. For example, mounted archery is a typical example of a national sport. In the north, animal husbandry was the main means of production, animals serving the most abundant production materials as well as the most powerful ways of transportation or labor. In particular, the domestication of a large number of horses ensured the development of mounted archery in northern ethnic groups. In addition, the vast grassland also created favorable conditions for horse training. However, there is no such geographical environment in southern China, so it is impossible for equestrian culture to develop rapidly. Even in the north, there exist some differences in equestrian culture in different regions. For example, the horses in Mongolia are specialized in speed or endurance, and they often run horses in competitions. Still, in Northwest China, equestrian culture pays more attention to the performance of skills or interesting folk activities apart from speed and endurance. Therefore, there are a diversity of horse-skills performances often seen, such as running horses to pick up Yuanbao or Hada, horse wrestling, and other activities such as girl chasing and goat holding. Also, in some desert areas in the north, the ethnic groups in this region must rely on camels to carry materials or use them to and from the desert. Therefore, the unique regional sports culture of camel racing has emerged.

In short, the emergence and formation of ancient northern national sports are affected by some unique and specific factors. The interaction of various factors can not only bring up the cultural advantages of national sports but also inevitably lead to the corresponding value paradox and irrationality. Although some cultures were reasonable and rational at that time, with the development and change of society, they gradually revealed some sense of irrationality. The ancient northern national sports are just a case in point. Due to the influence of politics, the economic system, and feudal culture at that time, the national sports produced and formed in slave society and feudal society must have corresponding characteristics of the times, such as unfair, entertaining, ceremonial, and so on. Now they have turned out to be the shackles of the progress of contemporary sports and modern people. In the Tang and Song Dynasties, the development of the polo of the ancient northern nationalities was so brilliant, yet it was abandoned later. Why? The discussion of such issues and the factors affecting the progress of ancient northern national sports are not only beneficial to the choice of the direction for the Chinese contemporary traditional national sports, but also to the transformation of national sports as well as the formation of a new sports environment.

NOTES

1. [Qing] Wang Xianshen, *Interpretation of Han Feizi's Collection*, proofread by Zhong Zhe, vol. 19, 1st ed. (Zhonghua Book Company, July 1998), 442–443.
2. [Russia] Plekhanov, *Anthologies of Plekhanov's Aesthetics*, translated by Cao Baohua (People's Publishing House, 1983).
3. *Lü's Spring and Autumn Annals*, collated and annotated by Chen Qiyou, vol. 5, 1st ed. (Xue Lin Publishing House, April 1984), 284.
4. [Jin] Ge Hong, proofread by [Ming] Cheng Yi, *Miscellanies of the Western Capital*, 1st ed. (Zhonghua Book Company, January 1985), 20.
5. Li Xueqin, ed., *Yu Dian*, vol. 3 of *Rectified Interpretation of the "Book of History"* in *Notes to the Thirteen Classics*, 1st ed. (Peking University Press, December 1999), 79–80.
6. Dong Meikan, *A Brief History of Chinese Drama* (The Commercial Press, 1950), 8–9.
7. [Qing] Qin Jiamo et al., *Eight Kinds of World Books*, annotated by Song Zhong, 1st ed. (The Commercial Press, December 1957), 38.
8. [Liang] Zong Lin, *Records of Jinchu Age · The First Secret Collection of Baoyan Hall*, 9; *A New Edition of Series Collection*, vol. 91 (Taipei Xin Wen Feng Publishing Company, 1985), 180.
9. Shanxi Team, Institute of Archaeology, Chinese Academy of Social Sciences, Shanxi Provincial Institute of Archaeology, and Linfen Municipal Bureau of Cultural Relics, "Excavation Report of Large-scale Building Foundation Site of Sacrifice Community in Taosi City Site, Xiangfen County, Shanxi Province," *Archaeology*, no. 7 (2004): 17.
10. Institute of Archaeology, Chinese Academy of Social Sciences, *Baoji Beishouling* (Cultural Relics Publishing House, 1983), 68.
11. Marx and Engels, *Selected Works of Marx and Engels*, vol. 4 (People's Publishing House, 1972), 19.
12. [USSR] М. Ильин and Е. Сегал, *How Man Becomes a Giant*, translated by Shizhi (San Lian Publishing House, 1950), 142.
13. [Song] Li Jingde, ed., *Quotations from Zhu Zi*, proofread by Wang Xingxian, vol. 23, 1st ed. (Zhonghua Book Company, March 1986), 556.
14. Shao Ying, "Archaeological Research on the Forms of Ancient Chinese Inscriptions" (Shaanxi Normal University, 2006), 9–35.
15. *Lü's Spring and Autumn Annals*, vol. 5, collated and annotated by Chen Qiyou, 1st ed. (Xue Lin Publishing House, April 1984), 284.
16. He Ning, *A Collection of Notes on Huainanzi*, vol. 11, 1st ed. (Zhonghua Book Company, October 1998), 793.
17. The time recorded in the ancient northern rock paintings in China ranges from the ancient time to the Ming and Qing Dynasties. This section mainly refers to the conclusions formed by various works or papers on the study of the age of the rock paintings, and selects works that reflect the less productive time of each nationality or region, which are of great help to the research on the origin and budding state of sports for the ancient northern groups.

18. Li Xiangshi and Zhu Cunshi, *Helan Mountain and Beishan Rock Paintings* (Ningxia People's Publishing House, 1993), 240–245.
19. Gai Shanlin, *Yinshan Rock Paintings* (Cultural Relics Publishing House, December 1988).
20. Zhang Songbai and Liu Zhiyi, "Investigation Report of Rock Paintings in Baichahe Basin, Inner Mongolia," *Cultural Relics*, no. 2 (1984): 70–76. They believe that the rock painting of Baichahe continued for a long time, and their upper limit may be related to the lower Xiajiadian culture in this area.
21. Sima Qian, *Book of Music*, vol. 24 of *Historical Records*, 1st ed. (Zhonghua Book Company, September 1959), 1214.
22. Li Xueqin, ed., *Yu Dian*, vol. 3 of *Rectified Interpretation of the "Book of History"* in *Notes to the Thirteen Classics*, 1st ed. (Peking University Press, December 1999), 79–80.
23. Li Xiangshi, "Rock Paintings of Helan Mountain in Ningxia," *Cultural Relics*, no. 2 (1987): 61–65.
24. Tang Huisheng and Zhang Wenhua, *Rock Paintings in Qinghai: A Study of Binary Opposition Thinking and Its Concept in Prehistoric Art*, 1st ed. (Science Press, 2001). Other rock art images of Gansu and Qinghai were also mainly collected from this work.
25. Gansu Institute of Cultural Relics and Archaeology, "Ten Years of Cultural Relics and Archaeology in Gansu Province," in *Ten Years of Cultural Relics and Archaeology* (Cultural Relics Publishing House, 1991).
26. Gansu Provincial Museum, "Ancient Rock Paintings in Black Mountain, Jiayuguan, Gansu Province," *Archaeology*, no. 4 (1990): 344–359.
27. Chen Zhaofu, *Ancient Chinese Minority Art* (People's Fine Arts Publishing House, 1991), 2.
28. Sun Jingchen, *History of Chinese Dance (Pre-Qin)* (Culture and Art Press, 1983), 14.
29. Su Beihai, *Xinjiang Rock Paintings*, 1st ed. (Xinjiang Fine Arts Photography Press, November 1994). The images of the Xinjiang section were mainly collected from this book.
30. Hu Bangzhu, "Rock Paintings in Kuluke Mountains," *Xinjiang Art*, no. 1 (1984): 17–23.
31. Marx and Engels, *Selected Works of Marx and Engels*, vol. 4 (People's Publishing House, 1972), 88.
32. [German] Ludwig Feuerbach, *Selected Works of Feuerbach Philosophy*, translated by Rong Zhenhua (The Commercial Press, 1984).
33. Yang Jinxiang, "Several Messages from Xinjiang Rock Paintings," *Xinjiang Art*, no. 1 (1987): 42–44.
34. [Qing] Chen Li, *Rite and Music*, vol. 3 of *Notes on Bai Hu Tong*, proofread by Wu Zeyu, 1st ed. (Zhonghua Book Company, August 1994), 95–96.
35. [Han] Sima Qian, *Biography of Xiongnu*, vol. 110 of *Historical Records*, 1st ed. (Zhonghua Book Company, September 1959), 2879.
36. Marx, *A Contribution to the Critique of Political Economy* (People's Publishing House, 1995).
37. Marx, "The Emergence of Capitalist Land Rent · Land Rent II," Chapter 47 in *Capital*, vol. 3, 1st ed. (People's Publishing House, June 1975), 892.

CHAPTER II

Initial Development of the National Sports in Ancient Northern China

THIS PERIOD MAINLY REFERS TO THE time from the Pre-Qin to the Southern and Northern Dynasties. Major ethnic groups include Buyeo, Goguryeo, Sushen, Yilou, Wuji, Xiongnu, Wuhuan, Xianbei, and some other ethnic groups of Western Regions. With the growth of social productivity, more and more types of sports activities took their shape in this period, forming the initial development period of sports activities in the northern ethnic groups of ancient China.

2.1 Sports Activities of Buyeo and Goguryeo

2.1.1 Sports Activities of Buyeo

Among the ancient ethnic groups in the hinterland of northeast China, Buyeo was one of the pioneers in establishing a regime.[1] Buyeo, in its glorious age, was close to Zhangguangcai Mountain and bordered Yilou in the east, which ranged from Shuangliao County to Baicheng City, Jilin Province in the west, reached Songnen Plain to the south of Lesser Khingan Mountains in the north, and extended to the north of Kaiyuan County, Liaoning Province in the south. Its center sat in Nong'an County, Jilin Province.

During the Han Dynasties, politics, economy, and culture of Buyeo were considerably developed. Politically, the clan system had been replaced by the regime organization. An army of more than 20,000 soldiers had been established, consisting of cavalries and infantries who were wholly armed with bows, arrows, swords, and spears. The social economy was comprised of two major production sectors: agriculture and animal husbandry, with agriculture serving the leading role. In terms of culture, the Buyeo people worshiped heaven in the first month of the Yin Calendar (the twelfth lunar month of the Han Dynasty), which was called Yinggu, the most solemn festival of the year when people dined and danced for days. Before military activities, they would offer sacrifices to heaven in order to predict whether the battle would succeed. The sports activities of the Buyeo were developed based on the social production, military, witchcraft, and festival activities described above.

Historical records show some evidence of the sports activities of Buyeo, such as "Dongming was good at shooting after grow-up. The king was jealous of his vigor and intended to kill him. Dongming escaped south to Yanshui River and struck the water with his bow. All the fish and turtles gathered and floated on the water. Dongming took the opportunity to cross the river. Finally, he went to Buyeo and crowned himself as the king." The historical record mentioned above depicts the legend of the founding of Buyeo. When Dongming grew up, he specialized in shooting, even shooting fish. Such skill is not innate and should require constant training. Buyeo people lived in flat land in the middle of the north branch of the Songhua River. They relied on farming and animal husbandry in the place which was famous for fine horses. They used bows, arrows, knives, and spears as weapons and were also good at singing and dancing. The historical record is described as follows, "Buyeo was located in the downstream areas of Yellow River Basin, where land was flat and open, and the soil was suitable for cereals. This place was also rich in fine horses, red jades, martens, monkeys, and pearls as big as wild jujubes; it was emplaced with palisades where there were palaces, warehouses, and prisons. Men were tough, strong, and brave, but careful and kind, never committing invading or plundering. They used bows, arrows, knives, and spears as weapons … Buyeo people worshiped heaven in the twelfth lunar month, which was called Yinggu, and celebrated for several days with food and music. At this point, criminal cases were decided, and the prisoners were released. There were also military sacrifices to heaven, in which soldiers killed cows and foretold good and bad luck with cow hoofs. Besides, people were keen on singing, and the sound of music was constant day and night."[2] Only from the literature recorded can we see that Buyeo people also did activities like hunting, training with horses and weapons, sports, and dancing of their own culture, while getting engaged in agricultural production.

2.1.2 Sports Activities of Goguryeo

Before the establishment of the Goguryeo State by Zhu Meng, the Goguryeo people were distributed as clans and tribes in the region from Xinbin Manchu Autonomous County in Liaoning Province to Ji'an County in Jilin Province. The Goguryeo State was established in 37 BC (the second year of the Jianzhao Period in the Western Han Dynasty). It was the second ancient clan to establish a state regime after Buyeo of the Huimo ethnic group. According to the legend, Zhu Meng, the founder of the Goguryeo clan, was born in Buyeo; when he was seven years old, he could shoot in unfailing accuracy with his self-made bows and arrows. Therefore, he was labeled the name "Zhu Meng" (literally meaning "good at archery" in the Buyeo language).[3] This legend indicates that the ancestors of the Goguryeo clan were good archers. Upon the state's founding, for the sake of development, Zhu Meng adopted a policy of expansion by annexing neighboring clans of the same ethnic group; shortly after the founding of the state, Zhu Meng personally visited the Feiliu State (located in the basin of the present-day Fu'er River) to display his might by shooting and archery, thereby forcing Song Rang, the king of the Feiliu State, to "surrender with his state" the following year. Later on, monarchs and vassals launched attacks again, demonstrating the courage and skill of the Goguryeo clan in the warfare. Fishing and hunting played an important role in the early social production of Goguryeo, too. In the early days, the Goguryeo people lived in the mountainous regions of the Hunjiang River Basin, where the land was scarce and barren, and hunting was a necessity to supplement their food and clothing, despite their efforts to cultivate the land. The Goguryeo people always valued hunting because it served two ends. King Shanshang (reigned from AD 197 to AD 227) was just such a good hunter "skilled at riding and shooting."[4] The livestock industry of Goguryeo was well-known in the Central Plains for the breeding of three-foot horses ideal for mountain climbing. The hunting picture unearthed at the Dance-themed Mound in Ji'an County of Jilin (see Fig. 2-1) illustrates the riding and shooting activities they were engaged in. This is a mural on the left wall of the main room in the Dance-themed Mound, which was built between the mid-3rd and mid-4th centuries in the Goguryeo period. In the upper right of the picture, a horseman is turning his head with his bow fully bent to shoot a running deer, and in the lower right of the picture, there are two horsemen in front of the mountain, with arrow cases hanging from their waists, galloping their horses and shooting a tiger with their bows. The picture reproduced the real hunting activities of Goguryeo.

Fig. 2-1 Hunting Picture of Goguryeo

The cultural customs of Goguryeo feature both their own ethnic characteristics and the influence of the Han ethnic culture. Though they had their own language, they did not have their own characters. Thus, they borrowed Chinese characters. According to *Historical Records of the Three Kingdoms*, in AD 372 (the second year under the reign of King Xiaoshoulin), the central government of the state "… established the Imperial College to educate the children."[5] Since then, reading became popular among the people of Goguryeo, and Jiong Halls (a type of large hall) were established in various places, where unmarried people had to study and practice archery. Apart from the *Five Classics*, other Han books were also imported, such as *Historical Records, Book of the Former Han Dynasty, Book of the Later Han Dynasty, Records of the Three Kingdoms,*

The Jin State in the Spring and Autumn Period, Yupian Dictionary, Zitong Dictionary, and *Zilin Dictionary*. In particular, *The Selected Works* compiled by Xiao Tong of the Liang Dynasty was the most favored one.[6] In the process of embracing the Han culture, the Goguryeo people, while incorporating their own local characteristics, also embraced Han sports culture, such as wrestling and mounted archery described in the historical records. According to such literature, there were sporting activities such as **mounted archery, beast fighting**, wrestling, *Tiaowan* (ball acrobatism), and wheel dancing, among which the latter two were obviously rooted in the Central Plains.

2.2 Sports Activities of Sushen, Yilou, and Wuji Clans

2.2.1 Sports Activities of Sushen and Yilou

The Sushen clan lived in the northeast near present-day Ning'an County, Heilongjiang Province. During the reign of Emperor Shun, there had already been the name of Sushen. As recorded in the *Historical Records · Chronicles of Five Emperors*, "**The territory of Emperor Shun covered five thousand** *li* (unit of distance, equal to 500 m) into the remote wild ... And to Shanrong, Fa, and Xishen in the north."[7] "Xishen" here was just Sushen. Yilou was the second clan name used by the **Sushen clan following the first name of Sushen. The Sushen people were off-springs of** Yilou, followed by other nationalities such as Wuji and Mohe. Generally, they were called Wuji in the Southern and Northern Dynasties, and Mohe in the Sui and Tang Dynasties.[8]

The Sushen people mainly lived on hunting while also beginning to live a more stable, primitive agricultural life with domesticated livestock. Sushen had connections with the dynasties in Central Plains in the early days, as recorded in the *Book of the Later Han Dynasty*, "When King Wu conquered King Zhou, Sushen came to pay tributes with stone arrowheads and thorn arrows."[9] As recorded in the *Historical Records*, "A falcon was shot and killed at the royal court of the Chen State. A thorn arrow of 1 *chi* and 8 *cun* long with a stone head penetrated its body (*chi* and *cun*, ancient Chinese units of length; 1 *chi* is equal to 33.33 cm, while 1 *cun* is equal to 3.33 cm). **King Min of Chen State sent someone to consult Confucius, who replied, 'This falcon came from afar, and the arrow was from Sushen.'** After Emperor Wu of the Zhou State conquered the Shang Dynasty, connections with various minorities were established. And ethnic groups from all directions were asked to pay tributes with their local specialties so that they would not forget **their duties and obligations. Therefore, the Sushen clan just offered the arrows of** 1 *chi* and 8 *cun* **with stone arrowheads. To highlight his great virtues, Emperor Wu gifted the arrows to his eldest daughter Daji. Later on, Daji married Duke Yuhu, whose manor was in Chen."**[10] According to both literature above, we can conclude that Sushen had a vassal relationship and frequent contact with the Zhou Dynasty, and Sushen's stone-head arrows were famous, indicating that Sushen had reached a certain level of skill in archery. Requirements for archery were particularly strict during the **Zhou Dynasty, and the ritual of archery was prevalent. Emperor Wu surprisingly gifted** Sushen's **arrows to his officials, indicating that** Sushen's archery level was also extraordinary, which exerted some impact on the Zhou Dynasty.

Yilou clan is said to have first appeared in the 1–2 century BC (Western Han Dynasty). According to *Biography of Yilou* in all historical records, "Yilou had already existed since the Han Dynasty, and it belonged to Buyeo." The activity area of the Yilou people was roughly the same as that in the time of Sushen, except that the southwest part was slightly reduced due to the invasion by the Buyeo people. The economy of Yilou included fishing, hunting, agriculture, animal husbandry, and handicrafts. Hunting and fishing still played a vital part in the social economy, with wild animals in the mountains and forests, and fish in rivers and lakes, remaining a key aspect of food sources. According to some literature and archaeological findings, the tribes that lived in the deep forests were mainly hunter-gatherers, while for the inhabitants of the areas around the rivers and lakes, fishing was the main production. Since these areas belonged to the sites of the Yilou period, "fish bones" were the most found among the various kinds of bone fragments with burn marks, and the pottery net pendants excavated were "prominent."[11]

The hunting tools for the Yilou people were still primarily bows and "thorn arrows with stone heads." Their bows were 4 *chi* long and as powerful as crossbows, and thorn arrows of 8 *cun* long with stone heads. They were passed down from the Sushen State. Yilou people were skilled at archery and would shoot into the eyes of the targets. The arrows were applied with poison so that all those who were hit would be killed without exception."[12] People of **Yilou often practiced** archery, so that their archery skills were superb without any missing. As recorded in the *Book of the Jin Dynasty*, "A Yilou person of the Sushen clan had the stone-head arrows, armor made of skins and bones, carrying a sandalwood bow of 3 *chi* and 5 *cun*. And the length of the stone-head arrows was about 1 *chi* and 5 *cun*. In the northeast of the state, there was a mountain producing stones as sharp as iron. Whenever people mined the stones, they would pray to the gods first."[13] It was also recorded that "Mahan people were brave in nature. When the nation called for active service or labor force, the young and powerful guys would carry huge loads on their backs without feeling pain. They were skilled at archery and defense. Though they would have to fight, they loved peace and generally believed in supernatural beings. Whenever they finished planting in May, they would gather together to dance for the worship of the gods. They also did so in October when the farming was done … Huihan State had similar customs to those of Mahan and shared the same weapons."[14] As recorded in the *General Review of Literature*, "Though Yilou people were small in number, most of whom were brave. They lived in the arduous mountains and were skilled at archery. Their bows were 4 *chi* long and as powerful as crossbows. Thorn arrows of 8 *cun* long with stone heads were used. The arrows were applied with poison so that all those who were hit would be killed without exception. The neighboring states were afraid of their bows and arrows but could not conquer them. And they looted neighboring states by boats from time to time, which resulted in the great panic and tension upon them."[15] In comparison with the Sushen period, the "stone arrowheads" made by the Yilou people were greatly improved and developed, which was not only reflected in the fact that all those that were hit would be killed by "the poisoned arrows" with no exception. In addition, we also found some round collar double-winged stone arrowheads imitating the metal tools as well as three-pronged bone arrowheads in the Dongkang site of Ning'an County about 1,700 years ago.[16] Yilou people raised horses "not for riding, but as their properties."[17] And they used horses to exchange for other things. "Yilou Mink," which was famous in history, reflected the fact that ferrets were hunted for their skins in order to pay tributes to the Central Plains and to exchange them with the inhabitants of the Central Plains or neighboring people. It was recorded in history that Yilou came to the Central Plains to pay tributes six times,[18] for example, in AD 262 (the third year of Jingyuan under the reign of **Cao Wei**). **Yillou offered tributes to Cao Wei with 30 bows of the state level, 300 stone arrowheads, 20 armors made of leather, bone, and iron, and 400 pieces of ferret furs. And Emperor Wei rewarded the "chicken, fabrics and silks" in return.**[19] Another example was that in AD 319 (the second year of Daxing), Yilou sent envoys to Eastern Jin with thorn arrows of stone heads,[20] which demonstrated the strength of Yilou's thorn arrows with stone arrowheads, the excellence of their manufacture as well as their high level of archery skills.

Nets and hooks were the main means of fishing for the Yilou people. They had become proficient in fishing methods such as netting and hooking. A large number of stone net pendants, together with fishnet clips and fine fish hooks, were unearthed from the site of Yilou. All the earthenware was handmade, and all the utensils necessary for daily life were manufactured, including pots, urns, basins, bowls, cups, stemmed cups, and pottery net pendants for fishing, which were unearthed at the same site.[21] As recorded in history, Yilou people were full of "courage and power," all wearing braids, who highly valued the young while looking down upon the old. With their excellent skills in boating and archery, they conducted unbridled attacks against the weak North Woju, who lived in the Tumen River basin with a relatively small number of people. As a consequence, North Woju people often had to hide in deep caves in order to protect themselves from the attacks, and only returned back to the villages in winter when the rivers froze over.[22] The description of "skilled at boating" indicated that the Yilou people had mastered the techniques of shipbuilding; however, the shapes and methods of manufacturing were still unknown. The workmanship of stone and bone tools had improved considerably compared with that in the time of Sushen. In addition to the round double-winged stone arrowheads imitating the metal tools, three-pronged bone arrowheads as well as stone knives mentioned above, they could also make armors with skin, bone, and iron.

2.2.2 Sports Activities of Wuji

The word "Wuji" literally means "deep mountain and old forest," which was used as a variation of the ancient Chinese character for the **Manchu language "Woji."** The name was given to the clan people who scattered in the deep mountain and dense forest to hunt for a living.[23] The social production of Wuji and Mohe made great strides compared to that of the Yilou period; however, in most areas, it represented merely some increase in quantity which had not yet reached the level enough to trigger social change.[24] Hunting was still one of the social productions on which they depended for survival, and was of greater importance in the northern and northeastern areas. Horned bows and thorn arrows were employed as their hunting tools as well as combat weapons. To enhance the lethality of their bows and arrows and to hunt giant beasts with large skins, thick furs, and meaty flesh, they used to "**produce poisons every July and August and apply them on arrows to shoot.**" The hunting activities of the Wuji at that time were different from the primitive hunting activities, with the greater purpose of conducting exchanges. Of the small beasts they hunted, the ferrets were most valued. In order to hunt more ferrets, Wuji people had a custom, in which it was said that if their parents died in autumn or winter, their bodies would be used as baits to "catch ferrets."[25] The ferret is a small, fur-trimmed animal, and for the relatively unproductive Wuji people, the ferret did not matter much in satisfying daily demands, but was more likely to be exchanged with or paid tribute to the Central Plains. To make the ferret furs more intact and thus more valuable, they must then improve their hunting skills, enhance their archery or capture training, and improve their archery accuracy as well as their ability to capture quickly and swiftly. As recorded in the *Book of the Wei Dynasty*, "People in the Wuji State were capable and vigorous ... who were skilled at archery. Their bows were 3 *chi* long, and their arrows were 2 *cun* long with stone heads."[26] As recorded in the *History of the Northern Dynasties*, "The Wuji State was occupied with thousands of capable soldiers who were courageous and daring. Particularly for the Heishui Tribe, all the arrows were equipped with stone heads, and everyone was skilled at archery and mainly relied on hunting." It could be seen that hunting was a necessity of their lives as well as an important part of the folk culture of their people.

The development of handicrafts in Wuji was also notable, with the manufacture of carriages and boats being the most prominent, and boats had been relatively used as common watercraft at that time. When Wuji's envoys paid tributes to the Northern Wei, a journey from its territory to the Taoer River was just covered by boats. As Yilizhi mentioned in Northern Wei, they had already discussed with Paekje that they were going to "conquer Goguryeo through waterways and by force," indicating that they already had ships that could transport a large staff within their territory.[27] People in Wuji were also able to process iron products, for example, iron adzes, knives, iron arrowheads, and iron band cards that were unearthed from the lower layer culture of the Suibin Tongren Site in Heilongjiang Province, which was found to be equivalent to those in the Wuji period.[28] At sites such as the Great Haimeng in Yongji County, Jilin Province, which belong to the remains of the Mohe clan, some iron weapons along with production tools were discovered, including knives, swords, daggers, spears, arrowheads, armors, harnesses, axes, adzes, etc.[29]

2.3 Sports Activities of Xiongnu

Xiongnu was an important ancient nomadic ethnic group in northern China. It originated in the area around Hetao and Daqing Mountains in today's Inner Mongolia Autonomous Region. During the Pre-Qin and Qin and Han Dynasties, the culture of Xiongnu was typical of northern nomadic steppe culture. During the Qin and Han Dynasties, Xiongnu established a strong slave regime, centered on "Touman City"[30] (which belonged to Chouyang County, Wuyuan Prefecture in the Han Dynasty and is now located in Baotou City, Inner Mongolia Autonomous Region) by Touman Chanyu, chief of Xiongnu at that time. This indicated that such northern nomads had made the transition from the military-democratic stage at the end of primitive society to the early stage of slavery. During the Qin and Han Dynasties, Xiongnu often launched wars against the Han regime and occasionally prevailed, signifying that Xiongnu had excellency in fighting tactics and techniques, which were inseparable from their training.

Archaeologists have found a great heap of stone, bone, and iron arrowheads in the northern, southern, and eastern regions of Mount Tianshan and the vast areas of the Altai Mountains, which not only proved the history of the use of bow and arrow by the ancestors but also provided some physical information for us to study the evolution of early bows and arrows. A number of rock paintings that depicted the hunting of Xiongnu, Turks, and Serbs using bows and arrows in ancient times have also been found in the southern foothills of the Karakorum and the Nilka County. According to related studies, these rock paintings could be dated from 3,000 to 5,000 years ago. More than 500 rock paintings have been found in Baishi Mountain, 3 kilometers east of Qincheng Town in Hami City, and rock paintings engraved on boulders have also been discovered in Zheyaogou, 12 kilometers southeast away. These rock paintings contain many images of archery, vividly reproducing the hunting and fighting scenes of the ancestors at that time. One of them is a lifelike picture of shooting a bow against a wild camel. According to the scientists, these rock paintings took their shape before Christ, indicating that Xiongnu had already started using bows and arrows earlier, and had sports activities like archery at that time. The following is an overview of the development of Xiongnu sports in three aspects.

First is the military organization of Xiongnu. The political system and organization of the ethnic group formed the basis for all political, military, and civil activities. Their most basic function was to direct and guide the actions and direction of ethnic groups, and it was within this framework that many policies and political objectives were implemented. The northern people evolved in their early development as a family unit, which progressed to clans, tribes, and tribal alliances later on. It was in this process of organizational refinement that the Northern ethnic groups evolved and grew, leading to the progress of the ethnic culture. Especially with the gradual refinement of such political and organizational forms, the ruling class was able to practice its strategy to a greater advantage, resulting in some indelible effects on the development of ethnic sports. As described in the *Historical Records*, Xiongnu could be endowed with a *hu* of wine (*hu*, an ancient drinking vessel) if they took the heads of their enemies in battle; besides, the spoils of war and goods they plundered would be their belongings, and the captured or plundered population would become their slaves. Such an incentive policy would definitely encourage a number of people to train hard and fight bravely; hence there was the saying, "A child can ride a sheep, shoot birds and mice with a bow, and when he becomes a young man, he can shoot birds and rabbits on which they could feed themselves. All the adult men can draw the bow and ride the horse with armor."[31] We can draw the conclusion that this aggressive training and growth of the Xiongnu cavalry force had much to do with the policy orientation of Xiongnu. The social organization systems of the northern ancient ethnic groups, such as Wangting (Ruling Center) of the Xiongnu, Meng'an Mouke (military establishment units) and Four-Season Nobo Institution of the Khitan, Meng'an Mouke of the Jurchen and the Eight Banner System of the Manchu, provided the political guarantees for the development of the sports.

The Ruling Center (Wangting) of Xiongnu was both an administrative organization and a military commander, with jurisdiction over pastoral production as well as a commanding function in warfare. The skillful riding skills of Xiongnu were accomplished under this organization, which also included the training of people of all ages in riding and shooting. The armies of Xiongnu were basically pure cavalry units that were equipped with much weaponry based on the demands of mounted archery. With these weapons, Wangting and its subordinate organizations would necessarily arrange corresponding training. For example, Modu Chanyu would lead the people in mounted archery training with the whistling arrow or apply lasso method in the battle, all of which must be trained regularly. Such activities were carried out under the organization of the Ruling Center of Xiongnu, which was employed in battle in the time of urgency or in casual folklore as part of the sports activities of Xiongnu. Although "the total population of Xiongnu was even fewer than one county of the Han Dynasty," Xiongnu, by virtue of its great military power and state machinery, not only conquered tribes, states, and peoples by force such as Dingling, Wusun, Donghu, Loulan, and Hujie, but also directed its attacks directly at the affluent Central Plains inland, and continuously invaded the central government of the Han Dynasty. Such a strong **military force could not have been achieved without the benefits of military construction.** The structure of Xiongnu regime was divided into three parts: the core part was the Chanyu Court, which served as the main body of the state headed by Chanyu himself, who had direct jurisdiction over the central part of the area where **Xiongnu people were active.** The **center of power was near** Yinshan Mountain in the present-day Inner Mongolia Autonomous Region bordered to the south by the Dai County (present Wei County, Hebei Province) and Yunzhong County (around present Togtoh County, Inner Mongolia) of the Han Dynasty. Second in power only to Chanyu was the **Left/Right King of Sage. The Left King of Sage was responsible for ruling the eastern territory of the** Xiongnu, which was bordered to the south by the Shanggu County of the Han Dynasty (present Huailai County, Hebei Province) and to the east by the Huimo **ethnic group.** The **Right King of** Sage was responsible for ruling the western territory of the Xiongnu, which was bordered to the south by the Shang County outskirt of the Han Dynasty (around present Yulin County, Shaanxi Province) and to the west by ethnic groups such as the Yuezhi, Qiang, and Di of the Qin-Han times. The areas ruled by Chanyu as well as the Left/Right Kings of Sage, formed both the political divisions of **Xiongnu and the construction of military organizations.** The entire society of Xiongnu was a huge barrack of soldiers living among the people, with cavalry as the mainstream of Xiongnu armies. As explicated in the *Book of the Later Han Dynasty*, "When excellent cavalrymen engaged in the wild, arrows were shot; the northern minorities were skilled at riding and shooting, which were short of by the army of Central Plains."[32] This **indicated that the** Xiongnu were quite adept at **mounted archery, which manifests a significant difference between the military culture of** Xiongnu and that of the Central Plains.

Modu Chanyu set up a political and military institution of certain levels according to the actual situation of the area under his jurisdiction and **Xiongnu society. To be specific: The Left/Right Kings of Sage, Left/Right Kings of Military and Administration, Left/Right Senior Generals, Left/ Right Senior Commandants, Left/Right Ministers, and Left/Right Courtiers were established from top to bottom under Chanyu. Cavalrymen were assigned to different levels, from Left/Right Kings of Sage to Left/Right Ministers in different numbers from ten thousand to several thousand. And the chief administrating the 24 ten-thousand cavalry troops was called "Chief of Ten-thousand Cavalry …" The Left/Right Kings of Sage and Left/Right Kings of Military and Administration had the top authorities. The Left/Right Courtiers assisted in the administration of the regime.** In addition, different official ranks were established under the 24 Chiefs of Ten-thousand Cavalry.[33] With such an integrated form of military-political organization, the vast civilians of Xiongnu society were, on the one hand, direct participants in productive labor and, on the other hand, to be organized into "armored cavalry" as members of the state army organization. Generally, civilians herded cattle and migrated for water and grass, living a life of nomadic pastoralism characteristic of the steppe culture, and in case of war, they would mount their horses and go into battle, becoming a powerful fighting force of Xiongnu army. The form and method of the military organization of Xiongnu had a profound influence on the northern steppes of China, and certain nomadic ethnic groups in later times imitated and inherited this institution to form their armies, such as the Mongolian army in the 13th century, which was organized according to the standards of ten, hundred, thousand and ten thousand men.

Second is the military equipment and mounted archery of Xiongnu. Iron weapons formed an important part of the military equipment of Xiongnu. According to the *Historical Records*, Xiongnu was able to produce their own iron weaponry around the 3rd century BC. In recent decades, archaeologists have unearthed in Xiongnu burials a large number of iron relics from Xiongnu era, such as iron harnesses, iron arrowheads, iron knives, iron swords, and iron smelting furnaces, which dated back to around the 3rd century BC or the time between the 3rd and 1st century BC.[34] The utilization of iron wares energized Xiongnu culture and contributed to the advancement of social productivity. Based upon some documents and archaeological excavations, bronze casting and iron manufacturing played a significant role in Xiongnu society. During the reign of Emperor Yuan of the Han Dynasty, Hou Ying, a military strategist, reported the situation of Xiongnu to the Han Dynasty, saying that Modu Chanyu, in the area of Yinshan, "made bows and arrows and attacked as bandits."[35] Iron appliances had penetrated multiple areas of Xiongnu society, covering iron arrowheads, iron swords, iron knives, etc., which were produced in large quantities. According to *Book of the Former Han Dynasty · Biography of Xiongnu*, Xiongnu once produced a treasured sword called "Jinglu." It was also recorded in history that Deng Zun, a great general of the Han Dynasty, defeated the army of Xiongnu, and captured "three thousand daggers."[36] This confirmed that the dagger could be one of the most commonly worn weapons and equipment of Xiongnu army.

When fighting, Xiongnu cavalrymen would wear protective armors. *Book of the Former Han Dynasty · Biography of Chen Tang* recorded that Zhizhi, Chanyu of Xiongnu, wore armor in the fighting. *Book of the Former Han Dynasty* also covered the wood manufacturing industry of Xiongnu as follows, "All excellent arrows were shot at the same time targeting the same aim, even the Gesi (leather armor) or Mujian (wooden shield) cannot stop them." (Note: Mujian is "a kind of protective tool like wooden shields.") And Gesi is "something protecting the body made of leather as armor," as marked by Meng Kang.[37] Therefore, it could be seen that Xiongnu already knew how to process the leather of livestock and build armor as well as other protective equipment. In addition to the soft armor made of leather, Xiongnu also produced iron fish-scale armor. Based on the gold eagle-shaped crown and crown belt ornaments unearthed at Aluchaideng, 40 kilometers southeast of the Hangwei Banner in the Inner Mongolia Autonomous Region, it is assumed that Xiongnu should have used helmets for protection in battle. Such physical protection measures have been passed down from generation to generation and then adapted to sports, such as fencing, Taekwondo, and martial arts.

Bows and arrows were the main military equipment of Xiongnu. When describing the weapons of Xiongnu, *Historical Records · Biography of Xiongnu* pointed out that "the long weapons of Xiongnu were bows and swords, and the short ones were the sword and iron spears."[38] The nobles and high-ranking military generals of Xiongnu also used a kind of arrow called Mingdi (whistling arrow); when a Mingdi was shot, it would make a sound, and thus commonly called the "Whistling Arrow." According to historical records, Modu, Chanyu of Xiongnu, once commanded the cavalry with whistling arrows in the battles.[39] Mingdi was not only of great significance during the Xiongnu period, but also passed down among the northern ethnic groups in ancient times. For example, the method of making Mingdi was recorded in the *Divan lgat at-Turk*, and the arrows were made and used by the northern ethnic groups until the Mongolian period.

In 1959, a burial tomb of a husband and wife was unearthed at the Site of Niya, Hotan (in the hinterland of the Taklamakan), with the accompanying bows, arrows, and arrow bags in the wooden coffin. The arrows had bone heads. The bows and strings were quite well made, indicating that the manufacture of bows and arrows was advanced at that time. According to historical research and investigation, it was concluded that the tomb was dated back to around the 1st century AD. Buried bows and arrows were also excavated from the site of the ruins of Shaibae in Shamupur Town, Lopur County, Hotan, in 1984. Accordingly, the tomb was believed to date from about the 3rd century BC to the 3rd century AD (This bow and arrow are now preserved in the Xinjiang Autonomous Region Museum). This indicated that the production of bows and arrows had reached a relatively high level. As an indispensable tool and weapon for Xiongnu, this bow and arrow were therefore buried with the man as one of his most valued artifacts.

The cavalry generals of Xiongnu were also likely to extensively use the lassoes on the battlefield. It was presumed that the Hun horsemen often used lassoes when fighting against their enemies. They would pull out the woven lassoes to bind and capture the enemies. Such methods of fighting were still in use among the Kuaihu people, descendants of the Northern Xiongnu. The method of making and using the lasso was to "take the leather string as a rope, throw it at people while riding a horse, and get it hit with greater hunting possibility."[40] Li Guangli, a great general of the Han Dynasty, was captured by the Huns with a lasso during a battle against Xiongnu, and he escaped by breaking free and leaped away. The lasso was probably first invented from the capture of unacclimated horses and then used in military training. Such lassos of Xiongnu were passed down among the northern ethnic groups until the Yuan, Ming, and Qing Dynasties. They were employed not only in warfare or in livestock production, but also in sporting activities. For example, in Jiaotao activity (taming a horse of 3–4 years old) which was typical among the Mongolians, "for all fierce and tough horses, if they were unyielding at the beginning in the herd, the children of the dukes or princes would carry long poles and colored rope, manage to jump over, climb onto or overtake them, and finally domesticate them. The more outstanding the horse was, the more people would join in taming it. Both the horses and the men were agile and brave, and the scene was spectacular."[41] Such Mongol sporting culture was definitely influenced by the lasso of Xiongnu.

To facilitate the march across the river, Xiongnu armies also innovated transportation means such as leather boats, rafts, canoes, and Magesong. According to historians, Xiongnu artisans used horse skins to build boats to cross the river, whose name was "Magesong" (horse leather boat).[42] In the eighth year of Yongping Period (AD 65), Xubugu Duhou Chanyu of the Southern Xiongnu contacted the Northern Wei Dynasty, plotted to defect, and crossed the river. "In the autumn, the Northern Wei Dynasty deployed 2,000 cavalrymen on the northern bank. And the Southern Xiongnu made horse leather boats and planned to cross the Yellow River at Shuofang. However, the Han army was solid like iron, and they had no choice but to return."[43] This indicated that Xiongnu was also proficient in equipped swimming.

Xiongnu was also known for their horses, which were strong and capable of running for hundreds of miles a day, and some could even run for thousands of miles. Therefore, with their valuable horses, the strong and brave Xiongnu armored cavalry was invincible and unstoppable in battles. Beyond the battles, they also competed in horse races. Until today, the northern steppe people still have the custom of horse racing.

Xiongnu placed great emphasis on mounted archery training. The geographical environment and nomadic lifestyle of the northern part of the country determined that "people never slacken their bows and horses never release their leashes."[44] The warriors incorporated into the armored cavalry were even more fierce, strong, and courageous in battles. It was admitted that Xiongnu's military quality stayed at a higher level among the nomadic groups in the ancient northern part of the country, which was closely related to the regular mounted archery training of the Xiongnu. Mounted archery was taught to Xiongnu children at a very young age so that they had an excellent foundation. *Historical Records · Biography of Xiongnu* described Xiongnu custom in this way, "A child can ride a sheep, shoot birds and mice with a bow, and when he becomes a young man, he can shoot birds and rabbits on which they could feed themselves. All the adult men can draw the bow and ride the horse with armor." This means that Xiongnu placed great emphasis on training their children from an early age to enhance their physical and competitive skills. According to the historical records, the general assemblies of the various clans of Xiongnu were held in the first, fifth, and ninth months of the lunar year, which were known as "Three Sacrificial Ceremonies." In addition, Xiongnu often organized group hunting activities, both for the instinctive need to "shoot livestock for a living" and for the military training purpose of practicing riding and shooting of Xiongnu soldiers. Therefore, *Book of the Former Han Dynasty · Biography of Xiongnu* called this "practicing riding and shooting." Xiongnu also trained their horses in battle formation and tamed them for obedience in groups. In the war between the Han and Xiongnu, Xiongnu once resorted to a four-sided formation to suppress the Han forces. The cavalry of Xiongnu were all white horses in the west, all green horses in the east, all black horses in the north, and all red horses in the south.[45]

Xiongnu not only trained their people in terms of skills but also strengthened their psychological development in order to motivate them to achieve more military achievements. As described in the *Historical Records*, Xiongnu could be given a *hu* of wine (*hu*, an ancient drinking vessel) if they took the heads of their enemies in battle. Besides, the spoils of war and goods they plundered would be theirs, and the captured or plundered population would become their slaves. Therefore, during the Qin and Han Dynasties, Xiongnu was regarded as a powerful ethnic group by the Central Plains as a nation that "fought offensively."[46]

Then there were other sports activities of Xiongnu. By the time of Xiongnu, some of the ethnic groups in the north had shifted from a hunting economy to an animal husbandry economy. The ancient northern region geographically determined the mode of production and living of people, and the hunting economy played an important part in the survival and development of the ancient northern people. The hunting economy was a relatively common but backward form of economy for the northern groups, which imposed constraints on surplus production and strengthened the constant necessity of hunting to obtain subsistence. During this long process, the northern people practiced such basic forms of human physical movement as being good at shooting, running, and jumping or acquiring a special skill in animals. As people transitioned from a hunting economy to an animal husbandry economy, their understanding and utilization of the world changed dramatically. First, the process of animal husbandry reinforced people's knowledge of animals and their use, which was considered as the beginning of the mastery of animals by human beings, exerting a profound effect on the development of mounted archery in particular. Second, people had relatively free time and a stable place to live in the animal husbandry economy, which happened to have provided time and space for the creation and progress of national sports. Huns utilized their free time to formulate the most ethnically distinctive riding culture, as cited in some documents, including sporting activities like Jiao-Di (ancient wrestling), horse-riding, and camel-racing. As recorded in *Book of the Later Han Dynasty · Biography of the Southern Xiongnu*, "According to the customs of Xiongnu, there are three sacrificial ceremonies each year, respectively on the day of Wu (the fifth of the ten Heavenly Stems) in the first, fifth and ninth months of the lunar calendar for people to offer sacrifices to the heavenly deities. Since Chanyu of the Southern Xiongnu had surrendered to the Han Dynasty, he took the opportunity to offer sacrifices to the emperor of Han, gathered all the ministries to discuss state affairs, and held horse and camel races to have fun."[47] It was also covered in the *Eastern View of the Han Dynasty* that Chanyu of the Southern Xiongnu sent in a memorial to offer up splendid camels. The Chanyu held three sacrificial ceremonies a year to offer sacrifices to the heavenly deities, on which horse and camel races were organized to have fun of them.[48] It can be seen that horse and camel racing were common sports activities among the ancient people in the north, and such activities were relatively common in the west during the Middle Ages. As a nomadic ethnic group in the north, Xiongnu had a strong cavalry force acting swiftly in battles, which necessarily required excellent control of horses and training of their galloping abilities. Therefore, horse and camel racing was an essential part of life among the Xiongnu people.

There were no dedicated settings for the early sport governing bodies by the ancient northern ethnic groups. The administration of sports was subordinated to other institutions, which were generally administrative or military in nature. For example, Xiongnu still inherited the organization of primitive societies at the time of transition between the Qin and Han Dynasties. The basic social unit, Zhang or Luo, became the basis for the rules of the Xiongnu slave regime and the organization of military and political power. Upon entry into slavery, it was under the supervision of the military slavery regime that adult civilian males were routinely assigned to "armored cavalry" of the Xiongnu army, which was the smallest unit for the collective training of the Xiongnu. Armored cavalry in the cavalry force of Xiongnu was organized according to the decimal system, in which there should be ten soldiers in every ten Zhang (Luo), and these ten soldiers formed a small fighting unit of armored cavalry, led by an official appointed by the state power called Shizhang (commander of ten cavalrymen). Ten such small units of armored cavalry were then combined together, totaling about 100 soldiers, which in turn, formed a higher level of the Jiaqi cavalry group, with one assigned Baizhang (commander of 100 cavalrymen), and ten such combat groups combined together, with a Qianzhang (commander of 1,000 cavalrymen), in turn, formed an even higher level of Xiongnu military unit. Typically, each Xiongnu tribe had about 5,000–6,000 members, from which 1,000 cavalrymen could be selected to form a combat group of a relatively higher level. The Qianzhangs were administrated by Xiongnu noblemen—the overlords. According to some records in the *Historical Records* and *Book of the Former Han Dynasty*, an overlord with relatively great power could rule over 10,000 cavalrymen. In comparison, an overlord with relatively small power could rule several thousand cavalrymen. Regardless of their power or strengths, the overlords were habitually called Wanzhang (commander of 10,000 cavalrymen) by the Huns. Each overlord had its own right to assign Shizhang, Baizhang, and Qianzhang. In the 13th century, Mongol also raised its army according to these standards of ten, hundred, thousand, and ten thousand cavalrymen. "Every ten soldiers selected from the households were combined into a basic unit, then such units formed a greater level, that is, from 10 to 100, from 100 to 1,000, and then to 10,000. The combat units of different levels had their own heads."[49] The various levels of armored cavalry mentioned here were set up as administrative and military organs, as well as organizations for physical education and training.

During the Qin and Han Dynasties, Xiongnu had already been the largest national military alliance in the northern part of China. From many aspects, such as the military equipment, army construction, and training system, it could be seen that the sports of Xiongnu had developed greatly compared to its earlier minority forms or alliances, such as Shanrong, Linhu, and Loufan. With the frequent contacts between Xiongnu as well as the Central Plains, as well as the constant conquests and mergers of Xiongnu with other neighboring ethnic groups, the sports culture of different nationalities would exchange with the above contacts, intentionally or unintentionally. It could be assumed that, in accordance with the great military power of Xiongnu, which conquered other ethnic groups, the sports culture of Xiongnu, both in its own nature and in its interactions with others, would have been much richer than what is currently recorded, which was subject to further archaeological research.[50] In particular, during the period of the Sixteen Kingdoms, many Huns had established separate regimes in the north and the Central Plains, ruling over the local Han and other ethnic minorities, during which sports and cultural exchanges were unprecedentedly flourishing. Later on, due to the integration of Xiongnu into the Han or other ethnic groups, these sports cultures necessarily spread to quite a few other ethnic groups in the vast area of the ancient north.

2.4 Sports Activities of Wuhuan and Xianbei

2.4.1 Sports Activities of Wuhuan

In the first year under the reign of Emperor Gaozu of the Western Han Dynasty (206 BC), the Donghu was defeated by Modu, the Chanyu of Xiongnu, and the tribes were dispersed. One branch fled to the Wuhuan Mountains (north of the Ar Horqin Banner of the present Inner Mongolia Autonomous Region, i.e., the southern end of the Great Khingan) and thus was labeled Wuhuan following the name of the mountain.[51] Since the collapse of the Donghu tribal alliance, two of its components survived in later times, Wuhuan and Xianbei. At that time, like Xiongnu, the Donghu was also a large tribal alliance. Wuhuan and Xianbei, on the other hand, were two relatively large tribal groups in the Donghu tribal alliance.[52] During the period from Emperor Wu's counter-attack against Xiongnu of the Western Han Dynasty, to the third year of Yongyuan under the reign of Emperor He in the Eastern Han Dynasty (AD 91), Wuhuan and Xianbei replaced Xiongnu one after another, when Geng Kui defeated the Northern Xiongnu at Jinwei Mountain (present Altai Mountain), forcing it to retreat westward to Wusun and then to Central Asia. Xianbei, in particular, became an important ethnic group in the north during the Wei, Jin, and Southern and Northern Dynasties.

Wuhuan and the Eastern Xianbei were originally distributed in the southeastern part of the Mongolian steppe in the basins of the Xar Moron River and Laoha River; Wuhuan was located in the south, or Laoha River basin while Xianbei was in the north, or Xar Moron River basin. The region was divided into three zones according to its topography: south of the Xar Moron River, a loess zone suitable for agriculture; west to the north of the Xar Moron River, a sandy zone of the same nature as the Mongolian steppe, suitable for nomadic herding; and east to the north of the Xar Moron River, a forested zone suitable for hunting. Therefore, Wuhuan people were engaged in three economic activities: farming, herding, and hunting. *Book of the Later Han Dynasty* recorded the Wuhuan people as follows: "… were generally skilled at mounted archery, and lived on hunting for birds and beasts. They gazed with water and grass, living impermanently. And they inhabited themselves in yurts with doors open eastwards towards the sun." "The women were skilled at embroidery and weaving coarse cotton cloth. And the men were capable of making bows and saddles, and wrought weapons with iron." Therefore, it could be seen that Wuhuan was an ethnic group skilled at mounted archery and fighting, whose sports were mainly shaped and developed in the process of production and life. The adults there would generally teach their children to ride horses, shoot arrows and hunt birds and beasts. Based on their general knowledge of production, some men could also make bows and arrows, saddles and bridles, and smelt copper and iron for weapons.

History showed that Xiongnu had conquered Wuhuan. In the fourth year of Yuanshou under the reign of Emperor Wu of the Western Han Dynasty (119 BC), Huo Qubing, general of the Western Han Dynasty, defeated the Xiongnu soldiers of the Left King of Sage, so that Wuhuan unshackled freely from the oppression of Xiongnu and came under the jurisdiction of the government of the Western Han Dynasty. At that time, Emperor Wu moved Wuhuan to stay in the five border counties of Liaodong, Liaoxi, Yuyang, Shanggu, and Right Beiping and set the post of "Military Guarding Officer" in charge of commanding the Wuhuan tribes that moved southward. In the 22nd year of Jianwu under the reign of Emperor Guangwu of the Eastern Han Dynasty (AD 46), Wuhuan took advantage of the internal strife in Xiongnu regime and launched a massive attack, forcing Xiongnu to flee to the north; and from then on, Xiongnu "was absent in the south of the desert." In the 21st year of Jianwu (AD 45), Ma Yuan was ordered to lead 3,000 cavalrymen out of Wuruan Pass to fight against Wuhuan. "Wuhuan perceived the attack and escaped in advance;" when Ma Yuan retreated, "Wuhuan made a back thrust to the back of Ma Yuan's troop so that Ma Yuan had to flee overnight. When he finally entered the pass, over 1,000 horses were killed."[53] In this battle, Wuhuan Army adopted the tactic of "tail attack." From the battle outside the Wuruan Pass, it could be seen that Wuhuan was adept at fighting.

Emperor Guangwu of the Eastern Han Dynasty changed the strategy and allowed Wuhuan to move into the border counties in the northern region, and set up a Military Guarding officer to take charge of Wuhuan in Shanggu and Ningcheng (now northwest of Xuanhua in Hebei Province) and to supervise its people. Since the Eastern Han, Wei, and Jin Dynasties, the Central Dynasty had continuously incorporated the Wuhuan people to enrich its military forces. One Wuhuan cavalry unit called the "Wuhuan Hu Cavalry"[54] was incorporated into the military organization of the Han Dynasty. As a special force of the Central power, such Wuhuan cavalrymen were often sent to the northern borderlands to attack other ethnic groups, such as Xianbei and Xiongnu. Wuhuan cavalry also served as an important military force during the suppression of the peasant rebellion in the interior. "When Yuan Shao controlled Heibei, who tried to pacify the Wuwan people in the three counties, he pretended to respect them but took their troops in secrecy."[55] At the end of the Eastern Han Dynasty, the troops of the nephew of Qiu Liju, a Wuhuan official of Liaoxi, gained strength and posed a considerable threat to Cao Cao's regime. In the eleventh year under the reign of Emperor Xian of the Han Dynasty, Cao Cao personally led an expedition to Wuhuan and defeated Tadun at Liucheng (present-day Chaoyang County, Liaoning Province), "he beheaded Tadun at Linchen, leaving the dead wild in the field. Su Fuwan, Lou Ban, Wu Yan, etc. fled to Liaodong but were all beheaded there. All the rest of the remaining just surrendered. And over 10,000 Wuwan settlements in Youzhou and Bingzhou moved to the Central Plains and followed the lords and marquises in the battles. From then on, the Wuwan from the northern three counties became well-known for their cavalry."[56] The Youzhou Cavalry became famous at the beginning of the Han Dynasty, as recorded in *Book of the Former Han Dynasty · Chronicles of Emperor Gaozu*, "in the fourth year under the reign of Emperor Gaozu, excellent cavalrymen came from Beiluo and Yan to assist the Han Dynasty."[57] The excellent cavalrymen were not first originated from Donghu.[58] As recorded in the *Book of the Later Han Dynasty*, Wu Ziyan once talked to Peng Chong, the prefecture Chief of Yuyang, "The excellent cavalrymen of Yuyang and Shanggu were renowned all across the country."[59] Such excellent cavalrymen should have been from Wuhuan. In the same book, it was recorded that when Emperor Guangwu launched a war against the powers in the north, Wu Han "often deployed 5,000 excellent cavalrymen as the commando, which turned out to be effective for several times." Therefore, the fame of the excellent cavalrymen was further highlighted. Wuhuan Cavalrymen were deployed in both Youzhou and Jizhou in the Eastern Han Dynasty and were under the administration of either the prefectural governor or the provincial chief. Each prefecture had about 3,000 cavalrymen.[60] This system remained unchanged from the Han Dynasty to the Wei Dynasty, the Western Jin Dynasty, and the Sixteen Kingdoms, with the only exception of the number of soldiers, which varied from one to the other. The Han regime repeatedly deployed the Wuhuan riders to attack other neighboring ethnic groups, establishing great military achievements; however, they were eventually unable to endure the cruel rule and rebelled, ending with Zhang Chun being killed by his subordinates.

It could be easily observed from the bravery and skillfulness of Wuhuan cavalrymen that they were superb in mounted archery, and perhaps more clearly from the story of Lu Xi's rescue of his wife below. In the 22nd year under the reign of Taihe, when Cao Cao attacked Hanzhong, "all the armies returned to Chang'an, and Lu Xi was ordered to station his troop in Chiyang to defend Lushuo. Lu Xi's wife was in Jinyang then. Lu Xi missed his wife and was afraid that he could not return to his homeland. Therefore, he just led 500 cavalrymen to defeat back to Bingzhou. He left all his cavalrymen in the valley and entered Jinyang to take out his wife just on his own. The defending troops found him only after he had left the city. The soldiers and the civilians were afraid of his excellent archery, so they gave up chasing him. Therefore, Zhang Jing was ordered to recruit Xianbei cavalrymen to chase after Lu Xi. With his wife adding the weight, the horse went slow. As a consequence, he failed to gather with his troops in the valley, but unfortunately was killed by the Xianbei cavalry on the way.[61]

The Wei Kingdom not only attached great importance to the building of cavalry in its armed forces but also acquired a large number of war horses from the frontier regions so as to further strengthen its cavalry forces. Thus, in the Three Kingdoms, the cavalry forces of the Wei Kingdom were not only numerically superior to those of other regimes but also superior to their opponents in terms of the quality of their cavalry and their bravery in battle. The cavalrymen of the northern ethnic groups like Wuhuan participated in the military battles in the Central Plains and demonstrated the unique skills of mounted archery, playing an active and effective role in the improvement of the mounted archery culture of China.

2.4.2 Sports Activities of Xianbei

Xianbei nationality was one of the ancient ethnic groups of the Donghu system of China. In the Pre-Qin period, Xianbei had led a nomadic hunting life in the central and northern parts of the Great Khingan. It emerged later than Wuhuan and began to manifest its presence in the early Eastern Han Dynasty. Xianbei was originally located in the southeastern part of the Mongolian steppe, like Wuhuan, and it was also an important part of the Donghu tribal alliance. After the Donghu was defeated, Xianbei also migrated northward to the Xianbei Mountains near the Hagul River in Inner Mongolia, north of the Wuhuan Mountains. During the reign of Emperor Wu of the Western Han Dynasty, Wuhuan moved southward, and the Xianbei clan also followed southward, who was stationed in the Xar Moron River Basin upstream of the Xiliao River. After the Eastern Han Dynasty and the Three Kingdoms period, Ji Tong, the governor of Liaodong in the Eastern

Han Dynasty, in alliance with Xianbei group, launched a converging attack against Wuhuan in the area around the Chishan Mountains. After Wuhuan was defeated, Xianbei gradually occupied large areas in the southern part of the desert. In AD 85, Xianbei united the states of Dingling, Southern Xiongnu, and the Western Regions to attack the Northern Xiongnu, resulting in the escape of its Chanyu westwards, thereafter occupying many areas in the northern part of the Mongolia Steppe. In the second century, all the remaining Xiongnu settlements in the steppe surrendered to the Xianbei. On this basis, Xianbei nationality established a military alliance of Xianbei clans headed by Tan Shihuai. At this point, Xianbei's influence spread from the east of Liaoning to the west of Gansu.

In moving towards the south and west, Xianbei merged with Xiongnu, Dingling (Gaoche), Wuhuan, Han, etc., forming many new ethnic groups. For example, the Xianbei people who lived in the steppe intermingled with the remaining Xiongnu and married its people; and in the south, Tiefu Xiongnu of Hu fathers and Xianbei mothers emerged. And in the north of the Yinshan Mountains, the ancestors of the Qifu Xianbei came into appearance through the fusion of Xianbei and Chile. In the area around the Xar Moron River, as the Yuwen clan moved from the Yinshan Mountains after the Southern Xiongnu and ruled over the local Xianbei people, the Yuwen Xianbei came into being. Tribal groups such as Tanshihuai and Kebineng, as well as the subsequent Yuwen, Murong, and Duan clans, were collectively called the Eastern Xianbei. After the northern Xianbei entered the homeland of the Xiongnu, they merged with the remaining people of Xiongnu and became the Tuoba clan with Xianbei fathers and Hu mothers.[62] And a branch of the Murong clan called Tuyuhun moved west and integrated with the local Qiang as well as others to become the Tuyuhun clan. When Tuoba Xianbei established the Northern Wei Dynasty and then unified the Central Plains, they took the name of Xianbei exclusively for themselves and called clans such as Murong and Duan as Dongbu, Baihu, or Tuhe, and Yuwen as Xiongnu.

In summary, Xianbei was a highly complicated tribal group, typical of the plurality of its ethnic origins.[63] The Xianbei successively established regimes in the north such as Dai, Former Yan, Western Yan, Later Yan, Southern Yan, Western Qin, Southern Liang, Tuyuhun, Northern Wei, Eastern Wei, Western Wei, Northern Zhou, and Northern Qi. Among the "Five Barbarians," Xianbei nationality was the ethnic group that had established the most regimes. It was also due to the internal migration and the establishment of power that Xianbei fused most rapidly and thoroughly with the Han people in the north.[64] In the process of integration of ethnic groups, not only the people, the carriers of sporting culture, communicated with each other, but also a few "representatives" of sporting culture, including the singing and dancing artists, were compulsorily arranged. For example, in the first month of spring in the first year of Tianxing, 360,000 civilians and officials in six prefectures in Shandong and handymen in Koryo, and over 100,000 craftsmen of all trades were transferred to convene in the capital.[65] There were many above-mentioned records during the Southern and Northern Dynasties.

It is well known that the Southern and Northern Dynasties were one of the prime periods of ethnic integration in China. From the historical records, there were dozens of ethnic groups and national powers that had relations with the Northern Wei from east to west and from south to north. For example, in the autumn of the fourth year of Yongping, states such as Qiuyanda,

Zhujupan, Boluo, Mojiatuo, Yipopuluo, Jusaluo, Shemi, and Luoletuo all dispatched ambassadors to make offerings.[66] Ethnic interactions such as these were plentiful during the North and South Dynasties. It was in such a rapid and radical fusion that the Xianbei sporting culture, on the one hand, clearly demonstrated its ethnic characteristics in some of its sports, and on the other hand, featured blended sports of Han nationality and other ethnic groups. In terms of sports, they not only inherited the sports culture of the Han and Jin Dynasties, introduced music and dance from the Western Regions, and exchanged them with the Southern Dynasties, but also dared to innovate, so that their excellent sports culture was passed down to the later generations. According to the historical data, the sports activities carried out by Xianbei nationality included hunting, swimming, gripping, Baixi (Jiao-Di, ropewalking, Changqiao, Yuantong, Tiaowan, etc.), archery, horse racing, martial arts, speed-race, climbing, *Jirang* (a throwing game), pitch-pot, chess, rope skipping, etc.

In the early days of the Xianbei, tribal alliances in the form of clan bloodlines gathered together to carry out production and military activities. After most of the "36 Clans with Top Contributions and 99 Surnames with Great Contributions" of Xianbei became extinct, the remaining clans merged with the remaining Xiongnu in the steppe of Mongolia, giving rise to the name of Tuoba Xianbei.[67] In addition, in the process of development, many Xianbei and non-Xianbei clans were united to form a new geo-based tribal alliance known as the "Eight Xianbei Clans." By the time the Northern Wei Dynasty was established, the form of "scattered clans and separated settlements" was gradually shaped. The army followed a special military administration, while recreational sports were under the jurisdiction of the ministries of Taiyue, Zongzhang, Guchui, etc. As recorded in the *Book of the Wei Dynasty · Musical Records*, "In the winter of the sixth year of Tianxing, ministries of Taiyue, Zongzhang, and Guchui were instructed to sort up the Baixi, including Wubing, Jiao-Di, Qilin, Fenghuang, Xianren, Changshe, Baixiang, Haihu, Zhuweishou, Yulong, Bixie, Luma Xianche, ropewalking, Changqiao, Yuantong, Tiaowan, Wuan, etc."[68] As recorded in the *Book of the Sui Dynasty · Etiquette VII*, "After Emperor Wenxuan of the Northern Qi Dynasty accepted the abdication, he asked to follow the Etiquette of the Northern Wei Dynasty in terms of its military system. The military rules and systems during the Heqing Period (the reign of Emperor Wucheng of the Northern Qi Dynasty) followed suit, in which 12 Royal Janissary Officials were set on both sides of the emperor. The military system further included various teams named Chiji, Tingshuo, Changdao, Xizhang, Dunsha, Xiongji, Geshou, Chichang, Jiao-Di, Yulin, Buyoudang, Mayoudang, etc."[69] It could be seen that in the Northern Wei Dynasty, sports activities were not administered by a special institution, but mostly subordinated to departments related to music and ritual. The Xixia regime also had institutions such as Fan and Han Musician Academy,[70] which were specifically responsible for "Baixi." Baixi included some sports and recreational activities such as dancing, singing for entertainment, and games, but this was not yet a specialized sports governing body.

The development of Xianbei sports was extremely attributed to the fact that Xianbei emperors and generals started to highlight the training of military force. They attached great importance to the training in martial arts and combat techniques in their normal social life, and often held gatherings to train martial arts and archery. They "offer sacrifices to the ancestors, the Heaven, the Earth, the Deities and the Ghosts." In the autumn, the horses are plump and sturdy … the people gather around to offer sacrifices around the wood. It was a custom of Xianbei passed down from ancient times. If no wood was available, a willow branch would be erected on the earth, so that the riders would circle around it for three circles as an alternative solution."[71] **The rise and unification of Xianbei in the north were closely related to their strict organization and incessant training.**

In the spring of the first year of Yanhe, an imperial edict was promulgated, "It's a great honor for me to shoulder this important undertaking from my ancestors and calm down the territories. But at this point, the entire country is falling apart. And I have launched repeated expeditions to attempt to quiet down the situation. Since the period of Shiguang, I have deployed tens of chariots. All officials, civilian or military, who took the dagger-ax and wore armor shared the pains and gains with me. With the help of the deities and the joint force of the generals and soldiers, we have finally defeated the enemies. However, we should not make abuse of force. Now, both major enemies were defeated. And we should follow the rules as now the world is back to peace."[72]

In August of the year of Kuichou (the 16th year of Taihe), an imperial edict was promulgated, "The laws of civil and military have been hand in hand since time immemorial. And we should also temper justice with mercy. Therefore, even those with the greatest benevolence, like the Three Emperors and Five Sovereigns, had to send armed forces. The emperors in the Xia and Shang Dynasties never abandoned armies and weapons. Though the world is peaceful, we should not forget about the war. If we fail to train civilians on how to fight, we'll lose control in the battles in the future. Therefore, the ranks of Sima (Great Master of War) were established in the Zhou Dynasty and Jiangjun (General) in the Han Dynasty, to strengthen both civilian and military governance and inspire awe throughout the country. Though the country highlights both civilian and military means to seek peace and prosperity, we should still not undervalue the role of military forces. We now have a complete system for the civilian administration but not a military one. Before teaching **mounted archery**, we should first instruct the significance of martial arts and build sites with low walls for **riding and shooting**. The martial arts lecture should include the battle formation drill, battle formation practice in the traditional form as well as the review of the 'Five Military Affairs.'"[73]

During the reign of Emperor Gaozu of the Western Han Dynasty, Tuoba Cheng was the eldest son of the Rencheng King Tuoba Yun. At that time, the number of soldiers under the Imperial Corps Commanders for directions (east, west, south, north) was insufficient to guard and defend the capital. Therefore, Tuoba Cheng presented a memorial to the emperor to select candidates for Grade II and Grade III officials from the eastern central belt (Yingyang Prefecture), south-central belt (Luyang Prefecture), south-central belt (Hengnong Prefecture) and north-central belt (Henei Prefecture) with great merits in order to be responsible for the task. Capable soldiers were deployed in permanent settings so that the root of the military system would be strong enough to support the weak branches. Empress Dowager Ling of the Northern Wei initially planned to agree to the proposal but gave up later on due to objections. Later on, Tuoba Cheng presented another memorial saying, "… It is the prime age of you to **bring your kindness and merits to the people. And you work so diligently on your official duties. However, if you focus on loads of the state, you would probably have noticed that** the systems are not yet unified. Therefore, we should promote virtue and select the talented, highlighting the roles of the officials; reward those with loyalty and purity, highlighting the system of official promotion; improve military strengths, cultivating courageous warriors; value the time and undervalue the money, as well as value the grains and undervalue the treasures. In the seven to eight years to come, the emperor will be young and strategic, the princes and marquises will remain powerful, the officials will be capable, the armies will be combat-worthy, and everything will be at its peak. However, we still face many enemies and hidden dangers, and if the prosperity trend does not last long, and internal conflicts are found, we will probably be at risk of being subjugated …[74]

In August of the fifth year of Zhengguang (AD 524), Yuan Zhi was seriously defeated in East Gansu, and he retreated to Qizhou. In the year of Bingshen, an edict was promulgated, declaring "the civilians in the towns should be registered in the army roll, and should be shifted to the civilian roll after the town is changed to the prefecture. They have practiced martial arts for generations and are thus courageous. And they should seek to serve the state after they're selected. Three or five most outstanding ones may be selected as permanent soldiers. With concerted and pioneering efforts, the betrayed parties would be eliminated for sure. They charged themselves against enemies, with the certainty of self-dependence and self-appreciation."[75]

The court also took advantage of the military institution for major rituals as a sign of strength. For example, in December of the year of Heping, under the reign of Emperor Gaozong, a parade was organized in addition to the grand ceremony to show off the military power. The rules were systematized, where the infantries were deployed in the south, and the cavalrymen in the north. They sounded their own drums and bells as rhythms. The clothes worn by the infantries were colored in green, red, yellow, and black. The shields, long spears, spears, and halberds were displayed in turns. The formation was changed into flying dragons and snakes in four categories and over ten patterns. The pace was intense and bewildering. After the performance, both troops in the south and north beat the drums while all the soldiers shouted to the greatest extent. Then six cavalrymen were picked to challenge the infantries, who managed to organize their defense against the attack. Finally, the North defeated the South. The scene was splendid. From then on, such performances became a tradition.[76] In terms of deployment, the focus on the coordination and cooperation of different military forces was apparently the result of long-term training; in terms of the scenes in which they were deployed, it indicated the great importance attached to military training.

Society at the time valued martial men and provided them with certain status. At that time, Emperor Shizong adopted an examination-based selection and promotion system, and Yuan Yong (King Gaoyang, surnamed Simu) presented a memorial claiming "… for those practicing martial arts with superior quality, they can be titled Yulin; those with medium quality, titled Hufen; and interior quality, Zhicong …"[77] It could be seen that people who took up martial arts were highly valued by the imperial court, which of course would arouse the enthusiasm of commoners to practice martial arts, which would certainly result in a prosperous scene of competing for training.

During the Northern Wei Dynasty, soldiers were recruited from the civilian population. In June of the first year of Jianyi (AD 528), Xing Gao, the governor of Hejian in Hebei Province, led more than 100,000 households of Hebei exiles to revolt in the North Sea of Qingzhou and appointed himself King of Han with the title of Tiantong. In the year of Wushen, Li Shuren, the East General and Jinzi Guanglu Official, was promoted as the Cheqi Grand General (for chariots and cavalry) to suppress the rebellion. An edict was promulgated to have the officials in charge recruit civilians exempted from grazing into the army. Anyone who was enrolled would be granted the Grade IX official ranking. In the year of Jiyou, an edict was further issued to recruit those with private horses into the army, offering a rank to a level higher than others as well as an official title with real power. The same incentives were also applicable to a common civilian. Those with superb martial arts skills would enjoy the above provision even if they didn't have private horses. And if one was skilled at any one among archery, long spear, or weight lifting and proved to be strategic and courageous, further promotion of ranking would be granted with an official title in real power.[78] This record indicated that there was a relatively large number of people skilled in martial arts, and of course that martial arts training was widely practiced by the people at that time.

Martial arts and mounted archery

Forums were established to teach martial arts and mounted archery. Mounted archery was the basis of the foundation of Xianbei state, which was highly valued by the successive emperors and prime ministers. Almost every year, there would be an open forum for lectures on mounted archery, which had been recorded since Emperor Pingwen. In the fifth year under the reign of Emperor Pingwen (Tuoba Yu), "military forces were trained, and martial arts were taught, seeming to get prepared to quell the chaos in the southern part of China." Emperor Zhaocheng (Tuoba Shiyijian, the second son of Emperor Pingwen) "gathered the military units on July 7th in the autumn in the fifth year to instruct martial arts and mounted archery, which became a tradition ever since."[79] On the day of Dingsi of July in the autumn of the second year of Yongxing (AD 410), Tuoba Si "practiced mounted archery in Bixi who still taught martial arts and fighting."[80] In July in the autumn of the third year of Shiguang (AD 426), a mounted archery platform was built in Changchuan, and the emperor personally climbed on the platform to view the scene of mounted archery. The princes and marquises shot on the horses, and those who hit the target were awarded different gold and brocades. In April in the summer of the fourth year of Shiguang, "armies were trained, and martial arts were taught." On the day of Jimao in July in the autumn, a platform was built in Zuoling for horse racing and mounted archery, and those who hit the target were awarded different gold and brocades. On the day of Jisi of July in the autumn of the fifth year of Taiyan (AD 439), the emperor visited the capital city of the vassal state, where he entertained the officials and discussed martial arts and mounted archery with them.[81] In July of the autumn in the second year of Xing'an (AD 453), a platform for mounted archery was built on the city's southern outskirt. On the day of Renzi in September, the emperor inspected the troops there. In March of the second year of Heping (AD 461), there was a mountain in the south of Lingqiu that was four hundred feet *zhang* (a unit of length equaling 3.33 m) high. The emperor asked the official to shoot the peak upwards, but no one succeeded in hitting beyond the peak. The emperor himself then bent the bow and shot the arrow. The arrow flew over the peak by more than 30 *zhang* and landed over 220 paces to the south of the peak. Therefore, a stone inscription was built to record this.[82] On the day of Renwu in July of the autumn in the fourth year of Heping, an edict was promulgated, declaring, "I hereby ordered that the officials shall organize the teaching of martial arts at Pingrang in the spare month in the autumn." On the day of Jiyou in the spring of the fifth year of Taihe (AD 481), the emperor taught martial arts on the north bank of the Tangshui River. On the day of Guihai in March, the emperor further taught martial arts on the north bank of the Yunshui River.[83] On the day of Dingwei of August in the eighteenth year of Taihe, the emperor personally visited the outlook platform and audited lectures on martial arts.[84] Since Taihe regime, historical records of the rulers of Northern Wei emphasizing and engaging in lectures on martial arts and mounted archery were rare, which happened to be the time when the Northern Wei was steadily declining. It also demonstrated a favorable social environment laid the foundation for thriving sports, which in turn exerted a great contribution to social progress.

The training of martial arts and mounted archery was highly valued, which can be seen from the proficiency of the emperors and generals. When the Jin Dynasty was at full strength, Xianbei made peace with Jin and sent his son (Emperor Shamo Khan) to Luoyang. Emperor Wen learned many things in Luoyang, which astonished the Xianbei people. "Upon hearing emperor's return, the founding emperor was greatly delighted and soon organized all the ministers to greet him at the Hall of Yin. While they drank fully and delightfully, the emperor looked up and spotted a flying bird, then he spoke to everyone present, 'I'll get the bird for you.' Then he pulled out the slingshot and shot, and the bird fell onto the ground in a second. At that time, there was no slingshot in the north. All the ministers at present were shocked, and they said to each other, 'The manners and clothes of the prince are just similar to those of the Central Plains, and his magic arts are also unrivaled. If he becomes the new emperor, probably he would renovate the original customs, and we will not make it accordingly. Anyway, he is different from other princes at home who kept a simple nature and customs.' Others agreed with this view. Therefore, they plotted to provoke him and returned together in advance."[85] Later on, the people all over the state found it difficult to understand this alteration, thus killing Emperor Wen. With the development of history, Xianbei people gradually realized the importance of Han culture to the development of their own people and were able to correctly treat and learn from foreign cultures, so that they consciously accepted the advanced culture and technology. Martial arts and mounted archery were highly valued by successive emperors.

Tuoba Yao had conferred the title of Henan King in the sixth year of Tianxing. At the age of five, he shot a sparrow in front of the late emperor, which greatly amazed him. When he grew up, his martial arts skills were superb, and he supervised the lectures on martial arts among the armies together with Yangping King (Tuoba Xi). All others admired his great courage. Following the death of the First Emperor, Tuoba Hun was conferred the title of Nanping King as the second son of Yangping King (Tuoba Xi); after the succession, he was further promoted to Pingxi General. Tuoba Hun was adept at archery and bird hunting and could kill the flying birds, greatly astonishing others around. The First Emperor Shizu ordered a shooting competition to see who could hit all the targets and get the full score. Tuoba Hun shot three without missing, which immensely delighted the emperor. Emperor Shizu admired Tuoba Hun's excellent skill and often asked him in the company. In addition, he also conferred a hundred horses and tens of servants to Tuoba Hun.[86] Situ Shi, the great-great-grandson of Emperor Pingwen, was courageous, strategic, and specifically skilled at mounted archery.[87] Tuoba Yi, son of Tuoba Tijun's grandson, was 7 *chi* and 5 *cun* tall with a grand appearance and handsome mustache. He was tactful enough to play the sword when he was just a child. In addition, his riding and shooting skills were also unique and excellent. Tuoba Yi had extraordinary physical strength with the bending power of the bow up to nearly 10 *dan* (a unit of dry measure for grain, equal to 100 *sheng*). Chenliu King Tuoba Qian also carried an extraordinarily long spear at that time. There was a saying by the people at that time, "The bow of King Wei, the spear of King Heng" (Tuoba Yi was conferred King Wei by the First Emperor). Tuoba Gan, son of Tuoba Yi, was smart and calm. He was skilled at horse riding and shooting and inherited the style of his father when he was young. Later on, Emperor Taizong succeeded to the throne, and Gan was conferred the titles of Inner General and Imperial General serving in the Imperial Guards. One day, Emperor Taizong toured the northeast of Baideng, and Tuoba Gan accompanied him on the horse. Two barn owls flew and called over them. Emperor Taizong ordered the guards around him to shoot them. But none of them succeeded. And the barn owls flew higher. Tuoba Gan offered himself to have a try and shot the two barn owls with two arrows. Emperor Taizong was satisfied and conferred him with imperial horses, bows, arrows, and belts to praise his skill. And thus, he was also called "Owl Shooting General" in the army. Tuoba Zhen, son of Tuoba Gan, was proficient in various dialects and skilled at mounted archery. He called over 30 barbaric chiefs from Xincai and Xiangcheng. Fully armed, Zhen prepared a feast in Zhouxi and had the guests enjoy the archery. He first selected over 20 guards around him and took the first in shooting without missing. His guards followed and no one failed. Chenliu King (Tuoba Qian) was the son of Tuoba Hege (son of Empress Dowager Zhaocheng). He was well-known when he was a child for his robustness and courage. Qian was tall and strong with incomparable martial art skills. The long spear seemed too thin and short for him, and he additionally placed a bell under the blade to increase its weight. His draw power of the bow was also times ordinary people. His weapons with such extraordinary power were specially marked by the weapon warehouse in the capital. In battles, Tuoba Qian often punctured the enemy and raised the body high with a long spear. Sometimes, he just dragged the spear on the ground and rode the horse to pretend to be retreating. The enemies would chase him but no one succeeded. Then Tuoba Qian shot them with his bow, killed two or three with just one arrow, and poked the bodies away with the long spear. Finally, he collected his long spear and left away.[88]

On the day of Gengzi in October of the winter in the third year of Jingming (AD 502), the emperor personally shot an arrow as far as 1 *li* plus 50 paces. The officials thereby recorded this event in the archery range.[89] Emperor Chu of the Northern Wei Dynasty, tabooed surname Xiu, styled Xiaoze, was the third son of Emperor Wumu (Yuan Huai), with his mother's surname Li. Emperor Chu had a composed personality with few words and was fond of martial arts.[90]

The emperor, who was good-looking, enjoyed literature very much. Meanwhile, he was able to cross a wall carrying a stone lion, and he was such a skilled archer who never failed to hit the target. The emperor once hunted in the east of Ye, and he galloped swiftly as if he were about to fly. A military governor shouted loudly behind the emperor, "Do be careful. If you fall off the horse, the General would not be happy with it!"[91] Yuan Qiong, styled Kongque, was quiet and inward but skilled at martial arts. He was also upright and honest. He would stay in the palace on days of rest and would never expose his breast and belly, even in hot summers.[92] Emperor Gao of Qi State (Xiao Daocheng) was fond of martial arts in his childhood. In the beginning, he was a little bit lazy. However, when he was enrolled into the army, he began to be diligent in demonstrating himself.[93]

In the training of martial arts and mounted archery, there were also techniques of exquisite. As recorded in the *Book of the Wei Dynasty*, Emperor Gaozu was very kind to his younger brother, who was second only to himself in age. However, Emperor Gaozu was aware of his greedy nature and often offered him deep warnings; although he would abide by them on the spot, he did not change his behavior in nature. Yuan Xi, the Xianyang King, expressed, "The court highlighted literacy and suppressed martial arts for quite a long period. But the soldiers from the settlements never stopped practicing martial arts. Now it's the end of the year, the right time to train the tactics. Different weapons, such as bows, arrows, shields, and spears were taught so that the soldiers could obtain related skills and face threats bravely. The edict says, "Martial arts, if taught without tactics, would be nothing. As long as we are going to march northwards, we should teach them and train them well so that we can stop the tensions."[94] Morality was also required in the mounted archery, just as what was recorded in the *Book of the Wei Dynasty*, "second, observe the morality" Emperor Gaozu once said, "Observe the morality through archery and then follow it by order."[95] This also indicates that Xianbei's acceptance of Confucianism in Central Plains had reached a fairly deeper level.

Riding race and performance are effective means to conduct training. Shooting was one of the six arts of Confucianism, which is regarded as an ancient ritual as well as a means of war. It is as solemn as an art, while cruel as a means of war. In the Southern and Northern Dynasties, the court followed the tradition of the archery culture of Han Confucianism, mainly in the form of group archery and single archery.

Group archery was a team competition in which participants were divided into two groups or two teams. Each player took a turn to shoot and was counted by the number of arrows he hit. The team with the higher total score would be the winner. There was also a special scorekeeper for such games. In the north, as some nomads moved into the Central Plains and those in power were mainly ethnic minorities, the trend of archery was even more prevalent. Some emperors of the Northern Dynasties often organized and participated in archery game activities. During the reign of Emperor Taiwu (Tuoba Tao), Tuoba Hun, the Nanping King, was excellent at archery. Once, Emperor Taiwu organized an archery race, and one team scored a series of hits and quickly got the total score. Emperor Taiwu then ordered Tuoba Hun to play, who hit three arrows in a row.[96] During the reign of Emperor Xiaowen (Yuan Hong), he once organized an archery game. One team was led by emperor personally, and the other by his younger brother, Pengcheng King Yuan Xie. At that time, the Left General of Martial Might, Yuan Yao, was on Yuan Xie's side, while the Right General of Martial Might, Yang Bo, was on emperor's team. The arrows hit the target so that a full mark was obtained. Emperor Gaozu said: "As the Left Team has obtained the full mark, the Right one must do so." Yang Bo replied: "With your special favor, I'll do my best." Then, he bent the bow and hit the target right, making the sores equal.[97]

Single archery game was based on individual players without any team or affiliation. The court of the Northern Dynasties also organized some single shots without counting the scores, and the rules were simple: some prizes were prepared, and whoever hit the target would be rewarded. During the reign of Emperor Gao Yan of the Northern Qi Dynasty, he banqueted and played archery with his ministers in the West Garden, and over 200 civil and military officials attended the event. Gao Yan ordered an arrow target to be set up more than 140 paces away from the banquet hall, stipulating that whoever hit the target would be rewarded with fine horses as well as gold and jade. One man shot the head of the beast on the target, missing the nose by just over 1 *cun*. At that moment, only one man named Yuan Jing'an had one arrow left. "The emperor asked Yuan Jing'an to shoot. Jingan behaved himself first, then bent the bow fully and hit just the nose of the beast. The emperor was so astonished that he conferred two fine horses, jade objects, silk fabrics, and other things."[98]

There was also a single archery game with a performative nature. According to the *Book of the Yan State* in Volume 744 of the *Imperial Digest of the Reign of Great Tranquility*, in Former Yan of the Sixteen Kingdoms, a man called Jia Jian possessed excellent archery skills. When he turned 60 years old, the Former Yan Lord placed a bull a hundred paces away and asked Jia Jian whether he could hit it. Jia Jian answered: "When I was young, I could possibly miss the target, but now that I am getting old and my eyesight is failing, so all I can do is to make the arrow hit." Minister Murong Ke burst into laughs after hearing that. Jia Jian began to shoot: the first arrow grazed the back of the bull, and the second grazed the bull's stomach; both arrows grazed the skin of the bull, yet both only shot off the hair of the bull without getting them injured. Murong Ke asked: "Can't you hit the bull?" Jia Jian said: "In the case of archery, what values the most is shooting without hitting, rather than hitting the target. The latter is not the least bit challenging." Then, he hit the body of the bull with just one arrow. Jia Jian's theory of "Missing matters more than hitting" reflected his deep comprehension of the secret of archery, and it was only this deep comprehension that endowed him with archery skills that had reached such an acme of perfection.

The development of Xianbei cavalry was dependent on the building of light horses and the supplies of horses in the army. Light cavalry facilitated quick and accurate attacks, as well as longer expeditions. Therefore Xianbei nationality, with its long experience in cavalry, applied this concept to the battle. In April of the summer in the second year of the First Emperor (AD 37), the emperor failed to keep up with his army provisions. He ordered Zhengdong General Dongping King Yuanyi to stop the encirclement around Ye and stationed at Julu so that they could gather and store the grains in Yangcheng. Pu Lin sent out more than six thousand infantry, waiting for the opportunity to attack the barracks. The edict ordered General Sun Fei to fight back with light cavalrymen. The emperor blocked the retreat route of the enemies with 5,000 warriors. In total, 5,000 were beheaded and 700 were captured alive, and then released with forgiveness. On the day of Xinchou in September of the autumn in the fourth year of Taiping Zhenjun[99] (AD 443), the emperor went to the south of the desert. On the day of Jiachen, they abandoned the loads and attached Ruru with light cavalry.[100]

Xianbei was an ethnic group on horseback, whose life and warfare were inseparable from the horses. Thus a debate was launched when Tuoba Tao planned to move the capital to the south. Emperor Gaozu intended to move the capital, near the Hall of Taiji, so he gathered the officials to discuss it. The edict then ordered Yuan Pi and others to state their opinions if they had any. Mu Pi, prefectural Governor of Yanzhou, offered: "Moving the capital is a big deal, and in my humble opinion, I don't think it's feasible." Emperor Gaozu responded: "Just let me know why." Mu Pi answered: "There are foreign invasions in the north, lower reaches of the Yangtze River in the south, an obstacle of Tuyuhun in the west, and trouble of Goguryeo in the east. The four directions have not yet been settled, and the nine territories have not yet been determined. Therefore, it's not feasible. The expedition move requires warhorses; without horses, nothing can work." Emperor Gaozu said: "You said there were no horses, which sounds reasonable. Horses are often found in the north, with the stables set up here. Why would you worry about running out of horses? Presently, our capital city is to the north of the Hengshan Mountains, far from Han's territory; and for that reason, I'm planning to move to the Central Plains."[101] In addition, for the purpose of gradual adaptation to ethnic life and warfare, Tuoba Tao also gradually expanded the farmland in the south into pastures. *Historical Records* are cited as follows: "After Emperor Gaozu came to the throne, he further appointed Heyang as a pasture, generally placing 100,000 horses in preparation for the vigilance of the capital. Every year the herds were moved from Hexi to Bingzhou, and bit by bit shifted southwards, so that they might be accommodated to the land and water to reduce casualties, while the pastures of Hexi grew even more fertile."[102]

Mountain climbing for hunting and touring

History books have documented a lot about the climbing and hunting activities of Xianbei emperors, and here are some examples. On the day of Bingwu (the first day) in January of the spring in the fourth year of Taian (AD 458), the ban on alcohol was launched for the first time. On the day of Yimao, the emperor visited the Guangning Hot Spring Palace, and then made a tour eastward to Pingzhou. On the day of Gengwu, the emperor visited the Huangshan Palace in Liaoxi, traveled for a few days to feast and drink, meeting with the elderly and inquiring about their sufferings. On the day of Bingzi in February, the emperor climbed up Jieshi Mountain to see the sea and feasted at the foot of the mountain with the officials, and conferred them with various rewards and promotions. Jieshi Mountain was renamed Leyou Mountain, and an altar was built on the beach to record the event. On the day of Wuyin, the emperor headed south to Xindu for hunting and toured Guangchuan. On the day of Dingwei, the emperor enjoyed mounted archery in Zhongshan.[103] On the day of Jiayin of August in the eighth month of Taihe, the emperor climbed Niutou Mountain.[104]

Weiqi (Game of Go)

In the Northern Dynasties, Weiqi (game of Go) was also prevalent. In the eleventh year under the reign of Emperor Taiping Zhenjun (AD 450), Tuoba Tao of the Northern Wei led a southern expedition and also sent people to borrow chess pieces along with other items from the Southern Song Dynasty. Tuoba Tao was so enthralled by the game of Go that he refused to listen to his subordinates' reporting while he was playing. On one occasion, Gu Bi, the Chief Imperial Secretary, had an important matter to present to the court, and Tuoba Zhuzheng happened to be playing the Game of Go with Liu Shu, a Government Affairs Consultant. Gu Bi had to wait outside, and after he had waited for a long time without seeing the end of the game, he barged in, grabbed Liu Shu by the hair, and pulled him out of his seat, slapping him while saying, "It is a crime of yours that the court does not function well." Tuobao Tao immediately put down the chess and said: "It should be my fault for not listening, and does this have anything to do with Liu Shu? Just go ahead!" Then he heard the report from Gu Bi.[105] In the Northern Wei Dynasty, Zhen Shen from Zhongshan was promoted to the rank of Xiucai (a title given to the one who passed the imperial examination at the county level), and he spent his days playing the game of Go, even all night long. When he played the game, he had a servant holding a candle to light up the room. The servant couldn't stay up much longer and dozed off. Zhen Shen then punched him with the cane. The servant couldn't stand it any longer, so he said, "You have bid farewell to your parents and become an official in the capital. If you read with a candle, I dare not shirk my guilt; yet playing the game of Go day and night is totally different. Is that your intention of going to the capital? So it is just unreasonable to punish me by the cane!" Zhen Shen was ashamed of what he said, and from then on, he concentrated on reading and studying.[106] In the Northern Wei Dynasty, Wei Zijian was a Front Army General who had not been promoted or transferred for ten years; he often played the game of Go with Li Shao, Li Yanhuan, etc., in his spare time in Luoyang. Some people advised him to make a change, yet he just replied: "The game of Go has involved too much when it comes to political integrity and bravery. And I'm not yet appreciated by the times, but I can gain much from the game of Go."[107] He found the game of Go inspiring in terms of timing, adaptability to circumstances, observation of situations, and courage to fight. One cannot obtain such a profound understanding if not playing this game for long and not pondering over it repeatedly. Yuwen Gui of the Northern Zhou Dynasty was "fond of music and playing the game of Go, and never tired of it."[108]

Pitch pot and Jirang

Pitch pot and Jirang can be traced back to the Spring and Autumn and Warring States Period. Pitch pot was first recorded in history as a ceremonial institution. The pitch pot is played to show the cultivation of etiquette of the host and guests. Though it is related to "fun," it has rituals in it. In the Northern Dynasties, Gao Cheng's sons, Gao Xiaohang and Gao Xiaocui, placed a small barrier in front of the pot to add difficulty. In the Pre-Qin Dynasty, the pots were filled with a certain number of small beans to prevent the arrows from jumping out. During the reign of Emperor Wu of the Western Han Dynasty, Guo Sheren improved the game of pitch pot by replacing the wooden arrows with bamboo arrows in order to increase their elasticity so that they would possibly jump out and return to the hands of the player, which was called "Xiao." (pattern) During the Southern and Northern Dynasties, there was another game called "Lotus Xiao," which was clearly not just catching arrows that bounced back. He Zhuo from the Qing Dynasty said: "Xiao was the formation that the arrows hang over the opening of the pot after bouncing out." The *Changes of Pitch Pot* by Yu Tan, Imperial Minister of State of Jin, recorded a skill called "Sword Xiao." "Sword Xiao" was perhaps the pattern that the arrow bounced back from the pot and hung on the ear of the pot, making a shape in which the sword hung on the ear of the pot. The greater difficulty of this technique determines the highest score awarded. By analogy, the "Lotus Xiao" referred to the pattern of the lotus when the arrow bounced out and hung on the ear. This skill, obviously much more difficult than the "Sword Xiao," was considered "superb." Thus, it appeared that the game of pitch pot contained two forms of skills, with the Lotus Xiao as a skill of unprecedented difficulty in the Wei, Jin, and Southern and Northern Dynasties. During the Southern and Northern Dynasties, in addition to the above techniques, there were also patterns such as "Leopard's Tail" and "Loong's Head." The details of these two techniques were not explicitly documented in the historical records. As described in the *Ode to Pitch Pot* by Sima Guang in the Song Dynasty: "Loong's Tail Xiao refers to the pattern that the tail of the arrow points directly to the thrower.; while the Loong's Head Xiao refers to the pattern that the head of the arrow points directly to the thrower."[109] The "Loong's Head" and "Loong's Tail" were highly possible to derive from the "Loong's Head" and "Leopord's Tail" of the Southern and Northern Dynasties. Plus, there were also some inventive ways to enjoy the pitch pot game. For example, as recorded in the *Book of the Jin Dynasty* in Volume 753 of the *Imperial Digest of the Reign of Great Tranquility*, "There's a singing girl in Shichong who was skilled at throwing the arrow beyond the screen barrier." There's another description in the *Records of Jinyang*: "Wang Hu was skilled at shooting arrows with eyes closed." It is well known that during the Southern and Northern Dynasties, Confucianism was favored by the ruling class of Xianbei. As part of Confucian rituals, the pitch pot had evolved significantly.

On the day of Bingshen in October of the winter in the third year of Yongping (AD 510), the edict was issued, "I, took the destiny to be enthroned for twelve years. I believe the benefits of Jirang and hereby order to teach and learn ..."[110] This indicated that Jirang was not only popular among the civilians but also highly valued by the emperors, which further demonstrated its great popularity at that time.

Chupu and Woshuo

Chupu had long existed in the Central Plains, which was developed soon after Xianbei's interactions with the Central Plains. In the Pre-Qin period, Murong Bao played Chupu with Han Huang, Li Gen, etc., in Chang'an. Murong Bao was seated, wearing a serious face: "People are saying that Chupu is efficacious. Who knows if it's true or not!" If it's a propitious sign of fortune, one should get all black successively three times." And he successively threw three times and got them all black![111] Zhang Senghao of the Northern Wei Dynasty was so crazy for Chupu that he would compete with anyone around him. Therefore, he was laughed at by others.[112] Zu Shan from the Northern Qi Dynasty often played with Chen Yuankang, Mu Zirong, Ren Zhou, and Yuan Shiliang.

On one occasion, they gathered together and took over a hundred bolts of fine silk for a gamble, in which they let their servant play Chupu to gain fun.[113] In the Western Wei Dynasty, Yuwen Tai had a banquet with his courtiers in Tongzhou (present-day Dali County, Shaanxi Province), where he brought out several bolts of brocade and miscellaneous damask, and ordered the generals to play Chupu to win them over.[114]

According to the *Book of the Wei Dynasties · Biography of Skills*, Woshuo "was created by the Hu who entered China later on." It was said that King Hu had a brother who was about to be killed. And he played this in jail, thinking that an odd number meant that he would be killed. Therefore, it can be seen that the game of Woshuo derived from the Western Regions, which was only popular in the north during the Southern and Northern Dynasties, with the earliest records dating from Emperor Wen of the Northern Wei Dynasty. It was also recorded in the same biography that "During the reign of Emperor Gaozu … Li Youxu in the Zhao State and Qiu Henu in Luoyang were skilled at Woshuo." After Emperor Xuanwu, Woshuo became popular in the north. He Shikai, a favored minister of the Northern Qi Dynasty, was a descendant of the Western Shanghu who was proficient in Woshuo. Emperor Wucheng, Gao Zhan, and Queen Hu were fond of such a game and often played with He Shikai, who was greatly favored by them. Han Feng and Mu Tipo were another two favored ministers in the Northern Qi Dynasty. During the reign of the Last Emperor Gao Wei, Shouyang was conquered by Wu Mingjiao, general of the Southern Dynasties. At that time, Han Feng was just playing Woshuo with Mu Tipo. Upon hearing that news, he said: "just let it be …," yet still with the Woshuo piece in his hand.[115]

Xianbei rulers were reluctant to accept the "tricks" from the Western Regions, who believed that they would affect social morals, and thus had them banned earlier. On the day of Wushen in January of the spring in the fifth year of the Taiping Zhenjun, an imperial edict was promulgated, saying, "The foolish people are ignorant, who believe in confounding demons, and keep books of sorcerers, prophecies, yin and yang, theologies, medicines, and tricks; some monks, by virtue of the falsehood of the opinions in the Western Regions, turned out to do strange and abnormal things. The only purpose was for politicization so that all could obey. From the princes down to the commoners, those who had private monks, sorcerers, and men of such "tricks" in their own homes were sent to the government and hiding of any kind was forbidden. The deadline was February 25th of this year. After such date, all those wanted would be killed, and the entire family concealing such people would also be killed. It is hereby announced for everyone to abide by." On the day of Gengxu, an imperial edict was promulgated, claiming "recently, the army and the state have been trapped by the multiple affairs, and they neglected the efforts on culture and education. Therefore, it's time to unify customs and set up guidelines for the country. It is an order that all the children from the imperial family to the ministers and officials should go to the Imperial College. Moreover, the children of the laborers and servants in their families should take the same occupations as their fathers/brothers, and they are not allowed to go to private schools. Whoever is against such rules would be killed, as their masters."[116] However, such a ban would not address the root of the problem. As seen above, these cultures at different times have been present in contemporary society to a greater or lesser extent.

Horse racing

In July of the third year of Shiguang (AD 426), a horse racing stage was built in Changchun, and the emperor personally climbed the stage to enjoy horse racing.[117] This was obviously a horse race. And according to historical records, the emperor (Xiaojing) was fond of literature and attached importance to appearance. In addition, he was able to cross a wall carrying a stone lion, and he was such a skilled archer who never failed to hit the target. The emperor once hunted in the east of Ye, and he galloped swiftly as if he were about to fly. A military governor shouted loudly behind the emperor: "Do be careful. If you fall off the horse, the General would not be happy with it!"[118] This is not a horse race; nevertheless, we can still see how fast it is on the horse. By contrast, a real horse race would be even faster and more intense.

Fast race

Yang Dayan, grandson of Yang Nandang[119] of Wudu. He was brave as a kid; he could leap and run as if flying. However, he was born of concubine and not well taken care of by the family. So he often felt hungry. During the reign of Taihe, he began to serve as a court official. At that time, Emperor Gaozu planned to launch a southern expedition, and ordered Minister Li Chong to select military officials. Dayan was eager to have this opportunity, so he pleaded: "Just let me show you a skill so that you can know me better." Then, he tied a long rope on his topknot and ran away. The rope was flying straight like an arrow, and even a horse could not catch him, which greatly astonished all at present. Li Chong said: "Probably no one could have had a skill like you in the past one thousand years." So, he was appointed as a military officer. Yang Dayan told his associates: "Finally, I have this opportunity so that I would not be as ordinary as you all." Later, he was promoted to Grand General. He followed Emperor Gaozu to fight against Yuan, Ye, Xiang, Deng, Jiujiang, and Zhongli and demonstrated his battle talents to a large extent. In the early years under the reign of Emperor Shizong, Pei Shuye surrendered with Shouchun. Yang Dayan and Kang Xisheng led the army to take first place and got it occupied. He then was conferred the title of Founding Chief of Ancheng County, governing three hundred households. In addition to the Zhihe General, he was also conferred other titles such as Fuguo General and Youji General.[120] Although Yang Dayan was not from Xianbei, his fast-running ability was actually amazing. He was promoted to general later on, focusing greatly on the training of racing with his soldiers, as he said, "the great achievement I have made can be attributed to the great condition I created for myself …," which also proved that he had played to his strengths. As proved by the facts, Yang Dayan's troops had made numerous military achievements, which certainly had much to do with his practices of training.

Rope skipping

The origin of rope skipping is still unknown. However, there is a record in the *Book of the Northern Qi Dynasty*: "At the end of the reign of Heqing, Wu Cheng dreamed that a giant hedgehog occupied Ye. So he ordered to kill all the hedgehogs in the city for extinction." The wise considered that the last emperor was acting as notorious as the hedgehog, which was a sign of the perishing of the state. In addition, the women all had their hair cut and shaved and wore false topknots. The topknots were inclined like flying birds towards the south. And the centers of the topknots faced west. Therefore, from the palace to other places, it was interpreted that the head of the emperor would be cut off, so that he should be heading westward to escape. And the knives were narrow and thin, which was interpreted as the destiny of the state being doomed. The children enjoyed jumping up and down with a rope in their hands while singing songs, which signified the ending of the emperor's rule. Therefore, probably all the destinies had their omens."[121] Jumping up and down with a rope is jumping rope, which is an activity performed by a single person. And the rope skipping discussed in the following section, as seen in the wall painting of a tomb of Liao unearthed in Xuanhua, was that one in which a man was jumping while the other two were waving the rope.

Sports activities in Baixi

Baixi were quite popular during the Han Dynasty, and it can be said that the sports activities covered in Baixi basically included entertainment, recreation, and fitness. This culture was spread through exchanges between the Central Plains and neighboring ethnic groups, and the acceptance of that culture by the Xianbei nationality was a must when Xianbei entered Central Plains. According to the historical records, in the winter of the sixth year of Tianxing (AD 403), ministries of Taiyue, Zongzhang, and Guchui were instructed to sort up the Baixi, including Wubing, Jiao-Di, Qilin, Fenghuang, Xianren, Changshe, Baixiang, Baihu, Zhuweishou, Yulong, Bixie, Luma Xianshe, rope walking, Changqiao, Yuantong, Tiaowan, Wuan, etc." The emperor offered a feast at the court, just like the tradition in the Han and Jin Dynasties. At the beginning of the reign of Emperor Taizong, it was further supplemented with full pieces of songs and the rhythms of bells and drums.[122] From the list above, the Baixi included sports activities such as Jiao-Di, ropewalking, Changqiao, Yuantong, Tiaowan, and Wuan. These activities were also performed in the court halls of the Northern Wei Dynasty court halls, thereby indicating their full acceptance towards the Han culture.

Xianbei nationality was a unique ethnic group in this period. In a relatively short period of time, Xianbei went from a primitive society to a feudal society, and became the first central government established by an ethnic minority; the whole ethnic group soon integrated into the Han and other ethnic groups. Therefore, its early sports mainly manifested in hunting and riding under the nomadic economy, in that the tribal leaders attached great importance to the development of mounted archery, and established a system conducive to the social development of nomadic economy, which facilitated the national economy to grow rapidly and thereby laid a solid foundation for the invasion of the Central Plains. Upon the establishment of the central government, apart from developing horse riding and shooting, Xianbei people quickly absorbed the sports of the Han and other ethnic groups, thus enriching their own, especially their sports culture, which was based on ethnic characteristics full of rich cultural connotations. In particular, it is closely related to its ethnic region, social development history, diverse ethnic cultures, and plain national concepts. Xianbei nationality came from the shores of graceful lakes, mysterious forests, and vast grasslands, all of which were closely linked to their excellent ethnic consciousness. Undoubtedly the Xianbei nationality has left precious wealth for the sports culture of the Chinese nation.

2.5 Sports Activities of Ethnic Groups in the Western Regions

Ancient records of the Northwestern ethnic groups already existed in the Pre-Qin period, but most are not detailed. The Central Plains' knowledge and understanding of the Northwestern ethnic groups began mainly after the journey of imperial envoy Zhang Qian to the Western Regions in the Han Dynasty, although these records were not as detailed as those for the North or Northeast. Due to the barrier of geography and natural environment, it is not as easy for the people in the northwest to have close contact with the Central Plains culture as those located in the north or northeast. The Northwestern ethnic regimes never occupied the Central Plains as the Northern or Northeastern ethnic groups did, which were yet deeply imbued with their culture while ruling over the Central population. From the view of integrating the entire Chinese ethnic groups, the Northern or Northeastern ethnic groups merged with the ethnic groups of the Central Plains more quickly and thoroughly than the Western ones. However, in the long history, the Western ethnic groups also had close ties with the Central Plains, interacting and influencing each other. Before and after Zhang Qian passed through the Western Regions, especially after the passage of the Western Regions, sporting activities there were introduced one after another, either officially or by folklore, and some of the best skills were absorbed by the Central Plains and then incorporated into the traditional sports, thus making them more exciting and enriching. For example, the sports in dynamic development, such as Dulu Xuntong, Tiaowan, Tiaojian, and Tasuo, were all based on the absorption of sports activities from the Western Regions.

It was believed that the Western Regions had links with the Central Plains long before the Qin and Han Dynasties, and they had sent some of their entertainers to the Central Plains. At the time of King Mu of Zhou, "people coming from the Western Regions brought in tricks about water, fire, metal, and stone."[123] During the Han Dynasty, there were even closer ties between China and the Western Regions, and vice versa. The Western Regions repeatedly paid tributes to the Central Plains with magicians and sportsmen of various types. "Originally, when the Han envoys arrived at the Parthia, the King of Parthia ordered 20,000 horsemen to welcome them in the east. Since the eastern part was far away from the capital, the group had to pass through tens of cities and exchange a lot with the people along the way. In 108 BC, Zhang Qian, the envoy of Han, returned. Later on, envoys from the Western Regions, who brought large bird eggs and magicians as gifts, were assigned to visit Han with Han's envoys. As for the small states in the west of Yuan State, such as Huanqian and Daiyi, and the eastern states of Yuan, such as Gushi, Hanshen, and Suxie, they all followed Han's envoys to pay tributes to the emperor.[124] In the first year of Yongning, "Yongyoudiao, King of the Dan State once again assigned envoys to the Han court to pay tributes. Musicians and magicians were presented. The magicians were skilled at performing conjuring tricks, jetting fires, and changing ox and horse heads. And they were also skilled at Tiaowan (ball throwing) with a count of several thousand. They called themselves the Romans. The Dan State was bordered by Rome in the southwest.[125] In the ninth year under the reign of Emperor Huan (Yan Xi), "Antoninus, the Emperor of Rome, assigned envoys to pay tributes with ivories, rhinoceros horns, and tortoiseshells, attempting the first contact between two empires."[126] As recorded in the *Imperial Digest of the Reign of Great Tranquility*, "Hu was having fun in the court hall, with acrobatics such as Gaogeng, Longyu, Fenghuang, and Anxi Wuan. There was a pole lifting with the forehead, or some would support the pole with the mouth, with birds flying around. Sometimes, a carriage was prepared, with one pole erected on the carriage and the other lying horizontally on top of it. The performers sat respectively on each end, jumping like birds or hanging upside down. Some acrobats acted like monkeys on the horse's rib, head, or tail, which was called Yuanqi (monkeys on the horse). Generally, such acrobatics and tricks originated in the Western Regions and were magic tricks brought in by the magicians. In the period under the reign of Emperor An of the Eastern Han Dynasty, India presented some acrobats who could cut off the hands and feet or split the stomachs.[127] There were numerous related exchanges between the Western Regions and the Central Plains, and in many cases, they influenced and inspired each other. The introduction of sports activities from the Western Regions into the Central Plains has contributed to the development of Chinese sports culture.

The traditional records were mainly about introducing Western magical arts and not much about the introduction of sports. In fact, the ethnic groups of the Western Regions had also created rich sporting cultures in their own territory, as known from the literature, including Jiao-Di (wrestling), martial arts, equestrianism, mounted archery, climbing, Tiaowan, Anxi Wuan, Tasuo, etc.

Xuntong, literally meaning pole climbing, was called "Zhuru Fulu" in the Spring and Autumn Period and "Dulu" in the period of Emperor Wu in the Western Han Dynasty. According to *Book of the Former Han Dynasty · Memoirs on the Western Regions*, Jinzhuo noted that, "Dulu, the name of a state." And Li Qi added: "Dulu, a man light in weight and skilled in pole climbing."[128] Based upon the description of *Book of the Former Han Dynasty · Geographia*, Yan Shigu noted, "People from Dulu State were adept at pole climbing, as was depicted by Zhang Heng in the *Verse of the Western Capital* that 'Dulu people, skilled at pod lifting as well as pole climbing' and 'it is the lightweight and robustness that endow them with superb talents in pole climbing.'"[129] This indicated that Dulu Xuntong was a climbing sport introduced by the Dulu State. The role climbing, role lifting, carriage pole tricks, and palm pole tricks were just the evolution of the Xuntong introduced from Dulu.

According to the *Government Affairs of Officials in the Han Dynasty*, "On the first day of the lunar year, the emperor came to the Deyang Hall and offered feasts to the guests. Sheli came from the east and played in the yard. When the feast was finished, all entered the gate of the hall to see the splashed water turn into a flounder, who jumped into and out of the water, rising mist. Then, a golden Loong of 8 *zhang* tall appeared. It came out of water and played in the yard under the sun. Besides, a rope was tied between two poles of several *zhang* apart, on which two actresses walked and danced. Tasuo (wire-walking) has been quite popular in the Central Plains since the Han Dynasty, which will be discussed in detail in the section related to the Uyghur.

Such activities introduced from the Western Regions also included flexible body skills, Anxi Wuan, etc. As recorded in the *Book of the Tang Dynasty · Musical Records*, "the musicians of Brahman stood upside down dancing, with knife beneath them. Then they lowered the body and moved quite near the knife. When the play proceeded, the knife was placed under the back and then on the belly with music being played. At the end of the music, they remained no hurt. Later they lay down, stretched their hands and feet, walked tiptoe, rotated their bodies and winded their body with hands, and swung for a long period without stopping. In addition, Anxi Wuan acrobat was found in many archaeological sites in the Central Plains, especially in the Han and Tang Dynasties. For example, the discovery of the five-fold superimposed Luohan in the Tang tombs in Chang'an (see Fig. 2-2[130]) showed that such activities were widely carried out in Chang'an, and well appreciated by the people in the Central Plains.

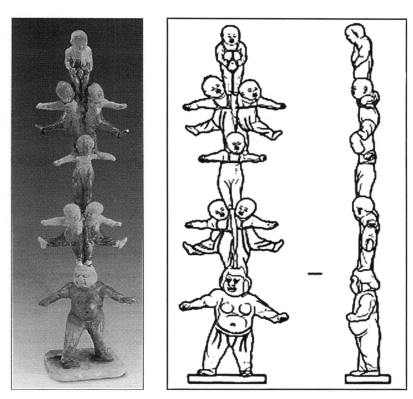

Fig. 2-2 Three-Color Acrobatic Figurines Unearthed in the Tang Tombs

Another example is Tiaowan (ball throwing). In the above literature, Haixi people were "skilled at Tiaowan who could count till several thousand," which indicated that their techniques were perfect. They could count several thousand without falling, demonstrating their perfect skills and sufficient physical strength. There have also been numerous archaeological finds of related images.

Relatively speaking, people of the Western Regions lived in a comparably harsher environment than those from the north and northeast, in which there were grassland oases, deep mountains and streams, and the Gobi Desert. Living in such an environment, people tried every means to struggle and adapt to the environment for generations; sometimes they had to fight against the war for survival, in which they developed strong bodies and spirits of martial arts. In addition, they could find joy amid hardship and create rich sports culture. Special attention should be paid to the profound equestrian culture associated with their lives and battles.

Zhang Qian's first mission to the Western Regions covered Dayuan, Yuezhi, Bactria (Great Xia), and Sogdiana. And it was said that there were still more states involved. After he returned to

Han, he described his experience of the Western Regions to the emperor as follows: Dayuan was in the southwest of Xiongnu, west of Han, thousands of kilometers away. Living on farming, the local people not only produced rice and wheat but also made wine. In addition, they were skilled at horse raising and riding, with the possession of many high-quality horses. They lived in towns and houses. There were over 70 cities and towns of different sizes with a total population of tens of thousands. Skillful in mounted archery, the troops used bows and spears as weapons. ... Wusun was about 1,000 kilometers to the northeast of Dayuan, living a nomadic life, and shared similar customs as Xiongnu. There were tens of thousands of people skilled in archery who were brave enough in battles. It once surrendered to Xiongnu, but later on, with the growth of internal power, they refused to obey the rule of Xiongnu anymore. Plus, Sogdiana was about 1,000 kilometers to the northwest of Dayuan, located next to Dayuan, which was a nomadic state with the same customs as the Yuezhi. There were about 80,000 to 90,000 people adept at archery. As it was a small state, Dayuan had to be subject to Yuezhi in the south and Xiongnu in the east.

Aorsoi was about 1,000 kilometers to the northwest of Sogdiana, a nomadic state with the same customs as the Sogdiana. There were over 100,000 people adept at archery. It faced the great lakes and had no steep mountains, situated near the North Sea (referring to the Caspian Sea). Da Yuezhi was 1,000–1,500 km to the west of Dayuan and on the north of the Gui River. It had Bactria on the south, Parthia on the west, and Sogdiana on the north. Yuezhi was also a nomadic state which migrated with the herds and enjoyed the same customs as Xiongnu. There were about 100,000–200,000 people skilled at archery. Yuezhi was formerly a powerful state which once despised Xiongnu. With the rise of Modu, he killed the King of Yuezhi and took his head as a drinking vessel. Yuezhi people once lived around Dunhuang and Qilian, and then moved further westwards after being defeated by Xiongnu. It conquered the Bactria and set the capital to the north of the Gui River. The small parts failing to escape, like the Nanshan Qiang, were called the Xiao Yuezhi.[131] As recorded in the *Book of the Former Han Dynasty*, the Western Regions was first visited under the reign of Emperor Xiaowu. In the beginning, there were 36 states visited, and then the number increased to over 50 later on.[132] The ethnic groups in the Western Regions were closely bordered by Xiongnu, and thus the sporting activities of Xiongnu were also present there. And features such as the emphasis on martial arts, riding and shooting, and fondness for fighting were commonplace among the people in the north.

In addition, the above revealed that the Western Regions produced famous horses in large numbers; for example, "Wusun has a large number of horses, and some wealthy people even own 4,000 to 5,000 horses." The horses bred by the Western Regions people were deeply treasured and favored by the Hans. The Han Dynasty also introduced horses of great quantity from the Western Regions. As a result, later on, "the emperor was fond of the horses, and numerous envoys were visiting with horses." The foreign missions were conducted in different sizes, from one hundred to several hundred, with great expectations to satisfy the emperor. They returned with roughly the same number of stuff that Zhang Qian brought back. Later on, the mission became more common until the power of Han declined, so the number of envoys decreased. The envoys sent by the Han Dynasty each year ranged from five or six batches to more than ten batches at their maximum. They returned back in eight or nine years when visiting faraway places, or came back in a couple of years from a place not far. "The numbers were large for both horses and foreign envoys coming and going. With the seeds brought back by the envoys, the emperor planted massive grapes and alfalfa near his residences."[133] "Numerous valuable horses of Pushao, Longwen, Yumu, and Hanxue were specifically for the royal palace."[134] Meanwhile, introducing horses from the Western Regions, the Han Dynasty also attached great importance to horse training, as well as the talents for horse selection and horse training. The court "once appointed two people familiar with horses as Military Officers in charge of the business of fine horses selection and training." In other words, they were responsible for reserving Dayuan horses and selecting top-quality ones. Later on, the troops of the Later Han defeated Dayuan, as was cited "Dayuan offered their excellent horses for Hans and took out food for the Han troops." The Han's troop selected and took away tens of top-quality horses and over 3,000 horses of medium quality and lower.[135] It is a fact that the states in the Western Regions were known for mounted archery, with more emphasis on the taming of horses and training of archery techniques. Many states in the Western Regions set up posts such as "Left/Right Riding Officials"[136] responsible for the training of the cavalry troops.

With the strengthening of the effective administration of the Western Regions by the Central Plains, the sports cultures of different regions and ethnic groups were exchanged during the frequent ethnic fusions. The magic and technique-based sports activities were widely generalized all across the country. For example, Chen of the Southern Dynasties greatly favored Xuntong, which integrated techniques, adventures, and excitement. Chen Shubao, the last emperor of Chen, often had entertainers in the imperial harem to perform for him. Another example is Shen Guang from Western Liang had an astonishing performance: Shen Guang was brave and nimble. He was skilled at taming the horse, which was incomparable at his time. Besides, he was good at writing and speaking and always thought about making contributions without sticking to the details. His stories were recorded in some historical records with only differences in details. His family was poor, and his father and brother had to live on copying books for others. But Shen Guang was unyielding and had young ruffian friends in company offering protection for him. Those young ruffians treated him much so that he could support his family, and never felt short of food and clothes. After the Chanding Temple was constructed, there was a flag pole of over 10 *zhang* high. The rope happened to break and became inaccessible, which troubled the monks a lot. Shen Guang noticed that and talked to the monks: "Just bring me the new rope and I'll do that for you." The monks were pleased to take out the rope. To their great surprise, Shen Guang held the rope with his mouth and climbed along the pole till the top. After he tied the rope, he released his hands and feet and then jumped directly down. He succeeded in landing with his hand and retreated for tens of paces. All people at present were astonished so that he was then entitled "Mortal Flying Celestial." During the period of Daye, Emperor Yang called the brave people all over the country to suppress Liaodong (the eastern part of Liaoning), and Shen Guang enrolled himself to join in. Among the tens of thousands of soldiers, Shen Guang was the most outstanding one. Whenever Shen Guang was about to set off, over one hundred people rode their horses to see him off in Bashang. He poured a bowl of wine and swore: "I'm determined to fight for the state, or I'd rather die on the battlefield in Koryo. If I chicken out, I would feel ashamed to meet you again." Shen Guang followed the emperor to attack Liaodong. They attempted to climb the city wall by ladders.

Shen Guang climbed up the pole of 15 *zhang* high, fought closely against the enemies, and killed more than ten of them. The enemies attacked him and forced him to drop before touching the ground. However, Shen Guang grasped a rope hanging from the pole and climbed up again. The emperor witnessed his performance and felt astonished yet delighted. The emperor promoted Shen Guang as Dafu (a senior official in feudal China) and also conferred him valuable swords and fine horses. Then Shen Guang was asked to be the knight beside the emperor thus establishing a close relationship with him.[137] The sports cultures of the Central Plains were also introduced westwards and integrated with those in the Western Regions, as proved in the massive cave and chamber cultures in Dunhuang.

2.6 Summary

The above sections only briefly describe the sports culture of some northern ethnic groups and provide a glimpse of the sports in the initial development stage. Research has shown that there is little historical information about the sports of northern ethnic groups in the Pre-Qin period, and there are even no detailed records of the sports activities of any ethnic group. Thus, it is only possible to discover from those scattered historical records that some northern ethnic groups may have such sports activities as singing, dancing, archery, and equestrianism associated with life and military affairs. *Book of the Later Han Dynasty* records that "Dongyi is populated with aborigines who are fond of drinking, singing, and dancing."[138] *Interpretation of Rites of the Zhou Dynasty* notes that "Dongyi people love dancing with spears, wishing to help crops grow." It is also recorded that "Dongyi's music is called Zhuchou, indicating that when it is the right time, everything will grow out of the ground." The above historical data shows that they are good at dancing, and the props, namely spears, held by the dancers, were used specifically for helping crops grow. It can also be seen that this dance is closely related to production, featured by the distinctive nature of witchcraft. Besides, it records that "The music of Dongyi is called Mo."[139] *Book of Music* has the following citation that "Wa musician is called Mao teacher," "Mo musicians with the instrument of Mao teach the music of Dongyi, and the music they play is often used in sacrificial events." "Mao" is an ancient flag decorated with yak tails on the flagpole. Therefore, the dance with Mao by Ji musician is a kind of witch dance. Regarding the lineup of musical dance, *Book of Music* records, "A Wa musician leads one Xiashi and 16 dancers, and a Mao musician leads four Xiashi and many dancers."[140] Thus, it can be seen that Dongyi's Mo music consists of lead dance and group dance, which integrates witchcraft and dance as a whole in harmony.

The northern ethnic groups had been in contact with the Central Plains for a long time. According to the *Discourses of the States · Lu Yu*, "Sushen paid tributes with Gushi and Shipan" as early as the time when King Wu successfully overthrew the Shang Dynasty.[141] Regarding musical dance, *Book of the Later Han Dynasty* records, "After King Taikang of the Xia Dynasty lost the morality, the barbarians began to rebel. After the reign of King Shaokang, the world obeyed Xia's ruling and paid tributes to the imperial court with their musical dances."[142] The book *Zhu Shu Ji Nian* (a chronicle) also records, "In the first year of the reign of King Fa, the barbarians paid tributes to the imperial court with local dances."¹⁴³ *History of Ancient and Modern Arts* also records, "The swing was originally a sports activity of **Shanrong, which was spread to China after** Duke Huan of Qi conquered Shanrong."¹⁴⁴ Shanrong is known as a minority in Northeast China in the Spring and Autumn Period, located between southwestern Liaoning and northeastern Hebei. In the 14th year of King Hui of the Eastern Zhou Dynasty (663 BC), Duke Huan of Qi conquered Shanrong and brought back the swing game, which thereafter became popular in Han and Tang Dynasties. All these showed that the sports and cultural exchanges among the northern ethnic groups had taken their shape since the Xia Dynasty.

From the perspective of the sports development of Buyeo and Goguryeo, Buyeo was an early-developed ethnic group with a low level of productivity and limited sports activities. The only sports events on record were restricted to production, life, and war-related themes. However, when this ethnic group developed itself into Goguryeo, its sports activities had evolved to a certain extent, rich in content and diverse in forms. In this period, its sports culture not only featured memories of production, life, religion, and war, but also manifested that people began to pursue individual development under the current level of social productivity and grand environment, thus endowing sports with more connotations.

From the Pre-Qin period to the Southern and Northern Dynasties, except that the Han Dynasties maintained their relative stability, the whole society was characterized by booming progress of different cultures and sharp disputes among separatist forces. The term "competition" can best describe the social situation in this period. In a society with backward productivity, economic and military power was the main capital available for effective competition. At this time, military power was largely manifested by individual abilities, such as the full use of personal strength and fighting skills, etc., which had turned out to be the main factor determining the outcome of the competition. Since the productivity of the northern ethnic groups lagged behind that of the Central Plains, this phenomenon of determining the outcome of competition by individual ability was even more prominent. For example, when Turks elected its king, Ashina's son was selected because he jumped highest among all the other sons.¹⁴⁵ For another example, Li Keyong, the leader of Shatuo, conquered the leader of Tatar with his superb riding and shooting skills. Surprisingly, the Tatars did not dare to harm him just because they were subdued by his bravery.¹⁴⁶ Although the above two cases are not precise enough to belong to this period, they share a similar social development status in a certain development stage, which is particularly prominent in this period, demonstrating that the phenomenon of subduing people with personal strength is widespread in the ancient northern ethnic groups.

Next, we are going to talk about the exchange of sports culture between Han and Hu nationalities in this period.

2.6.1 Exchange of Sports Culture Based on Mounted Archery between the Northern Ethnic Groups and the Han Nationality

The northern prairies in ancient China produced fine horses, and the people were doughty and brave and admired fighting on the horse. Therefore, the mounted archery culture can be regarded as an important feature of the sports culture of the nomads in the northern prairies, which was mainly reflected in the military, production, and religion as well as the folk custom of the northern ethnic groups. Equestrianism in the Central Plains was heavily affected by the northern nomads. After the equestrian culture of the northern nomads was introduced, it enriched the connotation of equestrianism in the sports culture of the Central Plains and significantly promoted the progress of ancient Chinese sports culture. Mounted archery is not only an important part of the equestrian culture, but also an ancient military sports activity. It includes riding and shooting skills, which are difficult to master, requiring highly skilled practice, mostly for hunting and military training. The mounted archery culture profoundly impacted the ancient northern ethnic groups and the Han people in the Central Plains in terms of politics, military, economy, culture, and customs.

According to the archaeological records, the use of bows and arrows existed in northern China as early as 10,000 to 20,000 years ago. In the microlithic cultural sites found in the northern prairies, extremely refined small stone arrowheads were unearthed, all made of hard-textured and beautifully colored silica stone materials, indicating that the northern nomads had a long history of using bows and arrows. After long-term exploration and practice, they gradually completed the process of transferring the use of bows and arrows from ground to horseback. Historical books often employ specific nouns such as "mounted archery," "archery and horsemanship," "draw a bow on horseback," "horseback kung fu," and so on to make the representation. Over time, the meaning of these words has also expanded. In many cases, wielding other weapons such as knives, lances, and long spears on horseback is also included within its meaning, which can be called mounted archery in a broad sense. The emergence time of mounted archery in China can also be roughly determined from the rock paintings excavated in archaeology. A lot of the rock paintings discovered in northern and northwestern China involve horse riding and hunting. This can be seen from the previous chapters, which provide a reference for solving the problem. Mr. Yu Xingwu once said, "Individual riding and mounted archery had become popular in the Shang Dynasty."[147] Therefore, mounted archery in the broad sense appeared 3,500 years ago at the latest. The bronze equestrian warriors unearthed in Ordos can be traced back to the Western Zhou Dynasty, together with the records of Humo and Tuhe cavalry going down to the south continuously, which further proved that cavalry had developed among the nomads in northern China from the Western Zhou Dynasty to the Spring and Autumn Period. The emergence of cavalry is an epoch-making event in the history of sports in China. Once mounted archery is employed in war, the knights on horseback are no longer hunters specializing in economic activities, but warriors engaged in military struggle. This marks the birth of a new event in Chinese history, i.e., the cavalry. In short, the birth of cavalry implies that the culture of mounted archery has shifted from labor production to military application, which also marks the beginning of formal and systematic training in riding and shooting techniques. The establishment of the cavalry unit signifies a great change in the mounted archery culture, which also turns out to be a potential driving force for the change in ethnic patterns.

The mounted archery culture of the northern ethnic groups was mainly developed in the prairies. It had borne a strong color of nomadic culture since its birth; for example, the people were good at riding and shooting, and they were usually brave in fighting. Using horses as carts and fighting with horses determine the characteristics of the equestrian culture of the northern ethnic groups. In the collision between the mounted archery culture of the northern ethnic groups and the sports culture of the Central Plains, they interacted with and influenced each other, learned from each other's strengths, and merged in the melting pot of a unified multi-ethnic country. Comparing the sports culture of nomads integrated into military activities with the sports culture of agricultural nationalities, the nomads are good at riding and shooting, doughty and brave, and highly flexible in horseback fighting. However, they have much less sophisticated weapons than agricultural nationalities, and they also lack heavy weapons, so they are generally not excellent at infantry war, especially weak in siege. The combination of military affairs and administration facilitates the migration of nomads; therefore, it is easy for them to adapt to the war environment, convenient for war mobilization, and simple to build up soldiers. In terms of these characteristics, the military culture of the agricultural nationalities in the Han region is much inferior to that of northern ethnic groups. The northern ethnic groups eat much more meat, so they are powerful. Because of the simple dietary structure, they do not need to carry large amounts of food, workforce, and animal-drawn carriers with them like the military forces of Central Plains during the operations. Therefore, they can act flexibly and quickly and are specialized in attacking and penetrating enemy positions. The agricultural nationalities are more advanced than the northern ethnic groups in weaponry, arms, and tactics, who have sharper and more sophisticated weapons as well as heavy equipment, so they are good at siege or defense.

The cavalry of the Central Plains was set up by King Wuling of Zhao in the Warring States Period by learning and summarizing experiences in battles with neighboring northern ethnic groups such as Loufan and Linhu. The reform of "shooting on the horse in Hu dress" initiated by the Zhao State is more than a simple military reform. Rather, it is a comprehensive, influential, and extensive reform of military, political, and cultural ideology in a more profound sense. After the middle age of the Warring States Period, cavalry became increasingly vital in military operations in the Central Plains. Chariot soldiers were gradually eliminated, and joint operations with infantry and cavalry became the main mode of military operations in China's feudal society. Therefore, all regimes must strengthen their cavalry training to fully play the potential role. Next, let's discuss it through the typical case of "shooting on the horse in Hu dress" in the Warring States Period.

The mounted archery culture of the ancient northern ethnic groups exerted a profound influence on the Han nationality in Central Plains in the Spring and Autumn Period and the Warring States Period. In the Spring and Autumn Period, Duke Huan of Qi "saved Duke of Jin, captured the King of Di, and defeated Humo and Tuhe. The horse-riding invaders were subdued."[148] The phrase "horse-riding invaders" in the literature is a direct written record of the nomadic cavalry in northern China in the early period. According to the historical records, "King Wuling of Zhao broke the established custom, changed to wear the Hu dress, and learned mounted archery, then defeated Linhu and Loufan in the north."[149] King Wuling of Zhao initiated this reform in order to strengthen the military power and defeat the cavalry of Donghu, Loufan, and Linhu. It is generally believed that Zhao was the first state to establish cavalry troops in ancient China. At that time, Zhao was surrounded by powerful enemies, with Qi and Zhongshan in the southeast, Han and Wei in the south, Qin and Linhu in the west, Loufan and Donghu in the north, and Yan in the northeast. Linhu, Loufan, and Donghu are known as Three Hu, who were all nomadic groups rising in the north and south of the desert as well as living on hunting animals, were good at mounted archery, bold and powerful, which posed a huge threat to the Zhao State. Since the Zhou Dynasty, Xiongnu had been in frequent conflict with the Central Plains, and sometimes a war was triggered. In the Warring States Period, "there were seven powerful states, three of which were bordered by Xiongnu."[150] The tribes around Zhao State were dominated by nomads who were all adept at mounted archery and often invaded the borders of Zhao with their cavalry. With an intimate knowledge of the superiority of the nomadic cavalry, King Wuling of Zhao believed that reforming the army with mounted archery was a way out to strengthen the military power. In the middle of the Warring States Period, King Wuling decided to initiate the reform of "shooting on the horse in Hu dress." He first asked General Lou Huan what Zhao should do in the face of powerful enemies around, and then he added, "We should wear Hu dress." Hu dress is the clothing of Hu people, including short clothes, belts, hooks, and leather boots. They are different from the wide clothes with long sleeves worn by people in the Central Plains, but they are convenient for riding and shooting. King Wuling of Zhao hoped to popularize Hu dress comprehensively among the military officers, soldiers, officials, and ordinary people throughout the country. Therefore, this reform enjoyed more extensive coverage. Some aristocrats, including Zhao Wen, Zhao Zao, Zhou Shao, and Zhao Jun, dissuaded him from popularizing Hu dress. King Wuling retorted them and argued, "The previous emperors adhered to the different conventions, so which one should we specifically follow? The rituals of predecessors varied from each other, and none of them inherited from one to the other, so which one should we specifically follow?" He also pointed out, "To change the country, we do not necessarily adhere to the ancient practices, since the saints do not rule the country by mutual inheritance." Regarding clothing, he said, "The style of clothes is only intended to dress people neatly, but not to judge the sages on the look." King Wuling received massive support from the ministers and refuted the accusations of some aristocrats.[151] Especially some influential aristocrats like Zhao Cheng also put on Hu dress, helping to promote Hu dress throughout the state. Later, after Zhao captured Yuanyang (now southeast of Hohhot, Inner Mongolia), King Wuling renamed it "Qiyi (cavalry base)" to train cavalry. A minister named Niu Zan opposed it again, saying that "A state must have fixed laws as the army must have unchanging rules. Changing the law will lead to chaos in the country, while changing the rules will weaken the army." King Wuling refuted, "The interests in ancient times and today differ from each other; the remote regions and the Central Plains possess different military weapons and equipment … You know the laws of the government, but fail to know the benefits brought by the military weapons and equipment … Now you take the government's laws to disrupt my reform. You are totally wrong!" Niu Zan hurriedly bowed down and said, "How dare I not obey your order?"[152] Because of the Hu dress reform, Zhao established a cavalry-based army, soon demonstrating its power in war. The following year after the reform, Zhao State launched an attack on Zhongshan and proceeded to Ningjia (now north of Huolu County, Hebei). Later, Zhao attacked the barbarian region westward and arrived in Yuzhong (now the northeastern bank of Hetao, Inner Mongolia), "opening up thousands of miles of land." The king of Linhu offered up fine horses to Zhao for peace. King Wuling ordered Zhao Gu, the prime minister of Daidi, to take charge of the barbarian regions occupied by Zhao and train cavalry for the central government. In the third year of the reign of King Huiwen (296 BC), Zhao finally occupied Zhongshan and drove its king to Fushi (now southeast of Suide County, Shaanxi).[153] While stepping up the attack on Zhongshan, Zhao State also attacked Xiongnu in the north, "expanding the land north to Yan and Dai." To the west, Zhao attacked Linhu and Loufan and reached Yunzhong (now Togtoh County, Inner Mongolia) and Jiuyuan (now Baotou City, Inner Mongolia). After the reform of "shooting on the horse in Hu dress," Zhao became the most powerful state except for Qin and Qi. This reform strengthened Zhao's military strength, and, more importantly, it promoted the transformation of China's ancient military system from chariot warfare to cavalry plus infantry warfare. Along with the progress of cavalry, the development of mounted archery was also accelerated in the Central Plains.

The reform of "shooting on the horse in Hu dress" had great influence and far-reaching significance for the later generations, which is mainly reflected in the following aspects:

First, the reform led to a change in the concepts of nationalities. In the Pre-Qin period, hundreds of schools of thought in the Central Plains culture were contending, and all vassal states were competing to occupy a leading position in politics, economy, and culture. In this period, the atmosphere of "scholar" culture was strong, requiring clearness, open-mindedness, and "high-end;" otherwise, it would easily be "judged" as heterodoxy. It was even more sensitive in dealing with ethnic issues. At that time, ethnic minorities were regarded as barbarians. The Central Plains represented the advanced culture which occupied a dominant position, while the surrounding ethnic minorities were "uneducated people," which represented backwardness and ignorance. Domesticating or attacking backward neighboring ethnic groups by advanced representative culture was easily accepted by the common people, but the Central Plains learning from the surrounding "fools" was regarded as "rebellious" at the time. However, after King Wuling practiced "shooting on the horse in Hu dress," Zhao State became more powerful, making a forceful strike on the northern ethnic groups and contending against Qin and Qi's attacks, which proved the success of the reform. This result was well recognized by the civilian, so other states began to follow Zhao's practice to establish their cavalry troops, which largely changed the traditional and secular national concepts of the Central Plains.

Second, the reform promoted mutual learning among different ethnic groups. In the Warring States Period, the cavalry often mingled with chariots for joint operations, called "light chariots and elite cavalry" or "chariots and cavalry." "The infantry stands on chariots, and the cavalry lines up nearby." As described in the *Six Arts of War*, a book on the arts of war completed in the middle Warring States Period, "Chariots, like the wings of an army, are used to assault fortified positions, break enemy ranks, intercept strong enemies, and cut off enemy's retreat. As the eyes of an army, the cavalry is used to track and chase defeated troops, cut off enemies' routes for providing foodstuff, and attack scattered enemies in escape." The ratio of chariots and cavalrymen should be adjusted based on the terrain of the battlefield in order to exert the advantages of different arms, the purpose of which is to maximize their strengths and avoid weaknesses. The book also notes that "for combat on flat terrain, five chariots form a row. Each row is forty steps apart from the rows in front and behind, and each chariot is ten steps apart from those on the right and left sides. The distance between each squad is 50 steps on all sides. Ten chariots form a *Ju* (a combat formation) for combat on steep terrain, and twenty chariots form a *Tun* (a combat formation). Each chariot is 20 steps apart from those in front and behind, and six steps apart from those on the right and left sides. Each squad is 36 steps apart from each other on all sides."[154] The distance between cavalrymen is reduced by half compared to that on flat terrain. In *Sun Bin's Arts of War · Eight Tactical Arrays*, it is also stated, "When fighting with chariots and cavalry, the troops should be divided into three parts, one part on the right side, one part on the left side, and one part at the rear. More chariots should be arranged for flat terrains, more cavalrymen for steep terrains, and more archers for narrow and dangerous places."[155] That is to say, it is significant to choose an advantageous ground based on the ratio of chariots and cavalrymen of both parties with the aim of defeating the enemy. The formation of chariots, cavalry, and infantry during the Warring States Period can be roughly perceived from the discovery of the Terracotta Warriors and Horses. In Pit 1, chariots and infantry are in alternate arrangements. In Pit 2, chariots and cavalry are in a mixed arrangement, with infantry on the front left, chariots on the right, and infantry following the chariots again. In this huge formation, various arms fight in concert, with infantry fighting against the enemy, chariots as the main attack force, and cavalry on the front, back, and flanks for support or chase. A pit of warriors constructs a complete combat system.

There are not many records of cavalry battles in the Warring States Period. The main reason is that cavalry rarely fights alone. There are only a few cases from which we can see how cavalry was used at that time. According to *Wu Zi · Encouragements*, Wu Qi once defeated the Qin army of 500,000 soldiers with 500 chariots and 3000 cavalrymen.[156] In the Battle of Maling, by using the method of reducing stoves, Sun Bin induced Pang Juan to give up his infantry and chase with cavalry only. Sun Bin set up an ambush on Maling Road and killed Pang Juan. That is a successful ambush battle, highlighting the use of terrain favorable to infantry so as to annihilate the enemy's chariots in one fell swoop. Another example is the Changping Battle, in which the Qin army pretended to be defeated and induced the Zhao army to chase. As a result, the Zhao army was intercepted by two cavalry units of Qin on the way, who stopped the entry of grains for the Zhao army, forcing their soldiers to become so fearful without fighting. Qin finally won a big victory by killing more than 400,000 soldiers of Zhao.

In the Warring States Period, part of the cavalry came from neighboring ethnic minorities. For example, at the beginning of King Wuling's reform of "shooting on the horse in Hu dress," he ordered "Zhao Gu, the prime minister of Daidi, to take charge of Hu affairs and recruit soldiers there." "In the second year of the reign of King Huiwen, King Wuling visited the newly occupied land, then left Daidi and met with the king of Loufan for recruiting soldiers."[157] "Recruiting soldiers" here means to recruit Hu soldiers to join the cavalry unit. Qin State also had Hu soldiers, as was cited in the *Historical Records · Biography of Zhang Yi*, "Qin was abundant in fine horses and numerous soldiers.[158] Many horses were able to jump for three *xun* (an ancient measure of length equal to about 8 *chi*)." The soldiers here mainly refer to the Yiqu people. As stated in the *Historical Records · Chronicles of Qin*, "In the 11th year of the reign of King Huiwen of Qin, Yiqu became a county of Qin … The King of Yiqu became affiliated to Qin as a minister."[159] Yiqu soldiers were originally good at mounted archery, who therefore mainly joined the cavalry. Until the Han Dynasty, the main sources of cavalry were still the frontier ethnic groups and those people who grew up there for generations. If the people of the Central Plains expected to join the cavalry, they had to "prepare armors and weapons, equip chariots and horses and practice archery."[160]

Due to the fact that the northern part of China is mountainous, it was particularly conducive to the light cavalry of Hu, but not to the chariots of the Central Plains. When the northern ethnic minorities attacked Qin State, they mostly used light cavalry, with changeable time and place plus fast-moving speed. The tactics of these ethnic minorities inspired Qin, who was good at absorbing foreign cultures. In particular, the miracle created by Zhao's cavalry provided an excellent opportunity for Qin, who had already satisfied the conditions for cavalry construction. As a result, Qin State quickly set up and developed a cavalry unit comparable to Zhao's, thereby repeatedly achieving meritorious results in wars.

The Central Plains not only learned mounted archery skills from the northern ethnic groups, but also researched them timely and effectively to form some theories of cavalry construction and training. In the discussions on the tactical principles of fighting under topographic conditions such as forests, mountains, rivers, and defiles in *Six Arts of War · Baotao*, it is stated that "if trees are sparse in the forest, use the cavalry to assist and place chariots in front. Fight when the terrain is favorable, and stop when the terrain is unfavorable."[161] Chariots and cavalry can also form a dark cloud-like array to shoot the enemy's flanks with powerful crossbows. *Six Arts of War · Quantao* discusses the characteristics, combat power, formation, and selection standards of chariots and cavalrymen of the three arms, including chariot, cavalry, and infantry. It argues the characteristics of three arms, "It is important that the infantry should be familiar with the changes of circumstance, the chariot should be familiar with topographic conditions, and the cavalry should be familiar with secret paths and routes."[162] Chariots are suitable for combat on plains, but must not be used in mountains, hills, grasslands, ditches, collapsing and ponding areas, and muddy areas, which are "fatal terrains" for chariots. Cavalry is suitable for attacking the advance forces of enemies in cooperation with infantry and chariots, striking the flanks of enemies, launching long-distance raids, and intercepting enemies' routes to provide foodstuff. However, it must not fall into "patios," "crypts," deep valleys, lush forests, swamps or low-altitude, moist and muddy areas, or the ambush by enemy chariots and cavalry, which are "fatal terrains" for cavalry. On flat terrain, one cavalryman can defeat eight infantrymen; on steep terrain, one can defeat four infantrymen. Chariots and cavalry are both powerful in the army. It is known that ten chariots can defeat 1,000 infantrymen, and 100 chariots can defeat 10,000 infantrymen; ten cavalrymen can defeat 100 infantrymen, and 100 cavalrymen can defeat 1,000 infantrymen.

Cavalry is highly mobile and is good at chasing enemies and defeated troops, cutting off enemies' routes for providing foodstuff, and attacking enemies' mobile forces. Chariots and cavalry were both technical arms of the time. They were strictly selected and paid well and were used as powerful strike forces at that time. The criteria for selecting cavalry are as follows: under 40 years old, more than 7.5 *chi* in height, stronger and more agile than ordinary people, able to shoot arrows on galloping horses, good at maneuvering forward, backward, leftward and rightward, capable of riding horses across ravines, hills, steep terrains, and rivers; one can chase strong enemies and disrupt the formation of enemies. Thus he can be named "Warrior Knight."[163]

Among all the states, Qin, Yan, and Zhao owned the largest number of cavalry because they had the most contacts with the neighboring ethnic minorities, each with more than 10,000 cavalrymen, followed by Chu and Wei with 3,000 and 5,000 respectively. The construction of large cavalry units of other states was all modeled on Zhao's practice to some extent, not only in the archery skills and tactics, but more importantly, in the spirit, concept, and cognition.

Third, the reform became a driving force for the change in ethnic patterns. Xiongnu is a nomadic nation in northern China, where people are good at shooting and riding, eating salty meat, and wearing clothes made of animal skins. In the late Warring States Period, Xiongnu entered the stage of slave society, in which the slave owners and aristocrats, relying on the strong mobility of cavalry, often went deep into the Central Plains to harass Qin, Zhao, Yan and other agriculture-oriented regions, plunder properties and compete for pastures, bringing huge trouble to the production and people's livelihood. At that time, all states were so busy with annexation that they had no time to deal with external factors; under this circumstance, they generally took a defensive position against Xiongnu and "built the Great Wall to resist." In the final stage of Qin's elimination of the other six states, Xiongnu took advantage of the warfare in the Central Plains and occupied "Henan" in the Hetao region, posing a severe threat to the Qin State. After unifying the six states, the First Emperor of Qin sent General Meng Tian with 300,000 soldiers to Hetao in the 29th year (218 BC) of his reign to eliminate this threat. The army "took back the whole land of Henan" and recaptured the Hetao region. After that, Qin State set up 34 counties there and reestablished Jiuyuan prefecture.[164] To further consolidate the rule over this region, in the 36th year of the reign of the First Emperor of Qin (211 BC), 30,000 inland households were relocated to Beihe and Yuzhong (now north of Ejin Horo Banner, Inner Mongolia Autonomous Region) to open up the wasteland. This large-scale immigration not only effectively stopped the looting of Xiongnu slave owners and aristocrats, but also promoted the development and ethnic integration of this region, a great move that had significant military and economic implications. Later on, particularly after the Han Dynasty established a large-scale cavalry force, more effective attacks and control were carried out on Xiongnu, and they were integrated into the Han as well as other neighboring ethnic groups. For more than a thousand years afterwards, the wars and exchanges between the northern ethnic groups internally and between them and the Central Plains were all closely connected with mounted archery. Through this method, the Chinese nation achieved rapid exchanges and integration between the ethnic groups, accelerated the change of ethnic patterns, and finally constructed the formation of a pluralistic and integrative Chinese nation.

In short, the complementation between the argo-pastoral economy and the husbandry economy in the Pre-Qin period facilitated the communication between the northern ethnic groups and the Central Plains. The sports culture generated under these two economic forms was also colliding with frequent exchanges among the ethnic groups. The sports culture that sprouted in the northern ethnic group in this period strengthened their physique and cultivated their militarism. The introduction of the mounted archery culture into the Central Plains greatly affected ethnic patterns and profoundly influenced the future of China.

2.6.2 Absorption of the Sports Culture of Han by the Northern Ethnic Groups

In ancient northern China, the development of the nomadic tribes from primitive social formation to the stage of class differentiation could be attributed to the improvement of their husbandry and hunting economy as well as the accumulation of material wealth as a result of private economy and inequality. In addition, the advanced farming culture of the Han nationality in the Central Plains was also an important influencing factor. No matter how strong the northern ethnic groups were in military strength in ancient China, if they intended to gain a foothold on the whole land, they must absorb the advanced culture of the Han region. History has proved that a politically, economically, and culturally advanced nation with a large population, regardless of whether it is in a dominant or dominated position, has always had a strong influence on the social progress of a backward nation; even if the backward nation is in a dominant position, it cannot resist this influence, regardless of the subjective wishes of its ruling clique.[165] Yelü Abaoji, the leader of Khitan, relied on the Hans to develop agriculture in the upper reaches of the Luan River, leading to an increase in strength. Later, he unified the nomadic tribes of Khitan. After founding the Liao Dynasty, he actively absorbed the progressive politics, economy, and culture of the Han nationality and finally initiated Khitan to dominate northern China for two centuries. In the construction of Zhongjing, Emperor Shengzong of the Liao Dynasty relied on "excellent workers" of the Han nationality in Yan and Ji regions, who imitated the style of Luoyang to build the city walls, palaces, pavilions, storehouses, and marketplaces of Zhongjing. The bronze and iron ware, paper, tea, and various necessities that Dangxiang (Tangut) and Tubo lacked were also obtained from the Han region through trade and other channels. In Jurchen, not only did the aristocrats actively study the Han culture and the Confucian way of ruling the state, but also many Jurchen commoners migrating to the Central Plains spoke Chinese, wore Han clothes, and changed to Han surnames in their contacts with the Han people. Although Emperor Shizong and Emperor Zhangzong of the Jin Dynasty repeatedly ordered not to forget the "national language and mounted archery" for fear that Jurchen would lose its inherent nature and its rule would be affected, they were still unable to reverse this trend. As a result, after the Jin Dynasty perished, those Jurchens who had moved to the Central Plains were naturally assimilated into the Han nationality.

The intimate relationship between the husbandry and hunting culture of northern ethnic groups and the farming culture of the Central Plains has been described since the legendary age. There arose numerous wars in the Spring and Autumn Period and the Warring States Period. The conflicts between different Han regimes in the Central Plains, between the northern nomadic tribes, and between the Han nationality and the northern ethnic groups all contributed more or less to the exchanges and cooperation among the ethnic groups, thereby promoting ethnic integration. Through trade and warfare, the agricultural culture of the Central Plains was spread to the northern nomadic regions, greatly improving the nomadic culture on its original basis. As stated in the *Historical Records · Trade*, "Tianshui, Longxi, Beidi, and Shangjun share the same custom as Guanzhong, yet they enjoy the geographical advantage of Qiangzhong in the west and the livestock of Rongdi in the north, thus forming the most developed husbandry in the world."[166] The non-governmental exchanges between the farming and nomadic cultures were mainly realized through those commercial activities at the beginning and then by war. From a cultural perspective, war is a form of cultural exchange, but it is only a partial reflection between nomadic culture and farming culture, and more importantly, the complementation of heterogeneous cultures and ethnic integration has been achieved in this process.

Since Xiongnu established a connection with the Han nationality, the Han region's material culture and spiritual culture had been continuously spread to Xiongnu through trade, gifting, and marriages, thus generating some significant impacts on the lives of Huns as well as the society of Xiongnu. According to the historical records, Xiongnu had captured many Han people at the border of the Han Dynasty, most of whom were farmers or craftsmen. After they arrived in Xiongnu, only a few joined Xiongnu's husbandry and hunting activities, and all the others were still engaged in agriculture and handicrafts. "According to the sickles and plow unearthed and some records about employing Han people to build buildings and store grains, the agriculture of Xiongnu was greatly influenced by the Han nationality. In addition, the agricultural techniques were disseminated from the Hans, and most of the laborers engaged in agriculture were also Han people." "According to the fact that many knives and swords resemble those of the Han style, it can be concluded that the Han culture greatly affected the iron culture of Xiongnu, and most of the blacksmiths at that time were also Han craftsmen from the Central Plains."[167] Since the Qin Dynasty, Han people had continued to escape to Xiongnu, many of whom were Han aristocrats and military generals. They participated in the political, military, and cultural activities of Xiongnu. Some literature shows that after Zhonghang Yue went to Xiongnu, he took up a civilian post. Zhonghang Yue had written letters in Chinese for the chief of Xiongnu and taught the Xiongnu people to learn Chinese characters and computing, and to distinguish people, animals, and place names.[168] There were also many Han people who surrendered to Xiongnu, who also spread Han culture and educated the Huns. In this way, Xiongnu not only obtained the wealth produced by these Han people, but also mastered advanced farming culture and production skills, farmer's customs, ways of thinking, ethics, etc., through frequent contact with the Han people, thus exerting a positive influence on the nomadic culture.

During the reign of Tan Shihuai, Xianbei people also attached importance to learning from the Hans. At the end of the Han Dynasty, some scholars and handicrafts men went to Xianbei, so that the Xianbei people learned from them the advanced knowledge of Han culture and further revitalized its education. Likewise, Xianbei also learned from other ethnic minorities the skills and arts needed. In terms of fishing, Tan Shihuai could actively learn from the ethnic groups in the eastern coastal areas of Northeast China and moved thousands of people who were good at fishing to Xianbei in order to teach them their fishing experience.[169]

Since the early days of its founding, Goguryeo had imitated the education system of the Central Plains to develop its own. In the 2nd year of the reign of King Xiaoshoulin (AD 372), Goguryeo "set up an imperial college to teach students." Goguryeo not only set up an imperial college in the capital city to educate the children of aristocratic families, but also established some official schools in various places during the Tang Dynasty, which were equivalent to the schools at the level of state, province, and county, as well prefecture schools established by the Tang Dynasty. According to the *Historical Records of the Three Kingdoms*, Goguryeo set up "Jiong School" in the capital in AD 372 and built a large house called "Jiong Hall" in local areas to teach Confucian classics to the children of aristocratic families. Also, according to the records of some ancient North Korean books, **Goguryeo** set official positions such as "Boshi of State School" and "Boshi of Imperial College" at that time, all indicating the existence of official schools in Goguryeo. All above are the particular proofs of existence for Goguryeo's "Jiong Hall." According to the historical records, "People loved books, even among those of low social status," "They built big houses in the streets, called Jiong Hall, where the children studied day and night before marriage. The books included *Five Classics, Historical Records, Book of the Former Han Dynasty, Book of the Later Han Dynasty* (by Fan Ye), *Records of the Three Kingdoms, Records of Jinyang* (by Sun Sheng), *Yu Pian, Zi Shu, Zi Lin,* and *Selected Works,* especially favored by the people. The "Jiong Hall" here is a form of a private school run in the Goguryeo era, which was built with funds raised from the government and ordinary families to educate children. The teaching content included reading and archery, which is similar to the six arts education in the Pre-Qin period of the Central Plains in terms of organization and content, which falls within the scope of the ancient education content in the Central Plains of China.

These include many examples of northern ethnic groups absorbing the Han sports culture, which will be briefly depicted in the following chapters. The most notable one is the spread of polo from the Central Plains to the northern ethnic groups. The love for polo and its extensive development among the northern ethnic groups are sufficient to prove the desire and reality of those northern ethnic groups to absorb and learn the sports culture of the Central Plains.

2.6.3 Integration of Sports Cultures among Neighboring Northern Ethnic Groups in Ancient China

Apart from the integration of sports cultures between the ancient northern ethnic groups and the Han nationality, sports cultures are integrated among the northern ethnic groups themselves. This phenomenon occurs more often in battles and migrations. As an earlier documented record cited, Xiongnu continuously conquered and annexed other ethnic groups around to form a national military alliance. When it comes to the Qin and Han Dynasties, Modu, the leader of Xiongnu, established a Chanyu sate, which annexed Donghu and defeated **Yuezhi**. After several decades till Emperor Wen of the Han Dynasty, the territory of Xiongnu extended to the Great Khingan Mountains in the east, Xinjiang and some parts of Central Asia in the west, and Lake Baikal in the north. "All nomadic tribes were unified as one, and the northern region was pacified."[170] As a consequence, Xiongnu became a unified multi-ethnic nomadic military alliance. China thus realized the unification of northern nomadic groups and the unification of agricultural regions between the north and south for the first time, forming two powerful regimes in confrontation. Since then, the northern regimes, from "Five Barbarians" (including Xiongnu, Xianbei, Jie, Di, and Qiang) to Shatuo, Khitan, Jurchen, Mongolia, Manchu, and other ethnic groups, had founded or unified as a country to confront the Han Dynasties in the south or unified the whole China in succession. Besides, some other northern and southern agricultural and nomadic nationalities **established frontier dynasties and nomadic khanates in different periods. In this process, nations** of kinds were ruled or merged by conquest or annexation, followed by cultural integration. As there are few records on the sports culture of northern ethnic groups, it is inconvenient to discuss more. It was not until the Song, Liao, Jin, and Xixia Dynasties that some clues could be vaguely found in the literature.

According to the archaeological data and literature study, the sports culture of the northern ethnic groups in ancient China was formed to adapt to their own social life. It featured relative unity and integrity, but could be decomposed and supplemented or became constantly updated and developed. Once different sports cultures come into contact, they naturally blend together. Therefore, in the development course of the ancient northern ethnic groups, they had early achieved the transition from the stage of sports culture exchanges between ethnic groups to the stage of not only creating their own culture, but also constantly communicating with each other, thus jointly creating the national culture. Together with the Han nationality, all ethnic groups created, promoted, and developed China's ancient national sports culture together with the Han nationality.

Arguably, sports culture exchanges among the ancient northern ethnic groups were omnipresent. When there were exchanges in remote antiquity, the sports exchange was also in its infancy, which became even more obvious when the ethnic groups entered the class society with conflicts of interest or connections. Especially when there were exchanges between the northern ethnic groups and the Central Plains, or when there were equal exchanges among several ethnic groups, sports, like other cultures or materials, became a part of the exchanges, and increasingly showed its prominent social functions. The development and prosperity of Chinese national sports mainly depend on the crystallization of national wisdom, which is also closely associated with the exchanges between different nationalities. No matter they are between ethnic minorities and the Central Plains, or between ethnic minorities on their own, there exist sports exchanges of various forms, for example, sports exchanges resulting from normal population movement in peacetime, sports exchanges promoted by means of Heqin (make peace with rulers of minorities in the border areas by marriage), sports exchanges arising from abnormal population movement during wars, or sports exchanges occurring in commerce among ethnic groups. The reform of "shooting on the horse in Hu dress" initiated by King Wuling of Zhao in the Warring States Period is just a case in point. In the Han Dynasty, the Central Plains and Wusun State established amicable relations, which was further embodied in the fact that the Han had several Heqin with Wusun. There were exchanges of wrestling between the two countries during the reign of Emperor Wu of Han, as shown from the Jiao-Di exchanges in the time of Emperor Wu. What's more, during the reign of Emperor Xuan of Han, there was also Heqin, which was recorded in detail in the *Book of the Former Han Dynasty · Memoirs on the Western Regions*. A lot of sports culture exchanges occurred along with this marriage.[171] There are a large number of records about Heqin between the Han Dynasty and Xiongnu, as well as between the Tang Dynasty and Turks. Every Heqin happens to be an important process of sports culture exchanges, such as the polo match associated with Heqin during the reign of Emperor Zhongzong of the Tang Dynasty. Sports exchanges in wars can also be found in history frequently. In peacetime, it is also common for people to move to different places. For example, Jin Midi was originally the prince of King Xiutu of Xiongnu. When King Hunye yielded to the Han Dynasty, King Xiutu was killed because of regret for the surrender, and Jin Midi, together with his mother Yanzhi and his brother Lun, yielded to Han. Jin Midi was good at breeding horses and therefore was appreciated by Emperor Wu of the Han Dynasty and permitted to follow the emperor. Later, when Ma Heluo and some other people rebelled, Jin Midi caught Heluo in the neck and threw him down in the place.[172] It can be seen that the exchanges of sports culture between the Han Dynasty and Xiongnu were already quite frequent at that time. In the Han and Tang Dynasties, a large number of entertainers from the Western Regions presented their skills in Chang'an, which can also be regarded as a kind of sports exchange in peacetime. In Shangjing, the imperial capital of the Liao Dynasty, different kinds of talents of the Han nationality, including eunuchs, officers from the national academy, magicians, musicians, wrestlers, Xiucai (Confucianism), monks and nuns, and Taoists,[173] gathered to engage in political and cultural activities, which is also considered as a mode of national sports culture exchange.

NOTES

1. Wang Zhonghan, *Chinese National History*, rev. 1st ed. (China Social Sciences Press, 1994), 141.
2. [Han] Fan Ye, *Biography of Dongyi*, vol. 85 of *Book of the Later Han Dynasty*, 1st ed. (Zhonghua Book Company, May 1965), 2810–2811.
3. Wang Zhonghan, *Chinese National History*, rev. 1st ed. (China Social Sciences Press, 1994), 145–147.
4. [Tang] Yao Silian, *Biography of Goguryeo*, vol. 54 of *Book of the Liang Dynasty*, 1st ed. (Zhonghua Book Company, May 1973), 803; [Jin] Chen Shou, *Book of the Wei Dynasty · Biography of Goguryeo*, vol. 13 of *Records of the Three Kingdoms*, 1st ed. (Zhonghua Book Company, December 1959), 843.
5. [Chao] Jin Fushi, *Memoirs of Goguryeo*, vol. 18 of *Historical Records of the Three Kingdoms*, collected by Kuijangge (Seoul University, Korea), 3.
6. [Later Jin] Liu Xu et al., *Biography of Koryo*, vol. 199 of *Old Book of the Tang History*, 1st ed. (Zhonghua Book Company, May 1975), 5320.
7. [Han] Sima Qian, *Chronicles of Five Emperors*, vol. 1 of *Historical Records*, 1st ed. (Zhonghua Book Company, September 1959), 43.
8. Wang Zhonghan, *Chinese National History*, rev. 1st ed. (China Social Sciences Press, 1994), 160, 420.
9. [Han] Fan Ye, *Biography of Dongyi*, vol. 85 of *Book of the Later Han Dynasty*, 1st ed. (Zhonghua Book Company, May 1965), 2808.
10. [Han] Sima Qian, *Confucius Family*, vol. 47 of *Historical Records*, 1st ed. (Zhonghua Book Company, September 1959), 1922.
11. Heilongjiang Provincial Museum, Heilongjiang Province, "Clearance of Neolithic Sites in Niuchang, Ning'an," *Archaeology*, no. 4 (1960): 22; Tong Zhuchen, "Distribution and Stages of Primitive Culture in Northeast China," *Archaeology*, no. 10 (1961): 562.
12. [Jin] Chen Shou, *Book of the Wei Dynasty · Biography of Dongyi*, vol. 30 of *Records of the Three Kingdoms*, 1st ed. (Zhonghua Book Company, December 1959), 847–848.
13. [Tang] Fang Xuanling et al., *Biography of Siyi*, vol. 97 of *Book of the Jin Dynasty*, 1st ed. (Zhonghua Book Company, November 1974), 2533–2534.
14. [Tang] Fang Xuanling et al., *Biography of Siyi*, vol. 97 of *Book of the Jin Dynasty*, 1st ed. (Zhonghua Book Company, November 1974), 2533.
15. [Yuan] Ma Duanlin, *Descendants · Yilou*, vol. 326 of *General Review of Literature*, 1st ed. (Zhonghua Book Company, September 1986), 2566.
16. Heilongjiang Provincial Museum, "Excavation Report of Dongkang Primitive Society Site," *Archaeology*, no. 3 (1975): 168.

17. [Tang] Fang Xuanling et al., *Biography of Siyi*, vol. 97 of *Book of the Jin Dynasty*, 1st ed. (Zhonghua Book Company, November 1974), 2534.
18. Yang Baolong, *About Sushen and Yilou* (China Social Sciences Press, 1989), 226–228.
19. [Jin] Chen Shou, *Book of the Wei Dynasty · Three Young Emperors*, vol. 4 of *Records of the Three Kingdoms*, 1st ed. (Zhonghua Book Company, December 1959), 149; [Tang] Fang Xuanling et al., *Biography of Siyi*, vol. 97 of *Book of the Jin Dynasty*, 1st ed. (Zhonghua Book Company, November 1974), 2535.
20. [Tang] Fang Xuanling et al., *Chronicles of Emperors*, vol. 97 of *Book of the Jin Dynasty*, 1st ed. (Zhonghua Book Company, November 1974), 152.
21. Dong Wanlun, *Outline of the Northeast History* (Heilongjiang People's Publishing House, 1987), 56.
22. [Han] Fan Ye, *Biography of Dongyi · Yilou*, vol. 85 of *Book of the Later Han Dynasty*, 1st ed. (Zhonghua Book Company, May 1965), 2816; [Jin] Chen Shou, *Book of the Wei Dynasty · Biography of Dongyi*, vol. 30 of *Records of the Three Kingdoms*, 1st ed. (Zhonghua Book Company, December 1959), 847.
23. Fu Sinian believed that during the Han and Wei Dynasties, Yilou people frequently "invaded" the North Woju, and many North Woju people were plundered into Yilou. Yilou then called himself after his name, that is, Wuji is a variation interpretation of Woju (see *Outline of the Northeast History*, vol. 1, 119). The present-day Wu Wenxian, etc. also shares a similar statement in page 52 of *A Brief History of Heilongjiang*.
24. Wang Zhonghan, *Chinese National History*, rev. 1st ed. (China Social Sciences Press, 1994), 422.
25. [Beiqi] Wei Shou, *Biography of Wuji*, vol. 100 of *Book of the Wei Dynasty*, 1st ed. (Zhonghua Book Company, June 1974), 2220; [Tang] Wei Zheng et al., *Biography of Dongyi*, vol. 100 of *Book of the Sui Dynasty*, 1st ed. (Zhonghua Book Company, August 1973), 1821.
26. [Beiqi] Wei Shou, *Biography of Wuji*, vol. 100 of *Book of the Wei Dynasty*, 1st ed. (Zhonghua Book Company, June 1974), 2220.
27. [Tang] Li Yan, *Biography of Wuji*, vol. 94 of *History of the Northern Dynasties*, 1st ed. (Zhonghua Book Company, October 1974), 3124–3125.
28. Zhu Guochen and Wei Guozhong, *Bohai History Manuscript* (Heilongjiang Provincial Cultural Relics Publishing and Editing Office, 1984), 7.
29. Gan Zhigeng and Sun Xiuren, *Outline of the Ancient Ethnic History of Heilongjiang* (Heilongjiang People's Publishing House, 1987), 242.
30. [Han] Ban Gu, *Geographia II*, vol. 28 of *Book of the Former Han Dynasty*, 1st ed. (Zhonghua Book Company, June 1962), 1620.
31. [Han] Sima Qian, *Biography of Xiongnu*, vol. 110 of *Historical Records*, 1st ed. (Zhonghua Book Company, September 1959), 2879.
32. [Han] Fan Ye, *Biography of the Southern Xiongnu*, vol. 89 of *Book of the Later Han Dynasty*, 1st ed. (Zhonghua Book Company, May 1965), 2961.
33. [Han] Sima Qian, *Biography of Xiongnu*, vol. 110 of *Historical Records*, 1st ed. (Zhonghua Book Company, September 1959), 2891.
34. Lin Wo, *History of Xiongnu*, rev. 1st ed. (Inner Mongolia People's Publishing House, 1979).
35. [Han] Ban Gu, *Biography of Xiongnu*, vol. 94 of *Book of the Former Han Dynasty*, 1st ed. (Zhonghua Book Company, June 1962), 3803.
36. [Han] Liu Zhen et al., *Biography of Deng Zun*, vol. 9 of *Eastern View of the Han Dynasty*, proofread and annotated by Wu Shuping, 1st ed. (Zhongzhou Ancient Books Publishing House, March 1987), 305.
37. [Han] Fan Ye, *Biography of the Southern Xiongnu*, vol. 89 of *Book of the Later Han Dynasty*, 1st ed. (Zhonghua Book Company, May 1965), 2961.
38. [Han] Sima Qian, *Biography of Xiongnu*, vol. 110 of *Historical Records*, 1st ed. (Zhonghua Book Company, September 1959), 2879.
39. [Han] Ban Gu, *Biography of Xiongnu*, vol. 94 (I) of *Book of the Former Han Dynasty*, 1st ed. (Zhonghua Book Company, June 1962), 3749.
40. [Tang] Fang Xuanling et al., *Biography of Lvguang*, vol. 122 of *Book of the Jin Dynasty*, 1st ed. (Zhonghua Book Company, November 1974), 3055.
41. Xu Ke, *On Etiquette*, vol. 2 of *Classified Anthology of Anecdotes of the Qing Dynasty*, 1st ed. (Zhonghua Book Company, November 1981), 495.

42. Tian Guangjin and Guo Suxin, "Xiongnu Relics Found in Aluchaideng, Inner Mongolia," *Archaeology*, no. 4 (1980): 333–338.
43. [Han] Fan Ye, *Biography of the Southern Xiongnu*, vol. 89 of *Book of the Later Han Dynasty*, 1st ed. (Zhonghua Book Company, May 1965), 2949.
44. He Ning, *Original Taoist Training*, vol. 1 of *A Collection of Notes on Huainanzi*, 1st ed. (Zhonghua Book Company, October 1998), 39–40.
45. [Han] Sima Qian, *Biography of Xiongnu*, vol. 110 of *Historical Records*, 1st ed. (Zhonghua Book Company, September 1959), 2879–2894.
46. [Han] Ban Gu, *Biography of Xiongnu*, vol. 94 (I) of *Book of the Former Han Dynasty*, 1st ed. (Zhonghua Book Company, June 1962), 3752.
47. [Han] Fan Ye, *Biography of the Southern Xiongnu*, vol. 89 of *Book of the Later Han Dynasty*, 1st ed. (Zhonghua Book Company, May 1965), 2944.
48. [Han] Liu Zhen et al., *Biography of Chanyu of Southern Xiongnu*, vol. 20 of *Eastern View of the Han Dynasty*, proofread and annotated by Wu Shuping, 1st ed. (Zhongzhou Ancient Books Publishing House, March 1987), 852.
49. [Song] Peng Daya, *History Department · Miscellany*, vol. 423 of *A Brief Account of the Black Tartar*, *Continuing Collection of Si Ku Quan Shu* (Shanghai Ancient Books Publishing House, 1995), 536.
50. For example, at the Meeting of Commemorating the 100th Anniversary of Mr. Ma Changshou's Birth and the Centennial Review and Prospect of Chinese Ethnology, professor Yang Jianxin of Northwest University made a report entitled "Archaeological Research on the Ancient Nomadic Cultural Settlement Sites." In his report, he talked about the Dongheigou site found in Gansu. He believed that this site might belong to the fixed residence of the Huns in the Han Dynasty. Sheep dibs and gyroscopes that gathered together were excavated in the tomb of the site. We know that sheep dibs is a common sports equipment of the northern nationalities, and it is unknown where the gyroscopes came from. However, through archaeological excavation, we can also conduct more research on the sports activities of the Huns.
51. [Han] Fan Ye, *Biography of Wuhuan*, vol. 90 of *Book of the Later Han Dynasty*, 1st ed. (Zhonghua Book Company, May 1965), 2979; [Jin] Chen Shou, *Book of the Wei Dynasty · Biography of Wuwan*, vol. 30 of *Records of the Three Kingdoms*, 1st ed. (Zhonghua Book Company, December 1959), 832; [Han] Sima Qian, *Biography of Xiongnu*, vol. 110 of *Historical Records*, 1st ed. (Zhonghua Book Company, September 1959), 2885.
52. Ma Changshou, *Wuhuan and Xianbei* (Guangxi Normal University Press, 2006), 104–105.
53. [Han] Fan Ye, *Wuhuan and Xianbei*, vol. 90 of *Book of the Later Han Dynasty*, 1st ed. (Zhonghua Book Company, May 1965), 2979–2982.
54. [Han] Fan Ye, *Officials · Sili Xiaowei*, vol. 27 of *Book of the Later Han Dynasty*, 1st ed. (Zhonghua Book Company, May 1965), 3612–3613.
55. [Jin] Chen Shou, *Book of the Wei Dynasty · Biography of Wuwan, Xianbei, and Dongyi*, vol. 30 of *Records of the Three Kingdoms*, 1st ed. (Zhonghua Book Company, December 1959), 831.
56. [Jin] Chen Shou, *Book of the Wei Dynasty · Biography of Wuwan, Xianbei, and Dongyi*, vol. 30 of *Records of the Three Kingdoms*, 1st ed. (Zhonghua Book Company, December 1959), 835.
57. [Han] Ban Gu, *Chronicles of Emperor Gaozu*, vol. 1 (I) of *Book of the Former Han Dynasty*, 1st ed. (Zhonghua Book Company, June 1962), 46.
58. Ma Changshou, *Wuhuan and Xianbei* (Guangxi Normal University Press, June 2006), 132.
59. [Han] Fan Ye, *Biography of Wu Gai Chen Zang*, vol. 18 of *Book of the Later Han Dynasty*, 1st ed. (Zhonghua Book Company, May 1965), 675.
60. Ma Changshou, *Wuhuan and Xianbei* (Guangxi Normal University Press, June 2006), 133.
61. [Jin] Chen Shou, *Book of the Wei Dynasty*, vol. 15 of *Records of the Three Kingdoms*, 1st ed. (Zhonghua Book Company, December 1959), 470.
62. Ma Changshou, *Wuhuan and Xianbei* (Guangxi Normal University Press, June 2006), 3, 26, 230.
63. Ma Changshou, *Wuhuan and Xianbei* (Guangxi Normal University Press, June 2006), 22–39; Wang Zhonghan, *Chinese National History*, rev. 1st ed. (China Social Sciences Press, 1994), 165–169.
64. Zhou Weizhou, *History of Tuyuhun* (Guangxi Normal University Press, June 2006), 1.

65. [Beiqi] Wei Shou, *Chronicles of Taizu*, vol. 2 of *Book of the Wei Dynasty*, 1st ed. (Zhonghua Book Company, June 1974), 32.
66. [Beiqi] Wei Shou, *Chronicles of Shizong*, vol. 8 of *Book of the Wei Dynasty*, 1st ed. (Zhonghua Book Company, June 1974), 204.
67. Ma Changshou, *Wuhuan and Xianbei* (Guangxi Normal University Press, June 2006), 264.
68. [Beiqi] Wei Shou, *Musical Records V*, vol. 190 of *Book of the Wei Dynasty*, 1st ed. (Zhonghua Book Company, June 1974), 2828.
69. [Tang] Wei Zheng et al., *Etiquette VII*, vol. 12 of *Book of the Sui Dynasty*, translated and annotated Shi Jinbo, Nie Hongyin, and Bai Bin, 1st ed. (Zhonghua Book Company, August, 1973), 280.
70. *Ministry of Organization*, vol. 10 of *The New Decrees of Tiansheng*, 1st ed. (The Law Press, 2000), 364.
71. [Han] Sima Qian, *Biography of Xiongnu*, vol. 110 of *Historical Records*, 1st ed. (Zhonghua Book Company, September 1959), 2892.
72. [Beiqi] Wei Shou, *Chronicles of Shizu*, vol. 4 of *Book of the Wei Dynasty*, 1st ed. (Zhonghua Book Company, June 1974), 80.
73. [Beiqi] Wei Shou, *Chronicles of Gaozu*, vol. 7 (II) of *Book of the Wei Dynasty*, 1st ed. (Zhonghua Book Company, June 1974), 170.
74. [Beiqi] Wei Shou, *Biography of Twelve Kings of Jingmu*, vol. 19 (II) of *Book of the Wei Dynasty*, 1st ed. (Zhonghua Book Company, June 1974), 479.
75. [Beiqi] Wei Shou, *Chronicles of Suzong*, vol. 9 of *Book of the Wei Dynasty*, 1st ed. (Zhonghua Book Company, June 1974), 237.
76. [Beiqi] Wei Shou, *Etiquette VI*, vol. 184 of *Book of the Wei Dynasty*, 1st ed. (Zhonghua Book Company, June 1974), 2810.
77. [Beiqi] Wei Shou, *Biography of Six Kings of Xianwen*, vol. 21 (I) of *Book of the Wei Dynasty*, 1st ed. (Zhonghua Book Company, June 1974), 554.
78. [Beiqi] Wei Shou, *Chronicles of Xiaozhuang*, vol. 10 of *Book of the Wei Dynasty*, 1st ed. (Zhonghua Book Company, June 1974), 258–259.
79. [Beiqi] Wei Shou, *Preface*, vol. 1 of *Book of the Wei Dynasty*, 1st ed. (Zhonghua Book Company, June 1974), 10–12.
80. [Beiqi] Wei Shou, *Chronicles of Taizong*, vol. 3 (I) of *Book of the Wei Dynasty*, 1st ed. (Zhonghua Book Company, June 1974), 50.
81. [Beiqi] Wei Shou, *Chronicles of Shizu*, vol. 4 (I) of *Book of the Wei Dynasty*, 1st ed. (Zhonghua Book Company, June 1974), 71–89.
82. [Beiqi] Wei Shou, *Chronicles of Gaozong*, vol. 5 of *Book of the Wei Dynasty*, 1st ed. (Zhonghua Book Company, June 1974), 112–119.
83. [Beiqi] Wei Shou, *Chronicles of Gaozu*, vol. 7 (I) of *Book of the Wei Dynasty*, 1st ed. (Zhonghua Book Company, June 1974), 150.
84. [Beiqi] Wei Shou, *Chronicles of Gaozu*, vol. 7 (II) of *Book of the Wei Dynasty*, 1st ed. (Zhonghua Book Company, June 1974), 174.
85. [Beiqi] Wei Shou, *Preface*, vol. 1 of *Book of the Wei Dynasty*, 1st ed. (Zhonghua Book Company, June 1974), 4–5.
86. [Beiqi] Wei Shou, *Biography of Seven Kings of Daowu*, vol. 16 of *Book of the Wei Dynasty*, 1st ed. (Zhonghua Book Company, June 1974), 395–400.
87. [Beiqi] Wei Shou, *Biography of Emperor Pingwen and His Descendants*, vol. 14 of *Book of the Wei Dynasty*, 1st ed. (Zhonghua Book Company, June 1974), 356.
88. [Beiqi] Wei Shou, *Biography of Descendants of Zhaocheng*, vol. 15 of *Book of the Wei Dynasty*, 1st ed. (Zhonghua Book Company, June 1974), 370–381.
89. [Beiqi] Wei Shou, *Chronicles of Shizong*, vol. 8 of *Book of the Wei Dynasty*, 1st ed. (Zhonghua Book Company, June 1974), 195.
90. [Beiqi] Wei Shou, *Chronicles of Three Dethroned Kings*, vol. 11 of *Book of the Wei Dynasty*, 1st ed. (Zhonghua Book Company, June 1974), 281.
91. [Beiqi] Wei Shou, *Chronicles of Xiaojing*, vol. 12 of *Book of the Wei Dynasty*, 1st ed. (Zhonghua Book Company, June 1974), 313.
92. [Beiqi] Wei Shou, *Biography of Emperor Pingwen and His Descendants*, vol. 14 of *Book of the Wei Dynasty*, 1st ed. (Zhonghua Book Company, June 1974), 351.

93. [Beiqi] Wei Shou, *Biography of Xiao Daocheng*, vol. 98 of *Book of the Wei Dynasty*, 1st ed. (Zhonghua Book Company, June 1974), 2161.
94. [Beiqi] Wei Shou, *Biography of Six Kings of Xianwen*, vol. 21 (I) of *Book of the Wei Dynasty*, 1st ed. (Zhonghua Book Company, June 1974), 537.
95. [Beiqi] Wei Shou, *Biography of Twelve Kings of Jingmu*, vol. 19 (II) of *Book of the Wei Dynasty*, 1st ed. (Zhonghua Book Company, June 1974), 468.
96. [Beiqi] Wei Shou, *Biography of the Seven Kings of Daowu*, vol. 16 of *Book of the Wei Dynasty*, 1st ed. (Zhonghua Book Company, June 1974), 400.
97. [Beiqi] Wei Shou, *Biography of Yang Bo*, vol. 58 of *Book of the Wei Dynasty*, 1st ed. (Zhonghua Book Company, June 1974), 1280.
98. [Tang] Li Baiyao, *Biography of Jing'an*, vol. 41 of *Book of the Northern Qi Dynasty*, 1st ed. (Zhonghua Book Company, November 1972), 543.
99. [Beiqi] Wei Shou, *Chronicles of Taizu*, vol. 2 of *Book of the Wei Dynasty*, 1st ed. (Zhonghua Book Company, June 1974), 29–30.
100. [Beiqi] Wei Shou, *Chronicles of Shizu*, vol. 4 (I) of *Book of the Wei Dynasty*, 1st ed. (Zhonghua Book Company, June 1974), 96.
101. [Beiqi] Wei Shou, *Biography of Emperor Pingwen and His Descendants*, vol. 14 of *Book of the Wei Dynasty*, 1st ed. (Zhonghua Book Company, June 1974), 359.
102. [Beiqi] Wei Shou, *Complete Book of Agricultural and Financial Records*, vol. 110 of *Book of the Wei Dynasty*, 1st ed. (Zhonghua Book Company, June 1974), 2857.
103. [Beiqi] Wei Shou, *Chronicles of Gaozong*, vol. 5 of *Book of the Wei Dynasty*, 1st ed. (Zhonghua Book Company, June 1974), 116.
104. [Beiqi] Wei Shou, *Chronicles of Gaozu*, vol. 7 (I) of *Book of the Wei Dynasty*, 1st ed. (Zhonghua Book Company, June 1974), 156.
105. [Beiqi] Wei Shou, *Biography of of Gu Bi*, vol. 28 of *Book of the Wei Dynasty*, 1st ed. (Zhonghua Book Company, June 1974), 691.
106. [Beiqi] Wei Shou, *Biography of Zhen Chen*, vol. 68 of *Book of the Wei Dynasty*, 1st ed. (Zhonghua Book Company, June 1974), 1509.
107. [Beiqi] Wei Shou, *Author's Preface*, vol. 140 of *Book of the Wei Dynasty*, 1st ed. (Zhonghua Book Company, June 1974), 2322.
108. [Tang] Linghu Defen et al., *Biography of Yuwen Gui*, vol. 19 of *Book of the Zhou Dynasty*, 1st ed. (Zhonghua Book Company, November 1971), 314.
109. Wang Liqi, *Za Yi*, vol. 7 of *Interpretations of Yan's Family Admonitions (Supplement)*, 1st ed. (Zhonghua Book Company, December 1993), 594–595.
110. [Beiqi] Wei Shou, *Chronicles of Shizong*, vol. 8 of *Book of the Wei Dynasty*, 1st ed. (Zhonghua Book Company, June 1974), 210.
111. [Tang] Fang Xuanling et al., *Notes of Murong Chui*, vol. 123 of *Book of the Jin Dynasty*, 1st ed. (Zhonghua Book Company, November 1974), 3080.
112. [Beiqi] Wei Shou, *Biography of Zhang Senghao*, vol. 76 of *Book of the Wei Dynasty*, 1st ed. (Zhonghua Book Company, June 1974), 1687.
113. [Tang] Li Baiyao, *Biography of of Zuting*, vol. 39 of *Book of the Northern Qi Dynasty*, 1st ed. (Zhonghua Book Company, November 1972), 514.
114. [Tang] Linghu Defen et al., *Biography of Wang Sizheng*, vol. 18 of *Book of the Zhou Dynasty*, 1st ed. (Zhonghua Book Company, November 1971), 294.
115. [Tang] Li Baiyao, *Biography of Han Feng*, vol. 50 of *Book of the Northern Qi Dynasty*, 1st ed. (Zhonghua Book Company, November 1972), 692.
116. [Beiqi] Wei Shou, *Chronicles of Shizu*, vol. 4 (II) of *Book of the Wei Dynasty*, 1st ed. (Zhonghua Book Company, June 1974), 97.
117. [Beiqi] Wei Shou, *Chronicles of Shizu*, vol. 4 (I) of *Book of the Wei Dynasty*, 1st ed. (Zhonghua Book Company, June 1974), 71.
118. [Beiqi] Wei Shou, *Chronicles of Xiao Jing*, vol. 12 of *Book of the Wei Dynasty*, 1st ed. (Zhonghua Book Company, June 1974), 313.

119. [Tang] Li Yanshou, *Chronicles of the Song Emperors*, vol. 2 of *History of the Southern Dynasties*, 1st ed. (Zhonghua Book Company, June 1975), 41.
120. [Beiqi] Wei Shou, *Biography of Yang Dayan*, vol. 73 of *Book of the Wei Dynasty*, 1st ed. (Zhonghua Book Company, June 1974), 1633–1634.
121. [Tang] Li Baiyao, *Chronicles of the Young Emperors*, vol. 8 of *Book of the Northern Qi Dynasty*, 1st ed. (Zhonghua Book Company, November 1972), 114.
122. [Beiqi] Wei Shou, *Musical Records V*, vol. 190 of *Book of the Wei Dynasty*, 1st ed. (Zhonghua Book Company, June 1974), 2828.
123. Yang Bojun, *Emperor Zhoumu*, vol. 3 of *Collected Annotations on Liezi*, 1st ed. (Zhonghua Book Company, June 1974, October 1979), 90.
124. [Han] Sima Qian, *Memoirs of Dayuan*, vol. 123 of *Historical Records*, 1st ed. (Zhonghua Book Company, September 1959), 3172–3173.
125. [Song] Fan Ye, *Memoirs of the South and Southwestern Barbarians*, vol. 86 of *Book of the Later Han Dynasty*, 1st ed. (Zhonghua Book Company, May 1965), 2851.
126. [Song] Fan Ye, *Memoirs on the Western Regions*, vol. 88 of *Book of the Later Han Dynasty*, 1st ed. (Zhonghua Book Company, May 1965), 2920.
127. [Song] Li Fang et al., *Musical Department VII · Youchang*, vol. 569 of *Imperial Digest of the Reign of Great Tranquility* (Zhonghua Publishing House, 1960), 2572.
128. [Han] Ban Gu, *Memoirs on the Western Regions*, vol. 96 (II) of *Book of the Former Han Dynasty*, 1st ed. (Zhonghua Book Company, June 1962), 3929.
129. [Han] Ban Gu, *Geographia II*, vol. 28 (II) of *Book of the Former Han Dynasty*, 1st ed. (Zhonghua Book Company, June 1962), 1671.
130. **Xi'an Cultural Relics Protection and Archaeology Institute, "Briefing on the Excavation of Tang Tomb (M31) in the Southern Suburb of Xi'an,"** *Cultural Relics*, no. 4 (2004): 31–61.
131. [Han] Sima Qian, *Memoirs of Dayuan*, vol. 123 of *Historical Records*, 1st ed. (Zhonghua Book Company, September 1959), 3160.
132. [Han] Ban Gu, *Memoirs on the Western Regions*, vol. 96 (I) of *Book of the Former Han Dynasty*, 1st ed. (Zhonghua Book Company, June 1962), 3871.
133. [Han] Sima Qian, *Memoirs of Dayuan*, vol. 123 of *Historical Records*, 1st ed. (Zhonghua Book Company, September 1959), 3170–3173.
134. [Han] Ban Gu, *Memoirs on the Western Regions*, vol. 96 (II) of *Book of the Former Han Dynasty*, 1st ed. (Zhonghua Book Company, June 1962), 3929.
135. [Han] Sima Qian, *Memoirs of Dayuan*, vol. 123 of *Historical Records*, 1st ed. (Zhonghua Book Company, September 1959), 3176–3177.
136. [Han] Ban Gu, *Memoirs on the Western Regions*, vol. 96 (II) of *Book of the Former Han Dynasty*, 1st ed. (Zhonghua Book Company, June 1962).
137. [Tang] Wei Zheng et al., *Biography of Shen Guang*, vol. 64 of *Book of the Sui Dynasty*, 1st ed. (Zhonghua Book Company, August 1973), 1513–1514.
138. [Han] Fan Ye, *Biography of Dongyi*, vol. 85 of *Book of the Later Han Dynasty*, 1st ed. (Zhonghua Book Company, May 1965), 2811.
139. [Qing] Sun Yirang, *House of Dilou*, vol. 47 of *Interpretation of Rites of the Zhou Dynasty*, proofread by Wang Wenjin and Chen Yuxia, 1st ed. (Zhonghua Book Company, December 1987), 1919.
140. [Qing] Sun Yirang, *Officials' Names and Descriptions of Duties*, vol. 32 of *Interpretation of Rites of the Zhou Dynasty*, proofread by Wang Wenjin and Chen Yuxia, 1st ed. (Zhonghua Book Company, December 1987), 1273–1276.
141. The Collation Group of Ancient Books of Shanghai Normal University, *Lu Yu*, vol. 5 of *Discourses of the States (I)*, 1st ed. (Shanghai Ancient Books Publishing House, March 1978), 214–215.
142. [Han] Fan Ye, *Biography of Dongyi*, vol. 85 of *Book of the Later Han Dynasty*, 1st ed. (Zhonghua Book Company, May 1965), 2807–2808.
143. [Song] Li Fang et al., *Siyi · Dongyi*, vol. 780 of *Imperial Digest of the Reign of Great Tranquility* (Zhonghua Publishing House, 1960), 3455.

144. [Song] Li Fang et al., *Preface · Hanshi*, vol. 30 of *Imperial Digest of the Reign of Great Tranquility* (Zhonghua Publishing House, 1960), 142.
145. [Tang] Linghu Defen et al., *Biography of the Turks*, vol. 50 of *Book of the Zhou Dynasty*, 1st ed. (Zhonghua Book Company, November 1971), 908.
146. [Song] Ouyang Xiu and Song Qi, *Biography of Shatuo*, vol. 218 of *New Book of the Tang Dynasty*, 1st ed. (Zhonghua Book Company, February 1975), 6157–6158.
147. Yu Xingwu, "Means of Transportation and System of Post Transmission in the Yin Dynasty," *Jilin University Journal* (Social Sciences Edition), no. 2 (1955).
148. Li Xiangfeng and Liang Yunhua, *Xiaokuang*, vol. 8 of *A Collection and Annotations to Guanzi* (Zhonghua Book Company, June 2004), 425.
149. [Han] Ban Gu, *Biography of Xiongnu*, vol. 94 (I) of *Book of the Former Han Dynasty*, 1st ed. (Zhonghua Book Company, June 1962), 3747; [Han] Sima Qian, *Biography of Xiongnu*, vol. 110 of *Historical Records*, 1st ed. (Zhonghua Book Company, September 1959), 2885.
150. [Han] Ban Gu, *Biography of Xiongnu*, vol. 94 (I) of *Book of the Former Han Dynasty*, 1st ed. (Zhonghua Book Company, June 1962), 3748.
151. [Han] Sima Qian, *Shijia XIII*, vol. 43 of *Historical Records*, 1st ed. (Zhonghua Book Company, September 1959), 1806–1810.
152. He Jianzhang, *Tactics of the Zhao II*, vol. 19 of *Notes on the Warring States Policy*, 1st ed. (Zhonghua Book Company, July 1987), 705.
153. [Han] Sima Qian, *Shijia*, vol. 43 of *Historical Records*, 1st ed. (Zhonghua Book Company, September 1959), 1813.
154. Referred from [Zhou] Lü Wang, *Quantao · Junbing*, vol. 6 of *Six Arts of War*, bk. 60 of *Four Series*, 1st ed. (Shanghai Bookstore, March 1989), 46.
155. Bamboo Slips Sorting Group of Yinqueshan Han Tombs, *Bamboo Slips from Yinqueshan Han Tombs*, "Sun Bin's Arts of War · Eight Tactical Arrays" (Cultural Relics Publishing House, 1985), 60–61.
156. [Zhou] Wu Qi, *Encouragements VI*, vol. 2 of *Wu Zi*, 6; Book 60 of *Four Series*, 1st ed. (Shanghai Bookstore, March 1989).
157. [Han] Sima Qian, *Shijia XIII*, vol. 43 of *Historical Records*, 1st ed. (Zhonghua Book Company, September 1959), 1811–1813.
158. [Han] Sima Qian, *Biography of Zhang Yi*, vol. 70 of *Historical Records*, 1st ed. (Zhonghua Book Company, September 1959), 2293.
159. [Han] Sima Qian, *Chronicles of Qin*, vol. 5 of *Historical Records*, 1st ed. (Zhonghua Book Company, September 1959), 206.
160. [Han] Sima Qian, *Biography of Zhang Yi*, vol. 70 of *Historical Records*, 1st ed. (Zhonghua Book Company, September 1959), 2295.
161. [Zhou] Lü Wang, *Baotao · Forest Wars*, vol. 5 of *Six Arts of War*, bk. 60 of *Four Series*, 1st ed. (Shanghai Bookstore, March 1989), 38.
162. [Zhou] Lü Wang, *Quantao · Chariots*, vol. 5 of *Six Arts of War*, bk. 60 of *Four Series*, 1st ed. (Shanghai Bookstore, March 1989), 47.
163. [Zhou] Lü Wang, *Quantao · Warrior Knights*, vol. 6 of *Six Arts of War*, bk. 60 of *Four Series*, 1st ed. (Shanghai Bookstore, March 1989), 47.
164. [Han] Sima Qian, *Biography of Xiongnu*, vol. 110 of *Historical Records*, 1st ed. (Zhonghua Book Company, September 1959), 2886; [Han] Ban Gu, *Biography of Xiongnu I*, vol. 94 (I) of *Book of the Former Han Dynasty*, 1st ed. (Zhonghua Book Company, June 1962), 3748.
165. Wang Zhonghan, *Chinese National History*, rev. 1st ed. (China Social Sciences Press, 1994), 443.
166. [Han] Sima Qian, *Trade*, vol. 129 of *Historical Records*, 1st ed. (Zhonghua Book Company, September 1959), 3262.
167. Lin Guan, *History of Xiongnu*, rev. 1st ed. (Inner Mongolia People's Publishing House, 1979), 138–140.
168. [Han] Sima Qian, *Biography of Xiongnu*, vol. 110 of *Historical Records*, 1st ed. (Zhonghua Book Company, September 1959), 2892.
169. [Jin] Chen Shou, *Book of Wei · Xianbei*, vol. 30 of *Records of the Three Kingdoms*, 1st ed. (Zhonghua Book Company, December 1959), 336–338.

170. [Han] Ban Gu, *Biography of Xiongnu I*, vol. 94 (I) of *Book of the Former Han Dynasty*, 1st ed. (Zhonghua Book Company, June 1962), 3757.
171. [Han] Ban Gu, *Memoirs on the Western Regions*, vol. 96 (II) of *Book of the Former Han Dynasty*, 1st ed. (Zhonghua Book Company, June 1962), 3905.
172. [Han] Ban Gu, *Biography of Jin Midi*, vol. 68 of *Book of the Former Han Dynasty* (Zhonghua Book Company, June 1962), 2961.
173. [Song] Ye Longli, *Chronicles of Khitan*, proofread by Jia Jingyan and Lin Ronggui, vol. 25 (Shanghai Ancient Books Publishing House, 1985), 238; [Yuan] Tuitui, *Geographia*, vol. 37 of *History of Liao*, 1st ed. (Zhonghua Book Company, October 1974), 441.

CHAPTER III

All-Round Development of the National Sports in Ancient Northern China

This stage mainly refers to the Sui and Tang Dynasties to the Song, Liao, Jin, and Xixia periods in the history of our country, mainly including the Koryo, Paekje, Silla, Mohe, Bohai, Turks, Huihu, Tuyuhun, Tangut, Khitan, Jurchen, and other nationalities. During this period, the sports activities of the northern nationalities were very rich, manifesting the scene of all-round development.

3.1 Sports Activities in Koryo, Paekje, Silla, Mohe, and Bohai

3.1.1 Sports Activities in Koryo, Paekje, and Silla

Koryo has a kind of stone sport, also known as stone throwing. *Book of the Sui Dynasty · Biography of Koryo* records that "at the beginning of each year, people gather together on Peishui, the emperor rides to pay a visit with his imperial guards. After the event, the emperor put his clothes into the water by which he divided the people into two parts, life and right, who threw stones at each other to splash water, shouting and chasing until they were asked to stop."[1] It can be seen that stone throwing has become a special sport of the Koryo people. It's massive and popular. In the army, a specialized stone-throwing unit has already become an essential part, and sometimes brave stone-throwers are temporarily recruited to form a stone-throwing army. For example, *Historical Records of the Three Kingdoms* records that "There are four buildings, in which the first is a crossbow building, the second is a ladder building, the third is a rushing building, and the fourth is a stone-throwing building." *Records of Taizu* contains, "recruiting stone throwers in the city and calling them stone throwers." It can be seen that stone throwing training was widely carried out in the folk at that time, which developed into a featured project of folk sports. Stone throwing has been passed down from generation to generation in the Korean Peninsula, although it has been banned because of its risks. For example, during the time of the Sejong Period in the Li Dynasty, throwing stones was banned for "casualties." The banner is that "the stone throwing in Dragon Boat Festival has existed since the ancient times ... Please stop the stone throwing in the army. If there are private combatants, they will be strictly prohibited."[2] However, it has been handed down with a strong vitality, and the Ruizong Dynasty remained the same: "The people in the city will train themselves in the shooting field, do stone throwing, and fight for the two formations, and there will be casualties."[3] Stone throwing can be used to practice martial arts, and it can also promote the national martial spirit, which once made the colonists feel terrified. "The old custom in the capital is to gather outside the South Gate and up and down the Wujiang River in the first ten days of the first lunar month. Teams throw stones to fight and gamble to win. The dead and wounded are set as usual. They did not disperse for more than ten days, and the fight was regarded as normal. However, the Japanese hate them for martial arts and send troops to stop them, but the practice still doesn't end. Finally, they were disbanded by attacking with shells."[4] Because the practicability of stone warfare in the actual military has been valued, it plays an important role in military combat. According to the historical records: "Our country's old custom is that on the sixteenth day of the first lunar month in Anton and on the eighth day of the fourth lunar month and Dragon Boat Festival in Gimhae, the young men gather together. They are divided into left and right teams to throw stones to decide victory or defeat. It's called a stone battle. The victor is recruited as the vanguard of the army, and the enemy is afraid to move forward due to his bravery."[5] In the Li Dynasty's struggle against the Japanese, the stone battle also played a huge role: "Quan Li defeated the enemy of Xingzhou ... the stone was used well in the battle. There were many stones in that place, so they used stones as a weapon to assist in the battle."[6]

Paekje is next to Silla in the south and Koryo in the north. "Paekje was from Koryo in the earliest days."[7] The people of Paekje are mixed, including the people from Silla, Koryo, Japan, China, and so on. Their clothing custom is somewhat similar to those of Koryo. "There are monks and nuns, temples and towers ... pitch-pot, Go, barnyard grass, grippe, beads-play, and other activities."[8] It can be seen that there is no shortage of these sports in Koryo. *Old Book of the Tang Dynasty* records that Koryo people like playing Go, pitch-pots, and other activities, and people can play *Cuju*.[9] *New Book of the Tang Dynasty* cited that Korean people like playing Go, *Cuju*, and pitch-pots.[10] These three are actually the sports culture of the Central Plains, and Koreans enjoy them very much. This shows that the sports culture of the Central Plains has profoundly affected the sports activities of the northern peoples at this time. The above-mentioned sports items have surpassed the scope of sports in the budding period, which already embodies the functions of fitness and entertainment. On the other hand, it also shows that their sports have been greatly developed at this time.

Koryo "go out and walk more quickly,"[11] and long-distance running is a major specialty of Koryo. In the Tang Dynasty, there were records of long-distance races between the people of Koryo and the Turks. *Old Book of the Tang Dynasty · Biography of Li Zhengji* contains that Li Zhengji was from Koryo. As the deputy general of Yingzhou, He entered Qingzhou from Hou Xiyi. Because Xiyi's mother was his aunt, he was recommended as the captain of Zhechong. During the Baoying Period, the armed forces were sent to suppress Shi Chaoyi. At that time, Turks were rampant, and all armies did not dare to fight. Zhengji expected to compete with the chief and beat him. All the soldiers stood up on the wall and said, "The latter will be taught a lesson." He defeated the chief, and the army burst into laughter. The chief was so ashamed and dismayed that he did not dare to be violent.[12] Running and jumping ability has been the basic qualifications necessary for soldiers since ancient times. It seems that the Koryo people's running ability in the barracks at that time was extraordinary.

Swinging is one of the favorite sports of Koryo women. In the old days, swing ropes were often tied to large trees on hillsides and riverbanks. During festivals, girls took turns in groups wearing bright national costumes. Later, a lanyard swing appeared. As early as the 13th century, it was recorded in the *History of Koryo · Biography of Que Zhongxian* that "in Dragon Boat Festival, Zhongxian set up a swing to play in the Bojing Cave Palace, and a banquet for four or more civil and military officials for three days."[13] In the 15th century, when the Chaoxian (Korean) ethnic group took its shape, there appeared a competition where the golden bell was tied to the swing, and the height of flying straight was measured to determine the winner. At that time, Li Dynasty writer Cheng Ni described the scene of swinging in a poem as "hands holding a colorful rope like a dragon flying, golden bells in the air ringing." In the Beijing Dragon Boat Festival of the 15th century, a magnificent swing playground was set up in the North Alley of Zhonglu Street in the city center. The citizens were divided into two groups to hold competitions. Women from all over the city poured there from all corners and formed a huge crowd. In the 18th century, the poet Shen Guangzhu more delicately portrayed the moving image of Chaoxian (Korean) women swinging on a swing: "Green taro skirts and white tari robes are shining on the **Dragon Boat Festival**. The swing rope of Tonghua courtyard is pushed into the air and flies close to the ground."

Rolling dice is a long-standing folk game activity of the Koryo people. It was spread as early as the Three Kingdoms era of North Korean history, and it was very popular at that time. This kind of game originated from the communication with the five tribes of Goguryeo, namely, the Nu, the Juenu, the Shunnu, the Guannu, and the Guilou family. The big circles of the five intersections of the dice game pattern represent the five tribes respectively, among which the Guannu family is the starting point and the end point. The series of small circles between the large circles represent the number of steps to be taken from one tribe to another. When organizing a dice game, the participating teams are generally divided into four or five groups, but the number of each group is not limited, which can be multiple or with only one person. Each group has one or more pieces, usually two. There are many shapes of chess pieces, but they need to be distinguished from each other. The number of moves a piece takes on the pattern is determined by the number of dice rolled. The dices consist of 4 round wooden sticks, the size of which can be freely chosen according to the size of the array. Among the four dices, a mark should be placed on the front side (section of a semi-circle) of one dice. There are certain rules about rolling dice, moving chess, and determining the outcome.

Martial arts (later developed into Taekwondo on the Korean Peninsula) is a set of self-defense techniques that use the instinct of the human body, which already existed at the time of Goguryeo. The embryonic form of martial arts comes from the defensive techniques adopted by humans in primitive society against beasts. The swift attack of the beast is difficult to judge, so the defensive action is instinctive. This instinctive defensive movement gradually evolved into the basic moves of modern Taekwondo: guarding, kicking (using the toes or surface of the feet), and treading (using the soles or heels). Around the 10th century, there was a dispute among the three kingdoms of Goguryeo, Silla, and Paekje on the Korean Peninsula. This situation of division has created favorable conditions for the development of martial arts. The original fighting skills developed into "Shu Bo." According to the historical records, there are two samurai fighting scenes carved on the ceiling of the performance hall in the early capital of Goguryeo: the martial arts in the Silla period continued its development as a "Hualang Dao" composed of the children of high officials. The martial arts at this time is called Shoupai Dao.

At the beginning of the 10th century in the Koryo era, martial arts had a relatively complete theoretical system, which played its value as a martial art. The martial arts fighters who were good at Shu Bo could also serve as military officers. According to the *Records of Emperor Taizong* of the Joseon Dynasty, "People fought by hands, and the three winners were requisitioned by the army." This shows that martial arts received attention in society at that time. Meanwhile, martial arts have also been widely popularized among civilians. *History of Koryo* has such a record that goes as follows: "Those who fight and gamble for money or things would be beaten with a hundred sticks till it is done." *An Overview of the History of the East* also records that every July 15th, the people of Jeolla and Chungcheong come to Yushan to fight for victory or defeat. In 1392, Koryo General Lee Sung-gye seized power and established the Joseon Dynasty. In order to restrain the political rights of warriors, a policy of advocating Confucianism was implemented. Therefore, Shu Bo suffered a great blow during the Joseon Dynasty. At that time, although military officers were selected by martial arts, they were more popular among the people as folk games.

3.1.2 Sports Activities in Mohe and Bohai

In the process of mutual merging into the various tribes of Mohe, two tribal alliance groups were formed in the early 7th century, with Heishui in the north and Sumo in the south, and the new titles of Heishui Mohe and Sumo Mohe were given. The people of Heishui Mohe are strong and fierce, without sadness and sorrow. They value the strong and despise the weak, and they are good at foot combat. So they are often a threat to the neighboring nations due to their bravery. *Book of the Sui Dynasty* contains that they are "good at riding and shooting."[14] *Historical Records* contains that "the Mohe people are brave and good at shooting. The bow is four feet long, like a crossbow. The arrow is made from paper mulberry, and the blue stone is the sickle."[15] "The people in Wuji state are very tough and often despise Doumolou and other states. There are thousands of outstanding soldiers in the Sumo department, who are very valiant. There are 7,000 outstanding soldiers in the Boduo branch. There are no more than three thousand outstanding soldiers in the five branches of Anchegu, Funie, Haoshi, Heishui, and Baishan, and Heishui is particularly strong. From the east of the Buddha Nirvana, the arrow is made of stone which is the most powerful. Everyone is good at shooting and often makes medicine in July or August and places it at the arrow, so that the beasts hit by the arrow die immediately."[16] *New Book of the Tang Dynasty* has recorded that "the people of Heishui Mohe are vigorous and good at foot combat ... specialized in shooting and hunting, and their stone arrowheads are two inches long."[17] *Old Book of the Tang Dynasty* also cites that "Heishui Mohe is in the far north, and the people there are very vigorous. They are always a threat to his neighbors due to their bravery … their weapons are bows and arrows."[18] From these records, it is easy to tell that people in Mohe are occupied with a fairly high level of archery skills, in that they could produce the world-famous bow and arrow stones.

The Bohai State was established in AD 696 on the basis of the two groups of Sumo Mohe who moved to the Chaoyang area of Liaoning Province, and part of the "Koryo Remains" in the late Sui Dynasty and the early Tang Dynasty. It was destroyed by Liao after 229 years. *New Book of the Tang Dynasty · Biography of Bohai* contains that "the things that are precious are the dodder of Taibai Mountain, the kelp of the South China Sea, the soy of Zhacheng, the deer of Buyeo, the pig of Zhengjie, the horse of Lvbin, the cloth of Xianzhou, the cotton of Wozhou, the silk of Longzhou, the iron of Weicheng, the rice of Lucheng and the crucian of Meituo Lake. Fruits are plums from Jiudu and pears from Leyou."[19] It can be seen that there is a complete range of social production in the Bohai region. Except for fishing and hunting, all the agriculture, animal husbandry, and handicrafts in the Central Plains at that time were available.

The Bohai people also raise horses, and the horses in the Suifen River Basin are the most precious. The horse is an important commodity traded between the Bohai people and the Central Plains. At that time, when Li Zhengji ruled the Shandong peninsula, "Bohai horses were traded year after year."[20] The fishing, hunting, and gathering industry still occupied a certain position in the early Bohai society. With the development of productivity, the Bohai people built a powerful army with "tens of thousands of outstanding soldiers."[21] It was later increased to hundreds of thousands.[22] Bohai people are also good at shooting, as evidenced in *History of Liao*, "Gao Mohan, also called Mingsong, from Bohai with great physical strength, is good at riding, shooting, and military affairs."[23]

Judging from the fact that the founding of the Bohai state was dominated by Sumo Mohe and some "Koryo Remains," they have both accumulated the culture of Mohe and Koryo. At that time, Koryo had in-depth exchanges with the Central Plains. Even the polo of the Tang Dynasty spread to Koryo. It is conceivable that Koryo's polo and other sports cultures, such as Budaqiu and wrestling, will also be introduced to the Bohai. Historical materials also record some sports activities in Bohai, such as playing polo, but relatively speaking, there are fewer records of Bohai people's sports activities in general. We can only understand their sports events from their economic patterns and living customs. For example, they are engaged in fishing, hunting, gathering, horse raising, polo, shipbuilding, and swimming, as well as the establishment of a comparatively powerful army. We can draw the clue that they have carried out many sports activities in production, life, and military activities. Fudging from all these sports activities, the Bohai did have a great development in sports compared with the Pre-Qin period or the early nationalities.

3.2 Sports Activities of Turks

Turks broadly include all the Turkic language-speaking tribes belonging to Tiele and Turks and refer to the Turkic tribe and Turkic Khanate in the narrow sense.[24] The ancestors of the Turkic tribe can be traced back to Dingling before the era. *Book of the Jin Dynasty · Biography of the Northern Di* called Dingling "Chile,"[25] and "Chile" and "Shele" in the book *Records of Murong Jun*.[26] *Book of the Wei Dynasty · Biography of Gaoche* labeled it as "Chile" and noted that Gaoche, probably the rest of the ancient Chidi, was originally called "Dili," while the north called it "Chile" and Central Plain named it "Gaoche" or "Dingling."[27] In the *Book of the Sui Dynasty · Biography of the Northern Di*, it is called "Tiele."[28] Dingling, Dili, Chile, and Tiele are all Chinese translations of the same Turkic name from different historical periods. In AD 732 (20th year of Kaiyuan), the Turkic Bilge Khan said in the *Turkic inscription of the Kultegin Stele* that "Huihe of nine clans all belong to my family."[29] Before the rise of Huihe, the Huihe of nine clans was originally the Tiele tribes. Bilge Khan confirmed that the Huihe of nine clans and the Turks derived from the same kindred; that is, Turks were originally a branch of Tiele, and the Turks originated from Tiele. In AD 487, the Turks were established by Avo Zhiluo, the chief of Fufuluo clan of Gaoche. In AD 745, the Turkic Pak-mei Khan was killed and declared dead. It lasted more than two hundred years in the north of China. With its powerful military power and neighboring regimes, it contended with the surrounding regimes and formed a rich sports culture. Due to the limited data on Dingling, Gaoche, Tiele, Chile, and Rouran,[30] I will not specifically discuss them here, but mainly focus on the sports culture of Turks.

As a nomad, the foundation of Turkic social life depends on animal husbandry. Because "the rise and fall of the Turks are only based on sheep and horses,"[31] the development of animal husbandry provides a reliable guarantee for the Turkic horse riding culture. According to *Book of the Sui Dynasty · Biography of the Turks*, at the time ofÏšbara qaγan, the Turks had an army of 400,000 cavalries. It can be seen that the armed forces of the Turkic Khanate, mainly formed by cavalry troops, are also in harmony with the northern nomads such as the Huns in history. In the third year of Emperor Wu in the Northern Zhou Dynasty (AD 568), after the Turks destroyed Ruru, there were places outside the Great Wall with hundreds of thousands of soldiers.[32] In the second year of Emperor Wen in the Sui Dynasty (AD 583), 400,000 riders entered from Lanzhou to Zhoupan led by Ïšbara qaγan Khan, who broke the army of Daxi Changru army and intended to enter the south.[33] During the Wude Period, "(Ton-yabghu) After Ton-yabghu became the khan, he merged with Tiele in the north, reached Persia in the west, and Libin in the south. All was within his territory, with hundreds of thousands of soldiers, dominating the Western Regions."[34] Turkic people live a nomadic life and attach great importance to mounted archery training for the adaption to the environment, meeting the needs of survival and power expansion. Turks "would rather be ashamed of defeat and die than sick to die."[35] Tribal life and military life are intertwined. As we all know, the Turkic army and Byzantium invaded Persia from 588 to AD 589; in the 11th year of Daye Period in the Sui Dynasty (AD 615), the Turkic army set up a siege in Yanmen and forced Emperor Yang to "hold Prince Yanggao and cry with swollen eyes."[36] In July of the ninth year of Wude (AD 626), the Turkic Illig-qaγan Khan sent troops to the Weishui Bridge, which was about 20 kilometers away from Chang'an, forcing Emperor Taizong of Tang to negotiate peace across the river.[37] Such a strong military force is closely related to the usual training of the Turks, showing the power of the Turkic cavalry. Historically, İstemi Ḳaġan's self-ruled soldiers had 100,000 cavalries.[38] And Tarduš qaγan Khan and Illig-qaγan Khan had more than 100,000 horses. The

Turkic slave-owners and nobles relied on this powerful cavalry force to invade the northern part of the Central Plains, plunder the Han population, and at the same time enslave and oppress other northern peoples such as Xi and Khitan. This has a lot to do with their strengthening of technical and tactical training, enhancement of weapons and equipment, and improving the quality of the population. The following discusses the development of Turkic sports from three aspects.

The first is the Turkic military organization. Although "the number of Turkic soldiers is less than one percent of the Tang's,"[39] they "merged with Tiele in the north, reached Persia in the west, and Libin in the south. All was within his territory, with hundreds of thousands of soldiers, dominating the Western Regions."[40] They entered the Central Plains many times and had a profound influence on both Sui and Tang Dynasties. Such a powerful military force has a lot to do with the military organization of the Turks. *Tung-tien* records that Tumen called himself Bumïn qaγan Khan, and his wife qatun. His son and brothers were called Teqin (a Turkic title, usually held by a prince who is not related to the Khan kingdom), and the leaders of other tribes were called She (the third highest title, usually held by other surnames). The highest rank was Qu Lvchuo, then Apo, followed by Jielifa, Tutun, and Sijin. In the beginning, the official titles were divided into ten levels, named after body, age, color, beard and hair, wine and meat, or animal name. A brave and strong person is called Shipolo, or Yinghufu."[41] In modern research, translations for those titles vary. For example, the translation of Tuli She is Zuoxiangcha or Zuoxianwang, and the translation of Datou She is Youxiangcha or Youxianwang, and so on.[42] From the perspective of the establishment of Turkic official positions, we can tell they are roughly similar to those of the Huns. Therefore, Turkic tribes also have similar organizational titles, such as Wanfuzhang and Qianfuzhang. For example, the 6th line of the northern side of the Huihe Bilge qaγan stele has the characters "Qianfuzhang in its inscription."[43] The military establishment of this decimal method has been among the various ethnic groups in the north since ancient times, such as Xiongnu, Rouran, Mongol, and Jurchen.[44] The Turkic Khanate was also organized based on the decimal method, which was applied not only to hunting activities, but also to military organizations.

The military organization of the Turkic state is integrated with its administrative organs, which corresponds to the organizational form of Xiongnu and others. In the mid-eighth century, the tens of thousands of Turkic soldiers of different surnames in Suiyechuan were "all in armor,"[45] which can further prove the unity of the Turkic soldiers and civilians at that time. Its supreme rulers consist of Khan and the Great Khan, and his children are called the Minor Khan. Khan's children are called "Teqin." For the leaders of other tribes, the Turks called them somewhat "She." Due to the vast territory of the Turkic Khanate, the Turkic Khan followed the method of Xiongnu Modu Chanyu (Batur Tangrikut) and divided its ruling area into the East and West. The eastern area was named "Turi," and the western area was named "Datou." According to the literature, "the leaders of other tribes are called 'She.'"[46] "Mosang set his brother Duoxiwei as the "Zuoxiangcha," and MojJu, the son of Qutlugh, as the "Youxiangcha," each leading more than 20,000 soldiers and horses." "Kultegin did not accept it, so he was appointed as Zuoxianwang, in charge of military forces." "Tengri, along with his uncles, took charge of military forces, the left section of which in the east was called 'Zuosha' and the one in the west was called 'Yousha.'" The elites are all included in these two Sha."[47] From the above several examples, it can be seen that those who are titled with "She" are all Khan's close relatives, i.e., the so-called "Khan's children and brothers."[48] The statistics show that during the period of the First Turkic Khanate (AD 552–630), there were 16 people who were known as the "She," among which 12 were born in the Ashina clan. Those with suspected descent cannot be titled "She." For example, Ashina Simo was not allowed to be called "She" because he "looked like a Northern barbarian, but not Turkic."[49] Turkic Khan adhered to the two principles of "genealogy" and "blood lineage" in selecting candidates for "She," which showed the characteristic of extreme xenophobia, and precisely reflected the importance of this position. For this reason, the Western Turkistan Khan divided the country into ten ministries and arranged ten "Shes," as recorded in *New Book of the Tang Dynasty · Biography of the Turks*, "The country is divided into ten ministries, each headed by one person. Each person is awarded only one arrow, called 'Ten She,' also called 'Ten Arrows.' As for the left and right, on the left, there are five divisions, with five 'chuai,' located in the east of Suiye. On the right, there are another five divisions, located in the west of Suiye. One arrow is one division, called the Ten Arrow Tribes."[50] These ten "She" are Khan's agents in ten military administrative units, who are chief executives in peacetime, and military commanders in wartime. Non-Ashna's immediate family members cannot be entrusted with this important task. It can be drawn that "Turks are not only shepherds, but also horsemen, horse dealers, veterinarians, and knights."[51] The unity of soldiers and civilians, with tribes, clans, clans, and other blood as ties connecting the soldiers together, is characterized by strong internal cohesion and combat effectiveness.

Through family-style training organized by tribes, the Turkic Khanate has a large number of soldiers, as many as "hundreds of thousands."[52] This huge team is basically composed of three parts, namely, guards, soldiers, and the Tuojie. According to *Book of the Zhou Dynasty · Biography of the Turks*, "The guards are called Fuli, from the clan of Ashina, so his nature remains unchanged." It can be seen that among the hundreds of thousands of soldiers in the Turks, some of them are the Khan's entourage, originally the soldiers of the Ashina clan, namely, the wolf clan, thus named "Fuli." As for Tuojie, historians at home and abroad have published some works on Tuojie's ethnicity and nature.[53] Roughly speaking, the army-men were composed of nine surnames of Zhaowu in Central Asia. The Turkic Khan relies on the Hu people, so the Turkic army is mixed with them. Especially in the era of Illig-qayan Khan (AD 620–630), the "Hu Branch" was established. The Hu people were even more domineering. "Illig-qayan Khan always appoints Hu people but alienates his kin. Hu people are greedy for meritorious advances with impermanent personalities; there were kinds of regulations to follow, and wars occur from time to time."[54] The "appointment of Hu people" actually became the reason for the "revolution of the military." It can be seen that the soldiers of Hu played a fairly important role at this time. During the period of Illig-qayan Khan, Tuojie participated in many specific campaign activities, which can be found in the following records, "In the last years of Wude, Turks reached Weishui Bridge with an army of 400,000 soldiers … Hu people were good at riding, so the war ended in a few days."[55] In the Turkic era, the word "Hu" is often used to refer to Soghdians, which is different from the Turkic or Mongolian-speaking races. The so-called "Hu" who is good at riding may be "Tuojie." According to *New Book of the Tang Dynasty · Biography of Zhang Xun*, "Zhang Xun ordered Nan Jiyun and the others to open the gate and attack Yan Ziqi's camp directly. They killed the general, and cut off the flag. A chief in armor led a thousand Tuojie cavalry, waving a flag and persuading Zhang Xun to surrender."[56]

Turkic people encourage their soldiers to fight and obtain spoils in battle. Emperor Taizong once said that the Turks "have no cost of building camps and transporting food." When the Turks went out for a cruise and captured nothing, they would slaughter one of their stallions to satisfy their hunger. If they needed a drink, they would squeeze their own mare's milk to quench their thirst. Turkic people, like the Mongols, "carry some livestock with them to provide food when going out to battle."[57] This is not difficult to understand. "Because the unity of soldiers and civilians itself contains the requirement for the self-sufficiency of sergeants, and the recruitment of the armymen is certainly self-supported." "Since soldiers have no pay, if Turkic rulers expected them to care for the war, the only way out was to allow them to divide the spoils." According to the historical records, the Turks "property looted all belonged to the generals and soldiers."[58] Further proof was recorded that "the Turks led troops out of the fortress and indulged soldiers in wanton plundering. There were no people or animals left behind for more than 700 miles from Jinyang."[59] Therefore, when the Western Turkic Yukuk Shad Khan "took too many spoils and refused to share," it "caused his General Nishuchuo to be so furious that he intended to seize them."[60]

The second is Turkic weapons and equipment. The main equipment of the Turkic army is war horses and weapons. *Tang Hui Yao* records that "the Turkic horse has excellent skills and strong muscles and bones. It can reach far, extremely useful for hunting in the field."[61] The physique structure and working performance of Turkic horses have been described in general here. The following are some supplements based on the archaeological data. The archaeological team of the Institute of Material Culture of the Soviet Academy of Sciences once excavated 23 remains of horses in the tombs of herders in Altai. A total of 12 sets belonged to the 7th and 8th centuries, namely the Turkic era, including ten limb bones and six skulls. According to Chalkin's research, 11 of these 12 horse skeletons can be classified as "grassland" horses with a body height of 134–142 cm, accounting for almost 92 percent of the total. Therefore, it can be determined that the basic body shape of the Altai horse group of the Turkic era was similar to that of modern Kazakh horses. The Kazakh horse, the so-called "Ili horse" in our country, is one type of fine horses.[62]

Wherever there are horses, there must be a harness, yet we can only cite those archaeological materials for reference due to the missing related literature. The saddle was not preserved long because of its material inconvenience, but horse titles and fetters have been unearthed. In the Turkic era, Altai's horse title was made of iron, paired and asymmetric. There are two loops, and the loop end is perforated. The buckle is made of iron, copper, or bone, and a live shaft is attached to the buckle so as to adjust the belt loose and tight.[63] Horse fetters can be divided into three types according to the unearthed tombs of Kulei tombs. One is the most popular type, characterized by 8-shaped fetters with wide fetters and small leather holes. The shape of the second type is slightly simpler, with a flat top at the ring hole and an open leather hole. There is also the most complicated shape, with a high nose above the ring hole and the leather hole horizontally open. These horse shackles are ingeniously made, with ring holes and shackles carved with patterns, and some of them are inlaid with grass and wood grain silver. The use of fetters is of great significance to the Turkic army, because when the knight's feet have the focus, they could change from slashing to cutting, thereby improving the killing effect.

The excellent weapons of the Turkic army, in addition to Rouran's "Duan Nü,"[64] also inherited the technical heritage of previous nomads,[65] which is related to the direct use of the subordinates' resources. The Turkic nationalities had mastered the forging technology before their rise, and provided Rouran with the forging labor in Gocho, Jinshan (now Altun Mountain), and other places,[66] who were much enslaved. After the Turkic Khanate was established, it conquered Xi, Khitan, Shiwei, Tatar, Huihu, and many other ethnic tribes by force, and often expanded outward. As far as weapons are concerned, Qïrqïz, who surrendered to the Turkic Khanate, produced a high-quality iron called "Gaza," which was considered the best raw material for smelting weapons. After the Turkic rulers discovered that "Gaza" was good enough to forge "sharp weapons," they ordered the Qïrqïz to offer on time every year, and then took advantage of the "Gaza" iron to manufacture weapons and equipment. Therefore, some of the sharp-edged weapons such as knives, swords, and spears employed in the Turkic army should be cast with the "Gaza" iron offered by the Qïrqïz. For example, "Whenever there is rain, there would be iron called Gaza, and the weapons made of Gaza are very sharp, which is often presented to the Turks."[67]

According to *Book of the Zhou Dynasty · Biography of the Turks*, the weapons used by the Turkic army "include bows, arrows, armors, spears, and swords." According to archaeological data, Turkic weapons are divided into four types: long-range weapons, guard weapons, short weapons, and long weapons. The long-range weapons include a bow arrow and a whistling arrow. The Altaic people used simple curved wooden bows in the early bronze and iron ages, and only started to use the more complicated bows till the 7th to 9th centuries. From the excavation of the Altai Turkic tomb, it can be seen that this kind of bow has a wooden frame, and the handle and both ends are lined with bones. When the unloaded string is laid flat, its length is 1.25 m, and the two ends bend into an M-shape when fully stretched. This bone-lined M-shaped bow has better range, strength, and accuracy than the ancient bow. Iron arrowheads are mostly triangular three-leaf ones. The arrowhead is perforated, with a drilled bony sphere at the bottom. When the arrowhead is shot, it makes a sound in the wind, thus called a "whistling arrow." This weapon was traced back to the period of Xiongnu. The second type is the guard weapon. Altai ancient tombs have not yet unearthed any armor worn by Turks, yet the literature covers this fact a couple of times. For example, Emperor Taizong said that Turks "used armor as a common clothing" and "thieves (referring to Turkic soldiers) competed to wear vests," etc. The third type is a short weapon. According to Altai Turkic tombs and some ornaments of Mongolian and Southern Siberian Turkic stone figures, we can classify sabers, daggers, and swords into this category. The saber has a straight handle, a cross-shaped wax (or a curved handle without wax), and a thick blade. The dagger is also with a straight handle, and the blade has a sharp edge. The sword is very well-made, with engraved patterns, which may be a foreign object worn by the nobles. The fourth type is a long weapon. At present, only two kinds of spear and horse-lock are known. The iron spear unearthed from the Altai tomb is shaped like a long-chiseled tube, and the spear is narrow and prismatic enough to pierce the armor.[68] A horse-lock is a lasso, which is the nomad's grazing gear as well as a weapon. Because of its value, Turkic law stipulates that those who stole horse-locks should be put to death.[69] The lasso existed among the Huns and was used in wars. The above-mentioned equipment of the Turkic army was quite superior under the circumstances at the time. With these types of equipment, the Turkic army was blessed with favorable conditions to carry out riding training or other skills training, which laid the foundation for the development of Turkic sports activities.

The third is Turkic riding and shooting training. Turkic cavalry, who was very powerful in the Sui and Tang Dynasties, often invaded the northern part of the Central Plains regime. Since the Turkic people are good at riding and shooting, the cavalry has become the main force of the Turkic military. "The number of Turks army is not up to one percent of Tang, yet they are powerful enough to fight against the Tang. They hunt along with water and grass without any fixed residence, and they practice martial arts to establish themselves safe and sound. When they are strong, they attack, while they hide when they are weak. Although Tang has more soldiers, it doesn't work."[70] Above is the analysis of Turkic military characteristics by Tun Yugu, a Turkic military strategist. "The Turks are good at riding and shooting. If the situation is favorable, they will move forward. If the situation is tough, they will retreat. They come and go like the howling wind and electricity. They use arrows as their military rations and armor as their usual uniforms. Their troops are not lined up, and they have no fixed camps, but rely on living quarters along the river and grassland. The Turks take sheep and horses as their military rations. They seek treasure when they win, and they are not upset even when they fail. They don't suffer exhaustion because they do not patrol day and night, and they have no worries about military expenses. In contrast, the Chinese army is exactly the opposite, which is why they can rarely win in their battle against the Turks."[71] Here, the Turkic military characteristics of mobility, flexibility, and suddenness are discussed and analyzed. "When it comes, it is like a sharp arrow, and it goes like a dead string." "It suddenly comes and goes, like clouds piling up and fog dissipating." Northern ethnic groups just take advantage of cavalry as their main force, characterized by rapid action and fierce attack, to give full play to their strategic tactics of sudden attack, long-distance assault, as well as encirclement and annihilation, which is the military culture tradition of the northern nationalities since Xiongnu. The best part is they can concentrate on superior forces, make a surprise attack, and specialize in quick battles and quick decisions. Regardless of the gains and losses of one specific place or one war, they always attack when the situation is favorable and retreat when the situation is unfavorable. Being well-informed, they can grasp the fighting opportunities well. All of these are the conditions brought to the military affairs by the unique riding and shooting of the Turks and other northern ethnic groups.

Turkic riding and shooting training is closely related to their nomadic life. In the tenth year of Emperor Wen's reign in the Western Wei Dynasty (AD 544), Yu Wenbi, in the beginning, served as an official in Zhou as Houmo and Chen Chang supervised the army, leading his troops to attack the Turks. He said to Chen Chang that "The Turks come and like a sharp arrow. If you intend to chase down, it will be difficult to catch up. You'd better choose some elite cavalry and go straight to the west of Qilian Mountains …"[72] Emperor Taizong once said that "The Turks are good at riding and shooting. If the situation is favorable, they will move forward. If the situation is tough, they will retreat. They come and go like the howling wind and electricity. They use arrows as their military rations and armor as their usual uniforms. Their troops are not lined up, and they have no fixed camps, but rely on living quarters along the river and grassland. The Turks take sheep and horses as their military rations. They seek treasure when they win, and they are not upset even when they fail. They don't suffer exhaustion because they do not patrol day and night, and they have no worries about military expenses."[73] Emperor Taizong's remarks were originally stated to overcome Wang Rengong's fear of the enemy, so he distorted Turk's mobility as unorganized. The similar situation basically corresponds with the following view of Tun Yugu, a Turkic military strategist at the beginning of the eighth century: "The number of Turks army is not up to one percent of Tang, yet they are powerful enough to fight against the Tang. They hunt along with water and grassland without any fixed residence, and they practice martial arts to establish themselves safe and sound. They move and hunt along with rivers and grasslands. When they are strong, they attack, while they hide when they are weak. Although Tang has more soldiers, it doesn't work."[74] It can be seen that the origin of the Turkic "military affairs" must be related to "shooting and hunting."

Xuanzang, a famous monk in the Tang Dynasty, once witnessed the hunting of Turks on his way to India to seek scriptures. He said that "when he arrived in Suye City, he happened to meet the Turkic İstemi Ḳaġan hunting. His horse was very strong. Khan was wearing a green silk robe with his hair exposed, and he wrapped his forehead with long silk. More than two hundred officials were wearing brocade robes, with their hair braided around the Khan. The rest of the army was dressed with coarse cloth, holding spears and bows. It is invisible at a glance."[75] İstemi Ḳaġan's hunting scale is so massive that it looks "invisible at a glance." This must be an organized hunting, and similar organizational forms exist in other nomads. For example, "the Mongols are very particular about hunting and fighting. First, they send people to detect the prey. After getting the report, they are ordered to set up fences to drive the beasts to a fixed place. This team is divided into 'Left Wing,' 'Right Wing,' and the 'Middle Army.' Each has a general to rule, with his wife and family in accompany."[76] Another example is that when the Jurchen hunt, "the yellow flag is placed in the middle as the 'Middle Army,' and the 'Left Wing' and the 'Right Wing' are marked with the red and white flags." "When preparing to start hunting, they choose a general among ten men, leading the other nine to go out and hunt. Each one in the team is responsible for his own duty, and the rules of hunting cannot be mistaken."[77] In other words, when nomads hunt around, they usually differ from each other in groups of ten. The Turkic riding and shooting activities mainly originated from hunting, so the Turkic rulers were able to confuse their opponents more than once by taking advantage of the characteristics of their own armies that were for both fighting and hunting. In the eleventh year of Daye, "Shibi Khan went hunting and arrived (Yanmen)."[78] In the first year of Zhenguan, "Illig-qaγan was afraid that Tang would initiate an attack when they were not ready, so he led troops into the territory of Shuozhou, claiming to go hunting, but actually it was for the purpose of preparation for war."[79]

Turks are not only good at riding and shooting, but they also actively learn from the Hans. For example, in the second year of the Northern Zhou Dynasty (AD 580), Zhangsun Sheng served as an official at the beginning as a sergeant of the Guardian. During Emperor Xuan's period, the Turks' İšbara qaγan asked to marry King Zhao's daughter as his wife. Zhou and İšbara qaγan both chose brave people as their messengers. Therefore, Zhangsun Sheng was appointed as the deputy for Yu Wenqing, and he was ordered to send the princess over for marriage. İšbara qaγan did not treat all the envoys well with courtesy except Zhangsun Sheng. Every time he was invited to hunt in accompany, he was asked to stay until the end of the year. Once, there were two eagles flying in the sky for a piece of meat when they were hunting. Išbara qaγan handed over two arrows to Zhangsun Sheng and said, "Please shoot them down." Zhangsun Shen rode and shot only once, and two vultures were hit at the same time. Išbara qaγan was so excited that he ordered all his sons, brothers, nobles, relatives, and friends to learn archery from Zhangsun Sheng.[80] As a result, Zhangsun Sheng not only conquered Turkic with his superb shooting skills, but also encouraged the Turks to take the initiative and learn shooting from him. Later in the Daye Period, i.e., in the tenth year of Emperor Yang of the Sui Dynasty, Rangan, the Turkic Jamï qaγan, came to Sui and attended a shooting ceremony at Wuan Hall. Twelve people who were good at archery were selected and divided into two groups. Qimin said that "I am able to meet the emperor because of envoy Zhangsun Shengm; hence I'd like to compete in shooting today by joining his side." The emperor agreed and provided six arrows to Zhangsun, each of which was shot right at the deer. As a result, Qimin's side won. Zhangsun Sheng was just the envoy to Turkic at that time.[81] The above can be regarded as a quite good sports cultural exchange. A similar story can be found in another case where the Turks were willing to learn from the Han nationality. When Cui Peng was Beishen General, Emperor Gaozu once hosted a banquet for Tarduš qaγan's messengers in the Wude Hall. There were pigeons squeaking on the beams of the house. The emperor ordered General Cui Peng to shoot down, and Cui Peng shot down with only one shot. The emperor was so pleased that he rewarded him with a lot of money. After the envoys returned, Khan once again sent a messenger to the emperor and said that "Please allow me to meet General Cui." The emperor responded, "It must be the reason that General Cui excels at archery." Later he dispatched General Cui Peng to the Turks. In Turkic, Khan ordered dozens of people good at archery to gather around. After throwing the meat into the wilderness to attract the birds, he ordered them to shoot, yet unfortunately, they all missed it. So he asked General Cui Peng to shoot once again, who shot several arrows one after another, and none of them missed. Turks applauded and admired the general's skills. Khan detained him in Turk for more than 100 days until the emperor presented a large number of colorful silk fabrics before he was dismissed.[82]

The fourth is some sports activities of the Turks that can be seen from the Turkic subordinates. For example, *Ce Fu Yuan Gui* notes that Bayegu is located in the east of Pugu, where the grass is flourishing, people are rich, and the land is mostly frosty and snowy. … People wear wooden shoes and chase deer on the ice. They make a living by farming, shooting, and hunting. They also produce fine horses and iron. The customs are the same as Tiele, but the language is slightly different. At the same time, it was recorded that Jiegu lies in the south of Boma State. Most people live near the water. They are tall and strong, with red hair and green eyes. If someone has black hair, it is considered ominous. People are brave and powerful, and their neighbors are all afraid of them. Their customs are roughly the same as those of the Turks … When hunting in this country, they ride horses, go up and down the mountain road, and chase after each other like flying.[83] *Tungtien* records that there was a state in the Sui Dynasty called Baximi or Bici, located in the south of Beihai in the Beiting period and southeast of the Jiegu, where there were scattered residents on the mountainside. It was more than nine thousand miles away from Dunhuang, where there was a commander, without being titled as the "king," leading more than three thousand brave men good at shooting and hunting. There was much snow in the country, so they often tied wood on their feet and rode on the snow to chase deer. The skis were shaped like a frieze but had a high top, the bottom of which was made of horse fur and tied to the feet like wooden shoes in order to slip smoothly on the snow. When it was downhill, they slipped easily to chase deer; when it was flat land, they walked with the help of a wooden pole like a boat floating; when they went uphill, they walked steadily holding the wooden pole.[84] In Marwazi's *Natural Attributes of Animals*,[85] it is stated that Kimak was also affiliated to the Turkic group, which was a nationality with neither villages nor houses, only forests and water plants. There was heavy snow in winter, and if someone went hunting, he would tie two wooden boards to his boots. Each wooden plank was 3 *wanchi* (1 *wanchi* is equal to about 45 cm) long and 1 *zha* (1 *zha* is equal to about 20 cm) wide, with one end bent like a bow. He just depended on this to cross over the snowy field, like a boat sliding on the water. The Bolgars, affiliated to the Turks, lived in a place where the snow had never melted. When they intended to travel, they would tie the femur of cattle to their feet with a pair of javelins holding in their hands. They inserted javelins back into the snow and pushed their feet to slide on the surface of the ice and snow. Amazingly they could walk a very long distance in a day with the wind.[86] From these records, it can be inferred that the Turks lived in the north, and their land had long been covered with snow; thus, skiing must have come into existence.

The fifth is the influence of the Central Plains on Turkic sports activities. Judging from the historical data, not only did the aforementioned Turks take the initiative to learn from the Central Plains, but the Han areas also realized the exchange of sports culture between the Central Plains and the Turks through various forms. For example, in the second year of Emperor Yang of the Sui Dynasty, when the Turkic Jamï qaγan came to the court, the emperor liked to show off. First, there were simulating animal performances and acrobatic activities on display, such as giant elephants on roller coasters, pulling out wells and planting melons, killing horses and peeling donkeys, and other strange performances, called Baixi (Variety Plays). During the Zhou Dynasty, Emperor Xuan favored Zheng Yi, and people who were good at acrobatics gathered together in the capital. At the beginning of the Kaihuang Reign, the entertainers were all sent out to gather around in the Eastern Capital. Initially, all the palace ladies came to watch besides the Jicui Pond in Fanghua Yard. The lynx show, which came from the west, was the first. After a while, it splashed the water into a flounder, jumped and sprayed into a mist of fog, and then turned into a yellow dragon 8 *zhang* long. The ropes were tied to the two columns with a distance of 10 *zhang*, and two dancers were asked to dance above them; they walked towards each other and then passed by, singing and dancing without leaning at all. Other performances include Xia Yu carrying a tripod, wheels, stone mortar, and large basin utensils playing in the hands while jumping. Besides, there were two performers, each of them lifting a large bamboo pole, on which someone climbed up and danced. From one pole to the other, they switched positions at a glance. There was also a huge legendary turtle carrying mountains, as well as magicians blowing fire. All those ever-changing acrobatics that were not available before surprised Jamï qaγan to the greatest extent. Since then, they have been learning acrobatics from the Hans. When the states paid the tributes in the first lunar month of each year, they always stayed until the 15th day to watch the performance. A theater was set up outside the Duan Gate, with hundreds of officials gathering in the stalls. From dusk to dawn, they were immersed in watching the acrobatics.[87]

Another example is that in June of the third year of Emperor Yang, he traveled north to Yulin County. In the year of Dingyou, Jamï qaγan came to the court for tributes. In Jiachen, the emperor hosted a large banquet for hundreds of officials while watching fishing out of the yellow river at Yubei Tower. In July of Xinhai, Jamï qaγan asked the emperor's permission to change their clothing and follow the rituals of Sui. In the year of Jiayin, the emperor held a big feast for 3,500 men from Qimin group and played Baixi in the east of the capital.[88] This is obviously Emperor Yang's intention to show off his strength to the Turks, by asking Yu Wenkai to set up the huge tent and play Sanyue (play). The effect is "all of them were pleasantly surprised, vying to offer tens of millions of cattle, alpacas, and horses to the Sui."[89]

During the Sui and Tang Dynasties, the Turks and the Central Plains fought for successive years. Many Han people entered the Turks through capture and surrender. According to the *Book of the Sui Dynasty · Biography of the Turks*, "The end of the Sui Dynasty was chaotic, and countless 'Chinese' returned, resulting into the scene of prosperity."[90] It can be seen that the prosperity of Turks is related to these "Chinese." "The Turkic Illig-qaγan attacked Mayi, relying on (Gao) Kaidao, who was good at managing troops and siege techniques, thus forcing Mayi to fall."[91] It seems that the Turks obtained effective siege methods with the help of the surrender troop from the Central Plains. In addition, the Turks in the north of Hedong Road in the Tang Dynasty were famous for producing bows,[92] which can be evidenced by Li Deyu's records that "obtained armor from Anding" and "invited people who made bows from Hedong."[93] It is known that the bow was an important weapon at that time. The odds are that a group of archers was taken into the Turks as Hedong has repeatedly been trampled by the Turks, which was very likely an external factor in promoting the development of bow-making techniques in Mobei. The relatively advanced Han's sports culture certainly must exert some impact on the Turks at that time, which should be multifaceted. Due to the limited data, no further discussion is made in this book.

3.3 Sports Activities of Huihu

Huihu has different translations in the historical records. They were called "Yuanhe" in the Northern Wei Dynasty, "Weihe" in the Sui Dynasty, and "Huihe" in the Tang and Song Dynasties. In October of the fourth year of Zhenyuan (AD 788) in winter, Bilge Khan of Huihe wrote a letter to the Tang Dynasty, requesting that Huihe be changed to Huihu, signifying "a light and swift turn like a falcon."[94] In the middle of the 9th century, after the Huihu were defeated by the Qïrqïz, the tribes separated and two branches moved westward, namely the Xizhou Huihu and Congling West-Huihu, who mainly settled in the Western Regions. These groups of people merged with the Turkic tribes that had been distributed to the north of the Tianshan Mountains and the western grasslands, along with the Hans, who had moved there since the Han Dynasty. They also multiplied and developed with the people of Yanqi, Kucha, and Yutian, who originally lived in southern Xinjiang, as well as the Tubo and Khitan people, who later migrated. After the Huihu moved west, immense changes took place in economics, politics, culture, religion, and social customs. During the Kara-khanid Khanate Dynasty, agriculture and handicrafts developed into the basic parts of social production, and settlement and urbanization have also become more popularized. Kashmir, Balchuk (Bachu), Balasagon, Falafu, Samarkand, and many other similar large economic, commercial, and cultural centers also took their shapes. With the strengthening of economic and trade relations between cities, together with the development of feudal ownership relations, Huihu entered a new period of prosperity on the basis of absorbing the Central Plains culture and Arabic civilization. During this period, the Huihu cultural model was manifested at the same level as the Kara-khanid Khanate and Qara-hoja.[95] **Kara-khanid Khanate was influenced by Islam and absorbed more nutrition from Arabic and Persian cultures; the Qara-hoja was more impacted by Buddhism and Manichaeism. However, these two types of culture share the same source and traditions, which are more influenced by the northern grassland culture, featured by the typical Chinese traditional culture.**

It is just based on the above-mentioned Huihu's ethnic habits in Mobei and the extensive national foundation that the Huihu has formed a wide variety of sports activities with a long history, such as riding, shooting, horse racing, polo, Dawaz, martial arts, and so on. **Huihu sports reflected the strong vitality of the historical development process, contributing to the civilization** of the ancient northern ethnic groups and a treasure in the treasure house of Chinese culture.

3.3.1 Riding and Shooting Activities

In the early days of the Huihu, they "had no permanent place and migrated with rivers and grasses,"[96] and engaged in nomadic production. Horses are the most important part of animal husbandry. Horses are of medium size and good at galloping. Huihu horses can be roughly divided into two categories; one is YORĜA, translated as "walking horse," whose pace differs from the normal breed. It can always make the rider feel a sense of pleasure, so it is often ridden by generals, chiefs, and nobles. The second is SÖKSÖK, a kind of flat running horse, or translated as "running horse," which is generally taken by the cavalier and military officers. Fast as it is, it can far be compared with BÄYGI, which is specially raised for horse racing.[97] The Huihu was still a nation that used bows and arrows very early. It is the special living environment that determines the fact that the Huihu are inseparable from the use of bows and arrows, the special production and living tools; they excel at riding and shooting. Archery consists of two types: step shooting and riding shooting. No matter it is for hunting or combat, riding shooting (mounted archery) is more deterrent than step shooting. As a specialty for the Huihu, riding shooting has long been valued since ancient times. In the Tang Dynasty, the Huihu helped Tang quell the rebellion many times,[98] and accordingly many characters came into existence due to their excellence in riding and shooting.

At that time, Li Maoxun was originally a descendant of Huihu Absi. During the period of Zhang Zhongwu, he and his marquis both surrendered. "He was a man of great courage, good at shooting, and capable of using weapons. Zhong Wu highly valued him and appointed him as a general to lead soldiers. Because of his great contributions in the battle, he was given a surname and first name as the reward."[99] In the Jin Dynasty, there were still Huihu people showing the characteristics of mounted archery, as was recorded in the *History of the Jin Dynasty*, "When Jin Aizong came to the throne for eight years (till the eighth year of Zhengda), thirteen captains were set up in the East Palace, each of which led about 10,000 army-men, who were usually strong, swift and excellent. Infantrymen carried weapons, armors, and grains that were up to 6 or 7 *dou* (1 *dou* is equal to 6.25 kg), and marched two hundred miles a day and night. There were about 8,000 people in the Zhongxiao Army, all of whom were looted and fled from Huihe, Hexi, and Zhongzhou. They all ride horses, and only those who competed successfully in riding and shooting can join the army.[100] Besides, there are also some records about mounted archery in *Happiness and Wisdom*, including many items regarding archery, such as arrows, bows, quivers, archers, archery masters, and so on. There also include some entries in the dictionary about Huihu archery competitions, such as "… always compete in archery," "he always competes archery with me," "he competed with me in archery," and so on. From the above mentioned, we can tell archery competition is a common activity of Huihu. Literally, some of their competitions are casual ones in their lives, while others are more formal and organized. Arrows are divided into clustered arrows, arrows without clusters, and others, as is noted in the dictionary, "people with arrows without clusters."[101] Of course, there are also many entries about bow and arrow making, such as "He bent the bow in a game with me,"[102] "Man carved the arrow," "With the arrow, … install the pointed tip, and put on the metal arrowhead," "Arrow with poison added to the arrowhead," "He furnished the arrow with feathers,"[103] "An archery bow made of wood," "He glued feathers on the arrow," "The arrow was feathered with the gum," "the arrow coated with gum," "the pointed end of the arrow shaft is inserted into the notch of the arrowhead," "the leather ring that fastens the arrow," "he tightened the bow, or the bow is wrapped with tendons."[104] We can draw the conclusion from the above records that the procedures for making bows and arrows at that time were more complicated, and people were very particular about making them. On the other hand, the way to forge a whistling arrow is as follows: hollow out a piece of wood and make it into a cone, penetrate it on three sides, and then install it on the arrow shaft; a whistle was made out. For example, the entry, "He asked to drill holes in the arrowheads,"[105] is the production of a whistling arrow, which was originally developed in Modu Chanyu (Batur Tangrikut) of the Huns. This culture was later passed down among the Huihu, which obviously reflects that this technology has been circulated by the northern peoples.

The Huihu have a tradition of fine-mounted archery, which is regarded as not only a means to obtain living materials, but also an important activity in their religious sacrifices. Wang Yande's *Journey to Gocho* in the Song Dynasty records that "in spring, residents often gather together to have fun, some shooting objects on horses with their bows, for eliminating the disaster."[106]

The above historical facts show that mounted archery is one of the oldest traditional sports handed down from generation to generation by the Huihu. This kind of sports activity inherited customs of life and military activities from the ancient Northern Xiongnu, Turks, Dingling, Khitan, and other nomads, and carried out extensive or organized sports activities during this period.

3.3.2 Horse Racing

There are a large number of entries related to horse racing in the *Divan lgat at-Turk*, which reflects the living customs of the Huihu and displays their national features of specializing in horsemanship. As the wings of Turks, horses are widely used in both agriculture and animal husbandry. Horses, among other things, are also indispensable for their production and daily life. Children have practiced horse riding since their childhood, and horse races are held at festivals or major events. The first is to tame the horses, which are "brilliant horses, untamed horses, uncontrollable horses."[107] "The brave horses are tamed."[108] They have to tame the wild horses before they can ride. Thus, taming is also a regular and indispensable work for the nation on the horse. Relevant records are followed: "This one who often makes his horse surpass (others)," "The rider galloped," "He and I raced," "The rope drawn on the edge of the court during the horse racing and polo,"[109] "In horse racing, his horse was agreed to take part in the race," "A good runner, namely a horse good at running, or the leading horse in the jockey club" and "He raced with that man in the horse racing."[110] According to these aforementioned records, it is not difficult to see that horse racing has become so commonplace among the Huihu, some of them casual, while others formal, like at the jockey club. In a word, Huihu's horse racing activities are carried out in a colorful manner.

The Huihu of the Kara-khanid Khanate and the Qara-hoja Khanate also enjoy some other sports activities such as Go, chess, running, swimming, wrestling, and polo. As cited in *Happiness and Wisdom*, "(As an envoy) one must be proficient in playing Go and chess, and be able to defeat his opponents and win. At the same time, he must be good at playing polo, have superb arrow skills, and be superior to others in hunting birds and beasts."[111] There are also a lot of entries in the *Divan lgat at-Turk*, such as "he out-competed him in the race,"[112] "good runner, fast runner," "run, run fast," "make a run, he makes him run"[113] and so on. At this time, several other regimes, such as Song and Liao, were neighbors with very rich sports cultures. For instance, their polo sport happened to be the peak of the Chinese polo development during that period. Both the Song and Liao emperors were keen to play polo. Since the Huihu often conducted political and economic relations with these regimes, they must send envoys to these places, so sports such as polo became one of the essential qualities of envoys.

3.3.3 Rope Acrobatics and Dawaz

Dawaz is one of the traditional sports that has been passed down from generation to generation, with a long history and strong ethnic color. It has become well-known in the world and presented as a skill activity that best demonstrates Huihu wisdom and superb techniques. Dawaz enjoys a quite long history, which is labeled as "Rope-walking," "soft rope," "Gaogeng," "Tasuo," and so on in some Chinese historical records; it is also called "rope acrobatics" or "rope play." Most historical records believe that acrobatics such as "Gaogeng" is "most likely to derive from the Western Regions."

In his epic *The Goddess of the White Turban*, Kurban Bharati described that during the early time when the Huihu still believed in Shamanism, the entertainers set up high ropes and hung five-color flags and drums in order to celebrate the harvest. They performed various thrilling moves on the high ropes to express their gratitude to god. The poem reads that: not far from the gravel-covered flat ground, the cable-walker erected a cable high up to the sky. The young man dancing on the rope was performing all kinds of thrilling moves. The five-color flag fluttered in the wind, and the Suona and tambourine played together. Joyous applause was dedicated to the performers, and people watched them rise to the sky step by step. The loud shouter was a shaman, expressing the moral of the rope play: the eternal yearning for the sky and the pious admiration for the blue sky. They prayed together, shaking their bodies and necks. The red cap was placed in their hands, and their hair swayed with their body. Today, archaeological discoveries show that there are paintings of Dawaz in the murals of Cave No. 77 in Kizil Thousand Buddha Caves (Qizil Ming Öy) near Baicheng County, Xinjiang. Among the figurines unearthed from the Astana tomb in the 7th and 8th centuries preserved by the Xinjiang Uygur Autonomous Region Museum, there are a pair of pottery figurines holding balance poles, with their feet raised high, which resembles today's Dawaz movements. In *Divan lgat at-Turk*, there is also a record of "Dawaz performed by people, which is performing acrobatics on ropes."[114] In the *Complete Collection of Chronicles* written by a Kashgar-born historian, there are the records as follows: "During the era of Timulkan, Dawaz is particularly prevailing. The two brothers, Ilchate and Dilchate, are both good at performing rope-walking skills. They led their apprentices to walk around the territory of Timulkan, performing rope-walking skills everywhere." There is a legend among the Huihu which goes like this: in ancient times, a demon appeared in the clouds above the city, who acted recklessly and often brought disasters to the people, making the whole city uneasy. People who suffered from it intended to make it eradicated, but it turned out to be a failure since the demon always hid in the clouds. People had no choice but to wait. One day, a young man named Ubuli came, who was determined to kill the demon and save the people. Ubuli erected several thick wooden pillars high enough to connect to the sky, which was grounded by the link of some thick cables. As soon as the demon appeared in the cloud, he dexterously stepped up and started a desperate struggle with the demon. Finally, he chopped off the head of the demon, helping people relieve themselves from suffering. From that time, Dawaz has become a symbol of heroes, and the story of it has been passed down till today.

Dawaz originated in the Western Regions and spread to the Central Plains in the Han Dynasty. *Book of the Jin Dynasty* records that "In the late Han Dynasty, the emperor arrived at Deyang Hall and received the tributes from other states. The lynx show, which came from the west, was the first. After a while, it splashed the water into a flounder, jumped and sprayed into a mist of fog, and then turned into a yellow dragon 8 *zhang* (1 *zhang* is equal to 3.33 m) long. The ropes were tied to the two columns with a distance of 10 *zhang*, and two dancers were asked to dance above them; they slid towards each other and then passed by, singing and dancing without leaning at all."[115] *Old Book of the Tang Dynasty* also cited that "most acrobatics are hallucinations, imported from the Western Regions, especially from Tianzhu (India). Emperor Wu of the Han Dynasty sent envoys to visit the Western Regions, and brought back those magicians who were good at hallucination back to the Central Plains ... There was also wheel playing, performed by the entertainer to toss the wheels in his hands and play acrobatics. Tousanxia is like the flying ladder show, and Gaogeng is probably the current rope acrobatics."[116] Wang Xuance of the Tang Dynasty wrote a book named *Records of the Travel to the West* after he visited the Western Regions as an envoy, in which he described the scene of "Tasuo" in the West: "In India in the fourth year of Xianqing (AD 659), the king ordered five female performers to play for the Han people. The five women played with three knives, adding up to ten knives. They also performed rope acrobatics, with their shoes on, throwing knives in their hands. Various acrobatics ... cannot be described in detail." Qiu Chuji, the ancestor of the Taoist Quanzhen School, traveled to and from the Snow Mountains during AD 1221–1223, whose disciple Li Zhichang recorded what he saw and heard during his itinerary and wrote in the *Changchun Zhenren's Journey to the West*. "Going from north to west for three days, to a city ... I saw a young child walking up high, dancing with swords in both hands." The Song Dynasty's *Book of Music* and other historical books all have records of "Gaogeng." *San Cai Tu Hui* said that "Baixi originated in the Qin and Han Dynasties, including Gaogeng and many other acrobatic forms that are too many to be listed. Now the acrobatics in the palace are just the same, most of which derive from the Western Regions."[117] From this point of view, the Huihu Dawaz is mainly inherited from the former Western Regions' Tasuo and Gaogeng, and this culture has been passed down to this day by the Huihus.

3.3.4 Martial Arts

Martial arts have also been developed among the Huihu. Many martial arts movements, such as turning, jumping, kicking, and hitting, are incorporated into the ancient traditional sports such as "Dawaz" of the *Huihu*. The Turpan Astana Tomb, built in the 7th-9th centuries AD, was also home to some **martial arts pottery figurines (preserved in the Xinjiang Autonomous Region Museum)**. The Huihu in the ancient city of Qitai has a tradition of practicing martial arts for a long time. It is they who inherited the martial arts of the boxer Tohti, and carried them forward. Among them, there are many people with special skills. Young people inherit the traditions of their ancestors and practice **martial arts all year round. They often perform their skills during festivals to enhance the entertainment atmosphere. The vigorous atmosphere of** martial arts fully manifests the impassioned, brave, and fearless character of the Huihu.

3.3.5 Swinging

Regarding the situation of swinging by the ethnic minorities in Xinjiang autonomous region, *Divan lgat at-Turk* has the following interpretation "Swing, the name of the game played by girls, tied the two ends of a rope to a piece of wood or Purlin. A girl sits in the middle, stomping the ground with her feet, so that she can sometimes rise and sometimes drop."[118] There is also a description of swings in the long poem of *Manas*. In the era of Aychoruk, young girls and boys came to meet. The full moon cast down the silver brilliance everywhere, the rope was tied to the poplar tree, and they flew the swings together high. The couple looked at each other in affection and quietly delivered the gift of love. The gift was wrapped in a white silk handkerchief, with a small note attached. When reading carefully, we discover it means "never change." This narrative vividly describes the love story in swing activities in simple and popular language. The long poem *Manas* was produced in the 11th century, so we can speculate that the Huihu already had the swinging events before that.

3.3.6 Ball Hitting

Divan lgat at-Turk records that "man hits the ball with a branch (branch stick), which is a typical game of the Turks. If one of the participants is willing to take the lead in the game, he hits the ball with a branch. Whoever hits the ball hard and strong, will become the man of kick-off."[119] Here, it is clearly stated that ball hitting is a game unique to the Turks; thus it should be distinguished from some other ball games in the Central Plains. The naming of this batting game and the rule of playing the game still remain unknown, which await to be verified.

In general, the sports activities of the Huihu have also gone through the stages of budding, initial development, and all-round development in the long history, then developed richly and colorfully during the Tang and Song Dynasties, forming an ethnic sports culture with distinctive characteristics and certain regional color in Northwest China.

3.4 Sports Activities of Tuyuhun

Tuyuhun, also known as Tuhun and Tuihun, is one of the ancient ethnic groups in the northwest of our country. It was originally a branch of the Murong tribe of Xianbei. Its ancestors led a nomadic life in Tuhe Qingshan (now northeast of Yi County, Liaoning Province). During the first four to ten years of the Taikang Period in the Jin Dynasty (AD 283–289), Tuyuhun, the eldest son of Xianbei Chanyu, was at odds with his younger brother Ruoluogui (Murongui), who succeeded Chanyu because of the high status of his mother. In order to open up new pastures, he led 1,700 households to separate them from Murong Xianbei in Liaodong,[120] and moved west to Yinshan Mountain, Inner Mongolia, in the present day. Around the year 313 (the end of the Yongjia Period in the Western Jin Dynasty), he went south from Yinshan Mountain, passed the south of Hetao, crossed Longshan Mountain, and reached Paohan (now Linxia City, Gansu Province) in Longxi.[121] In AD 317 (the first year of Jianwu in the Eastern Jin Dynasty), Tuyuhun was deceased, and the eldest son Tuyan succeeded in the throne. Tuyan set up its headquarters in Shazhou, imitating the tradition of Han emperors, named after his ancestors Tuyuhun, "also known as the country's name,"[122] and initially formed a set of simple political institutions to manage the country. From then on, "Tuyuhun" changed from a person's name to a surname, clan name, and even country name. Because it is located in the south of the Yellow River, and its leader was named the King of Henan by Bactria, Liusong, and so on,[123] it is also labeled as Henan State. In the long-term development, as early as the time when the Xianbei Murong clan of the Tuyuhun royal family and their tribes migrated to the northwestern border of China and settled down, they had absorbed a part of Xiongnu, the Achailuks. Therefore, the Northwest ethnic groups used "Achai," "Azi," "Zilu," and many other humble appellations for the Tuyuhun tribe. Tuyuhun was successively adjacent to the Northern Wei, the Western Wei, and the Northern Zhou. It bordered the Song, Qi, and Liang Dynasties in the south, and connected with the states of the Western Regions in the west. The territory of Tuyuhun stretched from Tao Shui in the east to Bailan in the west (today somewhere in Dulan County and Balong County in Qinghai Province), to Angcheng (today's Aba, Sichuan

Province) and Longzhu (today Songpan County, Sichuan Province) in the south, and to Qinghai Lake in the north. In its heyday, its jurisdiction was to the present Ruoqiang County and Qiemo County of Xinjiang Uygur Autonomous Region in the west and was adjacent to the Hexi Corridor across the Qilian Mountains in the north. The political center of the later period was Fusi City (15 *li* west of Qinghai Lake, the ancient town Tieboka, Gonghe County).

With continuous conquests, Tuyuhun was incorporated into the people of Tubo (Bailan, Shaqiang, Diqiang, Rong, etc.), Xianbei (Qifu family of the Western Qin and their commoners), Hun (Helian family of the Xia and their commoners), Han (Han-clan surname Zhang in Tuyuhun) and the Eastern Yilan (When Muliyan conquered Yutian State and Tuyuhun ruled the Tali Basin, there was a family of Kang surnamed in Tuyuhun, and the Chinese historical records labeled people under the Kang surname as Soghdians).[124] The Tuyuhun, originally a branch of Xianbei in Liaodong, gradually merged with the Qiang, Di, Han, Xiongnu (Hun), Hu of the Western Regions, Gaoche, and other ethnic groups into a new national community. During the Five Dynasties, the Tuyuhun people mainly gathered in Qinghai, Hexi of Gansu Province, the north and south of the Yellow River Hetao, and Shanxi Province. It was once affiliated to the Li family of Shatuo and the Shi family of Later Jin. At the beginning of the Tianfu Period, after the Khitan acquired the sixteen states of Yanyun, the Tuyuhun people began to become attached to it, with a Tuyuhun King's Mansion set in the Liao Dynasty.[125] After the 12th century, some of the Tuyuhun people in Hedong returned to the homelands of Gan and Qing, met with their peers in the Huangshui River Basin, and later merged with the Han people or other ethnic groups. In the Yuan Dynasty, the name of Tuyuhun was not recorded in history, yet there are natives of Xiningzhou in the old place, which is related to the Tu nationality today.

In the process of communicating with the above-mentioned ethnic groups, the Tuyuhun people not only learned the sports culture, such as *Cuju*, swinging, wrestling, and so on, but also created a sports culture with distinctive ethnic characteristics in combination with their own ethnic environment, such as mounted archery, equestrian and so on.

3.4.1 Equestrian

As Tuyuhun is located on the Qinghai Plateau, the natural conditions are not as good as the Mongolian grasslands in the north for the development of animal husbandry. However, the Tuyuhun people are good at exploiting rivers, lakes, and valleys to engage in animal husbandry, thus producing a number of horses, yaks, sheep, and camels. The horse breeding industry is particularly developed. Among the fine horses are "Longzhong" horse, "Qinghai horse," and Shu horse, which have been imported into the mainland in large numbers. Qinghai horses are produced in the Qinghai Lake area and mated between the breed of Persian horses from Central Asia and local stallions. Shu horses, small in size and resistant to high cold, are good at walking in the mountains. Many related historical records are as follows: "There are hills scattered around Qinghai as far as four thousand miles. Every winter, after the ice is sealed, the good-bred horses are placed in the mountains. When spring comes, the horses are all pregnant. The new-born horses are called Longzhong (meaning "the best breed of all"). Most horses are of fine quality. Tuyuhun once got a good **Persian horse and placed it in Qinghai. The horses born can travel thousands of miles** a day and thus called the Qinghai horse."[126] Although this legend may not be reliable, it is true that Qinghai has been rich in good horses since ancient times. For example, the well-known Hequ horses and Datong horses are all regarded as excellent horses throughout the world, most of which are presented to the imperial palaces of the Central Plains by the ethnic minorities of that region. **These horses are tributes, which were highly valued and appreciated by the emperors of the** past dynasties, who raised them as royal horses. Due to their excellent quality, Qinghai horses are **regarded as fine horses by all** ethnic groups, and usually receive strict domestication and training. In particular, Tuyuhun's contribution to this matter is outstanding. For example, since horses are an indispensable part of Tuyuhun's survival and development, Tuyuhun's penalties include "killers and horse thieves die, and the rest family must be expropriated for atonement, and punishment is imposed according to the crime. When punishing a person, he must be covered with felt on his head and hit from high with a stone."[127] Both the horse thief and the murderer were sentenced to death, which shows that the Tuyuhun people attach great importance to horses. During the centuries they lived in the Qinghai-Tibet area, they have contributed to the history and culture of **Qinghai**. They tamed the horses and introduced them to the Central Plains, which enriched the history of sports for the Chinese nation.

The dancing horse of Tuyuhun is a wonderful work of ancient national sports. The so-called dancing horse is the one that can perform dance performances or join dance competitions. In modern sports competitions, the equestrian "dressage" match is performed by the rider with his horse, while the ancient **dance horse is the** one listening to music and dancing itself. This kind of horse **dance is more difficult to control because it is not ridden by the rider**. Not only does it involve hard work in the process of training and taming, but it must also demand a strong rhythm **of drum music in company**. After a long time of training, **the horse will shape a fixed** dance step, or be able to listen to music and **dance**, thus forming **a stable conditioned reflex** to dance with music. Domesticated horses must continuously strengthen their coordination between dance steps and music. Therefore, it is a long-term training process that requires special personnel to get engaged.

Music is related to the nomadic economy and horse raising. What's more, music is mostly the "sound of the horse." Among the so-called "Northern Di Music" in the Sui and Tang Dynasties, there is Tuyuhun's "Horse Music," which goes under the jurisdiction of institutions that specialize in drums and other musical instruments. In the Tang Dynasty, "there are fifty-three chapters, of which six chapters are clearly related: Murong Khan, Tuyuhun, Buluoji, Princess Jvlu, Prince Baijing, and Qiyu."[128] It shows that there is the Tuyuhun branch in the Sui and Tang drum music, which was originally the Xianbei song since the Sixteen States Period. Since its "Horse Music" was introduced to the mainland, the dancing horse of Tuyuhun just set a precedent for Emperor Xuanzong to train the dancing horses.

First in the **Southern and Northern Dynasties, in the fifth year of Emperor Xiaowu (AD** 461), "Shiyin sent envoys to present dancing horses and sheep with four horns. Crown princes, princes, and nobles made a total of 27 dance horse songs."[129] This piece of historical data shows that when Liu Jun, Emperor Xiaowu of the Song State, reigned, Shiyin, the leader of Tuyuhun, took the initiative to make friends with the Song Dynasty, and he was highly appreciated by the Song

Dynasty. He was given various titles and entrusted with important tasks. In order to express his gratitude to the Song Dynasty, Tuyuhun did his best to look for exotic animals and pay tributes. In order to demonstrate his loyal, he presented some smart dancing horses as the main tribute. After the dancing horses were transported to the capital of Jiankang (now Nanjing, Jiangsu), Emperor Liu Jun was very pleased. Not only was he comforted by Tuyuhun's loyalty, but he was also amazed by this rare good horse in the world, so he ordered the princes and ministers to present articles and songs about dancing horses to express their joy. During this period, the agile Xie Zhuang made the first step in a short period of time. He first wrote an ode to dancing horses with more than 700 words, which not only described the scene of dancing horses, but also took it as an opportunity to cater for the court. After listening, Liu Jun was so happy that he also asked him to compose a dance horse song so that the Yuefu could add some tunes to sing. As for the event of Tuyuhun's offering of dancing horses to the Song Dynasty, historical data also cites that "Later, Shiyin become arrogant and disrespectful because he located strategically far. He sent messengers to make friends with the Song Dynasty and presented fine horses and sheep with four horns, and Emperor Ming offered him an official title."[130] Similar records for this incident can be found many times elsewhere. Here, "presenting a fine horse" corresponds to "presenting a dancing horse" in the *Book of the Song Dynasty*. During Kualv's reign, he sent envoys to the Western Wei Dynasty several times to build a friendship. In the more than 70 years of historical records, Tuyuhun has presented dance horses as valuable gifts several times in exchanges with various dynasties. It can be seen that Tuyuhun's dance horses are not few, or occasionally, but more. And the domestication activities are lasting. Undoubtedly, this event spread the sports culture of the Qinghai-Tibet Plateau with its regional and ethnic characteristics on the land of the Central Plains.

During the Sui and Tang Dynasties, Tuyuhun had a very close relationship with the Central Plains. Sometimes local specialties and dancing horses were also included in their tributes. There were many poems and essays in the Tang Dynasty that recorded horse dancing. In the middle of Shengli reign (AD 699) in the Tang Dynasty, poet Xue Yao's *Dancing Horse* detailed the grand scene of dancing horses in the Empress Wu Zetian era. This 300-word *Dancing Horse* vividly portrays the pattern, decoration, movement, and spirit of the dancing horse, which is regarded as an excellent work on dancing horses. During the Xuanzong Period, there were more records of horse dancing activities. "Qianqiu Imperial Festival is in August, and all the states come to Tang to worship and present. The south side of Huae Tower plays a grand ensemble, bringing joy and auspiciousness far and near. Xuntong of Dulu is no big deal, but Gongsun's sword dancing becomes even more impressive. After the dance, the horse needs to get prepared, as people begin to get dressed at the end of the music." The Tang poet Zheng Yu also wrote in his notes of the poem that "In the eighteenth year of the Kaiyuan era of the Tang Dynasty, the Ministry of Rites established the birthday of Emperor Xuanzong (the fifth day of August) as the Qianqiu Festival. At this time, the emperor usually treats the officials of Han nationality and other ethnic groups in the Qinzheng Tower with a variety of entertaining activities. For example, there is the Gongsun sword dance, graceful and vigorous; there is also the horse dance, in which the horse wears silk decorations with bells, raises his head, feet, and tail with hair flying, and moves with the music. The palace dancers are ordered to comb their beautiful hair in a bun, put on a malachite green dress, and wear beads and jade ornaments, like a neon feather robe. After An-Shi Rebellion, An Lushan privately took a few dancing horses back to teach, and then his Ministry General Tian Chengsi placed the horses on his behalf. The dancing horses danced as soon as they heard the drums in the army. The soldiers were very frightened and reported to Tian Chengsi. Tian Chengsi thought it was a demon, so he ordered the soldiers to beat the horse to death. From then on, the horse dance disappeared."[131] In Wang Jian's poem *In Front of the Tower*, "Qinzheng Tower in the Tianbao Period celebrated the Qianqiu Festival for three days a year. There were flying dragons and dancing horses, who raised their heads when they heard the sound of music," which depicted well the scene of horse dancing during the Qianqiu Festival held in front of the Qinzheng Tower during the reign of Emperor Xuanzong. In addition, Du Fu's poems such as "the cockfighting has just been given the brocade, the dancing horse got on the bed," and Li Shangyin's "Qinghai dance horse, Runan cockfight" as well as other verses all describe things related to dancing horses. The six poems about dancing horses described by the poet Zhang Yue of the Tang Dynasty depicted the grandeur of horses dancing from different angles, bringing us closer to the scene of horse dancing in the Tang Dynasty. Similar horse dancing activities described in many other poems are the vivid portrayal of Li Longji's life of luxury and wealth during his reign. They not only reproduce the vivid image of the dancing horse, but also cover a series of grand scenes of sword dancing, neon feather dancing, and fun with the envoys of various countries.

During the time of Emperor Xuanzong of the Tang Dynasty, "The chiefs of the tribes were feasted in Fu County, entertained by a series of relaxations such as Dry Boats, Xuntong, Rope-walking, Wan Sword, Jiao-Di, Horse-playing, and Cockfighting. Hundreds of court ladies were decorated with beaded jade robes, thundering and drumming to play Pozhen, Taiping, and Shangyuan music. Also, the elephants and rhinos entered the venue, dancing to the music. Some people worshiped and danced to the music. On every fifteenth night of the first lunar month, the emperor had great fun in the Qinzheng Tower, where nobles, ministers, and envoys all came to pay tribute, who were entertained by the singing and dancing of those palace ladies in front of the building."[132] "… Emperor Xuanzong once ordered four hundred dance horses to be raised, and he divided them into left and right branches, naming "Moujia Chong" and "Moujia Jiao." Whenever there were fine horses presented as tribute from the west, the emperor would conduct training on them, which could make the best of those horses. Through training, the horses were able to dance to the music. Therefore, Emperor Xuanzong ordered people to dress the horse in embroidered colorful silk, put a bridle made of gold and silver on them, and decorate the horse's mane, interspersed with beads and jade. The tune accompanying the horse dance is called Qingbei Tune, which is played dozens of times in a row. The horse holds its head high and shakes its tail, running around in tune with the music. Then he asked to set up a three-story plank bed and let the horse jump right away on it, spinning like a fly. Or he ordered the warriors to raise a couch with their hands, on which the horses were dancing. Several entertainers stood at the left, right, front, and back, wearing pale yellow gowns and jade ribbons with patterns on their waists, who were all selected beautiful young lads. On the Qianqiu Festival on the fifth day of August every year, the emperor orders the horse dance in front of Qinzheng Tower."[133] These records describe the number of dance horse training, the decorations, gestures, and musical effects during performances, and

Fig. 3-1 "Dancing Horse Cup" on the Silver Teapot

they also trace the dance horses scattered among the people due to the chaos of An Lusahn. The few horses that were taken by An Lushan were also killed when they heard the sound of drums and danced naturally. They were mistaken as enchanting behaviors by the stableman, and the dancing horses that passed from Tuyuhun to the Central Plains became extinct in the world. The historical records also stated that "in the beginning, the emperor drank at every banquet ... entertained by a hundred dancing horses holding cups to toast; he also let rhinos and elephants enter the venue to dance or worship. An Lushan was very happy when he saw it. When he captured Chang'an, he made an order to hunt down musicians, carry musical instruments and dancing clothes, and drive dancing horses, rhinos, and elephants to Luoyang."[134] This historical material echoes the previous paragraph, and the commentary also elaborates on the background of that time and some untouched facts, indicating the great influence and widespread of this widely praised horse dance. Regarding the materials about the Tuyuhun dance horse in the Central Plains, there is also the "Dancing Horse Cup" on the silver teapot unearthed in Xi'an. The dancing horse on the silver pot is well-proportioned and beautiful, with coordinated and elegant movements. It holds the Wannian Cup in its mouth, standing in front and sitting back, showing a vivid scene of praying for the emperor's longevity (see Fig. 3-1). The emperors of the Tang Dynasty not only found fun in Tuyuhun's horse dancing, but also displayed it as a fashionable culture to other ethnic groups. This not only proves the fact that these foreign sports activities prevailed in the Central Dynasty at that time, but also shows that the Tang Dynasty made full use of the sports culture of all ethnic groups to display and communicate in the national "grand assembly," reflecting the splendid culture of multiple ethnic groups.

3.4.2 Sports Activities in the Unearthed Coffin Board Paintings in Guolimu Township, Delingha City

In August 2002, on the Bayin River in Guolimu Township, Delingha City, Haixi Autonomous Prefecture, Qinghai Province, archaeologists excavated two ancient tombs and unearthed three coffins with exquisite-colored drawings on the coffin panels. Liu Chuncheng and others believe that Guo Limu's coffin board belongs to Tuyuhun.[135] These six groups of pictures are independent yet closely connected with each other. The content is rich and colorful, reflecting some of the folk customs of the Tuyuhun people, contributing a panoramic view of the social life of a nation and an era. There are many scenes reflecting their sports activities, such as hunting, riding, and shooting.

One of them is a **hunting picture** (see Fig. 3-2). This set of hunting pictures is intense and exciting. At the left bottom of the painting, there are three deer running like flying westward, and a young hunter behind who is chasing on horseback is trying to shoot. One deer at the bottom had been shot in the left heart, and the injured deer staggered away. On the upper left, three hunters on horseback are chasing two ferocious wild yaks, who are sprinting with their hoofs. The hunters are vigorously chasing, like three flying eagles. A bison on the right has been shot at the critical point, so the bull looks back. A hunting dog leaped to the side, blocking the way of the injured cow, and a hunter in front turned back and shot it dead. In the picture, five Tuyuhun hunters who rode on the straddle are particularly mighty and handsome, beaming with a focused and confident expression. They shoot with the bows in their left and right hand, displaying their proficient riding and archery skills, and reproducing the ethnic style of the Tuyuhun people who specialized in riding and shooting.

Fig. 3-2 Tuyuhun Hunting Picture

Hunting is the most primitive and basic lifestyle of human society, so it has become an important content of ancient rock paintings and tombs at home and abroad. In the rock paintings of Yeniugou, Golmud, and Haixi Prefecture, there are very vivid pictures of Qiang hunting. After entering the class society, hunting has become an activity of military and political significance in the upper strata of the ruling class. When Emperor Yang of the Sui Dynasty When Emperor Yang of the Sui Dynasty marched westward to Tuyuhun, he held a large-scale hunting campaign of 100,000 people in the area of Bayan Mountain in Hualong, now **Qinghai Province**. This conduct is not only a sign to show off his strength towards Tuyuhun people, but also sharpened their swords in the face of the battle. Tuyuhun was originally a group of archery, in which the people were "good at riding and hunting, with beef, mutton, and milk as their food."[136] **After Tuyuhun was founded, it often fought wars with the Northern Dynasties, Turks, Tiele, and so on. The wild** animal resources in its territory were extremely rich, which became an important resource for the Tuyuhun to live and fight in the war. Under such a grand background, the Tuyuhun people have developed a national character of being brave and good at fighting, adept at riding and shooting, and proud of self-sacrifice. Mounted archery has become a compulsory course for Tuyuhun men. In the Tuyuhun ethnic group, the level of archery skills is closely related to a person's social status, which accounts for the reason why Chinese Tu nationality worships the arrow god today. The hunting picture occupies a quarter of the whole in this group of coffin board paintings, and it is also placed in a prominent position, which indicates that hunting occupies a very important part of the life of the Tuyuhun people.

The second is the business picture. A strutting camel headed east with a lot of goods stacked on the saddle, behind which a rectangular cargo box was placed. In front of the camel, there were four riders marching in the shape of a fan. The camel is followed by several riders, who are dressed beautifully in robes with trim, a wide band tied around their waists, holding a quiver, and wearing a hat on their heads. The clothes and saddles of the riders vary from person to person. These riders shoulder the shared responsibility to protect the safety of the caravan. The Tuyuhun army is organized the same as other nomads, which is closely connected to the tribal clans. Warriors usually herd livestock for the tribal people. Once a war breaks out, the defense is needed, they will become soldiers. Their "weapons are bows, knives, armors, and spears."[137] It can be seen that the Tuyuhun people can fight at any time, many of whom can accomplish the important task of protecting the merchants."

Tuyuhun is a nation that is good at doing business. Historically, it is said that "the country has no fixed taxation, and it is levied from the rich and businessmen when needed."[138] That is, when necessary, taxes are collected from wealthy people and merchants for use by the state. During its heyday, Tuyuhun spanned the vast areas of Gansu, Sichuan, Qinghai, and Xinjiang. To the west, it reached Shanshan and Qiemo in southern Xinjiang. At this time, the Northern Silk Road was often blocked by the war. Yet, the Tuyuhun people make full use of the advantages of geography, language, and familiarity with borders near the Hexi Corridor and adjacent to Central and Western Asia. They also gave full play to their long-term contacts with the states of the Western Regions, as well as their friendly political resources with North and South Korea, and developed or participated in Sino-Western trade, gradually forming the Tuyuhun people's business concept of "business only" and "commercial exchanges," along with their strong business ability and unique cultural mentality. The Tuyuhun people often trade in the name of tribute to gain political protection. Therefore, the Tuyuhun paid "annual tribute" to the Southern and Northern Dynasties, even "three times." There are 66 tributes recorded in the history books to the Northern Dynasties and 37 times to the Southern Dynasty. A tribute is a large-scale legal business activity with armed protection. For example, in AD 553, Kualv Khan paid tribute to the Northern Qi and was robbed on the way by Shi Ning, the governor of Liangzhou in the Northern Zhou Dynasty. Shi Ning captured the tributary envoy, General Zhai Panmi, who was in charge of the protection, as well as 240 Hu merchants, 600 camel mules, and 10,000 pieces of silk. It seems that the size of this caravan is at least a thousand people. Usually, the caravan must be protected by knights or guards skilled in martial arts. For this reason, the Tuyuhun people have already developed the habit of conducting regular training in related skills in this regard.

The third is the sacrificial picture (see Fig. 3-3). A fat black yak was tied to a thick wooden stake. On the left side was a magnificent middle-aged man with a large spiral hat, a beard, and dressed in a fancy costume, standing on the top of a carpet with clouds. He aimed his bow at the cow's heart, ready to shoot. There was a beautiful girl standing behind, holding a bow and arrow, which seemed that there was still a whole set of procedures for shooting a cow to sacrifice the sky. Whether the woman's arrow was used for shooting cattle or for offering sacrifices is still unknown, but this must be a custom of the Tuyuhun at that time. In front of the yak, four women with different clothes and different hairstyles stood in a row, participating in the grand ceremony of offering sacrifices to the sky and ancestors of the Tuyuhun people. One of the women was holding a plate with three wine glasses on it, and the other was pouring wine. The Tuyuhun used three cups to pay homage to heaven and earth, which accords with the wine customs of the Tu people today. The Tuyuhun custom of killing cattle to sacrifice to heaven and ancestors can be found in Dulan Sacrificial Platform and No.1 Tomb. There are cow heads and hooves in the sacrificial pit, and the left section of tomb No.1, as high as 1.4 m, has some neatly stacked whole cow scapula and cow ribs. There are also 87 sacrificial horses in the sacrificial pit. This painting allows us to understand more about the Tuyuhun ancestors' ceremonies, such as the sacrifices being shot by people with noble status instead of being slaughtered, featured by the traditional ethnic culture.

Fig. 3-3 Tuyuhun Sacrificial Picture

Some sports in Tuyuhun are closely related to folklore and religion. It is known that folklore is a behavioral habit formed during the development of a nation, while religious belief is spiritual sustenance developed in the long-term development of each ethnic group. Both have shared an important position and function in ethnic life and social development. In the previous chapters, we have all involved sports activities in folklore and religious beliefs, which were embodied with a certain meaning, related to the origin of the nation, connected to the worship of ethnic totems, or inseparable from their production and life. All those exert vital impacts upon the cultural characteristics of ancient northern ethnic sports. For example, the legacy of "Achai Breaking the Arrow" was originally an allusion to teaching the Tuyuhun people, but then followed by the custom of the Tuyuhun people or the Tu people now worshiping the God Arrow. Achai succeeded his brother Shu Luogan in AD 417 and named himself General Piaoqi and Shazhou Governor. He expanded his territory with today's Gannan as the center. Taking advantage of the continuous battle between the Western Qin Dynasty and Northern Liang, Achai regained Qiangchuan and expanded its border to Longhe (now Songpan) and Pingkang in the south, and to the south of Ruoshui in the northwest. At the same time, "merging Diqiang, thousands of miles away, it is named Strong Power." The Western Qin appointed Achai as "General of the West, Anzhou Mu, and King Bailan." He determined that he would be good to the Southern Dynasties and be at peace with the Northern Dynasties in order to develop his own strength as a national policy. He once climbed the Xiqing Mountain, watched the source of the Dianjiang River, and searched for a passage to the Southern Dynasty. In AD 423, he sent envoys to Jiankang, and Liu Song Dynasty named Achai as "General Anxi, Governor of Shazhou, and Duke Jiaohe," which is the beginning of the Southern Dynasty, manifesting that Tuyuhun again seized the land of Jiaohe. In AD 426, Achai was seriously ill. Before he died, he summoned his children in the clan to leave a "legacy": he ordered each of his 20 sons to take an arrow and asked his younger brother Mu Liyan to take one and break it; the arrow was broken; he then ordered him to take 19 arrows together and break them all at one time; Mu Liyan failed to break them off. So Achai said, "You know that a single one is easy to be broken, but many are difficult to be broken. If you are united, you can make the country stable." Thus he educated the children to be united and protect the country as one. He died after speaking. With historical changes, Tuyuhun's prosperity and development during the Southern and Northern Dynasties benefited from the continuous practice of Achai's strategy of "standing together" to develop its strength. The legacy of Broken Arrow has been passed on from generation to generation as a precious spiritual treasure. The "arrow" in this legacy is still enshrined in the Tu people as a guardian of the gods. Today, the Tu people are also fond of practicing archery and organizing folk archery competitions.

Tuyuhun originally belonged to the Xianbei branch. Most of the Xianbei had been assimilated into the Han nationality during the Southern and Northern Dynasties. However, the environment of the Tuyuhun has changed due to migration. On the one hand, it retains the nomadic characteristics of the Xianbei people's riding, shooting, and hunting. On the other hand, because of the special geographical environment, it played an important role in the Silk Road and formed a new type of sports culture. The Tuyuhun horse dancing constructed a characteristic sports culture of the Tang Dynasty, based on the development of animal husbandry and combined with the music in the ideology. Without the evolution of productive forces and the exchange of music between ethnic groups, this kind of culture will lose its possibility of production and survival. Therefore, the formation of these ethnic sports cultures was deeply foregrounded under the corresponding historical environment. The Tuyuhun horse dancing fully reflects this phenomenon, with which the new sports culture has made greater progress compared with that of the earlier nations.

3.5 Sports Activities of Tangut (Dangxiang)

Tangut nationality, originated from Qiang people,[139] also known as "Dangxiang Qiang," was an ancient nomadic nationality living in Northwest China in the Ancient Middle Age. Its people originally lived in the Qinghai-Tibet Plateau in southwest China. Later, they reproduced and multiplied, gradually expanding to their surrounding areas. From the end of the 6th century to the beginning of the 7th, Tangut was successively affiliated to the Sui Dynasty (581–619) and Tang Dynasty (618–907). Starting from the middle of the 7th century, various branches were scattered in vast northwest regions under the support of the government of Tang. From the end of the Tang Dynasty through the Five Dynasties (907–960) to the beginning of the Northern Song Dynasty (960–1172), the regime of the Tuoba family of Tangut, being approved by the Central Plains Dynasty, continued to strengthen its military force in Xiazhou. After the establishment of the Northern Song, it began to break away from the domination of the Song and established a multi-ethnic feudal regime, Xixia—with Dangxiang Qiang as the main body, including Han, Tibetan, Uyghur, Mongol, and other ethnic groups. In the Yuan Dynasty (1271–1368), people of Xixia or Tangut were called Tang Wushi, one of the Semu People, whose upper class was highly valued by the Yuan government. When Xixia was subjugated, part of its people returned to their homeland in the southwest while most of them still stayed in Xixia or moved to various places, gradually integrating with the Han people and others. Dangxiang nationality, or Tangut, as a national community, later disappeared in history during the Yuan and Qing Dynasties (1616–1912).

Xixia Dynasty was officially founded by Li Yuanhao, the first emperor, in AD 1038 and was destroyed by the Mongolian Khanate in 1227. With a total of 10 rulers, lasting 190 years, it was co-standing with Liao (907–1125), Northern Song, Jin (1115–1234), and Southern Song Dynasty (1127–1279). Xixia fought against the big powers, even if it possessed a tiny territory. In a series of foreign wars, it won more and lost a few. As a small country located on the border, this powerful military force has closely related to the Tanguts' skillful martial capacity and durably martial spirit. During this period, due to the development of their own productive forces and the deep influence of the surrounding ethnic groups, the sports activities in the domination of Xixia have greatly evolved.

People of Dangxiang Qiang, unsophisticated and honest, have been keen on martialism since ancient times. It was recorded in the *Book of the Former Han Dynasty* that Tianshui and Longxi (both in Gansu Province) are filled with trees and mountains, and people use boards to build their houses. While in Anding, Beidi, Shangjun, and Xihe, close to Rongdi (the north region of China), people often practice combat, shoot, and hunt.[140] In the same book, it is also noted that Tianshui, Longxi, and Anding are located in the vicinity of Qiang and Hu people (the minorities in the northwest region), and people there usually were good at riding and shooting.[141] All the above shows that during the Qin and Han Dynasties, the Qiang and Hu people in the northwest were especially strong and interested in martial and shooting practice in order to defend. The government forced the troops stationed at the border to practice combat and pay attention to strength training and archery exercises in order to take precautions. *Book of the Later Han Dynasty* recorded that Xiqiang was close to Shu (ancient Sichuan Province) and Han barbarians in the south, Shanshan, Cheshi, and various states in the northwest. People living there were movable along with the rivers and grasslands. Xixiang was short of grain yet took animal husbandry as its main industry. Their custom of the clan is uncertain, and they usually take their father or mother's surname as their own name. After 12 generations of development, one can marry his stepmother after his father's death, and marry his sister-in-law after his brother's death. Thus, there is no single man or single woman left. Since there are no affiliations, the power matters. If you are strong enough, you will be a chief man; if you are weak, you need to attach yourself to others. Power is everything. There is no ban on killing for death. The soldier there usually lived in the valley instead of on the land. However, it is lucky to die in the battle yet ominous to die in illness. They can endure cold and bitterness like wild animals. Moreover, a woman who gives birth to a child without taking shelter from the wind and snow has the nature of strength and courage.[142] What can be reflected here is that in its early social organization, "the one with power and strength definitely is the hero"; due to the long-term restriction of the natural environment, people are urged to be "strong, firm and brave in nature." Based on the above-mentioned factors, the martial spirit of the Qiang people naturally formed and developed. At the time, sports are still in the initial stage. Before and after the establishment of the Xixia, Dangxiang Qiang's productivity increased rapidly, and its social and cultural levels were also promoted. Dangxiang Qiang then started to communicate with other surrounding ethnic groups, thus making positive contributions together to the all-round development of northern ethnic sports.

The records of Xixia in *History of Liao* are very detailed: People who are fifteen-year-old can be an adult, and if there are two adults in a family, one of them must serve in the army. One serving in the military for labor work is called One *Chao* and four for Two *Chaos*. The rest who has not entered the army can learn to shoot and combat. Everyone is accustomed to fighting with others. The one in the army is rationed one horse, one camel, and a tent. For the military training commissioner, he is rationed by one tent, one bow, one horse, five hundred horses, one camel, five flags and drums, a gun, sword, stick, bag, rain felt, spades, shield, iron strainer, etc.; for the people working under the prefectural governor, they are supported by a camel, three hundred arrows, and a set of curtains per person; for the remaining soldiers, three persons share one curtain. There are 200 gunners, known as "Poxi." The brave man is known as the "Zhuang Linglang." The preparation of rations does not last more than ten days. During the daytime, smoke is set off, and dust is raised when fighting; and at night, bonfires are lit to watch in rest. If a man or horse is captured, it will be shot and killed, known as killing ghosts and calling souls. The army there chooses the odd-number day to send troops for good luck. In many cases, the cavalry would always charge ahead, followed by an ambush of the infantry to break. Plus, the army men are wearing heavy armor and riding fine horses to fight. They, together with their horses, are tied together with a hook and rope, so that they will not fall off even if they are killed on the horse.[143] Xixia people have various army types and train themselves in various ways, such as "shooting dummy scarecrows" to practice archery. They award different titles to those who are skilled in riding and shooting. Clearly, people have the courage to fight and die without falling from their horses. How brave and strong they are! In the battle, hook and rope are also applied, which is very similar to the lasso used by the Huns. Presumably, this also requires them to practice frequently in order to acquire skills for the war. Besides, their sports activities are gradually enriched with the development of their groups and frequent exchanges with the surrounding nationalities, mainly including dance, riding and shooting, wrestling, *Cuju*, chess, boating, high jump, long jump, fast race, martial arts, etc.

3.5.1 Dance

Dance is not only a reflection of human spiritual life, but also an expression of physical exercise. Looking at the sports culture of all ethnic groups in ancient northern China, we found that there were basically different dances. "Dance" is recorded in both *Homonymy Research*[144] and *Wenhai Research*. In *Wenhai Research*, it shows that entertainers are called "Yue Ren" who bring "dance and happiness" to audiences; "Xi Shua" is interpreted as a game that makes one pleased; "Yu Le" is "dancing, entertainment and singing"; "Xi Nao" refers to playing, dancing, and playing games enthusiastically."[145] From the above interpretations related to Xi, we can see that the content of Xi is rich and colorful, including dance, frolic, cheer, etc. The Xixia regime attached more importance to "Xi" and set up some special organizations called "Fan and Han Yue Ren Institution"[146] that highly valued musicians. "King Liangzuo started to ask permission from the Song Dynasty and follow Song etiquette. He even appointed the entertainer Xue Laofeng as the Deputy envoy, entitled Zuosi Longzhong (a high-rank government official), etc."[147] It indicates that Xi (drama) in Xixia is popular, and the status of musicians there is important. The Xixia cultural relics unearthed from the Hei Shui City site in Ejinaqi, Mongolia, have musical instrument patterns and musical dance images. Plus, a Guanyin Picture (now in Russia's Hermitage Museum) unearthed in 1909 is 100 cm high and 59 cm wide. The lower right part of it shows Xixia providers and accompaniment of dances and musical instruments.[148] In the picture, the solo male dancer makes a leap: his arms are stretched, the right shoulder is shrugged, the left hand is drooping, the buttocks are left-handed, the right leg is raised, and the feet are tilted. Alongside are three people, one clapping his hands and two playing Hu music. A dance statue (now in the Inner Mongolia Municipality Museum) was unearthed in an ancient temple, 40 km east of Dalankubu Town in Ejinaqi. The dance sculpture has deep eyes, a rising head, and a beard full of cheeks, and it is barefoot like it is dancing.[149] What's more, there are two dancers on the "Induction Tower Stele of Liangzhou Huguo Temple" in AD 1094, and both are plump and fit, topless in the upper body, wearing gem-beaded crowns, and holding silk ribbons barefoot. They have well-proportioned movements, tilting left and right respectively, whose dances were bold and unrestrained, and whose expressions were nice and charming.

3.5.2 Riding and Shooting (Mounted Archery)

In history, all the northwest nationalities took riding and shooting as their strengths. Tangut (Dangxiang), a nomadic group in the ancient northwest region of China, is located in the present Gansu, Ningxia, northern Shaanxi, and Inner Mongolia regions. It is close to Qiang and Hu and usually practices military skills, riding, and shooting.[150] Therefore, the Tangut people are skillful at mounted archery. There are good bows and strong crossbows in Xixia. Generally, bows are made of "leather strings," "willow," as well as ox horns. *Wenhai Research* interprets "Zhang Gong" as: "Zhang refers to a bow made of strings to shoot"; "Gong," a string stretching in a bow; "Ba," a target point, shooting mark, and shooting place"; "She," is shooting a bow; "Jian," archery arrows; "Shi," also called "arrows." There is a kind of "three-edged arrow" in Xixia, which is interpreted in *Wenhai Research* as "an arrow with three-edges."[151] The explanation of "Ba (target)" in *Wenhai Research* indicates that there are special training or competition activities in archery far back in Xixia. People have hunting activities in autumn and winter, and a state banquet is held in October to start the hunting. *Translation and Annotation of Xixia Text Sheng Li Yi Hai* once recorded: "In the winter of October, the state banquet official Zaihui presented a horse to lead the soldiers to shoot eagles."[152] It can be concluded that autumn hunting in Xixia is somewhat attached to the color of military practice. The historical facts about the Tanguts' excellence in riding and shooting are stated as follows:

Firstly, some figures of Tangut nationality in history are adept at mounted archery. As stated in the *History of the Song Dynasty · Biography of Xia State*: "When Tuoba SiZhong, Taba Sigong's brother, attacked DongWei Bridge (now northeast of Chang'an County, Shaanxi Province) in the battle against Huang Chao, there was an iron crane on the bridge deck. Then Sizhong shot, but the arrow was drowned in the feather of the crane. The enemy was awed."[153] The story indicates that Sizhong is so strong in his arm and so excellent in his shooting. Afterwards, Li Qi, a poet in the Tang Dynasty, once wrote in his poem: "Flying through Bazhan, Hong'en, and Xiatai, towards heaven and from the sun."[154] It vividly depicts an image of a Tangut general who is capable of riding and fighting.

Li Jiqian, who laid the foundation for Xixia's establishment, is an outstanding leader specializing in mounted archery. Volume 3 of *Records of Xixia (Xixia Shushi)* wrote: "Li, being good at riding and shooting, once hunted accompanied with ten riders. Suddenly, a tiger came from the foot of the mountain, and Li ordered all his attendants to enter the cypress forest; he shot at the top of the tree with a bow, hitting the tiger's eye and killing it quickly, which produced his reputation."[155] It can be seen that Li Jiqian's extraordinary martial skills played a great role in establishing his prestige in the branches of Tangut. Plus, Yuanhao is even more of a leader who is excellent at leading troops to fight. "He was the first to fight bravely." He went on an expedition to Hexi to fight against Song and Liao Dynasties. After dozens of battles, he lived a life through various military wars and enjoyed a tenacious fighting spirit. Before sending troops, Yuanhao would lead the army to go hunting and jointly discuss military strategies with his subordinates. He took advantage of the strengths of all people and demonstrated the performance of bravery and wisdom. As recorded in the *History of the Song Dynasty*, Yuanhao would lead the army to go hunting before each war. Once he got something, he would dismount the horse, sit around while drinking, and cut fresh food, asking the opinions of his soldiers and gaining advantages from them.[156] Several Empress Dowagers of Xixia also possessed some extraordinary martial temperament. For example, Li Liangzuo's mother—Mozang Empress Dowager has conducted diverse battles, and Chongzong's mother, Liang Empress Dowager, also commanded many expeditions herself.

Not only can we see that the Tanguts are good at riding and shooting from the skills of their leaders of the Tuoba clan in Xixia, but also from the giant family of She clan in Hedong, which is the enemy of Xixia. The She clan has produced a lot of famous northwest generals in the Northern Song Dynasty for generations. In the wars against Liao and Xia, they built many outstanding achievements and thus were called "She Jia Jun (She family army)" by Khitan and Xixia. All of the family members in the group were good at riding, like She Deyi and She Keshi. *History of the Song Dynasty* cites the following: "Keshi, being brave before his twenty-year-old and capable of riding without learning." The reason why they could "ride without learning" is due to the fact that archery skills are considered to be family breeding, and even the kids could acquire it naturally in the immersion. Therefore, She Keshi was praised as "a Born General" by Guo Kui (a famous general in Northern Song).[157]

Mu Guiying and She Taijun (two famous women) in Chinese plays are generally considered Tanguts by Chinese historians. Mu Guiying, being reputed as a well-known female general, excels at riding and fighting and has mastered the exquisite skill of piercing a willow leaf with an arrow from a distance of a hundred paces. Moreover, as *Jin Cheng Sou Lue* recorded: "It is obvious that She Taijun is good at riding and shooting, and even her maidservants surpass others in these regards. She succeeded in fighting against the enemy Liang Hongyu (a famous female general in Southern Song Dynasty)."[158] To compare her with Liang, who defeated ten thousand Jin soldiers of Wuzhu's troop in Huangtiandang (located in Changjiang River), we can find out the popularity of She's fame in bravery and courage.

In the Yuan Dynasty, the number of people with brilliant archery in the Tangut clan was even more. Sandanba, a man in Pingxing, Zhejiang Province, was adept at sword-fighting, riding, and shooting. When fighting in Jiangnan (the south of the Yangtze River), he was nominated as "God of Ride" by the southerners because he shot the enemy quickly and accurately.[159] Plus, with excellent riding and shooting skills, Hashi Baduer was awarded the title "Baduer" (warrior in Mongolian) by Genghis Khan because he possessed incomparable courage and fought invincibly. Hu Yi, who served as the steward of Huizhoulu, was originally a military leader of Xixia, and also a man skilled in riding and shooting. When Hu Bilie (the founder of the Yuan Dynasty) was conquering Jiangnan, Hu Yi built a number of outstanding achievements with his superior martial arts. There were also a lot of famous and brave generals when Genghis Khan conquered the west, such as Chahan, Angjier, and Xililingbu, all of whom were amazing riders and shooters. Therefore, it was said that the Tanguts were the bravest and most brilliant men in martial arts when Genghis Khan conquered the west, which fully reflected the Yuan's highest compliments towards Tanguts.

Furthermore, "Dangxiang Horse" and "Xixia Bow" are two famous instruments. In the book of *Wenhai Research*, "Jun" refers to a horse or a fine horse; "Wu Ma" is also a horse; "Liang Ma" refers to a good horse like "Jun"; "Ju" shares the same connotation of "Wu Ma" and "Liang Ma" which indicates the most excellent one among horses.[160] The horse laid the foundation to establish a country for the Tangut nationality, and the Xixia regime paid special attention to horse husbandry and set up a special organization—the Horse Husbandry Department.[161] *The New Decrees of Tiansheng* in Xixia stipulates: "If the horses in the official pasture are not well raised, the punishment shall be more serious than that of stealing. If the horse becomes weak because of improper forage, both the horse breeder and the supervisor shall be punished. And they must hold guilty, taking the punishment ranging from stick beating to one year's hard labor, according to the seriousness of the crime.[162]

Tanguts clan attached great importance to mounted archery, and strengthened the horse-taming. In 1977, a painted wood painting was unearthed in Xixia No. 2 Tomb in Forest Farm, Wuling County, Gansu Province. It is 14 cm long and 8 cm wide (now in the museum of Wuwei District). In the picture, a horse driver runs in front of the horse with his face turning to the left, his head covered with short hair, and the lower ends of his hair on both sides tilted up. With a ruddy face, the man wears a Ru costume (a dressing pattern in Han Dynasty) with his sleeves folding up, wrapping girdle, and baring feet. Besides, he is holding a red-pole whip in his right hand and seizing a purplish red horse in his left hand; the horse is well saddled and is raising its head highly, swinging its mane, lifting its tail, and galloping its four hooves. The horse rider was fully absorbed, without panic, and effectively controlled the running horse. The picture, with its lively and lifelike image, reflects skillful horse riding, which is quite emotive.[163] Since the Tanguts moved to the north, their horses have become famous. Yuan Zhen, a poet of the Tang Dynasty, wrote that "one should buy Dangxiang horse in the north and capture Tubo hawk in the west."[164] In the Tang Dynasty, the commanders on the border did not hesitate to trade with armored weapons in order to obtain the "fine horse and sheep" of the Tanguts clan.[165] In the Song Dynasty, the "Dangxiang Horse" even was a rare and expensive commodity. Hong Zun, a native of the Southern Song Dynasty, said: "I have consulted the men who have great knowledge of horses: the horses from Xixia were the first-class, followed by that from tribes, and then Xihe horses bought from Tea and Horse Department, and the worst was Dusheng horse produced in Sichuan."[166] Obviously, "Dangxiang Horse" at that time was the best of all.

The horses domesticated in Xixia are extremely excellent, and their cavalry runs quite quickly like floating with strong combat effectiveness. In Emperor Taizong's regime (939–997) of the Song Dynasty, one hundred thousand elite soldiers and generals were mobilized to attack Li Jiqian in five directions. Yet the Tangut cavalry "rode lightly and quickly, intercepting in front and back, and running thousands of miles a day,"[167] which dragged the Song army to exhaustion and forced them to return without success. Su Shunqing, a poet of the Northern Song Dynasty, once made a sharp contrast between the cavalry of the Song and Xia in his poem *Qingzhou Defeat*. He wrote that the cavalry of the Song "rode fat horses, wore heavy armor, gasping for breath; with bows and arrows in the hands, some stumbled to fall into the deep valley … which caused its enemy into laughter." And the Xixia cavalry, in contrast, "lined up neatly, cutting off the access at the foot of the mountain, and the Song army was thus surrounded."[168] It is concluded that with fine horses, the Xixia army enjoys excellent riding skills, strict discipline as well as strong fighting capability.

The good making of the bow and arrow has a great impact on the accuracy of archery, just as riding depends on horses, so bows and horses complement each other. Having a fine horse without a fine bow is not enough, and vice versa; for both are indispensable. The Tanguts clan has been good at mounted archery since ancient times. Their hunting and fighting are not only highly related to good horses, but also good bows and crossbows. In Zhuang Chuo's *Ji Lei Bian*: "Xingzhou (now Yinchuan city) of Xixia produces good bows, which are bought by the central people with each costing lots of money."[169] In Kang Yuzhi's *Yesterday's Dream*: "Xixia has bamboo cattle (i.e., yak), weighing hundreds of *jin* (a unit of weight, equal to 0.5 kg), with its long horns in yellow and black alternating, who are excellent for making bows."[170] Yak horn is an excellent raw material for bow-making. It not only has good performance, but also is beautiful and durable. Yet, the general bow is still made of "dried willow strings." The most powerful bow in Xixia is the "Shenbi Bow (Magic Arm Bow)." Shen Kuo cited in *Annotations to Mengxi Bitan* that in the year of Xining, Li Ding "offered a kind of magic bow, which was actually a giant crossbow. When it was erected on the ground and loaded by stepping on its mechanism, it could penetrate the enemy's armor 300 paces away."[171] This magic arm bow is the so-called "Jue Zhang" in the Han Dynasty. It disappeared in Central Plains for generations, while Xixia possessed it exclusively. And then, it was introduced into Song as "Central's Excellent Object."[172] Xixia people are good at riding and shooting, so they would worship the Shenbi Bow. As *Translation and Annotation of Xixia Text Sheng Li Yi Hai* recorded: "In winter, Shenbi Bow should be worshiped first."[173] Its magic power forced Song to strengthen its shooting training, many records of which have been included in the *History of the Song Dynasty* many times.[174] Song imperial court once showed off his capability to use the bow through the performance of various kinds when receiving Xixia envoys. For example, in the *History of the Song Dynasty,* there are records that in the year of Zhidao, Zhang Pu was sent to offer good camels and horses. Emperor Taizong ordered a lot of people to appreciate in the back garden and then asked the soldiers to pull the strong bow of 2 *dan* (an ancient unit of weight, 1 *dan* is around 100 to 150 *jin*). The emperor smiled and asked Pu, "Can Qiang people withstand this?" Pu answered, "Qiang's bow is weak, and its arrow is short. When we see your bows, we have already escaped. How dare to fight?"[175] Zhang Pu's words naturally flattered Emperor Taizong. As far as the "Shenbi Bow" of the Tanguts found in archaeology is concerned, it by no means looked like what Zhang Pu said. The truth is it has a very large shape. During the reign of Emperor Shun, the Longxi earthquake caused the collapse of the wall of some official residences in Huizhou. There were more than 500 crossbows found, with a length of more than 10 *chi* for the long one, or 9 *chi* for the short one. Huizhou is the old territory of Xixia, and we can infer that these bows are undoubtedly a relic of Xixia. The ancient crossbows took 6 *chi* and 6 *cun* as the upper-class, 6 *chi* and 3 *cun* as middle, and 6 *chi* as the lowest-class.[176] The Xixia crossbows were more than 10 *chi* for long ones and 9 *chi* for short ones. A large number of such crossbows reflected not only the progress of the bow-making techniques of the Tanguts, but also the refinement of the archery skills of its people.[177] Judging from the fact that the Tanguts can make this huge bow themselves, we can conclude that their shooting skills have already reached a very high standard.

There are a large number of laws and regulations on bows and horses recorded in *The New Decrees of Tiansheng*, in which *Laws of Military Weapons Supply* are detailed in particular. Here are some excerpts:

War equipment

Zheng Jun (the first-class official): an official horse, a set of armor, a pie, a bow, 30 arrows, a gun, a sword, a long spear, and a full set of clasps.[178]

Zheng Fu Zhu (the second-class official): a bow, 20 arrows, a long spear, and a full set of clasps.

Fu Dan (the lower-class soldier): a bow, 20 arrows, a sword, a long spear, etc. Similarly, if bows and arrows are given, the clasps should also be given.

In addition, there are also other officials and guards who are basically the same as the above. The main difference in their weapons supply mainly lies in the number of arrows. The number of arrows rationed to other officials is usually based on their ranks:

Shi Cheng to Sheng Jian: 50 arrows
An Jian to Xi Jian: 100 arrows
Tou Zhu to Zhu Qu: 150 arrows
Yu Di to Zhen She: 200 arrows
Tiao Fu to Ju Xie: 300 arrows
Zhang Wei to Sheng Xi: 400 arrows
Mao Xun and above: 500 arrows[179]

At the same time, the law also stipulates that if the teams are good at shooting and winning the first prize, the weapons they hold will be offered as mentioned above, according to the categories of various departments. Among them, in addition to the previous 100 arrows with sufficient numbers, those with insufficient ones must be supported with another 100 accompanying with clasps to make sure they are fully prepared to join in a battle.[180] What can be seen is that the rulers of Xixia held archery competitions during military training and rewarded players in accordance with their achievement as well as their ranks, thereby encouraging the soldiers to strengthen their archery practice. In ancient ethnic groups, the hierarchy was clear-cut, and those who were good at shooting (those who carry out shooting are generally not equipped with arrows and horses like cavalry because their status is relatively low) could hold a hundred arrows, which signifies that the rulers attached great importance to shooting.

Genghis Khan paid special attention to the outstanding bow-makers when he conquered Xixia. In the *History of the Yuan Dynasty*: "After the establishment of Xixia, Emperor Taizu invited a diversity of craftsmen and Xiaochou (the grandfather of Tangwu people Duoluotai) who were good at making bows. Xiaochou was given the title of Qieyan Wulan because of their talents in bow making and was even asked to be the chairperson of one hundred bow craftsmen."[181] Xiaochou is from Tanguts clan and is good at making bows, and his grandson Kuokuochu is also engaged in bow-making and often presents the bows he makes to the emperor and thus gets rewards. It can be clearly seen that the Tanguts pass on the bow-making from generation to generation, who have made outstanding contributions to the development of crossbows in our country.

In addition, a kind of armored force called "Tieyaozi" appeared in the cavalry of Xixia. In *History of the Song Dynasty*, it is cited: "Tieyaozi march for a hundred miles, even a thousand miles as quickly as lighting and clouds."[182] The force moved so agilely and galloped amazingly fast, the records of which were considered the truth. There are also other records in the *History of the Song Dynasty*: "When the "Tieyaozi" troop of Xixia were crossing the river, they might win if they rushed to fight. When all of them crossed the river, they could not stop them. Xu Xi refused to listen. As expected, the Northern Song Army under Xu Xi's command was defeated, and a lot of generals and hundreds of soldiers died in this fighting.[183] "Tie" literally refers to the armor, while "Yaozi" indicates that the soldiers move as quickly as hawks so that they can "come and go like lighting." Xixia dispatched a lot of "Tieyaozi" soldiers each time, just like a forest of fighters. As for the costumes of normal Xixia warriors, there are some recorded in the *History of the Song Dynasty*: "The military soldiers wear the gold and black crown with silver, whose costumes are mainly purple with a silver ribbon. They are adorned with an awl, short knife, and bow bag attached to the belt. Their horse is decorated with leather saddle and red tassel, galloping and marching." The above is for ordinary warriors, not to mention Tieyaozi cavalry. Soldiers in the cavalry who are all excellent at archery are chosen from the offspring of aristocratic families. They are equipped with fine horses and the best armor, with which the troop's combat effectiveness is quite strong. When Yuanhao fought around his territory, he was very satisfied in all aspects but one regarding the battle with "Shan'e Troop," which is an excellent army force of Qiang people in the Hengshan region. But even this arm force cannot be compared with Tieyaozi cavalry. Yuanhao chose 5,000 men who were good at mounted archery and provided them with two *dan* of rice per month. Besides, three thousand cavalry soldiers were divided into ten parts. When dispatching troops, Yuanhao would call the chiefs of clans to gather and make a vow of blood with them, jointly swearing to carry out the cause of occupation and robbery."[184] Qiang people are good at riding and guerrilla warfare, and as early as the Pre-Qin period, they already formed a great military threat to the Central Plains. During the Xixia Dynasty, the Qiang people also exerted great military pressure on Xixia's military. Therefore, Xixia had to combat the Tangut military with its most elite troops. In many battles with the neighboring regimes, Xixia took advantage of Tieyaozi as its former army, clashing with the enemy lines by injecting strong bows. Their arrows were as intensive as rain, and then the infantry carried and rode in, leading to the enemy's failure in resistance. Therefore, Xixia army became invincible in many battles. There are a number of famous battles between Song and Xia in history, such as Dingchuan Battle,[185] Sanchuankou Battle, Haoshuichuan Battle, Lingzhou Battle,[186] and Yongle Battle.[187] The reason why the Song army suffered from the defeat is that Xixia enjoyed a powerful cavalry to pose attacks.

Not only the Song army but also the Khitan cavalry, who are good at shooting and equipped with three horses for each person, better than the Huihe cavalry in the Tang Dynasty, cannot be matched with Xixia's troops.[188] Thus, in the contests with the Xixia cavalry, the Khitan cavalry won less and lost more. Accordingly, there was a common saying at that time: "The Western soldiers are good at riding, shooting, and fighting, while the Northern ones are not comparable to them."[189] This indicates the excellence of Xixia's "Tieyaozi" cavalry in riding and shooting, as well as their power in overall strength.

In addition, there are also camel-riding troops in Xixia cavalry, equipped with a certain number of camels according to their military system. The first class has one, and riders under "Tuanlian" have five, and those under "Cishi" only have one. All of them rode camels to take a fight occasionally. In addition, "there is another troop called Poxi with 200 gunners, all of whom attached stones to the camel saddle, and threw them like boxing rain."[190] It is easy to see that Xixia is well-known for its camel cavalry in history.

3.5.3 *Cuju*

Sports activities like *Cuju* were recorded in *Wenhai Research*. "*Cu*" refers to "kicking with feet" and also means "jumping with feet and hands."[191] Such an activity was very popular in the Song Dynasty, and *Cuju* sports in Xixia should have been introduced during the Song Dynasty.

3.5.4 Yi Qi[192]

"Bo Yi and Xia Qi" both have been recorded a lot in *Wenhai Research* and *Homonymy Research*. "Yi" refers to "playing Qi and gaming, moving the Qi pieces"; "Qi" means "playing and moving the Qi pieces."[193] Judging from the unearthed Xixia cultural relics, its Qi activity has two forms: Weiqi (the game of Go) and Chinese chess.

The first one is Weiqi (Go). There are two kinds of Weiqi pieces found on the ground of No. 6 Mausoleum (originally No. 8 Mausoleum) in Xixia Mausoleum District at the eastern foot of Helan Mountain: it is black or dark blue. With round-shape, the Weiqi pieces are 1.1 cm in diameter, slightly bulging on one side, which were also unearthed in the stele pavilion; in the rammed earth of the tomb in this mausoleum, there is a blue piece, flat on one side, and bulging on the other, with a diameter of 1.2 cm. The various pieces were unearthed in Phase I culture (middle period of Xixia), Phase II culture (late Xixia), and Phase III culture (from Xixia to Yuan Dynasty) in Ciyaobao Xixia Site in Lingwu County, **Ningxia**. The Weiqi pieces in Phase I culture consist of a total of 261 ordinary pieces, printed pieces, and character-carved pieces. Except for one made of stone, the rest are all made of porcelain: there are 245 Type I pieces with round-shape, flat on both sides, with a diameter of 1.1–2.65 cm and a thickness of 0.3–1 cm; plus, there are two Type II pieces with round-shape, slightly convex on both sides, about 1.5 cm in diameter and 0.5 cm in thickness; finally, it has two Type III pieces with round-shape, slightly convex at the top and flat at the bottom, and one of them is cyan-white made of stone, 1.3 cm in diameter and 0.6 cm in thickness, and the other is white glazed, about 1.7 cm in diameter and 0.5 m in thickness. Besides, there are seven printed pieces with oblate-shape, flat on both sides, decorated with the same external thread pattern. Only one piece of them is single-sided printing, five are white, and one is black; the rest one is made of porcelain with a diameter of 1.4–1.8 cm and a thickness of 0.3–0.6 cm. Moreover, there are five white character-carved pieces with oblate-shape, flat on both sides, engraved with a character from the Heavenly Stems and Earthly Branches, such as "Bing," "Ding," "Ji," "Geng" and "Yin," with a diameter of 1.7 cm and a thickness of 0.4–0.5 cm. In the Phase II culture relics, there is only one type of Weiqi piece, with eight pieces of biscuiting, including seven white and one black with round-shape, flat on both sides, with a diameter of 1.5–2.9 cm and a thickness of 0.2–0.5 cm. In the Phase III culture, there are two kinds of Weiqi: ordinary and printed. It found ten biscuiting pieces, six of which are white and four black. Seven ordinary pieces are divided into four types: three Type I with round-shape, flat up and down, 1.8–2 cm in diameter; two Type II with round-shape, slightly convex on both sides, 1.6–1.7 cm in diameter; one Type IV piece with round-shape, slightly convex on both sides, 1.7 cm in diameter; one Type V with round-shape, with slightly sloping perimeter and a concave edge on top, 2.3 cm in diameter. Also, it has three printed pieces with oblate-shape, flat on both sides, with the same external thread pattern, 1.6–1.9 cm in diameter.

The second is Xiangqi (Chinese chess). In Phase I culture, there are two white chess pieces made of porcelain, oblate and flat on both sides. Both are character-carved; one of them is engraved with the word "Pao" (gun), 2 cm in diameter and 0.5 cm in thickness, and the other is engraved with the word "Huo" (fire), 2 cm in diameter and 0.4 cm in thickness.

According to a large number of Go and chess pieces unearthed from the Ciyaobao Xixia Site and other unearthed materials, we can infer that the residents there love Weiqi and Chinese chess. The pieces with the word "Huo" (fire) and the word "Pao" (gun) prove that there was indeed three-men chess playing in the Southern Song and Xixia Dynasties. The appearance of the three-men chess playing should be related to the influence of the tripartite confrontation of the "Three States" at that time, but the main reason may possibly be linked to the political situation from the 11th century to the beginning of the 13th century, when there were two tripartite confrontations: "Northern Song-Liao-Xixia" and "Southern Song-Jin-Xixia." Presumably, three-man playing could be a variant of Chinese chess.[194]

3.5.5 Fan Zhou

In *Wenhai Research*, it interprets "Fan Zhou" as: "it is used to cross the border"; the interpretation of "Chuan" (boat) is: "an object for crossing the river." Xixia people have a special way of crossing the river, i.e., sheepskin. *Wenhai Research* interprets "Pi Nang" as: "If the skin is not cut but peeled off as a whole, it is called "Pi Nang."[195] The place Jingji in Xixia is close to the Yellow River, with many canals and lakes, which undoubtedly endows a naturally convenient environment for its boating activities. In the book *Translation and Annotation of Xixia Text Sheng Li Yi Hai*, it is recorded that when a son crosses a river, the boat helps him transit so that the parents do not worry about him.[196] There is another record in the book that "the weather gets cold in October, the river starts to freeze, and November is even colder, in which the ice is so tough that ships are difficult to travel."[197] *The New Decrees of Tiansheng* clearly stipulates the building and management of ships.[198] From this point of view, Xixia attaches importance to boating and develops some boating activities for the purpose of both common life and military needs. However, we are not clear about the specific situation of Xixia boating activities till now, which still await to be further researched.

3.5.6 High Jump, Long Jump, and Racing

As mentioned earlier, Yang Dayan in the Southern and Northern Dynasties was a member of the Qiang nationality, who was highly appreciated by the army for his fast running. Similarly, there are many other talents of his kind in the Xixia army, which enjoys both powerful cavalry and considerable infantry. The *History of the Song* Dynasty quotes as follows: "Since ancient times, choosing cavalry or infantry has been depending on the terrain. According to the *Arts of War*: Fan soldiers are good at archery and rushing with strength, while Han soldiers excel at strong crossbows and special horns; so to speak, Fan is good at riding, and Han is skillful at shooting. And presently, the situation changed. People in the west of Hengshan tribe have a troop called "Bubazi," who go up and down the mountains at ease and wade into the stream amazingly fast like lighting; there is also the cavalry called "Tieyaozi" as mentioned before, marching all the time invincibly. When Xixia army encounters their enemy on the plains, they employ "Tieyaozo" to combat every time; and while in deep and dangerous valleys, they dispatch "Bubazi" to fight. All these are the war arts of the Xixia people."[199] The narration here clearly tells us that Xixia not only has cavalry, but also has the mountain infantry called "Bubazi," which play their part in "ambushing and covering attacks" in deep and dangerous areas in the valley. The infantry not only stand hard work and "walk for a hundred and thousand miles," but also "run fast like lightning or flying clouds." Thus, their capability to run or jump is extraordinarily awesome, which must be gained through strictly long-term training.

3.5.7 Martial Arts

There are few documentaries recording the level of bare-handed martial arts of the Tanguts. Only two words, "Jiao-Li" (wrestling) and "Xiangpu"[200] (Sumo), are included in *Wenhai Research*, explaining them similarly: two-person wrestling, which is called "Jiao-Li" and "Xiangpu." As early as the Western Zhou Dynasty, wrestling was a highly valued activity. In ancient times, "the emperor ordered the generals to train martial arts and learn shooting and wrestling."[201] The wrestling (Jiao-Li) here is to train the army with some unarmed fighting techniques. *Wenhai Research* interprets "wrestling" as "Sumo," which shows that "wrestling" in Xixia, like that in Han areas, has developed from bare-handed wrestling skill to a popular social sport. Its appearance in Xixia can reflect that the martial arts of Tangut nationality have already reached a higher level. Yao Sui praised that Suanzhi Weier "is so excellent at shooting and riding that no one can compare,"[202] while Yang Weizhen praised that Maili Gusi "had a strange talent from an early age who was good at fighting.[203] Judging from these above materials, we can guess there are still many other capable warriors who are adept at wrestling or eager to learn fighting skills. Qi Jiguang once said: "Wrestling or boxing does not seem to be an effective means of fighting in the war, yet it helps people exercise their muscles and bones, a fundamental part before learning a martial art. Generally, wrestling or boxing starts from playing with a fist, stick, sword, bow, arrow, etc., which are regarded as the source of martial arts,"[204] which thereby reflects that Tanguts' martial arts skill has reached a considerable level.

The sports development of the Tanguts has greatly related to their neighboring ethnic situation, which directly affects the possibility of their survival; thus in history some smaller nations are often likely to attach themselves to a larger one. Or a nation itself must strengthen its military strength, which to some extent is related to physical exercise. Take the Xixia established by Dangxiang Qiang as an example. From AD 1038, when Li Yuanhao officially proclaimed himself as emperor and founded the empire, till AD 1227, when it was destroyed by the Mongolian Khanate, Xixia was handed down to 10 rulers, lasting 190 years. It successively established itself as the dominant state, coexisting with Liao, Northern Song, Jin, and Southern Song Dynasties. Among all these separated regimes, Xixia is smaller than the regimes of Liao, Northern Song, Jin, and Southern Song in terms of territory, population, and financial resources. However, its lasting time is longer than that of Liao and Jin. Moreover, during its two hundred years of existence, it was always demonstrated as a big military power, invading the Song Dynasty in the south and Liao Dynasty in the east, and was at loggerheads with the powerful Jin Dynasty occasionally. In a series of foreign wars, there have been many victories and few defeats. As a small country located on the border, it can actually compete with the two big countries.[205] This situation not only benefits from its people's skillful martial arts and enduring spirit, but also, more importantly, from the ruler's correct ways of handling the relationship with the neighboring ethnic groups.

In fact, before competing with the above-mentioned regimes, Tanguts were attached to the Tang Dynasty and learned and borrowed the sports culture of the Central Plains during its process of attachment. Because people in this ethnic group were born good at martial arts,[206] the prevailing tendency of fencing in the Tang Dynasty was bound to be introduced into the nation. In particular, since the Tangut tribe often traded weapons with commanders in the border town and Han merchants, they were more likely to be affected in terms of fencing of the Tang Dynasty, which can be found from the excellent swords forged by the Dangxiang tribe. In Chao Buzhi's poem *A Song to Dai Siliang*, he highly praised Xixia's swords and broadswords.[207] At that time, the swords of Xia State were well-known all over the world, and they were so valuable that Emperor Qinzong of the Song Dynasty also carried one with him.[208] Therefore, in *Taiping Old Man's Sleeve Brocade*, "Khitan's saddle, Xia's sword, and Koryo's Mise porcelain are all the top-class in the world." In the mid-Tang Dynasty, the Tanguts had to trade with the commanders in border towns with fine horses and sheep because of their blunt equipment.[209] After the Song Dynasty, its sword was awarded the laudatory title of being the best in the world, which was mainly because the Tanguts promoted the continuous development of their military technology in order to strengthen the army and boost the country, and succeeded in employing military force to fight against its strong neighbors such as Song, Liao, and Jin. Fencing was introduced into the Tangut tribe in the Tang, and then further developed due to the needs of their nation. As a result, the art of fencing or swordplay has become one of their indigenous martial arts, part of which was also due to the environment.

The great development of Xixia sports precisely resulted from the strong military pressure around. Such phenomenon still exists in Khitan, Jurchen, and other ethnic groups. Relatively speaking, the martial spirit of the people from those ethnic groups located in the remote northwest is not as strong as that of the groups mentioned above. The reason lies in that the remote population may not have such great military pressure compared with other nationalities. Although there are also rivals such as Xiongnu and Wusun, their pressure is indeed much less than that of frequent and large-scale war affairs in the Central Plains and Northeast China.

However, the Central Plains, which is famous for its strong military power, had to change its traditional way of fighting and learn to ride and shoot from the "Hu people" under the attack of nomadic military forces in the north. Mounted archery put forward higher requirements than those of the original chariot warfare, especially for the capability of controlling horses. Therefore, under such a situation, it forced the people of Central Plains to repeatedly ride and practice their harnessing capability, such as cutting, stabbing, splitting, and other technical movements on the house, as well as other greater physical fitness training. This above phenomenon is exactly due to the surrounding environment of the states located around the Central Plains. Next, we will take a Zou Zhe (memorial to the throne) by Wihan during the period of the Five Dynasties and Sixteen Kingdoms as an example[210] to understand the impacts of the surrounding environment exerted on a nation's sports development. In this sense, we may feel the urgency of developing sports for safeguarding and developing a regime. At that time, Bai Chengfu, commander-in-chief of Tuyuhun, was threatened by the Khitan, so he asked his followers to attach to the Later Jin Dynasty. However, Emperor Gaozu believed that Later Jin was getting along well with the Khitan, so he would not accept Tuyuhun. At the time, An Chongrong, a governor in Zhenzhou, believed that Khitan was too strong to be a huge hidden danger to the Central Plains. Thus, he was prepared to attack Khitan, by secretly allying himself with Tuyuhun and even incorporating Tuyuhun's military force into the army. Under such circumstances, Wihan presented that the impossibility of fighting against the Khitan was mainly due to seven factors. "First, the Khitan was the strongest among all the tribal groups for years, and all the fine armor and warrior were in their army. Besides, Khitan had a vast territory, large popularity, and refined military equipment and horses. Second, the Central Plains' armor was not as superior as the Khitan's even though it was complete in form; there were a number of horses, yet poorly trained. Third, Khitan and the Later Jin Dynasty were still friendly countries, so it would not be wise to initiate the attack first. The fourth is that it is significant to fight at the correct time. Fifth, Khitan people were all good at shooting and were brave and capable of living in various bad environments. They were hard-working, regardless of coldness, frost, hunger, and thirst, all of which were far beyond the reach of the Central Chinese. Sixth, Khitan people were all good riders who benefited from the smooth land, while infantry of the Central Plains enjoyed fighting in narrow and dangerous areas. Seventh, when the battle broke out, the command was in power. The military officers and soldiers were asked to seek appeasement to seize the temporary peace. As a result, the border vassals and distant counties were even more rampant. The Central Plains looked tough on the surface yet soft inside, which is humiliating to bully the superior and surpass the inferior. In Wihan's view, Khitan cavalry troops are well equipped and conducive to the war. Although the troops of Later Jin were well equipped, their horses were not trained well, so they failed to compete with Khitan. Wihan then remonstrated to the emperor, "train and comfort the soldiers, raise the commoners, accumulate grain, gather people, and persuade farmers to learn to fight. With the nine-year accumulation, the soldiers will be ten times stronger, the ruler will have no internal worries, and the people will have spare capacity, so that we can keep observant and wait until they become weak and tired, and then initiate our attack. This plan is more effective, and I hope you may think it over, my majesty."[211] From this point of view, the Central Plains must "train and comfort the soldiers" and "persuade farmers to learn to fight" in order to fight with Khitan, that is, to strengthen military training. This is a typical case of strengthening sports training and enhancing military capabilities due to the surrounding environment.

From the perspective of these sports, we can also sense the national mentality of the Tanguts towards the Han nationality in the Central Plains. For example, before its establishment, Tangut group was famous for its brave, fierce, tenacious, and skillful fighting customs. After the establishment of the political power, it attached great importance to the martial arts, and employed military force to resist the Song, Liao, and Jin Dynasties, causing three parties daunting. Even after the demise of the Xixia regime, there was still the "brave and calm"[212] trend prevailing among the adherents of the Xixia in the Yuan Empire. It can be seen that from the rise of the Dangxiang and Qiang nationality to their disappearance, their martial spirit has lasted for a long time in the long historical period of eight centuries, which has closely associated with the mentality formed by the surrounding situation in which the Dangxiang clan is located. The story of "Shenbi Bow" that we mentioned before indicates that Zhang Pu's answers are naturally flattering to Emperor Taizong, which clearly reflects the mentality of the Tangut clan under such circumstances at that time. The ethnic group is in the midst of complex and powerful forces, which makes it difficult to survive without a certain military strength. At the same time, it is also self-destruction to blindly fight without a survival mentality. Therefore, the Tangut group strengthened its national military training internally, improved its national physique and martial arts capability, and organized the famous "Tieyaozi" and "Bubazi" troops with their strong attack power. Externally, they either took the attack as their defense or attached to different big powers, wandering among several major regimes.

The sports development is also helpful to the guidance of its ethnic policy, which mainly refers to the ruler's attitude towards sports. Judging from the emperors of the northern nationalities in ancient China, anyone who attached importance to the development of sports culture basically played a vital part in the northern society. For example, Tanguts advocate filial piety and treat their parents with filiality. They adhere to the principles of "five qualities and five virtues" and honor the rule of "being filial with good manners, bearing the responsibility towards the officials, and being diligent and loyal to the emperor." Besides, they believed in modesty and trust in relatives and friends, virtue, loyalty and diligence in affairs, sensitivity to litigation, and courage to fight the enemy, which are considered as the most important rules for them. If they fail to obey, they will finally destroy themselves, and their parents will also suffer from the consequence.[213] Therefore, they strictly obey their parents' words, because "filial sons inherit their parents' teachings, do good deeds and speak good words, learn literature and martial arts, and do not violate their parents."[214] Under such education and fumigation from the state to the family, Tanguts have formed tenacious and martial customs and traditions for generations.

In addition to maintaining their national integrity, the strong martial spirit is an important pillar for the Tanguts. Therefore, they put forward high requirements to themselves so that they maintain their noble sentiment and high morale. Some records were cited in *Translation and Annotation of Xixia Text Sheng Li Yi Hai*.

Besides, Tanguts also set laws for sports. The stipulation for weapons in *The New Decrees of Tiansheng* was mentioned earlier. From such rules, the dominant of Xixia held archery competitions during military training, rewarding the riders who achieved different outcomes or grades, to ensure and encourage them to strengthen archery practice by the law. Xixia State also has enacted legislative protection on individual legal responsibilities in Sumo wrestling. It is recorded in *The New Decrees of Tiansheng*: "The person who killed the other in Sumo by carelessness would be sentenced to three years; if one incited the player to kill another, he would be sentenced to three years, too; and the player's sentence depends on the judgment."[215] This law is the only literature on the protection of Sumo wrestlers found so far. From the records, we can see that there are also some bad phenomena in the sports activities carried out by these ethnic minorities in ancient times. What is commendable is that the imperial court has provided legal protection for the personal safety of athletes participating in the competition, has the legal basis of "no dead people in Sumo wrestling compete," and punishes those who kill people unreasonably or instigate others to kill people in Sumo wrestling.

During the Song and Xia Dynasties, the national contradiction was always in the dominant position, and the war was constantly going on, which stimulated the society's need for military skills. The shooting skill and *Cuju* in Xixia sports items are originally military exercises, which fail to discard the nature of military training. However, archery, *Cuju*, and Sumo all have the functions of practicing martial arts, entertainment, and bodybuilding. The game of Weiqi (Go) and Chinese chess are sole activities that encourage the players to give up strength, take in silence, and focus on pure entertainment. The shooting skills in martial arts can be carried out in the form of gambling, but the scale is very well-defined and clear. *The New Decrees of Tiansheng* stipulates that in archery competitions, shooters can bet on what they actually have. In archery, you should pay for what you lose to your opponent. It is forbidden to gamble on animals that they do not carry with them during the competition. It should be prohibited when the competitor gambles extra hard. If someone violates the law, those who gamble on what they owe should be convicted; those who have official ranks should be fined one horse, and the common people should be beaten by a rod 13 times. The property lost in the bet shall be returned to the owner[216]. The people who took part in the gambling were both common people and officials, which also showed that archery competitions were very popular in Xixia. *Translation and Annotation of Xixia Text Sheng Li Yi Hai* recorded that August is the national drama period and is equipped with a net of magpies and animals. August is the time when the nation gets its first frost and signifies a harvest season. The citizens celebrate together, acting and playing, as well as preparing for hunting in winter. These sports activities in Xixia reflect the spiritual pursuit of the people who love peace and enjoy a peaceful life. And the enactment of these laws and regulations guarantees people to enjoy this spiritual life.

3.6 Sports Activities of Khitan

The name of the Khitan nationality is first found in the *Book of the Wei Dynasty*, and there are many titles of this tribe throughout history. According to Mr. Ma Changshou, a diversity of tribes have experienced vicissitudes and moved from place to place, as the northeast of China has been a multi-tribe region since the ancient times. The tribes' names often follow their chief's name and change frequently.[217] Therefore, based on the historical records, we believe that Khitan people stem from Donghu people or from the Yuwen Division of the Xianbei ethnic group,[218] which is an ancient and powerful nationality in Chinese history. Khitan took its form in the middle of the 4th century. After the middle of the 14th century (i.e., up to the Ming Dynasty), the word "Khitan" disappeared from Chinese history, which lasted for about 1,000 years. For more than 200 years, the state of Khitan (also known as the Great Khitan State or Liao Dynasty), not only united for the first time all the ethnic groups in the vast northern region of China, but also broke through the barrier of the Great Wall for the first time, with the Han people moving north and the northern groups moving south, combining the nomadic economy in the north with the agricultural economy in the south of the Great Wall. The nomadic economy was injected with new blood and gradually embarked on the development path of integrating agriculture and animal husbandry. Khitan's political system and "custom-based rule" policy left a precious legacy to the rulers of later dynasties, thus enriching Chinese culture.

In the early years, the Khitan people were mainly engaged in nomadic life, supplemented by hunting. They lived a life of feeding animal meat, wearing animal skins, and dwelling in tents and carriages.[219] The nomadic economy offers the people a powerful army. After the establishment of the Khitan state, all sectors of social production, such as agriculture, animal husbandry, and handicraft industry, have prospered greatly, laying a material foundation for the development of sports in Khitan.

From the end of the 9th century to the beginning of the 10th century, with the rise of the Khitan nationality, a large number of Han soldiers and civilians in Hebei were captured, or they fled into Khitan territory. Therefore, the economic and cultural exchanges between the two nationalities entered a new era. With the increase of plundered and fleeing Han people, the nobles set 39 states and counties successively, which were scattered all over Liao's Shangjing, Zhongjing, and Dongjing. The Khitan people, who used to have no townships, began to build houses, city walls, and palaces after they were "taught by Yan people."[220] As a result, towns and villages appeared on the grassland, and the civilians began to live a settled life. "Everything was fully ready."[221] Khitan monarchs of all dynasties advocated Confucian thoughts, including loyalty, filial piety, benevolence, righteousness, self-cultivation, and family harmony, which encouraged Confucianism advocated by the Han nationality to spread and develop unprecedentedly among the Khitans. Yelü Hongji of Emperor Daozong of Liao once said, "I am no different from Central China in preserving cultural relics."[222] Another example is the painting of grassland scenery by Yelü Beishan, the son of Emperor Taizu Yelü Abaoji. His painting of "archery, snow-hunting riding and thousands of deer" were secretly kept by Song nobles.[223] In the imperial capital of Shangjing, there were all kinds of talents from the Han nationality, like eunuchs, academicians, performers, teachers, scholars (of Confucianism), monks and nuns, Taoists, etc.,[224] engaging in political and cultural work. After Shi Jin ceded the economically and culturally developed sixteen prefectures of Yanyun to Khitan in AD 936, it accelerated the process of Khitan people learning Chinese culture and thus pushed the exchange between nomadic culture and agricultural culture to a higher stage. At this point, the ancient northern ethnic sports culture has entered an all-round development stage.

The Khitans are nomadic people, who are featured by toughness, bravery, and full of vigor. From the emperors and generals to the common people, there are sports such as archery, equestrian, hitting the ball, wrestling, chess, rope skipping, etc.

3.6.1 Sese Ceremony and Mounted Archery

Mounted archery was the means of livelihood for the early Khitan people. *History of Liao* records as follows, "Shuomo people made a living with animal husbandry, like Han people living on farming, from generation to generation."[225] With the progress of society, riding and shooting have also become the basic skills to participate in the war. Khitan "is rich in horses and strong in soldiers; Khitan people trained running horses effectively in field and soldiers among the commoners; when the battle arises, all were summoned to gather, ready to fight; the Khitan migrated along the rivers and grassland, fed them on meat and cheese; they rode and hunted for making their living."[226] After the establishment of Khitan state, the political power gradually stabilized, and thus the sports developed in an all-round way. Shooting and hunting gradually became Khitan people's martial arts and entertainment sports activities (see Fig. 3-4).

Fig. 3-4 Riding and Shooting Picture in the Liao Dynasty

Willow-shooting is an ancient custom of nomadic people in the north, which originated from the "Die Lin" activity of Xiongnu and Xianbei. According to the records of *Historical Records · Biography of Xiongnu*, "When in the autumn, harvest season, the tribes gathered together, with herds of cattle, celebrating and feasting." Yan Shigu noted, "People who attended the sacrificial convention did fete around the trees, which has been handed down as the custom of Xianbei nationality since ancient times. If there were no trees around for sacrifices in autumn, willow branches are erected so that all the soldiers could ride around for three circles till the stop."[227] Xianbei has the custom of stacking willow branches when doing sacrifices. Khitan people originated from Yuwen of Xianbei nationality, and Yuwen people called themselves a group of Xianbei, so the Khitan people's willow-shooting may have come from Xiongnu and Xianbei.[228] However, Liao Dynasty endowed a somewhat new meaning to the willow-shooting. The nomadic hinterland of the Khitan nationality is in the Tuhe (now Laoha River) and Huangshui River (now Xilamulun River) basins, where there are many deserts, and the weather is dry and rainy. Nomadic life often relies on nature, and when there is drought, they can only pray for rain. However, willow trees have strong vitality, much related to the nature of water. With this feature, combined with the Khitan people's horse culture, willow trees achieve the goal of completing religious sacrifice and practicing martial arts.

Willow-shooting is a kind of sports activity for Khitan people to ride and shoot, which is mostly carried out at the same time as the Sese ceremony for praying for rain. *History of Liao* recorded it as follows, "In Sese ceremony, if people suffered from a long-time drought, they would choose an auspicious day to conduct willow-shooting activities in order to pray for rain. In the beginning, hundred-column willow branches were set up; and then the emperor started to sacrifice to the late emperors and did willow-shooting. The emperor shot fist, and then the princes and the ministers followed to shoot one after another. Those who won were required to dress in willow costumes, while those who failed wore the normal dress. On the other day, the willow tree branches were held up again in the southeast, accompanied by some wine and corn piled for sacrifice. The emperor and empress offered sacrifices to the East first, and then their children started shooting willows. The royal family, the princes together with their relatives, the ministers as well as all the proprietors would gain different rewards accordingly. If it rained for three days, the people would be presented with four horses and four clothes. Otherwise, it would not."[229] During the existence of the Liao Dynasty for over 200 years, there are more than 20 items that have recorded the events of willow-shooting activities, based upon *History of Liao*. It could be summarized that in real life, Liao Dynasty must have enjoyed more willow-shooting activities than the number of records.

Based on the records of willow-shooting in *History of Liao* and *History of the Jin Dynasty*, there is a set of relatively fixed patterns in the ceremony.[230] Firstly, before the competition started, emperors and generals first carried out symbolic sacrificial procedures, shooting willow in turns according to their grades. The emperor shot twice, the prince, the ministers, and the officials once. Secondly, Willow-Shooting Competition is detailed as follows:

(1) Competition Setting. Each willow branch to be shot with a handkerchief was stripped of bark a few inches from the ground. The man riding a horse first blazed a trail, then the other proceeded to shoot with a feather-free arrowhead.
(2) Method of judging the outcome. If the willow branch is broken and caught by one's hand, the winner will be given the official dressing. Broken and unable to take, it is ranked the second; broken on the green part but able to take, followed; if one missed the target, he was lost. If one loses, one must promise to bet on his official dress to the winner. Yet, after the competition, their respective costumes would be returned back.

(3) On the second day of Sese Ceremony, trees are planted for praying for rain in the first-half day and willow-shooting in the last half, which is featured by the nature of ceremony and military sports, usually played by the juniors.
(4) Time of willow-shooting. Generally, it is arranged from February to July, especially in March, April, and May.
(5) The arrow used for willow-shooting is called Hengcu Arrow (horizontal cluster arrow). This kind of arrow is flat-headed with a flat body, shaped by an inverted isosceles triangle, or a fan-shaped arrow, with the front end curved with a blade line. There is an arrow, about 11.6 cm long and 4.5 cm wide, unearthed from the Liao tomb in Faku, Liaoning. When unearthed, the arrow was in a container, which seemed to have special purposes.[231]

During the time the Khitans ruled the northern region, they continuously absorbed the customs and culture of the Central Plains, including holding some riding and shooting activities at some folk festivals. For example, during the "Chong Yang Festival" (Double Ninth Festival) each year, the emperor led his ministers and tribes to shoot tigers, and the man who got a few would be punished at the festival banquet. After shooting, he chose the highland to pitch the tent and poured chrysanthemum wine to officials of Fan and Han. During this festival, they would eat rabbit liver with a sauce made of deer tongue and drink Zhu Yu wine to eliminate disasters. The Double Ninth Day is recorded like this in the ancient book.[232]

Khitan also has another custom of riding and shooting, which is called "Taoli Hua." *History of Liao* contains that March 3 is celebrated as a national custom, on which people would carve wooden rabbits for shooting. The one who first shot the target was the winner, who would drink wine on the horse served by the loser down the horse. This activity was recorded as "Taoli Hua." "Taoli" refers to rabbit, while "Hua" refers to shooting.[233] This is different from the willow-shooting activity with a certain religious element, but "Taoli Hua" is a relatively fixed activity only with riding and shooting as its main competition forms.

The monarchs after the middle of the Liao Dynasty were lack of diligent administration and failed to win the trust of their people. Especially when it came to Tianzuo Period, the emperor's fatuity surpassed that of all his predecessors. As soon as Emperor Tianzuo ascended the throne, he prayed to Buddha for blessings. During his reign, he paid less attention to national affairs and appointed more unloyal officials. Besides, he did not deal with government affairs but indulged himself in hunting and debauchery. Even when Aguda of Jurchens attacked Ningjiang, he was still shooting deer in Qingzhou, "not caring at all" when he heard that. By AD 1121 (the first year of Baoda), Jurchens captured Shangjing, and many towns were lost successively. He was still addicted to shooting as usual. For example, in AD 1117 (the year of Tianqing), under the circumstances of the Yelüzhangnu Rebellion, the Jin soldiers took some territory of Liao, and countrymen revolted one after another; the Emperor Tianzuo still got indulged in hunting in different mountains in June, August, and September.[234] At this time, the sports events engaged by those aristocrats and the emperor were totally the media of their recreation, deprived of the nature of sports. It is precisely because the Khitan ruler failed to highlight the significance of sports activities towards military, but addicted himself to entertainment that the regime fell into collapse in the end.

3.6.2 Qi Activities[235]

According to literature records and archaeological discoveries in recent years, Weiqi, backgammon, etc., have been introduced to Khitan, and there are other simple chess activities among the Khitans.

Firstly, it is Weiqi (Go). It has a long history, which came into existence in China during the Spring and Autumn Period and the **Warring States Period approximately. The activities in the early** ancient times that were communicated between the Central Plains and its neighboring nationalities were accepted and popularized by the Khitan people. Since the liberation of China, chess pieces have been discovered many times in Liao tombs, proving that Weiqi in Liao Dynasty has become very popular. In 1954, Weiqi was unearthed from Xiao Xiaozhong's tomb in Xigu Mountain, Jinxi, **Liaoning Province. There were 76 pottery** chess pieces of black or white, round-shaped and pattern-printed. However, the number of **chess pieces was insufficient, and no chessboard** was found.[236] In 1966, some were unearthed in the tomb of Chang Zunhua in Chaoyang Textile Factory, in which the white pieces were exquisitely made of agate.[237] In 1977, a complete set of chess instruments was unearthed from a Liao tomb in Fengshou Commune of Aohan Banner, Mongolia. The chessboard is a square table with a height of 10 cm and a side length of 40 cm. The table was painted white, the wood rotten. The center of the table is 30 cm long and 30 cm wide, with 13 rows vertically and horizontally. There are 79 black pieces and 76 white pieces, 155 in total. There are spaces between pieces. When unearthed, black and white chess pieces were placed on the board in the form of a chess game in progress, and the chess pieces were all placed on the vertical and horizontal crossing lines of the board (see Fig. 3-5).[238] This reproduces the whole set of Weiqi and its practice in the Liao Dynasty for us.

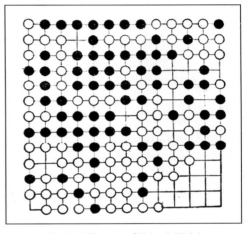

Fig. 3-5 Diagram of Khitan's Weiqi

The second is backgammon, a popular game in our country. It is said that it was introduced from Tianzhu and prevailed in the Southern and Northern Dynasties, Sui and Tang Dynasties. It was also introduced into Khitan. Because the display is like a chessboard, there are six directions on the left and the same on the right. The horse piece is tapered, 15 in black and 15 in white. The two players fight each other and move horse pieces by throwing dice. The white horse goes from right to left, and the dark horse goes the other way. The one first to move out all pieces wins. Such activity prevailed in the Liao court. *History of Liao* contains the event in September of the 6th year of Tonghe (AD 998), "in the year of Ding You, the Empress Dowager stayed in Han Dehang's mansion, and ordered her ministers to play backgammon for enjoyment. She would offer more rewards to those winners in the game.[239] In *History of Liao*, Emperor Xingzong along with his brother Chongyuan played backgammon even by taking the residents and territory as a reward. The emperor has repeatedly failed to compete, so he has already compensated several towns accordingly. And after several days, they re-competed with each other. The emperor was defeated one more time, so he decided to quit it forever.[240] It is obvious that Emperor Daozong played backgammon with his brother by taking some of his towns as a reward, which also has been cited in *Annotations to National Records of the Great Jin Dynasty*.[241] Also, *The Sketches in Jin Dynasty*, written by Hong Hao, recorded that the Khitan people played backgammon with the Jurchens, "After Liao Dynasty perished, Linya Daxi also surrendered. Later, he fought with Nimahe in backgammon, who intended to kill him but not saying a word. Daxi returned to his tent in fear, abandoned his wife, and fled by night with his five children."[242] While two sides were playing backgammon, one intended to kill the other to take advantage of the game. Thus, we can tell backgammon was also introduced during the Jin Dynasty. According to *The Sketches in Jin Dynasty*, "The backgammon was served in numbers, from 5 and 6, up to 10, in the tea house in Yanjing, and people enjoy playing as much as the people in the South who prefer a set of tea instruments placed in their tea house."

Backgammon was unearthed in China as early as 1971. In the Liao tomb excavated in Liaoning Province, a pair of lacquer wood backgammon was first excavated (see Fig. 3-6). The chessboard is rectangular, with a crescent-shaped pattern carved on each of the two long sides and a total of 12 round pits on the left and right (the so-called "shuang lu"). The carvings are painted white, and 30 tapered chess pieces, 15 in black and white, are piled up on the board. There are also two horn dice beside them, which have become rotten.[243] This is a backgammon set found in the tomb of Khitan women. Therefore, it can be inferred that backgammon was flourishing in the Liao Dynasty, which is also the manifestation of the influence of the Central Plains culture on Khitan people.

Fig. 3-6 Backgammon in the Liao Dynasty

The third is folk chess. In 1980, in the provincial cultural relic survey organized by the Liaoning Provincial Cultural Bureau, a stone chessboard was found in the Liao tomb in the Warring States Site in Jianchang County. The chessboard is carved with natural river pebbles. It is nearly square and flat on both sides, carved with characters on the outside of the chessboard. There are three characters on one side and one on the other, which are not recognizable. Among them, two characters linked may have some relation with the chess surface, which could be Khitan characters.

One of the chess games is still played by the local people, which is nicknamed as "tigers eating sheep." No one understands the content of the other side. We guess this may be the popular chess instrument for the local villagers, including Han and Khitan people, for their sports activities in spare time.²⁴⁴

3.6.3 Khitan Children's Rope Skipping

The sports activity of children skipping rope is recorded in Xianbei literature, but the picture of skipping rope was first discovered during the archaeology of Khitan. From the Liao tomb murals in Xuanhua, Liaoning, the children's rope skipping picture was drawn on the upper part of the wooden door in the back room of Zhang Kuangzheng's tomb. The picture consists of three Khitan children, one boy on the left and one on the right, wearing a red robe, swinging the rope up and down, while the other shirtless boy struggled to skip the rope (see Fig. 3-7).²⁴⁵ Judging from the current relevant materials, rope skipping was first recorded in the *Book of the Northern Qi Dynasty*, which has a close relationship with Xianbei nationality. And archaeological images were first discovered in the murals of Liao tombs in Xuanhua, which have a lot to do with the Khitan nationality. Because Khitan and Xianbei have a certain original relation, they have made great contributions to the development of rope skipping. Nowadays, the activity is still a traditional one loved by the general public in our country. It is very well carried out among communities and schools, giving full play to the characteristics of this competitive sport and the function of national fitness.

Fig. 3-7 Picture of Khitan Children's Rope Skipping

3.7 Sports Activities of Jurchen

Jurchen ethnic group, with its origin in the Mohe People, is related to Sushen People in the Pre-Qin period, Yilou in the Han-Jin period, Wuji in the North Dynasty, and Mohe in the Sui-Tang period.²⁴⁶ However, although the main source is the Mohe people, many other ethnic elements have been integrated or assimilated in the process of formation and development. Later, there were two groups joined the Jurchen Community. In AD 928 (the third year of Tianxian), Wu Qimai, Emperor Taizong of Liao, ordered Yelü Yuzhi to move the Bohai people southward. As a consequence, Bohai people either died in Silla or moved to Jurchen during their movement; the other part of the Bohai people who were "difficult to migrate"[247] stayed in the original place. Thus, when Bohai people in large numbers moved southward, the Jurchens quickly entered the old place of Bohai and co-habituated with the local Bohai. In the Liao Dynasty, except for those who are called Wure (transliterated) people in Jurchen's territory, the others were mostly called Jurchens by Khitan people, indicating that both parts of Bohai people had merged into Jurchen.[248] The people who joined the Jurchen nationality in the Jin Dynasty are as follows: first, a large number of Bohai people who were originally under the jurisdiction of the Liao Dynasty, like Tieli and Wure, later transferred to Jurchen before Liao's destruction. And after joining Jurchen, Tieli, Wure, and other groups' names disappeared. As a result, Bohai people intermarried with each other under the control of Aguda's thought of "Jurchen and Bohai belonging to one family." The title of Bohai perished in history after Emperor Shizong's domination. Obviously, they all became members of Jurchen. Secondly, after the Khitan uprising led by Yila Wowo and others was suppressed in AD 1163 (the third year of Dading), Emperor Shizong in the Jin Dynasty issued a decree to abolish the name of Meng'an Mouke and put them into a branch of Jurchen.[249] Later, when the Khitan people who took part in the Yila Wowo uprising moved to Shangjing, Jihzhou, Lizhou, and other places, Emperor Shizong explicitly told the minister in charge to make them co-live with the Jurchens, so that they could marry each other, gradually forming into a custom.[250] Many Khitans who mingled with the local Jurchens also became the native Jurchen people. Thirdly, the Jin Dynasty forced the captured Hans during the Southern Expedition to move to the "mainland" many times since Aguda, and most of them became slaves. During the nearly 100 years of historical evolution, many of Hans were gradually assimilated by the Jurchen people.

Positively, Aguda would trade his relation with the surrounding tribes by marriage in good times, while he would wage war in bad times. Internally, he developed farming to grow grain, trained soldiers, and herded horses, and externally, he would rely on some gold, pearls, and good horses to bribe other surrounding states in order to be on good terms. Eventually, Jin Dynasty was established. At that time, there were fewer than 10,000 Jurchen soldiers, but later they defeated the Liao army of ten thousand troops, whose morale was greatly boosted. All the great achievements of Aguda have much to do with his wise diplomatic strategy plus the internal policy of "training soldiers and herding horses." Well-trained soldiers and commanders are the magic weapons for him to win on the battlefield. *History of the Jin Dynasty* recorded that Jin Xing, who fought like a god and won many wars, was invincible and achieved tremendously within ten years. The reason for his success can be accounted for: he was calm and brave, and his brothers and sons were all excellent generals. The troops were well-trained and sharp-skilled. In addition, his land is small and thin, yet the men still work hard to provide themselves with food and clothing. Where there is a war, they could fight to capture and win. Efforts can help to prevent coldness and hotness, and they could work as a whole. Therefore, with ambition and bravery combined, with a strong army and concerted efforts, Jin state could organize all people from all walks of life to conquer and fight. In that sense, the weak become the strong, and the few may defeat the more, which is absolutely true. Therefore, in the 32 armies of the Jin Dynasty, most of them are named with "brave-like" characters, covering Shen Wei (God-like and powerful), Shen Rui, Shen Yi, Shen Yong, Shen Feng, Wu Sheng (mighty), Wu Wei, Wu Ding, Wu An, Wei Ding (powerful), Wei Sheng, Wei Xin Wei Jie, etc.[251] All of the above fully reflects the ethnic style and temperament of the Jurchen. Of course, this must be based on the emphasis of military training, especially the speed training that embodies "Shen (God)," the skill training that embodies "Wu (force)," and the strength training that embodies "Wei (strength)." In November, Emperor Shizong said to his minister, "I heard that Song army has been training their soldiers all the time. Now our army is idle. You'd better not believe that the world has been settled and there will be no war. Once there is a fight, the army can't be used. Can we not fail? Thus, there is a must for us to do training in time."[252] It can be seen obviously that they were also constantly watching the military training of the Song troops and tried to learn from military training. The Jurchen group organized their army into the military Meng'an Mouke, which was conducive to strengthening military training. Meng'an varies from level to level. For example, the four-class position was in charge of engaging military affairs, training martial arts, advising, and farming for defense; the five-class position, took care of the army's census registering and training affairs. And Mouke was affiliated to Meng'an.[253]

Jurchen's customs mostly followed Liao's and accepted the Central Plains culture during their long-term interaction with Song Dynasty. For example, in the process of attacking the Song Dynasty, they took advantage of the Song emperor's hobby to lure him into playing ballgames, thus making him a hostage. And then, Jurchen forced Song Dynasty to sign many treaties, demanding the Song to pay tribute to Jin. Among the tributes, there were many musicians and artists sent. For example, it is recorded in the *Southern Expedition Records* that Xiao Qing (envoy of Jin) said, On 22nd day, under the command of the general, I bought some gold and silver, and asked the Song emperor to play the ball. I then negotiated with the Song ministers, Wu Kai and Mo Zhu, and finally came to an agreement that the southern land of the river and Bianjing should belong to Jin. Besides, a number of maids were supposed to be sent to Jin, including two from the emperor's court, four from the imperial clan, 2,500 court maids, 1,500 women musicians, and 3,000 crafts …[254] These maids and artists are all representative groups of the Song Dynasty culture. As we all know, Song culture inherits the legacy of Sui and Tang, and the folk culture, including sports culture, is even more abundant than that of the Sui and Tang Dynasties. After these maids and artists entered the Jin Dynasty, they inevitably promoted the sports exchanges between Jurchen and Han nationality. Although there are few historical materials recording this phenomenon, we can still see that from Jin's imitation of the Han system that Jurchen was greatly influenced by the advanced culture of the Han nationality. Judging from a large number of historical materials about Jurchen's sports activities after the establishment of the Great Jin regime, Jurchen quickly changed from an early slave society to a feudal society, whose sports activities were deeply branded by Han and Khitan cultures.

Jurchen group organized its members into a military organization—Meng'an Mouke, which was not only a military bod, but also managed training and administration for sports development. As mentioned before, leaders in different positions in such an organization undertake different responsibilities[255]. However, no matter Meng'an or Mouke, one of their major responsibilities is to manage the army and train soldiers in **martial arts**. This also shows that **military training in the Jurchen nationality cannot be separated from such sports activities, and the sports have not been completely separated from the training as well**.

In its early development, the sports mainly included fishing and hunting, climbing, swimming, running, jumping, riding and shooting, wrestling, and other survival skills. With contacts and exchanges with other ethnic groups, particularly in the communication with Khitan, Tanguts, and Han nationalities, a large number of sporting cultures of northern nationalities and Han nationalities were absorbed, especially the introduction of military practical and recreational sporting cultures such as willow-shooting, polo, and Budaqiu, which promoted the economic and cultural advancement as well as enriched the life of the people among nationalities.

3.7.1 Climbing and Swimming in the Early Period

There is a record in *Annotations to National Records of the Great Jin Dynasty*, "Jurchen people are vulgar, brave and fierce, fond of fighting, and resistant to hunger, thirst, and suffering. They are good at riding, flying up and down the cliff, and even crossing the river without boats but by riding horses."[256] The **birthplace of** Jurchen is a regional environment with numerous mountains and rivers. In this environment, their early ancestors must practice their climbing and swimming skills to survive. At the same time, they also showed their brave national character and good quality of hard work, accounting for why Aguda defeated tens of thousands of Khitan troops with only thousands of Jurchen. The **nation was good at boating and swimming, especially in the war with the Song Dynasty**.[257]

3.7.2 Chess: A Popular Activity in Jurchen Group

It is recorded in the *History of the Jin Dynasty*: "Emperor Xizong was smart when he was a child. It happened that his father went south to the Central Plains, so he was taught by Han Fang, a Yan person, as well as one of the Chinese Confucian scholars. Later, he was able to write poems, compose elegant songs, make tea and burn incense, and play chess, losing the old style of Jurchen."[258] It can be seen that playing **chess is not their traditional culture but was introduced from the outside**. The Jin government set up a post as a chess player in the palace,[259] which displayed that this culture was valued and developed in the Jin Dynasty.

In the fourth year of Cheng'an, the Jin emperor said to the prime minister, "Someone showed me the eight-array diagram. How about it? I have read the *Outline Records of Military Affairs*, and many of the tactics of attack and defense recorded are difficult to implement." The prime minister said, "One military tactic is not able to adapt to all changing situations. Our army only takes Zheng and Qi to tackle everything in the face of the enemy's system." The emperor said, "It is not surprising to use two methods to fight since ancient times. Moreover, learning the ancient art of war is like learning to play chess. If one wants to use the old appearance to meet the enemy, he is careless. If what the enemy does is different from the old situation, we will be defeated. However, it is difficult to follow what is said in the martial arts classics. The more one knows it, the less one knows it."²⁶⁰ Obviously, chess-gaming had already existed in Jurchen group at that time, who were good at this skill and could link it to the art of war. Among the cultural relics unearthed in Xiangfen, Shanxi Province, there were also Jin people's chess-playing bricks (see Fig. 3-8).

Fig. 3-8 Picture of Two-women Chess-playing in the Jin Tomb²⁶¹

Surely, some Jurchen people were so addicted to chess that they neglected their riding and shooting. Warned by the Jin emperor, Fang (the son of Alibu) became Jingzhao Shaoyin (a government post) and then was promoted to the governor of the unified army in Shaanxi. Fang was engaged in financial bribes and failed to benefit the army. The emperor issued a decree saying, "When you arrive in Tiande, you'd better not follow your senior officials. Check the soldiers along the border, do not use cowards, and do not substitute servants for labor. In the tradition of Jurchen, people enjoy riding horses and shooting arrows at all parties. Now, playing backgammon on both sides should be completely prohibited, and learning to ride a horse and shoot arrows should be allowed. You may not summon trouble among the folks, taking the convenience of your post."²⁶² From this point of view, backgammon and chess playing were very common among Jurchen at that time. People loved it even more than their traditional riding and shooting culture.

3.7.3 Recreational Jumping and Throwing

History of the Jin Dynasty once recorded, "There is something urgent in Zhongdu, and a letter has been issued to the Donghua Gate to set up a recruitment office. People all over the country heard about it and some were entitled officials. As a result, people often showed off official positions and even sold them. Wang Shouxin, a village man recommended by Wanyan Yu to the imperial court, boasted that Zhuge Liang had no knowledge of military affairs. He instead recruited street rogues to enlist and taught them to jump, which was probably like children's play"; he used cattle heads and other objects as "magic objects," claiming to be able to repel the Mongols. But when they went out of the city, they did not dare to fight with the Mongolian army, so they had to kill some people outside the city to fulfill the mission, which was actually hilarious.²⁶³ This citation mainly describes some folk activities of that time. The author believes it is a kind of children's play, which shows that there were a large number of such sporting activities among the folk at that time (See Fig. 3-9 and 3-10).

Fig. 3-9 Brick Sculpture of Drum-beating and Dancing Child Figurine in the Jin Dynasty

Fig. 3-10 Brick Sculpture of Gong-beating Dance in the Jin Dynasty

3.7.4 Willow-Shooting in Religion and Sacrifice

The Jurchen's willow-shooting movement inherited the customs of Khitan, as the product of the combination of religion and folk customs. The ethnic group believed in Shamanism and placed arrows in the most prominent position in the ceremony of sacrifice. They also recited poems to the divine arrows for the sake of happiness and peace. Riding and shooting activities were always held in official or folk sacrificial ceremonies or other occasions. The official system is as follows: The emperor returned to his tent, got dressed, then started to play the game of willow-shooting and ball-hitting, which was borrowed from the Liao custom. After the five-day worship ceremony, two rows of willows were planted in the field. The shooter tied a willow branch with handkerchiefs, several inches from the ground, preparing for shooting. All the shooters took the order of superiority and inferiority. In each shot, a drum beating to cheer up, and with a ride as the lead, the shooter galloped the horse with no feather-free arrowhead arrow to shoot. If the willow branch was broken and caught by one's hand, the rider won. Broken and unable to take, the rider was ranked the second; the willow broken on the green part, or hit but not broken, or missing the target, the rider was lost.[264]

3.7.5 Riding and Shooting: Foundation of the Jurchens

Jurchen people live in the northeast corner of Khitan, where the land is suitable for farming, producing Ma Gu, ginseng, honey wax, north **pearl, raw gold, fine cloth, pine seeds, white aconite,** etc. There are many animals in the forest, such as eagles named "Haidongqing," cattle, horses, elk, deer, wild dogs, white swine, green rats, mink rats, etc., all of which are the hunting targets of the Jurchens. "They are brave and fond of farming, and moreover, they are good at riding, shooting, fishing, and hunting. Every time they see a trace of a wild animal, they can find its hiding place by creeping for it. And with birch bark as the horn, they can blow the sound of yo-yo, and shoot the moose." From this point of view, riding and shooting are two important skills of Jurchen, which reflects the folk characteristics of their "slow hunting (in peaceful times), quick fighting (in warring period)."[265]

Generally, their brilliant riding and shooting are well-known for Song people, so they employed many strategies in the battles. History recorded that Wanyan Hong Xiang attacked Yingzhou, conquered it, and rewarded a place called Yang Si. Zhang Jun, the Cardinal of the Song Dynasty, was assigned to follow the old style of imperial rule. He replied, "I would like to send an envoy to make the negotiation." At that time, Kuoli and Zhaba, members of Yiwowo group, played their tactics to attack Lingbi and Hongxian counties. Xi Ta, a governor of the Song, also rebelled against the Song Dynasty, and soon Suzhou collapsed. Kuoli and others said, "The northerners relied on riding and shooting to defeat and capture. This summer, it has been raining for a long time, and the bow is unavailable." Therefore, Li Shifu came to attack Suzhou with him[266]. It can be seen that Jurchen takes riding and shooting as its advantages to win the battle. However, according to their long-term experience of living in the north, Kuoli, a member of the Wowo Rebellion, believed that the glue of bows and arrows would be ineffective when affected by damp weather for a long time. These are demerits for the north to ride and shoot. It also shows that in order to give full play to the advantages of the army in the war, one must have a full understanding of such weapons.

Horse-breeding system in Jurchen group[267]

In order to establish a strong cavalry unit, the Jurchen people must strengthen its management of horse breeding. The group had a set of special systems in this regard. At the beginning of the Jin Dynasty, a group of animals grazed at the place of Zhu Mo, a place where there were no mosquitoes and where beautiful aquatic plants grew. During the reign of Emperor Tiande, five groups of pastoral houses were set up, all of which took the old name of the Liao Dynasty, such as Dihe Woduo, Wolibao, Pusuwo, Yan'en, and Wuzhe; each of them was governed by different officials. In addition, in each tribe, some slaves, servants, as long as housemaids were selected to manage animal husbandry. These people were called herders who were divided to feed horses, camels, cattle, and sheep, and eventually were rewarded according to their efforts. Later, they were increased to nine groups. During the Liao Rebellion, five disappeared, leaving only 1,000 horses, 280 cattle, 860 sheep, and 90 camels in the last four groups. Emperor Shizong set up seven places at that time, including Teman, Teman (in Fuzhou), Woduzhi, Pusuwan, Ouliben (changed into Wuxianwu Lugu in the third year of Cheng'an), Heluwan, and Yeluwan (in Wuping County located around Linhuang and Taizhou). In March of the 20th year of Dading Period (AD 1180), a group of pastoral officials was appointed to take charge, who were rewarded for their good performance and punished for their losses. In the 21st year (AD 1181), the three-year-old horses were bred by the Jurchens. The cattle were either cultivated by the commoners, or the sheep were raised by the farmers and sold to the poor households. The envoys were sent to check the actual number: if there was a shortage, the man in charge would be punished, and the shepherd should compensate for such loss, while those who hid the actual number would be punished as well. In the 28th year (AD 1188), after a long time of peace, the number of horses reached 470,000, the cattle reached 130,000, the sheep reached 800,000, and camels reached 4000. In the 5th year of Mingchang (AD 1191), the horses were scattered to be bred in Zhongdu, Xijing, as well as the east and west of Hebei. It is also ordered that those of other ethnic groups should raise horses; if some of them were dead, they would be replaced by the ones; while if they were needed by the court, the raiser should not hesitate to turn them in. That is the golden rule of raising horses in the Jin Dynasty. However, every big battle would require the commoners and the officers to hand in their rides for the soldiers. In the first year of Emperor Xuanzong's reign (AD 1217), it was decided that the governor would buy the enemies' horses from the civilian as well as the officials. "The first-class horse is worth fifty taels of silver, and the middle and lower levels would decrease by ten taels. If you didn't intend to pay, the two first-class horses would be replaced by the post of official, or middle level of three horses, or lower level of four horses, and so on. Whoever disobeys will be hanged." The emperor also sent officials to collect citizens' horses and set up the corresponding rewards. People offering more than 500 horses were rewarded with Qian Guan, more than 1,000 were rewarded with a government post, and more than 2,000 with two posts.

Martial arts election system in Jurchen group[268]

During the reign of Taihe, Jurchen formulated a military system. In the third year of Cheng'an (AD 1198), it was customized so that people under 45 years old could participate in the Jin Shi (scholar) examination. Ten days before the Fu Shi (government test) examination, the two officials were appointed to do a pre-test for good shooters. The rule of the shooting test is to set up a pile 60 steps, two poles setting opposite from the shooters 15 steps away. Two poles are 20 steps in the distance with a rope binding horizontally, 2 *zhang* away from the ground. Bows were not limited, only on the condition that they hit the target or not. Those who were skillful in bows and quick in shooting were the winners. Particularly, the one who could target two of every ten arrows, and fly his arrow under the rope to reach the pile is considered the winner. During the process, there would always be two supervisors named Txingsi monitoring the imperial test, till the completion of three tests in different forms. In the fourth year of Chengan's reign (AD 1199), Ja Xuan, minister of the Ministry of Rites, said: "In Celun Jinshi systems, the test-takers are asked to test shooting with bows and arrows, which turned out to be unreasonable and unfair for the ones under the age of 16. Those who ranked in the middle should not be given more posts or promoted." Another minister continued, "If the test is set according to the age, there must be some complaints. If they are young, learning will never be late. As for the rise and fall of the test afterwards, there is already a rule." Thus, the advice was taken and the rules still followed suit.

Wu Ju (Military system) was set up in the unification of the imperial system, and it was found in Taihe style, with upper, middle, and lower grades. "Any participant can hold a stone-strength bow, with the heavy bamboo arrow, standing one hundred and fifty steps away from the target. Among the ten shootings were one for Fu Shi (government test), two for Sheng Shi (government test), and three for Cheng Shi (routine test). Another 220-step stack was shot from a long distance, and one passing the test with one shooting would become successful. Within another hundred and fifty steps, there would be two lying deer with a height of 5 *cun* and a length of 8 *cun* every fifty steps. The test-takers would be able to shoot with a heavier bow and two big chiseled iron arrows. They were allowed to shoot four times in government tests, three times in provincial tests, and two times in routine tests, and one being able to shoot twice would be successful. Within another 150 steps, there are puppets with a height of 3 *chi* with 5-*cun* square boards on the left and right in every 30 steps. People are allowed to stab them with spears. The government test is conducted three times, the provincial test twice, and the routine test three times. One can stab one board in both left and right would be the winner. And then, the test-takers are asked to answer the questions about the law. One is labeled superior if he is capable of stating 5 out of the ten regulations. Yet, any error found in the routine test would be regarded as a failure. If one shoots with heavy bows of 8 *dou* with a long distance of two hundred and ten steps, and knows four of Sun and Wu regulations, he would be the middle winner. If one shoots with heavy bows of 7 *dou* with a long distance of two hundred and five steps, and knows three regulations, he would be the inferior. Interpretations of the law and stabbing board are similar to those mentioned before. Those who don't know regulations, though they are the best, should be degraded into the middle, and the middle goes to the lower. Anyone who gets middle and lower grades intends to try again should listen carefully." The above tests are step shooting, riding shooting, and riding stabbing. Surely, the government plan to select talents with both civil and military skills, so they can't be exclusively martial or literary.

In the second year of Yuanguang (AD 1223), Dongjing's chief commander Gesgu Lieya Wuta said: "Whenever the military officials enter the government, they are all under the jurisdiction of the patrol commandant army. Although this man is good at riding and shooting, having no experience of marching and no knowledge of army life, he may possibly lose once he faces the enemy. The chief would promote whoever had made an achievement in the battle" A minister alleged to the emperor: "The state has set up this Keju and Jinshi tests to recruit personnel for the army instead of selecting the talented people." Hence, he asked the people such as Dingyou, Daique, and others without a post to have a shot.

The above-mentioned horse herding and martial arts examination both show the Jurchen people's emphasis on riding and shooting. When Jurchen took its shape, its strength was very weak compared with its surrounding Khitan, Han, and Bohai people. In order to survive in the strong power, especially in the face of the strong cavalry troops from the Liao and Song Dynasties, it was necessary to vigorously develop **riding and shooting**. Therefore, all Jurchen emperors attached great importance to the training in **riding and shooting**. Even after the establishment of its state, they still did not forget to strengthen its practice.

First of all, emperors took the lead and practiced riding and shooting on their own. For example, Emperor Renxiao was good at both and was regarded as a top-class man in this regard. In each hunting competition, all the civilians would follow to watch him.[269] The second is to **carry out riding and shooting training in the Jurchen Meng'an Mouke**. History recorded that "it is a great **emphasis of its power, giving the kings the name of Meng'an, or the specified title. It is extremely strict to control its extravagance, prohibit its drinking, learn its riding and shooting, and store its grain essence.**"[270] In October of the 26th year of Dading (AD 1186), the emperor said to the ministers, "**The recruitment office is located in the narrowly situated southwest and northwest; the Meng'an people have no place to hunt and cannot enjoy riding and shooting. Hence, the emperor ordered each Meng'an official to encourage training in accordance with the time and trainer, and the one without managing training or failing to supervise would be punished.**"[271] The other is to include riding and shooting in the imperial examination in order to motivate people to strengthen their training. For example, "in the year of Mingchang, it is said that all the people are supposed **to know both civil and military affairs, so that Meng'an Mouke should participate in Jinshi, trying riding and shooting in the Celun system, and then being graded in corresponding degrees by their test performances.**[272] **In April of the fourth year of Mingchang (AD 1193)**, after winning Jinshi, a Jurchen still had to try the test of mounted archery. Whoever wins will be rewarded and promoted.[273] The last is about the rewards. According to the *History of the Jin Dynasty*, every town's defense army is tested every year. If there are outstanding shooters, the superior will be rewarded with four taels of silver, while the particularly special ones will be rewarded with twelve taels of silver. He has the chance of taking the post of guarding commander, and whenever he travels with his family to the capital, he is provided with six rations and four horses of hay every day.[274]

In order to improve the army's combat capability, Jurchen has certain requirements for the selection of soldiers. For example, at the beginning of its establishment, the army has 4,000 people. In the 22nd year, it was reduced to 3,500. Another guard army was set up in the capital. In the same year, Shangshu Department presented to the court that both imperial officers and guarding army should be set. The emperor responded, "You can collect 450 people and 120 horses, and divide them into three groups for altering. And when I enter the capital, they will stand as two patrols, with a change half a year. People in the patrols would be given the amount of 50, one and a half liters of rice, and enough hay for the horse per day. Meng'an Mouke officials could be about 40 years old, and soldiers above 30 years old."[275] It can be seen that as a commander, he can be older due to the need for experience, while the common officer should be a young man in his 30s or so. This is not only in the capital, but so is the case in other places. For example, in May of the fifth year of Zhenyou's reign (AD 1217), a minister named Wanyan Heda in charging of Yan'an government affairs and also taking the former post, presented to the court, "the defense troops of Henan and Shaanxi are all stationed in different regions, and there are the old and the young left in the barracks. It would be better to choose old adults as leaders who could supervise their children to learn **riding and shooting, which will be available in the future.**" The court took his advice.[276]

In order to improve the defense capability of the capital, the number of guard troops increased many times, to 5,000 and 6,000 in the fourth year of Cheng'an (AD 1199) of Emperor Zhangzong period. And there is another army called Vijie Army, in which thousands of crossbowmen joined in the year. There is a whole set of requirements for choosing a crossbowman: first, build a scale staff, which is 6 *chi* long, called Deng Zhang, measuring the people's height. The one who is as tall as 6 *chi*, capable of shooting with a 3-stone strength bow, and good at climbing is the selected one. Besides, he must excel at shooting skills, with six hits on the pile and two on the target. For the members of choice in Qin Jun, taking those who are good at riding and shooting with a height of 5 *chi* and 5 *cun*, Meng'an Mouke leaders would report their names to the Ministry of War; if it is not sufficient in number, the Dianjian Department and Xuanhui Academy will try to make up. There are also 200 guards serving the imperial court with weapons, who are chosen from the descendants of five-class to seven-class ministers, as well as some from royal clans. All of them are supposed to be around 5 *chi* and 6 *cun* in height, correspondingly decided by the test. Besides, there are also 200 imperial guards for a rainy day.[277]

After gaining power, not all people in the Jurchen groups maintained their ethnic characteristics of specializing in riding and shooting. For example, some nobles gradually led a debauched aristocratic life and refused to make progress, after accepting the Han culture, as is recorded in the *History of the Jin Dynasty* that the emperor asked: "There are many soldiers being dead and is lack of military materials, is it possible to make up for according to the position?" The one responded, "The children of rich families are too cowardly to be entrusted. When they are guarding, they are so insatiable that they cannot keep their fortunes. If we recruit brave people who are good at riding and shooting according to the number of material resources, and if the number is not sufficient, we will send soldiers to supplement them, then the government will receive effective results. Thus there is no need to worry about the dereliction of duty." The emperor obeyed him. The emperor agreed.[278] It can be seen that the children of rich families had degenerated and did not learn to ride and shoot at that time, like the son of Alibu mentioned before.

Because the Jurchen fought everywhere, the ethnic composition of its army was complicated. At the same time, most of the northern ethnic groups were recruited, so the soldiers were good at carrying heavy loads and rushing away. *History of the Jin Dynasty* recorded that it was eight years since the emperor (Jin Aizong) ascended to the throne. There are altogether 13 Duwei set in the East Palace (a place for future emperors), under each of which there were no fewer than 10,000 people. Soldiers in each Duwei were strong, superb, and extremely refined. Infantries carried armors, weapons, and grain, which weighed about 6 *dou*, and they were able to march around 200 miles a day. In addition, there were 18,000 members in Zhongxiao Army (loyal and filial troops), involving those from Huihe, Hexi, and Zhongzhou who were captured but fled back. Only those who were skilled at riding and shooting could be selected. Besides, there were totally another 200,000 members, including imperial guards, cavalries, military guards, and foreign soldiers.[279] The author believes that as a weak and small nation, the reason why Jurchen could have developed rapidly and then dominated the northern part of our country, is mainly due to the fact that they were acquainted with "expedition" and have trained themselves "strong and brave." Based on the literature, "Song Dynasty has a long history of peace. As a result, people are luxurious and comfortable, so they are not willing to learn riding and shooting. Song people also have no knowledge at all about our Jin state, which is good at expeditions and whose soldiers are strong and brave. I hope our need will be satisfied, which has never been heard in the past."[280]

In addition to the above-mentioned military riding and shooting training, there are also entertaining equestrian cultures among the Jurchen people, which can be seen from the archaeological relics in Xiangfen. From **willow-shooting in religious sacrifice**, mounted archery training in the military, and horse skill performance in life, it can be inferred that Jurchen's equestrian culture is extremely rich, which fully manifests the characteristics of northern national sports, and also reflects the vigorous development of northern ethnic sports in its comprehensive development period.

3.8 Summary

From Sui-Tang to Song, Liao, Jin, and Xixia Dynasties, all these periods are important for the integration of ancient northern nationalities in China, which is also the prime time for the integration of "Hu" and Han Dynasties. Surely, the northern ethnic groups in these periods have certain origin relations with the early Buyeo, Sushen, Xiongnu, and other **ethnic groups**. There is also somewhat inheritance in sports culture, which is developed with social progress. Especially in **the flourishing age of the** Tang Dynasty, the society was relatively stable and prosperous, in which all nationalities realized the inter-ethnic communication with Central Plains.

By the time of Song, Liao, Jin, and Xixia periods, there were mainly Tanguts, Khitan, Jurchen, and other ethnics, forming the relationship between the Han-dominated Song Dynasty and several northern ethnic regimes that rose alternately around, including the mutual exchanges between these northern ethnic groups. During this period, the areas under the jurisdiction of several ancient ethnic groups that established political power were basically the places ruled by the Tang Dynasty previously, which will inevitably retain the influence of the Central Plains culture. In this basic situation, several ethnic groups have set up separatist regimes successively, forming a strong **cultural collision. The culture of various** ethnic groups collided with the culture of the region they ruled, resulting in a distinctively regional and ethnic sports culture. Their productivity level has been significantly improved, and their sports activities are rich and colorful, involving a wide range of people in a period of all-round development. During these periods, sports activities not only retained the characteristics of production skills, but also showed more prominent military practicality. The entertainment and fitness were also enhanced in an all-round way, resulting in diversified sports characteristics that inherited the legacy of Sui and Tang Dynasties. Sports activities are reflected in people's production and life, military activities, entertainment and fitness, religious beliefs, and sacrificial activities, as well as other occasions. Many sports are closely related to other social cultures, especially the combination of sports activities and etiquette, which highlights an organic combination of ethnic customs and traditional culture, together constituting **the sports culture system in the ancient northern region, and profoundly affecting the formation and development of traditional Chinese sports.**

The great difference between some northern ethnic groups in these periods and those in the Pre-Qin and Southern and Northern Dynasties lies in their relatively high productivity and the effective establishment of state machines to manage tribes and other ethnic groups. In the past, there were also some nationalities who established their political power, but many of them were confined to the management of their own nation. For example, although the Xianbei people migrated to the Central Plains, their culture was quickly sinicized by the Han customs.

Besides, several major ethnic groups established their localized ethnic regime that faced off with the Song Dynasty regime of Han nationality. They took the initiative in politics, economy, culture, and other aspects, which played a positive role in maintaining their national cultural characteristics. At the same time, they also managed other ethnic groups, which was more conducive to exchanges, and promoted another form of ethnic integration in addition to the integration of Han people with other ethnic groups, which turned out to be significant in ethnic integration. Under the situation of continuous development of their own nation and continuous integration with other nations, sports culture has also been constantly exchanged and disseminated among various ethnic groups along with its carrier. According to the collection and analysis of some historical documents, the author believes that compared with the sports activities in the time between Pre-Qin Dynasty to the Southern and Northern Dynasties, the sports culture in northern China has been comprehensively developed at this time.

NOTES

1. [Tang] Wei Zheng et al., *Biography of Koryo*, vol. 81 of *Book of the Sui Dynasty*, 1st ed. (Zhonghua Book Company, August 1973), 1814.
2. *Records of King Sejong Zhuangxian*, vol. 44, June of the eleventh year, *Kuizhangge Chinese Literature* (Seoul National University, Korea).
3. *Records of King Ruizong Xiang Mourning for the King*, vol. 5, first year of May Wuzi, *Kuizhangge Chinese literature*, (Seoul National University, Korea).
4. Huang Xuan, *Stone Warfare Was Forbidden*, vol. 6 of *Meiquan Wild Records*, Quoted from Li Lianyou, "The Martial Arts of Korean Traditional Sports and Its Causes," *Journal of Chengdu Institute of Physical Education*, no. 3 (1993): 20.
5. Li Qiuguang, *Acrobatics*, vol. 18 of *Zhi Feng Lei Shuo*, a collection of *Outer Territory Poetry*, edited by Cai Zhenchu (Beijing Library Press, 2006).
6. *Records of the Great King Xuanzu Zhaojing*, vol. 35, 26th February, Yiyou article, *Kuizhangge Chinese Literature* (Seoul National University, Korea).
7. [Tang] Wei Zheng et al., *Biography of Paekje*, vol. 81 of *Book of the Sui Dynasty*, 1st ed. (Zhonghua Book Company, August 1973), 1818.
8. [Tang] Wei Zheng et al., *Biography of Koryo*, vol. 81 of *Book of the Sui Dynasty*, 1st ed. (Zhonghua Book Company, August 1973), 1818; [Tang] Li Yan. *Biography of Paekje*, vol. 94 of *History of the Northern Dynasties* (Zhonghua Book Company, October 1974), 3119, "especially good at chess."
9. [Later Jin] Liu Xu et al., *Biography of Koryo*, vol. 199 of *Old Book of the Tang Dynasty*, 1st ed. (Zhonghua Book Company, May 1975), 5320.
10. [Song] Ouyang Xiu and Song Qi, *Biography of Koryo*, vol. 220 of *New Book of the Tang Dynasty*, 1st ed. (Zhonghua Book Company, February 1975), 6186.

11. Wang Zhonghan, *Chinese National History*, 1st ed. (China Social Sciences Press, 1994), 148.
12. [Song] Ouyang Xiu and Song Qi, *Biography of Li Zhengji*, vol. 213 of *New Book of the Tang Dynasty*, 1st ed. (Zhonghua Book Company, February 1975), 5989.
13. [Chao] Zheng Linzhi, *Biography of Que Zhongxian*, vol. 129 of *History of Koryo* (Chinese Literature of Kuizhangge, Seoul University, Korea, 1957), 22.
14. [Tang] Wei Zheng et al., *Biography of the Dongyi*, vol. 81 of *Book of the Sui Dynasty* (Zhonghua Book Company, August 1973), 1818.
15. [Han] Sima Qian, "Xia Ben Ji" and "Justice" cited in the *Chorography of Records of Historians*, vol. 2 of *Historical Records*, 1st ed. (Zhonghua Book Company, September 1959), 54.
16. [Tang] Li Yan, *Biography of Wuji*, vol. 94 of *History of the Northern Dynasties*, 1st ed. (Zhonghua Book Company, October 1974), 3124.
17. [Song] Ouyang Xiu and Song Qi, *Biography of Heishui Mohe*, vol. 219 of *New Book of the Tang Dynasty*, 1st ed. (Zhonghua Book Company, February 1975), 6178.
18. [Later Jin] Liu Xu et al., *Biography of Mohe*, vol. 99 of *Old Book of the Tang Dynasty*, 1st ed. (Zhonghua Book Company, May 1975), 5358.
19. [Song] Ouyang Xiu and Song Qi, *Biography of Bohai*, vol. 219 of *New Book of the Tang Dynasty* (Zhonghua Book Company, February 1975), 6183.
20. [Later Jin] Liu Xu et al., *Biography of Li Zhengji*, vol. 124 of *Old Book of the Tang Dynasty* (Zhonghua Book Company, May 1975), 3535.
21. Tuitui et al., *Geographia*, vol. 38 of *History of Liao* (Zhonghua Book Company, October 1974), 456.
22. [Song] Ouyang Xiu and Song Qi, *Biography of Bohai*, vol. 219 of *New Book of the Tang Dynasty*, 6180; *Geographia*, vol. 38 of *History of Liao* (Zhonghua Book Company, October 1974), 456.
23. Tuitui et al., *Biography of Gao Mohan*, vol. 76 of *History of Liao*, 1st ed. (Zhonghua Book Company, October 1974), 1249.
24. Wang Zhonghan, *Chinese National History*, rev. ed. (China Social Sciences Press, January 1994), 326.
25. [Tang] Fang Xuanling et al., *Biography of the Northern Di*, vol. 97 of *Book of the Jin Dynasty* (Zhonghua Book Company, November 1974), 2549.
26. [Tang] Fang Xuanling et al., *Records of Murong Jun*, vol. 110 of *Book of the Jin Dynasty*, 1st ed. (Zhonghua Book Company, November 1974), 2838–2841.
27. [Jin] Chen Shou, *Biography of Gaoche*, vol. 133 of *Book of the Wei Dynasty*, 1st ed. (Zhonghua Book Company, December 1959), 2307.
28. [Tang] Wei Zheng et al., *Biography of the Northern Di*, vol. 84 of *Book of the Sui Dynasty* (Zhonghua Book Company, August 1973), 1879.
29. Han Rulin, *Turkic Inscription of the Kultegin Stele*, in *Han Rulin's Collected Works* (Jiangsu Ancient Books Publishing House, 1992), 390.
30. Zhou Weizhou, *Chile and Rouran*, 1st ed. (Guangxi Normal University Press, May 2006); Duan Lianqin, *Dingling, Gaoche and Tiele*, 1st ed. (Guangxi Normal University Press, December 2006).
31. [Later Jin] Liu Xu et al., *Biography of Zheng Yuanshu*, vol. 62 of *Old Book of the Tang Dynasty*, 1st ed. (Zhonghua Book Company, 1975), 2380.
32. [Tang] Linghu Defen et al., **Biography of Queen Ashina · Foreign Ministers Department · Tribute II**, vol. 9 of *Book of the Zhou Dynasty*, 1st ed. (Zhonghua Book Company, November 1971), 143–144.
33. [Northern Song Dynasty] Wang Qinruo, *Section of Vassal States · Preparedness III*, vol. 990 of *Ce Fu Yuan Gui* (Zhonghua Book Company, 1960), 11631–11632.
34. [Northern Song Dynasty] Wang Qinruo, *Section of Vassal States · Strong and Prosperous*, vol. 1000 of *Ce Fu Yuan Gui* (Zhonghua Book Company, 1960 Edition), 11733.
35. Wei Zheng et al., *Biography of the Turks*, vol. 84 of *Book of the Sui Dynasty* (Zhonghua Book Company, August 1973), 1864.
36. [Song] Sima Guang, ed., *Tzu-chih t'ung chien (A Comprehensive Mirror for Aid in Government)*, annotated by [Yuan] Hu Sanxing, vol. 182, 1st ed. (Zhonghua Book Company, June 1956), 5698.
37. [Song] Sima Guang, ed., *Tzu-chih t'ung chien*, annotated by [Yuan] Hu Sanxing, vol. 191, 1st ed. (Zhonghua Book Company, June 1956), 6019–6020.

38. [Later Jin] Liu Xu et al., *Biography of the Turks II*, vol. 194 of *Old Book of the Tang Dynasty*, 1st ed. (Zhonghua Book Company, 1975), 5188.
39. [Song] Ouyang Xiu and Song Qi, *Biography of the Turks II*, vol. 215 of *New Book of the Tang Dynasty* (Zhonghua Book Company, February 1975), 5052–5056.
40. [Northern Song] Wang Qinruo, *Section of Vassal States · Strong and Prosperous*, vol. 1000 of *Ce Fu Yuan Gui* (Zhonghua Book Company, 1960), 11733.
41. [Tang] Du You, *Border Defense XIII, Northern Di IV, Turks I*, vol. 197 of *Tung-tien*, proofread by Wang Wenjin et al. (Zhonghua Book Company, 1988, reprinted in 1996), 5402.
42. Ma Changshou, *The Turks and the Turkic Khanate*, 1st ed. (Guangxi Normal University Press, May 2006), 71.
43. Malov, *Ancient Turkic Inscriptions in Mongolia and Kirgiz* (С.Е.Малов:ПамятникДревнеАтюркскойписьменности Монголиии Кирґнзии), 1959, 39. Quoted from Cai Hongsheng, *Nine Surnames Hu and Turkic Culture in the Tang Dynasty* (Zhonghua Book Company, 1998 edition), 125.
44. [Japanese] Yanai Wataru, *Examination of the Yuan Dynasty System* (The Commercial Press, 1934), 34.
45. [Song] Ouyang Xiu and Song Qi, *Biography of Kang State*, vol. 221 of *New Book of the Tang Dynasty*, 1st ed. (Zhonghua Book Company, February 1975), 6246.
46. [Tang] Du You, *Border Defense XIII, Northern Di IV, Turks I*, vol. 197 of *Tung-tien*, proofread by Wang Wenjin et al. (Zhonghua Book Company, 1988, reprinted in 1996), 5402.
47. [Later Jin] Liu Xu et al., *Biography of the Turks I*, vol. 194 of *Book of the Old Tang Dynasty*, 1st ed. (Zhonghua Book Company, 1975), 5177.
48. [Tang] Du You, *Turks II*, vol. 199 of *Tung-tien*, proofread by Wang Wenjin et al. (Zhonghua Book Company, 1988, reprinted in 1996), 5453.
49. [Later Jin] Liu Xu et al., *Biography of the Turks I*, vol. 194 of *Book of the Old Tang Dynasty* (Zhonghua Book Company, 1975), 5163.
50. [Song] Ouyang Xiu and Song Qi, *Biography of the Turks II*, vol. 215 of *New Book of the Tang Dynasty*, 1st ed. (Zhonghua Book Company, February 1975), 5058.
51. Xue Zongzheng, *History of the Turks* (Chinese Society of Social Sciences, 1992), 746.
52. [Tang] Wei Zheng et al., *Biography of the Turks*, vol. 84 of *Book of the Sui Dynasty*, 1st ed. (Zhonghua Book Company, August 1973), 1864.
53. Shawan, *Historical Materials of the Western Turks* (Zhonghua Book Company, 1958), 127.
54. [Later Jin] Liu Xu et al., *Biography of the Turks I*, vol. 194 of *Old Book of the Tang Dynasty*, 1st ed. (Zhonghua Book Company, 1975), 5159.
55. [Song] Sima Guang, ed., *Tzu-chih t'ung chien*, annotated by [Yuan] Hu Sanxing, vol. 191, 1st ed. (Zhonghua Book Company, June 1956), 6019–6020.
56. Ouyang Xiu and Song Qi, *Biography of Zhang Xun*, vol. 192 of *New Book of the Tang Dynasty* (Zhonghua Book Company, February 1975), 5537.
57. [Sweden] Constantin Mouradgea d'Ohsson, *Histoire des Mongols*, translated by Feng Chengjun, vol. 1 (Zhonghua Book Company, 1962), 30.
58. [later Jin] Liu Xu et al., *Biography of Zheng Yuanshu*, vol. 62 of *Book of the Old Tang Dynasty*, 1st ed. (Zhonghua Book Company,1975), 2380.
59. [Song] Sima Guang, ed., *Tzu-chih t'ung chien*, annotated by [Yuan] Hu Sanxing, vol. 169, 1st ed. (Zhonghua Book Company, June 1956), 5238.
60. Ouyang Xiu and Song Qi, *Biography of the Turks II*, vol. 215 of *New Book of the Tang Dynasty* (Zhonghua Book Company, Feburary1975), 5059.
61. [Song] Wang Pu, *Zhufan Ma Yin*, vol. 72 of *Tang Hui Yao*, 1st ed. (Shanghai Ancient Books Publishing House, 1991), 1305–1308.
62. Xie Chengxia, *History of Horse Raising in China* (Science Press, 1959), 275–276.
63. [Su] Jishelev, *Ancient History of South Siberia*, translated by the Library of the Archaeological Institute of the Chinese Academy of Social Sciences (National Institute of Xinjiang Academy of Social Sciences, 1981), 519–520.
64. [Tang] Du You, *Border Defense XIII, Northern Di IV, Turks I*, vol. 197 of *Tung-tien*, proofread by Wang Wenjin et al. (Zhonghua Book Company, 1988, reprinted in 1996), 5402.

65. [Su] Jishelev, *Ancient History of South Siberia*, translated by the Library of the Archaeological Institute of the Chinese Academy of Social Sciences (National Institute of Xinjiang Academy of Social Sciences, 1981), 432–434.
66. Ma Changshou, *The Turks and the Turkic Khanate* (Guangxi Normal University Press, May 2006), 7.
67. [Song] Ouyang Xiu and Song Qi, *Biography of Qïrqïz*, vol. 217 of *New Book of the Tang Dynasty* (Zhonghua Book Company, February 1975), 6147.
68. [Su] Gishelev, *Ancient History of South Siberia*, translated by the Library of the Archaeological Institute of the Chinese Academy of Social Sciences (National Institute of Xinjiang Academy of Social Sciences, 1981), 511–522.
69. [Tang] Li Yanshou, *Biography of the Turks*, vol. 99 of *History of the Northern Dynasties*, 1st ed. (Zhonghua Book Company, October 1974), 3288.
70. [Song] Ouyang Xiu and Song Qi, *Biography of the Turks II*, vol. 215 of *New Book of the Tang Dynasty*, 1st ed. (Zhonghua Book Company, February 1975), 5052.
71. [Tang] Wen Daya, *Living Notes in the Great Tang Dynasty*, proofread by Li Jiping and Li Xihou, vol. 1, 1st ed. (Shanghai Ancient Books Publishing House, October 1983), 2.
72. [Northern Song] Wang Qinruo, *General Section · Strategies V*, vol. 365 of *Ce Fu Yuan Gui* (Zhonghua Book Company, 1960), 4344.
73. [Tang] Wen Daya, *Living Notes in the Great Tang Dynasty*, proofread by Li Jiping and Li Xihou, vol. 1, 1st ed. (Shanghai Ancient Books Publishing House, October 1983), 2.
74. [Song] Ouyang Xiu and Song Qi, *Biography of the Turks II*, vol. 215 of *New Book of the Tang Dynasty*, 1st ed. (Zhonghua Book Company, February 1975), 5052.
75. [Tang] Hui Liben and Yan Kejian, *Historical Biography II*, vol. 2 of *Biography of the Sanzang Master of the Great Tang Dazien Temple*, bk. 50 of *Dasho Newly Revised Tripitaka* (Japan: Taisho All Sutras Publishing Association, 1934), 227.
76. [Sweden] Constantin Mouradgea d'Ohsson, *Histoire des Mongols*, translated by Feng Chengjun, vol. 1 (Zhonghua Book Company, 1962), 156.
77. Mo Dongyin, *Manchu History* (People's Publishing House, 1958 edition), 64–65.
78. [Later Jin] Liu Xu et al., *Biography of Xiao Yu*, vol. 63 of *Book of the Old Tang Dynasty*, 1st ed. (Zhonghua Book Company, 1975), 2399.
79. [Song] Sima Guang, ed., *Tzu-chih t'ung chien*, annotated by [Yuan] Hu Sanxing, vol. 192, 1st ed. (Zhonghua Book Company, June 1956), 6046.
80. [Northern Song] Wang Qinruo, *Section of Envoys · Decree*, vol. 653 of *Ce Fu Yuan Gui* (Zhonghua Book Company, 1960), 7834.
81. [Northern Song] Wang Qinruo, *Section of Vassal States · Compliment*, vol. 974 of *Ce Fu Yuan Gui* (Zhonghua Book Company, 1960), 11440.
82. [Northern Song] Wang Qinruo, *Register Section · Archery*, vol. 846 of *Ce Fu Yuan Gui* (Zhonghua Book Company, 1960), 10046.
83. [Northern Song] Wang Qinruo, *Section of Vassal States · Customs III*, vol. 961 of *Ce Fu Yuan Gui* (Zhonghua Book Company, 1960), 11312–11314.
84. [Tang] Du You, *Border Defense XVI · Northern Di VII*, vol. 200 of *Tung-tien*, proofread by Wang Wenjin et al. (Zhonghua Book Company, 1988, Reprinted in1996), 5490.
85. Marwazi (SharafA1 Zamun TabirMarwazi, 1046–1120), the wife of the Persian Khorasan (Mave), during the period from the Ghaznavid Dynasty to the Seljuq empire, she was appointed as the imperial physician of the court. Her complete manuscript of two versions for *Natural Attributes of Animals* (including several chapters, 21 verses, in Arabic) was found in 1937, and the English translation was done by Englishman Vladimir Minorsky entitled *Marwazi's Views on China, Turks and India*, published by the Royal Asian Society in 1942.
86. The above is quoted from Xue Zongzheng's Notes, *Collection of Turkic Historical Materials in Turkic Literature Outside the History* (Xinjiang People's Publishing House, December 2005), 545–547.
87. [Northern Song] Wang Qinruo, *Section of Rituals · Music V*, vol. 569 of *Ce Fu Yuan Gui* (Zhonghua Book Company, 1960), 6832.
88. [Northern Song] Wang Qinruo, *Section of Emperors · Banquet*, vol. 190 of *Ce Fu Yuan Gui* (Zhonghua Book Company, 1960), 1299.
89. [Song] Sima Guang, ed., *Tzu-chih t'ung chien*, annotated by [Yuan] Hu Sanxing, vol. 180, 1st ed. (Zhonghua Book Company, June 1956), 5632.

90. [Tang] Wei Zheng et al., *Biography of the Turks*, vol. 84 of *Book of the Sui Dynasty*, 1st ed. (Zhonghua Book Company, August 1973), 1876.
91. Cen Zhongmian, *Collected History of the Turks (I)*, 149; according to page 40 of the same book, it is known that in the first year of Emperor Wu of the Zhou Dynasty (AD 578), although the Turks used "attack tools" when they were besieging Jiuquan, they did not win the battle.
92. [Tang] Zhang Jiuling et al., *Department of Shangshu Households*, vol.3 of *Tang Liu Dian*, bk. 595 of *The Complete Collection of Si Ku Quan Shu of Wenyuan Pavilion*, annotated by [Tang] Li Linfu et al. (Shanghai Ancient Books Press, 1987), 4.
93. Zhou Wei, *The History of Chinese Weapons* (Sanlian Bookstore, 1957), 217.
94. [Song] Sima Guang, ed., *Tzu-chih t'ung chien*, annotated by [Yuan] Hu Sanxing, vol. 233, 1st ed. (Zhonghua Book Company, June 1956), 7515; [Later Jin] Liu Xu et al., *Old Book of the Tang Dynasty*, vol. 195, 1st ed. (Zhonghua Book Company, May 1975), 5210.
95. Yusuf Haas Hajifu, "Foreword to the Translator" in *Happiness and Wisdom*, translated by Hao Guanzhong, Zhang Hongchao, and Liu Bin, 2nd ed. (Minzu Publishing House, April 2004), 3.
96. [Later Jin] Liu Xu et al., *Old Book of the Tang Dynasty*, vol. 195, 1st ed. (Zhonghua Book Company, May 1975), 5195.
97. Liu Yitang, *Uyghur Studies* (Zhongshu Bureau, April 1975), 333.
98. [Song] Ouyang Xiu and Song Qi, *Huihu I* and *Huihu II*, vol. 217 of *New Book of the Tang Dynasty*, 6111–6152.
99. [Later Jin] Liu Xu et al., *Biography of Li Maoxun*, vol. 212 of *Old Book of the Tang Dynasty* (Zhonghua Book Company, May 1975), 5983.
100. [Yuan] Tuitui et al., *Biography of Chizhan Hexi*, vol. 13 of *History of the Jin Dynasty*, 1st ed. (Zhonghua Book Company, July 1975), 2494.
101. For more information, please refer to Mahmud Kashgari, *Divan lgat at-Turk*, vol. 1 (The Ethnic Publishing House, February 2662), 160–195.
102. Mahmud Kashgari, *Divan lgat at-Turk*, vol. 2 (The Ethnic Publishing House, February 2002), 95.
103. Ibid., 95–368.
104. Mahmud Kashgari, *Divan lgat at-Turk*, vol. 3 (The Ethnic Publishing House, February 2002), 18–401.
105. Mahmud Kashgari, *Divan lgat at-Turk*, vol. 1 (The Ethnic Publishing House, February 2002), 24–419.
106. [Song] Wang Yande, *Journey to Gocho*, vol. 56 of *Notes of Various Kinds*, ed. Tao Zongyi, 1st ed. (Shanghai Ancient Books Publishing House, October 1988), 2609.
107. Mahmud Kashgari, *Divan lgat at-Turk*, vol. 1 (The Ethnic Publishing House, February 2002), 67.
108. Mahmud Kashgari, *Divan lgat at-Turk*, vol. 2 (The Ethnic Publishing House, February 2002), 30.
109. Mahmud Kashgari, *Divan lgat at-Turk*, vol. 1 (The Ethnic Publishing House, February 2002), 167–384.
110. Mahmud Kashgari, *Divan lgat at-Turk*, vol. 3 (The Ethnic Publishing House, February 2002), 8–70.
111. Yusuf Haas Hajifu, "The Wise Men Arguing on Who Should Be Sent as Envoys," chp. 33 of *Happiness and Wisdom*, translated by Hao Guanzhong, Zhang Hongchao, and Liu Bin, 2nd ed. (Minzu Publishing House, April 2004), 343.
112. Mahmud Kashgari, *Divan lgat at-Turk*, vol. 2 (The Ethnic Publishing House, February 2002), 193.
113. Ibid., 34–426.
114. Mahmud Kashgari, *Divan lgat at-Turk*, vol. 1 (The Ethnic Publishing House, February 2002), 421.
115. [Tang] Fang Xuanling et al., *Zhi · Yue II*, vol. 23 of *Book of the Jin Dynasty*, 1st ed. (Zhonghua Book Company, November 1974), 718; [Liang] Shen Yue, *Zhi · Yue I*, vol. 19 of *Book of the Song Dynasty*, 1st ed. (Zhonghua Book Company, October 1974), 546.
116. [Later Jin] Liu Xu et al., *Music Records II*, vol. 29 of *Old Book of the Tang Dynasty*, 1st ed. (Zhonghua Book Company, May 1975), 1073.
117. [Ming] Wang Yi and Wang Siyi, comp., *San Cai Tu Hui* (Shanghai Ancient Books Publishing House, 1988).
118. Mahmud Kashgari, *Divan lgat at-Turk*, vol. 3 (The Ethnic Publishing House, February 2002), 370–371.
119. Mahmud Kashgari, *Divan lgat at-Turk*, vol. 2 (The Ethnic Publishing House, February 2002), 22–23.
120. [Tang] Fang Xuanling et al., *Biography of Tuyuhun*, vol. 97 of *Book of the Jin Dynasty*, 1st ed. (Zhonghua Book Company, November 1974), 2541.
121. [Later Jin] Liu Xu et al., *Biography of Tuyuhun*, vol. 29 of *Old Book of the Tang Dynasty*, 1st ed. (Zhonghua Book Company, May 1975), 1073.

122. [Tang] Yao Silian, *Biography of Zhuyi · Henan*, vol. 54 of *Book of the Liang Dynasty*, 1st ed. (Zhonghua Book Company, May 1973), 810.
123. [Liang] Shen Yue, *Biography of Tuyuhun*, vol. 96 of *Book of the Song Dynasty*, 1st ed. (Zhonghua Book Company, October 1974, 2372–2373.
124. Muller, "General Survey of Tuyuhun Culture," translated by Guo Xiangdong and Rong Zhen, *Journal of Northwest Ethnic Studies*, no. 2 (1989): 233.
125. [Yuan] Tuitui et al., **Chronicles of Officials**, vol. 46 of *History of Liao*, 1st ed. (Zhonghua Book Company, October 1974), 758.
126. [Song] Yue Shi, *Xirong IX · Tuyuhun*, vol. 188 of *Notes of Peace in the Song Dynasty* (Zhonghua Book Company, photocopied in 1999), 8.
127. [Northern Qi] Wei Shou, *Biography of Tuyuhun*, vol. 11 of *Book of the Wei Dynasty*, 1st ed. (Zhonghua Book Company, June 1974), 2240.
128. [Later Jin] Liu Xu et al., *Music Records*, vol. 29 of *Old Book of the Tang Dynasty*, 1st ed. (Zhonghua Book Company, May 1975), 1072.
129. [Liang] Shen Yue, *Biography of Xianbei Tuyuhun*, vol. 96 of *Book of the Song Dynasty* (Zhonghua Book Company, November 1977), 2373.
130. [Tang] Li Yan, *Biography of Tuyuhun*, vol. 96 of *History of the Northern Dynasties*, 1st ed. (Zhonghua Book Company, October 1974), 3183.
131. [Qing] Zheng Yu · *Jinyang Gate Poems and Preface*, proofread by Peng Dingqiu et al., vol. 567 of *The Complete Collection of Tang Poetry* (Zhonghua Book Company, 1960), 6618–6623.
132. Zheng Chuhai, *Zibu · Fictionist*, bk.1035 of *Miscellaneous Records of Ming Emperor*, *The Complete Collection of Si Ku Quan Shu of Wenyuan Pavilion* (Shanghai Ancient Books Press, 1987), 515.
133. Zheng Chuhai, *Zibu · Fictionist*, bk. 1035 of *Miscellaneous Records of Ming Emperor · Supplements*, *The Complete Collection of Si Ku Quan Shu of Wenyuan Pavilion* (Shanghai Ancient Books Press, 1987), 503.
134. [Song] Sima Guang, ed., *Annals of the Tang Dynasty*, vol. 218 of *Tzu-chih t'ung chien*, annotated by [Yuan] Hu Sanxing, 2nd ed. (Zhonghua Book Company, June 1956), 6993–6994.
135. **Liu Chuncheng and Cheng Qijun, "The Spectacular Life of Tuyuhun People: A Study of Coffin Slab Paintings Unearthed in Guolimu Township, Delingha City," *Journal of Chinese Tu Nationality* (Winter 2004): 4–9. The coffin panel paintings in the text were copied by Liu Chuncheng. In addition, Xu Xinguo's article "On the Origin of Xitatu Tubo Coffin Plate Paintings" was published in** *Journal of Qinghai University for Nationalities* (Social Science Edition), no.1 (2007): 65–73. He believes that these paintings are the representation of Tibetan theme. Combining the discussions of Liu Chuncheng, Cheng Qijun and Xu Xinguo, and consulting relevant materials, the author believes that both from the view of both geographical location and customs, they are more in line with the history of Tuyuhun. Therefore, the author concludes that these coffin paintings must be based on the social lives of Tuyuhun.
136. [Northern Qi] Wei Shou, *Biography of Tuyuhun*, vol. 110 of *Book of the Wei Dynasty*, 1st ed. (Zhonghua Book Company, June 1976), 2240.
137. [Tang] Li Yan, *Biography of Tuyuhun*, vol. 96 of *History of the Northern Dynasties*, 1st ed. (Zhonghua Book Company, October 1974), 3186.
138. [Northern Qi] Wei Shou, *Biography of Tuyuhun*, vol. 110 of *Book of the Wei Dynasty*, 1st ed. (Zhonghua Book Company, June 1974), 2240.
139. Zhou Weizhou, *Tangut of the Tang Dynasty* (Guangxi Normal University Press, June 2006), 1–15.
140. [Han] Ban Gu, *Geographia II*, vol. 28 of *Book of the Former Han Dynasty*, 1st ed. (Zhonghua Book Company, June 1962), 1644.
141. [Han] Ban Gu, *Biography of Zhao Chongguo and Xin Qingji*, vol. 69 of *Book of the Former Han Dynasty*, 1st ed. (Zhonghua Book Company, June 1962), 2998–2999.
142. [Song] Fan Ye, *Biography of Xiqiang (Western Qiang)*, vol. 87 of *History of the Later Han Dynasty*, 1st ed. (Zhonghua Book Company, May 1965), 2869.
143. [Yuan] Tuitui et al., *Biography of Xixia*, vol. 115 of *History of Liao*, 1st ed. (Zhonghua Book Company, October 1974), 1524. Page 1530 collation notes: a. The rest of the people who shoot it are accustomed to combat. According to *Biography of Xia State*, vol. 486 of *History of the Song Dynasty*, 1st ed. (Zhonghua Book Company, November 1977).

144. Li Fanwen, *Homonymy Research* (Ningxia People's Publishing House, 1986); *Wenhai Research* and *Homonymy Research* are the Xixia literary classics compiled during the Xixia period.
145. Shi Jinbo, Bai Bin, and Huang Zhenhua, *Wenhai Research* (China Social Sciences Press, 1983), 412–484.
146. *The New Decrees of Tiansheng*, translated and annotated Shi Jinbo, Nie Hongyin, and Bai Bin, 1st ed. (The Law Press, January 2000), 364.
147. [Qing] Dai Xizhang, *Annals of Xixia*, proofread by Luo Maokun (Ningxia People's Publishing House,1998), 291–293.
148. Shi Jinbo, Bai Bin, and Wu Fengyun, *Cultural Relics of Xixia* (Cultural Relics Publishing House, 1988), 294.
149. Ibid., 312.
150. [Han] Ban Gu, *Biography of Zhao Chongguo and Xin Qingji*, vol. 69 of *Book of the Former Han Dynasty*, 1st ed. (Zhonghua Book Company, June 1962), 2998–2999.
151. Shi Jinbo, Bai Bin, and Huang Zhenhua, *Wenhai Research* (China Social Sciences Press, 1983), 399–545.
152. Luo Maokun, *Translation and Annotation of Xixia Text Sheng Li Yi Hai*, 1st ed. (Ningxia People's Publishing House, July 1995), 53–54.
153. [Yuan] Tuitui et al., *Biography of Xia State*, vol. 485 of *History of the Song Dynasty*, 1st ed. (Zhonghua Book Company, November 1977), 13985.
154. [Qing] Zhou Chun, *Continuing Collection of Si Ku Quan Shu*, vol. 2 of *Book of Xixia* (Shanghai Ancient Books Publishing House, 1995), 649.
155. [Qing] Wu Guangcheng, *Records of Xixia (Xixia Shushi)*, vol. 3 (Wenkuitang, 1935), 6.
156. [Yuan] Tuitui et al., *Biography of Xia State*, vol. 485 of *History of the Song Dynasty*, 1st ed. (Zhonghua Book Company, November 1977), 13993.
157. [Yuan] Tuitui et al., *Biography of Shekeshi*, vol. 253 of *History of the Song Dynasty*, 1st ed. (Zhonghua Book Company, November 1977), 8866.
158. [Qing] Kang Jitian, *Jin Cheng Sou Lue*. Treasured edition of Xiayin Hall in the Xinwei Year of Emperor Jiaqing Period.
159. [Yuan] Yang Weizhen, *Collected Works of Yang Tieya*, vol. 2, reprinted version of Hongzhi in Shuyun Mansion at the end of Ming Dynasty.
160. Shi Jinbo, Bai Bin, and Huang Zhenhua, *Wenhai Research* (China Social Sciences Press, 1983), 401–550.
161. *The New Decrees of Tiansheng*, translated and annotated Shi Jinbo, Nie Hongyin, and Bai Bin, 1st ed. (The Law Press, January 2000), 363.
162. Ibid., 580.
163. Museum of Wuwei District, Gansu Province, Ning Duxue, Zhong Changfa, "A Brief Report on the Cleaning up of Xixia Tombs in the Forest Farm in the Western Suburbs of Wuwei, Journal of Gansu Province." *Archaeology and Cultural Relics*, no. 3 (1980): 63–66; Chen Bingying, *Research on Xixia Cultural Relics* (Ningxia People's Publishing House, 1985), 196, 201; *Cultural Relics of Xixia*, 296, plate 91.
164. [Tang] Yuan Zhen, *Yuefu · Guke music*, vol. 23 of *The Collection of Yuan Zhen*, edited by Ji Qin, 1st ed. (Zhonghua Book Company, August 1982), 268–269.
165. [Later Jin Dynasty] Liu Xu et al., *Biography of Dangxiang Qiang*, vol. 198 of *Old Book of the Tang Dynasty*, 1st ed. (Zhonghua Book Company, May 1975), 5290–5293.
166. [Ming] Huang Wei et al., *Memorials Submitted to the Throne by Important Officials for Successive Dynasties*, 1st ed. (Taiwan Students' Publishing House, December 1964), 11.
167. [Song] Fan Zhongyan, *A Collection of Fan Wenzheng's Essays*. A block printed edition in the 10th year of Daoguang reign of the Qing Dynasty.
168. [Song] Su Shunqing, *Collected Works of Su* (Shanghai Bookstore, 1989).
169. [Song] Zhuang Chuo, *Ji Lei Bian*,1st ed. (Zhonghua Book Company, March 1983), 33.
170. [Song] Kang Yuzhi, *Yesterday's Dream* (The Commercial Press, 1930), 654.
171. [Song] Shen Kuo, *Annotations to Mengxi Bitan*, proofread by Hu Daojing,1st ed. (Shanghai Ancient Books Publishing House, September 1987), 628–629.
172. [Yuan] Tuitui et al., *Military Annals*, vol. 195 of *History of the Song Dynasty*, 1st ed. (Zhonghua Book Company, November 1977), 4862.
173. Luo Maokun, *Translation and Annotation of Xixia Text Sheng Li Yi Hai* (Ningxia People's Publishing House, 1995), 53–54.

174. [Yuan] Tuitui et al., *Military Annals IX · Training System*, vol. 195 of *History of the Song Dynasty*, 1st ed. (Zhonghua Book Company, November 1977), 4853–4876.
175. [Yuan] Tuitui et al., *Biography of Xia State*, vol. 485 of *History of the Song Dynasty*, 1st ed. (Zhonghua Book Company, November 1977), 13987. After this reception, Zhang Pu was forced to stay in Han as the Zhengzhou regiment trainer. In the spring of Xianping, following the relocation and restoration, Emperor Zhenzong granted him as the Xiazhou governor, Dingnan commander etc, to observe and dispose of envoys, who made great contribution to the local household, so that he was finally released.
176. [Song] Li Fang et al., *Imperial Digest of the Reign of Great Tranquility* (Zhonghua Publishing House, 1960), 1597.
177. [Qing] Wu Guangcheng, *Records of Xixia (Xixia Shushi)* (Wenkuitang, 1935), 17–18.
178. The translator believes that the clasp is probably a finger paddle for archery. *The New Decrees of Tiansheng*, translated and annotated Shi Jinbo, Nie Hongyin, and Bai Bin, 1st ed. (The Law Press, January 2000).
179. *The New Decrees of Tiansheng*, translated and annotated Shi Jinbo, Nie Hongyin, and Bai Bin, vol. 5, 1st ed. (The Law Press, 1st edition, January 2000), 223–230.
180. Ibid., 228.
181. [Ming] Song Lian et al., *History of the Yuan Dynasty*, 1st ed. (Zhonghua Book Company, April 1976), 3264–3265.
182. [Yuan] Tuitui et al., *Military Annals*, vol. 190 of *History of the Song Dynasty*, 1st ed. (Zhonghua Book Company, November 1977), 4720.
183. [Yuan] Tuitui et al., *Foreign Biographies II: Xia II*, vol. 486 of *History of the Song Dynasty*, 1st ed. (Zhonghua Book Company, November 1977), 14011–14012.
184. [Yuan] Tuitui et al., *Foreign Biographies I: Xia*, vol. 1485 of *History of the Song Dynasty*, 1st ed. (Zhonghua Book Company, November 1977), 13993–13995.
185. [Yuan] Tuitui et al., *Foreign Biographies II: Xia*, vol. 1486 of *History of the Song Dynasty*, 1st ed. (Zhonghua Book Company, November 1977), 14010–14011.
186. [Yuan] Tuitui et al., *Foreign Biographies I: Xia*, vol. 1485 of *History of the Song Dynasty*, 1st ed. (Zhonghua Book Company, November 1977), 13995–13998.
187. [Yuan] Tuitui et al., *Foreign Biographies II: Xia*, vol. 1486 of *History of the Song Dynasty*, 1st ed. (Zhonghua Book Company, November 1977), 14011–14012.
188. [Song] Ma Yongqing, *Nen Zhen Zi*, vol. 3, *The Complete Collection of Si Ku Quan Shu of Wenyuan Pavilion*, vol. 863 (Shanghai Ancient Books Publishing House, 1987).
189. [Song] Cai Xiang, *On Territory*, vol. 19 of *Duan Ming Collection* (World Book Company, 1986).
190. [Yuan] Tuitui et al., *Biography of Xia State II*, vol. 486 of *History of the Song Dynasty*, 1st ed. (Zhonghua Book Company, November 1977), 14028–14029.
191. Shi Jinbo, Bai Bin, and Huang Zhenhua, *Wenhai Research* (China Social Sciences Press, 1983), 440–536.
192. China Institute of Social Sciences and Archaeology, *Excavation Report of Lingwu Kiln in Ningxia* (China Encyclopedia Press, 1995), 75–77, 107, 133, 188–189, Plate 76, 103, 134; Ningxia Hui Autonomous Region Museum, "A Brief Report on the Excavation of Xixia No. 8 Mausoleum," *Cultural Relics*, no. 8 (1978): 60–68.
193. Shi Jinbo, Bai Bin, and Huang Zhenhua, *Wenhai Research* (China Social Sciences Press, 1983), 498–513.
194. China Institute of Social Sciences and Archaeology, *Excavation Report of Lingwu Kiln in Ningxia* (China Encyclopedia Press, 1995), 188–189.
195. Shi Jinbo, Bai Bin, and Huang Zhenhua, *Wenhai Research* (China Social Sciences Press, 1983), 535–546.
196. Luo Maokun, *Translation and Annotation of Xixia Text Sheng Li Yi Hai* (Ningxia People's Publishing House, 1995), 72.
197. Ibid., 53–54.
198. *The New Decrees of Tiansheng*, translated and annotated Shi Jinbo, Nie Hongyin, and Bai Bin, 1st ed. (The Law Press, January 2000), 393–394.
199. [Yuan] Tuitui et al., *Military Annals*, vol. 190 of *History of the Song Dynasty*, 1st ed. (Zhonghua Book Company, November 1977), 4720.
200. Shi Jinbo, Bai Bin, and Huang Zhenhua, *Wenhai Research* (China Social Sciences Press, 1983).
201. [Qing] Sun Xidan, *Collection and Interpretation of the Book of Rites*, proofread by Shen Xiaohuan and Wang Xingxian, 1st ed. (Zhonghua Book Company, February 1989), 491.
202. [Yuan] Yao Sui, *Stele of Duke Shi*, vol. 26 of *A Collection of Mu'an*, 1; vol. 233 of *Four Series*, 1st ed. (Shanghai Book Store, March 1989).

203. [Yuan] Yang Weizhen, *Epitaph*, vol. 24 of *A Collection of Dongweizi*, 6; vol. 245 of *Four Series*, 1st ed. (Shanghai Book Store, March 1989).
204. [Ming] Qi Jiguang, *New Version of Ji Xiao*, 1st ed. (Zhonghua Book Company, November 2001), 101–102.
205. [Yuan] Yu Que, *Collected Works of Mr. Qingyang* (Shanghai Bookstore, April 1985).
206. [Tang] Wei Zheng et al., *Book of the Sui Dynasty*, 1st ed. (Zhonghua Book Company, August 1973), 1845.
207. [Song] Zhao Buzhi, *Collection of Ji Bei Chao's Ji Lei* (Shanghai Bookstore, 1989).
208. [Yuan] Tuitui et al., *Biography of Wang Lun*, vol. 371 of *History of the Song Dynasty*, 1st ed. (Zhonghua Book Company, November 1977), 11522.
209. [Later Jin Dynasty] Liu Xu et al., *Biography of Dangxiang Qiang*, vol. 198 of *Old Book of the Tang Dynasty*, 1st ed. (Zhonghua Book Company, May 1975), 5290–5293.
210. [Song] Xue Juzheng et al., *Old History of the Five Dynasties*, 1st ed. (Zhonghua Book Company, May 1976), 1164–1165.
211. Ibid.
212. [Yuan] Tuitui et al., *Biography of Xixia*, vol. 115 of *History of Liao* (Zhonghua Book Company, October 1974), 1524.
213. Luo Maokun, *Translation and Annotation of Xixia Text Sheng Li Yi Hai* (Ningxia People's Publishing House, 1995), 72–75.
214. Ibid., 72.
215. *The New Decrees of Tiansheng*, translated and annotated Shi Jinbo, Nie Hongyin, and Bai Bin, 1st ed. (The Law Press, January 2000), 483.
216. [Soviet Union] *Xixia Code, The New Decrees of Tiansheng*, translated by E. H. Kechanov and Li Zhongsan (Ningxia People's Publishing House, 1988), 212; *The New Decrees of Tiansheng*, translated and annotated Shi Jinbo, Nie Hongyin, and Bai Bin, 1st ed. (The Law Press, January 2000), 363.
217. Ma Changshou, *Wuhuan and Xianbei* (Guangxi Normal University Press, June 2006), 185.
218. Wang Zhonghan, *Chinese National History*, rev. 1st ed. (China Social Sciences Press, 1994), 445–446.
219. [Song] Ouyang Xiu, *New History of the Five Dynasties*. 1st ed. (Zhonghua Book Company, December 1974), 886–887.
220. [Song] Xue Juzheng et al., *Biography of Khitan*, vol. 137 of *Old History of the Five Dynasties*, 1st ed. (Zhonghua Book Company, May 1976), 1830.
221. [Song] Xue Juzheng et al., *Biography of Lu Wenjin*, vol. 197 of *Old History of the Five Dynasties*, 1st ed. (Zhonghua Book Company, May 1976), 1295.
222. Zhang Zhiyong, "On the Absorption of Confucianism in the Liao Dynasty," *Journal of Research on the History of Khitan Jurchen in Liao and Jin Dynasties*, no. 1 (1989): 17–20.
223. [Yuan] Tuitui et al., *Biography of Yi Zongbei*, vol. 72 of *History of Liao* (Zhonghua Book Company, October 1974), 1211.
224. [Song] Ye Longli and Jia Jingyan, *Chronicles of Khitan*, proofread by Lin Ronggui (Shanghai Ancient Books Publishing House, 1985), 238; [Yuan] Tuitui et al., *History of Liao* (Zhonghua Book Company, October 1974), 441.
225. [Yuan] Tuitui et al., *The Biographic Sketches of Emperors and Tour Tables*, vol. 68 of *History of Liao* (Zhonghua Book Company, October 1974), 1037.
226. [Yuan] Tuitui et al., *Complete Book of Agricultural and Financial Records*, vol. 59 of *History of Liao* (Zhonghua Book Company, October 1974), 923.
227. [Han] Sima Qian, *Biography of Xiongnu*, vol. 110 of *Historical Records*, 1st ed. (Zhonghua Book Company, September 1959), 2892.
228. Feng Jiqin, "Some Sports among Khitans," *Journal of Seeking Truth*, no. 4 (1991): 84–87.
229. [Yuan] Tuitui et al., *Records of Rites I*, vol. 49 of *History of Liao* (Zhonghua Book Company, October 1974), 835.
230. Feng Jiqin, "Some Sports among Khitans," *Journal of Seeking Truth*, no. 4 (1991): 84–87.
231. Xu Bingkun, "Hengcu Arrow and Willow-shooting Ceremony," *Journal of Social Science*, no. 4 (1980): 126–128.
232. [Yuan] Tuitui et al., *Records of Rites VI*, vol. 53 of *History of Liao* (Zhonghua Book Company, October 1974), 879.
233. Ibid., 878.

234. [Yuan] Tuitui et al., *Chronicles of Emperor Tianzuo*, vol. 28 of *History of Liao*, 1st ed. (Zhonghua Book Company, October 1974), 336.
235. Feng Jiqin, "Some Sports among Khitans," *Journal of Seeking Truth*, no.4 (1991): 84–87.
236. Feng Yongqian, "Main Archaeological Discoveries of Liao Dynasty Since the Founding of the People's Republic of China," in *Collection of Liao and Jin History*, vol. 1. (Shanghai Ancient Books Publishing House, 1987), 323.
237. Zhang Bibo and Dong Guoyao, *The Cultural History of Ancient Northern China* (Heilongjiang People's Publishing House), 2001.
238. Aohan Cultural Center, "Liao Tomb of Baitazi in Aohan Banner," *Archaeology*, no. 2 (1978): 119–121.
239. [Yuan] Tuitui et al., *Chronicles of Emperor Shengzong*, vol. 12 of *History of Liao*, 1st ed. (Zhonghua Book Company, October 1974), 131.
240. [Yuan] Tuitui et al., *Biography of Luo Yiqing*, vol. 190 of *History of Liao*, 1st ed. (Zhonghua Book Company, October 1974), 1480.
241. [Song] Yuwen Maozhao, *Biography of Jurchens*, Appendiex I to *Annotations to National Records of the Great Jin Dynasty*, proofread by Cui Wenyin, 1st ed. (Zhonghua Book Company, July 1986), 589.
242. [Song] Li Xinchuan, *Chronological Records Since Jianyan* (Zhonghua Book Company, 1956), 11.
243. Liaoning Provincial Museum, Liaoning Tieling Cultural Relics Group, "Summary of Liao Tomb at Yemaotai in Faku," *Cultural Relics*, no. 12 (1975): 26–36.
244. Feng Yongqian and Deng Baoxue, "Important Findings of Cultural Relics Census in Jianchang County," *Journal of Liaoning Cultural Relics*, no. 1 (1980).
245. Hebei Provincial Institute of Cultural Relics, *Murals of Liao Tombs in Xuanhua* (Cultural Relics Publishing House, 2001).
246. Wang Zhonghan, *Chinese National History*, rev. ed. (China Social Sciences Press, 1994), 480.
247. [Yuan] Tuitui et al., *Chronicles of Emperor Taizong*, vol. 3 of *History of Liao*, 1st ed. (Zhonghua Book Company, October 1974), 30.
248. Feng Jiqin, "New Exploration of Jurchens of Changbai Mountain in the Liao Dynasty," in *Collection of Liao and Jin History* (Catalogs and Documentations Publishing House, 1987), 14.
249. [Yuan] Tuitui et al., *Emperor Shizong I*, vol. 6 of *History of the Jin Dynasty*, 1st ed. (Zhonghua Book Company, July 1975), 132.
250. [Yuan] Tuitui et al., *Biography of Tang Kuoan*, vol. 88 of *History of the Jin Dynasty*, 1st ed. (Zhonghua Book Company, July 1975), 1964.
251. [Yuan] Tuitui et al., *Military Annals*, vol. 44 of *History of the Jin Dynasty*, 1st ed. (Zhonghua Book Company, July 1975), 992–994.
252. [Yuan] Tuitui et al., *Chronicles of Emperor Shizong II*, vol. 8 of *History of the Jin Dynasty*, 1st ed. (Zhonghua Book Company, July 1975), 195.
253. [Yuan] Tuitui et al., *Chronicles of Officials III*, vol. 57 of *History of the Jin Dynasty*, 1st ed. (Zhonghua Book Company, July 1975), 1329.
254. [Song] Qu'an and Nai'an, eds., *A History of Jingkang · Southern Expedition Records*, noted by Cui Wenyin (Zhonghua Book Company, 1988), 135–136.
255. [Yuan] Tuitui et al., *Chronicles of Officials III*, vol. 57 of *History of the Jin Dynasty*, 1st ed. (Zhonghua Book Company, July 1975), 1329.
256. [Song] Yuwen Maozhao, *Annotations to National Records of the Great Jin Dynasty*, proofread by Cui Wenyin, 1st ed. (Zhonghua Book Company, July 1986), 551.
257. Ibid., 97–110.
258. [Song] Yuwen Maozhao, *Annotations to National Records of the Great Jin Dynasty*, proofread by Cui Wenyin, 1st ed. (Zhonghua Book Company, July 1986), 179.
259. [Yuan] Tuitui et al., *Chronicles of Officials*, vol. 58 of *History of the Jin Dynasty*, 1st ed. (Zhonghua Book Company, July 1975), 1347.
260. [Yuan] Tuitui et al., *Military Annals*, vol. 44 of *History of the Jin Dynasty*, 1st ed. (Zhonghua Book Company, July 1975), 997.
261. Tao Fuhai, Xie Xigong, "A Brief Report on the Cleaning Up of Jinyuan Tomb in Quli Village, Xiangfen County, Shanxi Province," *Cultural Relics*, no. 12 (1986): 47–52.

262. [Yuan] Tuitui et al., *History of the Jin Dynasty*, 1st ed. (Zhonghua Book Company, July 1975), 1812.
263. [Yuan] Tuitui et al., *Biography of Wanyan Yu*, vol. 104 of *History of the Jin Dynasty*, 1st ed. (Zhonghua Book Company, July 1975), 2301.
264. [Yuan] Tuitui et al., *Records of Rites · Worship Heaven*, vol. 104 of *History of the Jin Dynasty*, 1st ed. (Zhonghua Book Company, July 1975), 826–827.
265. [Song] Yuwen Maozhao, *Annotations to National Records of the Great Jin Dynasty*, proofread by Cui Wenyin, 1st ed. (Zhonghua Book Company, July 1986), 551–552.
266. [Yuan] Tuitui et al., *Biography of Geshi Liezhi Ning*, vol. 87 of *History of the Jin Dynasty*, 1st ed. (Zhonghua Book Company, July 1975), 1931.
267. [Yuan] Tuitui et al., *Military Annals*, vol. 144 of *History of the Jin Dynasty*, 1st ed. (Zhonghua Book Company, July 1975), 1004–1005.
268. [Yuan] Tuitui et al., *Electoral Annals I*, vol. 51 of *History of the Jin Dynasty*, 1st ed. (Zhonghua Book Company, July 1975), 1151–1152.
269. [Yuan] Tuitui et al., *Chronicles of Emperor Shizong*, vol. 6 of *History of the Jin Dynasty*, 1st ed. (Zhonghua Book Company, July 1975), 121.
270. [Yuan] Tuitui et al., *Military Annals*, vol. 44 of *History of the Jin Dynasty*, 1st ed. (Zhonghua Book Company, July 1975), 996.
271. [Yuan] Tuitui et al., *Biography of Emperor Shizong*, vol. 8 of *History of the Jin Dynasty*, 1st ed. (Zhonghua Book Company, July 1975), 194–195.
272. [Yuan] Tuitui et al., *Military Annals*, vol. 44 of *History of the Jin Dynasty*, 1st ed. (Zhonghua Book Company, July 1975), 997.
273. [Yuan] Tuitui et al., *Biography of Emperor Zhangzong*, vol. 10 of *History of the Jin Dynasty*, 1st ed. (Zhonghua Book Company, July 1975), 231.
274. [Yuan] Tuitui et al., *Military Annals*, vol. 44 of *History of the Jin Dynasty*, 1st ed. (Zhonghua Book Company, July 1975), 1007.
275. Ibid., 1001.
276. [Yuan] Tuitui et al., *Biography of Wanyan Heda*, vol. 112 of *History of the Jin Dynasty*, 1st ed. (Zhonghua Book Company, July 1975), 2464–2465.
277. [Yuan] Tuitui et al., *Military Annals*, vol. 44 of *History of the Jin Dynasty*, 1st ed. (Zhonghua Book Company, July 1975), 1001–1002.
278. [Yuan] Tuitui et al., *Biography of Wei Ziping*, vol. 89 of *History of the Jin Dynasty*, 1st ed. (Zhonghua Book Company, July 1975), 1977.
279. [Yuan] Tuitui et al., *Biography of Chizhan Hexi*, vol. 113 of *History of the Jin Dynasty*, 1st ed. (Zhonghua Book Company, July 1975), 2494.
280. *Expedition Records of the Great Jin*, vol. 1; *Hui Zhazi*, vol. 408 of *The Complete Collection of Si Ku Quan Shu of Wenyuan Pavilion* (Shanghai Ancient Books Publishing House, 1987), 846.

CHAPTER IV

Rise and Fall of the National Sports in Ancient Northern China

THIS PERIOD MAINLY REFERS TO THE Yuan, Ming, and Qing Dynasties. During this period, the northern ethnic groups are mainly Mongolian, Uyghur, and Manchus. The national sports are in their heyday. In the late Qing Dynasty, due to the influence of various factors at home and abroad, the northern national sports quickly went from prosperity to decline.

4.1 Sports Activities of Uyghur

Although the Uyghurs are in a relatively developed stage of the ancient northern ethnic society, due to various reasons, not many sports activities by Uyghurs are described in historical materials. According to the *Discovery Atlas of the Western Regions*, *Witness Notes of the Western Regions*, *Xinjiang Huibu Annals*, *Huijiang Annals*, *Xinjiang Archaeology*, *Records of Rites and Customs in Xinjiang*, and other works, among which there are very few about sports among Uyghurs, only a small amount of information can be compiled from some works to get a glimpse of the ancient Uyghur sports activities.

One of them is horse racing and mounted archery. Mounted Archery is a special feature of Huihu, and the Uyghur people maintained this traditional skill until the Qing Dynasty, as recorded by He Ning in Qing Dynasty in his book, "A few days later, old men and women in Huihe, freshly dressed and decorated, each with a paper flower on their hats, would go up to a high place outside the city, where the women gazed at the scene, and the men sped off to shoot. The 'Nulus' is a festival that the Kazak, Uzbeks, Uyghur, and Tatar peoples mark the day of the lunar spring equinox (around the 22nd day of March in the solar calendar) as the beginning of the new year and as the traditional spring festival."[1] According to the *Records of Rites and Customs in Xinjiang*, children under fifteen came to the clubhouse to enroll one by one, gathered tens of miles away, saddled, and stood at attention. The moment they heard the alarm, they were about to set out as fast as an arrow. The first to come would gain the first prize, being followed by the next forty riders (the rest are not registered). The first prize was worth a thousand gold, and the others were all prized differently, which was regarded as the great favorites by both near and far. In the middle of the Lunar New Year, Tang Gutui, the head of a thousand households, held a memorial ceremony on the anniversary of his father's death, and more than four thousand Russian relatives arrived as scheduled, with over three hundred houses occupied by bandits. The Chinese and Russian officials were both invited to the meeting, and they enjoyed the meat of presented horses and camels, and then one goat was given to each house to feed the servants. On that day, more than two hundred and fifty horses were raced. The first horse was rewarded with ten pieces of silver and five camels, and all the other horses were rewarded accordingly.[2] In the 17th century, after the appearance of muskets and the development of agriculture, mounted archery was not that common among the Uyghurs.

The second is the "Girl' s Chasing." The activity can also be called "Chasing Girls," which is carried out among multiple ethnic groups in many areas of Xinjiang. In addition to the Uyghurs, other ethnic groups in Xinjiang, such as the Kazaks and the Kirghiz, are also involved in this kind of sport. The origin of this activity is unknown, but it was better developed among the Uyghurs in the pastoral areas during the Qing Dynasty.

The third is the rope acrobatics and the Dawaz (A kind of acrobatic rope walking). During the Qing Dynasty, the performance of rope acrobatics prevailed among the Uyghurs, and their skills were exquisite. It is recorded in the *A General Survey of Imperial Documents* that the Hui were good at copper-rope walking. A copper rope with a diameter of 2 *cun* and a length of 1 *zhang*, or a hemp rope with a diameter of 2 *cun* and a length of 3 *zhang*, was used across the wooden frame, which was 2 *zhang* and 5 *chi* high. Another hemp rope was used to bind it to the ground, and a pole of olive wood was erected on one side, 60 *zhang* high. The Hui were dressed in color, holding a log in both hands, climbing on the slope of the rope bare-footed back and forth, and leaping on the rope. Then they also put on their boots and walk back and forth on the rope by stepping on the copper plate, or by stepping on a standing wood, 2 *cun* in diameter and 5 *cun* in height. One may walk, jump, leap, straddle and ride, or sit and rise, as if he were walking on level ground. The next person standing up is also dressed in colorful clothes, beating drums and making noise. After jumping, he hung his bow from the left and held an arrow on the right. With a wooden ramrod, he went straight up to the top of the rampart, setting up a small ball on the ground and shooting with his bow.[3] The rope acrobatics was inherited from the Huihu, which is clearly recorded in *Divan lgat at-Turk*.

Dawaz is an important part of traditional Uyghur skill sports, combining both sports and acrobatics, and it is distinguished from other sports activities by its unique ethnic style. Dawaz is a skillful sport that requires high theoretical and technical skills. It is a high-altitude performance, where maintaining the body's center of gravity and balance is crucial. Besides, it involves a high degree of danger, including the movements on the ground and in the air. Those that go to air consist of rope and lever movements, hoop movements, as well as some artistic performances, magic, and so on. Dawaz moves are complex and varied, combining sport, art, and acrobatics as a whole.

The fourth is swinging. Swinging is an interesting sports activity suitable for Uyghur people to carry out extensively. During summer and festivals, young men and women, as well as children of Uyghur, entertain themselves by tying ropes and making swings on grapevine trellises in the courtyard, on sturdy tree branches in orchards or streets, on trees in the field or on slopes. This activity is good for developing courage, daring, and flexibility in teenagers, as well as for promoting their overall physique. Young men and women can sing songs, single or in pairs, while swinging on the swing, which is very interesting. The proficient players can play such tricks as picking up objects from the ground, biting leaves in the air, hanging themselves on the swing upside down, and some can even perform difficult movements such as changing positions in the air. As for the history of swinging in Xinjiang, there is an explanation in *Divan lgat at-Turk*: "Swinging is a kind of fun for girls. Tying the ends of the string to a piece of wood or a moulding, one girl sits in the middle and stomps on the ground with her feet so that sometimes she rises and sometimes she falls."[4] The swing is also described in a long poem called *Manas*: "In the time of Aycholuk, the girls and the boys came together. The full moon shone down on the earth, and on the poplar tree, a rope was tied. They all floated on the swing. They were so much in love with each other that they secretly exchanged a gift of love. The gift was wrapped in a handkerchief with a note on it that read, 'Forever and ever.'"[5] This narrative, in simple and popular language, vividly describes the love story in the swinging activity. The poem *Manas* was written in the eleventh century, so it is not difficult to surmise that the Uyghur and Kirgiz people had been swinging before that time.

In the southern part of Xinjiang, there is also a type of swing called "Sahardi," or "Chakpilek" in Aksu, which means "turning swing" in Chinese. Sakhardi belongs to the same category as the swing, related to the pole technique of the Western Regions. According to the records in *Du Yang's Compilation of Collected Works*, in the Tang Dynasty, there was a woman named Shi Huohu from the Western Regions who could stretch five strings on a hundred-foot pole, with eight or nine women taking up one string each. This technique is quite similar to the Uyghur Sahardi (turning swing). According to the classic Uyghur narrative poem *Yusuf and Ahmet*, the two brothers, Prince Yusuf and Ahmet, were forced to leave their home because of a conflict between them and their uncle, Bogra Khan. They led some of their people to a place where they set up a turning wheel in the air to entertain the crowds, accompanied by drums and music, so that they could attract peasants and herders from all over the diaspora to join them and strengthen their power. The poem depicts the social life and historical events of the Uyghur people in the 13th century, which implies that Sahardi was born at least no later than the 13th century. Xiao Xiong in the Qing Dynasty wrote about it in a poem called *Frolic*, in which it describes as follows: "A swing swings with a slight shadow and a colorful dress sways in the wind. As the skill passed down to the west, beautiful lady loves to fly."[6] Sahardi is made up of a 15-or-16-meter-high spindle, a main wheel, and a wheel mast, connected by ropes. The spindle stands vertically on the ground, with the wheel mast attached to the bottom of the spindle, which rotates in the same direction when pushed by two groups (four people each). The top of the spindle is equipped with an epicycle and connected with the bottom wheel rod by silk, where the epicycle is driven to rotate whenever the wheel rod is pushed. Two long ropes are tied to each end of the wheel, attaching the player to it. When someone pushes the rod to rotate the wooden wheel, the person at the end of the rope turns around with it. The epicycle turns faster and faster while the person flies higher and higher. After people who push the rod let go of their hands, the person can still fly for a long time due to the inertial force.

In addition, from the ethnographic investigation, there were also sports activities such as wrestling and chess among the ancient Uyghurs, but owing to the lack of historical data, it is not possible to ascertain the form of these sports activities and the specific conditions in which they were carried out.

The Uyghur people mainly inherited the Huihu's sports culture. However, as the Uyghurs have undergone the change from nomadic pastoralism to sedentary life and from conquest to trade, some of them engaged in agricultural production must adapt to the sedentary life, change the content and mode of sports activities, and fortunately they have adjusted themselves and developed the sedentary life or trade with sports culture style in the Western Regions, while on the other hand, they have succeeded in the nomadic custom of riding and shooting.

4.2 Sports Activities of Mongol

The name "Mongolian" is derived phonetically from the word "Mengwu," which originated mainly from "Mengwu Shiwei," a branch of the Eastern Hu system, and also from the Xiongnu, Rouran, Xianbei, and Turk (they are all ancient nationalities in China) in terms of branch source.[7] According to the historical records, at the beginning of the 12th century, Temujin led the Mongolian tribes to defeat the four major tribes of Tatar people, Kelie, Merkit, and Naiman, unifying the Mongolian Empire. In AD 1026, he was crowned the Great Khan of Mongolia, called Genghis Khan, and established the Mongolian State, where the Mongolian national community was formed with it. Genghis Khan and his successors, Ögedei and Kublai Khan, conquered the Xixia, Jin, and Southern Song Dynasties, and established the Yuan Dynasty in Chinese history, which was unprecedentedly unified and ruled by ethnic minorities. The Yuan Dynasty collapsed in AD 1368, and the Mongolian feudal lords withdrew from the Central Plains. During the Ming Dynasty, the Mongolian region was divided into three major parts: the southern, northern, and western parts of the Mongolian Desert. The nomadic Mongolian herders in the southern and northern parts of the Desert were called Tatar in the Ming Dynasty, whose leaders were descended from the rulers of the Yuan Dynasty, the so-called Mongolian orthodoxy; nomadic herders in the western part of the Desert were the Wala (Oirat), also known as Western Mongolia, whose leaders were subjects of the Yuan rulers. In the early Qing Dynasty, Khalkha in the northern part of the Desert and the Mongolian lords of Erut (i.e., Wala of the Ming Dynasty) in the western part of the Desert and Qinghai were successively submitted to the Qing Dynasty. In order to strengthen its rule, Qing Dynasty set up a system of allied-banners in the Mongolian areas based on the eight-banner system of the Manchu.

When the development of sports in the north reached its peak, there was a special agency to manage sports training and competitions. From Yuan Dynasty to the reign of Emperor Renzong, a special wrestling management agency called the Yongxiao Office was set up, similar to the Sumo sheds of the Tang Dynasty and the Yuqian Zhongzuo Army Division in the Song Dynasty. It is responsible for recruiting, training, and organizing wrestling competitions. The administrative body of the northern national sports should be the "Wrestling Bureau" during the period of Yanyou. In the *Emperor Renzong III* of *History of the Yuan Dynasty*, it is recorded that in June of the sixth year of Yanyou, Wrestling Bureau was set, in which the Jiao-Di activities were included.[8] *Emperor Yingzong I* of *History of the Yuan Dynasty* shares a similar record that "(in June of the seventh year of Yanyou) about 120 Jiao-Di players were awarded a thousand coins."[9] This shows that Mongolian wrestling developed rapidly under the control of specialized institutions, and that the government invested heavily in it. Under these circumstances, the progress of Mongolian wrestling was bound to be very favorable. The good development of Mongolian wrestling today must have a great deal to do with the importance that the government at that time attached to, as well as the influence among ethnic groups.

In the Yuan, Ming, and Qing Dynasties, the sports culture of the Mongolian people developed rapidly with the embodiment of prosperity. In particular, on the basis of the excellent sports culture of the ancient northern peoples in wrestling, horse racing, and archery, the Mongols created the "Male Triathlon" and the sports culture in Nayadum Fair in accordance with the level of productivity, which has been influencing the political, economic, cultural and national spirit of the northern groups to date, and thus has become a major treasure of the northern peoples' sports culture.

4.2.1 Hunting and Martial Arts

It is well known that the early Mongolian people lived on nomadic hunting, the style of which motivated them to become extraordinarily agile in vision and hearing, good at keeping a lookout and scouting, as well as detecting and tracing. Mongols had a natural but amazing ability to recognize the presence of water and grass and the terrain; hence "hunting was enough to learn to fight," and "the Mongolians rely on hunting to send troops."[10] Mongol leaders took advantage of hunting as a way to teach martial arts and train their fighting skills. Each hunting trip lasted for months. Mongols were generally organized into warring groups of hundreds, thousands, or tens of thousands of men, and over an area of thousands of miles, all the tribes were united in a massive hunt. The Mongol chiefs consciously divided the hunting group into four parts: search, front guard, main force, and rear guard, and moved forward in this order. The search part in the shape of the sector is not only responsible for learning about the condition of water and grass in a pasture, but also for the task of detecting. The front guard part follows up on the information provided by the search section and reports back to headquarters. The main force follows families, children, livestock, and valuables, while the rear guard is mainly responsible for giving shelter and getting ready for coping with the "enemy" in case of a surprise attack. This kind of hunting is no longer a simple process of chasing, catching, rounding up, killing, or playing games; it is more like a process of learning about the terrain and seasons where wild animals appear, familiarizing themselves with the habits of those wild animals, and mastering the methods of hunting, which allow people to link hunting training and warfare, to combine pre-hunting preparation with pre-war reconnaissance, and to apply the techniques of analyzing, judging, and rounding up prey acquired in hunting to combat. As Genghis Khan said, going hunting is the proper duty of an officer in the army, and it is the duty of soldiers to be taught and trained, like hunters, in how to pursue and hunt prey, how to manage the formation, and how to round up prey in face of more people. Mongols hunted not only for the sake of hunting wild animals, but also to become accustomed to the hunting practice, familiarizing themselves with riding and shooting, and enduring hardships and difficulties.[11] The

National Palace Museum in Taipei houses a hunting picture of Kublai Khan, Emperor Shizu in the Yuan Dynasty (see Fig. 4-1), which depicts Shizu of the Yuan Dynasty, Kublai Khan, leading hundreds of officials riding and shooting in a suburban area.

Fig. 4-1 Hunting Picture of Yuan Emperor Shizu

4.2.2 Mongolian Horse Training and Archery Training

Since the Mongols hunt mainly on horses, horses have become an indispensable part of their daily life. This all resulted from the fact that horse possesses the power of high-speed and rapid impact, whose movement is relatively less affected by the terrain or the weather, contributing to the easy and wide access to the plains, plateaus, grasslands, and deserts. All above are the fundamental attributes of the horse. If we compare the Mongolian horse with other horses of the same period, we can say that the Mongolian horse is the strongest after training in the world. The Mongolian cavalrymen are the strongest in the world as well. Therefore, when the Mongols entered the war, they made full use of the horses' superiority. Each cavalryman has a maximum of five or six horses that take turns to keep up their strength. As it is said in *Translated Words*, "The Mongolian cavalrymen come, often in tens of thousands. The horses multiply like clouds and lightning, and the waves and currents were so overwhelming that the white moon was blinded and the hills were shaking."[12] The war horses could be changed at any time, thus maintaining high speed, endurance, and mobility in battle. When they retreat, the enemy is unable to catch up; when they attack, they take the enemy by surprise and force them unable to defend; they can advance or retreat, gather or disperse, appear or disappear, be far or near … and come as swiftly as the wind and thunder, but go as far as a thousand miles away. In particular, when decoying or encircling the enemy for a flank or belly attack, the army would change horses at any time to ensure safety and improve combat effectiveness. For example, in the spring of AD 1221, when Genghis Khan, who had already captured the city of Ṭālaqān, heard the news that the Mongolian army had been defeated by Jalalad, he led his troops and chased the enemy to the bank of the Shen River like lightning. He finally caught up with the Jalalad army, who were trying to escape from the Shen River, beat them, and then wiped them out.[13] There is no clear record of how long it took Genghis Khan to cover the 400 to 500 kilometers from Ṭālaqān to Shen River, but it can be concluded that the main reason for his victory was due to the fact that the horses galloped non-stop and the cavalrymen alternated from time to time, thus gaining time and changing from quantity to quality to win the last battle of the Western expedition.

Of course, in warfare, good horses alone are not enough; talents with the ability to fight are the most important factor. For this reason, the Mongols attached great importance to the militarization of the tribe and adopted a system where all the members of the tribe were supposed to be soldiers. Whoever is in the tribe, he must serve and pay tribute to his lords at regular intervals. In times of war, herdsmen had to follow the lords to go for a battle with their own horses and saddles, weapons, and food. "Families with sons over fifteen and under seventy, are all recruited to be soldiers. Whenever there is an issue, a tent is set up and every ten as a squad. They ride on the horse and fight in battles, or they get off the horse to conduct herding. When the children grow a little older, they will be enrolled. Day by day, they will become warriors one day."[14] "The system of the people's households, with ten men called 'ten households (platoon),' varies from ten to a hundred, from a hundred to a thousand, and from a thousand to ten thousand, each governed by its head."[15] The advantages of this type of organization were: the combination of the ordinary and the soldiers; the combination of labor and armed force; storing soldiers and food within the people; the combination of soldiers with the commoners; the combination of military and civilian forces; the combination of military and political forces, so as to achieve familiarity and solidarity with each other. The Mongols were a peasant army, performing all kinds of duties and handing everything distributed to them without complaints. They were also peasants, young and old, noble and low, acting in military service. And all became warriors in the battle, with bows and guns, killing the enemy as the situation demanded. Even in their migration, women drove dozens of ox carts, like a slowly advancing phalanx in the battle. Such clan-based armies, "whenever the task of fighting the enemy and suppressing the rebellion arises, they would requisition everything that is needed, ranging from weapons to flags, pins, needles, ropes, horses and animals like donkeys and camels, and every man must offer his share as required by the ten households or hundred households." It was just because of the close blood ties and mutual affection that the power to protect and support each other was extremely raised. Particularly when the war was fierce, or their friends or relatives were killed, the will to fight against the enemy shoulder to shoulder became even more multiplied. Even the ancient Iranian historian Juvayni could not help sighing in astonishment: "What army in the whole world can rival the Mongols?"[16]

The Mongolian army was unique in the quality of its soldiers compared to any other army in the world at that time. It is important to be capable of riding skillfully in battle, which is just attributed to the training of the Mongols from an early age. The Mongolian children were roped to a board and attached to a horse since childhood to follow their mothers in and out. At the age of three, they could gallop around with others, and at the age of four or five, they could hold four bows. When they grew up, they were able to gallop their horses as fast as the thunder, with their knees clamped tightly between the saddle, pulling and controlling the horses at ease, without falling at all. They could also stand on the horse without holding a whip, and twist and turn to the left and right easily. They are as light as flying wings and never get tired of the long ride. According to *Marco Polo's Travels*, "They have been playing with bows and arrows since they were children, so the bow was their most practiced weapon."[17] They are skilled in archery because they live by hunting. Even the women are as good as men at mounted archery. At a gallop, the cavalrymen could shoot from either left or right, or shoot towards the back, with each arrow aiming at the target. It is true that the Yuan Dynasty was founded on riding and shooting, so the rulers have always attached great importance to mounted archery. The bow and arrow were not only a hunting tool for the Mongols, but also a weapon for defending themselves or conquering others, as well as a prop used by herders in riding and shooting competitions. Thus, horsemanship and archery can be passed down and further developed.

After Genghis Khan unified the Mongolian tribes in the 13th century, Mongolian archery developed rapidly, and its practice became known throughout the world. According to *Marco Polo's Travels*, "When the Tatars fight, every soldier must carry sixty arrows. Thirty of them are small, and used to kill from a distance. The remaining thirty are larger with a broad blade, used at close range to shoot at the face and arms of the enemy, and also to break the string of the enemy's bow, inflicting severe damage on the opponent. When their arrows are exhausted, they will draw their swords and spears to slash each other."[18] The Mongols also trained themselves in other techniques, such as shooting and slashing. For example, in step shooting, they position both their front leg and back leg with wide steps and squat on their waist. They shoot one step at a time in that the body is stable and the force is smooth, so the shooting must be fierce and strong that it could even pierce the heavy armor. When they use the saber, they bend down and look straight at the enemy, pointing it at the horse; when the horse overtakes the enemy, they slash them. When the saber is lightly wielded, the wrist is strong enough. When the armor is loose, the arrow does not enter; while the waist is tight, it can move freely.[19] It can be seen that the Mongols' cultivation of combat skills was quite exquisite. Living in a historical environment after the Song Dynasty, where technology was flourishing, the Mongols stayed in a favorable position to inherit and learn advanced military weapons and equipment, and more importantly, to use them for their optimization.

In October, the Mongols opened a pallet farm in the city of Xijin (now Beijing), as recorded in the *Xi Jin Zhi*. On the Juan Day of the Imperial Court, the officers of the capital set up the shooting field outside the Donghua Gate, three places from south to north and north to south respectively, about three hundred paces away. The first station in the west is for the emperor and the princes, the second for the governors of the provinces and prefectures, and the third for the military officials. When these all be done, all the officials are awaiting orders. In the sixteenth year, Hanlin bachelor Yuelu Timur was promoted by decree to act as the minister, managing national history. On the following day, the emperor gathered everyone at the Western Palace, and asked the Crown Prince to open the battlefield for archery. When the command was granted, a hundred soldiers came from everywhere to reach the field, where they all adjusted to getting ready for shooting. The system is as follows: The prime minister received the bow, held the arrow, and knelt to advance towards the

Crown Prince. After the prince received the bow and arrow, he shot three times to the sky, higher and further, which was "archery the Wolf." After it was done, the prime minister, dukes, and other officials followed to shoot several arrows at the reed stack. When they were all done, a banquet was served with plenty of food and rewards. After the feast was over, Yuelu Timur was awarded a small ingot of silver for complimenting his achievements in managing state affairs.[20] It can be seen from the above literature that the sporting culture of this type of reed shooting is very similar to that of the Dangxiang people.

The Mongols also hold willow archery competitions. On the day of the Dragon Boat Festival, Zhennan King opened a square in front of his mansion and sat down with the princess and concubines, all of whom were covered by a large red golden umbrella. On the left side sat the princess, while other kings and princes sat on the right side. The kings toasted each other for the festivities. In front of them were three armies with banners in full view. The warriors were ordered to shoot the willows, whose strips had been removed 1 *chi* of green part and planted 5 *cun* into the ground. The shooter tied the willow branch with a handkerchief, and remembered what it looked like. The one who led the horse went first, followed by the ten thousand households with their bows, who fired their bows at the willow. The one who broke the willow's white would win, applauded by beating the gong and drum, and rewarded as before. Those who lost were also punished as usual. The ceremonial horse-riding is the same as the preceding custom, in which a warrior could best show off his military skills.[21] The Mongolians' willow-shooting of the Yuan Dynasty is similar to that of the Khitan and Jurchen. In fact, the culture of this kind of willow-shooting has been passed down among the northern peoples, and the above literature best indicates the important role of the willow-shooting competition. Evidently, there is somewhat difference between this and the Khitan's willow-shooting, in which the former focuses on martial arts, while the latter enjoys the religious significance of praying for rain. We may conclude that this cultural difference is mainly due to the different environments and political statuses of the two.

Not only do Mongols practice archery in warfare, but this skill is a must for every man, as evident in Mongolian marriage customs. It can be said that if a man does not have the ability to shoot an arrow, he not only has difficulty getting married in Mongolia, but is also despised by others. Therefore, riding and shooting culture, with its outstanding features, is ubiquitous and prominent among Mongolians.

4.2.3 Horse Racing

Mongolian horses are a resource of production and livelihood as well as a means of transportation and warfare. The Mongolian nomadic cavalrymen are all excellent riders who enjoy horse racing. There are three types of horse racing among the Mongols: walking, running, and jostling. Walking-horse racing is a race of steadiness, speed, and beauty, while Running-horse racing is a race of speed, endurance, and a prescribed course, with the winner being the first to reach the finish line. Horse racing was very popular in the military and upper-class society at that time and was handed down from generation to generation. With the ever-increasing popularity, horse racing also prevailed among ordinary people, with many horse racing scenes even at weddings. For example, in the procedure involved in the *Bride's Embarkation and Welcome on the Way*, there is a game of horse racing, in which the celebrant first rides the horse away quickly, and then the young man of the senders rides after him, picking the celebrant's hat into his hands with a horse whip until he tries to catch it. At that minute, the celebrant drives his horse away so that he fails. Another greeting boy attempts to pick up the hat of the celebrant, and again his horse is chased away by the following sender. The chase and catch just occur one after another until the next stage.[22] This folk culture on the Mongolian steppes later evolved into one of the three major competitions in the Nayadum and Oboo festivals.

It is a tradition of the Mongols to love horses and to ride well. They have been known as "the people on horses," and according to the *Customs* in *Classified Anthology of Anecdotes of the Qing Dynasty*, "Mongolian women in Qinghai must ride horses when they go out, for several miles away without using saddles. The Mongols used to perform the 'Ebo' ritual in the fourth month of every year. After the ritual, the young Mongolians gather at a predetermined place to wrestle and gallop their horses. Those who gallop are going to choose the fine horses for reservation. The distance is from 30 to 40 miles away to over 100 miles away, awaiting the order to compete ... When the horn rises up, the horses race one after each other to their whips, galloping towards 'Ebo,' and the one who gets first is the winner." During the rituals of the Qinghai-Mongolian alliance, "a horse racing meeting is often held to train the horses' feet to the best of their ability and to make the trip as far as possible. Afterwards, they would meet on the coast, step on a wilderness, and gallop across the countryside, competing to race and win. A bet is not taken in the race, but a red cloth will be covered on the winning horse's head, just for making a difference."[23] Such a long-distance and high-speed gallop requires both good horse training and regular exercise to build up the riders' physical strength and skills.

In the Yuan Dynasty, horse racing and military service were combined as an institution due to the popularity of Mongolian princes and nobles. Whenever a "Хурал (large gathering)" was held, horse racing was included as a part of the event. In the Qing Dynasty, according to the *Tactics* in *Classified Anthology of Anecdotes of the Qing Dynasty*, the Mongolian people, "regardless of the young and the old, male and female, are all good at riding a horse. And children of both genders from the age of five or six are able to ride horses and gallop across the countryside." As is also recorded: "Every year in April or May, after the festival of Ebo, the young men would gallop on horses to compete with each other. Everyone chose the fine horses, and gathered ten miles away, waiting for the order to fight to win. They would check on the cushion under the saddle, tidy up the armor, comb the horsehair, getting fully prepared for the race, so that they could easily control the horse and speed it up. At the sound of the horn, the horses galloped along with a ton of whips, racing towards Ebo. Five ranks would be presented for the winner, each getting silver cloth with somewhat difference."[24] In the section of *Bamboo* of *Songs of Frontier Fortress*, Lu Jianzeng wrote: "Every family grazes plenty of cattle and sheep, and the sunset over hills. Ebo knows the distance here and far. A rider is racing toward what he can see."[25] Xiao Xiong wrote in *Playfulness*: "Playfulness is nothing more than a competition, where people compete in horsemanship with each other for money. It is also a competition about hugging and falling."[26] These two poems sing high praise for the skillful riding and wrestling of the Mongolian people.

During the Qing Dynasty, there were special rules and regulations for horse racing in Mongolia. *Khalkha Code · Regulations on Horse Racing* (1729) cites another article about regulations on Horse Racing ("Zha Sa") as follows:

> "Whenever a race is run, there are four seats as witnesses in addition to the presiding officer. These witnesses who are to be badged, go to the starting place, show their badges, and set off. If they failed to do so and started halfway, they would be fined: one horse for the lord, one ox for the Taijii and tabun-ong, and one goat for the ordinary presiding officer.
>
> If a child who rides a horse runs earlier, the horse would be confiscated, and the child would be given a lash ten times. Horses may not be mistaken or misled away by any reason, or they shall have their horses confiscated. For those who join the race halfway, their horses will be confiscated, and they shall be fined nine cattle; besides, the rider would be given a lash ten times if he were a child. For those who lead a runner to start halfway, their horses will be confiscated, too. Anyone who came up to race without permission from the superiors ("zerlik"), except the presiding officer and the racers, shall have his horse confiscated."

The Mongolian *Regulations on Horse Racing* is the most detailed of all the above rules, covering everything from the venue, equipment, horses, judges, and athletes to the conduct of the race, the penalties for violations, and the rewards for the winners. It is rare to find such rules about sports competitions in the ancient northern grasslands, and it is even rare to have those rules seen in the Central Plains, which signifies that the sports development of ancient northern China has entered a period of prosperity.

4.2.4 Long-Distance Racing on the Prairie

"Gui You Chi" was the name of the Yuan Dynasty guard force made up of Mongolians who were able to run and walk. Later on, the name "Gui You Chi" was used as a synonym for the Mongolian long-distance race. The "Gui You Chi" guard force was formed by Kublai in the 24th year of Zhiyuan (AD 1287) of the Yuan Dynasty and led by the general commander of the army, who was responsible for the task of Metropolis (present-day Beijing) and Shangdu (Li Palace of the Yuan Dynasty, now Mongolian Zhenglan Banner Mandera Sumu). A long-distance race was held once a year, and it was so important that the emperor himself would attend the event and award prizes. Tao Zongyi of the Ming Dynasty wrote in his *Farming in Nan Villiage*: "'Gui You Chi' is the one who walks fast. Every year, when the race called 'Letting Go' is conducted, those who are quick on their feet will be rewarded. Therefore, the supervisory officials have all the racers assembled to the rope so that they can start off with no difference. The racers all would go for the long distance. In Dadu, the journey starts at Ho-hsi-wu (now 30 miles northeast of Wuqing County, Hebei Province, on the west bank of the Northern Canal). If it is in Shangdu, the journey begins at Nihe River (now east of Yihua East, Hebei Province). After six hours of marching, they traveled 180 *li* to reach the Imperial Palace, bowing down and reaching out to the emperor. The first to arrive was given silver cakes, while the rest were given satin."[27] Yang Yunfu of the Yuan Dynasty wrote a poem titled *Miscellaneous Chants of Luanjing* about the competition at Shangdu, in which he described: "The race is going on along the Luanhe river, all people gathering for the watch. Everyone in the race struggled to win as the first."[28]

"Gui You Chi" not only served as an important means of training and inspecting the physical fitness and long-distance running ability of the imperial guards, but also as an official race prescribed by the imperial court, playing the role of both military training and recreation. There are specifically the starting point, finishing line, distance, and time requirements for the race. "Gui You Chi" is an unprecedented ultra-long-distance race in the history of China, as well as a great initiative and contribution in the history of sports of the northern nationalities in ancient China.

4.2.5 Camel Racing

The famous Mongol Khanate General Zhaba'er was a brave and skillful cavalryman and archer, and was also a typical camel-riding general who had made tremendous achievements in the battles. "Every time Zhaba'er was surrounded by the enemy, he would fly out of the trap amazingly. Zhaba'er was capable of fighting on the camel, and no one dared to fight with him."[29] The above is a heroic image of him fighting on a camel recorded in the literature, which shows that there were some camel caravans in the Mongol army at that time who were very powerful and trained for a long time. The Galdan army possessed thousands of camels, which, in addition to carrying supplies, were also applied to fight in the war. These camel caravans became an important part of the Galdan cavalry, active in the north and south of the desert as well as in Xinjiang over the years. In the twenty-ninth year of the reign of Emperor Kangxi (AD 1690), the Qing army and the Galdan army fought a duel at Ulaan-butung (southeast of Dalinor in today's Hexigten Banner), and the camel cavalry suffered great losses.[30]

The camel, with its huge body, walks steadily. People can travel up to 80 kilometers a day on its back. With the resistance to hunger and thirst, cold and heat, as well as the capacity to bear the burden, capable of walking in the Gobi Desert, the camel is known as the boat of the desert, which has established outstanding achievements in the economic and military history of the Mongolian nationality. In the pastoral areas where camel herding is the mainstay, the herders respect the camel as the king of all animals. Camel racing thus becomes a traditional sport of the Mongolian people during their nomadic life. It is popular in Alxa League, Bayannur League, IH Ju League, and Xilin Gol League in Inner Mongolia, the Haixi Mongol, Tibetan, and Kazak ethnic groups in Qinghai Province, and Bayinguolin in Xinjiang, where men, women, and children of all ages are good at riding camels. All camels participating in the race must have been selected based on their figure and training. The large, well-proportioned body shape and long limbs are preferred. Besides, the camels must undergo rigorous training before they can compete in the race.

4.2.6 Mongolia Jamah and Horse Racing

"Every year, the Yuan emperor spent his summer in the capital Shangjing. He would hold a three-day banquet in the palace of palm trees to meet with the royal princes. All officials above the fifth rank were given gorgeous clothes in the same color to wear, riding the ornate horses to the banquet, where the extravagance can shockingly amount to trillions ..."[31] This is excerpted from the *Ode to Jamah* written by Zheng Yong at the request of Toqta, whom he followed to the banquet in the capital of Mongolia. The writer renders the complete set of scenes with hyperbole that he saw at the banquet, which is rich in content and detailed in the description. The full text of 1,130 words truly records and portrays the cause for writing, i.e., the venue environment of the banquet, the horses dressed up and arrayed on the flat slope, the features of officials' clothes dedicated to the banquet, competitive sports activities such as wrestling and archery, as well as a variety of acrobatic performances, instrumental playing and other joyful scenes in the banquet.

The emperor of the Qing Dynasty went hunting every autumn, for the purpose of showing martial arts or practicing archery. Indeed, it was used as a means of controlling Mongolia so that the Mongols would fear the imperial power but be grateful, obedient, and loyal to the emperor. *Miscellaneous Records of Yan Pu* recorded that every time the emperor arrived in Chengde, nearby Mongolian dignitaries would come to greet and visit him as usual. On the emperor's birthday in August, a large-scale drama performance was held in the temporary imperial palace, lasting for ten days, where all Mongolian dignitaries attended the banquet and were given a large number of brocades embroidered with decorations. In the hunting ground, there were 1,300 soldiers, all of whom were Mongolians. In hunting, they were responsible for serving at dawn. Dignitaries accompanied the emperor, carefully obeying his commands. After hunting ten times, they would definitely agree on a date for a banquet, which the emperor would attend in person. On the day of the banquet, the biggest yurt was set as the main hall, and four other yurts were placed nearby to entertain the dukes and high ministers who followed the emperor. Most of the music was played with orchestral instruments, which was pleasant to the ear. At the same time, there were wrestling and a variety of acrobatics going on. Mongolian wrestling is inferior to that of the imperial bodyguard, but the skill in acrobatics is superb. The tricks are: The rider needs to hold a long pole tied with a rope, hitch the rope to the horse's neck and put a saddle on the horse. When the horse was still not tame, the rider should clamp the horseback and whip the horse with all his strength until it quieted down. These are all Mongolian plays for viewing. Every year, not only the relationship between superiors and subordinates can be improved, but also the art of training horses can be acquired in the process of horse driving, which is of far-reaching significance. Since the four major tribes of Khalkha resided in the most remote areas of Mongolia, only one of them could come to meet the emperor every year. Hence each tribe could merely visit him once every four years, even though the emperor went out of the fortress every year. Sometimes the emperor went out once every two years, and it would take eight years for them to see the emperor. This is a long-term strategy for ruling Khalkha-Mongolians.[32] These were events of the Qing Dynasty when Mongolian wrestling was no longer superior to that of Manchu, but the horsemanship performance at the banquet shows that Mongolian's ability to tame horses is extraordinary, not to mention their impressive acts in historical records.

According to the *Classified Anthology of Anecdotes of the Qing Dynasty*, whenever the emperor went hunting, all Mongolian nobles and chiefs of 48 tribes would line up behind the sentinels and respectfully step into the banquet, performing martial arts merrily. Other officials would either perform some Mongolian sports activities or enjoy comprising the poems. On Jamah Day, children over the age of six or seven wore exquisite clothes and galloped on their horses without saddles and reins. The one who first arrived at the flag, which was planted a few miles away, gained the best reward, and the rest were offered rewards in varying degrees. On the day of performing Mongolian music, people played wind instruments made of reeds, which was extremely pleasant to the ear. After drinking for some time, princes and dukes performed Mongolian music with rhythmic beats in turns. On the day of wrestling, attendants competed in martial arts with bare hands. Both sides seized the opportunity to capitalize on the opponent's mistakes instead of relying on their courage alone. The winners were awarded unlimited wine or mutton soup that was ready-made. On the day of taming horses, the descendants of princes jumped onto the horse with long poles and colored lassos like lightning, and rode on the horse until it was tamed, though the ferocious horse was out of control as soon as it entered the herd. The scene involving indocile horses and gallant horse trainers is quite spectacular.[33] Banquets were mostly set up by emperors of the Qing Dynasty during the period of time when they toured Chengde or went hunting for the purpose of improving the relationship between Manchu and Mongol. During the whole process, a wealth of sports activities were arranged to demonstrate the training effects of Manchu and Mongol military and civilians.

According to the *Classified Anthology of Anecdotes of the Qing Dynasty*, "no matter how fierce and inferior a horse is, it can be completely tamed as long as the Mongols harness it. When they encounter a horse that cannot be controlled by the iron chain, they will use a pole tied with a rope to lasso the horse, in order to catch and ride it."[34] Since the Hun period, the northern peoples have continuously used the lasso, which also existed in Xianbei, Turk, Khitan, Huihu, Uyghur, and other ethnic minorities either as a harness or a military weapon. However, lassos in production in Mongolia were usually used in sports and entertainment to perform or compete on joyous festivals, which enriches the ancient northern national sports as a real innovation.

4.2.7 Bu Mu Ge[35]

Bu Mu Ge, also known as kicking Xingtou, is a long-standing Mongolian recreational activity. Xingtou is made from the bladders of cows or sheep, which are blown into a ball shape and kicked with the backs of the feet for fun. There are many different kinds of kicking, such as kicking with one foot, crossing one's feet, jumping and kicking with one's heels, and so on, similar to kicking the shuttlecock. Xingtou made of bladder is light in weight, inaccurate, and easy to break, so later they were made of leather and sewn into Xingtou, stuffed with cow's hair or other things.

Legend has it that Genghis Khan, after winning a great victory in the desert, unified tribes like the Tatar people, Markit, Taichiwu, and Kereid, and began a western expedition against the Naiman tribe. Genghis Khan's Mongolian army formed a dragon and snake formation, like a fierce tiger descending from the mountains, and plunged into the Altai Mountains to capture the Naiman barbarians. Then Genghis Khan pursued his army and unified all the tribes in the grasslands of Mobei. This expedition could be considered a victory start and a triumphant return. When he returned to barracks, he slaughtered cows and sheep and offered sacrifices to the heavens. To commemorate the success of the expedition, the ears of the bull's bones were dyed red with blood to represent the fire of eternal life and the symbol of success. The bones of the bull, which were kicked before the expedition, are then placed on the altar and prayed over with wine, and all the soldiers bowed to heaven. Since then, the Mongols have turned this activity into a sport, and every year they would have a competition to kick the bones of the bull. Since the entire skeleton has been dyed red, this sport is also called "kicking Wulan."

4.2.8 Mongolian Chess Shatar

Shatar is a unique form of chess in ancient Mongolian society, and it is a combination of the superior insight and wisdom of the Mongols, which fully reflect the characteristics of their own personality. The herders often play chess for entertainment, which exercises their intellect and enriches their lives. The Mongolian word for chess is Shatar, also known as Xital, different from Chinese chess or international Xiangqi; thus, it is also called Mongolian Xiangqi in Chinese. Legend has it that Genghis Khan was a man of military power, equipped with the military ability to train a strong army. He was also a man of unparalleled skill and ingenuity in the art of warfare. Mongolian chess was one of the methods he used to study military warfare. According to *Miscellaneous Records of Qiaoxi* written by Ye Mingli of the Qing Dynasty, the Mongolian Xiangqi chess system was: "The game was nine lines horizontally and vertically, all 64 grids, with sixteen pieces each including eight pawns, two chariots, two horses, two elephants, a cannon, a general … It is a chess-shaped game with no characters, with the pawn going straight all the way to the bottom, the horse running only horizontally, and the chariot marching or retreating in a straight line freely. When there was no way out, the outcome of winner and loser was determined."[36]

Mongolian chess pieces are divided into two colors: red and blue or white and black to distinguish between the two sides. There is a king ("Noyan" in Mongolian, in the shape of a crown), a female leopard, which is the king's butler ("queen" in chess), eight young leopards, which play the role of pawns, and two camels serving as the role of the elephant. There are also two horses (like cavalry) and two chariots (as a fortress). Lions or tigers on different sides share the role with the same function. Each side has sixteen chess pieces, big or small. The chess pieces, in the shape of figures, animals, and vehicles, may be solemn and serene, or new and lively, some glaring fiercely, some raising their heads high, appearing lifelike and eager to spring up. Some pieces are carved from wood, some from animal bones, while some are made from clay and fired. Most of the chess pieces used by herders in the Inner Mongolian Autonomous Region are carved out of Barin stone (a stone produced in Balin Right Banner of Chifeng City for carving craft products), with painted color, one on one side. The chessboard is painted on canvas, on animal skins, or temporarily on the ground, most of which are made of wood. The chessboard is a square made up of eight grids, both vertically and horizontally, with 64 grids in all, painted in two colors. The horizontal grids are separated by one grid between two sides, and so are the vertical grids. When viewed from an oblique angle, the grids of the same color are connected to the top.

When the game starts on both two sides, the usual rule varies from region to region. Generally speaking, at the beginning of the game, only the lion's pawn is allowed to go first. Sometimes, after both sides have agreed, the prince's pawn is allowed to go first. The first move can be two steps, but not followed by other movers later. When the pawn reaches the bottom of the line, it can be promoted to a lion and a powerless lion, and the powerless lion can only walk in a cart and diagonally one grid; the king and the cart cannot move; the horse or the camel can only move as a general yet not kill directly, but only if other pieces move first, they can kill next. A capturing of the opponent can be a draw. Usually, the winner is decided in a single game, regardless of time. In the Qinghai region, the rules of chess are that if the other side does not "check," the king cannot move, and both sides cannot take the other side's passers-by. In the Durbet Grasslands, the "horse" (the mare leopard, steward of the king) cannot kill the "king" because the "king" is supreme and cannot die under the hoof. Either side is not allowed to take all of the opponent's pieces, and one pawn must be left behind, which means that not all should be killed. In addition, there is a difference between a "big victory" and a "small victory." A "big victory" is when an army of one side enters the enemy's territory, the enemy "king" is killed successively (also known as "successive kill"), and all be checked finally. As for "small victory," there are two types: one is that one side captures the enemy's "queen," indicating that the enemy has lost his ability to command, and the other is that one side can directly check the enemy by one step.

4.2.9 Baoge Chess

There is a widespread recreation called "Deer Chess" among the Mongols. The Mongolian herders in the autonomous region of Inner Mongolia call the game of deer chess "Baoge Yinjilege," while in the Durbod grasslands, it is also known as "Bige Jilaga" because its pieces are made of femur bones. The history of deer chess is more than 1,000 years old, as illustrated by the discovery of a chiseled surface of a deer chessboard by the Inner Mongolia Cultural Relics Team. From 1948 to 1949, a piece of deer chessboard was unearthed from the site of the Ögedei Khanate Palace at Karakorum, the ancient capital of Mongolian Mongolia, in the territory of the People's Republic of Mongolia. The chessboard proves that deer chess was a palace recreation for 600 to 700 years. Deer chess is very interesting because of its long and steep paths, its diagonal intersections, as well as two "mountains" providing areas for the deer to play. Nowadays, deer chess is also very popular in the rural areas of Inner Mongolia and among other ethnic groups. In some places, it is called "Wolf-Sheep Predation," i.e., two "wolf" pieces and 24 "sheep" pieces.

4.2.10 Bulu Throwing

The word "bulu" is the Mongolian transliteration, meaning "to throw." It has a history of more than a thousand years, originating from the ancient life of hunting. According to *An Extra Introduction of Ji Lin*, "The culture is mellow and ancient, and the people are pure and honest; they often use sticks to throw and catch flying birds and beasts, whether on horseback or on foot, and they can always hit them exactly."[37] Bulu is the Mongolian hunter's hunting tool and self-defense weapon. It can be used to hit animals such as birds and beasts, like pheasants, rabbits, foxes, etc. Animals that are knocked unconsciously or killed with their fur intact can be hunted alone or in a crowd by bulu. In order to shoot accurately at prey and master the skill of bulu throwing, hunters usually focus on practicing bulu in accuracy and distance. Besides, they often compete with each other, gradually developing into a sports item that could be preserved as a means of physical exercise. Bulu throwing is known to have some effects on building physical qualities such as arm strength and dexterity.

The Mongolian people also have another story about bulu. Once upon a time, there was a beautiful princess named Hairitu, who was very fond of bulu and good at throwing bulu. At the age of 18, Hairitu's father, Baiyin Nuoyan, put a notice recruiting a son-in-law for her. He chose from many noble sons, but none of them was to the princess's liking. Baiyin Nuoyan said, "My girl, no matter how high the golden eagle flies, it has to find a home, and you need a companion when you grow up." The princess replied," I have the ambition to protect the frontier and the country, and I have been training bulu since I was a child. I would like to select a handsome 'Tulaga' from the commoners to guard the frontier with me." After hearing the daughter's reply, the lord shook his beard and said, "You're a girl without a dream! Let beggars match with beggars, and you are the princess of the lord. How can you get married to a commoner?" Then Hairitu answered, "Let the sons of the rich or powerful have a match with me on bulu. Whoever defeats me will marry me, and if there is none, I'd like to ask your permission to choose from the common people." The lord thought it would be inappropriate to force the princess, who was his only daughter, so he reluctantly agreed. Baiyin Nuoyan then ordered all the officials, military or civil, to gather together, decide the auspicious day, prepare for the fine horses, and settle the race affair. On the very day, the lord, dressed in an imperial robe and girded with a jade belt, sits on the viewing platform and waits for his chosen son-in-law to win the "tulaga." But despite the hundreds of bulu thrown from the horses, only one from Hairitu hit the target. The result of the competition was disappointing for Baiyin Nuoyan. The next morning, in accordance with the wishes of Hairitu, the lord issued another notice asking the young herdsmen to sign up for the bulu competition. As a result, a young man named Bateer won the "Tulaga," and the princess married him. However, just as Princess Hairitu was about to marry Bateer, the cruel lord, Baiyin Nuoyan, ordered her to kill Bateer. People felt so much sympathy for the unfortunate princess. Later on, the herdsmen of the grasslands decided to hold the bulu competition, a practice of martial arts and physical training on the one hand, and a tribute to the memory of Princess Hairitu on the other hand.

The early bulu was made of elm wood, but in order to increase its lethality, it was later replaced with the one with metal heads, which were covered with lead, copper, iron, and other metals or cast into the head pattern. The bulu is about 50 cm long, 6 cm wide, and 1.5 cm thick, with a curved head that resembles a hockey stick. Depending on its purpose and shape, bulu can be divided into three types: "Jirugen bulu," "Tuguliga bulu," and "Haiyamura bulu." "Girugen bulu" is a heavy and heart-shaped one of copper or iron, tied to the head of the bulu with a leather band. This type of bulu is specially made for fighting large animals, such as wolves and wild boars, and is more often used at close distances, generally less than 20 m. The "Tuguliga bulu" is made by carving a fine pattern on the head of the bulu and pouring melted lead into the middle of the pattern. Because of its light weight, it is made for shooting small animals, such as pheasants and wild rabbits. "Haiyamula bulu" is shoulder-shaped, with no metal added to the head of the bulu, which is used for daily practice.

The game of bulu throwing consists of two types: long throw and accurate throw. In some areas, some use bulu to hit a rolling ring or shoot a flying bulu in the air. For accurate bulu throw, it can be a horse shot or walking shot. The bulu in long throw is a flat "Haiyamula bulu" with a round handle and a weight of 500 grams, while the bulu in accurate throw is a round "Tuguliga bulu" with unlimited weight.

4.2.11 Mongolian Swinging

According to *Xi Jin Zhi*, the palace was the most beautiful during the Qingming Cold Food Festival. People were caught in gold brocades and tied with sachets of incense, and they were appealing to each other. The feast was going on, with plenty of food and drinks. Everyone, either nobles or from the middle class, enjoys a pleasant life. Swings, among other things, are appreciated by people from all walks of life, including the rich and the richer, to get rid of their worries and nostalgia.[38] From this, it seems that the Mongolian people had a certain scale of swinging in the area of Xijin, because it prevailed in both the royal palace and wealthy families.

4.2.12 Sports Culture in Nayadum

Historically, the Mongolian people had a nomadic life of living in a dome, drinking milk and vinegar, dressing in sheepskins, and migrating from one place to another. Most of the grasslands have left traces of Mongolian herdsmen, who are known as the proud sons of the grasslands, people who are good at riding and shooting. The Mongolian herdsmen have created and developed the "Men's Triathlon" with ethnic characteristics, namely, wrestling, horse racing, and archery, and the "Nayadum Fair," in which they compete in wrestling, horse racing, and archery. The Nayadum Fair is a festival of the Mongols featured by steppe ethnic groups, which is enjoyed by the majority of the Mongolian people. The "Men's Triathlon" and the "Nayadum Fair" are not only a valuable cultural heritage of the Mongols, but also play an important role in ancient Mongolian society.

The time from the 11th to 13th century was a prosperous period of political, economic, military, and cultural development of Mongolian society after the Mongolians changed their mode of production from a hunting economy to an animal husbandry economy. With the development of social politics, economy, and production technologies, the transformation of social system was accelerated. The original clans and tribes gradually disintegrated and entered into the war of tribal alliance and unification of the whole Mongolian nation. In order to preserve themselves or to swallow other tribes, each tribe joined an armed group composed entirely of all men. In the *History of the Yuan Dynasty*, it is written that "Families with sons over fifteen and under seventy, are all recruited to be soldiers. Whenever there was an issue, every ten were regarded as a squad with a leader. They ride on the horse and fight in battles, or they get off the horse to conduct grazing."[39] This organization is not only a production organization, but also a military one. In ancient times, when skirmishing was the main feature of warfare, strength, skill, and tenacity became the most important qualities for a soldier. Thus, it was the primary task for every tribe to train and select strong and brave men. For this reason, the "Men's Triathlon" was included as part of military training for its ability to nurture and develop the above qualities of strength, skill, and willpower, because they were essential on the battlefield. Another important historical reason for the rapid growth of "Men's Triathlon" was the fact that in the democratic elections of the Confederacy, only those who excelled in men's triathlon were qualified to be elected as the chief of the tribe. One of the reasons why Hutula was chosen as the leader of the Mongolian was that he was the best in the Men's Triathlon. In the subsequent battle to unify the whole Mongolia, Genghis Khan's generals, such as Qasar, Belgutei, Muqali, and Jebe, were all outstanding in men's triathlon, especially Belgutei and Muqali were famous wrestlers of the time. By the time of Genghis Khan's invasion and expansion, Mongolian society had become feudalistic. The progress of society and the development of culture and education did not diminish the social status of "Men's Triathlon," which remained to be one of the most important conditions for the selection of the chiefs and generals for the throne. In the *History of the Mongol Empire*, it is written: "If you defeated you in the long-distance archery, I would break my thumb and give up; if you challenged me you in hand=fighting, I would not rise from the ground but instead follow the imperial decree of our father Khan."[40] This fully demonstrates the importance of "Men's Triathlon" in ancient society.

After the unification of Mongolia by Genghis Khan and the expansion of political and military power, the sport of "Men's Triathlon" became more popular in the military. It is not only a means of training soldiers, but also an indispensable tool for regulating military thinking, stabilizing emotions, and encouraging morale. Therefore, whenever it came to the end of a victorious campaign or a reconditioning period of the army, a "Men's Triathlon" competition was held. According to the book *Badukhan · Nayadum in Mongolian Amy* written by the former Soviet historian Nai · Yang, the Mongolian army, after crossing the river in victory, organized a "Men's Triathlon" at the ceremony of welcoming soldiers at the foot of the Morro da Urca in Russia. The soldiers came from all directions by the thousands and sat in a big circle. After Badukhan and his generals had laid carpets and saddle mats on the slopes of Morro da Urca and settled down, bugles, gongs, and drums sounded loud and clear. The presiding person entered first, shouting: "Come on, fearless warriors, for the sake of your health, come and wrestle. It is time to test our will and measure our strength." The best of the wrestlers came in from everywhere, stretching out their arms and picking up a handful of earth or grass from the ground like eagles. The one whose shoulders failed to hit the ground in a three-round fight was hailed as a hero. They then embraced and caught each other, each trying to beat the other to the ground.[41] In addition to regulating the minds and emotions of the troops, the "triathlon" was also used to improve the strength of the troops, replenish the casualties of war and encourage the soldiers to continue fighting for the Mongolian ruling class.

In July, August, and September every year, the vast grasslands under blue skies and white clouds are in full bloom with fresh flowers and green grass, which is the golden time for fat cattle and strong horses. The annual Oboo festival, mane trimming festival, foal festival, and temple fair are all held during this time of year. The Mongolian people have been gathering and entertaining themselves since ancient times. Dressed in festive garb, herdsmen and herdswomen ride on steeds and carry bundles of blankets as they gather from all directions for a traditional event called Nayadum, which in Mongolian means "to play" or "to gather" and "entertainment." The Mongolian word for celebrations, parties, and festivals is "Nair," the movement of which is always associated with "Naiyi Day," so it is said that without "Naiyi Day," there would be no "Nayadum."[42] *Yessongge Stele* (also known as the "Inscription of Genghis Khan") describes the gathering of Genghis Khan with his subordinates, an event that included a lot of riding and shooting activities. According to *A Guide to Mongolian Customs* by Blo bzang chos ldan, the Oboo ritual is held in autumn, whose scale depends on the size of the place and the wealth of the people, and the main purpose of the ritual is to discuss the choice of pastures, the handling of various issues and matters within the jurisdiction. After the porridge at the feast, the horses are selected. The fastest horses and riders set off racing in 20s or 30s as a group from 15 miles away, and the winners of them would compete in the second race until the final round the best were selected. The winners would name their horses according to their color, and famous fine horses would value most of all. Horse traders are also willing to buy horses at high prices. In addition, there are various types of horses for different functions, such as walking, trotting, jockeying, and cantering.[43] Nayadum is a traditional festival of the Mongolian people, which was originally a folkloric ritual of sacrifice and entertainment, but later the significance of the ritual diminished, and it gradually evolved into a sports competition and exchange of materials.

Wrestling, horse racing, and archery have been used for recreation and martial arts by the nomadic peoples of the north since around the time of the Hun. That was inseparable from the tradition of ancient nomadic peoples of the north, who were good at fighting, riding, and shooting and engaged in hunting and animal husbandry. By the time of the Liao Dynasty, the three skills were widely spread among the commoners, which became the main content of Nayadum Fair. In the Jin Dynasty, a system of rewards, coins, and goods was established for the winners of these three arts. Before the 12th century, the **Mongol leaders, in addition to enacting laws, appointing officials, and distributing rewards and punishments, held large-scale Nayadum Fairs, which were mainly composed of wrestling, archery, and horse racing.** After Genghis **Khan unified the Mongolian** tribes and established the Mongolian Khanate in AD 1206, with the socio-economic development of the **Mongols, Nayadum** was held on the occasions of Ikh Khural, success celebration, flag sacrifice, title appointment, military and civilian reunion, and the marriage of sons and daughters of Genghis Khan, making the cultural life of the Mongolian people become richer and more active. *Yessongge Stele*, engraved in 1227, records the event of Genghis Khan's nephew, Yesongge, who shot arrows at a distance of 335 paces when he was hosting a banquet in 1225 on his way to the **western expedition. Thus, it can be seen that** mounted archery was a skill closely related to both the socio-economic life and the warfare of the current time.

In AD 1260, Kublai became the Mongol Khan, founding the capital Kaiping, moving to Yanjing (later called Dadu, now Beijing) in AD 1267, changing the name of the Mongol state to Yuan in AD 1271, conquering the Southern Song Dynasty in AD 1279, and then unifying the whole country. Nayadum was then more widely held under certain circumstances. In the thirteenth century, the traveler Marco Polo recounted how Princess Agianit of Khaidu chose her mate in a wrestling match:[44] Dressed in a magnificent pink wrestling costume, the princess overwhelmed all the handsome young men who came to fight her. She also bravely dashed through the "enemy lines" to recapture the opposing warrior from his horse. This means that even strong women could participate in the Nayadum in the **Yuan Dynasty.** After three generations of internal and external wars, the Mongols established powerful khanates in Asia and Europe, with the Yuan Dynasty as their leader. After the war for the throne of Great Khan and the war against the Southern Song Dynasty in the early Yuan period, the Mongols, who had lived in war for more than half a century, eventually found peace and settled down in a good environment for developing their culture and art. In the Yuan Dynasty, the Mongolian emperor followed the national custom of martial arts and included **wrestling as one of the main entertainments of the imperial court**. Therefore, **wrestling was performed at every entertainment banquet**. The grand banquet in Shangdu hosted by Kublai Khan, the founder of the Yuan Dynasty, was recorded in the book *Annals of Koubei Three Tings* as follows: "A thousand officials from all direction gathered around, the instruments of all kinds were playing with the wrestling competition held; the dancing girls in purple danced beautifully, all immersed in the heavenly ensemble playing the spring melody."[45] The emperor not only enjoyed watching wrestling, but also rewarded and appointed those who excelled in wrestling. In order to further promote the sport of wrestling, the Yuan Dynasty set up the **"Yongxiao Office"** to administer the **wrestling affairs of the whole country**.

The emperors of the early and middle Qing Dynasty valued and enjoyed wrestling. Mongolian wrestling was strongly advocated by Huangtaiji. In order to improve the wrestling skills of Manchu children, he ordered them to sincerely learn from the Mongolian wrestlers. Those outstanding wrestlers were heavily rewarded in order to further develop wrestling. As is recorded in *Secret Notes of Manchu Scripts* by Jin Liang, since Emperor Taizong rewarded three warriors, the Mongolian princes of the allied banners all followed the example of the Qing emperor, selecting their own famous **wrestlers and named them princes of the "Three Buku"** (i.e., wrestlers) to train. Wrestling competitions are held on the occasions of alliance meetings, temple festivals, and oboo ceremonies. In addition, every duke or minister of Mongolian alliance would perform archery, and wrestling activities with Manchu wrestlers for the Qing Dynasty. For example, Emperor Taizong, in the eighth month of the second year of Chongde Period, watched the envoys of the outer fiefdoms compete in archery and wrestling, as recorded in the *Records of the Qing Dynasty*: "In the eighth month of the second year of Chongde, in the imperial arena, people watched the foreign envoys compete in archery. When the greeting was done, the enjoys from outer fiefdoms started to compete in archery. Besides, warriors from two sides were going to wrestle."[46] **These practices and competitions** contributed to the development of men's triathlon and the advance in technology at that time.

During the Qing Dynasty, Nayadum was gradually transformed into an organized and purposeful recreational activity that was regularly convened by the government, with some changes in scale, form, and content of the activity. According to the *Annals of Ujimqin Custom*, in the fifth year of Emperor Kangxi's reign (AD 1666), the Qing government organized a grand assembly in Ujimqin Banner, where a wrestling match of 1,024 wrestlers was held, and a young wrestler won the first prize.[47] In the 25th year of the reign of Emperor Kangxi, the princes of ten banners, including the Hexigten Banner, Baarin Right Banner, Baarin Left Banner and the Alut Banner, and Zasak Noyan, held an important gathering in the Great Pella of the Hexigten Banner, during which a large-scale Nayadum activity named "The Ju Ud Pageant" was held. According to the records in *Mongolian Wrestling*, a wrestler named Booher Lama won the championship at the Nayadum Congress held in Khalkha in 1690.[48] In the 36th year of Emperor Kangxi's regime (AD 1697), when the chief of the Seven Banners of Khalkha returned from Duolun Nur to their pasture lands, he held the Seven Banners Nayadum. During that horse race, a shepherd named Gongger won the race with his only horse.[49] The sports described in these events were not all three men's sports as we know in modern times, but only one or two of them, suggesting that the number of sports in any of these events usually depends on the needs of the meeting. It has therefore been inferred that the ancient Nayadum fair was not entirely synchronized with the three men's skills, but was generally either horse racing, wrestling, or archery alone.[50]

In the 18th century, new development was found in the scope and content of the Nayadum. According to the relevant custom in the eighteenth century, the unified organization of the three skills competitions was recorded in the Banner Annals. For instance, according to the *Annuals of Baarin Right Banner*, which is recorded from the eighth year of Emperor Yongzheng (AD 1730) onwards, more than a thousand lamas from thirteen temples within banners concentrated at Daban Huifu Temple and attended the annual "June Temple Fair." The temple fair features both ceremonial rituals of the lamas and group activities of national culture, sports, and material exchange. There will be an endless stream of people rushing to the temple fair from Beijing, Tianjin, Tongliao, Chifeng, etc. All banners within alliance will participate in the festival for one month, sending fast horses, horse-riders, wrestlers, archers, and chess players.[51] As was recorded in the *A Chronicle of Alashan Customs*, during the reign of Emperor Qianlong, the third prince of Alxa, Lobsang Dorji, married a Qing princess and became a prominent prince. To celebrate the event, a huge festival was held in the 30th year of the Qianlong reign (AD 1766). Thousands of shepherds and herdsmen gathered at the event; people of the eight Sumus and officials of the banner's government office all took the initiative and the task of organizing three arts training, in which 32 wrestlers and 120 archers were selected from hundreds of pairs of wrestlers and hundreds of archers, and 80 fast horses were selected from hundreds of stallions. After the congratulatory ceremonies, there would be a three-arts tournament. The first went to the stallion race, in which 30 out of 80 fast horses were ranked, and then the blessings would be presented to the top horse, and a trophy, as well as other rewards, would be given to the winning horses by grades. The second was the archery race, in which each person galloped three times according to the rules. The riders would be ranked according to the number of hits on the nine targets, and the top winner would be rewarded with nine kinds of prizes, the rest awarded differently by rank. Besides, *Odes to the Arrow Players* would be sung and recited. The third was the wrestling race, in which the winner would also be awarded nine kinds of prizes, and others were awarded respectively based on their grades.[52] In AD 1771, when the Turehot tribe returned from the Volga River region through huge hardships after eight months, Emperor Qianlong held a grand gathering at the summer resort in September, where various cultural and sports performances, including archery, horse racing, wrestling, and hunting were included. Emperor Qianlong not only took part in the gathering in person, but also he rewarded all for their participation. It can be seen that Nayadum Fair, typical of men's three skills, was held everywhere at that time, ranging from palace banquets, alliance gatherings, Oboo ceremonies, and official promotions to the inaugural ceremony of Living Buddha hütügtü. In addition, the Nayadum Fair also includes performances of Mongolian chess and polo, singing folk songs, and playing folk musical instruments. Plus, the Mongolian princes and nobles of the

Qing Dynasty also held Nayadum every six months, one year, or three years on the basis of Sumu, banner, or alliance and awarded prizes and titles to the winners in different categories. In small tournaments, the winner was usually awarded a goat or some brick tea. In the larger tournaments, the winner was awarded a full-saddle horse, and in the alliance tournaments, in which a large number of wrestlers took part, the winner was awarded a white camel wearing a silver-nosed pot and carrying eighty-one pieces of jewelry and silk.

As a product of the will and interests of the entire Mongolian people, Nayadum has been passed down from generation to generation in small-scale activities among the diaspora. At the annual religious festival, young men and women gather from yurts and independently organize their own activities. The "men's triathlon" is not only a compulsory sporting event at a grand gathering, but also an opportunity and a condition for princes and nobles to choose an emperor's son-in-law for the princess and for common people to choose a son-in-law for the daughter. The emergence of this culture is inherited from the folklore and customs of various nationalities in the north. On this basis, with the progress and changes in politics, economy, and social life, the connotation of Nayadum has been renewed and enriched. Since the Qing government unified the whole nation, the political and economic ties between the regions have been greatly strengthened, and the culture of lamas, folklore, and materialism with the center on monasteries and temples has been fully embodied. Nayadum culture thus has gradually evolved into a miracle in the Mongolian grasslands.

4.3 Sports Activities of Manchu

Manchu nationality has a time-honored history. According to the historical records, Jurchens of the Ming Dynasty were the direct ancestors of the Manchu, as well as the descendants of some Jurchens of the Jin Dynasty. As stated in the *Chronicles of Ming Emperor Shenzong Xian*, Jurchens of the Ming Dynasty "were evil offspring of Sushen, who once lived in the territory of Jin."[53] Historically, after Jin State collapsed, about one million Jurchens still stuck to the Jurchen customs till the Yuan Dynasty. Till Ming Dynasty, they were divided into three parts by people in the Central Plains, namely, Jianzhou Jurchen, Haixi Jurchen, and Wild Jurchen. The birth of the Manchu is the outcome of intermarriage among Jurchen tribes led by Jianzhou Jurchen and other ethnic groups such as Korean, Han, Mongol, Xibe, Daur, and Oroqen. In AD 1616, Nurhaci founded the Qing Dynasty, which marked the birth of Manchu. In AD 1635, due to political needs, Huangtaiji, Emperor Taizong, explicitly ordered to change Jurchen into Manchu, which has been in use to the present.

When society developed to a certain stage, professional sports groups emerged. In general, the establishment of a professional sports team should be earlier than the establishment of a specialized management agency. The professional sports teams of ancient ethnic groups in the north already existed at the latest during the Northern Wei Dynasty, among which Baixi (folk performing arts, esp. acrobatics) group is a case in point. Of course, military training of the northern ethnic groups in ancient times was a major part of national sports. Though these military troops were non-professional sports teams, they laid a foundation for the establishment of a professional one. The **Dangxiang Nationality** (Tangut) set up a branch of armed forces called "Bubazi," and Mongol Nationality had army corps named "Gui You Chi." Both "Bubazi" and "Guiyouchi" mainly served armed forces, yet they still shared somewhat athletic favor, so they could be regarded as professional competitive sports teams in embryo. In the Central Plains, professional sports teams were found among the Hans in the Qin and Han Dynasties at the latest, while competitive sports teams were set up no later than the Sui and Tang Dynasties. However, in the history of the northern nationalities, competitive sports teams were not established until the Yanyou Period of Emperor Renzong, marked by the establishment of Yongxiaoshu, which further developed into Shanpuying, established by the Manchu. Men's triathlon constitutes the major part of training of the Mongol **professional competitive sports teams. These teams had their own competition systems, and held regular competitions.** After the Qing Dynasty was founded, the Mongols still highlighted professional sports training, hoping to win glory and status for their tribes by displaying their fine skills in Nayadum, Jamah, and autumn hunting.

Looking into the evolution of **Manchu** civilization, we can easily find that the Manchu culture reached a climax in the Qing Dynasty. As a representative of ancient northern sports, the development of **Manchu traditional sports was also in a flourishing stage in the Qing Dynasty**, of which one example was wrestling (called Buku in Manchu language). In the Shunzhi Period of the Qing Dynasty, the Manchu exceeded the Mongolians at **wrestling, ranking first in the whole country.** The wrestling boom among the Manchu in the Qing Dynasty promoted its own development in terms of titles, skills, wrestling suits, refereeing, etc., and thus laid the foundation for the formation of Chinese-style wrestling techniques and wrestling rules, making a tremendous contribution to the wrestling development in China as well as the rest of the world. Another **example is skating.** After the Qing troops entered the Shanhai Pass and founded the Qing Dynasty, the authority set ice-play as a national custom. Grand ceremonies were held in Beihai, Nanhai, and other places every winter. Emperors, nobles, and senior officials would come to review and appreciate these ceremonies. The Qing skaters had the top class skating skills and the best skating performance in the world back then. Amid the boom of skating sports, a host of recreational and competitive events that were popular among the masses came into emergence, such as **speed skating, figure skating, skating on a trolley, spinning top, bed-sled dragging, ice football** (*Cuju*), etc. At the same time, a group of skating equipment was invented, such as speed skating shoes, figure skating shoes, bed sleds, ice trolleys, ice tops, etc. Coupled with the development of other types of sports in the Qing Dynasty, it can be concluded that the ancient northern sports in the Qing Dynasty have reached their peak in terms of the events' organization and quality.

4.3.1 Thriving Riding and Shooting

The Jurchens had extremely low productivity in their early stage. In the 13th century, Jurchen tribes "had no towns or cities, and had to live by **hunting and migrate for water and grass. Therefore,** the Yuan authority set administrative institutions to govern the Jurchens, and ruled scattered Jurchen in accordance with their custom."[54] Under these conditions, riding and shooting only got initial development. It was not until AD 1616, when Nurhaci established the Later Jin Dynasty, the Manchu's mounted archery began to enter a fast track of development. Nurhaci, as a gallant warrior in battle, was good at riding and shooting on the horse. In the thirteenth year of the Wanli Period, Nurhaci launched an attack on Elehuan City, reigned by his enemy Nikan Wailan. Despite being badly wounded, Nurhaci still shot eight enemies to death by himself. "(In the seventh lunar month, 1585) The chest and shoulder of the Emperor Taizu of Qing (Nurhachi) were shot through by arrows, and the number of wounds from head to toe in him amounted to thirty. However, this did not intimidate the emperor, who went on valiantly to shoot eight enemies to death and beheaded one. Seeing how tough and formidable Nurhaci was, the rest of the enemies fled off. He also killed nineteen Han people, and captured six enemies with arrow wounds in the City of Elehuan."[55] According to the records in *Manchu* of the *Records of the Qing Dynasty*, in the fourth lunar month of 1585, Nurhaci led his younger brother Murhaci, and two retinues, Yan Bulu and Wu Lingga, to advance on the enemies with their bows and arrows and shot twenty enemy soldiers to death, frightening the rest of enemies. Eight hundred enemies were beaten by them four and had to cross the river and flee off.[56] What a miracle! Also noted in the book: In the fourth lunar month of 1588, Amin Zhezhe (daughter of Huerhan Beile), the granddaughter of Wanhan, tribal Chief of the Hada Tribe of the Haixi Jurchen, was sent by her brother Daishan to Nurhaci as a concubine. Nurhaci sat in wilderness with his retinues at Yudong, waiting to welcome Amin Zhezhe. At the moment, a person riding a horse with a bow on his back galloped by. Emperor Taizu asked the entourage who this guy was, and the retinues told the emperor: "He is Niu Wengjin from Dong'e Tribe of the Jianzhou Jurchen, the best archer in his tribe." Emperor Taizu then beckoned him over to have an archery contest with him. The target was a willow tree a hundred paces away. Niu Wengjin then dismounted his horse, and drew the bow to shoot. Three out of five were shot on the target, and two high or low were missing. Emperor Taizu, by comparison, succeeded five out of five successively. Taizu's arrows were shot into the same place, the hole of which was so deep into the trunk that it could only be pulled out by chiseling some pieces of wood on the willow tree.[57]

The development of mounted archery among the Manchu was firstly attributed to the importance attached to by the emperors. In 1636, Emperor Taizong succeeded to the throne, setting the title of his regime as Qing. One year before his enthronement, he abolished the title of his nationality, "Jurchen," and replaced "Jurchen" with "Manchu." During the reign of Emperor Taizong, the Manchu system gradually diverted from a slave society to a feudal society influenced by Hans. As the Qing regime governed more and more Han people, the shock of the Han culture was also becoming stronger and stronger. In that case, how to preserve the riding and shooting custom for the future Manchu generations living in affluence came to the agenda. In 1636, Emperor Taizong issued an imperial edict to all Gushan Beizi (a rank of the Manchu nobility below that of the Beile), quote: "When the Emperor of Taizu was on the throne, every time we heard that next day the emperor was going hunting, we would drill the falcons and kick Cuqiu the Emperor, getting fully ready for the following hunting. If anyone was not allowed to participate, he would implore for permission in tears. Kids today, however, channel their energy for traveling, frolicking, and idling around. Back then, our royal family of all ages, struggled to go hunting and felt excited about marching or hunting. At that time, there were few retinues, so everyone by himself herded horses, managed the harness, collected firewood, and cooked meals. Even under these harsh conditions, everyone kept loyal to the emperor. This, actually, is the very reason why our country could prosper and thrive. Today's royal members, instead, whenever there is going to be a march or hunt, will always find ways to excuse themselves, like his wife is ill, or he has family affairs to do. If all our officials seek easy life at home and loaf away their days like that, how can we prevent our country from decaying! How can we further prosper our country!"[58] Some Manchu started to wear Han clothes, and some totally discarded riding and shooting. To change the status quo, in the first year of the Chongde Period (AD 1636), Emperor Taizong convened a meeting with Princes, Beiles (a rank of the Manchu nobility below that of the prince), Chiefs of the Eight Banners, and officials in the Department of Supervision at Xiangfeng Pavilion. He asked one official to read out the *Chronicles of Emperor Shizong* of the Jin Dynasty. Huangtaiji took Wanyan Dan, Emperor Xizong of Jin, and Wanyan Liang as cases to give his officials a lesson. He noted: "You all listen carefully. Wanyan Yong, the famous, sagacious Emperor Shizong of Jin, was also well-known by Hans. He was posthumously reputed as Junior Yao Shun. I have read this book, feeling impressed. What's recorded in it is just refreshing, which makes me admire Emperor Shizong's governance. **The complete and fine laws, rules, and regulations developed in the regime of Wanyan** Aguda, Emperor Taizu of Jin, and Wanyan Sheng, Emperor Taizong of Jin, could have gone down in history. However, when it came to Wanyan Dan, Emperor Xizong of Jin, and Wanyan Liang on the throne, they just indulged themselves in alcohol, carnal desire, and frolic and were eroded by the corrupt customs of the Han people, neglecting the administration. After ascending to the throne, Wanyan Yong, Emperor Shizong of Jin, strove to follow Emperor Taizu and Emperor Taizong and dedicated himself to improving governance. He also imposed bans on some Han customs lest the future generations would follow, and always admonished his officials and royal family not to forget the forefathers' will and aspirations. Clothes and language were asked to be also in accordance with the old system. Riding and shooting were regularly practiced. Despite such strict regulations, later emperors of the Jin Dynasty still gradually abandoned riding and shooting, which became more or less deteriorating. It was not until the time when Jin State was on the brink of collapse that Wanyan Shouxu, Emperor Aizong of Jin, also the last emperor, realized that any dynasty with emperors indulging themselves in alcohol and women was doomed to become extinct. Bakeshi Dahai and Kūrcan advised me many times to replace the Manchu clothes with Han's. I rejected it. Then they thought that I was not willing to accept suggestions from officials. Imagine, when we are assembling now, wearing baggy robes with loose sleeves, arrows, and bows on the left and right of our backs, suddenly Laosa raid in, can we guys resist the attack? If we threw away our riding and shooting, wore baggy robes with loose sleeves, and were served meat by servants, what would it be like? **In terms of archery, we are no better than a left-handed man equipped with a bow for a right-handed.** So much that I've said is actually out of my concern for the future of our dynasty. If I myself don't follow our Manchu traditions, it is foreseeable that our descendants' archery skills will **taper off one day, and they may pick up Han customs. That is what I have been concerned** about all along. In the past, our soldiers all excelled at riding and shooting, which is why they could always annihilate enemies. No other troops can even match ours, because our troops were always praised as: "In defense, no other forces can topple; when charging, no one can stop. This time we marched from Yanjing to the border, and our troops would be slowed down by you eight senior officials. **Your conduct really crippled the morale of our army.**⁵⁹ Emperor Taizong attached great importance to archery, put it on top of everything, and ordered the descendants to abide by this principle. In April 1637, the second year of the Chongde Period of Emperor Taizong, Huangtaiji admonished his clansmen: archery is one of the fundamental businesses of our country. If you spend too much of your time on feasts and entertainment, you will certainly neglect practicing archery and martial arts. Soldier's training, as you know, holds the key to governing the country. I hope you can strengthen your riding and shooting practice, and train soldiers at the regular time. When going for a battle or a hunt, you're allowed to wear casual clothes; otherwise, court wear is still a must. Please be consistent with our set regulations. How could a Manchu emperor be assimilated into Han customs? My talk today should not only work for now. I hope you can keep my word in mind, pass it on to people around you, and make it be complied by our descendants. Forefathers' governing system must not be distorted or abandoned."⁶⁰

In Huangtaiji Period, young royal family members who were greatly influenced by Han customs did neglect some Manchu physical exercises. For instance, Beile (a rank of the Manchu nobility below that of the prince) Abatai refused to practice archery for the excuse of painful hands. In the seventh lunar month of 1635, the ninth year of the Tiancong Period of the Emperor Taizong of Qing, Huangtaiji reprimanded Abatai: "You always say your hands are too painful to shoot. **It seems that you can't stand toils. You know what? Labor makes your blood flush and makes you feel energetic.** You all idle around at home and avoid shooting and shooting. When occasionally exercising, how will you not feel pain? If you can strengthen exercise, and practice riding and shooting on a daily basis, these pains will disappear. Moreover, you command troops and you have responsibilities on your shoulders to take. If you don't take the lead in honing riding and shooting and practicing martial arts, how can your soldiers be keen on doing these? Can you defeat enemies **with your poor fighting skills? Is there something more important than** riding and shooting for a man? Plus, practice makes your riding and archery skills perfect. You'd better regularly practice on it."⁶¹ Emperor Taizong often admonished royal family members lest the misgovernment by Wanyan Dan, Emperor Xizong of Jin, and Wanyan Liang would recur in Qing's reign. In the second lunar month of 1641, the sixth year of Chongde Period of Emperor Taizong, Huangtaiji warned his Princes, Beiles (a rank of the Manchu nobility below that of the prince), and senior officials: "**Why don't you lead your men to practice riding and shooting? Those strong enough are able to practice with horn bows and feather arrows, while teenagers and children, with wooden bows and willow arrows. For those addicted to gambling, you must punish them seriously. Riding and shooting is the top event in our martial arts system; neglecting their practice is a crime even worse than taking opium.** The ban on opium is difficult to put into enforcement, for you also commit surreptitiously. But practice on riding and shooting must be strengthened. You must set an example and supervise and persuade each other."⁶² **Actually, early in the first lunar month of 1633, the seventh year of the Tiancong Period of Emperor Taizong, Huangtaiji ordered the officials: "You must take the lead in practicing riding and shooting assiduously, and urge your men to do it, no matter what ages they are, especially in springs, summers, and autumns. I will send an inspector now and then. If someone is found incapable of riding and shooting, his superior will be punished.**

Mounted archery is one of our nation's strengths, which has been verified in battles in particular. So you must double your effort in practicing it."⁶³ In this way, mounted archery was upheld by the Manchu owing to the promotion of Nurhaci and Huangtaiji, from which we can get a glimpse of Manchu custom: When a boy is born, a set of bow and arrow will be hung at the door to convey delight; women can ride as well as men; teens can race on horses, with bow and arrow on their backs; the Manchu betrothal presents are always saddles, helmets and armor, bow and arrow; at the engagement ceremony, armor, bow, and arrow will be presented to the bride's side before the groom enters the bride's house; at the wedding, the groom will shoot the sedan in which the bride is seated, in order to ward off evils.

In 1644, Qing troops entered the Shanhai Pass and set Beijing as the capital. Later more Manchu followed. As the unification of the whole country in the Qing Dynasty was further consolidated, the Eight Banner Soldiers were designated to garrisons in key towns throughout the country to strengthen national defense, and their families followed. Thus, the Manchu spread all over the country. It was at that time that royal rulers realized that: only when the Manchu language and customs like riding and shooting are well preserved, and when the Manchu ruling class is prevented from being "Hanized" (be assimilated into Han community), can the Qing authority rule the Hans as well as people of other nationalities in so large a territory. Prior Qing Emperors all issued decrees on these points. For example, Emperor Shizu admonished the generals and soldiers not to abandon mounted archery in peacetime. Later he even enacted detailed rules on archery practice, which were recorded in history books: generals and soldiers in Xianghuang Banner, Zhenghuang Banner, and Zhengbai Banner, shall practice mounted archery twice, and foot archery four times every month. All Cavalry Battalions in eight Banners, shall practice archery six times monthly, supervised by officials junior to the Chief Executive of the Banner. The specific time for fully armed foot archery in springs and autumns can be set by each Banner, for fully armed mounted archery shall be determined by officials from the Central Departments. Other troops, like Sentinel Battalions, Guard Battalions, and Specials Forces, shall practice foot archery monthly, and also shall hold armed archery practices in springs and autumns. Even for the Artillery Battalions, training for foot archery, mounted archery, and horseback skills, for six times respectively, is regulated."⁶⁴ In the ninth lunar month of 1655, the twelfth year of the Shunzhi Period, Fulin, Emperor Shizu of the Qing Dynasty, issued an imperial edict to the Ministry of War, noting: When selecting talents for state governance, we must attach equal importance to the capabilities in both civil and martial arts. This year, up to now, the candidates for the final round of Imperial Examination majoring in civil affairs, should come to participate in the exam together with the 220 candidates majoring in martial arts, and I will invigilate the final test in person. Foot archery and mounted archery go first, then the session on state governance. In the future, the final round of Imperial Examination should continue to follow suit."⁶⁵ We can tell that back then, even the civil majors were expected to be proficient in riding and shooting.

In 1690, the 28th year of the Kangxi Period, Xuanye, Emperor Shengzu of the Qing Dynasty, issued an edict, reading: "Mounted archery is one of the foundations of our Manchu nationality. Practicing riding and shooting never conflict with learning classics. Candidates majoring in civil affairs for the final round of Imperial Examinations should also be tested for riding and shooting proficiency. If some examinee failed to live up to the standards of martial arts even though he has already passed the Imperial Examinations, he would not be taken; if so, both the examinee and the invigilator would be punished severely."⁶⁶ In the 32nd year of the Kangxi Period of 1693, Xuanye, Emperor Shengzu, offered an instruction again: "I'm deeply convinced that mounted archery is a crucial business for revitalizing our country. Children and teens in different units in the Department of Royal Court Affairs should have coaches to teach them riding and shooting."⁶⁷ *Miscellaneous Records of Xiao Ting* records as follows: "In the middle of the Kangxi Period, government expenditure on official salary was huge. Therefore, to fix that, officials were all demoted. Princes born either from wives or concubines were all appointed with lower-grade titles. Other officials were demoted competitively to a lower level, too. In the test for translation, foot archery, and riding and shooting, those who

Fig. 4-2 Picture of Xuanye in Armor

performed well in all subjects could be reinstated to their former posts; otherwise, they would be further demoted, and the salary followed in decreasing."⁶⁸ Even the average officials, to maintain their posts, needed to take a test for mounted archery. From that, we can see that great emphasis has been laid on riding and shooting by the Manchu authority. Emperor Shengzu, Xuanye himself, also took the lead in practicing riding and shooting (see Fig. 4-2).

In 1726, the fourth year of the Yongzheng Period of the Qing Dynasty, Yinzhen, Emperor Shizong issued an edict: "In ancient times, archery was set as one of the six classical arts, reflecting its importance in the heart of ancient sages. Since the foundation of our dynasty, we Manchu have highly valued riding and shooting. Now no matter what age or position we are, we must all indulge in riding and shooting practice, and luckily most Manchu are proficient at them, which is unprecedented in history. Examinees must first be tested for riding and shooting capability. Those whose performance is up to the set standards can pass the exam. By doing so, we intend to exclude examinees who only study Confusion Classics but neglect mounted archery practice, thus making the skills of riding and shooting rusty. Even the lord in each Banner shall train themselves mounted archery monthly on the drill ground. We are going to achieve the goal that 'all our civil officials are also proficient at martial arts.' Enshrining these into law is of profound and far-reaching significance. Recently, some non-Manchu civil officials taking office are found to gradually get out of riding and shooting practice. If this trend is left alone, their archery skills will definitely become rusty in the future, which doesn't conform to the purposes of our legislation. From now on, non-Manchu civil officials under 60 years old are given two years to practice riding and shooting until they can get the hang of them. Two years later, for those who fail, local chief executives must report them to the central government. No cover-up is allowed. If I ascertain that some local chief executives commit shielding, both the official and executive shall be punished seriously."[69] "In 1727, the fifth year of the Yongzheng Period of the Qing Dynasty, Emperor Shizong inspected the field exam of the military examinees at Ziguang Pavilion, Yingtai. Emperor Shizong then ordered the Guard Battalions to perform foot archery. Back then, many Manchu warriors could manipulate a stone bow weighing kilograms of tensile force. Seeing this, the military examinees from all over the country were all amazed, letting out spontaneous praises. Those who achieve excellent grades in the exam will be appointed as gate guards in the palace, which is really a glory for the examinees. Generally, examinees from the northeast perform better than those from the southeast. Those who have been promoted to be the governors or the envoys of different divisions are selected from above. Obviously, the tremendous effects of the state's training have been well displayed.[70]

During the Qianlong Period of the Emperor Gaozong of the Qing Dynasty, there would be a test for royal family members in the middle of October each year. Princes, dukes, defense ministers, and senior officials would be tested for Qing Language as well as mounted archery. Princes are asked to first contest archery. Officials at lower levels would conduct the test in the same way. Those who performed outstandingly would be awarded peacock feather-decorated headgear and silk and satin. In contrast, for those who performed poorly, their salary might be suspended. Therefore, all royal family members diligently got engaged in practicing riding and shooting and learned the Qing language in an effort to maintain their fiefs. In the 18th year of the Qianlong Period of the Qing Dynasty, Emperor Gaozong issued an edict stating: "Mounted archery and the Qing language are the foundation of Manchu. This year I inspected the officials' archery performance, whose job was in general all right. Very outstanding ones have been appointed as guards and retinues, who have been distributed in diverse regions. If they have lousy riding and shooting performance, and refuse to work on them to make progress, once the cases are ascertained, we shall remove them from office and transfer the positions to others. Manchu officials in the Department of Defense in each province, if they were not admonished for practicing mounted archery as well as Qing language, might seek ease and freeloading, which are negative examples. Governors and chief executives in Eight Banners must urge their men to practice riding and shooting, as well as Qing language, so as to achieve proficiency. For officials who defy rules or still remain poor at them after practice, the governors and chief Executives must report them to me. They will be either dismissed or demoted."[71] Below are several pictures portraying Emperor Gaozong's archery (see Fig. 4-3, Fig. 4-4, and Fig. 4-5). Fig. 4-3 portrays that Emperor Gaozong Qianlong practiced archery and martial arts in a summer resort. In Fig. 4-4, Emperor Gaozong Qianlong has just shot two deer with one shot. Fig. 4-5 shows that Emperor Gaozong Qianlong was on a hunt in a suburb escorted by retinues.

In the fifth year of the Jiaqing Period of the Qing Dynasty, Yongyan, Emperor Renzong noted: "Mounted archery is of top priority for us Manchu. If Manchu channel all their energy to reading Confusion classics for the Imperial Examination, they will, without doubt, neglect riding and shooting, as well as martial arts, which doesn't conform to our purposes of sending Manchu to defend and guard. In the future, descendants of Manchu officials in Defense Departments must keep on practicing archery instead of only learning classics. Issue my edict to governors, chief

Rise and Fall of the National Sports in Ancient Northern China 185

Fig. 4-3 Painted Hanging Panel of the Emperor Qianlong Archery

Fig. 4-4 Picture of One Shot, Two Deers

Fig. 4-5 Picture of the Emperor Qianlong Archery

executives of the Banners, and officials at all levels: riding and shooting is the number-one priority in training youngsters. Those who are aimed at the Imperial Examination should also practice riding and shooting to their proficiency. Only in this way can we live up to the expectations and will of our late Emperors. Here are words, and I hope we Manchu can develop in more aspects and draw more life circles. Please do convey my words to them."[72]

In the 13th year of the Daoguang Period of the Qing Dynasty, Emperor Xuanzong noted: "After reading the quotations of our late emperors, I find that they all took riding and archery as the top priority for us Manchu. If Manchu spend their energy all on reading for examination, they will certainly neglect riding and shooting, together with martial arts. Descendants of Manchu officials in different provinces must not abandon mounted archery which is the foundation of Manchu. Governors, chief executives of the Banners, and officials at all levels should admonish their men to take riding and shooting as the number one priority. Those who are aimed at the Imperial Court Examination should also practice mounted archery to its proficiency at the same time. This is not only the holy will of our forefathers but also the law of our country. So we must follow these rules steadfastly. Moreover, Jilin is the birthplace of our Manchu and the Qing Dynasty, so it is more strategically important than other provinces. Under this circumstance, riding and shooting should be more strictly practiced here. There is no way that mounted archery should be neglected for the Imperial Court Examination. The situation is: people will all participate in the Imperial Court Examination for titles, and our country has been in peace for decades. Jilin is a place with fine folkways. How could it be addict to the bad custom of giving up the practice of riding and shooting? Now I am determined to add some exam centers for testing those examinees who are supposed to be both capable of reading literacy and mounted archery, which happen to conform to my purpose of educating Manchu."[73] Emperor Daoguang in 1842, reiterated in an edict that "Mounted archery is the most important groundwork of the Eight Banners." It was also stipulated that Manchu examinees who took part in the Imperial Court Examination could not pass the exam if they failed to ride and shoot. Male royal family members must practice riding and shooting since childhood. There are many other records left manifesting the emphasis placed on riding and shooting by the late Qing emperors. For example, as recorded in *Miscellaneous Records of Xiao Ting*: "After we entered the Shanhai Pass and took Beijing, In the beginning, the princes, dukes, and senior officials were all proficient in archery and the Qing Language. Later, they were somewhat eroded by Han customs, who pursued ease and extravagance, and rarely practiced riding and shooting. Knowing it was a crippling trend, Emperor Gaozong undertook reforms. Those with clumsy archery performance will be punished promptly or be demoted to low posts as punishment. At the province level and metropolitan level of Imperial Examination, only examinees passing the archery test can enter the exam room to sit for the examination. As a result of this rule, descendants of men of great merits all practice riding and shooting to their optimum."[74] On top of this, *Miscellaneous Records of Xiao Ting* also records: "At the beginning of the Qing Dynasty, fifteen men most proficient in riding and shooting among the dukes, senior officials, and military officials would be chosen as the archers in the Imperial Palace. They would be awarded peacock feather-decorated headgear. Whenever the emperors shot, they accompanied them as retinues. If the emperors asked them to shoot, they would show their archery proficiency in turns. They were called 'Top 15 Archers.'[75] Plus, "Regulations were formulated as follows: princes must start to learn riding and shooting from 6 years old; military men from the Eight Banners who are proficient in mounted archery and the Qing language will be selected to serve the Imperial Palace as guards in turns, or to teach little princes riding and shooting. These people are called 'Companions,' acting in the role of company, teaching, and protection.[76]

Mounted archery was also accommodated in the Imperial Court Examination in the Qing Dynasty. The Imperial Court Examination in the Qing Dynasty, back then, was the latest talent-selecting system evolving from that in Sui and Tang Dynasties, but in the Qing Dynasty, riding and shooting were laid more importance. The Imperial Court Examination was divided into four rounds in terms of the preliminary exam (named Tong Exam), provincial exam (named Xiang Exam), metropolitan exam (named Hui Exam), and palace exam (named Dian Exam). To be specific, Tong Exam was held every three years in three rounds, as were Xiang Exam and Hui Exam. Hui Exam was held in the ninth month of the following year after the Hui Exam, while Dian Exam was usually held in the tenth month of the following year after the Hui Exam. Those who passed the different levels of exams would be awarded corresponding titles, such as Provincial Level Knight (titled Wu Jvren) for Xiang Exam and Samurai (titled Wu Jinshi) for Hui Exam. Palace exam was held in the tenth month of the same year of the metropolitan exam, the results of which would be the very best (Zhuang Yuan), Runner-up scholar (Bang Yan), and the third winner (Tan Hua) in sequence.

The Imperial Examination usually included three rounds, which were successively composed of mounted archery, foot archery, and martial arts, as well as literacy.[77] "According to the examination rules, in both the first two rounds, examinees will be given nine shots opportunities respectively. In mounted archery, those who hit two out of nine can move to foot archery. In foot archery, those who make three out of nine are qualified for the literacy examination. In addition, after the foot archery test, there would be skill tests of drawing bows, wielding sabers, and lifting stones." To better select talents, in each round and test, there would be examinees being eliminated. It is a fact that examination rules varied in different times. For instance, in the seventh year of the Shunzhi Period of the Qing Dynasty (1660), the skill tests of drawing bows, wielding sabers, and lifting stones were suspended, but later resumed in the 13th year of the Kangxi Period (1674). There were some other changes in the examination system, too: target distance was changed to 15 paces for mounted archery and 80 paces for foot archery. In mounted archery, those who have three or more shots at a target out of nine are allowed to move to the next round—foot archery. In foot archery, whoever hits two or more out of nine are qualified. After mounted archery and foot archery, military examinees are asked to draw bows weighing 8 *jin*, 10 *jin*, 12 *jin* respectively, perform wielding sabers weighing 80 *jin*, 100 *jin*, and 120 *jin* respectively, and lifting stones of 200 *jin*, 250 *jin*, and 300 *jin*. Those who are qualified in the first two, i.e., drawing bows and wielding sabers, are accepted to attend the round of lifting stones. In the 25th year of the Qianlong Period (1760), archery opportunity was reduced to six from the prior nine, and another test was added, that is: to shoot the fur-wrapped ball from horseback. The ball with a diameter of 2 *chi* is made of leather or felt, which is put on a pedestal made out of clay along the bridle path. Examinees who shoot the ball down are qualified and capable. Those whose arrows stab into the ball yet not down from the pedestal will not be judged qualified. The arrowheads with the oblate head used in this ball-archery test are made of wood. In the archery test, examinees shoot six times altogether, three of which were hit and were qualified to step into the foot archery test. In the foot archery test, the target size was adjusted to 5 *chi* in height and 2.5 *chi* in width, and the target distance was adjusted to 25 paces away. Again, those who succeed in two out of six can further enroll themselves in the next round, including bow, sabers, and stones.

In the late Qing, firearms replaced riding and shooting as the most important part of battles. In the 12th year of the Guangxu Period of the Qing Dynasty (1901), Imperial Military Examination was abolished by Emperor Dezong, as read in the edict: "Imperial Military Examination is supposed to be further carried forward by us, since it has been tapped into for a long time. But now its drawbacks begin to emerge. Mounted archery, foot archery, sabers, and things like these are no longer used in battles. Therefore we should advance with the times and seek reforms. From now on, Tong Exam, Hui Exam, as well as Dian Exam in Imperial Examination are going to be abolished forever. All Wu Jvren and Wu Jinshi are assigned to be trained with the designated tasks. Those robust military test-takers should be conscripted into the Military Academy in each province, waiting to be further selected and trained when the respective provinces finalize their own tests and rules. Selection should be conducted afterwards so as to cultivate more talents."[78] Though the Military Examination System was repealed, mounted archery remains a custom of Manchu nationality, and then evolved into a traditional sport for entertainment and fitness, popular among people.

Traditional mounted archery has had eight sub-events since the Manchu entered the Shanhai Pass. First, shoot incense. It takes more techniques in this event than strength to shoot the incense into the sky at night; second, shoot silk fabric. Hang a small piece of silk fabric and shoot it; third, shoot "Aihang" (a cloth target). Sketch the outline of a target on a piece of cloth and shoot it; fourth, shoot the suspending ball. Put an earthen ball with a pair of pigeons caged in and shoot the ball. Once it gets shot, the ball will roll down and break, and the pigeons fly away; fifth, shoot a rice ball. In the Qianlong Period of the Qing Dynasty, a court artist gifted Emperor Gaozong eight paintings of events during the Dragon Boat Festival. One of those was titled "Rice Balls," on which four women were shooting rice balls. Besides, one of the other five women on the right was aiming at a rice ball on a plate on a high-heeled rack. Shooting rice balls was once popular entertainment in the capital Chang'an and the imperial palace of the Tang Dynasty. *Ten Bygones in the Kaiyuan and Tianbao Periods* records: "On the Dragon Boat Festival, people in the imperial palace would make rice balls and Zongzi, a traditional Chinese glutinous rice dumpling, which would be served on plates. People also made small and delicate bows out of animal horns to shoot rice balls and dumplings. The rice balls and dumplings were slimy and hard to shoot. Only those who hit the target were allowed to eat. This entertainment was popular in Chang'an."[79] People in the Qing Dynasty later picked up this entertainment form; sixth, shoot willow branches. After the heavenly worship ceremony, two rows of willows were planted in the field. The shooter tied a willow branch with handkerchiefs, several inches from the ground, preparing for shooting. All the shooters took the order of superiority and inferiority to get started. In each shot, a drum beating to cheer up, and with a ride as the lead, the shooter galloped the horse with a feather-free arrowhead arrow to shoot. If the willow branch was broken and caught by the hand, the rider won. Broken and unable to take, the rider was ranked the second; the willow broken on the green part, or hit but not broken, or missing the target, the rider was lost. This kind of willow branch archery event is similar to the Khitan willow-shooting. Thus, it is inferred that this similarity is derived from the Jurchen in the Jin Dynasty and then carried on as the Khitan customs, and the Manchu further inherited it from the Jurchen; seventh, play the blowgun. He Peilin introduced the blowgun in his article *On Blowgun*: "Initially, the blowgun was made of a reed stem for it is hollow. Afterwards, the bamboo pole was used as a blowpipe. The bamboo pole would be polished smooth inside and outside. Guys with a taste for exquisiteness would sheathe the pole in rosewood or padauk, and inlay a mouthpiece made of precious materials like jade or ivory. Later, the blowgun made of brass or red copper emerged. The length ranged from 3 *chi* to 5 *chi*, with a diameter of some 7 millimeters. The 'bullets' of blowgun—peas or adzuki beans, should be steeped in water one day before use to get swollen. When using the blowgun, the user put a bean, aimed the blowgun at the target, and blew it out through the pipe. Vertically the bean can be blown to a height of over 35 m. Some people used clay balls as 'bullets,' but having clay in mouths was not a good experience, so clay balls were barely used." In another book by Ruan Kuisheng—*Talks after the Tea*, as recorded in Volume 20: "Blowgun to shoot birds, fishing line to fish." This "blowgun" just uses arrows or small balls as projectiles, which are light and fast, but can't reach far. In the early Qing Dynasty, the monk Shi Yuanjing wrote a book titled *Ode to the Capital* to depict customs in Beijing. One poem in it, *Blowgun*, goes like this: "Blow the pipe lightly, and walk gingerly; sparrow and pigeons fall prey, have you ever experienced such joy?"; eighth, shoot a bullseye, also named Shooting Drum (She Gu or She Hu). In addition, the poem *Shooting Drum* written by Li Shengzhen vividly records that archery has developed into a folk game that was popularized among civilians. Another Qing scholar Zhen Jun in Volume 1 of his book *Tian Zhi Ou Wen* (*A Miscellany of Stories of Beijing*) records as follows: "In establishing the Qing Dynasty, bows and arrows played a pivotal role, and the Manchu are famous for their excellent proficiency in archery. Therefore, the Eight Banners took mounted archery as an important fundamental. Literati and officialdom also shot as entertainment, who usually owned their private archery range. They would often make appointments with good friends to shoot around. The archery target had several rings, and the innermost ring was called the 'goat's eye.' Manchu people practiced riding and shooting apart from learning classics. Recently the authority was selecting riding and shooting instructors through 'shoot bullseye' competitions. Only those who excelled at it would be standby candidates for future officials."[80] "General Guo Yiiting specialized in 'shoot bullseye,' who was labeled as 'Guo' goat's eye' as a compliment. The most capable archer's shot can even drive the target to fall apart, for it's made of leather rings sewed together. This is the highest level of archery, which is truly hard to get to."

Next, let's get a glimpse of Manchu mounted archery tradition from the perspective of hunting. Hunting is another approach to practicing riding and shooting. "Mulan" is interpreted as "Hunting Deer" in Manchu language, while "Qiuxian" means autumn hunting from the ancient rituals. Mulan Qiuxian is a mixture of Manchu language and Han Language. The emperor goes hunting in four seasons, namely spring hunting (Chuns Sou), summer hunting (Xia Miao), autumn hunting (Qiu Xian), and winter hunting (Dong Shou). By comparison, Manchu people hunt frequently all year long. Sometimes they leave in the morning and come back at night, and sometimes they go out hunting for two or three days. Hunts with such a time span were called "small hunts." Hunts in autumn or winter, called "big hunts," may last for about 20 days. Hunting trophies they gain are so numerous that they can't even be carried back by barrows and horses. The Manchu were noted as people of "Hunting State." Whenever it is time to hunt, no matter how large or small the number of participants for the hunt is, they will go out for a hunt, with no exceptions. When one hunting trip starts, each participant is endowed with a chance to give a shot at the opening. Ten people are included within a group, with one leader in each group. Each man in the group watches out for a specific direction in no mess. *Records of the Qing Dynasty · Manchu* records: "In the tenth lunar month, Manchu people will bring their three-year-old falcons and hounds to go out for hunting. Different groups of hunters will, by Banner, be allotted to different areas, which are called hunting grounds, regardless of terrains, plains, or mountainous regions. The hunters, in small or large numbers, are divided into two groups, from far to near, encircling their prey. This process is called "encompassing." Different hunter groups will share their trophies with each other."[81] Looking into the history of Manchu hunts, we can find that before the 17th century, hunting was only a productive labor carried out by Manchu ancestors for the needs of life. At the beginning of the 17th century, after the Manchu entered the Liaoning and Shenyang provinces, it has gradually become a nationality mainly engaged in agriculture, in which hunting was reduced to a secondary activity that supplemented living materials, while the military function was driven to be more prominent. From the founding of the Qing Dynasty to the Qianlong and Jiaqing Period, hunting has been regarded as a major event. The purpose of hunting is not to prey on animals, but to practice martial arts. During the Nurhachi administration, in order to meet the military needs, he emphasized that the Manchu should expand the territory by riding and shooting, so the Manchu must be strong with bows and arrows, and martial arts must not be abandoned. Hunting to them means practicing martial arts and improving archery skills; therefore, it's a means of preparing for warfare and training in riding and shooting. In the 10th year of the Tianming Period of Emperor Taizu (1625), Nurhaci led an entourage to go hunting from Shenyang city. He strictly readied armaments and hunting equipment, declaring bans and controlling the hunting process by the law of military marching. Detailed hunting regulations were also formulated: "The majesty likes hunting and marching, thus formulates a set of strict laws and regulations for hunting and marching ... When sending troops or hunting, discipline must be strictly followed and no hubbub is allowed ... It is said that noise will expose us to the enemy in battles; hubbub will scare away potential prey in hunting. When prey is encircled, no riding in the enclosure is allowed; if the prey comes forward, anyone should stand in place and shoot; if the prey escapes from the encirclement, anyone can quickly chase it on horseback, run to it and shoot it head-on. All hunters have the morale 'Why would I go on a hunting trip if I don't shoot animals?' Everyone must not hinder others from chasing the prey. When the fast hunters try to drive the prey back to the enclosure, the slower hunters should follow behind in an orderly manner. Anyone who passes by the prey is entitled to shoot or kill, and the meat of the prey should be shared by everyone. If a tiger is lying on the ground, you'd better stand still and inform others of its position; if you see a tiger running, ride after it and shoot it. When you miss a bear or boar in archery at the first shot, it is accepted if you can catch up with the bear or boar and kill it on the second try. If you fail to do it by yourself, you can ask others to 'co-kill' the prey. A co-killed prey should be divided equally by the co-hunters. If you refuse the assistance to cause the prey to escape, the helpers may gain the beast's flesh as compensation; any other who has captured the running prey is privileged to have it slaughtered and obtain the prey after informing the hunter. Above are the regulations for hunting.[82] Since then, hunting has been incorporated into Manchu military training system. Later, Huangtaiji, Emperor Taizong, carried on this system. In 1632, the sixth year of the Tiancong Period of the Emperor Taizong of Qing, Huangtaiji issued an edict to Beile (a rank of the Manchu nobility below that of the prince) and senior officials: Our ancestors regarded hunting as a kind of military training; thus discipline must be strictly followed in the hunt."[83] Xuanye, Emperor Shengzu of the Qing Dynasty, attached more importance to mounted archery and went hunting himself, "The emperor hunted all the way in the South Mountain of the frontier, then out of Shanhai pass, to Wula.[84] In June of the second year, he came to the outside of Gubeikou for hunting, which was where the hunting began. In 1681, the 20th year of the Kangxi Period, when Emperor Shengzu led his hunting team to the north of the Great Wall on a hunting trip, he issued an edict to designate this very hunting trip as the constant system. As Mulan Hunting Ground was built, the Manchu conducted hunting and practiced archery and martial arts frequently there and at a large scale. From 1681, the 20th year of the Kangxi Period, to 1820, the twenty-fifth year of the Jiaqing Period of the Qing Dynasty, in the course of some 140 years, 95 large-scale royal autumn hunting ceremonies happened in Mulan Hunting Ground, and each lasted for over 20 days. In the fourth lunar month of the 58th year of the Kangxi Period, Emperor Shengzu claimed to the imperial guards when he sojourned in the town: "I have learned riding, shooting, and hunting since a very early age. Up to now, with fowling piece or bow, I've hunted 135 tigers, 20 bears, 25 leopards, 10 lynxes, 14 elks, 96 wolves, 132 boars, and hundreds of deer, excluding more prey hunted in other hunting grounds. I once shot 318 rabbits in a single day."[85] We can clearly see that in treasuring mounted archery, Emperor Shengzu first set himself as a good example, excelling in riding and shooting.

The ruins of Mulan Hunting Ground are located in the present Weichang Manchu-Mongolia Autonomous County in Hebei Province, which is at the junction of the Great Khingan Mountains and Yanshan Mountains. Mulan Hunting Ground was 150 kilometers long from east to west and 100 kilometers wide from north to south, with a total area of 15,000 square kilometers. The northern part of Mulan Hunting Ground was the Bashang Grassland, and the southern was hills and basins. With dense forests and crisscrossed rivers, it was a good place for wild animals to live and breed. Emperor Kangxi selected this piece of land which was near Beijing to the south and Mobei (roughly Mongolia nowadays) nomadic regions to the north, to establish a hunting ground for the purpose of training soldiers. In the 21st year of the Kangxi Period, Emperor Shengzu issued an edict: "Hunting can train our soldiers and battle steeds, which is of great military significance. It must not be abandoned or carried out irregularly. We'd better hold "Big Hunts" in the eleventh lunar month and the last hunt of a year at the end of the twelfth lunar month. In springs and summers, we will decide to or not to hunt according to the condition of our steeds."[86] Emperor Kangxi talked about the significance of setting up a Mulan Hunting Ground on the way back to Beijing after the Duolun Alliance (1691, the 30th year of the Kangxi Period): "First Emperor of Qin built the Great

Wall to strengthen the northern border. We in the Qing Dynasty gave kindness to Horqin (referring to the Mongolian at that time), and they would like to help us defend the northern frontier, which is supposed to be stronger than the Great Wall."[87] Emperor Kangxi did exactly what he said. In the sixth year of the **Qianlong Period**, when admonishing the officials, **Emperor Gaozong** recalled the feats of the late emperors: "I inspect the hunts all over the country, because I'm afraid that officials at all levels would hunt for pleasure and not take it seriously. We must have a sense of risks and hardships, and be alert for dangers even in times of peace. Some officials in the capital went against my will and gradually slackened. This is a very serious matter. Now, it is the right time to rectify our laws and system and manage our military affairs with stringency. The memorial (from Congdong, a member of the Commission for Discipline Inspection) about "stopping the hunts just for the prey of heavenly harmony" was well received. I'd like to say that our forefathers trained troops via hunts in four seasons. Our military forces now are stronger than in any other periods of proceeding emperors. When the late emperors led troops to go out for battles, they were always invincible that no enemy troops could compete, which was attributed to their hard work in daily training. Our late emperors were so good at military strategies, and our prior troops united as one and were full of valor, which is why they swept all enemies. If we don't take each hunt seriously, or don't treasure it valuable, or even abandon it, our soldiers will become accustomed to ease, and their archery skills will gradually become rusty. **The annual hunt trips led by our late emperors were of great significance to the troops. More importantly, during the hunt trips, regulations and rules were so strictly followed, and government work was well handled, which were all exactly the same as in the capital. When the late emperors went to the order, they would always inspect Mongolian vassal states and show them much grace. What they did was actually implement a long-term strategy, farseeing and significant.**"[88] The practice has proved that our late emperors used the hunting activities of the **Manchu and Mongolian** people to connect national affection and strengthen unity, thus realizing the major strategy of "uniting the vassal states through martial arts," so as to stabilize the whole country. During the **Qianlong Period**, some officials believed that large-scale hunts were wasting manpower and money, and they submitted memorials to advise Emperor Gaozong to stop such hunts. In the sixth year of the Qianlong Period, Emperor Gaozong decreed to refute this idea: "**The country's army management and training must not be neglected or abandoned. I hold autumn hunts to train the army and pass on the autumn hunting custom of our ancestors. As you know, in the past, our ancestors held autumn hunts every year, and everything related, such as the hunt routes, would be scheduled in detail in advance. Therefore, this autumn hunting of mine will exactly follow the regulations of our late emperors.**"[89]

Miscellaneous Records of Xiao Ting included a detailed record of the hunting system in Mulan Hunting Ground: "Mulan Hunting Ground was 400 miles north of Chengde, which was situated in Linhuangfu in the capital Shangjing of the Liao Dynasty, under the administration of Xingzhou Vassal, where Wengniute Banner inhabited. In the mid-Kangxi Period, the seignior of Xingzhou Vassal presented this land to the Qing Dynasty as tribute, and Emperor Shengzu used it as a hunting ground, setting up Mulan Hunting Ground. Mulan Hunting Ground covered an area of 15,000 square kilometers, with dense forests, abundant water and grass, and a number of wild animals. The emperor designated the Mulan Hunting Ground as a place where we could train our army, strengthen the ties with the northern nations, and safeguard the northern territory. Therefore, the autumn hunt custom developed by Emperor Shengzu has been carried on by later emperors, and then written into law to be followed for good and all."[90] In each hunt, Mongolian vassal states would dispatch 1,250 soldiers, who were going to form a big circle in an encirclement hunt. In the circle, there were soldiers holding large yellow ensigns in the middle and soldiers holding red and white ones on the left and riding sides. All these soldiers obeyed the general of the middle troop. The enclosure ministers were either led by the princes and ministers from the court or the Mongolian princes and dukes. There were two kinds of hunts: one was half-surrounded, in which only a few hundred soldiers distributed in the woods formed a semi-enclosed circle to approach and prey; the other was encirclement. At around 4:50 a.m., led by the Manchu enclosure minister, the Mongolia ministers, the elites of Eight Banners and Battalions, and good archers from different vassal states, would set out from camps, and form a large hunt circle, which could reach as far as 30 or 50 or even 70 *li*. The soldier at which the circle was finally completed would hold up his hat with a whip and shout, "Hat." Other soldiers relayed the slogan all the way to the general. After the general confirmed that the circle had been completed, they would begin to encircle. And the time, usually, was near 9 a.m. When encircling from a place of around 10 *li* (a Chinese unit of length equal to 500 m) to the place 2–3 *li* to the camps, the general would locate a high land and put up a tent, which was called "Lookout Post." When the soldiers marched close to the Lookout Post, they were standing by, expected to shoot prey that escaped from the enclosure, but couldn't shoot animals inside. Before sunrise, the emperor would ride from the royal camp to the Lookout Post and shoot the wild creature one after other, in the company of Generals, ministers, officials, and groups of soldiers. Everyone on the spot, including the officials and soldiers from different vassal states, was fully impressed by the emperor's gallant performance and cheered on it loud and clear. Sometimes it was too dangerous to catch a tiger alive, so people would wait until the tiger was dead before acting according to the emperor's orders. After the hunt, the emperor would ride to the Lookout Post and watch other officials and archers hunt down the remaining animals. Sometimes if there were too many animals trapped in the hunting ground, the emperor would order the soldiers to open a gap in the ring of the encirclement, and let some animals flee. The hunters and soldiers in the outer circle still could not shoot the animals that were released. After the hunt was over, the emperor would return to his barracks, while soldiers from all vassal states also returned to theirs in order. It was usually till three to five in the afternoon that the daytime hunt was over. Besides, the schedule of a deer hunting trip was different from regular hunts. In deer hunts, the emperor would set out from camp and divide the guards and entourage into three teams. Each team stopped and was stationed at different distances from the barracks, like 10 *li*, 5 *li*, and then 2 to 3 *li*. Only a dozen of guards and retinues followed the emperor to look for deer. Gradually, the sound of deer, high and low, would be heard. Suddenly there was a gunshot, and everyone knew that it was the emperor who had shot a deer. Everyone was very delighted and impressed by the emperor's might. Following the emperor's order, the three teams rushed to the deer hunting site in order. The memorials presented by the officials during hunting would all be checked and replied by the emperor in his barracks.[91] From Fig. 4-6, we can get a glimpse of the scene of the hunt in Mulan Hunting Ground (see Fig. 4-6). This picture is based on the scene when

Emperor Qianlong watched an equestrian show at a summer resort. Inside, the warriors set off from the assembly area at the upper left and galloped past the emperor and senior officials in the file while performing various technical movements on horseback.

Fig. 4-6 Picture of the Hunt in Mulan Hunting Ground

Hunting is actually military training, which abides by strict regulations and penalties. The records in the *Examples of Qing Huidian* read: "These regulations were established in the early years of the Shunzhi Period of the Qing Dynasty. If a team of officers and soldiers at the hunting scene is scattered, and even remains a mess after being asked to tidy up, the leader of this team will be punished with the exemption of one month of salary; those who lag in carrying prey with horses and retrieving his arrows will be whipped 30 times; if a head pulls another man's arrow, which was found by others, he shall be fined one month's salary, and this man is given 27 lashes; if a rider disturbs the order in hunting ground, his superior's horse will be confiscated; if a person absents himself from his post without asking for leave, he will be whipped 50 times and his horses shall also be confiscated; anyone who shoots arrows from the other side of hill without notice will be whipped 30 times plus a penalty of 5 *liang* (a unit of weight, equal to 50 grams) of silver to the informant; if a person who abandons his companion and causes him to freeze to death, his leader will be given 70 lashes and fined for nine months' salary; for hunting in prohibited places, the principal offender gets 80 whips and the accessory gets 50 whips. Their prey shall be confiscated and their superior shall be fined one year's salary; Princes, Beiles (a rank of the Manchu nobility below that of the prince), Beizis (a rank of the Manchu nobility below that of the Beile), and Dukes (Duke is the fifth class of imperial kinsmen), who shoot other Princes, Beiles (a rank of the Manchu nobility below that of the prince), Beizis (a rank of the Manchu nobility below that of the Beile), and Dukes by mistake shall compensate 3,000, 2,000, 1,000 *liang* of silver respectively to them, and be fined two months' salary; if someone does not shoot animals, but instead shoot at random, he would be interrogated for his act; if he gets a soldier injured, he will be fined two months' salary … If Princes, Beiles (a rank of the Manchu nobility below that of the prince), Beizis (a rank of the Manchu nobility below that of the Beile), and Dukes miss-shoot a horse of their inferiors, they shall be fined a month's salary; if the horse is shot to death, the shooter shall compensate the owner for another horse of fine." Related regulations and rules have been continuously improved and perfected later.

After the emperor of the Qing Dynasty finished autumn hunting in Mulan Hunting Ground, according to the usual practice, the leaders of the Mongol Zhuosutu Region and Shaowuda Region (now Chifeng City in Inner Mongolia) would pay tribute to the Qing emperor in Zhang Sanying—the emperor's temporary dwelling place during a hunt, and the emperor would bestow on them a royal friendly banquet, labeled as "Four events of the banquet." In the 17th year of the Daoguang Period of the Qing Dynasty, Emperor Xuanzong formulated the following rules for the royal banquet and rewards: After the annual hunt in Mulan Hunting Ground, the leaders of the Mongolian Zhuosutu Region and Shaowuda Region will be offered a banquet. At the banquet, there will be six yurts and "nine white presents, i.e., one white camel and eight white horses," 18 saddled horses, 162 un-saddled horses, 18 bulls, 162 sheep, 81 vats of liquor, 27 banquet tables, 20 Buku (wrestlers), variable number of indocile horses, 20 riders, 250 racehorses … Then the emperor will bestow food on Mongolian Princes and Dukes and order the attendants and guards around to deliver liquor to the Mongolian Princes and Dukes for two rounds. After the meal, tea will be served. Then, wrestlers will perform wrestling, and Mongolian Princes and Dukes will perform riding horses. Now, the banquet ends. Then begins the well-prepared "Four Events of Banquet"—Jamah, Mongolian music play, wrestling, and lassoing horse. Jamah: Before the banquet, a hundred good horses will be in position 20 *li* from the banquet camp. Each horse's tail will be tied up, and stirrups will be removed. Hearing starting gun, children riders galloped out, following the set route to the banquet camp. The first 36 riders arriving at the camp will be awarded by the emperor. Mongolia music play: Before the banquet, there will be a band performance. The band is composed of four teams, each with four performers, playing Mongolian-style musical instruments. Mongolian young girls in costumes dance to the music with a bowl of liquor on their heads. When the music stops, the girls will bend down and deliver the bowl to the nobility, who will take over the bowl and drink it all. Wrestling: Two wrestlers take off their hats and put on wrestling shorts, employing various technical movements to throw the opponent down to the ground. Whoever hits the ground first loses. Lassoing horse: Before the banquet, the Mongolian will drive a group of three-year-old horses to the field. The Mongolian nobility with excellent riding skills will wear formal attire and ride horses, with horse poles in their hands, to chase the scattered horses. The horse caught will be bridled and saddled. Before the banquet ends, the two chiefs will pay tribute to the Qing emperor: one white camel and eight white horses, called "Nine White Presents," to show their loyalty. And the emperor of the Qing Dynasty will reward the Mongolian nobility for showing favor in return.

The emperor of the Qing Dynasty not only required the troops in the capital to participate in hunting as training, but also required Manchu officers and soldiers from other provinces to come to the capital and participate in state hunt and training. In the 41st year of the Kangxi Period, Emperor Shengzu issued an imperial decree: "Manchu officers and soldiers stationed in Hangzhou of Zhejiang Province, Jiangning of Jiangsu Province, and Xi'an of Shaanxi Province hardly go on errands and live in ease and piece. If this trend continues, they will inevitably fall victim to decadence and laziness, and then become slack. From now on, each of these three provinces shall send 24 young, sturdy garrison officials or soldiers proficient in riding and archery to the capital to participate in the state hunt. Even if their riding and archery skills are already excellent, they can be evaluated and ranked and stand by to be appointed." Later in the 50th year of the Kangxi Period, Jingzhou of Hubei Province was also accommodated into this system with a quota of 16 participants. Seeing that the system in which different provinces sent officers and soldiers to the capital to participate in the state hunt had achieved good results, Emperor Gaozong, in his first year of the Qianlong Period, decided to inherit the system established by Emperor Shengzu. In the third year of the Qianlong Period, Emperor Gaozong issued an edict to expand the quota: 24 garrison officials and soldiers must be sent to participate in the annual state hunt and training in the capital, among whom 8 are Han officials and soldiers stationed either in Jingkou (now a district in Zhenjiang, Jiangsu Province) or in Hangzhou, and 8 are Manchu officials and soldiers stationed in Zhapu of Zhejiang Province. Emperor Gaozong, in his sixth year of the Qianlong Period, asked the locals to follow the stereotyped system and take a shift for learning and training in hunting and ordered the participants to go hunting that year by issuing decrees to comply. There were certain requirements for the number of trainees sent by each administrative region. Hangzhou, Jiangning, and other regions have fixed quotas. But the following regions didn't send officials and soldiers to the capital as scheduled for different reasons, and they were: Fuzhou, Guangzhou, Zhuanglang, Liangzhou, Ningxia, and Chengdu, which were all remote areas and inconvenient to travel, Taiyuan, Cangzhou, Dezhou, Zhengjiazhuang (now in Zibo City, Shandong Province) and other places where were not densely garrisoned, border in Suiyuan (now south-central Inner Mongolia) which was of significant strategic importance. Only Tianjin, Qingzhou (now central Shandong), and other administrative regions closer to the capital sent 16 officers and soldiers respectively, and Henan sent 8 to participate. Rehe (including part regions of present-day Inner Mongolia, Hebei, and Liaoning) selected 24 officers and soldiers to stand by. In the third year of the Qianlong Period, a total of 144 garrison officers and soldiers were sent from various regions outside Beijing to participate in state hunt and training in the capital. The regions qualified to send men to the capital, and the quotas for each region changed every year accordingly.[92]

Before the Jiaqing Period of the Qing Dynasty, horse riding and archery were still the major means in battles, although firearms were in use. Hunting as a means of training troops was laid under great stress by the authority. Later, as firearms became more and more widely applied, the military significance of horse riding and archery tapered off. Thus later on, Emperor Xuanzong canceled the state hunt in Mulan Hunting Ground. According to *Tian Zhi Ou Wen (A Miscellany of Stories of Beijing)*: "From the establishment of the Qing Dynasty to the Qianlong and Jiaqing Period, hunting has always been a very important ceremony for troop training ... Since the era of Emperor Daoguang, hunting as a military training was abandoned, and state hunts were no longer held ..."[93] In summary, the rise and fall of Manchu mounted archery are closely related to the historical development of Manchu nationality, social needs in military, political, and educational aspects, the rulers' decisions, as well as the might of the dynasty. Mounted archery is an excellent Manchu cultural heritage, yet nowadays, it receives little attention in Manchu settlements with its sharp decline in popularity.

4.3.2 Cuqiu

"Cuqiu" means kicking the stone ball. According to the records in books created by folk artists during Tongzhi Period and Guangxu Period in the late Qing Dynasty, such as "One Hundred Pictures of Beijing Folk Customs," "Depiction of Scenery and Customs in Beijing," and "100 Folk Songs in Yantan," "Cuqiu" rules are as follows: two or more people are divided into two teams. **One person from team A first kicks one of the two stone balls to a certain distance, followed by the second ball. Team B then sends another, from the same starting line, to kick the second ball for two kicks. After the first kick, it is required that the second ball shall not go farther than the first ball or hit it. Then he kicks the second ball for the second time. If the second ball hits the first ball with the second kick, Team B wins; if the second ball goes farther than the first one or collides with it with the first kick, Team A wins; if the second ball fails to hit the first ball with the second kick, also Team A wins.**

Zhai Hao's *Customs Records* notes: **"Children use clay to make footballs, put one ball on the ground as a target, and kick another to hit it. The ball may also be earthen balls or even walnuts.** Cuqiu may be evolved from *Jirang*, which was a throwing game in ancient China in which you put a plank on the ground, and throw another plank at it at a certain distance, and you will win if you hit it. *Notes on the Age of Yanjing* notes that *Cuqiu* is a branch of *Cuju*, a traditional football game in ancient China. Whether Cuqiu (kicking a stone ball) is a variant of *Cuju* and *Jirang* or a combination of the two awaits further research to identify, because though both Cuqiu and *Cuju* involve kicking, the balls shapes of the two sports as well as their ways of kicking vary from each other. According to the *Notes on the Age of Yanjing*: "In the tenth lunar month, children from poor families carved out stone balls to kick. If one stone ball hit another, the kicker won. In cold winter in Beijing, hands and feet are prone to be frozen to chilblains. By kicking stone balls, children can invigorate the circulation of blood and keep warm. Thus, *Cuqiu* is somewhat like *Cuju*." Stone ball, commonly known as "kick the ball," is set with two iron balls, played mutually, and kicked to win, which was very joyful. The players chased and kicked the ball on the ice in winter. Of course, kicking the ball in the Qing Dynasty was inherited from prior dynasties, which can be supported by the details in Beizi (a rank of the Manchu nobility below that of the Beile). *Notes on the Age of Yanjing*: "**The sport of kicking balls was born in the Jin and** Yuan Dynasty, not in the Qing Dynasty."[94] In 1636, Emperor Taizong, Huangtaiji noted in his edict to Gushan: "In the Emperor Taizu's reign, whenever we were told to go out hunting the next day, we would train the falcons and play the stone ball for preparation …"[95] **The above records show that** *Cuqiu* originated in northern China, but the sports of ball-playing started later in the Central Plains and northern China in the Liao and Jin Dynasties. In the Qing Dynasty, *Cuqiu* was further developed with more innovation, which gained wide popularity.

4.3.3 Pearl Ball

In ancient times, one type of pearl, "Dongzhu," called "Tana" in Manchu language, was produced in northeast China. This kind of pearl was very precious because of its long growth cycle and low output. Therefore, it became a treasure that the Manchu paid tribute to emperors since ancient times. In the Qing Dynasty, the production of Dongzhu became less and less, so the Qing government strictly prohibited private collection of Dongzhu, and arranged for the Department of Royal Court Affairs to collect. Dongzhu pickers got salaries directly from the royal government, so the pearls they picked must be handed over to the court. According to the *General Annals of Jilin*, it was recorded that: "Huntong River, Wula River, and Ningguta River rich in Dongzhu. These pearls are round and crystal white. The larger ones may be 0.5 *cun* in diameter, and even the smaller ones are as big as soybean grains. They are evenly round and white, which can be as large as half an inch, and the small ones are like soybeans."[96] *A Brief Account of Ningguta* records: "The old city faced a river, in which there were many clams, thus producing a lot of Dongzhu. Each weighed 2 or 3 *qian* (a unit of weight equal to 5 grams). They were pink, blue, and white. Without imperial decree, no one can pick pearls privately. Some red pearls were as big as small meatballs, shining gorgeously."[97] Picking pearls was really a toil, and sometimes a life-threatening job. For example, *General Annals of Jilin* cites the following: "pearl collectors drowned during their work, but the government didn't give them rewards or condolences."[98]

How did the ancient Manchus gather pearls in the rivers, lakes, and seas in northeast China? *Annotations to Records of the Great Jin Dynasty* records that soon after Yelü Yanxi (the ninth emperor of the Liao Dynasty) ascended the throne, courts in central China sought luxury and extravagance, and pursued Beizhu (another name for Dongzhu). People in central and northern China all came to fairs at borders to trade pearls. Knowing about this, at first Yelü Yanxi planned to ban pearl trading at the border. But one of his counselors argued that: "The central courts exhausted their national treasury to trade useless things, which would weaken their national power, so it is a good thing for us." Yelü Yanxi accepted this suggestion. Gradually Yelü Yanxi became arrogant and indulgent and began to pursue pearls himself. Fine Beizhu, big as marble, small as a seed, were all produced in the rivers and seas of eastern and northern Liaoning. Every year on the 15th day of the eighth lunar month, when the moon shines brightly, it is a symbol of harvest year for pearls. Till the tenth lunar month, it is the right time to collect pearls. But as the weather becomes cold early in the north, the ice in the river has been quite thick in the ninth and tenth lunar months. Pearl pickers have to dig through the ice and dive into the icy river to pick pearls. By doing that, pearl pickers are more inclined to get sick. There is a kind of swan that eats mussels, so that the pearls are hidden in the swan's stomach. Interestingly, there is a species of vulture called "Haidongqing," which can prey on this type of swan. Therefore, afterwards people domesticate wild vultures, use vultures to catch swans, and then obtain pearls from the swans' stomachs.[99] *General Annals of Jilin* describes vividly and thoroughly the scene of pearl picking.

The ancient Manchu pearl pickers living in the Songhua River, Mudanjiang River, and Nenjiang River areas developed a game based on **pearl-picking activity**. They used the tool for plucking pearls—diddle-net, as a game tool to imitate the process of picking pearls. Initially, this game was played in the river and later moved to the shore: they also inflate the pig bladder as a ball and shoot it into the diddle-net for fun.

4.3.4 Ice Skating

The Manchus and their ancestors have been living for a long time in northeast China, where the ice freezing period each year lasts for more than half a year. Living in the snow and ice environment, in order to meet the needs of life, production, and military affairs, they have invented skating shoes, ice trolleys, bed sleds, and other equipment for ice transportation, thus acquiring various skating skills.

It is said that the Manchu invented skates early in the Jurchen period. Legend has it that when Wanyan Aguda, the leader of the Jurchens back then, later Emperor Taizu of Jin, united with other Jurchen tribes to fight against the Liao, which stationed massive forces at the confluence of the Songhua River and the Yitong River in Binzhou. In contrast, Wanyan Aguda had only three thousand soldiers camped by the Songhua River. Generals of Liao troops believed that Jurchens could not come because the heavy snow had paralyzed rivers and roads, so they stayed in the city un-vigilantly, having feasts and fun. One night, there were several Jurchen young men, each carrying a bag made of roe deer fur. They skated swiftly to the face of Aguda with their skating shoes squeaking on the ice, and said that they were sent from the Tieli Vassal State to transport arrows. Seeing the ice skates (roe deer fur boots with two small iron rods tied under the wooden sole) they wore, an idea occurred to Wanyan Aguda. Immediately he ordered people to make three thousand pairs of skating shoes as soon as possible to attack Liao troops stationed at Binzhou. Aguda's troops set off at night and arrived at Liao barracks at Binzhou in the early morning. When they launched an attack, Liao soldiers were still sleeping. Later, skates quickly spread from the army to the civilians, which became Jurchen's skating equipment.

Although the legend cannot be regarded as a historical fact, it is recorded in the book *Scripts in Manchu Language* that at the beginning of the 17th century, Nurhachi's troops once rescued Mogen City from a siege with the aid of Wula Skates. Here go the records: "In the Tianming Period of Emperor Taizu (1616–1626), Bargut Tribe besieged the city of Mogen. Fei Gulie, one of Nurhachi's generals, led his soldiers who wore Wula Skates and tugged artillery with bed sled and rushed along the ice on the Naowen River for rescue. They marched forward for 700 *li* in a single day. When the Manchu reinforcements arrived, Bargut soldiers didn't even notice. Until the Manchu soldiers fired the artillery, they were totally shocked and thought that the Manchu soldiers had fallen from the sky. Then, Mogen City was rescued from the siege."[100] Now some ancient skates are still preserved in the Palace Museum, but the differences between the Wula Skates and other ancient skates have not yet been verified. However, there are many records in ancient documents on the skates preserved in the Palace Museum. For instance, *Notes on the Age of Yanjing* records as follows: "The skates are made of iron, which is tied to the shoes with a rope. Once one starts to skate, it is difficult to stop; people with good skating skills are as agile as a flying swallow. The scene is very enjoyable."[101] Bed sled in the Qing Dynasty is also recorded in this book (see Fig. 4-7): "After the winter solstice, thick ice has formed on the lake and river, and there will be people playing on the bed sled in Shichahai, the moat of the Forbidden City, and Qingfeng Water Gate (also called the Second Water Gate). One person's pull can make a bed sled slide quickly. Bed sled is known to be made of wood with iron bars underneath, which can seat three or four people, with a length of 5 *chi* and a width of 3 *chi*. When the snow stops and the weather is good, people will play on the bed sled on ice in full enjoyment. After the beginning of spring, people can no longer play on the bed sled, because the weather is getting warmer and the ice layer becomes thinner. Once, a bed sled fell into an ice hole, and the dragging man ran away without rescue. In recent years, princes and senior officials who have done meritorious services or were awarded by the emperor have also been allowed to ride the royal bed sleds in Xiyuan. The royal bed sled is gorgeous and has a canopy to shelter from wind and snow. It was recorded in *Miscellaneous Copy of Yiqing Pavilion* that: "In the Ming Dynasty, people who are tasteful in Jishuitan in winter will tie more than ten bed sleds together, spreading blankets on them, bringing wine set, drinking and entertaining on the 'big' bed sled. It is one of the favorite activities of chivalrous men and gentlemen."[102]

Fig. 4-7 Picture of Bed Sled Game

Emperor Gaozong of the Qing Dynasty described the skates at that time in more detail in his work *On Ice-Play*: "The ice boot has a sharp runner. Some skaters wear leather knee pads and use leather to make the skates stouter. Some skating shoes have two runners, so that skaters are not easy to fall. Some skates are equipped with blades as runners, with which the skaters can go faster." Cao Yin of the Qing Dynasty wrote about the blades of figure skating skates in the *Three Poems on Ice Ball*: "The ice boots are very compact, and the tip of the metal blade is jagged ice picks,"[103] which is very similar to the blade of modern figure skates.

The Manchu ice-play are the representatives of the ancient ice games in our country. According to the *Secret Records of Manchu Old Archives*, the Manchu first held an ice-play meeting on the second day of the first lunar month in the third year of the Tianqi Period of the Emperor Xizong of the Ming Dynasty (AD 1623), when Nurhachi held the speed skating and ice *Cuju* and other games on the natural ice rink of the Taizi River (in present Liaoning). The participants were mainly Manchu and Mongolian nobles. Nurhachi and his Empress rewarded the contestants with silver (20 taels for the first prize winners and 12 taels for the second prize winners) in person. After the competition, a banquet was held on the ice as a token of congratulation.[104]

Emperor Shizu designated ice-play as a "national custom." Every year in the 12th lunar month, Qing emperor, princes, and nobles watched ice sports in three lakes, Beihai, Zhonghai, and Nanhai in Xiyuan (now Zhongnanhai). In *Ice-Play*, composed by Wu Shijian of the Qing Dynasty, he described Emperor Gaozong together with Empress Xiaosheng watching the ice game during the Qianlong Period, and the descriptions are as follows: "Emperor Gaozong and Empress Xiaosheng sit on the royal bed sled to watch the ice games, and the retinues held colorful flags. The yellow canopy is laid in the middle, under which sit on the majesty, marten fur-sheathed."[105] Every tenth lunar month, preparations for the ice sports meet will start: assemble athletes and arrange venues and equipment for competitions and performances. *A General Survey of Imperial Documents* records: "Every year in the tenth lunar month, each Banner by quota selects 200 excellent skating players from Sentinel Battalions, Guard Battalions, and other departments, and sends them to the capital for attending the annual royal ice games. Department of Royal Court Affairs prepares equipment such as skates, bows, arrows, and ball stands. After the winter solstice, the weather becomes cold and the lakes and rivers freeze, turning into natural ice rinks. Otherwise, people pour water on the ground to make an ice rink. When everything is ready, ice shows and competitions will begin. *A General Survey of Imperial Documents* continues: "After the winter solstice, the emperor will go to Yingtai and other places to arrange ice-play. Soldiers will be divided into two rows. The twelve in the front of each row wear a red and yellow mandarin jacket, and the rest wear red and yellow shoulder-length gowns. A total of 160 soldiers and 40 young children who are going to shoot the ball, all wear mandarin jackets with small flags on their backs as the symbol of their Banner—the color of the small flag is consistent with each of Eight Banners' representative colors. Players from Eight Banners shoot in sequence. After the competition, the emperor will reward three first prize winners with 10 taels of silver, three second prize winners with 8 taels of silver, three third prize winners with 6 tales of silver, and the remaining soldiers each with 4 taels of silver. These prizes are provided by the National Treasury of the Department of Royal Court Affairs."[106]

A Grand View of the Unofficial History of the Qing Dynasty records the grand occasion of royal ice games: "In the tenth lunar month every year, three lakes of Beihai, Zhonghai, and Nanhai in Xiyuan will have formed thick ice. On an auspicious day, the emperor will take the royal bed sled to watch ice games there. There is an iron bar in the middle of the bottom of the skates. Put it on with a powerful run-up and you can ride swiftly. The speed skating competition will be held on the first day of the games. At a distance of 2 or 3 *li* away from the emperor's bed sled, the soldiers will stand in the neat array and set up the big flags, and then the emperor would board the bed sled. Hearing a signal of gunfire, the soldiers will dash to the emperor at full speed. The guards and retinues around the emperor will help speed skaters to brake and stop when they approach the emperor's bed sled. Speed skating will reward the first and second prizes in different standards. The next day ball catch will be held. The soldiers are divided into left and right queues, the left in red and the right in yellow. One of the emperor's retinues kicks a ball into the crowd, and the soldiers scramble for it. The soldier who gets the ball throws it again like the retinue, and the soldiers catch it again. Next is the ball archery: "One soldier holds a small flag of which the color is consistent with the man's Banner and takes the lead; two soldiers carry bows and arrows behind him, forming a long queue. There are some two hundred soldiers holding the small flags, and the number of soldiers behind with bows and arrows double. As the queue winds on the ice, it looks like a dragon from a distance. A gate is set up close to the bed sled of the emperor, with two balls hung above and below it. The soldiers first shoot the ball below the gate, and the person who hits the target will be rewarded. Those who have given a shot shall get back in position in the queue. The child holds a flag at the end of the queue, just like a dragon's tail. According to the old system, each Banner has its own performance team, and the emperor will watch their performances in turn and reward them according to their performance." The ice game at that time lasted for a few days. Speed skating competition is on the first day, and the ball catch is on the second day, in which the score is evaluated by the times of catch. The ball archery contest goes on the third day. The entire ice games are immersed in a large-scale and splendid scene (see Fig. 4-8). This painting is background by Zhonghai, which depicts in detail the spectacular scene of the royal ice games in the **Qing Dynasty**, Which includes speed skating, figure skating, acrobatics on ice, ball archery, etc., reflecting that ice sports have reached a fairly high level in the Qing Dynasty.

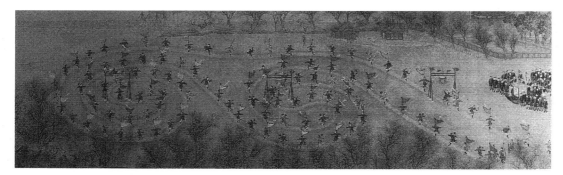

Fig. 4-8 Picture of the Partial Ice-Play

In 1792, the 57th year of Qianlong Period of Emperor Gaozong, Galun, the Chief Executive of Tibet, came to Beijing to watch a royal ice-play. He described: "Emperor Gaozong watched the skating show early in the morning at a large lake to the north of Baita Temple (now Miaoying Temple in Beijing). The ice on the lake was as flat and smooth as a mirror. When the emperor arrived at the lake, he boarded a sedan chair, which was slowly pulled by the manpower. When the sedan chair reached the center of the lake, firecrackers suddenly broke out from all sides. In the sound of firecrackers, more than 100 people wearing colorful costumes and flower crowns dashed to the emperor and knelt before him as a salute. They each carried a bow and arrows and wore skates with metal blades. Sliding on the ice, they were as agile as fish in the water or swallows in the air. At the same time, they shot the bouquets that hung in the distance. When a bouquet was shot, it burst out the sound of firecrackers. What an amazing scene!"[107]

Ice-play is a means of training the soldiers of Eight Banners. *Notes on the Age of Yanjing* reads: "Quoted from *Examinations of Old Stories* that every year in the 11th lunar month, the royal family will hold ice games on the frozen lakes in Xiyuan. It is both a kind of non-serious military training and a national custom. The emperor also rewards the contestants."[108] The scale of ice-play was very large. Speed skating, which can improve the combat capability of the speedy march on ice for the troops, thereby it has always been the main focus of the emperor's inspection.[109] The emperor of the Qing Dynasty, who often highlighted the power of bows and arrows to stabilize the country, then added ball archery to ice games.

During the Kangxi and Qianlong Periods, the heyday of the Qing Dynasty, ice-play gradually evolved from "military parades" to "entertainment performances." At that time, a large-scale group of calisthenics named Bai Shan Zi was added into ice games, which absorbed some movements from martial arts and acrobatics, and the difficulty of the movements and the artistic level reached their peak in ancient times. The performers perform 24 difficult moves (see Fig. 4-9). The performance was neat and uniform, and the scene was spectacular and enjoyable. For example, the event "One skater, thirteen movements" was a kind of single skating, in which the performer must perform thirteen figure skating movements innovated by himself. The outstanding performers of this event included Xigui, who was titled "Swallow on Ice" by Emperor Gaozong, Haiying, who invented backward skating, and Yang Erli, who was famous for his performance of Big Bell.

Fig. 4-9 Pictures of Some Speed Skating and Figure Skating Movements in the Qing Dynasty

The Qing government has a Special Force specializing in ice skating. Soldiers in this troop were called "Skates," and skating coaches were called "Skates Coach." The soldiers of the Specials Forces are mostly strong and agile, excelling at a certain field, most of whom were selected from the Eight Banners. They were appointed to the different troops based on their expertise. Every four battalions constitute one Group (Yi), with its own head; every two make up one Guidai, with its governor. Each battalion is in charge of five squads, each with its own captain in a number of 25 soldiers." So altogether, there are 5,000 soldiers in the Specials Force.

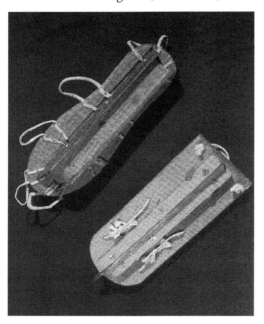

Fig. 4-10 Picture of Skates in the Qing Dynasty

In order to better organize large-scale ice-play, the Qing government established a special organization called "Skates Department." During the annual troop-inspection period (the tenth, eleventh, twelfth, and first lunar month), the Skates Department would select 1,600 excellent skaters from Eight Banners" Specials Force (200 per Banner), to form the "Intrepid Skates Battalion," which was under the direct leadership of the Skates Department. The Intrepid Skates Battalion would organize intensive training, host ice games and performances, and take responsibility for the emperor's inspection. After the inspection period, the soldiers of the Intrepid Skates Battalion would return to Specials Force in Eight Banners, and continue their daily training. Skating in the Qing Dynasty reached its climax in terms of skate equipment manufacturing (see Fig. 4-10, which are collected in the China Sports Museum), the scale of ice-play, skating technical movements, and the administration of ice shows, which were of the first class in the world at that time.

At the end of the Qing Dynasty, internal and external troubles gradually deepened, and national and military power was weakened. As a consequence, skating lost its material and spiritual foundation. Skates Department, the organization for ice-play, was closed down, and the system of royal ice games was abolished. Yet, skating, as an entertaining and competitive sport, was still enjoyed by the Manchu and northerners, who even excelled at it, so skating was widely developed among the people. "Around the Beihai Bridge, the scenery is picturesque. The west wind is blowing. The surface of the frozen lake is smooth as a mirror. Tens of thousands of people crowd to watch skating." As we can see, this poem is a true record of the scene in that masses of ice skaters frolicked on the ice despite the icy weather.

4.3.5 Pair Skating

"Pair Skating," as a traditional sport, is evolved from pair skating in ice skating. Dating back to its history, we can find that pair skating has long been one of the military training items of the Eight

Banners' soldiers, which intended to improve the soldiers' ability to coordinate operations and rescue the wounded. *A General Survey of Literature in the Qing Dynasty* incorporates works of court painters of the Qianlong Period, which records as follows: "In the tenth lunar month every year, the emperor would review the skating performance of the Eight Banners' soldiers on the icy Beihai, which was considered as a training and drill as well. The number of soldiers who participated in each inspection reached 1,600 (200 per Banner), which was unparalleled in the world at that time. During the inspection, soldiers were divided into two groups, performing at the same time. Every soldier wore a small flag on his back to identify his Banner and also to help the scorekeeper record. In addition to speed skating, the review items also included figure skating, as well as other types of ice competitions." In the last years of the Qing Dynasty, the military schools organized by the Westernization Group, such as the Beiyang Marine Academy, incorporated Pair Skating into its physical education class. In Pair Skating, two people, side by side, with their inner side legs bound together, skate forward in perfect coordination. It was very similar to a three-legged race, very unique. During the ice-free seasons in spring, summer, and autumn, training was carried out on land, so the "Pair Skating" was labeled as "Pair Running." At the end of the Qing Dynasty, in the military schools set up by the westernization movement, such as the Beiyang Naval Academy, "Pair Running" was just included in their sports class.

In addition to the Manchu sports mentioned above, the rulers of the Qing Dynasty also promoted both the military and civilians specialized in competitive sports, in order to strengthen physical fitness and improve combat capability. The historical record goes as follows: "In the past, during the Dragon Boat Festival, the imperial court would race dragon boats and initiate soldiers to compete in willow-shooting, which were intended to train the navy and army. People now are just not aware of its meaning. The custom of willow-shooting has disappeared, and the dragon boat race still remains, yet it is more entertainment-oriented than before and lacks military significance. Now the government should restore the old customs by asking the navy to practice boat races at the Dragon Boat Festival. More boats can be built, and more bows and arrows can be made. On that very day, all officials and citizens were ordered to come and watch the games, in which the navy and land forces would give their full play. The authority shall reward the outstanding soldiers and encourage citizens to donate money and materials to those who performed well. Through the initiatives from both government and civilians, soldiers will unceasingly sharpen and improve their skills. In the long run, the significance of these activities will be beyond anything."[110] The authority tried every means to train the military and civilians, especially by means of the sports featured folklore characteristics, so as to encourage more people to get in and thereby achieve the expected results.

The items of martial arts in the Imperial Examination of Martial Arts in the Qing Dynasty also reflect the level of sports training in both theory and practice at that time. The rulers of the Qing Dynasty attached great importance to the development of martial arts, and included it in the Imperial Examination. In addition to various types of martial arts practiced by folks, the Imperial Examination included many other events. For example, in the 24th year of Guangxu Period, Emperor Dezong decreed to reform the system of the Imperial Examination for Martial Arts, changing the examination items, in the martial forms of riding, shooting, stone lifting, etc. "The imperial examination system was set up to give civilians the opportunity to come to the fore, enter the upper classes of society, and change their fates. As for training in the Imperial Examination for Martial Arts, it should be based on the intention of developing the talents for the country. The First (Tong Shi), Second (Xiang Shi), and Third Round (Hui Shi) of Imperial Examination for Martial Arts should follow the old system, testing events items like the long-handle saber, riding, mounted archery, stone lifting, foot archery, etc. Both the rewards and punishment systems should be set up, followed strictly by the administration at all levels. No cheating is allowed. ... After the candidate is enrolled, he must be sent by his affiliation to the National Artillery Battalions for practice. As for the establishment of provincial military academies, provincial governors are entitled to have the final say. All qualified candidates for the Imperial Examination of Martial Arts who have not yet enlisted in the army should be assigned to the nearest army school to study different subjects and train skills of various kinds, such as riding, shooting, lifting, and fighting, which are all expected to resist invasion."[111] It can be seen that "selecting military talents through the Imperial Examination of Martial Arts" was a standing mechanism in the Qing Dynasty. There were state Artillery Battalions and provincial military academies, and the form was responsible for instating qualified candidates like Wu Jinshi, and training them afterwards.

In addition to the above-mentioned mechanism of "selecting military talents through the Imperial Examination of Martial Arts," the use of talents was also very methodical at that time. People of different ages, weights, and physiques had different functions: "The selection of soldiers must be based on their physical characteristics, and they will be incorporated into different arms of services and equipped with appropriate weapons. In terms of soldier selection, you must first know how to classify them before you can do a good job and then make the best use of them. Years from 20 to 40 is one's prime of his life, and his physical condition begins to decline after the age of 40. But even men between 20 to 40 years old, should be further classified and equipped with appropriate weapons according to their height, weight, physique, etc., so as to give full play to their potential. Generally speaking, soldiers with sharp eyesight and long limbs are suitable for bows and arrows, those with short stature are suitable for shields and knives, and those of short fuse with scary faces are suitable for pistols and broadswords. All weapons must be wielded by soldiers who are strong and endurable, as youngsters and teens have not yet fully developed their muscles and bones. If asked to practice these items, they will exhaust themselves and collapse very soon. Tall and strong soldiers would better use shields of 2 *chi* in diameter and short swords, charging into the battlefield to fight the enemy at close range. So the key to selecting soldiers is to first accurately identify which kind of weapon is suitable for them, and then let them practice this weapon till he becomes skillful. Those who know this fact and do it well are the ones you can discuss military training with."[112] At that time, classifying people according to their physical characteristics was an indispensable prerequisite for selecting soldiers. People in the Qing Dynasty realized the law of physical growth and development, and applied this law well to soldier selection so as to make full use of human resources.

Zhao Yi, in the Qing Dynasty, had his own views on martial arts training. He said: "In peacetime, the military officers wear gorgeous costumes, leading easy lives. Without leaders charging ahead, the soldiers of course will lack courage and incentive to advance, so they cannot be blamed for failing to render meritorious service. But cultivating strong soldiers from scratch is very costly. So the authority recruits soldiers from the civilians, trains them, and gives them favors so that they can safeguard the governments in emergencies. Famous generals in the Southern Song Dynasty, such as Han Shizhong, Yue Fei, and Wu Lin, trained their soldiers with fighting tactics. Qi Jiguang ever held the belief that soldiers must be trained regularly to be sturdy and strong. So everything is for training soldiers. When Qi Jiguang first served as an army commander in Zhejiang, seeing that soldiers were not trained well and their combat ability was low, he dispatched 3,000 outstanding soldiers from Yiwu to teach these bad-trained soldiers how to use various weapons. Afterwards his troops became very powerful.[113] It can be seen that proficiency in martial arts is acquired through diligence. Reading the imperial edict below, we may have a deeper understanding of the training of martial arts, including riding, shooting, and stabbing, in the Qing Dynasty: "In terms of training soldiers, daily training must be effective, and every soldier must be able to contribute." In my humble view, physical strength, if used every day, will continue to strengthen; otherwise, it will gradually decline. Training should be conducted anytime and anywhere, morning and evening, here and there. Firstly, in practicing archery, the fist and wrist must be strong and stable. The key is to draw the bow in a standard manner. Soldiers should be taught to put their bodies and feet in the right place. In each round of training, soldiers were asked to draw a bow with each hand respectively a hundred times, and both hands a hundred times, with a maximum of 300 hundred times. The archer must keep his shoulders horizontal and upper body straight, gathering strength from every part of the body and putting it on the bow. The left and right sides should be evenly skilled. When the fist and wrist are stable, the bow force will naturally increase, and the archery will be more accurate. Secondly, in practicing firing with a rifle, the elbow, waist, and abdomen must be strong and stable. The key to firing with a rifle lies in holding. Train the soldiers in the positions of standing and twisting waists. Let them hold a heavy brick in the left hand for 20 seconds to simulate the posture of holding a rifle. With the stability of elbow and waist, he can shoot nicely and well. Thirdly, in practicing riding, the legs must be strong, and the center of gravity is set on the feet. The key to riding is the legs and feet. So, make more wooden horses, 5 *cun* higher than the average real horses, and equip them with saddles and stirrups. First, ask the soldiers to practice mounting the wooden horse through stirrups without grasping the saddle and practice on both sides. Then ask them to mount via saddle instead of stepping on the stirrups twenty or thirty times each round, and the distance from the horse is a little farther than usual. Such training can strengthen the soldiers' legs and feet to be strong, agile, and stable on horseback, and further skilled at archery in all directions on horseback. Lastly, as for the spear, it is the basic training item for archers. Spearing doesn't need too much skill, as long as it's accurate and powerful at a close distance in battles. The spear practice of shielding soldiers is very simple and flexible, so no further training is added in this regard. The above-mentioned training should not be overdone to exhaust the soldiers, nor should they be out of practice or insufficient practice. As long as the soldiers keep training, they will absolutely make progress every day.[114] This paragraph clearly narrates and reflects the military training practice in the Qing Dynasty, indicating a proper case to stand for the training level at that time.

Therefore, it can be concluded from the above literature that since the prosperity of the northern national sports in the Yuan and Qing Dynasty, these nationalities have formed sports training methods and theories to guide the development of sports in their time.

In addition, in the Qing Dynasty, there were also some other sports such as Galaha, flying kites, swinging, and dragon boat racing. These sports emerged like blooming flowers, and contributed to the evolution and prosperity of national sports in China. From the above, it can be seen that Manchu sports in the Qing Dynasty were very rich, some of which have not yet been sorted through. From the history of various ethnic minorities in China in ancient times, we can infer that no ethnic group had such a rich sports culture as the Manchu. Even the Manchu, given its productivity level, is not supposed to be so rich in sports. However, this is purely true. The rich sports culture of the Manchu, can be attributed to the reference and integration of various ethnic cultures in ancient China.

4.4 Decline of Ancient Northern National Sports

The 19th century was a period when Chinese society was greatly influenced by Western countries, and a period when Chinese society suffered from turbulence. The overseas students sent by the Qing Dynasty, who were deeply affected by the Western culture, gave rise to a giant wave of reforms after return; Western Christians who came to China propagated advanced culture; the Western invasion of China particularly, forced the Qing rulers in large degree, to have realized that traditional cold weapons could no longer adapt to war. Driven by both internal and external factors, the Qing rulers replaced traditional mounted archery training with the more advanced military form. Since then, traditional national sports in northern China have gradually declined.

The first hit was the most characteristic riding and shooting culture. By the end of the Qing Dynasty, the mass use of rifles transformed traditional war forms. Riding and cold weapons such as arrows, spears, and swords were no longer the main combat tools. So the Qing government increased its investment in guns and cannons, and reduced investment in training such as riding and shooting. The training of horses was also not as developed as before; as a result, national riding and shooting culture gradually went downhill. At that time, areas still maintaining archery culture well were mainly Mobei, as well as the livestock areas in Gansu, Qinghai, and Xinjiang, because these were places impacted relatively late and less by the Western sports culture. However, due to the lack of attention from the Qing government and backward economic development in these areas, the progress of riding and shooting culture was also restricted.

Secondly, official wrestling was in decline. In the face of both domestic and external troubles, the Qing government had no energy to develop wrestling, but channeled great attention to military gymnastics training. "Shanpuying," the royal professional wrestling body, and Skates Department, were both disbanded, which reflected the huge transition of the Qing authority's emphasis on these sports. Wrestling was just maintained in some remote areas in the north and carried out by the commoners. For example, the Mongolian nationality has all along retained wrestling, and Beijing folks have also carried out wrestling activities, which have, to some extent, inherited these national sports.

Moreover, many other traditional sports of ethnic groups have lost their developing foundation. At the end of the Qing Dynasty, the ruling class was corrupt and incompetent; domestic uprisings emerged one after another, local regimes asserted independence, and foreign powers continued to invade, leading to continuous wars and national turmoil, in which people suffered a lot. In addition to the official training on the use of rifles and artillery, the ancient northern national sports were mainly conducted by the local organizations, the populace as well as people who were dragged out in degradation, all of which helped to carry forward the above sports to a certain extent. Against this backdrop, the ancient northern ethnic sports gradually declined.

4.5 Summary

During this development stage, Mongolian and Manchu built up the regimes of the Yuan and Qing Dynasties, defining the boundary of China's territory in ancient times and realizing the climax of ethnic integration. The productivity level was further improved, and the agriculture and animal husbandry economies effectively complemented each other. In this period, sports activities were rich and colorful, and people from all walks of life participated actively. Organization and management of sports were relatively systematic, and new sports events continued to emerge. Ancient northern ethnic sports culture thus became unprecedentedly inclusive and prosperous. However, on the other hand, at the end of the Qing Dynasty, the government was corrupt and incompetent, thereby leading to weak national power and suffering livelihood, which further led to the rapid decline of northern national sports from prosperity; second, the widespread use of firearms pushed some former military practical training to a secondary position; third, the introduction of modern Western sports had a huge impact on northern national sports. In a sports system that has not yet matured and is easily impacted by the above factors, these northern national sports were gradually neglected and then abandoned by the government and eventually declined.

NOTES

1. [Qing] He Ning, *A Brief Account of the Three States*, 1st ed. (Taipei Cheng Wen Publishing House, March 1968).
2. [Qing] Wang Shuzhan, *Records of Rites and Customs in Xinjiang*, 1st ed. (Taipei Cheng Wen Publishing Company, March 1968), 19–20.
3. [Qing] Ji Huang et al., ed., *Yue Kao XXI · San Yue, and Bai Xi · Huibu Musicians*, vol. 175 of *A General Survey of Imperial Documents*, bk. 635 of *The Complete Collection of Si Ku Quan Shu of Wenyuan Pavilion* (Shanghai Ancient Books Publishing House), 824.
4. Mahmud Kashgari, *Divan lgat at-Turk*, translated by Xiao Zhongyi et al., vol. 3 (The Ethnic Publishing House, February 2002), 370–371.
5. Lang Ying, *On Manas* (Inner Mongolia University Press, 1999).
6. [Qing] Xiao Xiong, *Miscellaneous Poems in Western Xinjiang · Xiyue* (1934).
7. Wang Zhonghan, *Chinese National History*, rev. 1st ed. (China Social Sciences Press, 1994), 585–587.
8. [Ming] Song Lian et al., *Emperor Renzong III*, vol. 26 of *History of the Yuan Dynasty*, 1st ed. (Zhonghua Book Company, April 1976), 589.

9. [Ming] Song Lian et al., *Emperor Yingzong I*, vol. 27 of *History of the Yuan Dynasty*, 1st ed. (Zhonghua Book Company, April 1976), 603.
10. [Sweden] Constantin Mouradgea d'Ohsson, *Histoire des Mongols*, translated by Feng Chengjun, vol.1 (Zhonghua Book Company, 1962), 156.
11. [Iran] Juvayni, *History of World Conquerors*, tranlated by He Gaoji, revised by Weng Dujian, vol. 1 (Inner Mongolia People's Publishing House, 1980), 29–30.
12. [Ming] Yin Geng, *Translated Words*; Shen Jiefu, *Collection of Records*, vol. 56 (1938), 29.
13. [Iran] Juvayni, *History of World Conquerors*, translated by He Gaoji, revised by Weng Dujian, vol. 1 (Inner Mongolia People's Publishing House, 1980), 95–156.
14. Ding Qian, "Grand Ceremony of the Yuan Dynasty," *Zhejiang Library Journal* 7, no. 2 (1915).
15. [Song] Peng Daya, *Hei Da Shi Lue*, vol. 423 of *"History Department · Miscellany" of Si Ku Quan Shu* (Shanghai Chinese Classic Publishing House, 1995), 536.
16. Juvayni, *History of World Conquerors*, translated by He Gaoji, revised by Weng Dujian, vol. 1 (Inner Mongolia People's Publishing House, 1980), 32.
17. [Italy] Macro Polo, *Marco Polo's Travels*, translated by Feng Chengjun, vol. 1 (Shanghai Book Store Press, 2000), 24–26.
18. [Italy] Macro Polo, *Marco Polo's Travels (II)*, translated by Feng Chengjun, vol. 4 (Shanghai Book Store Press, 2000), 784–785.
19. [Ming] Yin Geng, *Translated Words*; Shen Jiefu, *People in Min'e Moutain*, vol. 56 of *Collection of Records* (The Commercial Press, 1938), 20.
20. [Yuan] Xiong Mengxiang, *Records of Xi Jin Zhi* (Beijing Ancient Books Publishing House, 1983), 211–212.
21. Ibid., 204.
22. Rong Suhe, Zhao Yongxian, Zalaga et al., Chapter 2 of "Wedding Message" in *History of Mongolian Literature*, vol. 2, 1st ed. (Inner Mongolia People's Publishing House, December 2002), 69–99.
23. Xu Ke, *Customs*, vol. 5 of *Classified Anthology of Anecdotes of the Qing Dynasty*, 1st ed. (Zhonghua Book Company, October 1984), 2214–2215.
24. Xu Ke, *Tactics*, vol. 6 of *Classified Anthology of Anecdotes of the Qing Dynasty*, 1st ed. (Zhonghua Book Company, August 1986), 2989.
25. [Qing] Lu Jianzeng, *Songs of Frontier Fortress · Bamboo*.
26. [Qing] Xiao Xiong, *Playfulness*, vol. 3 of *Miscellaneous Poems in Western Xinjiang* (1934), 36.
27. [Ming] Tao Zongyi, *Gui You Chi*, vol. 1 of *Farming in Nan Villiage*, 12th ed. (Shanghai Bookstore Publishing House, 1985), 24.
28. [Yuan] Yang Yunfu and [Qing] Bao Tingbo, *Miscellaneous Chants of Luanjing* in *Zhi Bu Zu Zhai* (1921).
29. [Ming] Song Lian et al., *Biography of Zhaba'er Khwajah*, vol. 20 of *History of the Yuan Dynasty*, 1st ed. (Zhonghua Book Company, April 1976), 2961.
30. *Records of Emperor Shengzu Ren*, vol.148 of *Records of the Qing Dynasty*, 1st ed. (Zhonghua Book Company, September 1985), 632.
31. Li Xiusheng, *Ode to Jamah*, vol. 1761 of *A Collection of Essays in the Yuan Dynasty*, 1st ed. (Phoenix Publishing House, December 2004), 869–870.
32. [Qing] Zhao Yi, *Miscellaneous Records of Yan Pu*, vol. 1, 1st ed. (Zhonghua Book Company, May 1982), 13–14.
33. Xu Ke, *Feast in Mongolia*, vol. 2 of *Classified Anthology of Anecdotes of the Qing Dynasty*, 1st edition. (Zhonghua Book Company, November 1981), 495.
34. Xu Ke, *Tactics*, vol. 6 of *Classified Anthology of Anecdotes of the Qing Dynasty*, 1st ed. (Zhonghua Book Company, August 1986), 2989.
35. 4.2.7–4.2.10 in this section mainly refer to Professor Xu Yuliang's *History of Chinese Minority Sports* (Central University for Nationalities Press, October 2005), 86–94.
36. [Qing] Ye Mingli, *Miscellaneous Records of Qiaoxi* (Zhonghua Book Company, 1985).
37. [Qing] Sa Ying'e, *An Extra Introduction of Ji Lin*, vol. 8 (Wen Hai Publishing House, 1974), 10–12.
38. [Yuan] Xiong Mengxiang, *Analysis of Xi Jin Zhi* (Beijing Ancient Books Publishing House, 1983), 203.
39. [Ming] Song Lian et al., *History of the Yuan Dynasty*, vol. 98, 1st ed. (Zhonghua Book Company, April 1976), 2508.
40. [France] René Grousset, *History of the Mongol Empire*. Similar descriptions are found in section 14.

41. [USSR] Nai · Yang, *Badukhan · Nayadum in Mongolian Amy*, quoted from Xu Yuliang, *Sports History of Ethnic Minorities in China*, 76.
42. Rong Suhe, Zhao Yongxian, and Zha Laga et al., *History of Mongolian Literature*, vol. 2, 1st ed. (Inner Mongolia People's Publishing House, December 2002), 138.
43. [Qing] Blo bzang chos ldan, Chapter 42 of "Zhama Fair and Oboo Festival in the Temple" in *A Guide to Mongolian Customs*, translated by Zhao Jingyang (Liaoning Ethnic Publishing House, 1988).
44. [Italy] Marco Polo, *Marco Polo's Travels*, translated by Feng Chengjun (Shanghai Bookstore Press, 2000).
45. [Qing] Jin Zhijie, *Art and Literature III*, vol. 14 of **Annals of Koubei Three Tings** (Taipei Cheng Wen Publishing House, March 1968), 11–13.
46. *Annals of Emperor Taizong*, vol. 18 of *Records of the Qing Dynasty*, 1st ed. (Zhonghua Book Company, September 1985).
47. Fu Rongga et al., *Annals of Ujimqin Custom* (Inner Mongolia People's Publishing House, 1992), 194.
48. [Mongolia] Ji Damdin, Chapter 2 of *Mongolian Wrestling*, complied by Brintgus and Gao Cai,(Inner Mongolia Culture Press, 1983).
49. [Mongolia] Re Galindibu and Re Wusuhu Bayaer, *Three Kind of Arts on the Prairie* (Inner Mongolia Education Press, 1984), 53.
50. [Mongolia] Re Galindibu and Re Wusuhu Bayaer, *Three Kind of Arts on the Prairie* (Inner Mongolia Education Press, 1984), 3.
51. **The Compilation Committee of Baarin Right Banner Annals,** *Annals of Baarin Right Banner* (Inner Mongolia People's Publishing House, 1990), 424.
52. Song Rubu and Siqin Bilige, *A Chronicle of Alashan Customs* (Inner Mongolia People's Publishing House, 1989), 269–309.
53. Institute of History and Literature of Taiwan Academia Sinica, *Chronicles of Ming Emperor Shenzong Xian*, vol. 444, printed copy (1962), 2.
54. [Ming] Song Lian et al., *Geographia II*, vol. 59 of *History of the Yuan Dynasty*, 1st ed. (Zhonghua Book Company, April 1976), 1400.
55. *Emperor Taizu Alone Fighting 40 Warriors*, vol. 2 of *Records of the Qing Dynasty · Manchu*, 1st ed. (Zhonghua Book Company, November 1986), 34.
56. *Emperor Taizu Defeating 800 Warriors*, vol. 2 of *Records of the Qing Dynasty · Manchu*, 1st ed. (Zhonghua Book Company, November 1986), 33.
57. *Emperor Taizu Shooting in the Field*, vol. 2 of *Records of the Qing Dynasty · Manchu*, 1st ed. (Zhonghua Book Company, November 1986), 35.
58. *Chronicles of Emperor Taizong Wen*, vol. 30 of *Records of the Qing Dynasty · Manchu*, 1st ed. (Zhonghua Book Company, June 1985), 386.
59. *Chronicles of Emperor Taizong Wen*, vol. 32 of *Records of the Qing Dynasty*, 1st ed. (Zhonghua Book Company, 1st edition, June 1985), 404.
60. [Qing] Ji Huang et al., *Complete Collection of Si Ku Quan Shu of Wenyuan Pavilion*, vol. 141 of *A General Survey of Imperial Documents* (Shanghai Ancient Books Publishing House, 1987), 111–112.
61. *Chronicles of Emperor Taizong Wen*, vol. 24 of *Records of the Qing Dynasty*, 1st ed. (Zhonghua Book Company, June 1985), 313.
62. *Chronicles of Emperor Taizong Wen*, vol. 54 of *Records of the Qing Dynasty*,1st ed. (Zhonghua Book Company, June 1985), 729.
63. *Chronicles of Emperor Taizong Wen*, vol. 13 of *Records of the Qing Dynasty*,1st ed. (Zhonghua Book Company, June 1985), 179.
64. [Qing] Zhao Lian, *Miscellaneous Records of Xiao Ting*, proofread by He Yingfang, 1st ed. (Zhonghua Book Company, December 1980).
65. *Chronicles of Emperor Shizu Zhang*, vol. 93 of *Records of the Qing Dynasty*, 1st ed. (Zhonghua Book Company, August 1985), 734.
66. *Chronicles of Emperor Shengzu Ren*, vol. 140 of *Records of the Qing Dynasty*, 1st ed. (Zhonghua Book Company, September 1985), 533.

67. *Chronicles of Emperor Shizu Zhang*, vol. 159 of *Records of the Qing Dynasty*, 1st ed. (Zhonghua Book Company, September 1985).
68. [Qing] Zhao Lian, *Princes Demoting Their Titles of Inheritance*, vol. 7 of *Miscellaneous Records of Xiao Ting*, proofread by He Yingfang (Zhonghua Book Company, December 1980), 204.
69. *Chronicles of Emperor Shizong Xian*, vol. 148 of *Records of the Qing Dynasty*, 1st ed. (Zhonghua Book Company, October 1985), 726.
70. [Qing] Ji Huang and Cao Renhu et al., *Selection VII*, vol. 53 of *A General Survey of the Literature of Dynasties*, bk. 636 of *The Complete Collection of Si Ku Quan Shu of Wenyuan Pavilion* (Shanghai Ancient Books Publishing House, 1987), 391.
71. [Qing] Ji Huang and Cao Renhu et al., *Military Test XIV*, vol. 192 of *A General Survey of the Literature of Dynasties*, bk. 636 of *The Complete Collection of Si Ku Quan Shu of Wenyuan Pavilion* (Shanghai Ancient Books Publishing House, 1987), 391.
72. *Chronicles of Emperor Renzong Rui*, vol. 62 of *Records of the Qing Dynasty*, 1st ed. (Zhonghua Book Company, June 1986), 832.
73. *Chronicles of Emperor Xuanzong Cheng*, vol. 247 of *Records of the Qing Dynasty*, 1st ed. (Zhonghua Book Company, October 1986), 717.
74. [Qing] Zhao Lian, *Sticking to the Origin*, vol. 1 of *Miscellaneous Records of Xiao Ting*, proofread by He Yingfang (Zhonghua Book Company, December 1980), 16.
75. [Qing] Zhao Lian, *Good at Archery*, vol.1 of *Miscellaneous Records of Xiao Ting*, proofread by He Yingfang (Zhonghua Book Company, December 1980), 373.
76. [Qing] Zhao Lian, *Communicating*, vol.2 of *Miscellaneous Records of Xiao Ting*, proofread by He Yingfang (Zhonghua Book Company, December 1980), 432.
77. [Qing] Zhao Lian, *Selection*, vol. 180 of *Miscellaneous Records of Xiao Ting*, proofread by He Yingfang (Zhonghua Book Company, December 1977), 3172.
78. *Chronicles of Emperor Dezong Jing*, vol. 485 of *Records of the Qing Dynasty*, 1st ed. (Zhonghua Book Company, 1st edition, July 1987), 412.
79. [Five Dynasties] Wang Renyu, *Ten Bygones in the Kaiyuan and Tianbao Periods* (Shanghai Ancient Books Publishing House, 1985), 83.
80. [Qing] Zhen Jun, *Tian Zhi Ou Wen (A Miscellany of Stories of Beijing)* (Beijing Ancient Books Publishing House, 1982).
81. *Records of the Qing Dynasty · Manchu*, vol. 2, 1st ed. (Zhonghua Book Company, November 1986).
82. [Qing] Gao Zongchi, *Chorography in the Qing Dynasty · Rituals*, vol. 2 of *All-Encompassing Library*, compiled by Wang Yunwu (The Commercial Press, 1935).
83. *Chronicles of Emperor Taizong Wen*, vol. 21 of *Records of the Qing Dynasty*, 1st ed. (Zhonghua Book Company, July 1985), 279.
84. Zhao Erxun, *Chronicle 65 · Qiu Xian*, vol. 90 of *Manuscripts of the Qing History* (Zhonghua Book Company, October 1977), 2668.
85. Chronicles of Emperor Shengzu Ren, vol. 285 of *Records of the Qing Dynasty*, 1st ed. (Zhonghua Book Company, July 1985), 781.
86. [Qing] Kun Gang et al., *Ministry of War · Hunting*, vol. 770, bk. 18 of *Examples of Qing Huidian* (Zhonghua Book Company, 1994), 14254.
87. *Chronicles of Emperor Shengzu Ren*, vol. 151 of *Records of the Qing Dynasty*, 1st ed. (Zhonghua Book Company, June 1985).
88. *Chronicles of Emperor Gaozong Chun*, vol. 136 of *Records of the Qing Dynasty*, 1st ed. (Zhonghua Book Company, June, 1985).
89. [Qing] Kun Gang et al., *Examples of Qing Huidian*, vol. 770 (Zhonghua Book Company, 1994), 14259.
90. [Qing] Zhao Lian, *Mulan Hunting System*, vol. 7 of *Miscellaneous Records of Xiao Ting*, proofread by He Yingfang, 1st ed. (Zhonghua Book Company, December 1980), 219–221.
91. Ibid.
92. [Qing] Kun Gang et al., *Ministry of War · Hunting*, vol. 770, bk. 18 of *Examples of Qing Huidian* (Zhonghua Book Company, 1994), 14256–14265.

93. [Qing] Zhen Jun, *Tian Zhi Ou Wen (A Miscellany of Stories of Beijing)*, vol. 1 (Beijing Ancient Books Publishing House, 1982), 12.
94. [Qing] Fu Cha Dun Chong, *Notes on the Age of Yanjing · Kicking Balls* (Beijing Ancient Books Publishing House, 1981), 86.
95. *Chronicles of Emperor Taizong Wen*, vol. 30 of *Records of the Qing Dynasty*, 1st ed. (Zhonghua Book Company, June 1985), 386.
96. [Qing] Li Guilin and Chang Shunxiu, *Records of Tianzhang*, vol. 6 of *General Annals of Jilin* (Jilin Literature and History Publishing House, 1986), 96.
97. [Qing] Wu Zhenchen, *A Brief Account of Ningguta* (Zhonghua Book Company, 1985), 170.
98. [Qing] Li Guilin and Chang Shunxiu. *Records of Imperial Edict*, vol.1 of *General Annals of Jilin* (Jilin Literature and History Publishing House, 1986), 15.
99. [Song] Yuwen Maozhao, Appendix I of "Memoirs of Jurchen," in *Annotations to the Records of the Great Jin Dynasty*, proofread by Cui Wenyin, 1st ed. (Zhonghua Book Company, July 1986), 589.
100. Refer to *Scripts in Manchu Language · Wula Skates*, vol. 38 of *The Continuing General Survey of the Literature of Dynasties*.
101. [Qing] Fucha Dunchong, *Notes on the Age of Yanjing · Ice Skates* (Beijing Ancient Books Publishing House, 1981), 91.
102. [Qing] Fucha Dunchong, *Notes on the Age of Yanjing · Bed Sled* (Beijing Ancient Books Publishing House, 1981), 91.
103. [Qing] Cao Yin, *Collection of Jian Pavillion · Three Poems on Ice Ball*, vol. 2 (Shanghai Ancient Books Publishing House. 1978), 432.
104. Jin Liang et al., ed. *The Secret Records of Manchu Old Archives*, printed copy (1929).
105. [Qing] Wu Shijian et al., "Ice-Play," in *Qing Gong Ci*, included by Wu Shijian et al. (Beijing Ancient Books Publishing House, 1986).
106. [Qing] Ji Huang et al., *Yuekao XXI · Ice Game*, vol. 175 of *A General Survey of Imperial Documents*, bk. 635 of *The Complete Collection of Si Ku Quan Shu of Wenyuan Pavilion* (Shanghai Ancient Books Publishing House, 1987), 823.
107. [Qing] Galun, *Biography of Rdo-rings-bstan-vdzin-dpal-vbgor*, cited from Xu Yuliang, *History of Chinese Minority Sports* (The Ethnic Publishing House, 2005), 61.
108. [Qing] Fucha Dunchong, *Notes on the Age of Yanjing · Ice Skates* (Beijing Ancient Books Publishing House, 1981), 91.
109. [Qing] Kun Gang et al., *Music Department · No. 250*, vol. 533 of *Examples of Qing Huidian* (Zhonghua Book Company, 1994), 12108.
110. [Qing] He Changling, *On Battle Tactics II*, vol. 71 of *A Collection of Essays on National Affairs during the Ming Dynasty*, printed copy (Taipei Wenhai Publishing House, 1966), 2.
111. *Chronicles of Emperor Dezong Jing*, vol. 430 of *Records of the Qing Dynasty*, 1st ed. (Zhonghua Book Company, September, 1985).
112. [Qing] He Changling, *On Battle Tactics II*, vol. 71 of *A Collection of Essays on National Affairs during the Ming Dynasty* (Taipei Wenhai Publishing House, 1966), 1–2.
113. Ibid., 4.
114. [Qing] He Changling and Yang Fang, Training Tactics, vol.71 of *A Collection of Essays on National Affairs during the Ming Dynasty* (Taipei Wenhai Publishing House, 1966), 8–9.

CHAPTER V

Origin and Evolution of Wrestling in China

5.1 Germination and Formation of Wrestling in the Qin and Han Dynasties

5.1.1 Germination and Formation of Pre-Qin Jiao-Li

In ancient times, wrestling, one of the most primitive and ancient sports of mankind, was also called Jiao-Li, Jiao-Di, Sumo, etc. In primitive societies with underdeveloped productivity, hunting activities carried out by humans for survival, or the behavior of competing for food between individuals was mainly manifested as a kind of vigorous activity. When there were no better tools for these events, humans mainly relied on their own limbs to complete, such as fighting between people and beasts. When human beings were occupied with free time after satisfying their food needs, the elders started to teach children and youngsters skills to fight beasts or fight between people. At this time, such sorts of conscious teaching activities were the educational forms for human motor skills, which involved the skills of physical confrontation, which is the embryonic form of sports. Before humans could use weapons universally or proficiently, the human group's acquisition of food or territory, or the establishment of an individual's image in the group, was mainly determined by the ability of physical activities to use force in reality. The man who owned greater strength or was enabled to use skills reasonably to win in a fight would naturally become the object of worship at that time, and may also become a role model for others.

Wrestling could be dated back to the ancient age. In primitive society, hunting was the main means of survival for human beings. Therefore, humans often had to fight with wild beasts. Only by winning the battle can they protect themselves and get prey. For this reason, people need to compete with each other in strength in order to select the most courageous and powerful man to hunt. Based on this speculation, wrestling activities have been presented in primitive society. In ancient times, mankind constantly acquired and summarized the knack of winning through strength and skill in the long historical process, and imparted it as educational content to future generations for improving collective competitiveness and viability. In the patrilineal clan society where hunting was the mainstay, these forms of educational activities must be more common. In the history of written records, the earliest accurate citation of wrestling (Jiao-Li) in the ancient literature in China was in the *Book of Rites · Yue Ling*,[1] which was written in the Warring States Period, stating: "(In the first month of winter) The emperor ordered the generals to teach martial arts, learn to shoot and fight, and wrestle." This demonstrates that wrestling has become one of the important items of military training at this time, but the origin of wrestling should be more aged than that. Chang Renxia discussed in the chapter "Da Nuo and Jiao-Di" in the *Two Oldest Dances in China* that: "Another dance that has existed in primitive society is Jiao-Di. It is a fighting dance between people, which drove from the Yellow River Plain in central Hebei, where the ancient Chinese culture developed. This dance came into being in the primitive tribal conflicts."[2] Huikang Yesou mentioned in "*Shi Yu*": "Today a child leaned over, touched the ground with both hands, and made a bullfight with his head touching and fighting with each other, which is so-called the ancient 'play of horns' … Another version is that: Chiyou had horns on his head, fighting with the Yellow Emperor. In the Chiyou play of the Song Dynasty, people wore ox horns to match with each other.[3] In the *Book of the Han Dynasty · Chronicles of Emperor Wu*, Wen Ying commented "Jiao-Di" and claimed that: "The two are wrestling with the horns, hence the name Jiao-Di (Jiao means horns homophonically), which is a kind of acrobatic form of fun."[4] From these materials, we know that wrestling has been presented differently in different scenes. For example, a man must wear a mask while dancing. While during the competition, men meet each other face to face in the company of music. Based on Wen Ying's comment, at this time, Jiao-Di was no longer a single form of wrestling, but a comprehensive sports activity that included competition skills. It involves a long process from dancing to wrestling with somewhat sports characteristics. In the beginning, dance-like wrestling and competitive wrestling co-existed. Probably after the Han Dynasty, the artistic style of wrestling dance faded, and the competitiveness gradually strengthened.

Competitiveness naturally demands the choice of powerful Hercules. Wrestling was originally an entertainment for folks in their leisure time. However, the strong men or Hercules in the wrestling became the bodyguards of the feudal lords in the Warring States Period. "*Han Feizi*" recorded it as follows: "Shao Shizhou came to Jinyang and served as the guard for Zhang Xiangzi. In Jinyang, there was a strong man Niu Zigeng invincible in strength. Shao failed to compete with him. So he presented to the Lord: "The reason why you employed me to serve as the bodyguard is just because of my strength. Now there is another who is more powerful than me, and I would like to recommend him."[5] During the Spring and Autumn and the Warring States Period, Jiao-Li and Jiao-Di were still necessary training items for soldiers of various states to prepare for fighting, and the training was mainly practice-oriented. This kind of practicality has existed since the Zhou Dynasty. After Qin unified the Six Kingdoms, weapons of all states were removed, so martial arts had to be exercised mainly with bare hands. At this time, wrestling and warfare were gradually separated. On the one hand, wrestling was employed as a means of military training. On the other hand, it became a sports activity enjoyed by the ruling class. Of course, it was also entertainment and exercise for the folks in their leisure time. *Book of the Former Han Dynasty · Records of Criminal Law* stated: After the Spring and Autumn Period, the small and weak states were annexed and merged to form the Warring States Period. Some martial etiquette was added either for fun or to boast with each other. In the Qin Dynasty, its name was changed to "Jiao-Di," and the etiquette of the former dynasty was drowned in unrighteous music.⁶ The second Qin emperor especially enjoyed *Jiao-Di*, as was recorded in the *Book of the Former Han Dynasty · Biography of Li Si*: "The second emperor of the Qin Dynasty intended to punish the prime minister, but he worried that the situation was not suitable. At that time, someone reported to the emperor that Li Si's third son, Sanchuan County Chief Li You, had a good relationship with Chen She, who was a rebel. So the emperor sent someone to investigate if the message was true. Li Si got the news. At that time, Qin Emperor was watching wrestling game in Ganquan Palace. So Li Si could not enter to explain."⁷ The story went that someone reported to the emperor that Li Si's son Li You had some contracts with the rebel Chen She. Upon the news, Li Si went to see the second Emperor of Qin for an explanation, but the emperor refused to meet him because he was enjoying *Jiao-Di* play at that moment, from which we can see how obsessed the second Emperor of Qin was with Jiao-Di.

However, Jiao-Di at this time was also a kind of entertainment activity, including Jiao-Li, which was the same concept as the Baixi (Variety Plays) in the Han Dynasty. It is recorded in *Shi Wu Ji Yuan* that Jiao-Di is just Sumo today. *Story of Emperor Hanwu* cited Jiao-Di was formed during the period of Six Kingdoms. *Historical Records* recorded the second Emperor of Qin stayed in Ganquan as a fan of Jiao-Di. This book also noted that during the Warring States Period, wrestling was expanded with more favor of entertainment. Two wrestlers were fighting with each other for fun. Emperor Wu of the Han Dynasty is fond of this game.⁸ From this perspective, the game of Jiao-Di that Emperor Wu of the Han Dynasty later enjoyed was the "acrobatics" type of wrestling which the second Emperor of Qin was keen on. In addition, we can also have some understanding of Jiao-Di in the Qin Dynasty from the archaeological materials. In 1975, a wooden grate with colorful paintings was excavated from the tomb of the Chu State in Fenghuang Mountain, Jiangling County, Hubei Province, which has an image of the Jiao-Di (see Fig. 5-1),⁹ in which a judge stands on the right of the picture, while two other athletes on the left are competing. The costumes of the three are similar, except that the judge wears a narrow white waistband, and the two athletes wear a wide waistband which is black and white. All three are shirtless and bare-legged and wear triangle shorts. One attacks with his right hand under the armpit of the other, while the other

Fig. 5-1 Picture of Jiao-Di in the Wooden Grate of the Chu Tomb

attacks the upper part of his rival. At the same time, both of them trip each other with their feet. The scene is very lively and tense. There is a hanging curtain-like streamer on the upper part of the screen, indicating that this is an official game on a dedicated corner stage. The two athletes don't display mutually the posture of hugging their waists and legs, which are more flexible in their angular movements.

5.1.2 Jiao-Di Interaction between the Han Dynasty and the Northern Minorities

Han Dynasty was a very important period in the historical development of our country. On the basis of the unified multi-ethnic country of the Qin State, Han Dynasty made a significant contribution to the development of the Chinese nation. Liu Bang established the Western Han Dynasty in 202 BC, with Chang'an being the capital. At the beginning of the Western Han Dynasty, the society was desolate and dilapidated, with serious damage to production, economic development, and the people's livelihood. Through a series of reforms, production was gradually restored, and social and economic development was promoted, leading to the panorama of the famous "governance of Emperor Wen and Emperor Jing." Liu Che, Emperor Wu of the Han Dynasty, was a very courageous monarch. Internally, he developed the economy, cracked down on local separatist forces, and strengthened centralization. Externally, he carried out military attacks on Huns, who were the strongest power in the north, and implemented a linkage policy against the small states in the Western Regions.

During the Western Han Dynasty, the surrounding ethnic minorities mainly included Xiongnu, ethnic groups in the Western Regions, Yue, Southwest, Southeast, and Northeast ethnic groups, among which Xiongnu posed the greatest threat to the Han. From Emperor Gaozu to Emperor Jing, the Huns had continuously waged wars against the Han Dynasty, who tried to ease the conflict by "Heqin (make peace with rulers of minorities in the border areas by marriage)." During the reign of Emperor Wu, the Han launched a large-scale war against the Huns based on its strong economic strength. Through Zhang Qian's envoy of the Western Regions plus a series of strategies, the Han Dynasty defeated the Huns and thus established a relationship with the ethnic groups of the Western Regions, which was of great significance to the formation of China's national pattern. Sports fellowship, among other things, is one of the effective strategies adopted by the Han Dynasty.

Emperor Wu of the Han Dynasty was a man of great talent in handling matters. For a seemingly simple match like Jiao-Di, the emperor practiced it quite differently from the second Emperor of Qin, who fully enjoyed the privileges of the aristocracy and appreciated the show exclusively. Emperor Wu instead not only maintained the dignity of the nobility, but also had a concern for the common people. He hoped that people would enjoy themselves and they could also witness how prosperous the country he ruled was, so that they could live and work in peace and contentment. *Book of the Former Han Dynasty · Chronicles of Emperor Wu* recorded: "In the spring of the third year under the reign of Emperor Wu (108 BC), Jiao-Di play was widely appreciated by the people coming three hundred *li* (unit of distance, equal to 500 m) away."[10] In the same book, it was recorded that in the summer of the sixth year of Yuanfeng (105 BC), Emperor Wu of the Han

Dynasty held a Jiao-Di competition for the folks: "In the summer, people enjoyed Jiao-Di play at the Pingle Hall in the capital."[11] Shanglin refers to the Shanglin Garden, which was the Chang'an Garden in the Han Dynasty, and Pingle Hall was right located in Shanglin Garden. There were a lot of people who watched Jiao-Di in the spring of the third year of Yuanfeng. Although the literature seemed to be exaggerating, it was enough to see the political enlightenment of Emperor Wu and the prosperity of the whole country. In the sixth year of Yuanfeng, Jiao-Di match was held at the Pingle Hall in Shanglin, where the space was limited, but it was available to the people in the capital. It was also an amazing scene. In addition, from the above two materials, we can see that during the reign of Emperor Wu of the Han Dynasty, it was likely that Jiao-Di match was frequently held in both spring and summer. The custom was later spread to the Sui, Tang, Five Dynasties, and Song Dynasty. In the Sui and Tang Dynasties, it was then introduced to Japan. Until modern times, Sumo wrestling in Japan still competes twice a year in spring and summer, which will be discussed later.

The Han Dynasty not only held the Jiao-Di match on schedule, but also regarded *Jiao-Di* as an important entertainment event for treating guests from Xiongnu and Wusun at that time. In *Biography of Zhang Qian* of *Book of the Former Han Dynasty*, it was cited as follows: At that time, the emperor went for the inspection on the seaside several times and always asked the foreign guests to follow. He would pass those more populated towns and places and distribute gifts and money generously to the locals for the display of wealth and generosity of the Han Dynasty. Meanwhile, Jiao-Di play was held on a large scale, and antiques and novelties of various kinds were on display. More spectators were attracted to watch. Under that circumstance, the emperor would give rewards such as wine and meat, impressing foreign visitors with the accumulation of warehouses in which the goods were stocked and piled. For that reason, the foreign guests were greatly awed by the vastness of the Han Dynasty. With the magic added to the show, Jiao-Di plays changed accordingly every year, which started to prosper since then.[12] Here is a general description of the situation when Emperor Wu of the Han Dynasty showed off the power of Han towards Xiongnu and Wusun through the boasting display of Jiao-Di. This may seem to be a simple boost of the Han Dynasty's affluence, but its far-reaching significance is beyond the end. Jiao-Di here should be within the Yuanfeng Period (110–105 BC).

In October of the winter in the first year of Yuanfeng, Emperor Wu prepared to patrol the border and decreed that "The Nan Yue rebel and the East Ou rebel have been condemned, while the West barbarians and North barbarians are not fully convinced. I am going to patrol the border and lead the troops all by myself to rally the morale. Twelve generals are going to be assigned, and I am the commander in chief." This patrol started from Yunyang, north to Shangjun, Xihe, Wuyuan, out of the Great Wall, north up to Chanyutai, and to Shuofang next to Beihe. Armed with 180,000 cavalries, with the banner stretching more than a thousand *li* long, which formed a huge threat to Huns. Emperor Wu sent an envoy to inform Chanyu: "The emperor of Nan Yue is in grave danger. If ChanYu is able to fight, our emperor must be waiting at the border. If Chanyu is not strong enough to fight, come and surrender as soon as possible! How come you hide in the cold land of Mobei!"[13] The Huns were smitten with fear. After his return, he worshiped the Yellow Emperor at Qiaoshan and returned to Ganquan. Since then, Emperor Wu had repeatedly patrolled during the Yuanfeng Period (See Table 5-1 below for details).[14]

Table 5-1 Statistics of the Patrols of Emperor Wu in the Han Dynasty

Patrol Time	Patrol Site
In October of the winter in the first year of Yuanfeng	Started from Yunyang, north to Shangjun, Xihe, Wuyuan, out of the Great Wall, north up to Chanyutai, Shuofang next to Beihe. Then returned to Ganquan.
In January of the spring in the first year of Yuanfeng	Then patrolled until the sea in the east.
In April of the Summer in the first year of Yuanfeng	Climbed up to Mount Tai and offered sacrifices to heaven there, then patrolled until the sea in the east to Jieshi. The emperor patrolled from Liaoxi and went through the nine areas in the north. At last, returned to Ganquan.
In October of the winter in the second year of Yuanfeng	Patrolled at Yong County and worshiped at Wuzhi.
In the spring of the second year of Yuanfeng	Patrolled at Goushi and then went to the Donglai.
In April of the Summer in the second year of Yuanfeng	Sacrificed the heaven on Mount Tai on the way home. Then the emperor went to the Huzi river and arrived at the Yellow River.
In January of the spring in the third year of Yuanfeng	Patrolled at the Ganquan Palace to give banquets to foreign guests.
In October of the Winter in the fourth year of Yuanfeng	Patrolled at Yong County and worshiped at Wuzhi. Through Huizhong road, the emperor patrolled northward to Xiaoguan pass, went through Dulu, Mingze, back to the capital from Dai, and reached Hedong.
In the winter of the fifth year of Yuanfeng	Patrolled to the south to hunt and reached Shengtang County. He visited the Temple of Yao and Shun on Jiuyi Mountain and then climbed Tianzhu Mountain.
In April of the summer in the fifth year of Yuanfeng	Patrolled at Jingyang and returned back to Ganquan.
In the winter of the sixth year of Yuanfeng	Patrolled at Huizhong.
In March of the spring in the sixth year of Yuanfeng	Patrolled at Hedong.

In 119 BC, Emperor Wu of the Han Dynasty ordered Wei Qing and Huo Qubing to lead 50,000 soldiers respectively to go through the desert from the north to attack Yi Zhicha's offensive troops from Youbeiping and Dingxiang and killed more than 70,000 people, which dealt a heavy blow to the Huns. After this failure, the Huns withdrew from Hetao area and its west regions. Historically, it was said that "the Huns fled far away, and there was no minor royal court in Monan."[15] In 114 BC (the third year of Yuanding in the Han Dynasty), Yi Zhicha succumbed to death. Zi Wuwei Chanyu (114–105 BC) and Sun Wushilu Chanyu (105–102 BC) successively sat on the throne.

At this time, the production and development of animal husbandry of the Huns were severely restricted, because they were far away from the mountain areas with abundant water and grass. The Han Dynasty took advantage of the "Huns Left-land" that was captured to make the Wuhuan tribe (formerly living in the Liao River Basin and Laoha River) migrate to the outside of the five counties of Shanggu, Yuyang, Youbeiping, Liaodong, and Liaoxi. In order to spy on the Huns for the Han Dynasty, Zhang Qian was also sent to the Western Regions to contact the Yuezhi and Dayuan clan, and to dismantle the alliance between the Huns and Wusun with the princess, the wife of Wusun Kunmo. The four counties of Jiuquan, Wuwei, Zhangye, and Dunhuang were set up in the homeland of King Hunxie to cut off the communication between the Huns and the Qiang. Under such circumstances, the Huns' power was declining. However, the power of the Huns at that time could not be ignored, for it still posed a great threat to the Han Dynasty.

When banqueting "foreign guests," on the one hand, the Han Dynasty has fully demonstrated its strength and power to those small states attached to the Huns through Jiao-Di competition. The purpose was to show that Han Dynasty had the ability to compete with the Huns and protect their interests, so that they could draw closer to the Han Dynasty, isolating themselves from the Huns, or forming a pincer against the Huns. On the other hand, it also demonstrated to the Huns the mental state of the soldiers and civilians of the Han Dynasty, so as to form a kind of deterrence to combat their arrogance and reduce the military pressure of the Huns on the Han Court. Historical facts have proved that the differentiation of the Huns in the later period and the eventual integration of the Huns with the Han nationality or other ethnic groups exerted a significant impact on the formation and development of the Chinese framework. Certainly, there were also ethnic groups such as Wusun and Da Yuezhi who established the relationship of domination and subordination with the Han Dynasty. They jointly attacked the Huns and stabilized the situation of the Han in the north to a certain extent, which created a strong and relatively stable social environment for the progress of the Han Dynasty. It can be seen from the above documents that Emperor Wu of the Han Dynasty did have the intention of receiving foreign guests with Jiao-Di plays, and achieved the expected results. We can clearly understand from the literature that Emperor Wu not only demonstrated the spiritual mentality of the soldiers and civilians of the Han Dynasty through Jiao-Di, but also allowed "foreign guests" to appreciate the accumulation of the palace and warehouses, and visit vast and fertile land of the Han Dynasty, all of which have manifested towards "foreign guests" the richness and strength of the Han Dynasty from multiple levels, leading them to "awe."

Under the potential military pressure of the northern Huns, such a practice also existed during the reign of Emperor Xuan of the Han Dynasty. *Book of the Former Han Dynasty · Memoirs of the Western Regions* wrote that (Emperor Xuan of the Han Dynasty) in the second year of Yuankang, Wusun Kunmi submitted a memorial to Emperor Xuan through Xiaowei Chang Hui, "I would like to take Yuan Guimi, the grandson of the Han Dynasty, as the heir to the throne, and let him also marry a princess of the Han Dynasty for a closer relationship, so as to break the relations with the Huns. And a thousand horses and mules will be the dowry." Emperor Xuan appreciated Wusun's great achievements in the current time, and resolutely broke off the old relations with the Huns, so he sent messengers to Wusun to receive the bride-price. Kunmi, together with the crown prince, the generals, and Duwei (title of the military officer under general), formed a delegation of more than 300 people to meet the young princess in the Han Dynasty. Emperor Xuan took Princess Jieyou's sister Xiangfu as the princess, and arranged for more than 100 officials and maids of honor to live in Shanglin Garden and learn the Wusun Language. Emperor Xuan personally went to Pingle Hall to meet the Huns and foreign monarchs and entertained them with Jiao-Di plays. As an important ally of the Han Dynasty in the Western regions, Wusun formed the "Kundi" with the Han Dynasty at the end of the 2nd century BC.[16] Therefore, to protect Wusun was to maintain the rule of the Han Dynasty in the Western regions. In 71 BC (the third year of Emperor Xuan), the Han Dynasty dispatched Duliao General Fan Mingyou, Qian General Han Zeng, and Pulei General Zhao Chongguo to lead the troops and fight against the Huns together with Wusun. Because the Han soldiers failed to arrive at their destination within the scheduled time, Xiaowei Changhui and Wusun joined forces to attack the court of Youguli King. They enslaved more than 39,000 people, including Huyandi Chanyu and his wife, Juci (princess), Mingwang, Liyi Duwei (title of the military officer under general), Qianzhang, and soldiers, as well as more than 700,000 cattle, sheep, horses, camels, donkeys, mules, etc.[17] Chanyu was so furious that he attacked Wusun in the winter and captured quite a lot. But when they were going to return, the weather happened to be freezing. With heavy snow falling suddenly, a large number of people and animals froze to death. So Dingling took advantage of the momentum to attack the north, with Wuhuan invading the east and Wusun assaulting the west, which hit Huyandi Chanyu with a heavy blow. In 68 BC, Hu Yanyandi Chanyu died, and his brother Zuoxianwang succeeded to the throne, known as Xulü Quanqu Chanyu (68–60 BC). It was under this historical background that Wusun made his marriage to the Han Dynasty. Therefore, Emperor Xuan of the Han Dynasty found it difficult for Wusun to refuse the marriage due to his new achievements. And this time, the place of seeing off was at Pingle Hall of Shanglin Garden, where Jiao-Di plays were often held.

That was a larger see-off scene, including Kunmi, the prince's generals, and Duwei, as well as all the envoys, in the number of over 300. It also involved more than one hundred officials and maids that Emperor Xuan arranged for the princess. Of course, there were other officials or imperial secretaries in accompany. In any case, more than 300 people from Wusun previously and a hundred from Han Dynasty will leave for Wusun. Isn't this a great communication of sports? Before leaving the frontier fortress, it was heard that Wusun Kunmi Wengguimi was deceased. According to Cenzou's living will, Wusun noble, the son of Li Cenzuo, Nimi, will become Kunmi, the king of Wusun. Chang Hui submitted a memorial to Emperor Xuan: "I suggest leaving the young princess in Dunhuang temporarily." Chang Hui rushed to Wusun and blamed him for not establishing Yuanguimi as Kunmi, "… and we will pick the young princess back to Chang'an later." This matter was discussed among the ministers and Xiao Wangzhi also argued, "Wusun has both ends, with whom it is difficult to make a contract. Princess Jieyou has been in Wusun for more than 40 years. The relationship between the two states is not close, and the border has not been peaceful, which has been proven. Up to now, the princess could return to Chang'an because Yuanguimi's status was not established. There is no place to make an apology to Wusun; instead, a blessing for the Han Dynasty. If the princess doesn't return, corvee will rise again."[18] Emperor Xuan accepted this advice and took the princess back to Chang'an.

Participants in this event included not only the above-mentioned people, but also the Huns' envoys and the monarchs of various states. Why did the Han Dynasty come to show Jiao-Di in such a scene? The author believes that, on the one hand, this may be a custom at that time; on the other hand, more importantly, it was determined by the environment and role played by the Han Dynasty in the north. During the reign of Emperor Xuan of the Han Dynasty, the Huns in the north were still powerful. However, the Han Dynasty had established relations with Wuhuan, Wusun, Da Yuezhi, Daxia, Dayuan, etc. At this time, the Han needed to establish an image to the minorities in the Western Regions and other regions, maintain its great power style, unite and protect the weak, and strike and divide the strong.

So, what was Jiao-Di in the Han Dynasty like? This is rarely recorded in the literature, with only a few records in Zhang Heng's *Ode to Chang'an*. The fact is that the emperor arrived at the Pingle Hall, opened the tent, and sat inside to watch the wonderful performance in the front square. *Ode to Chang'an* also talks about the situation and costumes of the Jiao-Di athletes.[19] Strong men like Zhonghuang and Yuhuo in ancient times, who were naked, wearing a crimson kerchief on the head, with their hair combed like a pole standing upright on the top of their heads, reach forward, pushing and fighting each other to compete. This record is very similar to the image of Jiao-Di in a mural unearthed in the Eastern Han Dynasty tomb of Dahu Pavilion in Mi County, Henan Province, in 1961(see Fig. 5-2). As can be seen from the picture, the competition was carried out on a platform. Two athletes were bare-chested and bare-legged. One was wearing a black belly protector and red shorts, and the other was wearing a red belly protector and black shorts. With their hair braided in a mane, they were about to fight each other. Judging from the standing posture and demeanor of the two, they do not necessarily have to hug their waists and legs when fighting but instead act by chance and attack mutually. This form of Jiao-Di is analogous to the Jiao-Di on the zodiac-shaped seals in the Palace Museum (see Fig. 5-3). In Fig. 5-3, one player is holding his opponent's left foot with his right hand, while the other is struggling to break free, awaiting an opportunity to counterattack. The two players do not use the posture of hugging the waist and legs

Fig. 5-2 Part of the Mural of Jiao-Di

Fig. 5-3 A Seal of Jiao-Di

of their opponents. Thus, we can draw the conclusion from the above information that Jiao-Di in the Han Dynasty followed the features and techniques of Qin Jiao-Di movements.

So, did Wusun and Xiongnu have the sport of Jiao-Di? If so, what would it be like? The answer should be yes. Jiao-Di is a very primitive sports activity for human beings, which just depends on how much we know about these nationalities. Only from the above-mentioned that the Huns, Wusun, and other foreign guests from various states who have been invited to watch the Jiao-Di play in Pingle Hall of Shanglin Garden by the Han Dynasty, we can infer that apart from the Han court itself, competitive sports like Jiao-Di were also popular in Huns, Wusun, and other places. As a result, the Han Dynasty would hold major events in Pingle Hall of Shanglin Garden, on the one hand, to compete with and boast its power to other states, and on the other hand, to strengthen the friendship with Huns and Wusun.

We have not yet mastered the detailed materials of Wusun, but we had access to a wresting bronze plaque of the Huns[20] (see Fig. 5-4) in the Han Dynasty unearthed in Keshengzhuang, Chang'an County, Shaanxi Province in 1955. The plaque shows two Huns tying horses to a tree, starting to compete in wrestling or to train Jiao-Di. From the clothing, we can see they are wearing trousers and short boots, but bare to the waist. From a technical point of view, it seems that both are grabbing each other's legs or waist, with the intention of throwing their opponent down. On the one hand, the bronze plaque of the Huns' Jiao-Di reflects the nomadic lifestyle of the people: the horses tied to the trees are leisurely, while the owners of the horses are engaged in wrestling. On the other hand, it can be seen that Jiao-Di play must be very popular among the Huns. Obviously, this is a cultural relic discovered in Shaanxi Province, yet it was brought into the Central Plains by the Huns. Similar bronze plaques are collected in numbers in Ningxia Museum,

Fig. 5-4 Bronze Plaque of Jiao-Di of Huns in the Han Dynasty

which is obviously modeled on the life customs of the Huns or typical of the most common life of the people. The movement form of Jiao-Di play can be seen from the decoration of this plaque, which can be concluded to be a classic representative of the wrestling by the northern peoples in our country. This type of wrestling enjoys a fixed form of hugging and uses force techniques and relative strength to throw the opponent down. Clearly, there is a certain difference with reference to Jiao-Di in the Han Dynasty.

Regarding the sports exchanges between the Hans and Xiongnu and other ethnic minorities, there are not many records in the literature, but we can have some understanding through the population migration among the ethnic groups, as the population migration is often accompanied by the cultural exchanges between different nationalities. If it involves the migration of nobles or the number of people involved in migration is particularly large, the degree of cultural exchanges between ethnic groups must be more profound and more influential. During the Pre-Qin and Qin Dynasty, the Huns were very active in the north and often launched attacks on the Han Dynasty, robbing the population and materials of the Han. Till the Han Dynasty, this practice was still followed. But at this time, the Han Dynasty had gradually shifted from defense to offense, thus forming a two-way communication between the Han and Xiongnu.

Xiongnu, living in the north of the Han nationality, were nomadic people in the north of ancient China. It emerged during the Warring States Period, as a military alliance formed in the third century BC after a long-term struggle and integration of the various ethnic groups in the north and south of the desert, known as Guifang, Xunzhou, and Xianyun. During the Modu Chanyu period, Xiongnu successively conquered many neighbors: they destroyed Donghu to the east, Yuezhi to the west, merged with Loufan in the south, and served Hunyu, Qushi, Dingling, Gekun, and Xinli in the north. Later Yuezhi was eliminated, and Loulan, Wusun, and their neighboring ethnic groups were put down. Huns were in charge of the land from Liao River in the east, to Congling in the west, from Lake Baikal in the north, to the Great Wall in the south.[21] In a sense, the Huns in the Han Dynasty were already a mixed-ethnic community.

It is recorded that the Huns would reward the soldiers with the captured items and take the captured as slaves when they fought.[22] According to the historical records, the number of Han people who had been taken captives was more than 100,000 from the Huns' war and extortion against the Han till Emperor Zhao.[23] In addition, the Huns also took a lot of people from other tribes as captives. For example, in the early Eastern Han Dynasty, tens of thousands of "captives" took advantage of the split of the Huns and fled collectively. Among these fleeing slaves, there were those from Xiyu, Dingling, and Qiang tribes, which totaled tens of thousands of households.[24] If there are five people per household, there will be tens of thousands in total, who turn out to be the main source of Huns' slaves. In addition, slaves in Huns could also be bought from their neighbors. For example, in the Eastern Han Dynasty, Qiang people sold large numbers of looted Han slaves to the Southern Huns.

Besides, some Han aristocrats or officials flowed to Xiongnu. For example, in the early Western Han Dynasty, Han Xin fled to the Hun when Emperor Gaozu of the Han Dynasty destroyed the seignior of other surnames. Zhong Xingyue of the Han nationality even became a state master in

Huns. In 123 BC, Qian General Zhao Xin[25] led more than 3,000 cavalries to attack Huns, yet almost the entire army was wiped out. Zhao Xin was forced to surrender to the Huns. According to the classification of the above groups, the author believes that the sports activities that were taken to the Huns by people like Han Xin and others must be mainly recreational; while others brought forward to Huns by the group represented by Zhong Xingyue, Zhao Xin and the captured soldiers were mainly military training events with some competitive features.

Of course, a large number of Huns also entered the Han region during the constant wars and other contacts. For example, a tomb of the Huns in the early Western Han Dynasty was discovered in Kexingzhuang, Chang'an County, Shaanxi Province, with two open-cut bronze plaques ornamented with Jiao-Di designs. The seals of official name of the Eastern Han Dynasty were found in Dongsheng County, Inner Mongolia, as well as Yulin County and Xi'an City, Shaanxi Province. A tomb of the Southern Huns in the Eastern Han Dynasty was discovered in Shangsun Jiazhai, Datong County, Qinghai Province, in which a bronze seal of "Han and Huns Belonging to the Han Dynasty" was unearthed.[26] All these illustrate the presence of the Huns in the territory of Han. There also recorded a large amount of information in historical material as follows: In 126 BC (the third year of Yuanshuo in the reign of Emperor Wu of the Han Dynasty), Junchen Chanyu died and his brother Yizhicha Chanyu succeeded. Prince Yu Dan, the son of Junchen Chanyu, bent down and fled to Han, who was named Zhi'anhou by the Han Dynasty. In 124 BC, the Han Dynasty sent Wei Qing, Su Jian, Li Ju, Gongsun He, and other generals with a troop of more than 100,000 soldiers to defeat Youxian King. The King was defeated with a loss of over 15,000 men and women, over ten dukes, and a large number of Hun's captives. In 121 BC, Emperor Wu of the Han Dynasty ordered General Huo Qubing, Heqihou Gongsun Ao, Bowanghou Zhang Qian, and Langzhongling Li Guang to strike attacks from Longxi, Beidi, and Youbeiping respectively. Huo Qubing encountered Hunxie King and Xiutu King in Mount Yanzhi, Juyan, Qilian, and other places. He defeated all of them and captured more than 38,000 people, including Chanhuan, Qiutu King, Jiju King, Yanshi Chanyu, Queen mother, prince, minister, general, Danghu, Duwei, etc. Yizhicha was furious and intended to kill two Kings, yet Hunxie King then led more than 40,000 people to surrender to the Han. The Han conferred him Puyinhou, in charge of some places beyond the Great Wall, such as Longxi, Beidi, Shangjun, Shuofang, and Yunzhong, and thus a "subordinate state" was set up.[27] In 51 BC (the third year of Han Ganlu), Huhanye Chanyu came to Chang'an to make a pilgrimage to Liu Xun, Emperor Xuan of the Han Dynasty.

Huhanye's surrender to the Han Dynasty was a major event in the history of the Huns. It was not only a product of the class struggle in the Huns' society, but also the result of the development of relations between the Han and Xiongnu. It not only announced the end of the war between Xiongnu and Han nationalities, but also claimed the replacement of a new situation of cooperation between the two nationalities. It also broke the old tradition of "Hu and Yue's refusal in surrender to the Hans" since the "Three Dynasties (Xia, Shang, and Zhou)" and opened up the precedent that the north national regime started to accept the rule and leadership of the Central Plain Dynasty. At the same time, it promoted the political, economic, and cultural exchanges between the north and the Central Plains, strengthened the centripetal force and cohesion of the northern minorities, and contributed to forming favorable conditions for further reunification.

In AD 46 (the 22nd year of Jianwu in the Eastern Han Dynasty), Huduershidao Gaoruodi Chanyu died, and his son Zuoxian King, Wudadihou, who died later, succeeded. Afterwards, his brother, Zuoxian King, ascended the throne called Punu Shanyu. Youaujian King named Bi was unable to succeed and became resentful. At the time when the Huns were "suffering from drought locusts in successive years, thousands of miles of land failed to harvest, vegetation withered, people and livestock suffered famine and plague, and more than half of them died." Punu Chanyu was afraid of Han, so he waited for an opportunity to send envoys to Yuyang for marriage. Then, Guo Heng, a Han person, was secretly sent by Bi to Xihe with a map of Xiongnu and asked the governor of Xihu to surrender. The matter was known by Liangguduhou, who persuaded Chanyu to kill Bi during the alliance in the Dragon City in May. Bi was very frightened, so he summoned 40,000 to 50,000 people from 8 tribes in the south of his jurisdiction to murder Liangguduhou, who heard the news and rushed to report to Chanyu. Consequently, Chanyu sent troops to fight with them. Later, seeing that Bi led the soldiers in numbers, Chanyu did not dare to act rashly. Yet Bi came to realize it was difficult to be on the same side with Chanyu at that time. In AD 48 (the 24th year of Jianwu in the Eastern Han Dynasty), under the support of 8 tribes, he followed the title of his ancestor Jihoushan as Huhanye Chanyu, and announced, "I wish to surrender forever" in Wuyuansai (now west of Baotou city, Inner Mongolia Autonomous Region).[28] In AD 50 (the 26th year of Jianwu Period), Huhanye Chanyu sent his son to serve the Han court again. Since then, the Huns have been split into two parts: the Southern Xiongnu and the Northern Xiongnu. In that case, the Huns were weakened again, which became a new turning point in its decline. The attachment of the Southern Xiongnu is not only an inevitable trend of the social and historical development of Xiongnu, but also related to the influence of the advanced economy and culture of the Han nationality. Since AD 18, Huhanye Chanyu Bi has been stationed in the south of Xiongnu and led eight tribes of herdsmen who have lived in Beidi, Shuofang, Wuyuan, Yunzhong, Dingxiang, Yanmen, Dai, Shanggu, and other counties for a long time. Because of the profound impacts of the Han economy and culture, the desire to reconcile with the Han people is also stronger. Under the historical conditions at that time, it was obviously a progressive phenomenon.

Due to the frequent looting of the North Xiongnu, some folks gradually became war-weary, and they intended to get rid of their fetters and go south to the Han. After the two battles mentioned above, people escaped from the North to join the South Huns from time to time. For example, in AD 83, there were 38,000 people in Wuyuansai, including Master Jiliusi of Sanmulou; since AD 85, the "73 batches" of people such as Lord Cheli and Zhuobing entered the South one after another. Due to the continuous increase in the number of fugitives and the severely weakened power, the enslaved people of all ethnic groups took the opportunity to rebel and resist. Punu Chanyu was forced to move far away due to internal and external difficulties. In AD 87, Xianbei invaded the left land of Huns and attacked the North Xiongnu, beheading Youliu Chanyu. The North Xiongnu was in great chaos. A total of 200,000 people from 58 divisions, including Qulan, Chubei, and Huduxu, went to Yunzhong, Wuyuan, Shuofang, and Beidi County respectively to attach the East Han Dynasty. It happened to be the time Xiulanshi Zhuhoudi Chanyu succeeded shortly (AD 89–93), who submitted a letter to the Eastern Han Dynasty, "I wish to defeat the Northern Xiongnu and integrate the South and North as one."[29] Huchuquan was the last Chanyu of the Southern Xiongnu. After being in power, he was repeatedly attacked by Xianbei. In AD 216, Huchuquan turned to Cao Cao. In order to weaken his power, Cao Cao divided him into five parts and selected a distinguished man as the commander for each. At the same time, some Han people were appointed as Sima for supervision. Although the Xiongnu tribal organization was still preserved in name, its power had all fallen into the hands of the Cao Wei Dynasty, only with its title Chanyu remaining. The Southern Huns state itself has perished in essence.

Judging from the above-mentioned surrenders and attachments of Huns nobles, or military and civilians, the scale is quite large and its level is relatively high. Hundreds and thousands of them surrendered to the Han Dynasty, from Chanyu to the commoners. What they brought to the Han was a large number of northern ethnic culture, among which there must be a lot of sports culture. For the Huns, "When they were kids, they could ride sheep, draw the bow and shoot birds and mice; when they were teenagers, they would shoot foxes and rabbits or feed on them. Soldiers could pierce the bows, capable enough to be armored riders. It is a common custom that people feel free and enjoyable in good times, regarding shooting animals and birds as their business, while it is natural for them to be trained with fighting skills for the wars. The long weapon is the bow and arrow, and the short one is the sword."[30] Another example: Jin Midi was the prince of Xiutu of the Huns. When Kunye King was attached to the Han Dynasty, Xiutu King was killed by Kunye King because of the regrets of King Xiutu, the father of Jin Midi. Together with his mother and his younger brother Lun, Jin Midi entered the Han mansion and served the Han court. He was good at raising horses, so he was appreciated by Emperor Wu of the Han Dynasty, in accompany with the emperor all the time. Later, Mang Heluo and others conspired, and they were seen through by Jin Midi. "Midi had to disclose Heluo and grabbed him, 'Mang Heluo is rebellious!' The emperor was startled, and the guards attempted to draw swords to kill him. Emperor Wu immediately stopped and told them not to use the sword to avoid hurting Jin Midi. In a few rounds, Midi caught Heluo and threw him down in the face of the emperor. As a result, Heluo was brought to justice."[31] This shows that the Huns are very capable of wrestling, whose wrestling style is similar to that of the Han people. The Huns are powerful and capable of riding, shooting, and fighting animals, which is inseparable from their training since they were young. Therefore, when they entered the Han region, they would inevitably bring about a large amount of sports culture. Now we are trapped in poor documentation, and thus little is known. The author believes that with archaeological excavations, there will be greater discoveries about the sports activities of Xiongnu.

Jiao-Di competition that prevailed throughout the country during the Qin and Han Dynasties was not only different from that of the Huns at that time, but also very different from the wrestling prevailing today. In general, Qin and Han Dynasties held large-scale competitions in the spring and summer, in which the participants were strong men with no tops on, and the competition skills were mainly pushing and punching. Of course, everything in the world cannot be immutable, which always develops and evolves with the advancement of history. In short, Jiao-Di activity in the Qin and Han Dynasties differs from today's wrestling. It either moves from Han to Huns or vice versa. Whatever the case may be, it is an integral part of the cultural exchange and integration of the Chinese nation, contributing tremendously to the increase of national physique and ethnic exchanges.

5.2 Development of Sumo from the Wei and Jin to the Tang and Song Dynasties

5.2.1 Sumo during the Wei, Jin, South, and North Dynasties

The wrestling of the Central Plains in the Wei and Jin Dynasties was basically inherited from the Han Dynasty. At this time, the name "Sumo" emerged. In Wang Yin's *Book of the Jin Dynasty*, there is an item that says that two counties of Yingchuan and Xiangcheng both claimed to meet, as they meant to play for fun (note in the text: Jiao-Di play). Taishou (governor) of Xiangcheng blamed Liu Zidu, saying, "The people of your county are not as good as those of Yingchuan in terms of Sumo." Zidu replied, "Sumo belongs to an inferior art, which can't be used for judging the strength and weakness of two states. Why not talk more about the strategies of governing a state as well as losses of the characters."[32] It can be seen from this record that: First, "Jiao-Di" was called "Sumo" in the Wei and Jin Dynasties; second, Sumo was a popular game among the people, and people in Yingchuan and Xiangcheng counties often carried out this event. Third, "Sumo" was regarded as "inferior art," which was basically neglected during this period. One thing can be seen from the *Book of the Jin Dynasty · Chronicles of Emperor Wu*: "(the first year of Emperor Wu of Taishi Period in the Jin Dynasty) In December, Yuefu, Mili, and Baixi (Variety Plays) were forbidden."[33] At that time, both Jiao-Di and Sumo were included in the Baixi (Variety Plays), so the entertainment Sumo was inevitably banned. However, it can be drawn from the literature that in the first year of Taishi, the edict was issued that the plays for fun must be prohibited, while Jiao-Di as a competitive form of entertainment was still favored when Sima Yan had just become the emperor. It was recorded in *Book of the Jin Dynasty · Biography of Yu Chan* that Yu Chan, with the courtesy name of Zhongchu, came from Yanling of Yingchuan. His grandfather Yu Hui served as Anbei General (Anbei Zhangshi), and his father, Yu Dong, was noted for his bravery. During the reign of Emperor Wu, there was a Hu man from the Western Regions, strong and swift, invincible in wrestling, and no one was able to compete with him. The emperor recruited warriors, but only Yu Dong was selected, who eventually killed the Hu, the news of which shocked people near and far.[34] This record corresponds to the former document that Yingchuan was popular with Sumo activities, and also filled with people who were good at Sumo. In this story, how could Emperor Wu yield to the Hu person from the Western Regions? Otherwise, how could he boost his morale and face the military pressure from all sides? In the first winter of the first year of Taishi, Emperor Wu led tens of thousands of men, including officials, Southern Chanyu of Huns, and four foreign tribes, to set up altars in the southern suburbs for ceremonial.[35] At this time, how can he let the Hu person be so domineering in the capital? So Emperor Wu issued an edict to recruit warriors, hoping to defeat the Hu. Yu Dong, the father of Yu Chan, was known for his strength and was selected. As a result, he defeated the Hu man in a Sumo wrestling. This tells us that Sumo in the Jin Dynasty was enjoyed by the people and respected by the emperors; it also shows that the Sumo activities in the Western Regions were extraordinary at this time. However, due to a lack of relevant records, it is impossible to clarify the overall situation in terms of its motive forms and development.

After the Rebellion of the Sixteen Kingdoms, the Central Plains was divided into the Southern and Northern Dynasties. The wrestling in the Southern Dynasties basically followed the Wei and Jin Dynasties. For example, *Book of the Sui Dynasty · Etiquette VII* recorded: "After Emperor Wu came onto the throne from Emperor Wenxuan of the Qi Dyansty, the guards still followed the proceeding system, including the official system and the guarding system. There were 12 Yulinlang teams of guards directly led by the generals. Besides, there were also many other teams, including the short-spear team, long-spear team, long-sword team, shield team, halberd team, animal team, red-cloak team, Jiao-Di team, Yulin team, walk team, horse team, taking on their own responsibility."[36] Therefore, it can be seen that during the period of Emperor Wu in the Liang Dynasty, such sports as Jiao-Di not only existed but also remained in large numbers. A "wrestling team" only for the imperial kinsmen is just a case in point. Now that Emperor Wu period is like this, to say nothing of the South Qi. To summarize, wrestling in the Southern Dynasty not only followed that of the Wei and Jin Dynasties, but also developed for its own purpose.

Now it is time to discuss the Jiao-Di sports of Goguryeo. First, the relationship between Goguryeo and the Central Plains Dynasty should be clarified. Before the relocation of the capital (Pyongyang), Goguryeo was bounded on the east by the Sea of Japan, on the west by the Liao River, on the south by the Han River, on the northeast by Zhacheng (now Huichun City, Jilin Province), and on the northwest by the left bank of the second Songhua River.[37] Goguryeo considered Geshenggu City as its capital first and then moved to the inner city (now east of Ji'an County, Jilin Province). In addition to being stationed in various places, the Goguryeo people mainly lived in the Yalu River Basin and Huifa River in the upper reaches of the Songhua River, centered in Ji'an County, Jilin Province. Before the founding of the Goguryeo state, Goguryeo people were already residents in the territory of the Han Dynasty. After the founding, Goguryeo established a "vassal" relationship with the Han Court and became the principality of the Han Dynasty. During the Three Kingdoms period, Goguryeo became affiliated to Cao Wei Dynasty. In the Jin Dynasty, Murong clan of Xianbei rose up and developed eastward, so the two sides launched a fierce battle over the Liaodong region. After Murong Huang built the Former Yan, he attacked Goguryeo. In AD 340, Goguryeo sent the eldest son to pay respect to Murong Huang.[38] In AD 342, in order to eliminate the menace from the rear and further develop towards the Central Plains, Murong Huang dispatched 15,000 soldiers to attack the north, and led 40,000 soldiers in person to attack the south, so as to directly attack the capital of Goguryeo, Wandu (now in Xitonggou, Ji'an County, Jilin Province). After moving the capital to Pyongyang, all the kings of Goguryeo maintained a vassal relationship with the Central Plains Dynasty until the early 7th century. The state of Goguryeo was destroyed by the Tang and Xinluo coalition forces in AD 668. After the destruction of Goguryeo, the Goguryeo clan disintegrated. Tang Dynasty then received a total of 697,000 households, which was the total number of households in its territory, including many non-Goguryeo households. It is estimated that the total sum of households of Goguryeo nationality at that time would not exceed 150,000. There are four destinations for those households, namely, being moved to Central Plains, classified as Silla, or migrated to Mohe and Turks. After Emperor Taizong of the Tang Dynasty acquired ten cities, such as Xuantu, the number of households who moved to the Central Plains arrived at 70,000, and they moved to the three prefectures of Liao, Gai, and Yan in AD 645 (the 19th year of Zhenguan Period).[39] In the second year after the demise of Goguryeo Kingdom, Emperor Gaozong of Tang moved 38,300 households to the open areas of the Yangtze River, the south of the Huai River, and other places of Jingxi.[40] Nearly 200,000 migrated people were supposed to be the main part of the Goguryeo ethnic group to be relocated this time. Most of the Goguryeo people who moved to the Central Plains were later assimilated into the Han nationality.

Jiao-Di sports of Goguryeo have not been recorded in the historical records, but archaeological materials provide us with a vivid picture. The first is the Jiao-Di mural unearthed from the "Dancing Tomb" in Donggou, Ji'an County, Jilin Province (see Fig. 5-5). At the lower part of caisson ceiling of the main wall in the chamber of the "dancer," there are two Jiao-Di players in the middle of the picture who are naked and barefooted, only with shorts on. They stand opposite to each other, preparing for the attack. Judging from their preparation position, the way they will play is relatively free, unlike the Huns' fixed posture. How-

Fig. 5-5 Jiao-Di Mural Unearthed from the "Dance Tomb"

ever, if we link it to the Mongolian wrestling activities discussed later, we will see that this is a more typical pre-match form of northern peoples, i.e., northern peoples like Mongolia will always have the action of imitating animals (such as eagles) before wrestling. It can also be seen in Fig. 5-5 that these two wrestlers are imitating a certain action, which is the typical feature of northern ethnic wrestling.

The second is the Jiao-Di mural unearthed in the "Jiao-Di Tomb" in Ji'an County (see Fig. 5-6). This painting is painted on the east wall of the tomb, in which there are two sturdy Jiao-Di athletes who are naked to the upper body and wear shorts underneath under a big tree. There also stands an old man with a cane in his right hand on the right side of the picture. He is pointing with his left hand to the athletes. From the scene in the picture, we may find out it looks like a training scene of Jiao-Di. Their actions are two people cuddling their waists and shoulders, which is very similar to the Huns' Jiao-Di. The four athletes in the two paintings are painted vividly. From their facial expressions to their strong and prominent muscles, it can be seen that they are good at Jiao-Di. In Fig. 5-5, there are horses running behind the two athletes, which shows that they are receiving training in the field instead of a formal competition. From Fig. 5-6, we can tell they might be trained in the stockade. The third is that Goguryeo's wrestling murals are also found in the tomb of Changchuan No. 1 in Ji'an (see Fig. 5-7). It can be told from this mural that the two wrestlers are wrestling, and their movements are very similar to the postures of the Huns, characterized by the northern national wrestling style.

Fig. 5-6 Jiao-Di Mural Unearthed from the "Jiao-Di Tomb"   Fig. 5-7 Jiao-Di Mural in Goguryeo

According to the above information, Goguryeo established a relationship with the Central Plains in the Han Dynasty, and also interacted closely with other ethnic groups in the north. Judging from the Jiao-Di form of the two murals above, Goguryeo's Jiao-Di movement was mainly affected by the exchanges with other ethnic groups in the north, which was particularly influenced by the Huns system. Of course, Goguryeo was also greatly affected by the Central Plains, especially when it was subordinated to the Central Plains; various cultures flooded to Goguryeo. For example, there is a record in *Book of the Later Han Dynasty · Memoirs of Goguryeo*, "Emperor Wu destroyed Korea and took Goguryeo as the county affiliated to Xuantu Prefecture, bestowing a number of musicians and players."[41] This indicates the affiliation between Goguryeo and the Central Plains at that time as well as the contacts between the two places. Of course, Goguryeo was also deeply influenced by the grassland culture. For example, the political organizations of Goguryeo share the same form as the Huns, including imperial titles at different levels.[42] From the above three murals, it can be seen that the Goguryeo people are fond of the Jiao-Di sports extremely. The sport is highly popular in Goguryeo, whose form of movement is mainly inherited from the tradition of the northern ethnic groups.

The Northern Dynasties were dominated mainly by the Xianbei people. The migration of the Xianbei from North China to the west brought not only North China's sports culture, but also part of the homeland of the Huns. They combined with the elements of the Huns and many other ethnic groups, and co-lived with the Han people. Thus, what about their wrestling sport? Does it follow the Sumo wrestling that prevailed in mainstream Chinese wrestling or the Huns' Jiao-Di? The discussion will be shown below.

Book of the Wei Dynasty · Biography of Xi Kangsheng contains: "Xi Kangsheng was rough and tough. Even Yuan Yi was afraid of him, and Xi Kangsheng felt uneasy. In March of the second year of Zhengguang, Emperor Xiaoming met Empress Dowager Hu in the Xilin garden. The civil and military officials sat down aside, drinking and dancing. It was Xi Kangsheng's turn to dance, who performed a dance of strength. Every time he turned around, he looked at Empress Dowager Hu, raised his hands, danced to his feet, glared, and nodded to her as if he would kill."[43] "Dance of Strength" is the jumping posture before the game, which is similar to Fig. 5-5. It can be seen from the Dunhuang murals that "raising hands and dancing feet" is the preparation posture of Sumo, which is the typical feature of **wrestling in Northern Dynasties. There are also some archaeological pictures as solid proof of Sumo of the Northern Dynasties. For example, the embossment Jiao-Di painting of the Northern Wei Dynasty was unearthed in Datong City, Shanxi, in 1970. On the stone brick (see Fig. 5-8), music and dance, beasts, strong men, and other images are embossed on its surrounding and the sides. One corner of the inkstone is embossed with a** *Jiao-Di* **image, in which there are two** *Jiao-Di* **players with long hair, bare legs, shorts, burly and strong physique. The two are tightly cuddled together, with the movements of hugging the waist and shoulders. Besides, in the embossment of Fudi Reservoir, Yijun County, Shaanxi Province, there are also images of Sumo wrestling in the Western Wei Dynasty (see Fig. 5-9). In the picture, two Sumo wrestlers are naked in shorts, which illustrates that they are in the middle of a competition. They are bound to each other and they trip with their feet.** The form of Jiao-Di in this painting is relatively free, inheriting the style of the Wei and Jin Dynasties. **Sumo figures from the Northern Zhou period can also be seen in the 290th mural of Mogao Grottoes in Dunhuang, Gansu Province (see Fig. 5-10). Although the characters in this painting are not from the Northern Zhou, it naturally reflects some conditions at that time as a work of the Northern Zhou Dynasty.** The Sumo picture is on the upper level of the west slope of the cave, which embraces one of the stories of the Buddha. In the picture, Prince **Xudana grabs the Prince of the Devil's neck with his left hand and Prince of the Devil's right ankle with his right hand, and he is about to throw Prince of the Devil to the ground. Both Prince Xudana and Prince of the Devil are topless, with only shorts on. The main** wrestling movements are still grappling, sharing the same characteristics as those in the Wei and Jin Dynasties.

Fig. 5-8 Jiao-Di Embossment Inkstone

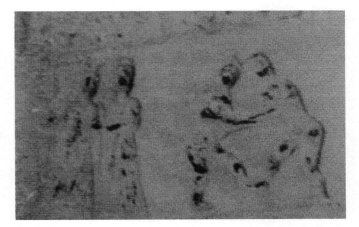

Fig. 5-9 Image of Sumo in the Western Wei Dynasty in the Embossment of Grottoes

Fig. 5-10 Sumo Figures from the Northern Zhou Period in Dunhuang Mogao Grottoes

Book of the Northern Qi Dynasty · Emperor Xiao records as follows: "Emperor Wenxuan Gao Yang was so addicted to *Jiao-Di* in his senior ages, and he stripped to play Sumo even in front of servants and women when he was in the house of his noble relatives, which seemed acts of obscenity."[44] Through the wrestling dress and wrestling movements, it can be illustrated that there is not only the wrestling style of the northern peoples mainly represented by the Huns, but also the influence of the Han culture, which was inherited from the Wei and Jin Dynasties. Therefore, both styles of wrestling co-existed at this time. In the *Book of the Sui Dynasty · Etiquette VII*, it is also recorded that after Emperor Wenxuan succeeded the throne, the guards followed the etiquette of Wei, including the official system and the guarding system. There were 12 Yulinlang teams of guards directly led by the generals. Besides, there were also many other teams, including the short-spear team, long-spear team, long-sword team, shield team, halberd team, animal team, red-cloak team, Jiao-Di team, Yulin team, walk team, and horse team.[45] We can thus conclude that the Northern Dynasty has also had a royal "wrestling team" since the Northern Wei Dynasty, and this etiquette system is similar to that of the Southern Dynasty.

5.2.2 Development of Sumo in the Sui and Tang Dynasties

In the early years of the Sui and Tang Dynasties, folks loved Sumo wrestling. *Book of the Sui Dynasty · Biography of Liu Yu* contains that people in the capital city played Jiao-Di, competing and rivaling each other until the 15th day of the first lunar month in recent times. As for the waste of financial resources, a document by Liu Yu suggested banning the show, which wrote, "I can see the wrestling scene in capital and other places in other parts of the country. Every night on the 15th day of the first lunar month, the streets are blocked, the drums are deafening, and torches are shining on the earth. People wear animal faces and men are in women's clothes, singing and dancing in acrobatic forms. What a weird scene it is. People at home and abroad have observed it and have never avoided it. They have exhausted their resources and competed in this period. The whole family is involved, regardless of age and gender. Men and women are mixed regardless of being high or low, and there is no distinction between monks and laymen. As a consequence, evil acts are born, and so do thieves arise. It is not unhelpful for education, but indeed it hurts people. Please enact the edict to the world and ban it immediately." The emperor issued the edict for approval.[46] It was during Emperor Wen of the Sui Dynasty that Liu Yu requested to ban the Jiao-Di pageant. The Jiao-Di play described here requires makeup, which is an ornamental activity accompanied by music and similar to the traditional Jiao-Di play since the Qin and Han Dynasties. Because he mentioned "since the recent times," he meant the time must be before the Sui Dynasty and must have been in existence for a long time. The article fully demonstrates that the activities of Jiao-Di are extremely popular in the capital and outside the city. Some people compare them unrealistically with each other so that it costs a lot of money. And "Jiao-Di doesn't make distinctions between the high and the low, involving both men and women. As a consequence, evil acts are born …" From this point of view, there were still some women who participated in this kind of sport. In particular, when they joined this sport, their clothes were not as tight and formal as usual. Hence, it will be more likely to feel shameful due to the possible exposure. He said, "Please enact the edict to the world and ban it immediately." This shows that people all over the country have the habit of watching Jiao-Di plays. Jiao-Di pageant can gather people from all walks of life together, which is highly boisterous. The competition mentioned here usually takes place in the first lunar month, which is very similar to the Sumo in the Han Dynasty held in spring and summer, which happens to be the time when traditional festivals of the Han culture take place in the Central Plains. Moreover, the truly competitive Jiao-Di activity is still developing among the folks.

Although Emperor Wen of the Sui Dynasty restricted the Jiao-Di play due to Liu Yu's letter, it was actively advocated by Emperor Yang of the Sui Dynasty. *Book of the Sui Dynasty · Emperor Yang* (in the first month of the spring in the sixth year of Daye) records that Jiao-Di was on show at Duanmen Street, where the world's wonderful arts and tricks were displayed till a month later. The emperor in plain clothes went to watch it many times.[47] The fact that "The emperor in plain clothes went to watch it many times" indicates that this kind of play isn't performed for the emperor or high-ranking officials, but one of the entertainment for the folks. It also shows that Jiao-Di play at that time was very common among civilians. This incident is similarly recorded in the *Tongjian Chronicles · Death of Emperor Yang in the Sui Dynasty*. There is also such a record that says, "It has become a regular activity every year," which means that this has become a convention held every year since then. During this period, Jiao-Di plays were also held in the first lunar month, which lasted for a long time. Certainly, Sumo was only part of the Jiao-Di plays.

There is such a record in the *Continued Biography of Eminent Monks Vol. 35 · Sensation · Interpretation of Dharma in Tang Fahai Temple* which notes that there was a son of Tao in the Sui Dynasty, a native of Benqin County, who was thin and weak, despised by others. Later he became a monk called Fatong. After being bullied, he told Guanyin what had happened. One day, he returned home to visit his mother. He slept under a tree and salivated massively. His mother thought he had a nightmare and screamed to wake him up. Fatong replied, "Just now, I dreamt that someone gave me three pieces of fragrant donkey tendons. I had just finished one piece when you woke me up. Unfortunately, I can't have the remaining two pieces." Fatong felt that he had strength at once and had no difficulty in lifting things. At that time, a Taoist of Xifan wrestled with people at the North Gate, and no one could beat him. Emperor Wen was worried and issued an edict to wrestle with the Hu people.[48] Although this story is mythological, it also conforms to the reality of Buddhist culture at that time. A Taoist whose Sumo wrestling is so advantageous, so it is not normal for people from the Western Regions to develop Sumo wrestling. Likewise, this is also the practice of the Central Plains emperor to deal with foreign competition, as the emperor would not easily lose the honor and dignity of Central Plains. In the third year of Daye, Emperor Yang went to the eastern capital. Pei Ju had seen a great number of "barbarians" coming to Luoyang to pay tribute. Thus he tried to persuade the emperor to popularize the arts and plays all over the country. Then kinds of acrobatic activities, including Jiao-Di plays, were everywhere in Luoyang. The display well boasted the strength of Central Plains to the minor ethnic tribes, yet it ceased one month later.[49] Pei Ju was very smart and saw that many "barbarians" came to pay tributes to Luoyang, so he suggested emperor to collect unique skills across the country, including Jiao-Di play. In this way, not only strange skills were possessed, but also the prosperity of the Central Plains could be widely manifested. The display that lasted tens of days well boasted the power of Han to the ethnic groups in the Western Regions. Pei Ju's move won the heart of Emperor Yang, who spoke to Yu Wenshu and Niu Hong: "Pei Ju knows what I meant well, and everything he submitted happened to be my will. He just took the words out of my mouth. Who can be like this unless he is devoted to serving the country?"[50] This best shows that in the period of Emperor Yang, both the emperor and officials fully realized the importance of handling the relationship between the ethnic groups, and also understood that sports performances can achieve favorable results. Here, it also confirms that wrestling in the Sui Dynasty as a common activity has penetrated into the lives of the people. Otherwise, how could it be possible to recruit unique skills and arts across the country? How can this grand event flourish for a month without regard to its rich content and large population?

Of course, it can be seen from the above documents that the content of the Jiao-Di play at that time was a large-scale pageant, including wrestling and other skills. It is true that wrestling is the highlight of the play that can win people's favor most.

From the early Tang Dynasty to Emperor Xuan Li Longji, Jiao-Di movement was promoted as important as it was in the Sui Dynasty. In *Tang Huiyao · Armies in the Capital*, the situation of *Jiao-Di* in the army is as follows: "At the end of Tianbao, the emperor appreciated the peace of Central Plains and cultivated culture and education, abolished the military armaments, destroyed the weapons, so as to weaken the powerful. Therefore, those who hold weapons were convicted, those who conspire prophecies were sentenced, and those who practice bows and arrows were guilty. Only the border states had heavy troops, and the Central Plains were wrapped in the middle so that the weapons were confiscated, indicating that they would not be employed anymore. People did not know the sound of war until they became old. All the soldiers and guards of the six armies were just common city residents and training-less. Rich people sold colorful clothes and ate delicious food. The stronger were immersed in wrestling, tugs of war, Qiaomu (Wood-lifting), and Kangtie (Iron-Carrying) all day long. When An Lushan rebelled, they failed to take the weapon and fight."[51] During the Emperor Xuanzong period, the country was relatively peaceful, with an emphasis on civil administration and a ban on martial arts, so the capital army was not allowed to use weapons.

Therefore, the guards and soldiers of the six armies, like other people in the capital, did some business if they were wealthy. Even the relatively strong men could be trained only through Jiao-Di, tug-of-war, wood-lifting, and iron-carrying to their satisfaction. Jiao-Di here obviously refers to the sport of wrestling. A similar record is also covered in the *New Book of the Tang Dynasty · Records of the Soldiers*: "Since Tianbao Period, archery system has been declining and the soldiers have begun to lose their military training. For eight years, Li Linfu advised the emperor to stop the entertaining practice as there were no official soldiers to be on employment. Later, there were only a small number of soldiers and officials left, and all other stuff prepared for military wars, such as weapons, carrying horses, and food were not available. Therefore, at that time, people in the government took turns to guard, who were either called 'servant officials' or 'guardians of the emperor' at this time. Wei Zuo served others with children slaves, and people in the capital were all shameful of that. When they insulted each other, they would say that they were officials. All the soldiers and guards of the six armies were just common city residents. The rich sold colorful clothes and ate delicious food, while the stronger were immersed in wrestling, tugs of war, Qiaomu (Wood-lifting), and Kangtie (Iron-Carrying) all day long. When An Lushan rebelled, they failed to take the weapon and fight."[52] Under this circumstance, most soldiers could not do business. As they had nothing to do, the game of Jiao-Di became everything to them, so wrestling became fairly popular in the heyday. Meanwhile, Jiao-Di activities carried out in the army could also be seen in Tian Hongzheng's army during the reign of Emperor Muzong: Liu Wu rebelled against the army and beheaded the leader of the army, Li Shidao. He then claimed to Hongzheng he would surrender with two states to offer. In the beginning, Liu Wu subdued the enemy and drank heavily in the army. For three days, he set up Jiao-Di plays for fun. Tian Hongzheng was greatly appreciated by the show, in which Liu Wu fought hard to show his competing skills, so that everyone knew how brave he was.[53] It can be seen that the Jiao-Di play was very prevalent in the army of the Tang Dynasty, which was not only used for military training, but also a performance item in the army. It is featured not only by competition but also by the function of entertainment.

The prevalence of the Jiao-Di movement in the Tang Dynasty was inseparable from the advocacy of emperors. For example, there are records in history that Emperor Xuanzong, Jingzong, and Wuzong all advocated Jiao-Di. *Old Book of the Tang Dynasty · Chronicles of Emperor Muzong* reads: "(in February of the 15th year of Yuanhe, AD 820) the amnesty was granted to the world at Danfeng Palace. After the announcement was completed, all kinds of acrobatic players were arrayed along Danfeng Gate, and the emperor took a look. In Dinghai year, the army of Zuoshence watched Jiao-Di and the acrobatic plays till the late afternoon. (In June) For three days, the officials and soldiers would go to Jiuxian Gate to watch Jiao-Di and acrobatic plays."[54] It is recorded in the *Old Book of the Tang Dynasty · Chronicles of Emperor Jingzong* that (In June, the second year of Baoli) the emperor inspected the musical workshops of the army located in the inner gardens. There were a variety of plays, such as the donkey bow and Jiao-Di. When it came to the climax, some people played broken heads and arms till one and two o'clock at night. *New Book of the Tang Dynasty: Biography of Liu Keming* cites: "Liu Keming, in accompany by Emperor Jingzong, watched Jiao-Di in the palace. The head and arms of those players were executed, with the blood flowing on the court. The emperor was so excited that he was awarded a lot, and the play lasted till late at night."⁵⁵ In *Tzu-chih t'ung (A Comprehensive Mirror for Aid in Government) · Emperor Wuzong in the First Year of Huichang*, the records are as follows: "The emperor was very fond of hunting and martial plays. (Note: Martial plays refer to ball-kicking (polo), mounted archery, hand-fighting (Sumo or Jiao-Di), etc.) Wufang kids were allowed to enter the palace and awarded tremendously."⁵⁶ From the above-cited information, it's obvious to see the prevalence of Jiao-Di in the Tang Dynasty and the situation advocated by the ruling class. In the competition, the wrestlers wrestled barehanded, and deaths and injuries accompanied from time to time, reflecting the fierce match at the time. It was not an ordinary performance but a life-and-death struggle.

Jiao-Di movement not only prevailed in the central army of the Tang Dynasty, but also in remote areas. There was such an event cited in the Protectorate mansion of Chanyu—Zhenwu Army (now somewhere in Horinger County, Inner Mongolia). *Taiping Collections · Zhenwu Jiao-Di People* notes that during the Guangqi year, Wang Bian, the envoy of Zuoshence army, went out of Zhenwu and held a banquet. After the musical play, he asked to show *Jiao-Di*. There was a very strong man coming from a neighboring state to compete here. More than a dozen people of similar physical appearance and strength in the army could not beat him. The general then selected three soldiers to battle with that man successively, but the man still won, which amazed all. The general and the guests all made a high compliment upon him. At that moment, a scholar sat on the table and suddenly got up to inform the general, "I can defeat this person." The general was quite surprised by the scholar's words, but he agreed to his request for his insistence. The scholar stepped down, entered the kitchen, and came out after a while. Then he covered his clothes, clenched his left hand, and moved forward. The strong man smiled and said: "well, one finger of mine can wrestle you down!" Waiting for the strong man to approach gradually, the scholar darted out his left hand only to throw him suddenly down to the ground. Gales of laughter erupted from the seats as the scholar slowly walked out of the ring and washed his hands before returning to his seat. The general questioned, "What kind of trick?" He replied, "A few years ago, I met the man in a restaurant. He got close to the table and stumbled. A companion said, 'He is afraid of sauce, and will fall as soon as he sees it.' I heard and remembered. I went to the kitchen just now, asked for some sauce, and held it in my hand. This person fell by himself as expected when he saw the sauce. Think of it as the adding laughter to this party." A judge aside witnessed this matter. How wonderful this man is in the article! Even a dozen strong soldiers in the army can not beat him (From *Yutang Gossips*).⁵⁷ The article also states that this person does not have a fixed residence and has been seen in another restaurant by the scholar. It is possible that there still exist people who work for Jiao-Di plays or other competitions for a living.

In the Tang Dynasty, there were "Sumo sheds" in the musical workshops, which was an organization that specialized in managing and recruiting Sumo wrestlers. In *Notes of Jiao-Li · Archaeology*, it was cited as follows: "Meng Wanying claimed to be a native of Hu County, Jingzhao. During the Xiantong Period of Emperor Xizong in the Tang Dynasty, he was selected from a number of children to go into the workshop. When he was just 14 or 15 years old, people older than him were afraid of his agile punches and kicks. When he grew up, he often won competitions and received great rewards. That's how the name 'Wanying (all-won)' came to be. After getting old, (Wu Suqian) the king asked him to teach others."⁵⁸ "Sumo sheds" are the official Sumo management agency that appeared in the mid-Tang Dynasty, which is equivalent to the Left and Right army mentioned in the *Old Book of the Tang Dynasty*. The establishment of this kind of specialized management organization has actually been included in the previous article. For example, the "wrestling team" during the Qi and Sui Dynasty was a professional institution. "Wanying" is just his stage name, from which we may know his achievements in Sumo wrestling. This stage name is rarely recorded in the Tang Dynasty literature, but there are many records in the Song Dynasty.

In the later Tang Dynasty, the emperor was very keen on wrestling and even waged wrestling competitions with official positions as stakes. Of course, this was very absurd. However, it is reflected that Jiao-Di was still relatively popular in society at that time, according to the literature records. The case in the *History of the Old Five Dynasties · Biography of Li Cunxian* says Li Cunxian, who came from Xuzhou, had some talents and was good at playing Jiao-Di. At the beginning of the year, in the feudal residence of Emperor Zhuangzong (Li Cunxu), wrestling was always held at the banquet. The emperor asked his man to compete with Wang Yu in Jiao-Di, who repeatedly won the game. Emperor Zhuangzong boasted of his ability and said to Li Cunxian, "Let's have a competition. If you win, you will be rewarded a county." So they had a competition Instantly. Cunxian won the game and thus was appointed as the governor of Weizhou.[59] Sumo wrestling is also popular in all parts of the south, as is recorded in the *Notes of Jiao-Li · Origin: Between Poyang and Jingchu*, the great pageant would be held in May, in which people would play in water or race across the river. In the housing block, people were delighted with wrestling (Sumo). In Shu County, the young and rich set up society to recruit the brave and the strong from Qiaoshi and collected money to prepare wine and food. Probably in the Lantern Festival, they would meet at the plains in front of the mountain. At that time, the green grass looked like a green carpet. There were so many people who watched the match. A pair of rivals would fight first, and the winner would be rewarded by society, and then he would gather the horse riding away. There were a lot of spectators in the field and just a few in the alleys. It would last from the Lantern Festival till May.[60] These materials also indicate that the time of the Sumo wrestling match is from January to May. The competition is organized by the folk society, from which the rewards for the winners are provided. Special venues are built for a one-on-one fight. The southern wrestling had been developed so well and passed down to the Jin and Yuan Dynasties that the ruling class had to ban the wrestling of the Han for their own dominance.

From the Wei, Jin, Southern, and Northern Dynasties to the Sui, Tang, and Five Dynasties, Chinese wrestling is rough as follows: First, the wrestling movement in the Central Plains was very popular throughout the whole country, ranging from Wu and Shu state in the south to the Zhenwu Army in the north. The second is that the form of competition and the attire of the wrestlers are mainly inherited from the Huns among the northern ethnic groups, while the Han area is mainly inherited from the Qin and Han Dynasties. Third, the competition time happens to be the same as that in Qin and Han Dynasties. Spring Match is in the first month, while the summer match is in May. Fourth, there has been wrestling competition in arenas in folklore, in which the winner is usually rewarded.[61]

In addition, the situation of wrestling in the northern areas during the same period is also worth thinking about. *Continued Biography of the Eminent Monks: Biography of the Tianzhu Monk*

Lenamanti of Yongning Temple in Luojing recorded that Lenamanti was an Indian monk who lived in Yongning Temple in Luojing. He was good at Buddhism. Qiwu Huaiwen, the prefectural governor of Xin Zhou, was smart and knowledgeable in nature. He was very concerned every time the state purchased the instruments used in the palace, paying attention to both public and private benefits, which were widely appreciated. In addition, he also ordered to repair Yongning Temple. Knowing the fact that Lenamanti was a man of great attainments, Huaiwen sent some food and pay to him, expecting a chance to meet. However, Lenamanti just ignored him. So he has a grudge against him. At that time, there was a guest from the state of Ruru in Xuanwu Hall, Luonan, who was an old friend of Lenamanti in the Western Regions. He rode a horse and wore fur clothing to rebuild the temple. The two talked and laughed, clapping their hands all day. Besides them, Huaiwen didn't understand their language. So he said to Lenamanti, Ruru was a troublemaker. He came here to make offerings hoping that he could give some advice, but he never said a single word at all. This was the man of the northern minorities, with a human face but a beastly heart, who killed animals and ate them raw. There was nothing left to be desired. Unexpectedly, he was in the opposite. Lenamanti replied, do not take him lightly. Even if you have read thousands of books, it may not be enough to compete with him. Huaiwen responded, it was known that he spent money on horses and wrestlers.[62] Ruru is from Rouran, which is an ethnic group in the north of our country in ancient times. Huaiwen scolds Ruru people who only know about wrestling and horse racing, which provides us the enlightenment that the Rouran exerted somewhat influence upon the Central Plains at that time, and their wrestling was as prevailing as horse racing. From the current literature and archaeological materials, it is still impossible to know the wrestling form of Rouran people.

5.2.3 Sumo Movement Recorded in the Song Dynasty

The Song Dynasty's records of wrestling are more detailed, such as *Dongjing Menghua Lu* by Meng Yuanlao, *Meng Liang Lu* by Wu Zimu, *Old Story of Wulin* by Si Shui Qiang Fu, *Ducheng Jisheng* by Guanyuan Naide, and *The Prosperity of the Old Man in West Lake*. These works have very detailed records of Sumo in the Song Dynasty, providing us with precious materials for studying the history of ancient wrestling. We can learn about the specific situation of the official Jiao-Di employed by the emperor and the private Jiao-Di in the folklore through the relevant records.

The first is the official Jiao-Di, as recorded in *Jiao-Di*, Volume 20 of *Meng Liang Lu*: "Jiao-Di is the synonym of Sumo, also called 'wrestling.' In addition, at the imperial court meeting, holy festival, and the ninth of the royal banquet held Sumo wrestling which is named 'Neidengzi,' attended by those non-commoners. The official Jiao-Di is under the command of the head of the imperial Zhongzuo army, and those who are strong enough will be selected for the quota at Yuanyu Palace. Whenever there were suburban worship and Mingtang ceremony or dedication to the ancestral temples, the emperors would all drive off. And the carriages are driven by the Left and Right Army with top hats before carriages. The wrestlers are fluffy, with fists clenched. In the event of the sacred festival and the royal banquet, the Left and Right Army Sumo wrestling, Neidengzi, will be adopted. There are supposed to be 120 people, including twenty working on the custody, ten pairs of upper and middle classes, eight pairs of a lower class, and five pairs of swords and sticks. The rest are alternates. Once every three years, the department will compete for the next entry. From the custody to the Neidengzi, it's also changed once every three years. When the emperor selects Sumo wrestling players, the silver and silk will be rewarded then they will also be appointed as the custody officer or the head of the army by the department."[63] This information introduces Song's official Jiao-Di in detail. First of all, the changes in the name of Jiao-Di are well covered. Secondly, it states that Jiao-Di players are selected from the army and are managed by a special institution. The task of the Jiao-Di team is to perform at court banquets, the emperor's birthday, sacrifices, and other festivals, and to act as guards when the emperor visits out of the palace. There is a limit to the quota for the official management of Jiao-Di team, including a total of 120. Among them are 20 in official custody. The athletes of Jiao-Di are divided into three classes, including super, middle, and lower par, with ten pairs of upper and middle classes, eight pairs of lower classes, and five pairs of swords and sticks. To sum up, there is a total of 66 people and the rest are alternates. These players will compete in front of the palace every three years. The goodwill upgrade and be rewarded, either serving as custody personnel or working in the military offices of various states to act as the head. In this way, they spread the Jiao-Di movement from the palace to wider places and military barracks. Once every three years, such a speed of talent exchange is not simple. Once the Jiao-Di players who are under the jurisdiction of the original division serve around, it is bound to select the new players from the army again. Such an incentive mechanism contributes greatly to strengthening the Jiao-Di training among the sergeants and soldiers. It is conceivable that Jiao-Di movement of the entire official system must have been well-developed at that time. We all know that this phenomenon already existed in the Tang Dynasty, as mentioned earlier in the story of Meng Wanying.

Then there is the Jiao-Di in the folklore from *Jiao-Di*, Volume 20 of *Meng Liang Lu*. This book introduces the situation of local wrestling. The author said that folk Sumo wrestlers are generally spontaneous entertainers, who are people of different careers gathering together and earn money through performances. In this kind of scene, first some women engage in routine sparring to attract some audience, and then the most spectacular and exciting fight (wrestling) is revealed for people to watch, hoping that the audience can donate money. The author also described the situation at that time by taking the wrestling in Huguo Temple as an example. An open-air arena was built at a higher place in the south of the temple for competition. Participants must be selected from the county or state with strong arm strength, and the winner can win the rewards, such as flags, silver glasses, colored satin, brocade jacket, official currency, and horses. During the span of Jingding, under the rule of Jia Qiuhe, Han Fu, a man from Wenzhou, won a wrestling competition and got the first reward. Jia appointed him as the Junzuo in assisting the army affairs. In Hangzhou, there are men, like Zhou Jikuai, Dong Jikuai, Wang Jikuai, Sai Guansuo, Redhair Zhu Chao, Zhou Mangchong, Zheng Boda, Ironsmith Han Tongwang, Yang Changjiao, etc., and women like Sai Guansuo, Xiao Sanniang, Hei Sijie, all of whom won from the wrestling competitions in the folklore and became famous.[64] This source describes the condition of Jiao-Di plays among the commoners. It can be said that folk Sumo wrestlers are usually spontaneous entertainers who come together from different careers to earn money through performing. Such scenes begin with some women performing set sparring to attract some spectators, and then the most spectacular and exciting competing intercourse (wrestling) is revealed for people to watch, with a view to the spectators donating coins. The author also described the situation with the example of the scrimmage conducted at the Huguo Temple. An open-air arena was built at a higher place on the south side of the temple for wrestling competitions, in which the winners were rewarded. Another example, in the Jingding Period (under the reign of Emperor Lizong, Zhao Yun), a man named Han Fu from Wenzhou won first place in a wrestling match and thus was directly appointed as Zengbu Junzuo by Jia Qiuhe, who was in power at the time. This is a typical example of local government officials selecting talents through wrestling competitions, as well as promoting officials and increasing their posts. This is also a choice for ordinary people to go to the official career. Then, under such a mechanism, there must be many civilians who hope to achieve this leap through such training. Therefore, wrestling sports in folklore are carried out vividly. Here the author also mentioned many other wrestlers in Hangzhou City, and some of them have stage names that are very distinctive. The author lists the names of the wrestlers in *Meng Liang Lu*, *Notes of Jiao-Li*, and *Old Story of Wulin* as follows (see Table 5-2).

Table 5-2 Summary of Some Excellent Wrestler's Names in Selected Literature

Reference	Names of the Excellent Wrestlers			
Notes of Jiao-Li	Li Qingzhou	Wang Yuzi	Wang Basi	Li Chenzi
	Shen Guizi	Shi Yanneng	Liu Xianzi	Wang Sheng
	Yao Jieer	Zhang Qiongyuan	Xie Jian	
Meng Liang Lu · Jiao-Di	Han Fu	Dong Jikuai	Wang Jikuai	Redhair zhu Chao
	Yang Changjiao	Zhou Jikuai	Sai Guansuo	Ironsmith Han Tongwang
	Zheng Boda	Zhou Mangchong		
Old Story of Wulin · Jiao-Di[65]	Wang Jiaoda	Zhang Guansuo	Zhuang Daoshan	Liu Zilu
	Lu Dalang	Tie Banta	Sai Xiansheng	Jin Chongwang
	Sai Banta	Cao Tielin	Sai Jiaoda	Sai Guansuo
	Zhou Heida	Zhang Jiaoda	Liu Chunge	Cao Tiequan
	Wang Jikuai	Yan Guansuo	Han Tongzhu	Han Tieseng
	Wang Saige	Yi Batiao	Wen Zhouzi	Han Guiseng
	Hei Balang	Zheng Pai	Chang Huazi	Xiao Zhuge
	Zhou Senger	Guang Datou	Jin Shouge	Yan Tietiao

(Continued)

Reference	Names of the Excellent Wrestlers			
Old Story of Wulin · Qiao Xiangpu	Wu Dangshan	Gai Laizhu	Dong Jikuai	Dong Jiaoda
	Zhou Banta	Zheng Sanzhu	Zhou Chongwang	Xiao Guansuo
	Xiao Heida	Ruan Shege	Fu Maixian	Zheng Baida
	Yuan Yutou	He Ertou	Yuan Yangtou	Yi Tiaohei
	Yi Tiaobai	Dou Menqiao	Bai Yugui	He Baiyu
	Ye Mingzhu			
Old Story of Wulin · Nüzhan	Han Chunchun	Xiu Lebo	Jin Lebo	Sai Maoduo
	Yao Liuniang	Hou Beijiao	Nü Jikuai	

Part of the names of the above-mentioned wrestlers are stage names or are based on "birthplace" (such as Li Qingzhou, Wu Dangshan, etc.), "physical characteristics"(such as Yao Jieer, Li Changzi, Yang Changjiao, etc.), or "craftsmanship features" (such as Dong Jikuai, Han Tongzhu, etc.), to name just a few. From the novices whose stage names are based on craftsmanship features, some of the movement techniques of wrestling at that time can be understood. The first is to win quickly in wrestling, i.e., to end the match at the fastest speed through a few lightning moves, such as Dong Jikuai, Wang Jikuai, Zhou Jikuai, and Nü Jikuai, etc. The second is to push the opponent backward with a strong force and knock him down to the ground so that he can beat the opponent, such as Zhuang Daoshan. The third is to manage stabilizing the center of gravity during the game to prevent from falling over the opponent, such as Tie Banta, Zhou Banta, etc. Fourth, the wrestler picks up the opponent as a whole during the game and throws him down after leaving the ground, such as Yi Batiao, etc. These technical movements show that the requirements of wrestling moves at this time are relatively flexible, and it is not necessary for athletes to compete in a certain fixed posture, which is similar to today's freestyle wrestling.

5.3 Prevalence of Wrestling in the Liao, Jin, and Xixia Dynasties

Liao, Jin, and Xixia are three regimes respectively established by the Khitan, Jurchen, and Tangut in the Song Dynasty. Well, how is the Song's prosperous wrestling sport going in Liao, Jin, and Xixia? "Wrestling" is called "Balisu" in Jurchen language.[66] Jin culture is first inherited from Liao and then Song.

Wrestling was very common in the Liao Dynasty, established by the Khitan. *History of the Liao Dynasty · Chronicles of Emperor Taizu (I)* records: "(Taizu) In the first month of the spring of the eighth year, He Lu served as Yilijin of Diela Division and Hulie as Tiyin. Yuguli tribe, Telimin captured 17 people who were from the rebellious tribes, such as Buhu and Yali, and the emperor made the interrogation himself. Considering that the captives were related to several families and some were coerced into joining the rebel party, they just killed the head of Buhu and released the rest. Yu Yue along with Huage repeatedly plotted tricks, yet they were forgiven by the emperor a couple of times. Unfortunately, Huage was reluctant to correct the error. So the emperor called the old officials to rectify his sins and kill his sons, and distribute his wealth to the guards. There were more than 300 people who rebelled against the court and the case got closed. The emperor took into account that human lives were at stake and that they could not return back to life, so he hosted a banquet for a day in the hope of comforting the souls of the dead. The emperor let them follow their usual hobbies, some singing, some dancing, some playing archery or **wrestling after drinks till to their content."**[67] The records reveal that Emperor Taizu asked 300 criminals on the verge of punishment to follow their own favorite hobbies in life. Their choices after drinking were singing, dancing, and doing archery or Jiao-Di. Each criminal satisfied his own wishes. It can be seen that wrestling is very pervasive and prevalent among the Khitans.

During the reign of Emperor Taizong of the Liao Dynasty, Jiao-Di play was included in the banquets and pilgrimages, embedded into a major part of the spectacle. *History of the Liao Dynasty · Chronicles of Emperor Taizu (I)* records: "(Taizong Tianxian) In the first month in the spring of the fourth year, the state ministers, together with envoys of various states, watched Paiyou and Jiao-Di plays. It was also recorded that: (in June of the seventh year of Tianxian), Emperor Taizong watched the Jiao-Di plays." In the above two records of watching Jiao-Di plays, one was in the first month of spring, and the other was in June in the summer. That is to say, the wrestling in the Liao Dynasty court was also held in spring and summer, which is similar to the time the wrestling match held in the Han and Tang Dynasties.

In the *The Continuing General Survey of Qinding*, the information on the birthday banquet of the emperor of the Liao Dynasty and the **banquet to entertain Song envoys is recorded**. The performances performed at the banquet included Jiao-Di, Zaju (variety plays), etc., and a diversity of musical instruments, including Chinese lute, Sheng, Chinese zither etc., were followed one after another as the drinks proceeded. "On emperor's birthday, wine feast went with Bili in the first round, and then the song, Pipa playing in the third round with some tea and refreshments. When it came to the fourth round, Que entered and then solo Sheng, drum, and flute in the fifth round, followed by Chinese zither and Zhu Ball in the sixth round. The final round ended with Jiao-Di."[68] Similar events about feasting the envoys from the **Song Dynasty were recorded**. The two banquets mentioned above are both large scenes with high specifications. There are nine rounds of the drinking game in the second event, and a series of performances or competitions are held in the process, which is similar to the etiquette of the **Song Dynasty**. The previous quote in *Meng Liang Lu* cited that Sumo was held in the ninth line of wine banquet of the Song, which is consistent with the records of *History of the Song Dynasty*. Although the 19th program of the Song banquet in *History of the Song Dynasty* was Sumo wrestling, it was only performed during the ninth line of the wine order as the final program of the banquet. The etiquette of the Liao banquet is relatively simpler than that of the Song, yet the drinking game also contains nine lines, and Jiao-Di is listed as the final performing entertainment, too. The final programs are usually the most exciting. It is conceivable that both the Song Dynasty and the Liao Dynasty attached importance to the Jiao-Di plays.

From the above literature, we can easily see that the Liao Dynasty paid as much attention as the Song to Jiao-Di, and more documents are presented as follows. *The Continuing General Survey of Qinding* cites: "Liao Dynasty has its national music. On the first day of the first month, palace Yayue (elegant music) is used when the court celebrates, and Dayue (grand music) is used at Yuanhui. After the grand music is performed, Sanyue (folk music) follows, and Jiao-Di ends."[69] When the emperor confers titles of nobility on the empress, all kinds of entertainments, such as Jiao-Di plays and acrobatics, will be played for fun. In October (the tenth year of Chongxi), Prince Kulu Galisheng, the prime minister of the north, and the emperor's son-in-law Saiyin Baning greeted the emperor at his first banquet. The emperor appointed his guards to wrestle with Han people for fun.[70] Why are there records of the Han people wrestling with the guards of Liao in the literature? As we know, the relationship between the Northern Song and Liao was very close at that time. Regardless of the war, the two had frequent contacts and exchanges. So how did the Han people wrestle with the guards of the Liao? It is necessary for us to understand what the Jiao-Di of the Liao Dynasty is like and how they play the game. There is a record in Zhang Shunmin's *Huamanlu*: When the northern captives entertained the southern envoys, there were more than 300 people involved in the queue who danced and played nonstop till they halted stumbling and shrinking. Jiao-Di prescribes that the one who falls to the ground is the loser. The two hold each other tightly, intending to throw the opponent down but not getting at it. A small piece of object covered their breasts, and if they were exposed by chance, they would walk away with both hands covering their face, feeling deeply ashamed.[71] These pieces of materials clearly reflect some key information about the Khitan tribe's wrestling at that time. First, falling to the ground is regarded as a failure in the game. Secondly, the two hold each other tightly, intending to throw the opponent down but not getting at it, which is obviously different from the tactics of the Tang and Song Dynasties' Sumo that determines the winner in a quick way. On the contrary, it is very similar to today's Chinese wrestling and Mongolian national-style wrestling. Third, some small objects are used to cover the player's breasts, which seems like the costume of wrestlers. Jin Qicong believes that it must be a hard object used to cover the player's chest, which can only be made of leather.[72] However, it is not stated whether they wear clothes, and evidence still remains to be found. In 1931, an octagonal white clay pot of the Liao Dynasty was unearthed at the Dongjing site in Liaoning (now Liaoyang City, Liaoning Province) (see Fig. 5-11-1 to Fig. 5-11-4), which turned out to be a very precious cultural relic for the study of Khitan wrestling. The Japanese, Torii Ryuzo, once wrote the article *Khitan's Jiao-Di*.[73] He believes that the painting on the pot is the image of a Khitan child wrestling, typical of a comic strip. Torii Ryuzo's explanation is as follows: In the first picture, two Khitan children who wear something similar to a belly band opposite each other, waiting for the game. The second picture draws these two Khitan children, who wear short sleeveless coats and belly bands, raise their hands, and exercise their feet to make preparations. In the third painting is that the game is about to start, and the two are yet twisting together. Besides, there are two other people aside, holding flowers in their hands, who seem to be referees. The fourth picture is a scene of tense fighting with each other, with the Khitan child on the left twisting with his two hands and pushing the opponent to the ground by his feet.

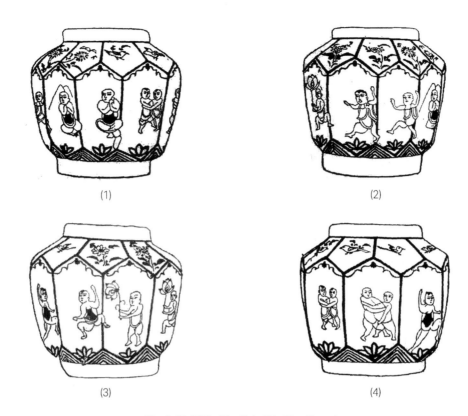

Fig. 5-11 White Clay Pot of the Liao Dynasty

Based on the above literature, Jin Qicong also has the following views. He believes, firstly, the short sleeveless coat proves that the wrestlers wear clothes during the Balisu competition. This kind of coat is the predecessor of the "Zhuoduoge" worn by Mongolian national wrestlers today. Secondly, Khitan children wear their belly bands, which are explained by Torii Ryuzo as "a small piece of object used to cover the breasts." Or besides wearing costumes, there are other breast-shielding things on their chests when Khitan wrestle. However, these covers are gradually eliminated, with only short sleeveless coats remaining. The sleeveless costume of Khitan is very likely to be made of leather, which later evolved into the "Zhuoduoge" worn by Mongolian warriors today. Therefore, the following conclusion can be drawn: in the "Balisu" played by the Khitan people in the Liao Dynasty, players wear short sleeveless coats with their breasts covered. The form of the match is different from Sumo but similar to today's Chinese wrestling and Mongolian national wrestling.[74]

The author argues that Japanese scholar Torii Ryuzo's views are open to question. First of all, he regarded the pictures on the clay pot as a comic strip, which paved the way for his improper explanation later. He used these pictures as a comic strip and described them like a story. Didn't he make sure this was a real story? According to his views, if you look closely at the two people in Fig. 5-11-1 and the other two in Fig. 5-11-2, they are clearly not the same. He also said that the third painting describes that the competition is about to start, and the players have not yet been twisting. And the fourth one is a scene of intense fighting with each other. As a matter of fact, the four pairs of eight people in the above four pictures are eight different players, which can be told from their figures, costumes, and hairstyles. Since it is not a series of stories, it certainly cannot be used to explain Khitan's wrestling. The real wrestling scene of this clay pot just happens to be in the fourth (Fig. 5-11-4). Yet there is also a certain gap compared to the understanding of Jin Qicong in terms of the costumes worn by the two contestants. From this picture, it can be clearly seen that both players are topless, so there are no sleeveless coats or any covers. In addition, from the fourth picture, Khitan's wrestling movements mainly inherit the form of the Huns, which requires hugs. However, from the picture, it can be seen that their movements are flexible and also apply tripping movements. Of course, the pot only painted Khitan children, yet we can extrapolate the Khitan people's love for wrestling and the grand development of the sport.

The Khitan people's wrestling movement can also be confirmed by other materials. For example, *History of the Liao Dynasty · Geographia* reads that during the period of Guangshun, Hu Qiao cites the following: "If you go to the West Building of the capital, you can see there are huge markets where people trade and use cloth instead of money. There are all kinds of occupations, including eunuchs, Hanlin scholars, technicians, staff from teaching workshops, Jiao-Di players, Confucianism believers, monks, nuns, and Taoist priests. The majority of the above are those from Bing, Fen, You, and Jiu."[75] This corresponds to the above-mentioned fact that "the emperor ordered guards to wrestle with the Han people" in October in the tenth year of Chongxi, including the wrestling between the Khitan and the Han. The reason why they can compete on the same stage is that their sports must have something in common. Some scholars believe that the Khitan itself originated from the ancient Huns or Xianbei in our country.[76] Although this view is still controversial, in any case, the Khitan is indeed inseparable from the Huns and Xianbei. During the Qin and Han Dynasties and the Southern and Northern Dynasties, these two ethnic groups conducted in-depth cultural exchanges and extensive ethnic integration with the Han, so the Khitan is no exception under the influence of the Han to some extent. Therefore, the wrestling activities they carried out, whether from the literature or from the archaeological pictures, not only maintained the form of wrestling of the northern people, but also were affected to a certain extent by the wrestling of the Han people, especially in terms of some wrestling customs. For example, wrestling is usually arranged in the first month or June in summer or popularized in some grand banquets.

Jin was a government established by the Jurchen tribe in the inheritance of some Liao customs. Jin was influenced by the Song Dynasty on the one hand and shared great similarities with the Khitan in many aspects on the other hand. The wrestling competition of the Jurchens should be similar to that of the Khitans, and the situation is as follows. *History of the Jin Dynasty · Biography of Bendu* contains: "Ang, whose real name was Bendu, was the grandson of Emperor Jingzu and the son of Xiewo. When he was a child, he served Emperor Taizu (Wan Yanmin). Taizu ordered several people to wrestle with each other. At that time, Ang was fifteen years old. The emperor asked him, 'Can you do this?' He answered, 'I dare not disobey the order.' Then he won six people successively. Emperor Taizu said amusingly, 'You are my clan brother and stay with me from now on.' After a few days, Ang was given gold medals and ordered to serve as the guard for the emperor."[77] *History of the Jin Dynasty · Biography of Arthan* contains: "Arthan was a member of the Wendihan tribe. … Arthan was a very filial son who was good at giving favors, hunting, and playing Jiao-Di and Cuju."[78] *History of the Jin Dynasty · Biography of Shi Morong* includes as follows: "Shi Morong served as the guard in the second year of Tianjuan (AD 1139). Emperor Xizong held the banquet for feasting and ordered Zuo Wangyuan to wrestle with Shi Morong. It turned out that Shi Morong won six or seven strong wrestlers successively. Delighted Emperor Xizong was, he proposed him a toast, granted him gold coins, and promoted him to the Suzhi General."[79] *History of the Jin Dynasty · Biography of Pucha Shijie* contains: "Pucha Shijie, whose real name was A'Sa, was from Woduhe in Hesuguan and later moved to Liaoyang. He served in Zongbi's army as a man of great power. And every time he wrestled with other warriors to bet on sheep, he always won. Even a four-year-old bull could be punched to die by him. There was a food truck stuck in the marshland, and seven bulls couldn't pull out. It happened that Shijie pulled it out from the marshland by force only with his bare hands."[80] *History of the Jin Dynasty · Records of Hailing* cites as follows: "(the third year of Zhenyuan) In June, the emperor climbed the Baochang Gate to watch the Jiao-Di play, and the people appreciated it. Also documented is that in the first year of Zhenlong, on the occasion of the emperor's birthday, Song, Gaoli, and Xia states all dispatched envoys to present congratulations. In the second year, they gathered to watch the Jiao-Di plays."[81] *History of the Jin Dynasty* was written by one person, but why is "Jiao-Li" or sometimes "Jiao-Di" respectively used to describe the wrestling in the above information? As mentioned earlier, Jiao-Li is a kind of wrestling that is known for its strength, and Jiao-Di is a general concept that includes not only wrestling but also other acrobatics, operas, paiyou, and so on at that time. The above documents show that the Jurchen's wrestling was noted for their strength before Hailing King Wan Yanliang, i.e., whoever has the greatest strength can basically have the advantage. For example, the author clearly described in the *Biography of Pucha Shijie* that Pucha Shijie could box a four-year-old cow to die, and pull a cart with grains that failed to be pulled out by seven cows from the marshland, which demonstrates the strength of Shijie explicitly. However, Arthan was also a Jurchen who lived before the time of Hailing King. Why was his wrestling recorded as Jiao-Di? As we know, Arthan followed Sagai and Wodai against other tribes since he was 17 years old. Then he also attacked Goguryeo many times and achieved numerous military exploits, capturing a lot of Goguryeo folks. At that time, Goguryeo people were deeply influenced by the culture of the Sui and Tang Dynasties. According to previous research on Goguryeo's wrestling, its wrestling was also affected by the Sui and Tang Dynasties. Of course, Arthan was just a case in point, who employed his strength and skills flexibly in wrestling and thus became absolutely famous. In addition, Jin had been deeply influenced by the Han culture from the time of Emperor Taizu via Taizong to Emperor Xizong, and "followed the old style of Jurchen."[82] When it was in the reign of Hailing King, he adopted a total sinicization policy. For this purpose, he did not hesitate to destroy Shangjing to stop Jurchen's homesickness. Hailing King loved wrestling and vigorously promoted Jiao-Di, even setting up wrestling competitions for the folks to watch. It can also be seen that wrestling at this time mainly advocated the style of the Han Dynasty, contributing to the more prosperous development of the sport.

Moreover, Hailing King imitated the time of the Han, Sui, and Tang Dynasties, and applied wrestling to political communication. For example, on the birthday of Hailing King, Jiao-Di plays were served to treat the envoys from Song, Goguryeo, and Xixia. It is well-known that China was divided into several major political powers represented by Jin, Song, and Xixia at that time, and Jin was the most powerful among other states. However, the Song state, located in the Central Plains, was rich in fertile fields and water, which is conducive to developing agriculture vigorously. As a result, it was economically strong, posing a huge threat to Jin. Therefore, Jin needs to demonstrate its strength in a variety of ways, thereby consolidating its position.

There are some notes which prove that Emperor Zhangzong in the Jin Dynasty once ordered the prohibition of wrestling. *History of the Jin Dynasty · Zhangzong (II)* contains: "(the 4th year of Mingchang) In March of Renshen year … the civilians who worked on Jiao-Di and weapons were convicted. (the 6th year of Mingchang) In May of Yisi year, some people gathered together to practice martial arts during breaks in farming. Benlu Tixingsi observed the situation and punished those lazy people."[83] Emperor Zhangzong mainly forbade Jiao-Di activities in the Han region, which happened in the fourth year of Mingchang. At that time, when Tixingsi[84] of all regions went to court, Emperor Zhangzong asked about the situation in various places. The emperor believed it was because Tixingsi had failed to do his work well that the social order of regions remained messy. In addition, the internal situation of Jin was no longer sound during the reign of Emperor Zhangzong. Mongolia rose from the north of Jin, and the emperor feared that the Han people would gather to resist again. Therefore, Emperor Zhangzong forbade the Hans to engage in Jiao-Di, as well as the use of spears and sticks. Instead, he encouraged the Jurchens to strengthen their military practice and increase their fighting ability so as to prevent the Hans from resisting. There is no record of the effects of Jin's prohibition on Han's wrestling, which can only be inferred. Yet, according to the instructions of the edicts when Emperor Shizu and Emperor Renzong of the Yuan Dynasty once again banned wrestling, we can infer that Jin's ban on Sumo has achieved the expected results. Of course, the folk customs that have prevailed for years could not be prohibited once and for all by the feudal emperor with a single edict. There were still many civilians engaged in the Jiao-Di plays. However, wrestling, as the former dominating form of the national mainstream games, for the first time encountered huge political pressure.

As mentioned above, Khitan's wrestling is not a system of its own, which failed to follow the kind of costume proposed by Jin Qicong. As Mr. Jin noted, Jin's wrestling activities were inherited from the Liao Dynasty.[85] So what exactly is the wrestling activity in the Jin Dynasty? A pair of Sumo clay figurines in Weinan County, Shaanxi Province, in 1986 (see Fig. 5-12) are the solid proof. The two figures have typical physical characteristics of Jin nationality, who are topless, bare-legged, barefoot, wearing triangle shorts, and are in the state of preparing for the competition. According to the *Proofs of the Annals of Great Jin*, Yellü Dashi was independent of the Liao emperor and claimed to be the emperor. Xu Kangzong was sent out to visit Jin State to extend the congratulations as the Song envoy. … the furnishing custom of Xu's Mansion basically corresponds to that of Khitan, yet other celebrating events such as acrobatic plays, Jiao-Di, cockfighting, and *Jiju* share a lot in common with the Song Dynasty. After the entertainment, a couple of female dancers on the stage were holding two mirrors up and down, the gestures of which were quite unique.[86] The above records depicted the scene of congratulation when Xu Kangzong was sent as an envoy to the Jin state. It can be seen that the residence of Xu shares the similar furnishing custom with the

Khitan, while all other acrobatic activities such as Jiao-Di, cockfighting, and *Cuju* are the same as those of the Song Dynasty, which fully demonstrates that Song exerted tremendous effects on the cultural rituals of Liao and Jin.

Fig. 5-12 A Pair of Jin Sumo Clay Figurines in Weinan, Shaanxi Province

Combining the above discussion, the author believes that the northern peoples were deeply influenced by the local wrestling in early development, and their wrestling styles have mainly inherited the form of the Huns. Once these ethnic groups, such as Xianbei, Khitan, and Jurchen, have in-depth exchanges with the Central Plains, and especially a large number of people entered and lived in the Central Plains, they would inevitably be influenced by the wrestling culture of the Central Plains and gradually acquire the Central Plains' wrestling. Therefore, no matter whether it is for the Central Plains or the northern groups, their sports culture learns from each other in the process of national exchanges, which forms part of the connotations embedded in the Chinese nation's sports culture.

The Tanguts of Xixia also have wrestling in their development. "Sumo" in *Wenhai Research* is explained as "competition with each other"; "Jiao-Li" is interpreted as "Sumo or wrestling, a kind of hostile fight"; "Xiangzhengqiu" is interpreted as "Sumo, contending with each other."[87] Currently, there is no document about the Sumo wrestling of Xixia people. However, there are laws to follow on individual legal responsibilities in the process of Sumo wrestling. *The New Decrees of Tiansheng* contains: "A person who causes the death of his opponent in a wrestling match will be detained for three years in accordance with the law on the condition that it is not an intentional homicide, which implies that no one is allowed to die in a wrestling match. If in the course of their Sumo match, someone abets the wrestler resulting in the death of his opponent, he is sentenced to three years in prison, and those who are involved are convicted accordingly based on the law of accessory."[88] The above law is the only available document on the protection of Sumo wrestlers. From these records, we can also see that there were some undesirable phenomena in the physical activities of ethnic minorities in ancient times. What is commendable is that the government provided somewhat legal protection for the personal safety of players participating in the competition. There are legal grounds for claiming that "Sumo does not kill the people" and for punishing those who unreasonably kill their opponents during a match or who instill others to kill during the Sumo. Due to the insufficient documentary records and archaeological findings regarding Dangxiang (Tangut) wrestling, the author feels humbled to make any comments on it; thus, future research remains to be conducted.

5.4 Rise and Development of Mongolian Wrestling

Mongolian wrestling has a long history whose birth is closely related to the survival and development of the ancient Mongolian people. In the book *Mongolian Boke (Burk)*, the Mongolian Zha Mirza believed that "Mongolian Boke was developed during the primitive Stone Age when humans fought with their bare hands against wild animals."[89] Today, various types of Burk entrance dance still remain the moves of beasts, for example, the camel pose and the eagle-like dance used as the march-in ceremony by Mongolia, the eagle dance used as the march-in ceremony by Xilinguole League of Inner Mongolia, and the dear-like dance of Hulun Buir League. Traces of the ancient origins of wrestling with ferocious beasts can still be seen in the game rule: "The winner is determined in one fall, regardless of body weight." As the Mongols expanded from east to west, they were naturally influenced by the original Huns, Turks, and Uighur cultures. Moreover, when the Mongols of Borjikin emerged, they were directly influenced by the culture of the Kelie and Naiman tribes, who had long-term relationships with Uighur and Western Liao. Wrestling in the Western Regions has been recorded in the Jin Dynasty and the Southern and Northern Dynasties, such as the wrestling between Yudong of the Western Jin and Jianhu (Strong and healthy Huns) of the Western Regions described above and the scene of Gao Chuo, the king of Nanyang, being culled by a Hun wrestler named He Weisa. All of these demonstrate the development of wrestling activities in the Western Regions during this period. And their wrestling style may be affected by the Central Plains wrestling, in accompany with the relatively free and lively movements. Research has also shown that Mongolian wrestling has its own prominent features based on the impacts of other ethnic cultures.

The Secret History of the Mongols records the wrestling match between Belgutei, the younger brother of Genghis Khan, and Bulibokuo, who came from Zhuerqi: "One day, Genghis Khan asked Bulibokuo to fight with Belgutei. In the beginning, Bulibokuo knocked Belgutei down with one hand and one foot, causing him to be unable to move. At this moment, Bulibokuo pretended that he was no match for Belgutei and then fell over. When Belgutei was subduing Bulibokuo, he looked back at Genghis Khan. As soon as Belgutei saw Genghis Khan biting his lower lip, he immediately took the cue, and then put his knee on Bulibokuo's back, grabbed his neck with both hands, and finally broke his back with a hard push. 'I wouldn't have lost the game, but for fear of Genghis Khan, I pretended to have lost my strength, yet unexpectedly costed my life,' said Bulibokuo."[90]

There is no clear description of the details of the wrestling movements here, but it can be seen that the Bulibokuo is relatively strong, so he could knock Belgutei down only with one hand and one foot. However, Bulibokuo pretended to fall down because he was scared of Genghis Khan; thus, Belgutei got a chance to ride over him again. It can be said that this is similar to modern wrestling but different from the former ones. A similar story happened during the Taizong Period. As recorded in *Histoire des Mongols*, written by Constantine d'Ohsson, Ogodai Khan was interested in watching wrestling. At that time, there were many strong men in Mongolia, Qincha, and Han. He heard that the strongmen of Persia were good at fighting, so he ordered Colmahan to send them over. Then Colmahan sent 30 Persian strongmen to Mongolia. Two of them were very famous; one was Pile, and the other was Mohammed Schah. After Ogodai saw them, he highly praised Pile for his strength. But Iltchidai, a general of Ogodai Khan, said: "I am afraid that the travel expenses and honorarium for inviting them here were spent in vain." Ogodai responded: "If you don't believe in their abilities, let some of your strong men come here and play Jiao-Li with them. If your men win, I will give you five hundred silver coins, but if your men lose, you owe me five hundred horses." The next day, Iltchidai sent one of the strongmen in his troops to compete with Pile. When they were wrestling, the Mongolian strongman threw Pile to the ground. But Pile said banteringly: "Hold me tight, or I will get free." As soon as he finished speaking, he immediately threw the Mongolian warrior to the ground. He used so much strength that the sound of bones colliding could be heard. Ogodai Khan stepped forward and said: "Hold him tight." and then went back to Iltchidai, "is this man really paid in vain?" Later he ordered Iltchidai to honor the bet immediately, and in order to reward Pile heavily, he gave him another five hundred silver coins.[91] This story reflects that the outcome of wrestling at that time depended on whether the player could subdue the opponent even after the opponent fell. The Mongolians' wrestling is very different from that of the Qin, Han, Tang, and Song Dynasties. Of course, it can be seen from the above that the Mongolians had both strength and skill in wrestling at that time, and actually more on strength. For the strongman, strength is of course the most important element, while Ogodai Khan heard that the Persian warriors were "good at wrestling," which implies that they were able to wrestle with reasonable force and tactful skills. Both strength and skills would make wrestling become more appreciative, which accounts for why ancient Chinese wrestling was appreciated by the emperors as well as people of all dynasties. The materials quoted above also show that the Mongolian rulers convened a large number of wrestlers from all over the world, regardless of ethnicity. There are Mongolians, Qincha, Hans, Uyghurs, and Persians. And with the power of Mongolia at that time, those wrestling elites could gather together for competition and communication at any time. The above is a case in point. The Mongolians themselves loved wrestling and were always tolerant of the cultures of the various nationalities they ruled; thus, they could co-exist at the same time. It can be said that for a long time, the Yuan Dynasty was a period of the convergence and fusion of various wrestling forms throughout the country.

At the same time, in order to rule the Yuan Dynasty, it was inevitable that the southern wrestling sport was banned. In the 21st year of the Yuan Dynasty, it was suddenly banned. According to the *Institutions of the Yuan Dynasty · Criminal Department*, the main reasons for banning wrestling were that the untouchables didn't work, went around all day long, and some even learned wrestling and played rods. If the things reported were true, both the teacher and the student would be beaten with a plank 77 times. And all the property of the reported person would be rewarded to the person reporting. From then on, no one dared to act tough, and no one dared to teach the skills of fighting.[92] In the fourth year of Yuanyou, the civil idolatrous procession was also prohibited. In the sixth year of Yuanyou, it is strictly prohibited to set up a gathering venue for mass games. This is obviously a supplement to the prohibition of wrestling, since the ancient idolatrous procession mainly referred to the wrestling procession, while the mass competition mostly referred to wrestling games. Wrestling, which existed in the south of the Yuan Dynasty, suffered a great blow after Emperor Shizu and Emperor Renzong twice banned it. Since then, the wrestling that flourished in the Central Plains from the Qin and Han Dynasties through the Sui, Tang, and Song Dynasties has been dominated by the Mongolian wrestling that emerged in the Yuan Dynasty.

Yuan Dynasty banned wrestling in the south, mainly because of the fear that the remnants of the Song Dynasty would gather around to resist. However, they have been vigorously developing wrestling in the north. For example, in the wrestling exhibition game described in *Two Sumo Poems* written by the poet Hu Zhiyu in the Yuan Dynasty, the poem wrote: In the sound of music, the two players wearing embroidered short vests, and arms wrapped in red ribbons, staring at each other, attack viciously without giving way.[93] And the rulers of the Yuan Dynasty have no limit to the rewards of wrestlers. In the 14th Chapter of the *History of the Yuan Dynasty · Shizu XIV* recorded that, in February of the 30th year of the Yuan Dynasty, the Hui Boke, Ma Conmousha, and others offered pearls, asking for tens of thousands of silver coins. Kublai Khan said: "Pearl is of no use to me. I'm saving the money to help the poor."[94] According to the *History of the Yuan Dynasty · Wuzong*, in June of the 11th year of Dade, Ma Conmousha, the commander-in-chief, was awarded the title of Pingzhang Governor (in charge of governmental affairs) because he had won a couple of wrestling matches.[95] The second part of *History of the Yuan Dynasty · Wuzong* records that in April of the third year, wrestler A'li was granted a thousand tales of silver and four hundred ingots of banknotes.[96] "Buku" is also a Mongolian name for a wrestler, which tells us that during the rule of Kublai Khan, there were also outstanding wrestlers among the Hui people, who were highly valued by the emperor. Ma Conmousha was appreciated by Emperor Shizu (Kublai Khan) for being a well-known wrestler, and under the rule of Emperor Wuzong (Külüg Khan), he won many times in wrestling, so he was appointed as Pingzhang Governor. A'li also was rewarded with a lot of money for his excellent performance in wrestling matches.

By the time of Emperor Renzong, a special agency for wrestling, the Yongxiao Office, had been established. It was responsible for recruiting, training, and organizing wrestling matches, the same as the "Sumo sheds" in the Tang Dynasty and the "Head of the Military Division of the Imperial Army" in the Song Dynasty. It was recorded in the *History of the Yuan Dynasty · Renzong (III)* that in June of the sixth year of Yanyou, Yuan Dynasty established the Yongxiao Office, which made the wrestlers affiliate to this institution.[97] Moreover, it is recorded in the *History of the Yuan Dynasty · Yingzong* that in June of the seventh year of Yanyou, more than one hundred wrestlers were rewarded with a lot of money.[98] This shows that under the management of a special agency, Mongolian wrestling had developed rapidly, and the government had invested heavily in it. Under such circumstances, the momentum of Mongolian wrestling was bound to be extremely gratifying. The success of today's wrestling must be closely related to the attention and influence of the government at that time. The emperors of the Yuan Dynasty attached great importance to wrestling for a long time. We can not only find this from the above-mentioned rewards to wrestling, but also see their consistent support for wrestling from the following sources. As recorded in the *History of the Yuan Dynasty · Biography of Wang Yue*, one day, Emperor Renzong was watching a wrestling match in the West Garden, planning to reward the players with good silk. When Wang Yue arrived and saw the emperor from a distance, he asked: "What is the point of this?" Hearing this, Emperor Renzong immediately stopped the reward. Wang Yue was an important minister who assisted the emperor from the time he was still a prince.[99] Also, as recorded in the *History of the Yuan Dynasty · Biography of Gai Miao*, in the sixth year of Zhizheng, Gai Miao was promoted to serve as the imperial censor and was soon appointed to the post of governor and head of the Central Secretariat. When Toghon Temür planned to reward the wrestlers again, Gai Miao said that "the famines throughout the country have not yet been cured; how could wrestling be so generously rewarded?"[100] This is another example of preventing the emperor from granting generous rewards to wrestlers.

We have already talked about the form of wrestling in the Mongolian period above, but in the process of long-term national communication and integration, especially when wrestling was banned in the south and vigorously developed in the north, what exactly was the Mongolian wrestling sport like in the later period? We couldn't find it in the official history, but there exists some relevant introduction in the *Timur Devrinde Kadistan Semer-Kand's Seyahat Ruy (Journey of Clavijo from Cadiz to Samargand)*. This book recorded how the Spanish envoy Clavijo was entertained by Timur's grandson Pir Mirza in the capital of Samarg when he was sent on a diplomatic mission to the Timurid Empire established by the Mongolian in Central Asia: "In a red silk tent, Pir Mirza was sitting on a low seat, with many people sitting around. … The soldiers were wearing sleeveless leather pouches. At this time, the two Hercules were holding each other in a fierce struggle, and then Pir Mirza ordered them to end it quickly, so one of them caught the other and lifted him up, and then threw him to the ground."[101] Judging from the athletes' clothing and movement techniques described in this wrestling record, it must be a cuddle wrestling, especially in terms of durability. These are exactly the same as the current Mongolian form of wrestling. However, this form is not commonplace in Central Asia. The Timur Empire must use this type of wrestling as a cultural event of the Mongolian nation and perform it at large banquets. The wrestling of the Timur Empire was inherited from the imperial court of Ilkhanate, which itself followed the form of the Yuan Dynasty.

The Mongolian Boke, horse racing, and archery are common skills that men must master. Whenever there is an alliance, temple fair, or sacrificing, there must be an exhibition match of Boke (wrestling). As recorded in the "Tactics" of *Classified Anthology of Anecdotes of the Qing Dynasty*: "The Mongols would offer sacrifices to Ebo in every April, after which, the young men would wrestle and ride horses to compete. The wrestlers stood in two columns, one at east and one at west. And the competitors would jump out and fight with bare hands. The battle went on fiercely. The winner would finally lift the loser up for comfort. The chief official sat high above the gate to watch. The best winner who could win ten players would be regarded superior, other winners ranking down from the second to the fifth, awarded differently."¹⁰² This custom of wrestling matches was especially popular in the north and south of the Desert area. *Sports Weekly (No. 48) of Tianjin In 1932* recorded that, starting from June 15th of the summer calendar, Mongolia held wrestling exams for five days, and participants were selected and sent to Kulun by Lamas. At that time, the Living Buddha would be in the center of the hall, and the Lamas would sit next to him. A circle would be drawn on the ground first. The wrestlers would not be accepted if they were out of the circle, no matter how brave they were. The strongmen were forbidden to be naked, so they wore leather clothes and long leather boots. During the wrestling, the most frequent kicks were repeated. The purpose was to shake and force the opponent to fall down to the ground. The landing of the legs and knees was not considered a loss, but not when the palm touched the ground.¹⁰³ This record not only implies that the wrestling of Mongolian nationality is characterized by body clinching and foot stumbling, but also shows the historical fact that in Mongolia, sports and religion have become intertwined.

Most famous wrestlers in the early Qing Dynasty were Mongolians. As recorded in Jinliang's *Secret Records of Manchu Old Archives*: "(The first month of the sixth year of Tiancong) Temudherus of Arub and Durma of Turbank Kukter wrestled at the gathering place. Durma won, Temudherus lost. Then Mendu wrestled with Durma; Mendu won while Durma lost. Mendu, Durma, and Temudherus, three strong men, then knelt in front of the emperor, waiting to be named. Mendu was officially titled 'Alsalan Tuxietu Buku' and awarded a leopard skin jacket. Durma was given the name 'Za Buku' with the reward of a tiger skin jacket, while Temudherus was given the name 'Barbatulu' and awarded with a tiger-skin coat, a knife, a piece of silk, and eight pieces of blue wool cloth. It was also stated that in the future if anyone continued to call them by their original names instead of their official titles, that person would be punished."¹⁰⁴ The names entitled to these three Hercules, if translated into Chinese respectively, are the strong man of Tuxietu tribe like a lion, a man of strength like an elephant, and a man of courage like a tiger. There is also a similar record in the *Donghua Lu*: these three are all Mongolians, strong and excellent at wrestling.¹⁰⁵ In fact, in ancient Mongolia, the winners of various wrestling competitions were given different titles. For example, the champion of 64 wrestlers was called "način" (falcon), the champion of 256 wrestlers was called "ĵayan" (elephant), and the champion of 1,024 wrestlers was called "arslan" (male lion).¹⁰⁶ Therefore, it is said that the name given to Mongolian Boke by the Manchu rulers above-mentioned is based on Mongolian culture and customs.

When the Manchus wrestled with other tribes outside Shanhai Pass, most of the representatives of the strongmen sent by the Manchus were Mongolians. For example, it is written in the *Donghua Lu* that in the first month of the eighth year of Tiancong, the emperor in the central hall ordered Alsalan along with three other Beile (a rank of the Manchu nobility below that of the prince) to select six Hercules for wrestling. Alsalan was not sure whom to choose, so he raised them up and threw them down one by one. People all said that he was very powerful¹⁰⁷. Although this Alsalan uses the Manchu name, he is actually a Mongolian named Mendu actually in the previous quotation.

In the Qing Dynasty, the Mongols were the main objects of the Qing government's pacification, so Manchu and Mongolian wrestlers often competed. Every year after the emperor's Mulan

Qiuxian (Deer-hunting in autumn), he must hold a grand banquet at Longhua Palace in Hebei Province, rewarding people with merits in hunting and entertaining Mongolian princes and nobles plus foreign envoys. In addition to holding activities like horse racing, Shibang (Mongolian Music Event), and lassoing horses, the banquet also carried out the **wrestling competition. Therefore, Manchu and Mongolian wrestlers performed on the stage and shared their skills.** The "Four Events of the Banquet," which is now in the collection of the Palace Museum in Beijing, truly depicts the **Manchu and Mongolian wrestlers in the match at that time.** In addition, after Mongolian princes and nobles had an audience with the Qing emperor, Mongolian wrestlers would compete with Shanpu Camp wrestlers "for advantages and disadvantages," demonstrating the exquisite skills of wrestling. During the Qing Dynasty, Mongolian wrestling had great development. During the reign of Emperor Kangxi of the Qing Dynasty, the well-known wrestler Buhabatsang was born in **1668 in a village in the New Mongolian Autonomous County of Liaoning today.** Under the influence of the environment, he had practiced martial arts since his childhood. When he was 14 years old, he used to fight against injustice with fists and sticks. When he was more than 20 years old, he was able to lift up two stone lions weighing more than 300 kg in front of the prince's mansion and waved them from side to side. People in the village all sang high praise of him. To celebrate his defeat of the emperor's wrestler in the capital, the prince built a temple in his hometown and named it "Pengzeng Temple" after his original name, so that his achievements could be passed on to future generations.

The Mongolians take wrestling as one of the activities in major festivals and sacrificial ceremonies. For example, when the princes and nobles held a banquet, they all carried out wrestling competitions in order to cheer. *Xinjiang Atlas · Tianzhang (III)* has some more detailed **records: "The Mongols placed great importance on the wrestling, which was bound to take place at banquets, so the court trained excellent wrestlers, namely 'Buku,' meaning 'Boke' in Mongolian. When wrestling, the wrestlers took off their hats and wore shorts to compete in pairs.** The winner was determined by the fact that he could throw his opponent down to the ground with bare hands. If yes, he would be rewarded with a glass of wine. Erut took off his coat and rushed towards his opponent. He grabbed him and refused to let him go free even though his opponent had fainted; he firmly pressed the opponent's head and shoulders down to the ground, so that he was claimed to win the game. Erut was highly praised for his strength and awarded the sheep's waist and arms ..."[108] There is also a record in *Records of Rites and Customs in Xinjiang*: "The Mongols would offer sacrifices to Ebo every April, after which, the young men would wrestle and ride horses to compete. The wrestlers stood in two columns, one at east and one at west. And the competitors would jump out and fight with bare hands. The battle went on fiercely. The winner would finally lift the loser up for comfort. The chief official sat high above the gate to watch. The best winner who could win ten players would be regarded superior, other winners ranking down from the second to the fifth, awarded differently."[109] Erut wrestling holds that the winner must hold the loser to the ground, till the loser cannot struggle to get up again; thus, the winner is determined.

There were two ways of wrestling at that time: one was "when wrestling, the wrestlers took off their hats and wore shorts to compete in pairs. The winner is determined by whether he could throw his opponent down to the ground with bare hands"; another is that the wrestler took off his coat and rushed towards his opponent; he grabbed him and refused to let him go free even though his opponent had fainted; he firmly pressed the opponent's head and shoulders down to the ground, so that he was claimed to win the game. The former Soviet Union historian Nai · Yang described the Mongolian wrestling skills in more detail in the book *Batu Army · Mongolian Army Naadam*:

"Thousands of soldiers came from all directions and sat in a big circle. After the Batu army and his generals sat down on the carpets and saddle pads laid slopes of Varka, the bugles, gongs, and drums sounded in unison. The presiding wrestler entered the arena first and shouted: Come on! Fearless athletes, come and throw for health! The time has come to test our will and our strength. Those excellent wrestlers entrust their horses to trustworthy warriors and enter the arena from everywhere. They jump, stretch their arms, and pick up a handful of soil or grass from the ground, shaped like an eagle … Let's start now! Batuhan is watching you; the young and fearless can be rewarded. In the three rounds of confrontation, those who do not land their shoulders on the ground are hailed as heroes. Then they held and caught each other, trying to throw their opponents down to the ground. Onlookers cheered their respective wrestlers for victory. Around each pair of wrestlers, the two-judge officials kept running, shouting, and encouraging their wrestlers. The winners leaped and sat in the promoted seat with snacks and delicious food around. They grabbed them, first bringing them to their mouths and then lifting them to heaven for gratitude, which endowed them with the gift of victory. They also sprinkled them among their friends for cheering. In the final round of the competition, there was a wrestler named Taogerule, who was tall, burly, and majestic in shape. He lifted his opponent highly and then threw him down to the ground, who jumped frantically because of victory. The loser, however, lay on the ground and cried motionlessly. Taogerule approached him and asked, 'Why are you so sad?' He replied, 'If I die here, I will be happy. Because I didn't die, what else can I be happy about?' After hearing this, Taogerule picked him up and said: 'This is our loyalty to the prosperity of the Mongolian Emperor's undertaking!' Then, the two exchanged their hand knives, embraced and kissed each other like brothers, leaving the arena hand to hand. Afterwards, a small group of knights came forward and reported: Blessed Batuhan ordered me to come and deliver the decree. He boasted of your bravery and fearlessness and enlisted the two of you into the Mongolian Guards."[110]

The number of participants in Mongolian wrestling must be a power of 2, such as 32, 64, … 512, 1,024, and so on. The rule follows the single elimination system with no time limit. And the winner is determined by only one game; half of them are kicked out in each round. The ranking is based on the champion and runner-up. For example, when the champion and runner-up are determined in the ninth round of the competition, those who were defeated by the champion in the eighth round are the third, those who were defeated by the runner-up are the fourth, those who were defeated by the third in the seventh round rank the fifth, while those who were defeated by the fourth rank the sixth. Athletes compete on flat grass regardless of their weight and the size of the field. Any part above the knee landing on the ground is lost. There are many technical movements, including 13 basic movements such as catching, pulling, tearing, pushing, and pressing. During the competition, wrestlers can do hundreds of movements. They can either grasp each other on their shoulders, hold on waists, or drill under the opponent's armpit to attack; yet they are not allowed to hold or grasp the opponent's legs, nor can they kneel down to throw. To sum up, they mainly win based on wrist strength and leg skills. Mongolian wrestling has always been divided into three types: large, medium, and small, according to size. The large size involves about 1024 or 512 people, the medium 256 people, and the small 128 or 64 people.

Mongolian wrestling costumes are featured in national characteristics. Wrestling costumes are made of cloth or leather and decorated with shiny copper or silver nails. A scarf-like "Xifang Buge" (made of blue, red, and yellow cloth; blue symbolizes the sky, red the sun, and yellow the ground) is usually attached to the waistband of the wrestling suit. In order to prevent injury accidents caused by leg-wrapping movements in fighting, and also to prevent the clothes from sticking to the body when sweating heavily, the players generally wear fat wrestling pants made from white cloth. Besides, there is another pair of wrestling "trousers" without crotch, embroidered with various ethnic patterns, which possess the function of protecting legs and knees. In order to prevent slipping or rupture of boots, wrestlers generally reinforce their Mongolian boots or riding boots with the help of strong leather straps before the fierce battle. A colorful "Jingga" made of five-color tassels was around the neck of the wrestler, which indicates the ranking he has ever achieved. The more ranks, the more color bars.

The entrance ceremony at the beginning of the game was very interesting. The burly wrestlers in special gold costumes lined up in a vertical line, with their waist and chest straight and arms stretched out, swinging up and down slowly, like an eagle spreading its wings. They seemed exceptionally vigorous. They jumped to the rostrum in accompany with greetings and applause and then clapped their hands on their knees and bowed. In the official competition, some elders were specially invited to sing to add some fun. The singing started, and the athletes from both sides jumped into the arena. Jumping is another characteristic of Mongolian wrestling. In the entrance ceremony, the jumping out is high and fast in a longer span, which is regarded as a preparatory activity before the fierce competition. Conversely, the jumping out is slow and relaxing at the end, a good finishing activity for the human body. The jumping includes the lion dance, eagle dance, and wheel dance. As the wrestling songs were sung three times in a row, the wrestlers of both sides knelt on the shoulders of the two assistants with two hands and one leg. In an instant, the wrestlers jumped out and started fighting. The one being thrown to the ground was the loser. The winner helped hold the loser up, and both of them danced to the rostrum to register their ranking. Meanwhile, they grabbed a handful of milk, cakes, and sweets on the table and threw them into the sky and the crowd while eating, then slowly jumped back to the arena.

In Mongolian wrestling, two wrestlers are equally competent. Therefore, the battle may last for a comparatively long time. Under this circumstance, whoever falls to the ground or lands his palm on the ground would be the loser. Mongolian wrestling is very similar to the one in the Liao and Jin Dynasties, which is characterized by certain inheritance. In addition, according to documentary records, Mongolian wrestlers' costumes have broken the tradition of being topless with only shorts on in the Han and Tang Dynasties. Instead, they attached a long cloth bag around the waist, called "Dalian (girdle)," which was passed down to the Qing Dynasty and further evolved into the specialized wrestling costume of today. Mongolian wrestling, like other types of wrestling, requires good coordination of the athletes between their hands, waist, and legs, and the athletes are supposed to fully demonstrate their strength and skills in confrontation. Engaging in wrestling can enhance physical fitness, develop physical qualities such as strength, agility, speed, and endurance, as well as cultivate people's wit, courage, and tenacity.

After the fall of the Yuan Dynasty and the rise of the Ming Dynasty, Zhu Yuanzhang, the first emperor of the Ming Dynasty, expected to carry forward the cultural customs of the Han nationality. He endeavored to restore the old system of the Tang and Song Dynasties in terms of clothing, etiquette, and customs. At the same time, he tried to inherit and carry forward the excellent culture produced in the process of national integration in the Yuan Dynasty. It is acknowledged that the cultural exchange and integration of various ethnic groups in China is the law of historical development. During the 90 years that the Yuan Dynasty ruled the whole nation, Chinese wrestling was greatly influenced by Mongolia, such a nationality with brilliant traditions and passion for wrestling, even though Yuan failed to exert more effects on Chinese Confucianism. Under this circumstance, it turned absolutely impossible for Zhu Yuanzhang to restore the etiquette and cultural customs of the Tang and Song Dynasties. It has been proved that apart from the forced imitation of the Tang and Song in terms of clothing, its etiquette has not been abolished. Instead, it continued to follow those of the Yuan Dynasty.[111] Zhu Di, the son of Zhu Yuanzhang in the Ming Dynasty, was stationed in the north. Most of his subordinates were Mongolian and Wuliangha people. They put an emphasis on northern customs, and even the horsemanship and willow-shooting in the army followed the ones in the Yuan Dynasty.[112] Therefore, the restoration of the culture of Tang and Song advocated by the Ming Dynasty actually produced a new culture that combined the culture of Tang, Song, and Mongolia.

Ming emperors liked to watch wrestling. According to historical records, Emperor Wuzong of the Ming Dynasty was an emperor who enjoyed traveling in disguise and seeking pleasure. According to the *History of the Ming History · Biography of Liu Jin*, Liu Jin used to engage in some games, for example, hunting, singing, dancing, wrestling, etc., to induce the emperor to travel in disguise. The emperor was so pleased that he gradually trusted him and appointed him as an internal official to supervise the regiment.[113] Besides Emperor Wuzong of Ming, King Fu at the end of the Ming Dynasty also loved this game in Jiangnan. *History of the Ming History · Yuan Jixian* records that in the first month, Yuan Jixian said: "New Year's Day is a day when ministers should kowtow to the ground and raise their glasses to celebrate. It is also a time when your majesty should learn from the pain and experience the hardships. Now your majesty didn't get revenge successfully, you'd better refer to the spirit of King Xuan of Zhou, who asked about time for court before daybreak, and that the behavior of later monarchs who drink and play all night should be stopped …."[114] *History of the Ming Dynasty · Biography of Jiang Bin* records as follows: "Jiang Bin was aware that he and Qian Ning could not coexist. But considering that Qian Ning was surrounded by his supporters, Jiang Bin had to manage the border forces to stabilize his position. Jiang Bin praised so much the bravery of the border troops that he even believed they could overtake the city troops. He asked the emperor to permit the drills with each other. All officials offered their advice one after another, including Li Dongyang, a grand scholar, who even detailed ten disadvantages of this move in his letter, but the emperor ignored them. The troops of Liaodong, Xuanfu, Datong, and Yansui were transferred to the capital, known as the 'four border troops,' under the jurisdiction of Jiang Bin. The soldiers swaggered around the city and kept training in the barracks in accompany with the occasional wrestling."[115] There are not many records of wrestling in the Ming Dynasty, and thereby it is difficult to comment on its development. It can only be concluded from the existing literature that wrestling was also practiced in the Ming Dynasty as it was in other dynasties; some were used for palace entertainment, and some for military training.

5.5 Prosperity of Wrestling in the Qing Dynasty

5.5.1 Rise of Buku in the Qing Dynasty

The name "Buku" was transformed from the sound of Mongolian "Boke" in the Yuan Dynasty. In the Qing Dynasty, it referred to the wrestlers or strong men. Sometimes wrestling is also called "Buku." The Buku movement in the Qing Dynasty was also represented by ancient Chinese sayings such as "Jiao-Di," "xiangpu," or "xiangbo." It is written in *Notes on Returning to the Fields* by Liang Zhangju that "every time old friends in the mountains come to visit, they like to ask about the imperial court to enrich their knowledge. Someone asked what Buku is, and I replied that Buku is interpreted as kicking feet in the official language. Healthy children in their teens are selected to fight with their bare hands. The strength of their feet counts, and winning or losing is determined by whether any one of them touches the ground. In the early years of the reign of Emperor Kangxi, the emperor took advantage of this technique to collect Oboi. Therefore, wrestling is performed in every banquet held in the palace now."[116] From this record, we can infer the following: Firstly, Buku, spoken by the Manchus, is what we call wrestling; secondly, Buku sports does not carry any equipment but only hand-to-hand combat; thirdly, Buku sports emphasize both skill and strength, yet mainly on the strength of the feet as well as the skill of the foot movement, which accounts for the name of "Liaojiao (kicking feet)"; the fourth is to determine the winner of the Buku game, mainly based on whether the opponent's upper body touches upon the ground; fifthly, Buku game is very popular in the Qing Dynasty. Regarding the above points, more supporting literature is shown as follows.

The formation of the Manchus was achieved by Nurhachi (Emperor Taizu of the Qing Dynasty) of Jianzhou Jurchen on the basis of the long-term economic, cultural, blood relationship, and geographical exchanges, along with the multiple military mergers and political alliances among the tribes of Jurchen in the Ming Dynasty. The Manchus nationality that established the Qing had a close relationship with the Jurchen nationality in the Jin Dynasty. After the fall of Jin, for the Jurchen nationality in the northeast, the Yuan Dynasty adopted some policy for the Jurchen nationality in the northeast, that "they could still maintain the old customs, and live in places with water and grass, with hunting as their career; they stayed in the market-free and city-free regions, with herdsmen officials set to govern those with the remaining old customs …"[117] The customs and habits of Jurchens were also influenced by the Mongols. After the establishment of the Ming Dynasty, the court set up a capital command department and a guard station in the northeast, following the old system of the Yuan Dynasty entirely. After the orthodox reign of Emperor Yingzong in the Ming Dynasty, Oirat also started to raise cattle in the East. Later, the Jurchen people threw away all their imperial letters and edicts, then even discarded their writing and simply adopted the Mongolian language. Therefore, the Manchu culture is still on the basis of inheriting the Jurchen, to a large extent affected by the Han and Mongolian ethnic groups, and it has absorbed the culture of the Han, Mongolian, and other ethnic groups at the same time. After entering Shanhai Pass, as a ruling nation, Manchu also incorporated the excellent culture of other nationalities, creating a favorable environment and condition for the formation of the integrated pattern of the Chinese nation.

As a nation that developed at a later stage, wrestling played an important role in its evolution. After Jurchens established the "Later Jin" regime in the northeast, they changed the name of Jurchens to Manchus. In order to annex various tribes of the same nationality and further expand the scope of influence, wrestling was once vigorously advocated. As Zhao Yi said in the poem *Scene of the Siege · Sumo Wrestling*, "Wrestling has been passed down since ancient times. Among all the games, it is the only thing that comes into the army ... The country values it for its profound meaning, so it is vigorously pursued."[118] This record shows that the wrestling of the Manchus is still inherited from the Jurchen, who was deeply influenced by the Han culture in the Central Plains. The main purpose of their development of wrestling is to prepare for the war, which accounts for the profound intention why it is attached to great importance.

As mentioned earlier, when the Manchus matched with other tribes outside the Shanhai Pass, most of the wrestlers sent to the ring were Mongolians. When it came to the time of Taizong of Chongde Period, Buku game of Manchus emerged. It is recorded in the *Records of the Qing Dynasty*: "(In August of the second year of Chongde) the emperor led Prince Heshuo, Duke Duoluo, Doroi Beile (a rank of the Manchu nobility below that of the prince), and Gushai Beizi (a rank of the Manchu nobility below that of the Beile) to set out from Huaiyuan Gate to compete shooting in the martial field in the morning. The emperor sat in the yellow tent, and the four sub-tribes, as well as the Bahrain tribe, presented to pay tribute. Because the concubine of Guanju Palace gave birth to the prince, they sent envoys to offer camels and horses to congratulate him. The emperor decreed to initiate the shooting among different tribes thus he could select those who were good at archery. Each time there were ten men competing in each banner, divided into left and right wings. Those who lose will be punished by offering cattle and sheep. Prince Heshuo, Duke Duoluo, Doroi Beile (a rank of the Manchu nobility below that of the prince), and Gushan Beizi (a rank of the Manchu nobility below that of the Beile) personally led the shooting. Beile (a rank of the Manchu nobility below that of the prince) and Beizi (a rank of the Manchu nobility below that of the Beile) of the right wing shot the most, winning two cows and 20 sheep. The emperor then ordered Hercules on both sides to step out and compete wrestling. This time, Beile (a rank of the Manchu nobility below that of the prince) and Beizi (a rank of the Manchu nobility below that of the Beile) on the right lost and thus returned one cow and two sheep that they had previously gained from the left side. Then the emperor asked Prince Heshuorui Dorgon, Princie Heshuoyu Doduo, Doluo Beile (a rank of the Manchu nobility below that of the prince) Haoge, Doluoraoyu Beile Abatai and others on the left wing to compete archery. The losers stood while the winners of the archery contest on the right feasted. After the banquet, the emperor ordered the foreign Beile (a rank of the Manchu nobility below that of the prince) and other envoys to sit in sequence and set a banquet for them."[119] The emperor also asked those in each banner who were good at archery to perform shooting and wrestling. These men must undoubtedly be Manchus. After that, the subordinate Han army, also started to acquire wrestling, as was recorded in *The Strategy for the Founding of the Qing Dynasty*: "(In October in the third year of Chongde) Emperor Taizong personally led troops to fight the army of Ming Dynasty and marched in three directions ... In the year of Dinghai, Emperor Taizong went out from Huaiyuan Gate and marched toward the martial field to inspect the two troops led by the Han army ministers Shi Tingzhu and Sima Yuan. The emperor asked them to try artillery fire, archery, and wrestling, and then entertained them."[120] The above is the wrestling activities beyond the Shanhai Pass. In the beginning, Mongolian wrestlers were recruited as Hercules, which proves that the Manchus followed the form of Mongolian wrestling. Later, Manchus soldiers and Han soldiers all practiced Bobu (wrestling).

After entering Shanhai Pass, the Qing Dynasty still followed the old customs. Every time the envoys of the Mongolian tribes came, the imperial court would hold a wrestling match between the Manchus and Mongolian Hercules. Everyone, including emperor and princes of the Qing Dynasty, enjoyed wrestling and practiced it personally. *Miscellaneous Records of Xiao Ting · Prince Huishun* records the following: "Although Prince Huishun failed to join the army because of his age, he was born with great strength. No one could defeat him ... During the Shunzhi Period, the envoys of Khalkha came and wrestled with the ministers, and no one could defeat them. After hearing that, Prince Huishun entered the court under the guise of a guard and mixed himself in the crowd. No surprise that he succeeded in defeating his opponent casually in the competition. The emperor was so pleased that he presented Huishun with countless rewards. At that time, he was only 20 years old."[121] It is also cited in the *Miscellaneous Records of Zhuywe Pavilian* written by Yao Yuanzhi that Kangxi was only eight years old when he became the emperor. At that time, his minister, Oboi, was powerful and quite arrogant. He was even more unscrupulous because the emperor was young. Kangxi chose some young and strong guards in the imperial court and asked them to play wrestling games with him. Even if Oboi sometimes entered the court, Kangxi did not shy away from it. Therefore, Oboi felt the emperor was very weak and easy to deal with, thus slowly letting down his guard. One day in the face of Oboi in the court, Kangxi ordered these young guards who had practiced wrestling to seize Oboi. More than a dozen eunuchs immediately caught Oboi, and then he was executed. Oboi, who was roasted with power, was finally held in the hands of a dozen young eunuchs. Only then did he know the emperor's intentions. All the things the emperor had done before were to make him let down his guard.[122] The story of Kangxi plotting wrestlers to catch Oboi was widely spread among the people, and it can be seen that after entering Shanhai Pass, wrestling was still utilized for the war and capture.

Also, as stated in *Miscellaneous Records of Xiao Ting*, the records are: "Generals who have commanded the army for generations said that fighting the enemy was like wrestling. If you feel that the situation is wrong, you must fight your opponent with all your efforts; otherwise, you will lose."[123] It can be seen that wrestling in the Qing Dynasty was always associated with war, and the government attached great importance to wrestling training and development. Later, the Qing Dynasty also set up the "Shanpu Camp" to train wrestlers, whose duties were similar to the "Yuqian Zhongzuo Army Division" in the Song Dynasty and the "Yongxiao Office" in the Yuan Dynasty. Wrestlers were divided into three classes: first class, second class, and third class. Shanpu Camp's wrestlers had a limit of two hundred, and young men who were not enlisted were called "Taximi." Shanpu Camp not only managed wrestlers but also managed "Yong She (courage Shooting)" and "Pian Ma (horse skills performance)." "Yong She" referred to hard bow shooting, while "Pian Ma" was also called "Pian Tuo (camel skills performance)," which was to practice the leap-over skills over horse or camel on the battlefield. All these fully prove that wrestling in the early Qing Dynasty, like other practices, was used for war. However, during the reign of Emperor Qianlong, wrestling became more entertainment-oriented than war-oriented compared with what was employed before. As recorded in *Miscellaneous Records of Xiao Ting · Shanpu Camp*:

> "The wrestlers in the Shanpu Camp were the best warriors in the Eight Banners. Wrestling was performed at every grand banquet and occasionally used to compete with other tribes. The winners would be rewarded with tea. Emperor Gaozong of the Qing Dynasty was fond of wrestling very much. The most famous wrestler, among other things, is Dawuge Haixiu, who was even called directly by the emperor. Some soldiers were chosen as guards because they were brave and well-trained. Soldiers in the Shanpu Camps were also required to practice wrestling, and it was not until Wenyuan Gaoning took office in the Imperial Guards Section that it was abolished."[124]

At this time, wrestling was often carried out among different nationalities, which was of great benefit to the development and communication of this activity. In addition, like the Tang and Song Dynasties, the Qing government often employed or promoted some wrestling experts to be senior officials in the court. Under this mechanism, the development momentum of wrestling was bound to be gratifying. Especially within the government, this phenomenon was even more commonplace. Therefore, the wrestling activities of the Manchus were held more effectively than those practiced by the Mongolians, who loved wrestling. In the Qing Dynasty, as for the match between Reheman and Mengbuku during the Qianlong and Jiaqing years, Liang Zhangju commented that "Although Monoglia Buku is not that superb in the imperial court, it is particularly good at horse plays."[125] It's for sure that different rulers in different social environments embrace different views towards cultural values. Therefore, in the later period, some people regarded wrestlers as lowly soldiers, some of whom were even dismissed for practicing wrestling. *Miscellaneous Records of Xiao Ting · Ma Zhuangjie* records: "When Ma Biao ranked third in the martial arts during the Renshen Period of Emperor Qianlong, he was dismissed because of wrestling with his colleagues."[126] Qiu Rixiu of the Qing Dynasty watched Elute Mongolian wrestling and commented, "Those who surrendered became slaves, and those who wrestled were even more ugly." At this time, wrestling was not as highlighted as it was in the early Qing Dynasty, but until the end of the Qing, Shanpu Camp still existed, and routine matches were still held.

Shanpu Camp in the Qing Dynasty not only conducted wrestling training and competitions, but also had the duty of guarding the court, catching criminals, and subduing strong bandits. Many of the wandering heroes were conquered by Shanpu Camp During the Qing Dynasty. Some Russians came to China and bullied the folks relying on their physical strength. The warriors of Shanpu Camp had once subdued these Russians with their super martial arts. Chen Kangqi records in *Records of Lang Qian II* that "when the Russian emissaries entered the capital, the emperor selected several strong wrestlers from the Shanpu Camp to serve them at the embassy. As soon as the Russian emissaries along with their soldiers went out, the wrestlers of the Shanpu Camp would follow. When they occasionally bullied the people, the wrestlers would kick them from behind, so that they could not get up. Though big and strong, their butts were tied with cloth, so that they were unable to lift their feet. From then on, they obeyed the law."[127] It can be clearly drawn that mastering wrestling skills can be enabled to cope the strong opponents. The superb skills of wrestlers' feet can clearly be witnessed here.

There are precious cultural relics of Shanpu Camp in our country, from which we can get a glimpse of the scene of wrestling training in the Qing Dynasty. This is a picture of Shanpu Camp wrestling in the Palace Museum (see Fig. 5-13), with the theme of the wrestling training in Shanpu Camp. The picture depicts the emperor, accompanied by the ministers, visiting Shanpu Camp and watching the training of wrestlers. As you can see in the picture, this was a closed venue, in which all officials were standing around the emperor, and three "coaches" were positioned in front of the emperor, wearing official hats and the same clothes as wrestlers. In other words, they were dressed in short sleeves on the upper part of the body, open without buttons, exposing their chests with wide waistbands attached; they wore baggy trousers and boots on the lower part of the body. The only difference lies in that three "coaches" wore robes, as well. At that moment, dozens of wrestlers on the field were performing wrestling, whose movements and postures varied from each other in terms of technical performance. Besides, on the left side of the picture, we can find several other wrestlers engaged in strength training. For the upper limb, some pushed and carried the bells, some lifted stone locks, and some did handstands; for lower limb, the wrestlers mainly dealt with equipment training such as bells. This painting conveyed to us a lot about wrestling during the Qing Dynasty.

Fig. 5-13 Shanpu Camp Wrestling

Origin and Evolution of Wrestling in China

Since the Kangxi Period, wrestling in the Qing Dynasty was evolving step by step to today's Chinese wrestling. This kind of evolution can be seen in Gu Qian's[128] poem *Pu Jiao Xing*:[129] "After the emperor ordered to select the warriors from the Eight Banners Army, the wrestlers, dressed up with short shirts and narrow-sleeved wrestling suits, rubbed their hands and looked for opponents to compete. The two sides peered at the other side warily and failed to start easily. They suddenly grabbed his opponent and twisted together, with their iron arms and copper legs tripping over each other. They looked like they were about to fall but still held on. The two wrestled as fiercely as a bear, jumping around like a Pixiu (a legendary fabulous wild beast). Sometimes a fat man pressed a thin man under his body, or a short man threw a tall one down. They insisted until it ended in failure. The audience of the whole army cheered and applauded the brave. This free wrestling and skillful techniques of wrestlers are all similar to today's wrestling."

Oubei Poetry · Sumo, written by Zhao Yi,[130] also recorded the wrestling situation in Qianlong Period, which is regarded as valuable literature for studying the evolution of wrestling in the Qing Dynasty to today's Chinese style. Zhao Yi took advantage of the long ancient poems to describe the wrestling sports he witnessed in "Mulan Hunting."[131] He described the competition venues, wrestlers' costumes, technical movements, victory or failure verdict, etc. This not only allowed us to understand the development of wrestling in Qianlong Period in details, but also provided us with the evolution and progress of wrestling during that period. The author believes that there is a cultural relic that can best correspond to this poem, which is "The Four Events of the Banquet (partial)" in the collection of the Palace Museum (see Fig. 5-14). This picture truly records the grand occasion of Emperor Qianlong when he feasted with his officials at Chengde Mountain Resort. We can tell that in the scene of wrestling activities: the emperor was sitting on the seat

Fig. 5-14 Four Events of the Banquet (Partial)

while the officials were watching; there was a carpet placed in the center of the venue, on which an orchestra was playing music, and beyond that stood the "foreign guests"; there were three pairs of wrestlers in the venue engaged in wrestling competition. If you look closely at the three pairs, you can see there were some huge differences among them. The first pair was on the right side of the carpet, wearing shorts, topless and barefoot, characterized by the typical wrestling in the Tang and Song Dynasties and before that; they were playing "Sumo" (similar to today's international classical wrestling) competition. Wrestler is claimed to win when he puts his opponent down to the ground, especially when the shoulder is landed on the ground. The second pair is on the carpet, who wore white yokes, trousers (the colors of trousers vary between the two wrestlers), and boots. What they were doing was "Buku" (similar to today's Chinese wrestling).[132]

In addition, we can further clarify the literature on wrestling in the Qing Dynasty, from the "Woodcut Wrestling Pictures of the Qing Dynasty" collected by the Palace Museum (see Fig. 5-15). Some of the technical movements of wrestling in this picture have many similarities with those in the "Four Events of the Banquet."

Based on the above research, the author summarizes several issues about wrestling in the Qing Dynasty as follows:

The first issue is about the type of wrestling. Wrestling in the Qing Dynasty was influenced by the wrestling of Khitan, Jurchen, Mongolian, and Han nationalities. Although all wrestling forms are roughly the same, they also reveal certain differences. As we can see from the "Four Events of the Banquet" (see Fig. 5-14), there are varieties of wrestling in the same venue: one is the wrestling that has been passed down and then lasted and reformed since the Pre-Qin period. For example, the type of wrestling on the right of the carpet in the picture (labeled as classic wrestling); the second is the transformation and development of wrestling based on the ancient wrestling culture of the North in the Qing Dynasty. For example, the form of wrestling performed by the two pairs of wrestlers on the carpet in the picture (labeled as freestyle wrestling). From the "Shanpu Camp Wrestling" picture (see Fig. 5-13), the wrestling in Shanpu Camp is just "freestyle wrestling."

The second issue is about the wrestler's costumes. The costumes of "classical wrestling" in the Qing Dynasty are consistent with those from the Pre-Qin to the Song and Yuan periods, basically topless, wearing a waistband and shorts. The costumes of "freestyle wrestling" in the Qing Dynasty were quite different. Wrestlers wore white double-breasted girdles, trousers (the colors of trousers vary between the two wrestlers), and boots. The "girdles" worn by the wrestlers are just like what Zhao Yi described in his poem, "The clothes just reached the bottom, two crotches leaked out, ten layers of cloth were sewn with a thousand threads." The color was white, which was the so-called "white clothes as white as herons" in the poem. "These people wear white blouses and short sleeves, but they are sewn with seven or eight layers of cloth, tough and durable."[133] It can be seen that the wrestling clothing is very exquisite; at the same time, it shows that during wrestling, there are also movements of pulling and tearing. The costumes of wrestlers are very similar to those of Mongolian wrestling today, from which we can draw the conclusion that Mongolians vigorously developed wrestling under the rule of the Manchus, and they mutually influenced each other in a profound way. Moreover, our current Chinese-style wrestling costumes basically follow this type of Qing Dynasty.

Origin and Evolution of Wrestling in China

(1)

(2)

This picture shows the close combat moves. Two wrestlers with bun braids at the back of their heads are wearing short jackets with a pouch attached and wide waistbands. One is in black boots and the other in white boots. The wrestler on the left stands up straight, using the cover-collar move to grab the opponent sideways with his right hand. The wrestler on the right shrugs and holds his stomach, arches his waist and crosses his legs, and grabs the under-sleeve of the person on the left. The two sides seem to be fighting to determine the outcome.

This picture shows the moves of grabbing the leg. The wrestler on the right leans forward and picks up the left leg of the wrestler on the left with both his hands, trying to turn the opponent down. The wrestler on the left crosses his legs, grabs the opponent's waistband with his left hand, and grabs his shoulder with his right hand. It seems that even if the wrestler is overturned by his opponent's leg-slip style, the opponent would not take advantage of it but definitely fall afterwards.

(3)

(4)

This picture shows the moves of tripping. According to the rules of wrestling, after the two sides start a fight, two wrestlers can bump, push, and throw. Some are good at strength, while some win as a result of dexterity. This engraving shows a pattern known for skills. The wrestler on the left grabs the opponent's left leg with his right hand and reaches into the opponent's left placket with his left hand. He grabs his opponent's clothes, lifts him up, and then throws him down to the ground, placing the opponent's hands on the ground so that he has to lie down on the side.

This picture demonstrates the moves to twist the arm and elbow. The wrestler on the left twists the opponent's arm with both his hands, and at the same, time he hooks up, picks up the opponent's right knee, forces his upper body forward, and intends to press the opponent to the ground while his body is leaning. The wrestler on the right has lost his balance and bent his knees and legs. When he is unable to use strength, his failure is set.

Fig. 5-15 Woodcut Wrestling Pictures of the Qing Dynasty

(5)   (6)

This picture shows the kneeling move. Both sides grab their chests and hold their backs in a wrestling posture. The left leg of the wrestler on the left side is upright, while the right leg is lifted up, with the toe hooking the ankle of the opponent's left leg. The left hand pulls the opponent's shoulder and neck, and the right hand twists the forearm as if to push the opponent down. Even hooked in left leg, the wrestler on the right bends his right leg in a half-squatting shape and grasps the opponent's chest with his left hand and the waistband with his right hand. The two fall into a stalemate.

This picture is a hook move, a pattern dominated by hooks and throws. Although the wrestler on the left turns sideways and embraces the opponent with his hands, he also shows signs of failure. The wrestler on the right grabs his opponent's armpit clothes and back waistband with his right hand, and hooks the opponent's right thigh with the lower right leg. The wrestler on the left has been lifted. It seems that the opponent could throw him down to the ground with just a little more effort.

(7)   (8)

This picture shows the big tripping move. The moves of both sides are almost the same. Both take the skills of under-sleeves and side-door movements, grabbing the sleeves and pulling the chest with all strength. The wrestler on the left employs the big trip move to lean over, while the one on the right pulls with a bow, attempting to pull the opponent over and trip him down to the ground under his feet.

This picture displays a big back span move, which reflects the quick grappling skills. The wrestler on the right has been picked up by his opponent and lost focus. The wrestler on the left grabs his opponent's clothes behind his back with both his hands and bows his head forward, acting a big back straddle to lift the opponent. He holds his breath as if he would throw his opponent over the shoulder.

Fig. 5-15 (*Continued*)

The third issue is about the venue. Official wrestling in the Qing Dynasty generally had dedicated venues. For example, there were specialized training venues at the official site of Shanpu Camp. The emperor also had a special place to watch wrestling matches. Even when he was traveling, he would choose the venue carefully. For instance, "Four Events of the Banquet" reflects that Emperor Qianlong was watching a wrestling game in Chengde Mountain Resort, and he had to choose a relatively wide flat area with a carpet placed on it. Wrestling competitions before the Qing Dynasty generally set venues, which can be learned from the previous discussion. Some were setting arenas, and occasionally the emperor watched the wrestling in disguise in the street, or sometimes enjoyed it in a special "garden." In general, from the Pre-Qin Dynasty to the first generation of the Qing Dynasty, wrestling competitions usually required special venues.

The last issue is about the technical moves and the referee. Looking up the *Wu Ti Qing Wen Jian · Wrestling*,[134] we can find that the wrestling movements in Shanpu Camp of the Qing Dynasty include names such as "hook," "kanzi," "kick," and "biezi." Today these names are still used in Chinese wrestling. From *Shanpu Camp Wrestling* to *Woodcut Wrestling Pictures of the Qing Dynasty* of the Qing Dynasty, we can clearly see that these former wrestling technical movements are still common in modern Chinese-style wrestling. For example, the standing technique is one of the basic wrestling techniques seen in these two pictures, including one-legged wrestling with the head inside, one-legged wrestling with the head outside, two-legged fall backwards, and one-armed leg swings. There are also various moves such as cross fall, big back, stumbling, and kicking. It can be seen from the pictures that there is no referee in this spectacle wrestling match, and both sides acquiesce to an established fact or the onlookers like those civil and military officials in the crowd are the judges. However, there should be a referee in the official game, which must be further proved. It is recorded in the *Civil Society Guide to Peiping* that every December 23, Qing emperor would watch a wrestling competition in front of the inner court's Yangxin Hall, which was known as "Liao Zao." On the ninth day of the first lunar month, he would watch the wrestling between the Shanpu Camp players with the foreign wrestlers at Ziguang Pavilion in Zhonghai, which was called "Ke Zao." The wrestlers among the foreign guests were mostly Mongolians. Because Mongolians were always aggressive, they would try to wrestle in order to show off when they paid tributes. While wrestling, they wore a girdle in short boots. The wrestling ground was covered with a large blanket, and three rounds determined the outcome.[135] From here, we can clearly discover the classification, competition suits, venue conditions as well as competition system of wrestling in the Qing Dynasty. The clothing and venue of the competition are the same as the above-mentioned. It is worth noting that the Qing Dynasty called the wrestling appreciation in the palace "Liao Zao" and called the foreign competition "Ke Zao," which is obviously to have divided wrestling into different types, adapting to the exchanges between different ethnic groups. At the same time, it also clarifies the condition for a player to win on the basis of two-out-of-three competitions.

5.5.2 Historical Contributions of Manchu Wrestling

As mentioned above, due to the great importance attached to wrestling by the emperors of the Qing Dynasty, Manchu wrestling had a complete set of management mechanisms. It established an organization and training body (Shanpu Camp), in which **Manchu wrestlers often discussed** with Mongolian about their skills. As a result, Manchu **wrestling flourished, whose technical skills** improved rapidly. During the Shunzhi Period, Manchu wrestling skills surpassed the Mongolians, **ranking first in the country. In short, the vigorous development of Manchu wrestling in the Qing Dynasty made a significant contribution to the formation of Chinese-style** wrestling.

Firstly, it endowed the origin of the name "wrestling." In the Ming Dynasty, the name of the wrestling sports was still commensurate with Jiao-Di, which was only used as an item of entertainment. During the Qing Dynasty, many literati translated the Manchu Buku into "Liao Jiao," "Sun Jiao," and "Shuai Jiao." It can be corroborated by the following records: "Buku was also called 'Liao Jiao'…" "The nineteenth day of the first lunar month is called 'Yan Jiu.' Every time 'Yan Jiu' arrived, the emperor would set up a banquet in the imperial hall to watch the entertainment and wrestling. Most Qing emperors enjoy wrestling." Jiao-Di was called Liao Jiao, Sun Jiao, and Shuai Jiao, which brought not only the change of name, but also the fundamental changes in wrestling techniques, rules, and training in the **Qing Dynasty.** The word **Shuai Jiao** (wrestling) came into being as a result of the development of Manchu wrestling techniques in the Qing Dynasty.

Secondly, Manchu wrestling in the Qing Dynasty established the main technical characteristics of Chinese wrestling, which is known for its foot strength. "Buku is also called Liao Jiao, which **was originally a hand-to-hand fight, mainly relying on foot strength. The success or failure is** determined by whether the wrestlers touch the ground. Although wrestlers with the special **wrestling suit are equipped with somewhat hand moves …, more emphasis is on foot.** That is, foot strength is the most important of all. There are moves such as walking, squatting, stomping, **rolling, backing, and straddling."** The above records indicate that the Manchu wrestling technique in the Qing Dynasty was mainly based on footwork. It is well-known that the main techniques of Chinese **wrestling are featured by tripping, big fit, small fit, big whip, hook picking, hooking,** wiping the neck and feet, rubbing the feet, pulling the feet, raising the feet, and buckling the legs. **There is a saying about Chinese** wrestling which goes as follows: Hands are two doors, while the legs count. It is clear that Chinese-style wrestling techniques further evolved on the basis of Manchus wrestling techniques in the Qing Dynasty.

Thirdly, Manchu wrestling suit of the Qing Dynasty established the style of Chinese wrestling **suits.** The Manchu wrestling costumes of the Qing were all white-cloth short shirts with narrow sleeves, and the collar and placket were sewn tightly with seven or eight layers of cloth, for the purpose of being tough and durable. Article 20 of Chapter 6 of the *Chinese-Style Wrestling Competition Rules* stipulates: "Wrestling suits are made of six layers of cotton-padded clothes, with collar, chest, and under-sleeves sewn more tightly." It can be easily seen that Manchu wrestling suits in the Qing Dynasty share basically a lot with those of Chinese-style wrestling suits in practice **and specifications. Besides, long pants and high-top shoes with soft soles are required during the** competition for both types of suits.

Fourthly, Manchu wrestling in the Qing Dynasty laid the basic rules for the outcome of Chinese **wrestling.** Whoever landed on the ground first was the loser. The following literature is the evidence: "Prince Huishun pretended to be a guard and entered the court, mixing among the soldiers. When he fought with the envoy, he threw his opponent casually down at one go …

Taking off their hats and short sleeves, the two competed against each other, and determined the winner by throwing each other to the ground with bare hands." "The fighters fought barehanded, and focused on their foot strength. The success or failure depended on whoever touched the ground." In Article 7 of Chapter 2 of *Chinese-Style Wrestling Competition Rules*, it stipulates: "If you throw your opponent, one point shall be scored for keeping his hands, elbows or knees on the ground, and two points shall be scored for keeping his torso on the ground, and three points shall be awarded for keeping his rear torso or head on the ground while another still remains standing." We can clearly see that in Chinese-style wrestling, the one who falls will be the loser, but the points vary depending on the body part that touches the ground. In Chinese-style wrestling, a single fall doesn't mean failure. Each match is divided into three rounds, and each takes three minutes. The final cumulative scores determine the outcome.

In short, the robust development of Manchu wrestling in the Qing Dynasty promoted the rapid improvement of its wrestling techniques, perfected the competition scoring rubrics of wrestling, and laid the foundation for the progress of Chinese-style wrestling techniques as well as the formulation of competition rules.

5.6 Summary

The wrestling culture of China is formed by the mutual influence and integration of the wrestling cultures of various nationalities, dominated by the Han nationality. Generally speaking, wrestling is dominated by the Han nationality. However, in some specific projects, on the basis of inheriting Chinese culture as the mainstream, some ethnic minorities, combined with the actual situation of geographical environment and the current situation involved, have promoted the development of China's wrestling to its optimum and thus made outstanding contributions to the progress of traditional Chinese sports culture.[136]

There are still some differences between the Central Plains and the northern nationalities in terms of wrestling. First of all, the origin of Jiao-Di in the Central Plains is closely related to early hunting, but the later evolution is mainly affected by the war. For people with great mobility or adaptability, both sides should seek relatively flexible and free forms to attack each other. Especially in war, there is no restriction of rules, so sports techniques have no fixed moves. This very form has exerted some impacts on the Jiao-Di plays of the Central Plains as well as the northern nationalities. However, its final direction mainly evolved into a form of strong fighting martial arts. On the other hand, the earliest targets of the northern ethnic groups are mainly animals, which do not possess the same flexibility and adaptability as human creatures. Therefore, to subdue animals, people should firmly hold their vital parts and resist with force. The battles of northern nationalities are basically carried out on the horse, while Jiao-Di is mostly practiced on the ground. Therefore, it is said that the origin of Jiao-Di mainly lies in the confrontation with animals in the process of hunting. As for the horse wrestling that was later followed by the Northwest Nationalities, it has become an innovation in people's entertainment after the development of national culture. In the early growth of strength training in the ancient northern nationalities, or in the competition, wrestling was mostly practiced in a relatively fixed form of cuddling, which eventually evolved into recognized modern wrestling.

From the third century BC to the beginning of the tenth century, Chinese wrestling was represented by Jiao-Di and Sumo in China. After the fall of the Tang Dynasty, China entered a state of multi-ethnic regimes and multi-regional divisions. The Central Plains culture and the northern minority cultures collided strongly. Therefore, at that time, China's wrestling was quietly evolving. The prohibition and ban of southern wrestling in the Jin and Yuan Dynasties had a great impact on China's wrestling, so the popular wrestling in the southern market slowly declined away in the historical stage. It was at that time that the wrestling featured by the northern grassland culture as its mainstream developed vigorously. Manchu wrestling in the Qing Dynasty could not have evolved into today's Chinese-style wrestling without the long-term historical contributions of all ethnic groups in ancient China, especially the great influence exerted by the two forms of wrestling at that time, namely the Sumo in the Han Dynasty and the wrestling in the animal husbandry regions in the north. Manchu is a nationality that is good at learning and absorbing other advanced cultures, and Manchus were constantly experiencing the conquest of war and the mergers of culture. After the integration of wrestling culture, on the basis of the absorption of wrestling techniques in the Han-Tang Dynasties and Jin-Yuan Dynasties, wrestling sport in China went through long-term development and eventually finalized in the Qing Dynasty, which is also in line with the historical law of the formation of the Chinese national pattern.

Buku has a unique Manchu style with the skills specialized by the Manchu people. Liang Zhangju wrote in his book entitled *Notes on Returning to the Fields* that "Someone asked what Buku was, and I replied that Buku is its name in Mandarin language, which is translated into Liao Jiao. Picking strong and healthy children in their teens to fight each other with bare hands, and paying great attention to the strength of their feet. Winning or losing is determined by whether to touch the ground."[137] Zhao Yi wrote in *Miscellaneous Records of Yan Pu*:

> "Buku, or kicking feet, is originally a barehanded fight. It depends on the strength of the feet, and the victory depends on the landing of the opponent. At first, both wrestlers intend to take advantage of the lax time to win, then the two scuffle together, with their feet tripping each other; once the wrestler loses his balance, he will be thrown to the ground; whoever falls to the ground decides the game, in that the loser is determined. The winner drinks and then goes away."[138]

This form of wrestling mainly focuses on the use of foot techniques. Once the loser falls to the ground, he is prohibited from initiating another attack, which is very similar to modern Chinese wrestling.

Mongolian tribes are all very fond of wrestling, and wrestling competitions are held at large banquets. According to the *Chronicles of Rehe*, when the Manchus wrestle, their upper limb moves include pressing, dragging, holding, and persisting; the techniques of the lower limbs involve twisting, squatting, stepping, and opening the foot. Each wrestler tries to throw the other to the ground in a stunt with his head and shoulders down on the ground. The game ends in accompany with the winner smugly drinking a bowl of mutton soup and then stepping away. The traditional method of Manchu wrestling is that "at first both wrestlers intend to take advantage of the lax time to win, then the two scuffle together, with their feet tripping each other. Once the wrestler loses his balance, he will be thrown to the ground; whoever falls to the ground decides the game, in that the loser is determined. The winner drinks and then goes away." The Manchu wrestling recorded in the *Chronicles of Rehe · Sumo* is that "the two sides took off their hats and short sleeves, and competed against each other. Once one side landed, the winner was decided, thus rewarded with wine."[139] Later, the wrestler wore girdles densely sewn with the cloth.

In the early Qing Dynasty, wrestling matches were often held in the army, which was not only for training and improving soldiers' unarmed combat skills, but also to satisfy the interests of the Manchu nobility. In the second year of Chongde, a collective wrestling competition was held in August. Emperor Taizong led the upper-class nobles to launch an archery competition in the martial arts field first, "then he divided them into the left and right wings and ordered them to wrestle with each other. The loser offered cows and sheep as a punishment ... and then he ordered wrestlers from both sides to wrestle. The king, Beile (a rank of the Manchu nobility below that of the prince), and Beizi (a rank of the Manchu nobility below that of the Beile) of the right side, who had lost, gave back an ox and two sheep to the left side."[140] In order to encourage the soldiers to improve their wrestling skills, the competition was no longer about drinking alcohol, but about rewards and punishments like cattle and sheep.

When Emperor Taiji of the Qing Dynasty succeeded to the throne, in order to further advance the Central Plains, he strengthened military training on the one hand, "practiced martial arts with wrestling and other games,"[141] and trained soldiers' strength and unarmed combat skills; On the other hand, in order to stabilize the north, he endeavored to reinforce the unity with other ethnic groups, especially the Mongolians. At this time, wrestling became one of the important means employed by the rulers of the Qing Dynasty to "practice martial arts and threaten other minorities." Emperor Taizong consciously trained wrestling players, and repeatedly asked them to compete with Mongolian and other ethnic players who were good at wrestling. In AD 1632, Emperor Taizong held a grand event to celebrate the arrival of Mogolia Beile (a rank of the Manchu nobility below that of the prince), Nomuqi, Ubashi, etc. The emperor personally reached the martial field, "he led the princes and his ministers to pay homage to the heaven, and then held a music and dance feast. He also ordered Nomuqi and others to play archery, and selected some Hercules to wrestle."[142] In this way, Emperor Taizong demonstrated his goodwill and enhanced the friendship between the two peoples of the north.

During the Shunzhi Period, Prince Huishun Hu Sai, who was less than 20 years old, had a very important wrestling match with Khalkha's messenger. Hu Sai was very brave and good at wrestling. Khalkha was a famous and powerful tribe in Mobei, which was one of the main objects for the unity of the Qing rulers. This tribe was skillful at wrestling, so the emperor arranged a match for them and watched it in person. "No one could defeat them. After Prince Huishun heard about it, he asked Prince Lilie for help, who asked him to disguise himself as his guard, enter the court, and hide in the crowd. When Prince Huishun competed with the envoys, he threw them down at one go casually. The emperor was so pleased that he awarded him a lot of rewards."[143] The victory of the competition symbolizes the strength and dignity of the nation. The Manchu prince was able to throw the Khalkha's wrestler over, which was to form a deterrent to the Khalkha tribe for the external world and convinced the civil ministers for the inside country. Therefore, the emperor was particularly happy to the extent that he generously rewarded him. Through friendly games and generous rewards, their ethnic relations grew closer. At the same time, it was also through these numerous competitions that Qing Dynasty borrowed the techniques and spirit of wrestling from other ethnic groups, which paved the foundation for the shaping of Chinese wrestling today.

Folks wrestling, taken as an activity of physical exercise, recreation, and networking, was commonly known as "private wrestling" or "private practice" in the Qing Dynasty. The fifth volume of *Notes on Returning to the Fields* recorded that Buku was translated into "Liaojiao," in which "the wrestlers fight each other with bare hands, with the focus on the strength of their feet. Winning or losing is determined by whether to touch the ground." The term "Guan Tui" may come from "focus on foot strength." Wrestling performers on various occasions also belong to the "private wrestlers." In the Qing Dynasty, there were wrestling venues in and around the capital, such as Tianqiao, Niujie, East Fourth, West fourth, Earth Altar, Moon Altar, Chaoyang Gate, Xizhi Gate, Haidian, Qinglong Bridge … and market, temple fairs, etc. Some places were settled with several wrestling courts, commonly known as "Jiao Wozi (wrestling nests)." So was the similar situation in Tianjin. Since the dissolution of the government-run Shanpu Camp in the late Qing Dynasty, most of the original wrestlers turned to be teachers or "buskers" in the Baoding area of Beijing and Tianjin; thus, folk wrestling became more and more prosperous.

In the wrestling and Sumo of the Han nationality, the wrestlers usually fight with their arms and employ their waist power to win over the opponent. In the wrestling of the Mongolians, the wrestlers can still fight after falling down, which is slightly different from Buku. Boku is Manchus wrestling, but still shares some similarities with Jiao-Di and Sumo of the Han Dynasty. Han wrestling, with a time-honored history, has many schools, the styles of which vary endlessly, and the attack and defense techniques are comprehensive, characterized by the combination of skills and strength. In particular, the traditional Jiao-Di plays allow arm-wrestling, one extra set of attacking abilities over the earlier form. Therefore, Han-style traditional wrestling was favored and valued by the Manchu Boku players. Buku gradually absorbed the essence of Jiao-Di plays and altered the original single-foot attack. In this way, Buku and Jiao-Di took their strengths from each other, integrated and connected, so that their competition regulations began to be consistent.

To sum up, the author believes that Buku was a popular wrestling style in the Qing Dynasty, which borrowed and adopted Jiao-Di and Sumo wrestling techniques of the Han nationality, thus merging into a form of skills and strength. In addition, the northern nationalities inherited and developed the wrestling form represented by Huns' Jiao-Di in their long-term growth. In the Qing Dynasty, as the Manchus absorbed and applied some of the Mongolian technical characteristics in the continuous exchange of wrestling with the Mongolians, it eventually evolved into a modern Chinese wrestling form. Thus, the wrestling sport in our country has been created and perfected by all ethnic groups in the long history of development.

NOTES

1. [Han] Zheng Xuan, *Yue Ling*, vol. 17 of *Collation and Interpretation of the "Book of Rites,"* 1st ed. (Peking University Press, December 2000), 644.
2. Quoted from *Guangmin Daily*, July 28, 1982.
3. [Ming] Huikang, Yesou, *ShiYu*, vol. 3, *Summary of Notes and Novels*, bk. 12 (Jiangsu Guangling Ancient Book Engraving and Printing Agency, 1984).
4. [Han] Ban Gu, *Chronicles of Emperor Wu*, vol. 6 of *Book of the Former Han Dynasty*, 1st ed. (Zhonghua Book Company, June 1962), 194.
5. [Qing] Wang Xianshen, *Wai Chu*, vol. 12 of *Interpretation of Han Feizi's Collection*, proofread by Zhong Zhe, 1st ed. (Zhonghua Book Company, July 1998), 295.
6. [Han] Ban Gu, *Records of Criminal Law*, vol. 23 of *Book of the Former Han Dynasty*, 1st ed. (Zhonghua Book Company, June 1962), 1085.
7. [Han] Sima Qian, *Biography of Li Si*, vol. 87 of *Historical Records*, 1st ed. (Zhonghua Book Company, September 1959), 2559.
8. [Song] Gao Cheng, *Wrestling and Play*, vol. 9 of *Shi Wu Ji Yuan*, 1st ed. (Zhonghua Book Company, April 1989), 492.
9. Cultural Relics Team of Hubei Provincial Bureau of Culture, "Important Cultural Relics Unearthed from Three Chu Tombs in Jiangling, Hubei Province," *Cultural Relics*, no. 5 (1966): 33–55.
10. [Han] Ban Gu, *Chronicles of Emperor Wu*, vol. 6 of *Book of the Former Han Dynasty*, 1st ed. (Zhonghua Book Company, June 1962), 194.
11. Ibid.
12. [Han] Ban Gu, *Biography of Zhang Qian*, vol. 61 of *Book of the Former Han Dynasty*, 1st ed. (Zhonghua Book Company, June 1962), 2697.
13. [Han] Ban Gu, *Chronicles of Emperor Wu*, vol. 6 of *Book of the Former Han Dynasty*, 1st ed. (Zhonghua Book Company, June 1962), 189.
14. The following materials were all selected from *Chronicles of Emperor Wu*, vol. 6 of *Book of the Former Han Dynasty*.
15. [Han] Ban Gu, *Biography of Xiongnu*, vol. 94 of *Book of the Former Han Dynasty*, 1st ed. (Zhonghua Book Company, June 1962), 3770.
16. [Han] Ban Gu, *Memoirs on the Western Regions*, vol. 96 (II) of *Book of the Former Han Dynasty*, 1st ed. (Zhonghua Book Company, June 1962), 3903–3905.
17. [Han] Ban Gu, *Biography of Xiongnu*, vol. 94 of *Book of the Former Han Dynasty*, 1st ed. (Zhonghua Book Company, June 1962), 3786.
18. [Han] Ban Gu, *Memoirs on the Western Regions*, vol. 96 of *Book of the Former Han Dynasty*, 1st ed. (Zhonghua Book Company, June 1962), 3906.
19. [Liang] Xiao Tong, *Ode to Chang'an by Zhang Pingzi*, vol. 2 of *Selected Works*, 1st ed. (Zhonghua Book Company, November 1977), 26–28.
20. Fengxi Excavation Team of Archaeological Research Institute, "A Briefing on the Excavation of Fengxi, Chang'an, Shaanxi Province," *Archaeology*, no. 5 (1959): 516–530.
21. Bai Shouyi, Gao Min, and An Zuozhang, *Medieval Times · Second Edition · Qin and Han Periods (I)*, vol. 4 of *General Chinese History*, 1st ed. (Shanghai People's Publishing House, November 1995), 130–137.
22. [Han] Sima Qian, *Biography of Xiongnu*, vol. 110 of *Historical Records*, 1st ed. (Zhonghua Book Company, September 1959), 2892.
23. This number was counted according to the *Historical Records · Memoir of Xiongnu, Book of the Han Dynasty · Biography of Xiongnu, Book of the Han Dynasty · Chronicles of Emperor Wu, Book of the Former Han Dynasty · Chronicles of Emperor Zhao*.
24. [Jin] Chen Shou, *Book of the Wei Dynasty · Biography of Wuwan, Xianbei and Eastern Barbarians*, vol. 30 of *The History of the Three Kingdoms*, noted by Pei Songzhi, 1st ed. (Zhonghua Book Company, December 1959), 858–859.

25. Zhao Xin was originally from Xiongnu, who later defected to the Han Dynasty and was given the title Xihou. After subordinating Zhao Xin, Yizhicha Chanyu named him "Zici King" because he had been in the Han army for a long time and was familiar with the situation of the Han army. Chanyu also took his wife as his sister and tried to use him to fight against the Han army.
26. Bai Shouyi, Gao Min, and An Zuozhang, *Medieval Times · Qin and Han Periods (I)*, vol. 4 of *General Chinese History*, 1st ed. (Shanghai People's Publishing House, November 1995), 83.
27. [Han] Sima Qian, *Biography of Weiqing and Huo Qubing*, vol. 111 of *Historical Records*, 1st ed. (Zhonghua Book Company, September 1959), 2931–2934.
28. [Song] Fan Ye, *Biography of Southern Xiongnu*, vol. 89 of *Book of the Later Han Dynasty*, 1st ed. (Zhonghua Book Company, May 1965), 2942.
29. Ibid., 2950–2952.
30. [Han] Sima Qian, *Biography of Xiongnu*, vol. 110 of *Historical Records*, 1st ed. (Zhonghua Book Company, September 1959), 2879.
31. [Han] Ban Gu, *Biography of Jin Midi*, vol. 68 of *Book of the Han Dynasty*, 2961.
32. [Qing] Huang Shuang, *Book Wang Yinjin*, vol. 11 of *The Compiled Nine Old Jin Books* (Ancient Bookstore, 1984).
33. [Tang] Fang Xuanling, *Chronicles of Emperor Wu*, vol. 3 of *Book of the Jin Dynasty*, 1st ed. (Zhonghua Book Company, November 1974), 53.
34. [Tang] Fang Xuanling, *Biography of Yu Chan*, vol. 93 of *Book of the Jin Dynasty*, 1st ed. (Zhonghua Book Company, November 1974), 2385.
35. [Tang] Fang Xuanling, *Chronicles of Emperor Wu*, vol. 3 of *Book of the Jin Dynasty*, 1st ed. (Zhonghua Book Company, November 1974), 50–51.
36. [Tang] Wei Zheng, *Etiquette VII*, vol. 12 of *Book of the Sui Dynasty*, 1st ed. (Zhonghua Book Company, August 1973), 279.
37. According to *Biography of Goguryeo*, vol. 100 of *Book of the Wei Dynasty*, 2215; *Annals of the Jin Dynasty*, vol. 114 of *Tzu-chih t'ung (A Comprehensive Mirror for Aid in Government)*, 3579; *Memoirs of the Eastern Barbarians*, vol. 220 of *New Book of the Tang Dynasty*, 6185.
38. [Chao] Jin Fushi, *Memoirs of Goguryeo*, vol. 18 of *Historical Records of the Three Kingdoms* (Kuizhangge, Seoul University, Korea), 1.
39. [Song] Sima Guang, *Annals of the Tang Dynasty*, vol. 198 of *Tzu-chih t'ung (A Comprehensive Mirror for Aid in Government)*, noted by [Yuan] Hu Sansheng, 1st ed. (Zhonghua Book Company, June 1956), 6230.
40. [Chao] Jin Fushi, *Memoirs of Goguryeo*, vol. 22 of *Historical Records of the Three Kingdoms* (Kuizhangge, Seoul University, Korea), 10–11.
41. [Liu Song] Fan Ye, *Records of the Eastern Barbarians · Goguryeo*, vol. 85 of *Book of the Later Han Dynasty*, 1st ed. (Zhonghua Book Company, May 1965), 2813.
42. See Zhang Ying, Ren Wanju, and Luo Xianqing, *Ancient Official Seals Unearthed in Jilin Province* (Cultural Relics Publishing House, 1992); Hua Yan and Jie Yong, "Several Bronze Seals Unearthed in Ji'an, Jilin," *Northern Cultural Relics*, no. 4 (1985).
43. [Beiqi] Wei Shou, *Biography of Xi Kangsheng*, vol. 73 of *Book of the Wei Dynasty*, 1st ed. (Zhonghua Book Company, June 1974), 1632.
44. [Tang] Li Baiyao, *Chronicles of Emperors · Emperor Xiao*, vol. 6 of *Book of the Northern Qi Dynasty*, 1st ed. (Zhonghua Book Company, November 1972), 80.
45. [Tang] Wei Zheng, *Etiquette VII*, vol. 12 of *Book of the Sui Dynasty*, 1st ed. (Zhonghua Book Company, August 1973), 280.
46. [Tang] Li Yanshou, *Biography of Liu Yu*, vol. 77 of *History of the Northern Dynasties*, 1st ed. (Zhonghua Book Company, October 1974), 2624.
47. [Tang] Wei Zheng, *Chronicles of Emperors · Emperor Yang*, vol. 3 of *Book of the Sui Dynasty*, 1st ed. (Zhonghua Book Company, August 1973), 74.
48. Quoted in [Song] Weng Shixun, *Annotations to the Notes of Jiao-Li*, 1st ed. (People's Sports Publishing House, September 1990), 50.
49. [Later Jin] Liu Xu et al., *Biography of Pei Ju*, vol. 63 of *Old Book of the Tang Dynasty*, 1st ed. (Zhonghua Book Company, May 1975), 2407.

50. Ibid.
51. [Song] Wang Pu, *Armies in the Capital · Miscellaneous Records of the Army*, vol. 72 of *Tang Huiyao*, 1st ed. (Shanghai Ancient Books Publishing House, 1991), 1539–1540.
52. [Song] Ouyang Xiu and Song Qi, *Records of the Soldiers*, vol. 50 of *New Book of the Tang Dynasty*, 1st ed. (Zhonghua Book Company, February 1975), 1327–1328.
53. [Song] Ouyang Xiu and Song Qi, *Biography of Tian Hongzheng*, vol. 148 of *New Book of the Tang Dynasty*, 1st ed. (Zhonghua Book Company, February 1975), 4783.
54. [Later Jin] Liu Xu et al., *Chronicles of Emperor Muzong*, vol. 16 of *Old Book of the Tang Dynasty*, 1st ed. (Zhonghua Book Company, May 1975), 476–479.
55. [Song] Ouyang Xiu and Song Qi, *Biography of Liu Keming*, vol. 280 of *New Book of the Tang Dynasty*, 1st ed. (Zhonghua Book Company, February 1975), 5883–5884.
56. [Song] Sima Guang, *Annals of the Tang Dynasty*, vol. 246 of *Tzu-chih t'ung (A Comprehensive Mirror for Aid in Government)*, noted by [Yuan] Hu Sansheng, 1st ed. (Zhonghua Book Company, June 1956), 7957.
57. [Song] Li Fang et al., *Jiao-Di Players in Zhenwu*, vol. 500 of *Records of the Taiping Era*, 1st ed. (Zhonghua Book Company, September 1966), 4101–4102.
58. [Song] Weng Shixun, *Annotations to the Notes of Jiao-Li*, 1st ed. (People's Sports Publishing House, September 1990), 77–88.
59. [Song] Xue Juzhen et al., *Book of the Tang Dynasty · Biography of Li Cunxian*, vol. 53 of *History of the Old Five Dynasties*, 1st ed. (Zhonghua Book Company, 1976), 721–722.
60. Weng Shixun, *Annotation to the Notes of Jiao-Li*, 1st ed. (People's Sports Press, September 1990), 95.
61. Jin Qicong, "Chinese-Style Wrestling Originated from Khitan and Mongolia," *Journal of Inner Mongolia University* (Philosophy and Social Science Edition), no. 3–4 (1979): 227.
62. [Liang] Hui Jiao et al., *Continued Biography of Eminent Monks*, vol. 26 of *Collection of Eminent Monks Bibliography*, 1st ed. (Shanghai Chinese Classics Publishing House, December 1991), 321.
63. [Song] Wu Zimu, *Jiao-Di*, vol. 20 of *Meng Liang Lu*, 1st ed. (Sanqin Publishing House, May 2005), 318.
64. Ibid, 318–319.
65. [Song] *Performers and Artists · Jiao-Di*, vol. 6 of *Old Story of Wulin*, collected by Sishui Qianfu, 1st ed. (Zhejiang People's Publishing House, February 1984), 112–113.
66. *History of the Jin Dynasty · Mandarine*, 1st ed. (Zhonghua Book Company, July 1975), 2893.
67. [Yuan] Tuitui et al., *Chronicles of Emperor Taizu (I)*, vol. 1 of *History of the Liao Dynasty*, 1st ed. (Zhonghua Book Company, October 1974), 9.
68. [Qing] Zhai Huaifu et al., *Yuekao · Sanyue Baixi · Liao*, vol. 119 of *The Continuing General Survey of Qinding*, bk. 629 of *The Complete Collection of Si Ku Quan Shu of Wenyuan Pavilion* (Shanghai Chinese Classics Publishing House, 1987), 399–400.
69. [Qing] Zhai Huaifu et al., *Yuekao · Cubuyue*, vol. 118 of *The Continuing General Survey of Qinding*, bk. 629 of *Si Ku Quan Shu of Wenyuan Pavilion* (Shanghai Chinese Classics Publishing House, 1987), 392.
70. [Qing] Zhai Huaifu et al., *Yuekao · Sanyue Baixi · Liao*, vol. 119 of *The Continuing General Survey of Qinding*, bk. 629 of *The Complete Collection of Si Ku Quan Shu of Wenyuan Pavilion* (Shanghai Chinese Classics Publishing House, 1987), 399–401.
71. [Ming] Tao Zongyi, Chapter 120 of *Three Kinds of Shuo Fu*, vol. 3 of *Shuo Fu 120*, 1st ed. (Shanghai Chinese Classics Publishing House, October 1988), 856.
72. Jin Qicong, "Chinese-Style Wrestling Originated from Khitan and Mongolia," *Journal of Inner Mongolia University* (Philosophy and Social Science Edition), no. 3–4 (1979): 231.
73. [Japan] Torii Ryuzo, "Khitan's Jiao-Di," *Journal of Yanjing*, no. 29 (1941): 210–213.
74. Jin Qicong, "Chinese-Style Wrestling Originated from Khitan and Mongolia," *Journal of Inner Mongolia University* (Philosophy and Social Science Edition), no. 3–4 (1979): 232.
75. [Yuan] Tuitui et al., *Geographia I · Shangjing Road*, vol. 37 of *History of the Liao Dynasty*, 1st ed. (Zhonghua Book Company, October 1974), 441.
76. Wang Zonghan, *Chinese National History*, rev. ed. (China Social Sciences Press), 446. There are so-called four sources about the origin of Khitans. One is from Donghu or Yuwen Xianbei, as recorded in *Book of the Wei Dynasty, Tongtian, The New History of the Five Dynasties, Annals of Khitan State, History of the Liao Dynasty,*

etc.; the second is from the Huns, as recorded in *The Old History of the Five Dynasties*, *Ce Fui Yuan Gui, Song Hui Yao, Annals of the Nine States*, etc.; the third is the integration product of Huns and Xianbe; and the fourth is from the minor tribes of Xianbei who are not their lineal descendants.

77. [Yuan] Tuitui et al., *Biography of Benzhu*, vol. 84 of *History of the Liao Dynasty*, 1st ed. (Zhonghua Book Company, July 1975), 1885.
78. [Yuan] Tuitui et al., *Biography of Arthan*, vol. 81 of *History of the Liao Dynasty*, 1st ed. (Zhonghua Book Company, July 1975), 1816–1817.
79. [Yuan] Tuitui et al., *Biography of Shi Morong*, vol. 91 of *History of the Liao Dynasty*, 1st ed. (Zhonghua Book Company, July 1975), 2027.
80. [Yuan] Tuitui et al., *Biography of Pucha Shijie*, vol. 91 of *History of the Liao Dynasty*, 1st ed. (Zhonghua Book Company, July 1975), 2020.
81. [Yuan] Tuitui et al., *Chronicles of Hailing*, vol. 5 of *History of the Liao Dynasty*, 1st ed. (Zhonghua Book Company, July 1975), 104–106.
82. [Song] Yuwen Maozhao, *Emperor Xizong Xiaocheng (VI)*, vol. 12 of *Proofs of the Annals of Great Jin*, proofread by Cui Wenyin, 1st ed. (Zhonghua Book Company, July 1986), 179.
83. [Yuan] Tuitui et al., *Chronicles of Emperor Zhangzong (II)*, vol. 10 of *History of the Liao Dynasty*, 1st ed. (Zhonghua Book Company, July 1975), 228–236.
84. Tixingsi was mainly local officials, especially for the Han Dynasty. In *Chronicles of Emperor Zhang (II)*, vol. 10 of *History of the Jin Dynasty*, it is stated: "The original intention of my special establishment of Tixingsi was to reassure the people. And now it has been five years, but the results have not turned out to be very obvious. The reason is that most officials don't know what their jobs are for, and many works are so trivial that officials in some states and counties fail to do. People in Shandong are having trouble getting enough to eat. I once sent emissaries to disaster relief, but because the officials did not fulfill their duties, it has come to this point. We should reflect on our past mistakes and correct them."
85. Jin Qicong, "Chinese-Style Wrestling Originated from Khitan and Mongolia," *Journal of Inner Mongolia University* (Philosophy and Social Science Edition) (1979): 233.
86. [Song] Yuwen Maozhao, *Ji Year · Emperor Taizong Wenlie I*, vol. 3 of *Proofs of the Annals of Great Jin*, proofread by Cui Wenyin, 1st ed. (Zhonghua Book Company, July 1986), 40.
87. Shi Jinbo, Bai Bin, and Huang Zhenhua, *Wenhai Research* (China Social Sciences Press, 1983), 456–508.
88. *Mistaken Fighting for Doumen*, vol. 14 of *The New Decrees of Tiansheng*, interpreted and noted by Shi Jinbo, Nie Hongyin, and Bai Bin, 1st ed. (The Law Press, January 2000), 483.
89. Zha Mirza, *Mongolian Boke*, quoted from Xu Yuliang, *History of Chinese Minority Sports*, 38.
90. *The Third Edition of Four series of Books (VIII)*, vol. 4 of *The Secret History of the Mongols* (Shanghai Bookstore, reprinted from the The Commercial Press's in 1935, 1985), 29.
91. [Sweden] Constantine d'Ohsson, *Histoire des Mongols (I)*, translated by Feng Chengjun (Zhonghua Book Company, 1962), 231.
92. Chenyuan, *Criminal Department XIX · Prohibition of Acquiring Guns and Rods*, vol. 57, bk. 18 of *Institutions of the Yuan Dynasty* (Zhonghua Book Company, 1983), 50.
93. Hu Diyu, *Two Poems of Sumo*, quoted from Kuang Wennan, "The Development of Martial Arts in Liao, Jin, Xixia, and Yuan Dynasties," *Journal of Chengdu Sports Institute*, no. 1 (1994): 18.
94. [Ming] Song Lian et al., *Emperor Shizu (XIV)*, vol. 17 of *History of the Yuan Dynasty*, 1st ed. (Zhonghua Book Company, April 1976), 371.
95. [Ming] Song Lian et al., *Emperor Wuzong (I)*, vol. 22 of *History of the Yuan Dynasty*, 1st ed. (Zhonghua Book Company, April 1976), 481.
96. [Ming] Song Lian et al., *Emperor Wuzong (II)*, vol. 23 of *History of the Yuan Dynasty*, 1st ed. (Zhonghua Book Company, April 1976), 524.
97. [Ming] Song Lian et al., *Emperor Renzong (III)*, vol. 26 of *History of the Yuan Dynasty*, 1st ed. (Zhonghua Book Company, April 1976), 589.
98. [Ming] Song Lian et al., *Emperor Yingzong (I)*, vol. 27 of *History of the Yuan Dynasty*, 1st ed. (Zhonghua Book Company, April 1976), 603.

99. [Ming] Song Lian et al., *Biography of Wang Yue*, vol. 178 of *History of the Yuan Dynasty*, 1st ed. (Zhonghua Book Company, April 1976), 4141.
100. [Ming] Song Lian et al., *Biography of Gai Miao*, vol. 185 of *History of the Yuan Dynasty*, 1st ed. (Zhonghua Book Company, April 1976), 4261.
101. [Spain] Ruy González de Clavijo, *Timur Devrinde Kadistan Semer-Kand's SeyahatRuy · Samargand (II)*, translated by Yang Zhaojun (The Commercial Press, 1944, Reprinted in 1997), 141–142.
102. Xu Ke, *Tactics*, bk. 6 of *Classified Anthology of Anecdotes of the Qing Dynasty*, 1st ed. (Zhonghua Book Company, March 1986), 2989.
103. *Sports Weekly*, vol. 48 (Tianjin, 1932).
104. Jin Liang, *Secret Records of Manchu Old Archives · Emperor Taizong's Rewards to Hercules*, quoted from Jin Qicong, "Chinese-Style Wrestling Originated from Khitan and Mongolia," *Journal of Inner Mongolia University* (Philosophy and Social Science Edition), no. 3–4 (1979): 240.
105. [Qing] Jiang Liangqi, *Donghua Lu*, proofread by Lin Shuhui and Fu Guijiu, vol. 2, 1st ed. (Zhonghua Book Company, April 1980), 33.
106. Rong Suhe, Zhao Yongxian, and Zha Laga et al., *History of the Mongolian Literature*, vol. 2, 1st ed. (Inner Mongolia People's Publishing House, December 2002), 148.
107. [Qing] Jiang Liangqi, *Donghua Lu*, proofread by Lin Shuhui and Fu Guijiu, vol. 3, 1st ed. (Zhonghua Book Company, April 1980), 35.
108. [Qing] Yuan Dahua et al., *Xinjiang Atlas · Tianzhang III* (Shanghai Chinese Classics Publishing House, October 1992).
109. [Qing] Wang Shuzhan, *Records of Rites and Customs in Xinjiang*, 1st ed. (Chengwen Press, March 1959), 7–8.
110. [Soviet] Nai · Yang, *Batu Army · Mongolian Army Naadam*, quoted from Xu Yuliang, *History of the Chinese Minority Sports*, 76.
111. [Ming] Hu Guang et al., *Chronicles of Emperor Taizuo*, vol. 73 of *Ming Shi Lu* (Shanghai Bookstore, 1984). The original records are: In the year of Xinhai (March of the fifth year of Hongwu), the emperor asked the department in charge of the etiquette to reset the rites between the officials and citizens. Before that, the officials would kneel on one knee to show their manner, and kowtow to show their respect. After kowtowing, they would again kneel on one knee. The lower official would stretch their hands later and step back before the higher official. The emperor hated this ritual and asked to abolish it since he took the place. However, this still existed. Therefore, this behavior was set to be the official behavior.
112. [Qing] Liu Xianting, *Guangyang Miscellany*, proofread by Wang Beiping and Xia Zhihe, vol. 1, 1st ed. (Zhonghua Book Company, July 1957), 25–26.
113. [Qing] Zhang Tingyu et al., *Eunuchs (I)*, vol. 340 of *History of the Ming Dynasty*, 1st ed. (Zhonghua Book Company, April 1974), 7786.
114. [Qing] Zhang Tingyu et al., *Biography of Yuan Jixian*, vol. 277 of *History of the Ming Dynasty*, 1st ed. (Zhonghua Book Company, April 1974), 7087.
115. [Qing] Zhang Tingyu et al., *Biography of Jiang Bin*, vol. 370 of *History of the Ming Dynasty*, 1st ed. (Zhonghua Book Company, April 1974), 7786.
116. [Qing] Liang Zhangju, *Oboi*, vol. 5 of *Notes on Returning to the Fields*, 1st ed. (Zhonghua Book Company, August 1981), 80.
117. [Ming] Song Lian et al., *Geographia (II)*, vol. 59 of *History of the Yuan Dynasty*, 1st ed. (Zhonghua Book Company, April 1976), 1400.
118. [Qing] Zhao Yi, *Oubei Poetry*, vol. 1, bk. 2 of *Wan You Wen Ku* (The Commercial Press, 1935).
119. *Chronicles of Emperor Taizong*, vol. 38 of *Records of the Qing Dynasty*, 1st ed. (Zhonghua Book Company, June 1985), 498–499.
120. [Qing] A Gui et al., *The Strategy for the Founding of the Qing Dynasty*, vol. 26 (Taipei: Wenhai Press, 1966), 5.
121. [Qing] Zhao Lian, *Power of King Huishun*, vol. 2 of *Miscellaneous Records of Xiao Ting*, proofread by He Yingfang, 1st ed. (Zhonghua Book Company, December 1980), 42.
122. [Qing] Yao Yuanzhi, *Miscellaneous Records of Zhuye Pavilian*, proofread by Li Jiemin, vol. 1, 1st ed. (Zhonghua Book Company, May 1982), 1.

123. [Qing] Zhao Lian, *Two Dukes Arguing about the Battle*, vol. 3 of *Miscellaneous Records of Xiao Ting*, proofread by He Yingfang, 1st ed. (Zhonghua Book Company, December 1980), 457.
124. Xu Ke, *Tactics · Wrestling in Shanpu Camp*, bk. 6 of *Classified Anthology of Anecdotes of the Qing Dynasty*, 1st ed. (Zhonghua Book Company, March 1986), 2886–2887.
125. [Qing] Zhao Yi, *Mongol Horse Plays*, vol. 1 of *Miscellaneous Records of Yan Pu*, 1st ed. (Zhonghua Book Company, 1982), 12.
126. [Qing] Zhao Lian, *Ma Zhuangjie*, vol. 4 of *Miscellaneous Records of Xiao Ting*, proofread by He Yingfang, 1st ed. (Zhonghua Book Company, December 1980), 86.
127. [Qing] Chen Kangqi, *Records of Lang Qian II*, vol. 9, 1st ed. (Zhonghua Book Company, March 1984), 481.
128. Gu Qian (AD 1646–1712). His courtesy name is Zhiyan. Gu was from Wu County, Jiangsu Province. Afterwards, Gu moved to Daxing County. In the Kangxi Period, Gu became an official and undertook many imperial positions. Gu was good at writing poems, whose poem collection is named *The Collection of Fengchi Garden*, from which the poem *Pu Jiao Xing* was selected.
129. Gu Qian, "Pu Jiao Xing," noted by Liu Ping, *Sports Culture Guide*, no. 4 (1985): 32–33.
130. Zhao Yi (1727–1814). His courtesy name is Yunsong, with Oubei as his literary name. Zhao was from Yanghu (Now Changzhou), Jiangsu. Zhao became Jinshi in the 26th year of Qianlong Period. Zhao has written *Reading Notes of Twenty-Two Historical Books* and *Oubei Poetry*.
131. Zhao Yi, *Hunting Scene · Sumo*, vol. 1 of *Oubei Poetry*; Wang Qihui and Liu Shaoping, "Zhao Oubei's (Sumo) Poem," *Sports Culture Guide*, no. 3 (1985): 37–38.
132. Cui Leiquan, *Catalogue of Chinese Ancient Sports Relics* (Zhonghua Book Company, September 2000), 96.
133. [Qing] Zhao Yi, *Miscellaneous Records of Yan Pu*, vol. 1, 1st ed. (Zhonghua Book Company, 1982), 13.
134. *Wu Ti Qing Wen Jian · Wrestling* (The Ethnic Publishing House,1957).
135. Li Jifang, "From Gradual Recovery to Unprecedented Development of Wrestling in Ming and Qing Dynasties: A Brief History of Chinese Ancient Wrestling," *Chengdu Sports College Journal*, no. 2 (1984): 10.
136. **Mr. Jin Qizong was the first to study the wrestling history of ethnic minorities in northern China in ancient times. His research was very comprehensive and profound. His work** *Chinese-Style Wrestling Originated from Khitan and Mongolia* **was published in the** *Journal of Inner Mongolia University* **(Philosophy and Social Sciences), no. 3–4 (1979). This paper comprehensively expounds the wrestling of** *Khitan* **and Mongolia. This section refers to Mr. Jin's early achievements and research scope in some degree, and further collects new documents and archaeological materials, thus shedding some lights on new viewpoints and issues.**
137. [Qing] Liang Zhangju, *Oboi*, vol. 5 of *Notes on Returning to the Fields*, 1st ed. (Zhonghua Book Company, August 1981), 80.
138. [Qing] Zhao Yi, *Miscellaneous Records of Yan Pu*, vol. 1, 1st ed. (Zhonghua Book Company, May 1982), 13.
139. [Qing] He Shen and Liang Guozhi, *Chronicles of Rehe · Sumo* (Tianjin Ancient Books Publishing House, December 2002); *Department of History · Geographia*, bk. 730 of *Continuing Collection of Si Ku Quan Shu* (Shanghai Ancient Books Publishing House, 1995), 806–807.
140. *Chronicles of Emperor Taizong Wen*, vol. 38 of *Records of the Qing Dynasty*, 1st ed. (Zhonghua Book Company, June 1985), 499.
141. *A Grand View of the Unofficial History of the Qing Dynasty · Qing Dynasty*, 1st ed. (Shanghai Bookstore, June 1981), 42–43.
142. [Qing] Ji Huang et.al., *Tian Li*, vol. 155 of *General Survey of the Literature of Dynasties*, bk. of *The Complete Collection of Si Ku Quan Shu of Wenyuan Pavilion* (Shanghai Ancient Book Publishing House, 1987).
143. Xu Ke, *Tactics*, vol. 6 of *Classified Anthology of Anecdotes of the Qing Dynasty*, 1st ed. (Zhonghua Book Company, March1986), 2863.

CHAPTER VI

Origin and Evolution of Polo in China

6.1 Origin of Polo

6.1.1 Three Views on the Origin of Polo

Before the 21st century, there were three academic views about the origin of polo. Firstly, polo could have originated in Persia and was brought into the Chinese Central Plains through the region of Tubo (present-day Chinese Tibet). Secondly, polo could have originated in Tibet, and was passed into the Central Plains during the early Tang Dynasty. The last view is that polo could have originated in the Central Plains.

The view of polo's origin in Persia was mainly presented by professors Xiang Da and Luo Xianglin. They believed that polo originated in Persia and spread into China through Turkestan, and then flourished in the early Tang Dynasty. There are three facts that support their argument: First, in ancient times, this sport was first called "Polo" according to Du Huan's book *Jing Xing Ji*, which records that "There was a polo forest, and beneath it was there a court for playing ball" in Ferghana. Xiang Da and Luo Xianglin reasoned that the court must be a polo field. Secondly, they concluded that after polo spread into China, since the pronunciation of "polo" did not exist in the Chinese language, "polo" was called "gui" in Persian instead. In the Tang Dynasty, it was called "da gui" (play ball), so they deduced that the Chinese word "毬," pronounced the same as "Polo" in Persia, proved that Chinese polo spread from Persia. Lastly, the professors pointed out that "'Qiu' is not recorded in ancient Chinese documents. So the Chinese polo family of games was influenced by the Western Regions during the Sui-Tang Dynasty."[1]

Hao Gengsheng also held the view that polo originated in Persia, as stated in his book *An Introduction to Chinese Sports*. He stated that 900 years ago, a Persian writer documented that in about AD 600, the last emperor, named Khosrau Paiwis, during the Sassanian Dynasty, married a Christian woman, Silain, who organized a group of noble women to play a polo game with a "Xia" team.[2] Hao Gengsheng concluded that polo spread from Persia to Turkestan, then to Tibet, and subsequently to Central China, where it became popular.

The view that Chinese polo originated from Tubo is mainly represented by professor Yin Falu, whose ideas were drawn support from other scholars later on. From studying phonetics, professor Yin raised doubts about Professors Xiang and Luo's view about "gui." He further proved that the Persian word "gui" is a phonetic translation of the Chinese word "毬 (Qiu)," and proved "波罗 (Po Luo)" through the English word "polo," which means playing a polo game. Most importantly, it is also pronounced the same as the Tibetan words "Polon" or "pulu." Accordingly, he inferred that polo originated in Tubo, and then spread into the Central Plains in the early Tang Dynasty.[3]

The theory that polo originated in the Central Plains is mainly based on the document *Essay on the Famous Capital*, written by Caozhi in the Han-Wei Dynasty. For the lack of evidence, as well as disagreements among the scholars on the meaning of *Jiju*, we still encourage more solid data to support and supplement, even though it was widely agreed upon by academia.

6.1.2 A New View on the Origin of Polo: Pluralistic Pattern

It is evident that there are many different views of the origin of polo. Some are more probable than others, with polo sports existing in some definite regions, but there is not enough evidence to overturn the other theories. Besides, most authors have insisted on their particular views, which makes it very difficult to determine the truth. According to much research, we have discovered that there are a variety of possibilities about the origin of polo. Perhaps polo did not originate in one place, but instead may be started in the Central Plains, Turk, Tubo, or Persia. It is possible the Tubo or Persia polo did not come from the Central Plains, and the Chinese polo did not come from Tubo or Persia. The forms of poll throughout these regions vary from place to place, yet during the Tang Dynasty, polo of various kinds gradually evolved into convergence through communication and integration.

Persia as the source of ancient polo
Some scholars insisted that polo originated in the Central Plains. This view ignored the possibility that polo perhaps originated in Persia. The article "Polo" included in *Diaz Lessons of Kashmir*, written by Muhammad Akram Khan in 1992, quoted the views of *Hunterland of Asia*, which documented the excitement of Alexander the Great receiving a polo ball. It implied the game of polo was an old sport in Persia. It was alleged that Emperor Akbar liked playing polo in the Mughal Dynasty. When the sky went dark, he would call for lights to be lit, so he could continue to play polo. According to the evidence from Wazir Ghulam Mehdi, polo was played in Iran early in 600 BC, which reached peak popularity during the Mughal Dynasty.[4] Thus polo existed in Persia well before the Common Era (Before Christ), and it became popular as history progressed. Of course, this view still needs more research to test its validity. Chinese records about Persian Polo are mainly in Du Huan's book *Jing Xing Ji*.[5] Du Huan said in his book, "Ferghana was a thousand miles south of Talas, separated by mountains to the east, and more than 2,000 miles to Shule, and over 1,000 miles to the west to Chaj. There were dozens of cities and tens of thousands of soldiers. In the tenth year of the Tianbao era of the Tang Dynasty, Princess He Yi got married here. There was a polo forest, and beneath it was a court for playing ball."[6] The author goes on to describe Persian Polo,

culture, and customs, "The name of the king of the Tazi, "Akula," and the capital was here. The women of the kingdom were tall, elegant, and well-dressed. When they went out, they would cover their faces. The women, irrespective of their rank, worshiped heaven five times a day, ate meat and made fasts, and killed people as a merit. They (Persians) wear silver belts and silver swords and forbid all forms of alcohol and music ... They were driven by camels, which were small in shape, but capable of walking a thousand *li* in one single day with only one hump in the back. And the horse was claimed to be the creature bred by a dragon and horse, who had a small belly but long legs. A fine foal was able to run a thousand *li* in a single day. ... Milu State was located more than 700 *li* from Yamei State, which enjoyed ball festivals and swinging festivals ... Tazi built its town here and then prospered through more exchanges with other regions."[7] From this quotation, we can infer a few intriguing points.

First, there were drums and music while they were playing polo in the Tang and Song Dynasties. Meanwhile, in Persia, people were not permitted to drink alcohol or listen to music. It shows there were major differences between the Persian and Chinese versions of the game. Secondly, there was a ball playing festival, which means the ball sports lasted a long period of time, becoming an integral part of the culture. Du Huan did not indicate the origin of polo in *Jing Xing Ji*, but referred to this sport in terms of the polo culture in the Tang Dynasty. This shows that Chinese polo was a native sport, rather than imported to China. Moreover, Persians, from ancient times, were nomadic horse riders, possessing strong economic and military power. They dominated Central Asia and had essential advantages in playing polo. It is possible that polo originated in Persia, yet there is no conclusion.

Northern Pakistan as the source of ancient polo

Northern Pakistan includes Baltistan (the second Tibet), Gilgit, Hunza, and Chitral,[8] which is surrounded by the Karakoram Mountains, the Himalayas, and the Hindu Kush Mountains. There, the mountain peaks and the harsh climate made it almost inaccessible. In early times, people lived a nomadic life, struggling through the hardships of the barren wasteland. They also had a good command of horsemanship, which built a good base for the game of polo.

According to the No.171 cliff carving in Ahmad Hasan Dani's book *Chilas: The City of Nanga Parvat*, on the top central portion of the engraving, three men were seen riding horses with long rods in their hands. Between the two huge men, there was something resembling a ball. Professor Dani states that this cliff painting is a prehistoric picture found near Djias, complete with horses, a ball, mallets, and mounted horsemen who seem to be hitting the ball.[9] Mohammed Hassan Hassrat wrote a book entitled *The Civilization and Culture in Baltistan* in 1995. It states that most researchers share the view that polo is a Balti word that originally means ball. "... Among young people, both Tiakoo Polo and Bentho Polo are popular. ... Children play a similar game to football called Kang Polo if it is made of cloth, or Ko Polo if it is made of leather." In the paper *Northern Festivals and Culture*, Muhammad Akram Khan also indicated Polo is a Balti word. The Balti language has the word "Polo," which means "ball," the round part of the willow or tree tumor. Perhaps the word "Polo" originated from this source. Remarkably the game of polo in northern regions (Pakistan) does not come from the Balti or the British. Polo has different names depending on where in the northern region you sample. In the Giselle Mountains of Gilgit, polo is called "Balah"; in the Astor area, it is known as the "Thop"; in the Gerais Valley and Yaghistan, it is called "Halo." Another essay *Polo* (1992), written by Muhammad Akram Khan, recorded that polo was called "Chogan" in Persian, "Balah" in Krishna, and "Mentho"[10] in Balti.

As the summary above proves, polo is not the chief term in the northern reaches of Pakistan for the horseback-riding ball game; it also means other types of ball games. To differentiate according to regions, materials, or rules of play, people add descriptors to the name to restrict or modify the game. Certainly, it has no relation to the "Polo-forest" speculated above, but instead clearly a local culture.

Turks as the source of ancient polo

The Turks of northern China were a powerful nomadic tribe living in the north and west of the desert and Central Asia. *Divan lgat at-Turk* recorded, "Turks shot the ball with a large branch fork (Chazi stick). It was a game unique to the Turks. If someone wants to begin a match, he will hit the ball with Chazi. The person who hits the ball most fiercely will be chosen for the opening kickoff."[11] It is clear that the game of Turkish polo is very unique and different from the ball games in the Chinese Central Plains.

In Muhammad Akram Khan's paper "Polo," he recorded that Iranians and Turks loved to play polo when they were not at war.[12] In Muhammad Ashraf's book *Indian Society in the Middle Ages*, he noted that "Turks were more invested in this sport (polo)." One of the symbols in the royal office was a polo mallet and a golden ball. Although the regime fell to the Afghans later, support for the game of polo did not falter.[13] This record shows how important the game of polo was among the Turks. To a certain extent, it was the specialty of the Turkic civilization, a highlight and pride of the local culture. According to these resources, we cannot deny the existence of polo or the origin of polo in Turkish because of their cultural traditions and living environment.

Clues to the origin of polo in Chinese Central Plains

Based on the available documents, polo may have existed in the Central Plains in the Han Dynasty. In the *Miscellanies of the Western Capital*, it was recorded that Han Emperor Liu Ao liked playing ball, but his ministers thought that playing ball might hurt his health, thus not suitable for the emperor. The emperor replied, "I do like it very much. We could choose the one that is similar but not laborious to play." Someone then made Tan Qi and presented it to the emperor for play. The emperor was so delighted that he awarded the man lamb, purple silk shoes, and costumes for the pilgrimage.[14] The Song Dynasty scientist Shen Kuo made an explanation and identification of this historical material. He wrote in the *Miscellanies of the Western Capital* that "Han Emperor Liu Ao had a crush on *Cuju*, and sought for a similar but labor-saving substitute, and got the 'tan qi,' which is a game hitting a relatively small ball. The game 'tan qi' is in no way similar to *Cuju*, but it is quite similar to *Jiju*, which is suspected to be a biographical error."[15] Shen Kuo clearly suggested that playing tan qi was "quite similar to playing *Jiju*," arguing that Liu Ao's hobby was playing polo rather than kicking a ball. Huang Chaomei of the Song Dynasty also stated on this issue: "Today, people also take *Cuju* as *Jiju*; this is the reason *Cuju* and *Jiju* integrate as one. Shen Cunzhong is to hit the *ju* indicating to hit the wooden ball, which is said to be different from *Cuju*. Thus, to view it as the error of the biography is totally incorrect."[16]

In the Han Dynasty, polo-like activities were recorded in some literature. For instance, *Cuju* as the subject was collected in the *Book of the Former Han Dynasty: Annals of Arts and Culture*. Although this monograph was lost, there are still some to be seen by the later generations in some works. *Shi Ji Suo Yin*, written by Si Mazhen in the Tang Dynasty, and *Historical Records of Justice*, written by Zhang Shoujie, are cases in point.[17] Later Han, Li You wrote in *An Inscription about Ju City* that "Round ball and square wall, Just like yin and yang of the Eight Diagrams picture. The rules of the game are just like the moon in the sky. Running its track relatively as two and six fairly …" In the article, the poet described the so-called "Ju city" as the polo field. "City" means the high walls around the field, just like the border around the city. Similarly, there are also "square walls" in the "round ball and square wall." In ancient China, ball games such as *Taju* in the Warring States Period, Balloon in Tang, Building ball in Song, and *Cuju* in Ming were all played without walls. Only polo played on horses was circled by a low wall in a three-sided course. Han Yu's poem in the Tang Dynasty has ever shared a similar description that in the play field, a thousand steps were level, with short walls encircling around on three sides.[18] It further corroborated that the polo field was quite large and flat, surrounded by short walls in three directions. *An Inscription about Ju City*, noted by Lee You (about AD 55–135) in the middle period of Later Han, pointed out the detailed rules of the polo game, which proves that polo had long taken its existence.

We can also explore the Han Polo game from later literature. Cai Fu was a Tang Dynasty poet who wrote a poem entitled *Playing Polo*. It recorded a scene in which rich people, like Liang Ji and Dou Rong, played polo in the Deyang Palace during the Han Dynasty. His descriptions included the riding venue, the horseback riding attire, the polo rod, and so on.[19] Interestingly, the author of the poem referenced another resource *Xu (Preface)*, which discusses how the emperor would use polo as a way to train his troops. Since Liang Ji and Dou Rong were from military families, using polo in this way is fairly natural.

Polo artifacts of the Han Dynasty unearthed in Dunhuang provide persuasive evidence that the game of polo in China may date back to the Han Dynasty. In 1979, archaeologists discovered a Mid-Han spherical object in the war tunnel ruins in Dunhuang City in the northwest Gansu Province. The ball had a diameter of 5.5 cm, was filled with silk floss, and was tied by a twisted rope with sclerotium and linen cloth lanyards. At present, although there are different views on this kind of spherical object, many polo researchers believe that it should be reasonable to regard it as a polo ball.[20] In ancient Chinese polo activities, polo ball was a kind of "soft ball (ruan qiu)" wrapped in leather outside and padded with hair inside. In addition, the word qiu (毬) in "da qiu (打毬), another name for polo that appeared as late as the 5th century AD, is constructed "with the left side deriving from the word 'mao wan (毛丸),' namely 'mao (毛).' And the right side for nub is based on the techniques for hitting and chasing with a ball and a staff, that is 'qiu (求).'"[21] This is also the evidence that the "mao wan" ball was used in early polo.

The balls found in Dunhuang archaeology are basically consistent with the above documents, and also consistent with the description of polo ball "as small as a fist" recorded in some ancient Chinese books. Combined with the custom of polo in ancient military activities in northwest

China, we can reasonably infer that the balls found in Dunhuang archaeology are polo themselves. Certainly, this archaeological discovery has helped us trace the origin of polo back to the Eastern Han Dynasty, which is also congruous with other well-known literature, such as the *Miscellanies of the Western Capital, Cuju, An Inscription about Ju City, Playing Polo, Song of Cuju*, and others. In a word, Chinese polo already existed during the period of Eastern Han.

During the Qin Dynasty, a turbulent time full of war emerged, and the vassal states scrambled to form cavalries. In order to enrich the country and strengthen the army, King Wuling of Zhao personally advocated "Hu clothing," practiced riding and shooting, and established the cavalry as the main weapon at that time. By the Han Dynasty, after hundreds of years of horse riding training, there were powerful cavalry troops in the Central Plains. The cavalrymen rode well-trained steeds and waved iron halberds to fight. But despite this, kickball was still very popular. Thus, professor Tang Hao believed that football was a kind of military sport in the Han Dynasty. When football competitions ended, the guards or soldiers who left the pitch last would ride on horseback and fiddle the ball with the weapons they had on hand before putting the ball away. This very act could be the start of "Riding Ball Play (polo)" in China. Gradually from then on, polo became more formal.[22] The polo rod decorated with the crescent-shaped design shares some similarities with the spears, as well as the legs and feet when they extend in an angled way. It is not for sure they are definitely linked with each other, but at least it helps us understand the evolution from football or kickball into polo.

In the Western Jin Dynasty, Lu Ji's *Song of Cuju · Preface* records the case of *Cuju*: "There are Hanzhang Ju Room and Lingzhi Ju Room at the gate of the Anhan Palace. There are Ju rooms in the street and filled in the city." Another poem by King Dong'e (Cao Zhi), "Lian Qi Ji Rang (riding to play *Cuju*), does it mean playing polo ball?"[23] Tang Hao, Weng Shixun, and Li Guohua have discussed polo. Tang and Weng thought it was playing polo, but Li denied it. In *Essay on the Famous Capital* of Cao Zhi, we can find the description "Lian Pian Ji Ju Rang."[24] Regarding these two documents, there is much debate in academic circles on whether the text should be "Lian Qi Ji Rang" or "Lian Qi Ji Ju Rang." Some people think that if it is "Lian Qi Ji Rang," this document records not polo, but an ancient sport called "Ji Rang." But those who hold this point of view cannot explain the "Lian Qi Ji Rang" as a whole. By contrast, those who claim that this sentence should be regarded as "Lian Qi Ji Ju Rang," although they can link "Lian Qi" and "Ji Ju" to explain playing polo, fail to explain the following word "Rang."

"Lian Qi" generally refers to a group of horses. For example, it is recorded in the *Continuation Notes on Baopuzi* that "when a man of great talent lived in the world, he did great things with outstanding talents when he was an official, and when he retired, he followed the example of Lord Tao and Lord Bai to set up a family business; being an official, he must make the country strong, and after retirement, he must earn more fortune. Therefore, in the old days, people must choose fertile land in order to gain profits, and they would cultivate and harvest diligently. The beans sown in the wilderness grew lushly, the dense and beautiful vegetables grew thrivingly, the harvested barley filled thousands of granaries, and the warehouses were full of grain. When he went out, he took many horsemen with him to go hunting, and when he came home, he wore the dress of a prince and enjoyed fine food."[25] According to *A Collection of Jin Literature*, the gentry of Shu

County, Guanghan and Jianwei often visited each other, kept personal friends in the city, formed cronies, talked a lot when they were together, and rode in and out of the city with a hundred riders.[26] *Biography of Zhang Zai* in *A Collection of Jin Literature* also described the grand occasion of "Lian Qi."[27] In the Jin Dynasty, it was recorded in *The Feeling of Marriage* by Zhang Hua that: "The marriage is to find an auspicious time when even the most outstanding talent will be present. The couples were handsome, beautiful and generous, beautiful in appearance and rich in family; the wedding stretched a street, horse after horse, and the whole city was in bustle and hustle."[28] Therefore, if the phrase is "Lian Qi," it means that many riders are engaged in a certain activity together, so that the following phrase, either "Ji Ju" or "Ji Rang," can be explained and understood as a polo match.

In fact, it is a consensus among scholars that the terms "Ji Ju" and "playing polo" both refer to the ancient sports of polo playing. Some of the information in the *Song of Cuju · Preface*, such as the "Hanzhang Ju Room and Lingzhi Ju Room" and the "Ju City," as well as the author's intended theme of *Song of Cuju* are about this, primarily a reflection of the Ji Ju event. The author followed up his previous section with Cao Zhi's poem, in which the question was asked, "Lian Qi Ji Rang, does it mean playing polo ball?" This is a clear indication that what is talked about here is more like "Cuju" rather than "Ji Rang." In the absence of sufficient material to fully grasp the original sentence of the *Essay on the Famous Capital*, I believe that it is still plausible to infer that the *Essay on the Famous Capital* is about playing polo by focusing on the keyword "Cuju." In addition, the phrase in the *Essay on the Famous Capital* reads: "The cock fights in the eastern suburbs, the horse walks among the long rowan. In front of me passed the two hares. With arrows and bows in hand, I take the long drive up to the southern mountains." What's more, we can also find clues in some archaeological images from the Tang and Liao Dynasties (see Fig. 6-1 and Fig. 6-2). These pictures show that even during the Tang and Liao Dynasties when polo was very popular, the game did not necessarily have to be played on a special field, but on flat ground in the mountains.

Fig. 6-1 Pictures of Polo Playing in Prince Zhang Huai's Tomb in the Tang Dynasty

Fig. 6-2 Polo Playing in the Liao Dynasty[29]

In 1976, archaeologists unearthed a picture of horse riders (see Fig. 6-3) from the tomb of Xu Minxing, who lived through the fourth year of the reign of Kaihuang of Sui (AD 584) in the Yang Village of Jia Xiang County in Shandong Province. The picture was painted on the west wall of the tomb. There are two men standing on each side of a saddled horse. One man is standing in front of the horse, holding the bridle in his hand, and the other is standing behind the horse with a polo rod. This picture demonstrates a vivid scene of a game of polo. The archaeological findings suggest that polo emerged before the Tang Dynasty on the one hand, but also had a great impact on people's lives. The tomb paintings found on this archaeological dig set a precedent in Chinese polo history. It directly proved that polo game was not brought from Tubo or Persia in the early Tang Dynasty era, but rather existed in China far earlier than the Tang Dynasty.

Fig. 6-3 Mural of Horse Riders Preparing for Polo

Based on the above arguments, it can be determined that China polo originated during the Eastern Han Dynasty. However, after reading through a large amount of literature, one could hardly discover the information about polo during the period of the Wei and Jin Dynasties, which is fully consistent with the historical development of the time. In fact, polo was not the only sport that saw a steep decline in written records when compared to the Han or Tang Dynasties; thus, fewer sports were mentioned during the Wei and Jin Dynasties in general. Wei, Jin, and Southern and Northern Dynasties were periods in Chinese history when the nation came together as a whole amidst the frequent flames of war and ethnic strife. At this stage, the nation's government was unstable both from inside and outside, and the person in power was frequently changed from one to another. During wartime, people could hardly afford food and clothes; how could they pay for expensive polo activities and gear? Besides the cost, horses were constantly needed in battle, so they quickly became precious commodities. Who could spare a horse for a game of polo? Additionally, polo required high-level horse training and extensive venues, not to mention the upkeep cost for the fields, horses, and equipment. Of course, the noblemen mentioned above, Dou Rong, Liang Ji, and Cao Zhi, had the resources and status to enjoy luxury sports, such as polo, and supported a lavish lifestyle. Yet with the establishment of the Tang Dynasty, the economy returned to a state of normalcy, and the Tang renewed diplomatic relations with the surrounding states. Thus once again, polo became a prominent part of daily life.

Chinese Central Plains polo not introduced from Persia or Tubo[30]
The origin of Chinese Central Plains polo is first of all related to the development of riding skills. Secondly, it is connected to the rise of kickball in the Warring States Period. Lastly, a local sports culture based upon the socio-economic and cultural prosperity in the Han Dynasty contributed to the local progress of polo. In past studies, polo was said to originate from Persia or Tubo mainly because of the records from Du Huan's book *Jing Xing Ji* and Feng Yan's book *Feng Shi First-Hand Accounts*. Here more discussion is about the latter work:[31]

Research on the origin of polo in the past has been closely related to the work *Feng Shi First-Hand Accounts · Playing Polo* in the Tang Dynasty, which is regarded as the initial study of China polo. Because of the lack of convincing information, most scholars believe that the above work was the earliest known record of polo. In the book, "Xifan" and "Tubo" were named, which initiated the researchers to explore the origin of polo. Among past studies, it has been quoted that "Emperor Taizong often inspected Anfu gate ... the majesty burned the ball apparatus as a form of self-admonition," which indicates that polo rose in the Central Plains during the early Tang Dynasty. This passage is also quoted as evidence that the game of polo passed through "Xifan" to the Central Plains. Additionally, some researchers cite the following, "During the Jingyun Period, a Tubo emissary was sent to welcome Princess Jin Cheng ... Emperor Xuanzong played the game of polo, like the wind and lighting. Being an uncontested winner from the east to west, the emperor was invincible in the field. Even the Tubo can hardly beat him." According to the literature mentioned above, most researchers inferred that the "Xifan" is Tubo, where people had a good command of polo. Mr. Wang Yao has ever argued that Tubo people were noted for their skills in polo games, which was highlighted in both Tang and Xifan as a sport activity. Both the government and the public are competing for it.[32] The author believes that it is necessary to study the origin of polo by studying *Feng Shi First-Hand Accounts · Playing Polo* again.

As for the records in this book, the author here will discuss two main issues. First, in reference to "Xifan," here referring to the Tubo people, the people in Northwest China or Persian, is still being debated in the academic community. The scholars who advocate for Perisa as the origin of polo generally insist on "Xifan" standing for the Western Regions or Persia, not Tubo specifically, as recorded in Luo Xianglin's paper. Those who advocate that "Xifan" here refers to Tubo specifically, were mainly based on the records of ball competitions between the Central Plains and Tubo.

In fact, "Fan" is a generic name given to national minorities outside the Central Plains or newcomers. In *Ce Fu Yuan Gui, Old Book of the Tang Dynasty, New Book of the Tang Dynasty*, and other history books, we found that Tang Dynasty usually used "Fan" to refer to the Northern or Western nations, such as Tanguts, Tuyuhun, Turks, and Khitan.[33] However, whenever Tubo is involved, it is called "Tubo" instead of "Fan," replacing "Tubo." Since the two terms "Xifan" and "Tubo" appear in the same article, it definitely means that the two terms refer to two different people.[34] Therefore, we can conclude the person from "Xifan" does not refer to the Tubo (Tibetan) people but to the Northern or Western people in the Tang Dynasty. Thus, following this logic, polo was not passed to the Central Plains by way of Tibet.

The second piece of evidence is the polo match between the Central Plains and Tubo. In the third year of King JingLong's reign (AD 709) in November, Tubo sent envoy Shangzanduo and others to the Central Plains to marry Princess Jincheng. Emperor Zhongzong in the Tang Dynasty feasted the group in the court of the palace. A polo match was requested by the envoys of Tubo in politeness. Thus, the emperor was satisfied with the request and ordered the consort Yang Shen to assemble a team against Tubo, while he along with other officials presided over the game.[35] This historical event was recorded in the *New Book of the Tang Dynasty* and *Feng Shi First-Hand Accounts*.

Initially, the Tang emperor only wanted the polo game played as a performance, but the Tubo envoys' request changed the show into a competitive match. Clearly, by the Tang Dynasty, polo was quite popular, while people of Tubo were also good at playing polo. Tubo ended up beating the Central Plains in the preliminary round, showing its superb skills in high-level polo. However, regardless of how outstanding Tubo's polo technique was at that time, it could not be compared to the Tang Dynasty. From the literature, we can see that the only way Tubo was able to win the first round was mainly because Emperor Zhongzong ordered the polo players to "test" their technique, which shows the great wisdom of the emperor to some extent. The following match illustrated the true level of the Tang's polo, in which the Tang team of four defeated Tubo of 10. Why was the emperor so confident? As the common phrase goes, "Know your enemy and know yourself, and in 100 battles, you will never be in peril." After Emperor Zhongzong "tested" the strength of Tubo polo, he had a good command of mutual strength and determined to have only four against Tubo ten, which showed that he saw Tubo was far behind Han in the polo game.

Throughout the whole *Feng Shi First-Hand Accounts*, the author believes that Mr. Feng described an overview of the history of polo from the reign of Emperor Taizong to Daizong in the Tang Dynasty in conciseness. He also reckoned the possible evolution of polo. Therefore, we are not able to conclude that polo was introduced into Central Plains through Tubo. Instead, we can come to the conclusion that polo is a type of local sports culture in Central Plains based on our discussion.

To demonstrate the view on polo's origin from Persia, Luo Xianglin also cited information from *A Collection of New and Old Book of the Tang Dynasty · Xirong II*: "The emperor of Anguo State presented to the emperor two Persian horses and one embroidered *qu qiu* (woolen ball), tulip and refined sugar; later presented one big textile *qu qiu* and one embroidered *qu qiu*, hoping to be awarded robes, armors, and weapons ..."[36] This also corresponds to the records in the *New Book of the Tang Dynasty*.[37] Mr. Luo commented that "despite no historical records on its way of use, the balls presented by Anguo State were offered along with famous horses, which undoubtedly were similar to polo balls. Although Emperor Taizong of Tang Dynasty had ordered people to learn playing polo (da qiu), such a game did not gain much popularity at that time because the ball used must still come from the Western Regions. Thus, until the Kaiyuan Period under the reign of Emperor Xuanzong of Tang Dynasty, *qu qiu* (woolen ball) was still present in the tributes from Anguo State." In fact, it was quite common for the states in the Western Regions to present fine horses to the emperor, so to infer the origin of polo from the mere concurrent description of ball and horse was obviously unreasonable. Besides, was the *qu qiu* the same as polo game ball? In many ancient classic books, the character *qu* was used most commonly along with the character *shu*. *General Introduction about Customs* recorded, "knitting woolen blanket is called *qu shu*." Therefore, the "big *qu qiu*" and "embroidered *qu qiu*" in *A Collection of New and Old Book of the Tang Dynasty* vary greatly from the polo depicted in other literature as well as on the relics and murals. *Qu qiu* appeared to be a handiwork of the herdsmen rather than polo.

As for the above-mentioned viewpoint of Hao Gengsheng, we have searched the Chinese classics *Old Book of the Tang Dynasty · Xirong* and *New Book of the Tang Dynasty · Western Regions* and found that one name sounding like Khosrau Paiwis was Peroz,[38] who lived between the 7th and 8th century rather than the 6th century. Supposing that polo was introduced from Persia and thrived in the early Tang, the time, however, does not correspond to the event. It is recorded that from AD 651–798, Tazi had sent emissaries to China more than 36 times.[39] A large number of Persians have settled in Central Plains. For example, since the period of Tianbao, "Hu people have stayed in peace for a long time or more than 40 years ... they are reluctant to go back, ... with fields and houses ... as many as four thousand."[40] Although not all of the Hu people here are Persians, we can imagine that there are many of them. There was a sum of Tazi people and Persians living in Yangzhou up to the first year of Shangyuan Period under the reign of Suzong of Tang Dynasty (AD 760).[41] The Persians, having lived in Chang'an for a long time, found their way to the core of the government, serving as important secretariat positions or even prime minister wielding military and political power. From this point, the imperial members that were sent as hostages to Tang Dynasty to show their loyalty, or came over and pledged allegiance to Tang Dynasty, would without doubt carry a large entourage who were prominent and representative of Persian culture. However, isn't it strange that there were no records mentioning that Persians had played polo games in China or Chang'an? Besides, Mr. Luo confused facts by using "gui" to prove the origin of polo from Persia. It is known that "gui" shares the pronunciation of Chinese character "Ju" which existed prior to the Warring States. If the Persians had called polo "gui," this might have been due to the influence of Han culture. Moreover, the British scholar Kimberley discussed in his work published in 1936, the polo match in Persia was called "Chaugan,"[42] having a similar pronunciation to Chinese ancient "ju gan," namely ball rod. All of these demonstrated that the polo game in China had exerted great influence all over the world.

Another aspect of interest is the diaphone problem of *po luo* or *bo luo* (in Chinese pinyin), mentioned both in the "view on polo's origin from Persia" and "view on polo's origin from Tubo." It is also based on such diaphone that many scholars inferred polo originated from Persia or Tubo. Nevertheless, Zhang Guangda believed from the perspective of phonetic and material object studies that the angular cups among the silver and gold objects introduced from the Western Regions were diaphones of pʻuala, pʻuala, and pĭeuăk, closer to Sogdian language.[43] Combined with the above explanations about the characters *po luo*, such as "*po luo* means measuring in Tang," and "gold Boluo suggests tiger skin," it appears that *po luo* does not necessarily denote polo game of the Tang Dynasty.

There are no known links between the polo of Central Plains and Polo pronunciation. The author trawled through myriad literature from the Pre-Qin period to the Sui and Tang Dynasties, and summarized records related to the word *bo luo*. Statistically, this word was found present back to the Pre-Qin period, mainly used as a religious term, place name, or country name. Along with the elapse of time, it started to be used as the name of people, trees, and objects in the Sui and Tang Dynasties. Nevertheless, no Chinese literature has covered the relationship between *bo luo* and polo.

Besides, as described earlier, Mr. Yin Falu held that the word *bo luo* stemmed from the English word "polo," which was pronounced the same as the Tibetan words "polon" or "pulu." To this end, he inferred the polo game originated from Tubo and was brought to the Central Plains in the early Tang Dynasty and then flourished. Mr. Wang Rao also wrote a paper on the origin of polo and espoused the "view on polo's origin from Tubo." He held that polo could be traced back to Tubo and was gradually spread westward to Central Asia and Europe. To bolster his argument, he drew on the word "po-lon" from *Mahavyutpatti*, the collection of Tibetan terms completed in the 8th to 9th century, and quoted materials from the *New Book of the Tang Dynasty · Tubo*, stating that "in the third year of Xianqing Period under the reign of Emperor Gaozong of Tang, (Zanpu of Tubo) presented gold *Ang*, and gold *poluo* to request the emperor for granting an imperial marriage." Wang explained that here gold *poluo* meant gold ball, which could only be the transliteration of the Tibetan "polo."[44] Such argumentation based on phonetics appeared reasonable but could not stand further speculation. For example, if the Tibetan words "polon" or "pulu" had referred to current polo and the Western countries also had borrowed its transliteration, such appellation must have been quite mature at that time; if the polo game was introduced from Tubo to the Central Plains, why its transliterations "boluo" or "pulu" were not used directly to call the current polo game in the Central Plains, or why was "play qiu" or "hit qiu" in literature not called "play boluo (pulu)" or "hit boluo (pulu)? This was obviously the result of cultural differences and efforts to corroborate history merely from phonetics would lead to nowhere. To be noted, either "polon" or "pulu" in Tibetan is actually the umbrella term of all kinds of balls and spherical objects. In Lhasa, the term came from the word *pa luo*, where "pa" indicates circular objects and "pa luo" means circular objects made of leather. Therefore, the inference that polo game spread from Tubo to the Central

Plains seemed far-fetched. Additionally, it is said that Mr. Yin Falu had abandoned such a view.[45] Also, some of the murals from the Sui Dynasty unearthed recently featured playing polo, which further proved the existence of polo game before the Tang Dynasty and negated the view of polo being spread from Tubo to the Central Plains in the early Tang Dynasty.

6.1.3 Exchange and Fusion of Multi-Source Polo

The polo culture in the Central Plains, Turk, Tubo, and Persia had manifested unique characteristics prior to their encounters. According to the records of Du Huan, Persian polo game had no music in company; the polo game in northern Pakistan, as documented in various Urdu books, used balls mainly made from willow trees or burls, of relatively hard texture and round shape; while in the Chinese literature, polo in Central Plains had a close connection to music, and that the balls were soft and sewn with cloth or leather, like the kickball in *Cuju*.[46]

The exposition about the Central Plain polo from Persia by Chinese scholars basically expands along the following line: "There was a polo forest in Ferghana" as described in Du Huan's book *Jing Xing Ji* → "beneath the forest was there a court for playing ball" → Chinese polo → British "polo." As a matter of fact, the word "polo" did not appear when polo sport came into being. It has been a matter of the 19th century that the British used it to refer to polo sport. Therefore, some people pointed out that it is reasonable not to believe polo came into being in Britain just because the British called the game polo.

Of course, we also have reason to believe that the word "polo" came from Tibet in China or other countries or regions in Asia. The period from the 19th century to the first half of the 20th century saw the British Empire's expansion of colonies around the world at its peak, so it was quite easy for them to bring the polo culture back to Britain. When the British were building colonies in Asia and brought polo games to their homeland, polo sports had been on the wane in China in Qing Dynasty but were flourishing in India and Pakistan. In terms of pronunciation and form, the polo culture introduced to Britain from Asia in the 18th century should belong to the multi-source fusion of polo culture amidst the Central Plains, Turk, Tubo, and Persia, contributing to the polo culture in Northern Pakistan.

More information of this kind can be traced from the records in the *Chronicles of Kings* (or *Book of Kings*). Persian poet al-Firdawsi (AD 920–1020) once created such a national epic with 60000 double lines, which includes three parts: myth and legend, warrior story, and historical story. In the chapter "Warrior Story," there were two pieces involved polo play, namely "Sharvosh's Ball Performance" and "Sharvosh Playing Polo."

The first two parts are imaginative creations under a strong national rejuvenation mood, which cannot be used as a historical reference. Therefore, scholars believe that "the historical background described in the *Chronicles of Kings* is not consistent with the real history."[47] The author believes that no matter what the historical authenticity of the epic is, we can draw a conclusion from the original intention of the author's creation, as well as the age and environment he lived in, that it is more likely that there is such a wonderful polo game in the author's real life, rather than the only description of Sharvosh's superb polo skills. Sharvosh, described by al-Firdawsi, was a national hero needed by Persians at this time. Different from the other three tragic heroes, he still showed the heroic spirit and brave spirit of Persians in a land of justice under the rule of others. In al-Firdawsi's era, Persians wished to promote this spirit. Therefore, it is reasonable and understandable for him to express and exaggerate the polo-playing activities that were characterized by courage and power in his era. Accordingly, we can infer that he endowed his historical expectations with things in reality; thus, the description of polo in the poem is absolutely true. In fact, *Divan lgat at-Turk* completed in 1074 by Mahmud Kasgari, a descendent of Turk living in almost the same period as al-Firdawsi, also provided some information about playing polo, which might have some connections to the afore book.

We could get a glimpse of the polo activity during the al-Firdawsi period, for example, match in groups, kickoff by dignitaries, beating drums and changing horses during the match, as well as bountiful awards after the match. Such procedures and requirements bore a resemblance to the polo of Central Plains documented in the literature of the Tang Dynasty.

The exchange and fusion of polo culture of the China Central Plains with those of Turk, Tubo, and Persia mainly occurred during the Tang Dynasty. Different from other forms of music, art, materials, goods, or other acrobatics in terms of exchanges, polo is an elegant and expensive sports activity, barely accessible to artists or merchants. Built upon powerful economic strength, the polo culture should also be buttressed by the relatively stable social environment and developed through exchanges mainly via the court, dignitaries, and militaries. Although Turk, Tubo, and Persia had exchanges with the Central Plains in commodity, culture, and military before the Sui and Tang Dynasties, the chaotic military separation at that time confined the development and exchanges of polo culture. The peace and prosperity of the Tang Dynasty not only created conditions for the polo game to flourish in the Central Plains but also fostered the environment for its exchanges among the Central Plains, Turk, Tubo, and Persia. Particularly, the Northern Silk Road in the Tang Dynasty further drove its exchanges. Combined with the intimate bonds between Tubo and different nationalities on the Pamirs, the invasion of the Western Turk into Northern Pakistan as well as the strategic position of Northern Pakistan as the stronghold along the ancient Northern Silk Road grew Northern Pakistan into a hub for polo exchanges. In light of the dissemination and exchanges of the Chinese polo game, the continuous spreading of polo culture to the Western Regions in the Tang Dynasty, Song, Liao, and Jin Dynasties and Mongolian period greatly contributed to its lasting prosperity there. It was the polo game after cultural exchanges and fusions among the Central Plains, Turk, Tubo, and Persia that was brought to Britain, so the British polo game is closer to the basic sports form of multi-sources.

6.2 Methods and Rules of the Ancient Polo Game

6.2.1 Ancient Polo Techniques

Polo is very much appreciated, with its quick and graceful movement. It has been recorded that "*qiu* (polo ball) is like a star/rod is like a moon/galloping horse goes straight to *Xue* (goal) with the wind," therefore it has been sung and praised by countless literati, "A man borrowed a good horse and ran to and from; the dust flew behind the horse in the field, and the ball was flying with the rod." However, there is a slight difference between the horse on the battlefield and the horse for batting, so more practice is needed as usual. Just as *Han Yu Playing Polo* writes, "You can't idle away to learn to wield spears. Instead, you can try practicing horses in a flat field."[48] Sun Yanqian was a military general on the battlefield, but he was killed while playing polo. Ancient polo games allowed absolute freedom. The collision, on the one hand, leads to fierce confrontations in the whole court, but on the other hand, it causes inevitable danger and injury. The impact of strong horses, the hitting of a rod, and the high-speed shooting of the ball will bring unexpected danger to people. There were polo accidents happening one after another during the Tang Dynasty. For instance, Zhou Bao, the batter, lost his eyes because of playing ball; on the equestrian course of the Pinglu Army, Zen General, Liu Wu, hit Governor Li Shigu upside down; Tian Wei, the son of Tian Chengji as well as Zhu Youlun, the son of Zhu Quanzhong, all died under the horse because of polo play, and so on. Polo is a highly skilled sport activity, which requires participants to have good physical fitness, agile skills, and quick response, but also withstands strong bumps and sudden collisions. Polo is not only very athletic, but also requires comprehensive skills. A good polo player needs to master riding skillfully, such as controlling the horse with one hand, being able to gallop quickly and freely, and using his staff at ease to hit good shots on horseback; at the same time, a good polo player must skillfully hook up the ball and finally made it with the high accuracy even under the other side's siege.

There are many sorts of strokes in polo. When the ball hits the ground, one needs to bend down and fiddle with it, sometimes bending low to the horse's belly; when the ball flies in mid-air, one can also swing arms from side to side to meet it. From Tang poetry, we can spot some wonderful scenes with these techniques. These riding skills may look dazzling, but they can't be accomplished in a single stroke. Perhaps striking the ball should be practiced like what is said in *Miscellaneous Notes of Youyang*, "At the early years of Jianzhong Period, there was a general surnamed Xia in Hebei, who could pull a hundred grams of bows. He used to stack a dozen copper coins on the *Cuju* Court, then galloped on horseback and shot copper coins with a *Cuju* rod, hitting one at a time to make it fly as far as 6 or 7 *zhang*. His skill was so exquisite."[49]

Polo also pays attention to the skills of dribbling, robbery, hooking, and the ability to break through. Zhang Hu's poem[50] and Zhang Jianfeng's poem[51] both recorded this artistic chant of intercepting the ball. The poets accurately capture the various sports skills of polo between the lines and reproduce the movement skills of dribbling.

Polo is a collective sport between people and horses, which requires mutual cooperation and tactics. It does not only need to have a strong sense of sports, but also demands the coordination of men and horses. There are principles for all to attack and defend when playing polo. Plenty of notes were recorded in *The Complete Collection of Tang Poetry* and *The Complete Collection of Tang Literature*, which reflect the ancients were well-trained in playing polo and cooperating with each other in harmony.

6.2.2 Equipment and Venue for the Ancient Polo Sports

Polo horse

Polo requires a person to ride horseback on the field, so participants first need to be proficient in riding, and it is only possible to hit the ball when the riding skills reach a certain level. Those who are skillful in riding are often easy to play their skills on the court and steal the ball. Of course, the horses who take part in the game also have to go through strict selection and training, and a good horse is a basis for winning the game. When the Tang poets described the equestrian match, they all preferred good horses first. Yan Kuan in the *Playing Polo in Huaqing Hot Spring* in *The Complete Collection of Tang Literature* depicted all the fine features characterized by polo horse, and the same was found in the poem of Yang Juyuan. From the above literature, we can fully appreciate the valiant and heroic bearing of horses on the playing field, which also demonstrates that the horse is considered a prerequisite for the batter to play his best.

In the Tang Dynasty, good horses were also chosen from all over the country in order to prepare for the royal ball game. Tang Emperors were fond of playing polo, which became the fashion of the day. They also paid attention to the selection and training of horses, especially Emperor Xuanzong, who even sought out those who knew horse scriptures to give lectures. In the Tang Dynasty, the emperor was particularly interested in the selection and training of good horses. According to *Annotations to Tangyulin*,

> "The majesty was keen on polo, and raised some horses in the inner stable. Yet, the horses kept in the inner stables were not quite suitable. Then, Emperor Xuanzong said to Fan Chuo, 'I have been eager to have good horses for a long time, but who can understand the horse scriptures?' Fan Chuo replied, 'The prime minister is good at horse scriptures.' Xuanzong said, 'I have chatted with the Prime Minister and related that. Apart from political affairs, I have studied all of his secondary studies, but I have not heard he knows the horse scriptures. How do you know this?' Fan Chuo replied, 'I see the Prime Minister's horses on the sandbank every day, and they are all good horses, so I am sure he is well informed.' The emperor laughed."[52]

The above literature shows that the imperial family of the Tang Dynasty had a number of excellent horses through tributes from all over the country, which is also in accordance with Wang Jian's poem: "The imperial horses were brought up, and I'd like to try out myself; the horse can predict easily where the ball is going. I cannot wait to ride without untying red tassels."[53] This is a wonderful depiction of the imperial horse playing polo.

According to the demands of the game, the tail of the horse was wrapped in a special way (see Fig. 6-4), the methods varying from dynasty to dynasty. The tail of the horse can be tied to avoid accidents, such as a horse startling due to a stroke to the ponytail and the sight blocked by the ponytail.

Origin and Evolution of Polo in China

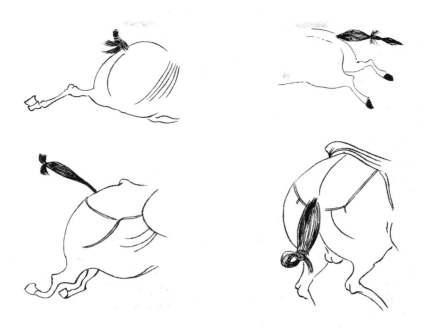

Fig. 6-4 Pictures of Horsetail for Polo[54]

Polo ball

In the Tang Dynasty, ball was also called *ju*, made of whip wood, just as the size of a fist, round and spherical. When Tang poets chanted poetry, they always adopted the word "star" to denote the ball, as was found in the poems of Yu Xuanji, Cai Fu, He Ning, and Lady Flower. In conclusion, the word "star" reflects the pattern of the ball as well as its rapid movement. In order to make the ball easy to recognize, people in the Tang Dynasty colored the ball, which is also known as a colored ball or a painted ball. Some poetic lines of Wang Lingran and Shen Quanqi are both manifestations.

The ball of polo is different from the ball of *Cuju*. *Ju* is a soft, bulky ball used for kicking. On the one hand, the polo ball has to be small in size in order to make it easier for the player to hit with his staff. On the other hand, its appearance has to be painted so that it can be easily identified. Ancient polo balls are made of wood and leather. The leather ball is filled with hair inside the cowhide and sewn into a round ball, and another kind is sewn outside the wooden ball and wrapped in a layer of cowhide. There are also polo balls painted with colors or patterns on the surface, usually labeled as painted balls, red lacquered balls, and white lacquered balls. The white lacquered balls possess the same color as those used in modern polo matches. The Song Dynasty inherited the Tang convention. "The inner attendant sent out a vermilion lacquered cone and threw it in front of the temple"[55] in the *History of the Song Dynasty* and "polo was as small as a fist, easily hit with a light touch"[56] in the *History of the Jin Dynasty* are clear evidence. Above is the convention after the Tang Dynasty. The researchers measured the ancient polo's diameter to be about 8.5 cm, which corresponds to the 8.5 cm diameter set by modern international equestrian rules.

Polo mallet (or Polo club)

The ball club, also known as *Juzhang*, is made of leather, several *chi* long, and slightly curved at the bottom to form a hooked spear. Compared with the description of ball, Tang poetry described the staff as the "moon," with kinds of expressions about the moves of wielding, beating, striking, and hitting.

The club is used to carry and hit the ball, which can be divided into the grip handle, rod body, and bottom. The wider part of the front pole, which is slightly bent, is mainly used for pressing, and the bottom of the pole is usually for hitting. In the literature, it is called "Juzhang," "Yuezhang," "Qiuguai," "Huazhang," and so on. The handle and body of the club are cylindrical and painted with patterns. The bottom is an elbow in the shape of a semi-crescent moon. The club is generally made of rattan, wood, or leather. From the literature, we can view that the shapes of staffs used in the Tang, Song, Liao, Jin, and Ming Dynasties are different (see Fig. 6-5). The ball club of the Tang Dynasty is decorated with patterns, with the top curved like a crescent moon, which is named "moon staff." The angle between the club arc and the straight bar is about 90 degrees, and the length is about one-seventh of the straight rod.

Fig. 6-5 Polo Club in Different Dynasties

The club in the Song Dynasty is longer than that in Tang Dynasty, and the bending arc at the end of the bar is larger, about 140 degrees of the angle with the straight bar. Its length is approximately one-ninth of that of the straight bar. Not only the shapes of the clubs in the Ming Dynasty are different, but also the materials selected differ from each other, which can be roughly divided into three kinds. One is the color painting club, made of tough, high-quality wood, on which all kinds of patterns are drawn with color pigment; the other is the leather club, wrapped on the surface of the rod by cowhide to make it more durable and delicate; one more type is the rattan club, which is made of rattan bars, more resilient and easier to swing. Polo sports held in the modern world, generally select the rattan rod.[57]

The production of the club is more fastidious, laying emphasis on delicacy. From many illustrations in the lines of *Note of Playing Polo* by Tang Caifu or "Worshiping Heaven" in the *History of the Jin Dynasty*, we can see that the ball rod also needs to be exquisitely decorated, representing the shape of the moon. It seems that "*qiu* (polo ball) is like a star, and the rod is like a moon." Murals of Li Xian playing polo in the Tang Dynasty, Cao Yijin's travel map of Cave 100 Mogao Grotto, and Cave 61 of Vimalakirti studying and sharing the sutra all present the ball rod in the shape of the full moon. Accordingly, some poems share the description that "the crescent moon flew to draw the head of the staff," as was seen in Yan Kuan's *Playing Polo in Huaqing Hot Spring*.

As a result of the popularity of hitting the ball, there are craftsmen who specialize in making ball clubs, among which there is emerging a number of skilled craftsmen. With the related records, kicking the ball was getting quite prevalent at that time, especially the high-quality staff become precious. It is recorded in *The Collection of Legendary Stories* by Du Guangting in the Tang Dynasty that Su Xueshu likes drinking and enjoys singing "Dreaming of the South." He was quite good at making polo clubs, innately made and well-decorated outside. Every time he made mistakes, he would exchange his club for money and get paid for the wine.[58]

Polo court

The court, also called Ju field, is a place specially used for playing polo. Having been artificially constructed, the ground usually becomes flat and clean. *Playing Polo in Huaqing Hot Spring* depicts the high level of construction and maintenance of the course at that time. Before the match, people need to clean up the ground so that no speck of dust is found in the air.[59] Sometimes the only way to do that is to pour oil on it. For general areas, it is just all right to clean the ground as smooth as a sharpening stone, not to mention to pour some oil. It is shown that the specifications of the local site and the capital are relatively different. In the Tang Dynasty, the field was particularly managed and regularly strengthened for maintenance. *Tzu-chih t'ung chien (A Comprehensive Mirror for Aid in Government)* includes the following: "Hundreds of people are involved in the overhaul of the polo course. Emperor Xianzong asked his prime minister, Zhao Zongru, 'I was told that you made weeds grow all over the polo court in Jingzhou. What happened?' Zongru replied, 'I am to blame. Even so, the weeds couldn't obstruct the ball play.'"[60] The record shows that the court was maintained in someone's charge. Yet the length and width of the field and other facilities are not clearly defined in the Tang Dynasty. The only thing we roughly know about them is from a poem by Han Yu, "Polo is played every corner of the town. The field is as vast as thousand paces, and as smooth as a carpet. Three sides are surrounded with short walls, drums beating, and flags fluttering." The field that Han Yu writes about is Xuzhou field, which depicts its vastness in terms of thousands of paces, further proof of its scale; besides, there are low walls on three sides of the field to keep out pedestrians and out-of-bounds ball, and one side left must be the entrance. It is recorded in the literature that the walls of the ancient polo ground needed to be built with stone, earth, and brocade, as is cited in the "Records of Later Liang" of *Tzu-chih t'ung chien (A Comprehensive Mirror for Aid in Government)*, "In the first year of Longde, the emperor of Shu (Wang Yan) often came to brocade walls to play polo." The low walls of brocade prevent injury to people, and also make the field look gorgeous. Flags are also erected around the field as a sign, and drummers beat drums and trumpets to boost morale. What's more, most of the fields are equipped with a grandstand for spectators to watch the match. The field where the emperor appeared is named Jiangwu Xie, which sets a throne furnished with elegant facilities. All these can help us verify the specifications and facilitates of the Tang Dynasty field just this much.

There are mainly three types of ancient equestrian courts. The first is the so-called "street playing polo," which takes the main road as the playing field. There were a group of players playing polo in the street of Shengxian Attic under the reign of Emperor Taizong, which belongs to this kind, as was recorded in *Feng Shi First-Hand Accounts*; the second category is the inner field. The Tang Dynasty city implemented the Lifang Unit (township) system, which required that the field must be as smooth as a sharpening stone so that the ball could run freely. There are records in *Research on the Township of Capitals* that both the emperor and the ministers, along with officials of various levels, built their own polo court in extravagance, and examples are Wu Chengxun and Yang Shenjiao. Thereby, it is no surprise that the extravagance of pouring oil on the ground could be seen; and the third one is the jungle field. Emperor Xuanzong of the Tang Dynasty built a field under the jungle at the foot of the Huaqing Pool hot spring. *Playing Polo in Huaqing Hot Spring* also depicts the background of polo play that antiquity trees and overlapping green hills are behind the horses. It seems that the field must be chosen from the natural environment of the jungle.

There are also pavilions at the side of the field for convenience to view, similar to today's grandstand. For instance, it is cited in *Playing Polo in Huaqing Hot Spring* that there are two groups of people at present in polo match: one is the audience and the cheer-leading team; the other is the participants. The emperor came to the pavilion in person for the watch. In *Feng Shi First-Hand Accounts*, there are also records about the pavilion in Liyuan theatre: "During the Jinglong reign of Emperor Zhongzong of the Tang Dynasty, Tubo sent envoys to welcome Princess Jincheng to Tibet. Emperor Zhongzong 'greeted the guests with the ball game' in the pavilion of the Liyuan theatre." Shen Quanqi, Wu Pingyi, and Cui Zhuo all had their poems on them of polo play. It can be seen that there are also pavilions in the Liyuan theatre. Besides, some Dunhuang lyrics have also shown that the royal palace court also has a building similar to the pavilion.

The exact location and number of ancient polo courts in ancient China can be hardly known from the limited literature. Nanliang, Sizhou, Xuzhou, Kaifeng, Yuanzhou, Pencheng, Caizhou, Luzhou, Xingzhou, Fanyang, Chengdu, Guangzhou, Guizhou, Chang'an, Dunhuang, Turpan, and other regions are all equipped with polo courts. Chang'an City in the Tang Dynasty is one of the largest and most concentrated places in the whole country. Many courts were built in the royal palace, such as the courts of Hanguang Palace, Linde Palace, Qingsi Palace, Zhonghe Palace, and Feillong Courtyard, as well as the court in the residence of Left and Right General. In 1956, Xi'an construction workers accidentally excavated a square stone at the site of the Hanguang Temple of Daming Palace in Chang'an City, on which was engraved "Hanguang Palace and polo field were built in the month of Yimo in the year of Xinhai during the reign of Dahe of the Tang Dynasty." In addition to the royal fields, princess, nobility, and the emperor's son-in-law have ordered to construct their own private courts. According to the "Biography of Princess Changning" in the *New Book of the Tang Dynasty*, "Princess Changning ... asked to build a polo court in the west corner of his palace." Also, *Tzu-chih t'ung chien (A Comprehensive Mirror for Aid in Government)* cites as follows: "The emperor is fond of playing polo, and so are other royal family members. For example, Wu Chengxun and Yang Shenjiao poured oil on the ground in order to make it flat and smooth."[61] Generally speaking, the administrative units at the state level of the Tang Dynasty all built the courts for local polo activities, and even the emperor supervised the maintenance of the local courts. Based upon the volume of "Supplement to the History of the Tang Dynasty," we can find the following conversation: Emperor Xianzong asked his prime minister, Zhao Zongru, "I was told that you made weeds grow all over the polo court in Jingzhou. What happened?" Zongru replied, "I am to blame. Even so, the weeds couldn't obstruct the ball play." After the Mid-Tang Dynasty, all generals of vassals had their own military polo field, used as a place for both hitting the ball and training troops. At the same time, there are also scenes of playing polo without the field, just playing anywhere randomly in the Tang Dynasty. The records can be found in *Feng Shi First-Hand Accounts*, "In Luoyang city, youngsters are playing polo everywhere in the street, even blocking the road," even though such free play is rare after all.

There were also strict grades in ancient polo fields, which can be divided into royal, military, and civilian. The royal field is for the exclusive use of emperors, members of the royal family, and ministers, such as the Liyuan Theatre Court in the Tang Dynasty, the Hanguang Palace Court, and so on. In addition to playing ball, the military field is also used to train the army, proclaim orders, appoint and remove, reward, and punish generals and soldiers, which serves as the central venue for military activities. For instance, the garrison of Dunhuang, in ancient times, took advantage of polo as a means of military training to improve the physique of the generals and soldiers. They built a specialized court for the polo play. Dunhuang Literature p. 3239, p. 3451, p. 3773, etc., had related similar records about the polo game in terms of its venue, constructs, and other related facilities, as well as the joyful scene when the polo was played.

Polo goal

The goal of the ancient polo court is composed of a single goal and double goals. According to *History of the Jin Dynasty*, the single goal is set at the south side of the court, in which two teams are required to hit the same goal, and whoever hits the goal will score; while the double goals are set in both sides of the court, in which two teams attack the other goal. In Zhang Ku's poem, it refers to a goal scored with an oblique angle at a long distance. Some goal is a few meters away from the two wooden pillars, the top engraved a dragon or small red flag, the root planted in a lotus-shaped stone base, and the body surrounded by colored silk. In another goal, wooden boards were inserted between the two wooden posts, and a round hole was made at the bottom of the board, labeled as ball room. From the literature records, the height of the goal is more than 3 m, engraved with the golden dragon on the top, sitting at the bottom of a lotus stone.[62] This height happens to be highly consistent with the modern rules of the polo goal. The width of the ancient goal is 5 *pace*, or about 7.5 m. For this, the British rule is 8 yards, while the Chinese is 8 m. Thereby, the height of the modern polo goal is similar to that of the ancient one through the above statistics.

Dunhuang lyrics cite, "*qiu* (polo ball) is like a star/rod is like a moon/galloping horse goes straight to *Xue* (goal) with the wind." Here, "Xue" refers to polo goal or net. When polo is shot, it must go to the hole in the ground, which is a jungle field rule. Tang poems in their prosperous time did not contain either goals or nets till the middle of the Tang Dynasty, goals became popular, with a hole behind the goal. This is what Zhao Song called "crossing the door and entering the Yu," as recorded in *Reminiscences of the Eastern Capital*. Here Yu must refer to "Xue," i.e., goal. Although the size of the "hole" is unknown in the literature, we can conclude its diameter is no more than

1 *chi* long. In addition, we can also spot clues from some Ming Dynasty paintings. Pictured here is Emperor Xuanzong, Zhu Zhanji (see Fig. 6-6), surrounded by ministers, watching the polo match. From the painting, we can't clearly view the manner of the horseback player, the shape of the polo goal, and so on.

Fig. 6-6 Emperor Seeking Pleasure (From the Imperial Palace)

Polo costume

In order to facilitate the sports, the player usually wear uniforms, and two teams are required to wear the garment in different colors to stand out the difference. In the Tang Dynasty, officials in Chengdu paid tribute to the court with uniforms sewn by brocade craftsmen, as was cited in "Chronicles of Emperor Jingzong" in the *Old Book of the Tang Dynasty*, "Governor Du Yuanying of Xichuan paid tribute with colored paintings and 500 polo suits." Here more than 500 sets of polo suits were a great number, which shows obviously that the royal court paid attention to the outfits in huge demand. Besides, the polo painting of Li Xian Tomb was occupied with all kinds of polo costumes, including narrow-sleeved robes of various colors, black boots, and headscarves, all of which are true of current polo outfits. Poems like *Chang'an Lads* by Li Kuo have all proved that there are special clothes for playing.

    The ancients are very particular about their polo garments. The suit is usually made of brocade embroidered with flowers and worn with a belt inlaid with beads and jade. In ancient times, jerseys were called "pleats," "embroideries," and "brocade clothes," divided into long gowns and coats, with round collars and narrow sleeves. The shirts are not only gorgeous in color, but also colorful in patterns, including floral texture, cloud patterns, wild goose grain, etc. Dunhuang remaining documents S. 2049 and p. 2544 "*Flying · Rod Polo*" quote that "Take off the purple robe and put on the brocade suit …,"[63] which means that in ancient times, when playing polo, one must take off the scarlet robe, and put on a round-collar and narrow-sleeved suit with the brocaded flowers. Right here is just the polo suit that the polo player wears. *Reminiscences of the Eastern Capital* shows that players wear red or blue "brocade coats." Wang Fu, a poet of the Ming Dynasty, described the polo costume in the form of a "brocade robe with narrow sleeves" in his poem *Enjoyments in Dragon Boat Festival*.

    Besides clothes, polo outfits also include hats and shoes, i.e., turban and boots, in addition to Hanyao, a kind of waist guard (see Fig. 6-7). The turban is made from silk, brocade, and cloth; the interlining is made from paulownia, gauze, and hemp. When playing polo, the commonly worn turbans are the long turban, rolling turban, and folding turban. With a turban on, one must look vigorous and agile. Plus, the turban has a certain protective effect.

Fig. 6-7 Hanyao (Waist Ornament) in *Tang People Playing Polo* by Li Gonglin[64]

Besides, boots are the shoes of the nomads from the north, which are usually sewn in cowhide, and later spread to the Central Plains. From the numerous archaeological excavations, it can be found that northern officials, nobles, and warriors were all wearing long boots or black leather boots, when they were in the polo game. In ancient times, knee-high leather boots were worn for polo games, known as "black leather boots." They were made from six pieces of cowhide, also known as "six-sewn boots." Black leather boots have an upturned toe and a soft or hard sole. With the boots on, it can protect your legs from injury on one hand; on the other hand, it's convenient to pedal when riding a horse, so as to master the balance. From Tang to Khitan and then to Jurchen, people playing polo were all dressed like this. And so were the people in the Song Dynasty (see Fig. 6-8).

Fig. 6-8 Song People Playing Polo

6.2.3 Rules for Ancient Polo

Polo sports require a certain quality and breadth for the court. The participants usually compete in two teams with equal members in most cases. Yet sometimes, the number is not equivalent, which is reflected in the case when Emperor Taizong sent Princess Jincheng off to the Shanglin Palace when the polo was being held. A goal is set on the field. Each player rides a horse and holds a staff to fight for the ball. Whichever team scores more goals will win, while the less team will lose. The sport of polo in the Tang Dynasty was one of the highest competitive events of that time, which already followed the strict competition rules and complete movement procedures. Polo in the Song, Liao, Jin, Yuan, and Ming Dynasties all originated from the Tang Dynasty, whose rules were much the same as the way they took.

Vol. 253 of *Tzu-chih t'ung chien (A Comprehensive Mirror for Aid in Government)* documents the entire course of a polo match of the highest standard enjoyed by Emperor Xizong at that time, which was noted by Hu Sansheng.[65] His annotations are basically true of the local polo match. Since the emperor has come to watch the polo match in person, the entrance ceremony, as well as the salutation session, must be especially solemn and grand. The polo match watched by the emperor is assumingly the highest level of all. In the match, the generals are divided into two teams, who begin to hit the ball under the order of the head coach. *Playing Polo in Huaqing Hot Spring* describes similarly the starting action of fighting for the ball first and then conflicting. When the emperor went out to watch, there would be a certain amount of rewards for each match, which were usually announced before the match to encourage competition. Wang Jian cites in his poem: "Nobody dares to take the lead, and the emperor is watching at the gate. Some new brocades are available for the winner from afar, lifted out and placed in front of the horse." It just describes the scene of this royal reward.

From the above categorical exposition of the horse, ball, polo club, polo court, polo goal, polo players, and polo costume, we can basically explore the rules and methods of Tang Dynasty Polo, which helps to make an overall panorama of polo sports.

6.3 Spread, Development, and Evolution of Polo in Ancient China

6.3.1 Spread of Polo

Spreading southward in the Tang Dynasty

A person who is anonymous in the Song Dynasty documented in his works, *The Story of the Five Kingdoms,* that one day, a military governor, Yang Xingmi, in the Huainan area during the late Tang Dynasty, *huiju* on the square and watched one of his subordinates, Jin to play under his guidance.[66] The so-called *huiju* is playing polo. Since then, people in the Huainan area of China started to indulge in playing polo, spending money lavishly, which is incomparable to any other region. An article in a book named *The Whole Story of Tongjian Chronicles*[67] told a story where in the second year of Tianyou of Emperor Zhaoxuan, a local official named Situ, who was credulous, advocated a leisurely lifestyle and enjoyed going out for playing and drinking. ... He ever had fun day and night by drinking and lighting about-one-meter-long-layout candles to play polo even when his father just passed away. His extravagance in playing polo could be compared to that of Emperor Jingzong in the Tang Dynasty, which proved that people in Huainan during the late Tang Dynasty were obsessed with polo.

In the south of the Yangtze River, the culture of playing polo in Jinling, the capital of the Southern Tang Dynasty, was the most prosperous. Jiangnan polo was probably introduced from Huainan, then to the entire country of the Southern Tang Dynasty. *Nan Tang Anecdotes* recorded that:

> "An emperor of the Mid-Southern Tang Dynasty, at his early age, promised to one of his attendants, 'I would buy silver boots for you when I became rich and in power.' At the beginning of his reign, he ordered princes and his former staff to 'hit *ju*' so as to entertain during the break from his holding court. When talking about his promise, he underscored the commitment to substituting 15 kg gold for silver boots."[68]

Similar records about Emperor Xuanzong can also be found in this work, "The beginning of the reign of Emperor Xuanzong was in its heyday. He indulged in entertainment and playing ball all day long. He idled away so much that he even forgot to deal with national affairs. Once at a feast, a man came forward to criticize his misconduct. The emperor came to his senses and rewarded him with gold and silk to praise his courage." From this, we can tell that people in the south of the Yangtze River are fond of playing polo. Besides, people in Changsha were also keen on "Hitting the ball (playing polo)." Wangyi, an assistant of the Changsha military general, ever got married to the daughter of the general thanks to his superior skills in playing polo.

Li Zhao's book *Supplement to the History of Tang Dynasty*[69] documented the following conversation: "Emperor Xianzong asked his prime minister, Zhao Zongru, 'I was told that you made weeds grow all over the polo court in Jingzhou. What happened?' Zongru replied, 'I am to blame. Even so, the weeds couldn't obstruct the ball play.' The emperor was wordless on hearing that. At that time, most officials of vassals were fond of playing ball and a polo field was built in Jingzhou. On hearing Zhao's dislike for polo play, people considered it weird and ominous, so they charged the prime minister with his inaction to let 'the weeds grow in the polo court.' The emperor was curious to know the reason why." From all the above, it could be seen that playing polo was widespread and prevailing at that time.

Similar records can also be found in *A Collection of New and Old Books of the Tang Dynasty*, *New History of the Five Dynasties*, *The Complete Collection of Tang Literature*, etc. In addition, playing polo also became popular among women in Chengdu, ranging from the street to the royal palace, which can be verified by *Palace Poems*, a book written by Lady Flower. She described the scene of women playing polo with the following poem, "Near the pool was lying a polo court, asking everyone to play the ball. First, to the gallery of the orchestral scene, with the music going on and on. Fear of taking the lead in the ball, waiting for the emperor to come for play. The wine was served ready by my wife, in one voice greeted the majesty to come. Since teaching the maids how to play, women jump on horseback for fun. The superior tries to figure out who is who and the maids struggle to win all the way."[70] It can be seen that polo in Jiannandao was very popular at this time. What's more, according to the *Records of the Natural Scenery and Folk Traditions of Guilin*[71] by Mo Xiufu, a writer of the Tang Dynasty, there were polo courts in Guilin, which proved officials in Lingnan West Road played polo at that time.

Spreading northward and eastward
Polo was popular in Luoyang, Kaifeng, Xuchang, Linhuai, and other counties in Henan Province. *New History of the Five Dynasties*[72] quoted that one emperor of the Later Tang Dynasty ever founded four polo courts in one open space, which is proof of the popularity and practice of playing polo among people in Luoyang. According to *Yunxi Friend's Topic*[73] (a noted novel written by Fanshu in the late Tang Dynasty mainly recording poetry responsory and funny anecdotes of the poet in the Tang Dynasty), governor Li Shen of Tang Dynasty discovered an existing polo court in Kaifeng when he was in charge of the place, which demonstrates that playing polo was ever prevailing here. In addition, according to *Huangchao Rebellion*,[74] a historical event recorded in the book *The Whole Story of Tongjian Chronicles,* Xuchang (belonging to Xuzhou in the Tang Dynasty) had a polo court which is big enough to accommodate 3,000 soldiers. Such a huge polo field demonstrated it was popular to play polo in Xuchang at that time. The book also included a story that a local governor ever dined with 1,000 men and enjoyed performances in a polo court in Linhui, which confirmed polo must be frequently played in the time of peace. In addition, in the book entitled *Works of Han Changli* (Hang Changli is also known as Hanyu, one of the famous poets in the Tang Dynasty),

> "Han begged again to ban the polo play till the petition was accepted. ... Those who are against polo play were concerned about its harm, not only to our face, but also to the body. You might listen or not cause you might consider, 'If I keep practicing, I may not get injured; if I were skillful and agile, how could I get injured?' Well, my point is we'd better think about it the other way around. Horses are not like human beings but instead creatures who are changeable with no reason and exhausted when they get tired. There are rules for riding those horses, which must be strong and healthy when they are young, yet they will be abandoned and forsaken when they get older. A fine horse can be usable for at most three to four years. Anyway, what matters is how people take advantage of them."[75]

Han advocated that although polo was necessary for troops training, this intense exercise like polo would do harm to the body, so he passionately proposed to the local governor to abandon polo play. From this, it is concluded that the governor in Pengcheng (Xuzhou in Jiangsu Province) was so obsessed with polo.

Polo was also very popular in Hebei Province during Ancient China. *A Collection of New and Old Books of the Tang Dynasty · Biography of Liuwu*[76] documented that Liu Wu, the grandson of Zhengchen, "... made a rush when playing polo and knocked the horse down." Li Shigu, a military and civil governor of Pinglu (now south and east of Hebei Province and Chaoyang of Liaoning

Province), came to rage and intended to kill him. Liu endeavored to contradict Li by trying to excuse him. Surprisingly, Li was amazed at his courage and exonerated him and even ordered him in charge of soldiers later." This proved polo was prevalent in Hebei during the Tang Dynasty. Besides, according to *New Book of the Tang Dynasty · Vassal Town · Biography of Li Baochen*, Li Baochen, a military and civil governor of Jizhou, took control of six vassals such as Heng, Ding, Yi, Zhao, Shen, and Ji and led an army of 50,000. Being powerful, he remained a relative to other generals like Xue Song, Tian Chengsi, Li Zhengyi, and Liang Chongyi by means of marriage. His younger brother Baozheng, son-in-law of Chengsi, once played polo with the son of Chengsi, Wei. Unexpectedly, the horse startled and killed Wei. Chengsi was so furious that he imprisoned Baocheng.[77] Before that, Baocheng assigned his brother, Baozheng, to take charge of polo sports in Weizhou because his brother had been engaged in polo, which was a sign of the prevalence of polo in Jizhou (Hengshui in Heibei now). "Biography of Weibo" in the same book also shared the similar event of Tian Ji'an, the grandson of Tian Chengsi, the military and civil governor of Weibo (now south of Hebei and north of Shandong). "Tian Ji'an abode by his father's career at an early age because he was afraid of Princess Jiacheng due to her strictness. With no other special talent, he simply followed laws. When the princess died, he began to indulge himself in playing polo and drunken debauchery," which showed that polo was also prevailing in Weibo at that time. According to *Tzu-chih t'ung chien (A Comprehensive Mirror for Aid in Government)*,[78] when the prefecture chief of Changshan (Zhending County of Hebei), Wangpo was to surrender to the rebels, all his commanders flew to rage, spurred horses forward to hit the ball and trampled him to death. After An-Shi Rebellion was pacified, Changshan, as a previously military strategic location, was taken charge of by Li Baochen, the place which must flourish necessarily with polo. From all the above, most militarily strategic places in Hebei Province learned the skills of polo. Besides, it is recorded in the *Miscellaneous Notes of Youyang* that "General Xia, a man of extraordinary strength, could shoot the bow weighing hundreds of *Jin*. He ever hit ten piles of copper coins on horseback with polo rod, one pile copper flying up to 6 or 7 *zhang*, which was a magnificent scene."[79] His wonderful skills in hitting copper coins with polo a rod indicated he was technically accomplished in playing polo. The emergence of this new thing is just an innovation. By far, it is hard to deny that polo came into being just in this way.

Polo also spread to Koguryo, Korea, Balhae Kingdom, and Japan. After playing polo was introduced into the three Kingdoms of Korea in the Tang Dynasty, it prevailed in Korea. However, polo had once vanished in the early of the Li's Dynasty. By March 1425, the training institute was set up, which was ordered to restart the polo practice. Also, polo was listed as one item of the martial arts examination. When it came to Emperor Zhengzu, polo was designated as one of the 24 martial arts recorded in *General Records of Martial Arts Atlas*. The three states of Korea attached great importance to the development of polo, mainly based on its function of military training and entertainment. Playing polo was of special significance to the training of cavalry, which played an important role in improving cavalry's physical qualities and combating effectiveness. For example, during the reign of Emperor Ruizong in Korea, when summing up the reasons for the failure in the battle against the Jurchen nationality, Marshal Yin Guan said: "The reason for my defeat is that enemies rode horses while our soldiers marched on foot. As a result, they are invincible."[80] When many officials repeatedly remonstrated with the emperors in Li's Dynasty about their ardent love for playing polo, Emperor Shizong explained, "Polo play is to practice combating. Those who were good at hitting balls would be adept at riding and shooting, so that they could be selected from martial arts contests. A man must be capable of riding, even more than shooting. This is all about martial arts. The prosperity of the former dynasty was also due to the practice of martial arts."[81] As a result, polo play was listed as an indispensable part of military examinations ranging from the preliminary exam and re-exam to the final palace exam. What is more, the serving military officers are required to take a riding and polo exam in front of the emperor when attending a re-exam for promotion held per decade. The private examination system impelled aristocratic children to practice polo and martial arts, and also drove the commoners to practice so as to grasp a promotion later. All the above advanced the development of polo locally. What's more, polo, as a kind of recreational activity loved by ancient Korean emperors and subjects, was developed among Koryo and Koreans. In ancient Korea, most emperors were fond of playing polo, who either participated in person or watched for fun, to the extent of intoxication, as is described in the following quotes, "a Korean teenager was so excellent in playing polo, which amazed the emperor, who appraised his wonderful performance and exclaimed, "Is it with the help of God, or is that magic?" More records are as follows: "Emperor was so good at playing polo that no one can compete."[82] "King Zhonlie asked Huchi and Yingfan to play polo in two teams, and the winner was rewarded silverware."[83] In addition, there are those who have been exonerated for playing polo well. Hitting the ball (playing polo) and other activities have become an integral part of life, and its custom has gradually taken shape. At the initiative of the kings, polo prevailed among the aristocrats. For example, Cui Yi, a Korean minister during the reign of Emperor Gaozong in the Koryo Dynasty, ever seized neighbors' lands to build a polo court, as flat as a chess-board covering hundreds of meters from east to west. Each time they played polo, he would order people to dust with water beforehand.[84] According to *History of Koryo*, "Xinwu ever led his subordinates to play polo in the street."[85] With a preference for polo among emperors and senior officials, building polo courts became a common practice. A polo game would be held at each Dragon Boat Festival when aristocrats would grasp the opportunity to compete on livestock extravagantly. *History of Koryo* recorded, "Emperor Gaozong elected Ziyuan as the crown prince when Zhongxian and Zhongcui empowered soldiers into the Privy Council and ordered the guarding generals to station their troops in the polo court. And then Zhongxian pleaded with the emperor to dismiss a eunuch named Min and other more than 70 people."[86] "King Zhonglie ever dined with 2,000 monks in the center of a polo court."[87] In the period of the reign of Emperor Minzong and Emperor Xianzong, "10,000 monks were granted to dine in the polo field to carry out the Buddhist activities." "30,000 monks were also invited to have meals for three successive days in the polo court."[88] As described above, it is evidently seen that the polo court was so vast at that time in Korea. Of course, the street was also one of their choices of playing ground. Sometimes, they would watch playing polo in the streets. In the accounts of *History of Koryo* and the novel *Yulou Dream*, the dignitaries also trained a wide range of women to play the ball for entertainment. Some women's batting skills have also reached the acme of perfection, from which it is not difficult to see the social atmosphere and progress of polo sports at that time.

In the Tang Dynasty, polo sports became popular all over the country, and quickly spread to the minority areas in the north. As the local regime of the Tang Dynasty, polo was also popular in the Balhae Kingdom, then spread overseas. After the introduction of polo into Balhae Kingdom, it was soon carried out in the upper class in Shangjing (located in Inner Mongolia) and other places. At the Site of Shangjing, the lacquered bone polo ball unearthed at the Site of Shangjing was about 8 cm in diameter, which is similar to the wooden polo ball unearthed in central China.

The book *Classics Collection* in Japan documented that in the 15th year of Emperor Taizong (AD 727) in the Tang Dynasty, Japanese Mikado, Saga Tennō received a polo team from Balhae Kingdom. In addition, in AD 821 (the first year of Changqing during the reign of Muzong), Wang Wenzhu, envoy minister of Balhae Kingdom, visited Japan. The following year (AD 822), Japanese Mikado, Saga Tennō, held a polo match between the two sides before the banquet for the Balhae diplomatic delegation in the Fengle Hall. When watching the match, the emperor wrote a poem entitled *Watching Polo in Early Spring* to describe the players' adept and superb skills. It can be seen that polo was not only introduced to the Balhae Kingdom, but also introduced to Japan and loved by Japanese Mikado. It can also be seen that China's polo culture has exerted a great impact on its neighboring countries. The very poem not only manifested that the skills and rules in Balhae and Japan are basically consistent with those of the Central Plains in the way of fierce competition but also showed that polo has already reached a certain technical level in Balhae Kingdom and Japan.

The Khitan polo probably originated from Balhae Kingdom. After Liao Dynasty destroyed Balhae Kingdom, Balhae people were forbidden to play polo. It is said that a Khitan person ever snatched the good horses in a polo match to return home with them. This shows that Khitan polo was already introduced long before the founding of Liao, and probably came from Balhae Kingdom. In AD 926, after conquering Balhae Kingdom, the Khitan rulers in Liao Dynasty moved the descendants of the Balhae state to Dongjing (now Liaoyang City) and ordered them not to play polo. Xiao Xiaozhong, an officer in charge of civil and military affairs in Dongjing in the Liao Dynasty, immediately recommended Emperor Xingzong Yelü Zongzhen, "Dongjing is the most important town where there were no birds and animals to catch. Without polo, how did we practice martial arts? And as the sovereign for all, emperor possessed all, including all places and things in the country. Thus it is unnecessary to distinguish one from the other, so it is advisable to loosen banning polo for Balhae people."[89] As a result, Emperor Xiaozong accepted Xiao's advice, and thereby, polo became widespread in the Liao Dynasty and even was carried over into Qin and Yuan Dynasties.

In the Liao Dynasty, polo was not only popular among the people, but also was held by emperors and nobles. *History of the Liao Dynasty · The Biographic Sketches of Emperors and Tour Tables* repeatedly recorded Khitan emperors hitting *ju* namely playing polo. For example, in the late lunar March of the third year of the Yingli Period in the reign of Emperor Muzong (AD 983), the emperor hit the ball in Yingzhou (the northwest of Shanxi Province)[90], and then in the lunar September of the sixth year and the lunar January of the 16th year, he also hit the ball. In lunar July of the first year and lunar August of the third year of Tonghe Period of the Emperor Shengzong of Liao, the emperor hit *ju* (the ball) in groups along with dukes. The Song people also had records of the Khitan people playing ball. Kong Pingzhong ever mentioned in *Tan Yuan* that Zhang An'dao had ever stated, "As a newly-summoned envoy to Liao State, I saw the Liao's emperor playing polo in the court, and with his remarkably distinguishing accessories, I identified the man as the emperor. Dare not to speak it out openly, and I only could repeatedly refer to his flawless skill."[91] According to the *Continuation of the Extended Version of Tzu-chih t'ung chien (A Comprehensive Mirror for Aid in Government)*, in lunar August of the second year of Baoyuan Period (the eighth year of Chongxi under the reign of Emperor Xingzong of Liao, or AD 1039), Nie Guanqing, an officer of Song's Ministry of Defense went on a mission to Liao. He saw the emperor enjoy hitting the ball in the palace court, and he was also ordered to compose a poem by the emperor. Due to his excellent poem, he received some favored treatment and entertainment.[92] A majority of Khitan people in the Liao Dynasty were good at playing polo, especially those among the high-ranking officials and aristocrats. For example, Yelü Yali, the second son of Emperor Tianzuo, "was fond of hitting the ball at high speed."[93] "Sa Ba was incorruptible, upright, handsome, and good at polo and archery."[94] "Xiaole Yinnu was also pampered by Emperor Daozong thanks to his aptitude for hitting *ju* (playing polo).[95] Whenever Yelü Tabuye was galloping on, the ball was well controlled by him at ease."[96] Gu Die, "with his muscular strength, was good at hitting *ju* (playing polo)."[97]

Emperor Shengzong in the Liao Dynasty was excessively addicted to playing polo, so Ma Dechen, an official in charge of admonition and arbitration, submitted a memorandum to the emperor and offered some reasonable suggestions to the emperor, where he earnestly proposed "As far as I know, you would snatch each break from handling state affairs to take pleasure in hitting the ball (playing polo). I think it is inappropriate in three ways. The first inappropriateness lies in that Your Majesty and courtiers are to contend for the upper hand in two groups, and when you, the emperor catches the ball, the courtiers will try to seize it; while you lose, the courtiers are pleased. The second one is that once the competition for a win is aroused, etiquette and looks are left behind in the course of hitting and intercepting the ball back and forth. And if much attention is paid to the game, it would be very likely to touch your clothes and even your body, which is difficult for you to blame the courtiers for their impoliteness. The third is that the way of seeking entertainment is to belittle imperial dignity. Yet even if the ground is flat and firm, horses are fine and trained. Will you, the majesty get hurt once a horse is frightened out of control, or everyone run in a rush and clash? Will the empress dowager be scared and panicked? Your Majesty, I hope you keep in mind the duty to our country's development and prosperity. Please end such a dangerous game."[98] On reaching, the advice was happily accepted by Emperor Shengzong. What Ma Dechen stated was good and right, which was greatly appreciated by the emperor. In fact, we can see from this remonstrance the khitan rituals between emperors and ministers on the one hand, but also some information like polo court, technical movements, etc.

In the Liao Dynasty, there were many polo courts built in multiple cities. For example, according to *History of the Liao Dynasty · Geographia*, in Xinjin Fu in Liao's Nanjing (now Beijing), "The three outer doors had been respectively named as Nanduan, Zuoye, and Youye. Later, Zuoye was renamed as Wanchun, and Youye was renamed as Qianqiu. There are towers on the city gates, a polo court in its south, and Yongping Pavilion in its east."[99] "That polo field in Khitan is flat and solid" is mentioned above in Ma Dechen's petition to Emperor Shengzong. It can be seen that the polo field requires leveling, which is conducive to the regular movement of the ball: secondly, it is necessary to be solid to ensure the horse runs smoothly. Khitan requirements for the court are very similar to those of the Tang Dynasty. For example, with the aim of a flat and firm field beneficial to polo game, Yang Shenjiao of the Tang Dynasty built the court by sprinkling oil. The batting skills mentioned above, like "jumping on the horse, swinging the rod, and galloping wildly," best indicate that polo playing was carried out on the horse; namely, it was an integration of equitation and ball play.

Some archaeological findings as to Khitan playing polo reflect polo sports ever flourished in Khitan. The first one is *Scrolls of Bian Qiao Alliance*, drawn by the painter Chen Jizhi in the Liao Dynasty. The scroll is ink-on-paper. The original, with a length of 36.2 cm, and a width of 77.9 cm, is now stored in the Palace Museum in Beijing. It is drawn on the basis of the historical event of the alliance between Li Shimin, Emperor Taizong of Tang (AD 627–649), and Turkic Khan Jieli in the ninth year of Wude Period (AD 663) on the Weishui Bridge in the west of Chang'an City, in which a polo match between Tang and Liao was depicted. In the painting, several riders were on horseback holding the rods, spurring horses, and contending to hit the ball, the scene of which is exciting and spectacular.[100] The second one is a *Mural of Preparing for Polo with a Club in Hand* (see Fig. 6-9), unearthed from the No. 1 mural of Liao Dynasty in Xuanhua City, Hebei Province, in 1998. The mural was painted on the southeast wall of the tomb, 40–41 cm high. In the picture, a coachman holds a rod in his left hand and leads the horse with the right hand, a boy behind the horse standing with two long handle polo rods in both hands. The whole picture should show the ready-riding scene before a polo game.[101] The third one is the mural of playing polo scene. In 1990, No. 1 mural tomb of the Liao Dynasty was unearthed in Baoguotu Town of Yunhan Banner, Inner Mongolia Autonomous region. The picture located on the west wall of the tomb is 180 cm wide and 50 cm tall. From left to right, there are five contestants all playing polo on horseback. The movements and costumes of the characters in the picture, as well as the ball and the shape of galloping horses, are clearly discernible. It definitely shows that a fierce polo game is going on.[102]

Fig. 6-9 Mural of Preparing for Polo with a Club in Hand

Polo was quite popular in Jurchens before the founding of the Jin Dynasty. When Koryo broke the promise and invaded the borderland of the Jurchen in the fourth of the Emperor Kangzong of Yuan (AD 1107), Aguda, Emperor Taizu was playing polo on the court, waiting for his brother, Wosai's triumphant return from the counterattacks. During Wosai marching against Koryo, Aguda, Emperor Taizu dreamed, "Today news of victory will arrive," and then got up to have his subordinates make preparations for waiting on the polo court. After reaching the field, he captured two river deer when the emperor shouted, "The warfare will be ended." Before his words were finished, the report of victory was reached. Everyone at present was in great surprise.[103] From this story, we can tell that Jurchen has a long history of playing polo.

Polo sports are carried out among Jurchens, mainly thanks to the active advocacy of emperors and aristocrats. Jurchen emperors from Emperor Taizu to Aizong, aristocrats, and even other subjects were all very fond of polo. The imperial clansman of the Jin Dynasty, Andahai, also known as Alutan, the second son of Wanyan Zongxiong, was as prudent and steady as his father. At the age of 15, Emperor Taizu granted him a first-grade umbrella. Up to over 20, he won three successive games in a royal polo match. All participants at present and other royal members were amazed at his performance. When Andahai reverentially offered the winning items as the head of the team, Emperor Taizong happily exclaimed, "my grandson made many contributions to today's success, and you deserve it."[104] And then, he got a more generous reward from the emperor, which showed Emperor Taizong's deep affection for polo as well as his praise of the promising young people from the imperial family. In addition, Jin Dynasty even arranged some significant activities on a polo court. For example, on the sixth day of lunar December in the fifth year of Tianfu Period, Emperor of Jin, Aguda by himself, launched a military attack against the Liao Kingdom. When the army entered Juyong Pass and reached Yanjing at about 4 p.m. In the capital of Liao, Empress Dowager Xiao led Xiao Gan and the rest of his men to flee after hearing the news of the fall of Juyong Pass. Before they had escaped away about fifty *li*, the army of Jin rangers had already traveled to the city, so Liao's Premier Zuo Qigong and Yu Zhongwen walked out of the Danfeng gate to surrender and worship Jin's emperor on a polo court. The emperor in military uniform was seated in the Hall of Longevity and worshiped by all surrenders.[105] Common people were permitted to watch the emperor playing polo is also a great characteristic of Jurchen people. In the lunar September of the second year of Zhenyuan Period of Hailing King, Wanyan Liang of Jin, allowed common people to watch his playing polo in Changwu Hall.[106] In the fourth month of the lunar calendar in the 25th year of the Dading Period (AD 1185), Emperor Wanli came to the martial arts hall to play the ball and permitted people to watch.[107] In the third lunar month of the first year of Mingchang Period, the emperor had already played the ball in Xiyuan, where about a hundred officials gathered to view.[108] In the fifth lunar month of the first year of Mingchang Period, the worship ceremony was first held in Xi Yuan, followed by willow-shooting and polo game. The civilians were allowed to present and watch.[109] Most emperors in the Jin Dynasty were keen on playing polo, as was seen from much literature: in the fifth lunar month of the 24th year of Dading Period, Emperor Shizong visited Shajing, in which he feasted the officials and organized the polo game for fun. It has already become a custom as scheduled.[110] In the fifth lunar month of the fourth year of Xingding Period, Emperor Xuanzong, Wanyan Xun, was playing polo in the Hall of Linwu.[111] Emperors of Jurchen liked playing polo so much, and they attached great importance to its development, which would inevitably affect the whole society. Someone who built a court riverside was dismissed because of its disturbance upon people. For example, in the second year of Mingchang, the chief of Guangning Prefecture was dismissed from office eventually, just because he built a polo court near the river, which disturbed the people around.[112]

It is inevitable that there were casualties in polo, so some petition believed that it was dangerous to play polo to the extent that they raised objections. In the lunar April of the eighth year of Dading Period in the Jin Dynasty, when Emperor Shizong hit the ball in Changwu Hall, Ma Guizhong remonstrated, "Your Majesty is the Lord of the world, shouldering the responsibility of inheriting and maintaining Jin's reign. Hunting and hitting the ball are both dangerous. We'd better take a lesson from the accident that the Crown Prince fell from his horse the day before yesterday and stop playing polo." Emperor Shizong refuted, "My forefathers pacified the country by force. How can I soon forget to exercise because of peace? During the reign of Emperor Xizong of Jin (AD 1141–1149), polo was ever forbidden. At that time, people all thought it was wrong. I saw the scene with my own eyes, so I ordered the country to play polo again to practice martial arts."[113] Ma Guizhong exposed the disadvantages of playing polo by taking the example of the crown prince's falling from a horse in his expostulation in order to request to ban people from playing polo. However, as rulers, they considered things in all-round way, so Emperor Shizong quoted the unsuccessful event of banning polo in the period of Emperor Xizong to elaborate on the real effects of polo. From this point of view, we can summarize that polo did not lose its nature of martial practice when passing from the Han Dynasty to Khitan and then to Jurchen.

From some anecdotes of playing polo, we can also see the love of polo among Jurchen people. For example, Wanyan Wolibu, the second son of Emperor Taizong, died from playing polo. On the 21st of lunar June in the fifth year of Tianhui Period, when Wobuli got the news that Zhaogou, Prince Kang ascended the throne, he met Zhanhan, also named Wanyan Zonghan, a famous royal general, in a meadow to discuss sending back the Emperor Huizong of Song, but Zhanhan did not agree to it. Later, Wanyan Wolibu caught a bad cold and died because he took a cold shower after playing polo.[114] Another example, Atuhan, a military officer, is talented, versatile, filial, benevolent, athletic, and adept at hunting. He could always excel at Jiao-Di (wrestling), *jiju* (polo), and hunting.[115] Also, Emperor Shizong of Jin just met his confidant while playing polo. His Queen Zhao Sheng was seen by chance when he was in charge of Dongjing (Nanjing). "When playing polo, Emperor Shizong of Jin felt shocked at seeing her, then had her meet his mother, Queen Zhenyi, in the palace. Zhaosheng was quiet and elegant, without indulgence and arrogance."[116] Besides, Hailing King enriched his power and usurped the throne by playing polo. Zhang Zhongpu, the head of Dading County, said to Hailing, "I dreamed that you were playing polo with our emperor and that when your house rushed past, the emperor fell from his horse." Hailing King was overjoyed at it.[117] Hailing King and Xiaoyu plot to murder Zongben and Bingde, fearing that such loyal ministers as Zongben and Bingde didn't have the intention to rebel. Since it was known that Xiaoyu had a good relationship with Zongben, it was credible for Xiao to report the rebellion to the imperial court. Zongben was invited to play polo. When Hailing King ascended the building first, two military officers of his were sent to assassinate Zongben halfway.[118] In lunar September of the sixth year of Zhenglong Period in the Jin Dynasty, Hailing King commanded Gao Cunfu, a deputy Liushou (an official in charge of military defense of the town) of Dongjing, to serve his own daughter in the emperor's harem. It happened that Wanyan Yong, Lishou of Dongjing, was manufacturing some weapons in secrecy. Cunfu discovered and said publicly, "Why does Liushou need to manufacture weapons?" He privately sent a man to leak the news to Hailing King. Then, he started to plot a conspiracy to kill Yong under the guise of playing polo, with the local official Li Yanlong.[119] In addition, there were also deaths in the court. In the lunar June of the fourth year of Dading Period in the Jin Dynasty, Liu Wei deceased. When playing polo in Xuanwu Palace, the emperor granted his prime minister, Liu Wei, the posthumous name "Anmin" after hearing his death.[120] Mouyan, a military officer, was honest, brave, and good at playing polo and hunting. Although he is not as intelligent as his father, he is as brave as Xiao Zhiyun.[121] Polo horses are also used as rewards awarded by dignitaries. For example, Emperor Shizong ever awarded his queen's brother coins and polo horses for his contribution to the reign, and also conferred the title Prince Renguo on his wife, along with a reward of a lot of gold, twenty brocades, and two polo horses.[122]

The popularity of Jurchen people playing polo also has a lot to do with their political orientation. Playing polo was an indispensable part for the candidates for the Final Round of the Imperial Examination in the Jin Dynasty. Since polo can practice martial arts, it is bound to be valued and stressed by the ruling class, even included in the Final Round of the Imperial Examination for the candidates. According to *History of the Jin Dynasty*, in lunar December (the seventh year of Taihe, AD 1207), the emperor issued a decree discussing the possibility of exemption from archery and polo competition.[123] This indicates that before then, the two competitions had been unalienable for such exams. Perhaps since the imperial court started to attach less importance to this sport, common people became less interested in it. Till the Emperor Xuanzong period, polo gradually declined in the Jin Dynasty. During Xingding Period, people playing polo were even punished.[124] It is likely that Chinese polo has started to decline since then.

Playing polo in Jurchen originated from the Khitan and continued to Han Dynasty. According to some historical records: in lunar May of the second year of Tianhui Period, the national envoy went to the Song Dynasty to inform the news that Emperor Taizong had been enthroned of Jin, so Song State sent Xu Kangzong to Lailiu River to congratulate the enthronement. Without imperial palace, Jin entertained the envoys with traditional Khitan etiquette in their residence, in which lights were decorated, drinks were offered, and Jiao-Di play, cockfighting as well as polo game were held, all of which were identical to the Central Plains.[125] The skills and rules of polo in the Song Dynasty were stated clearly, as mentioned earlier in the section of "Polo" in the *History of the Song Dynasty · Military Rites*. In addition, polo also exists in educational workshops and other institutions, as was recorded and described in the volume of "Musical Records" in the *History of the Song Dynasty*.[126] Song Dynasty attached great importance to the rituals of playing polo. Apart from the national laws, there were also some special works, such as *Rituals of Polo*, written by Zhang Zhifang, and *Notes on the Rituals of Polo*, by Li Yong. The rules for Jurchen women have been discussed in the previous part and will not be repeated here.

There are two ways for Jurchen people to play polo. One is the two-door game, and the other is the one-door game. The contestants are arranged into Team A and Team B. The two-door was set with two goals at opposite ends of the field. They strike each other, and each wins by shooting into the door. In the one-door game, two blocks, with a hole at the bottom as the goal and a net as the pouch, were placed south of the court, and the two teams shared to strike a ball. The person who gets the polo ball hit into the net pouch would be the winner. The Jurchen woman painted the polo red to make it easier to identify. The polo club was usually made of wood, but there was also another kind wrapped in leather. The club had a length of few *chi* with crescent-shaped end. The court was usually managed by a special staff. According to *History of the Jin Dynasty*, in lunar May of the fourth year of Dading Period (AD 1164), innocent prisoners were set free in the field as servants.[127] Of course, there is no need to be strict about the court just for the purpose of training or playing. For example, Guo Yongan, a military general, short and beardless, liked hanging out with frivolous youngsters and playing polo, which was regarded as a disgrace for a general.[128]

What's more, there are etiquettes in the field. For example, according to *History of the Jin Dynasty*, prince's saddle was painted with gold and silver. "Zhangni," the article hanging on both sides of horse's belly to stop dust, was purple cloth decorated with brocade. The bridle was wrapped in gold and silver ornaments. The imperial people who made many contributions, such as empress dowager and grandma-empress, were allowed to use golden flowers in their "Zhangni." If granted royally on the court, they were not restricted.[129] It seemed that the court was a rather fair place where the gap between the monarch and his subjects was bridged.

Most of the archaeological findings of the Jin polo are concentrated in Shanxi Province, mainly as decoration in tombs carved on bricks. Among them, the brick sculptures of polo portraits unearthed in Quli Village, Xiangfen County, Shanxi Province, in 1983 are more representative. All the painted bricks were used for the tomb building. There were a total of four painted bricks portraying polo play, with a width of 21.5 cm and a height of 25 cm, standing side-by-side as decorations for the lattice door in the tomb chamber. The images of playing polo are all sculpted reliefs. In the four pictures, the batters were dressed in robes with soft towels on their heads, ready to hit the ball, the horses galloping.[130]

Some individual data showed that the Mongols of the Yuan Dynasty also played polo, but the records are rare and scattered and difficult to form a theory. Here are a few examples to explore the history of Mongolian polo. Zhu Youdun cited in the preface of his book *One Hundred Poems about Yuan Palace*,

> "There are no sufficient statements about the court events in the Yuan Dynasty. However, the things written here can also be referred to by historians. In the first year of Yongle Period in the Ming Dynasty (AD 1403), a seventy-year-old female servant granted to us by the emperor, once the nanny of one queen of Yuan, was most knowledgeable about what had happened in the Yuan Palace. After conducting some careful investigation in combination with some informed details, I wrote the book *One Hundred Poems about Yuan Palace*, in which all recorded things did happen in the Yuan Palace, and some of them are still unknown to the outside world due to the absence of historical records. What matters is these things are able to be widely known by later generations. In the lunar February of the spring in the fourth year of Yongle Period (AD 1406), I completed this at Lanxue Xuan."[131]

One poem described, "In March, all princes in scarlet are filing out of the palace gate. Shooting the willow and hitting the ball on horseback are like meteors flying in the eastern garden. The scenery near the east wall is the most peaceful, and in the early autumn, one can enjoy the pool and the pavilion. Servants clean the yard each day because officials frequently come here to play polo."[132]

In the fourth year of Yongle in the Ming Dynasty (AD 1406), 38 years away from the end of the Yuan Dynasty, the old lady was as old as 70. Born in the early years of Emperor Hui of the Yuan Dynasty, she lived through half of the Yuan Dynasty, witnessing about 40 years of the dynasty. In addition, as a nanny of one empress in the Yuan Dynasty, she was most familiar with things that had happened in the palace, so works reflecting palace life at that time, written by Zhu Youdun, must be very reliable and valuable. Zhu's poems tell us that it was customary for the princes and soldiers of the Yuan Dynasty to organize activities of shooting willow and playing polo each spring. Shooting willow, as a custom originally from Khitan, was later transmitted to the Jurchen. When the Mongols conquered the Song, Liao, and Jin Dynasties, they inherited the shooting willow event from Khitan, as well as polo which was transmitted from the Han Dynasty to the Khitan and Jurchen. In the Yuan drama, there is also a line referring to shooting willow and playing polo: A petty official and a supervisor with his soldiers defeated enemies who violated the northern border. The emperor and officials welcomed the triumphant return with a great banquet, willow-shooting, and polo games.[133] Drama, though as a performance on stage, is a reflection of the real world. The truth is Yuan Dynasty carried on the traditional custom of shooting willow and playing polo in the Dynasties of Liao and Jin.

Polo playing in Yuan Dynasty is also found in some poems. For example, Yang Weizhen's *Selected Poems of Yuan Dynasty · Music Ballads in the Army* stated, "The road in front of the gate winding, and the sun setting down the slope of the Futu Mountain; two tall players in white on horseback have loosened bridles, returning after they finished the polo game."[134] Sadula's poem entitled *Imperial Guard's Parade* described the scene of guards playing polo, "A 15-year-old guard with jade belt in fine clothes played polo in the eastern garden high-spiritedly, then he rode the horse to a gallop with a cloud of dust."[135] What's more, Dai Liang's poem *Inscription on Picture of Playing Polo* also depicted it as the following, "Hu nationalities have never been seen playing polo before, in which riders and horses were spinning like gusts. Flashing in the court was like flying while the first three struggled to gallop their horses. And two others followed to turn over surprisingly, looking back and forth, raising a cloud of dust, and initiating the goshawk to fly forward. Immersed in riding and shooting, he could hardly expect whose hand the ball would fall into."[136] According to the *New History of the Yuan Dynasty,* in the 13th year of Zhiyuan Period, an officer named Dadali was ordered to guard the town of Jiande. Soon, Quzhou and Wuzhou started to rebel, and Suduo was asked to conquer them. Dadali was feasting Suodu in shooting field. When the rebels were about to come, they were still taking delight in playing polo with their fellowmen, pretending not to know. Then Dasali, along with Suodu, conspired to take troops underground and suppress the enemy down. As a result, the territory recovered to its stability.[137] There are very few records of polo playing in the Yuan Dynasty. However, we can still get some information from the sparse literature. Polo playing in the Yuan Dynasty was, in general, not as popular as that in the Liao and Jin Dynasties. In the archaeological findings of the Yuan Dynasty, there is also a picture of playing ball on a lion, a pattern carved on the tomb tower of Lingyan Temple in Changqing County, Shandong Province. It depicted the lion rider hitting the ball by raising his rod.

Spreading to the Western Regions

The origin and techniques of polo discussed above have more or less covered the spread of polo in the Western Regions. Numerous historical accounts show that polo was indeed spread to the Western Regions, which the author will clarify in detail in the following section *Polo's Development in the Exchanges Among Nationalities in the Western Regions*.

The author believes that the spread of polo to neighboring areas in the Tang Dynasty is also related to the system appointing a large number of officials from minorities and frequent personnel redeployment, apart from its entertaining and appreciating charm and military training value. Human beings are both creators and messengers of culture. From the prosperity of polo in the Tang Dynasty, we may form the judgment that anyone who had been an official or ever lived in Chang'an (especially the upper and middle class of society, businessmen, army men, etc.), must be informed of polo game and also that the higher his official position was, the more he knew about polo. Besides, there were many officials from ethnic minorities in Chang'an during the Tang Dynasty, who must have played a great role in promoting the spread of polo. For example, *New Book of the Tang Dynasty · Biography of Li Zhengji* recorded that Li Zhengji, from Koryo, was successively appointed as deputy general in charge of Yinzhou (Chaoyang in Liaoning Province), then Duwei (military officer), governor and many other official positions.[138] From the previous statements, we know that Xue Song, Li Baochen, and others all enjoyed playing polo. Li Zhengji, such a prominent minority official in charge of civil and military affairs in Zizhou and Qingzhou (located now in Shandong Province), will inevitably be affected so that he would also start engaged in polo sports, and then spread it around. Tang officials in Chang'an include not only the southern ethnic groups, but also the northern Turkic ethnic minorities, Tuyuhun, Uyghur, and Tiele ethnic groups from the Northwest, and others in the Western Regions.

6.3.2 Development of the Ancient Polo

Rise of polo in the Tang Dynasty

In the first part of this chapter, we already stated that Chinese polo may have existed in the Han Dynasty. However, being insufficient in literature materials, its development has rarely been known, so here we mainly talk about the development of polo during the Tang Dynasty rather than during the Han Dynasty and Sui Dynasty. Many reasons could contribute to the flourishing of polo in the Tang Dynasty. For example, the ruling class in Tang attached great importance to horse raising since Emperor Gaozu Li Yuan, which placed necessarily the material foundation for the development of polo. Compared with other sports, the practical and recreational features help polo be advocated and played in person by the supreme ruling class, army generals of the army, and other folks. In the following section, two aspects will be mainly discussed: one is that polo is an important means of military training, and the other is that social stability and economic prosperity are the basis of polo development.

The royal aristocrats and courtiers in the Tang Dynasty were fond of playing polo, and the initiator was Emperor Taizong. In the early Tang Dynasty, Emperor Taizong realized that it was necessary to train and possess a powerful cavalry force to fight against frequent nomadic attacks on the borders. In that sense, polo, with its competitive and entertaining features, is the best means to train cavalry. During the Jinglong Period of Emperor Zhongzong, some theatrical pavilions were luckily used to watch polo games, from which liberators started to compose poems, contributing to a new wave of fads. Later, during the reign of Emperor Xuanzong, he put great effort into promoting polo to wider popularity. It is reported that Emperor Xuanzong was adept at playing polo when he was a prince, and his exquisite skills in polo even out won Tubo players. *Feng Shi First-Hand Accounts* written by Fengyan, a writer in the Tang Dynasty, also recorded, "Hitting the ball (playing polo) is a frequently performed sport in the army, which cannot be abandoned, but even more thriving" This sentence well explains the reasons for the popularity of polo in the Tang and Five Dynasties. Although playing occasionally injured players and horses, it still flourished as a "regular game" to train riding skills. During the Tang and Five Dynasties, not only imperial aristocracy and playboys were adept in it, but also local officials of all levels, along with soldiers, frequently practiced it. The major reason for polo's popularity is an imperial edict issued by Emperor Xuanzong in the sixth year of Tianbao (AD 747), which extended the polo game popular among civilians and aristocrats to the army for drilling soldiers. Yan Kuan has ever given an account of the edict issued in his *Playing Polo in Huaqing Hot Spring*.

Cuju was popular in the Warring States Period as well as Qin and Han Dynasties, while polo playing was prevalent in the Tang Dynasty. Both of them could be used to train soldiers, but the cultural connotations vary from each other due to their historical backgrounds. First of all, from the Western Han to the Tang Dynasty, various kinds of music and dance introduced from the Western Regions were welcomed, and even greatly advocated by the rulers at that time. In Chang'an, Tartar's lifestyle was popular and popular. As Guanlong military aristocracy came to power from the Northern Dynasty to the early Sui and Tang Dynasties, martial arts were highlighted while playing polo naturally became a trend. Second, the rise and growth of military cavalry at that time were complementary to polo play. During the Warring States Period, the cavalry army was still in its childhood. The main force of the army was chariots and attached infantry. In terms of quantity, infantry took the majority. Until Emperor Wu in the Han Dynasty, the cavalry, characterized by light weight and rapidity, as the main force of the army, galloped in the war with the Huns. In the late Han Dynasty, with the rise of private soldiers of the Three Kingdoms, the cavalry gradually declined.[139] Until the period of the Sixteen Kingdom, Southern and Northern Dynasties, and then the Sui Dynasty, a large number of heavily-armored cavalry took their shape, influenced by Xianbei's cavalry. In the early Tang Dynasty, under the influence of Turkic cavalry, light-armored cavalry was active on the battlefield.[140] Light-armored cavalry can give full play to the cavalry's advantages of fast mobility and long-distance attack, whose advantages are suitable for the strategic needs of the vast territory in the Tang Empire. Since the rulers of the Tang Dynasty at the very start realized that the military training of cavalry was an important basis for the construction of cavalry, they began to promote polo sports in the Tang Dynasty just in order to serve the military training.

Therefore, in the last year of Emperor Gaozu, "shepherd supervision system" was established. And Taipu Temple, in charge of horse breeding, possessed a complete set of managerial systems and professional staff responsible for the herding, management, and training of horses. According to the *New Book of the Tang Dynasty · Military Records*, over about 40 years from Emperor Taizong to Emperor Gaozong, the number of horses in the Tang Dynasty increased rapidly from thousands to roughly 706,000, most of which were used for cavalry.[141] Therefore, in the infantry era, hitting the ball on foot (*Cuju*) was used to drill soldiers, while in the Tang Dynasty, the development of personal skills, as well as the breakthrough ability of the cavalrymen, were both attached to importance. Thus, naturally much importance was given to polo in the training of troops.

Since An-Shi Rebellion in the Tang Dynasty, a large number of vassals rose. "They occupied strategically difficult terrains, with their lands, their people, as well as their soldiers, and their wealth."[142] A powerful vassal state has its crack forces; likewise, brave commanders have no weak soldiers. All vassal states applied polo play to training their cavalry. Since then, playing polo has been endowed with a new cultural significance. In the Tang Dynasty, a military commissioner or army officer, though illiterate, could still be promoted thanks to the strength of his expert skills in playing polo. According to some historical records, during the reign of Emperor Wuzong, Zhou Bao, along with Gaopin, was appointed as the army general by virtue of being good at playing polo in selecting guards for vassal states.[143]

In Dunhuang area of the Tang Dynasty, the popularity of playing polo was related to military training. In AD 848, Zhang Yichao recaptured Dunhuang and counties along Hexi Corridor after driving away Tubo. According to historical records, "Zhang Yichao ever reformed his army and constantly strengthened to build his cavalry."[144] At this time, Guiyi Amry in Shazhou not only took a large number of horses, camels, cattle, and sheep from Tubo, but also built the polo court in Dunhuang. During the Guiyi Amry period in Shazhou, the court was mainly used for military training as well as the declaration of the edict, banquets, and other purposes. Even the ceremony of appointing military commissioners was also held on the polo field, and playing polo has become an activity used to entertain foreign guests. Influenced by the trend of training soldiers with polo, there are a large number of polo-playing materials in Dunhuang literature.

In addition, Tang Dynasty was an important highly-developed period in the course of feudal society in China. Political stability and economic prosperity provided a strong political and material foundation for the rapid development of Tang culture, and the whole social culture and social life thrived. In particular, the rulers of the Tang Dynasty were good at summing up and drawing lessons from the experience of feudal rulers in governing the country, vigorously advocating enlightening policies, implementing the policy of opening to the outside world, and extensively exchanging and absorbing the material culture of the ethnic minorities around. It was this stability and prosperity that facilitated sports in the Tang Dynasty unprecedentedly, thus contributing to another peak since the Han Dynasty. In short, the spread and progress of polo in the Tang Dynasty expanded the influence of Chinese sports, bringing about a profound influence upon various minority areas and neighboring countries or regions, and composing a glorious chapter for the revitalization and development of ancient Chinese national sports.

Development of polo in Song, Liao, Jin, and Mongolia

Song Dynasty carried on the leisurely climate of the Tang Dynasty and created a breeding ground for polo and a solid basis for sports development. Throughout the history of ancient Chinese sports, there is no denying that the Song sports were rich and colorful. In particular, the boom of commerce in the Song Dynasty, to a large extent, drove the development of its urban areas, so it was more inclined to form an urban culture. In the Song Dynasty, commercialization was richer than its previous dynasties, and even richer than that in the period of the Republic of China. It is the urban prosperity that gathers all kinds of people in the city, forming its metropolitan culture. It is worthwhile to point out the night market life in the Song Dynasty was more abundant and lively than that in the Tang Dynasty. Moreover, a commercial network frame provided a new way to spread culture; thereby, polo gained its rapid development to such an extent that it fully realized the exchanges and dissemination through its constant contact with the neighboring minority regimes.

Khitan people and Jurchen people, as two peoples on horseback, mounted archery is one of the most basic parts of their lives and education. Both nationalities enjoy a custom of regular riding and shooting, thus forming the national characteristics more suitable for carrying out polo sports. Most of the customs and traditions in Jurchen are inherited from Khitan, so in the following section, polo in Jurchen will be taken as an example to illustrate the influence of riding and shooting customs upon polo development.

Jurchen people, led by their leader Wanyan Aguda, destroyed the Liao and Northern Song in a few decades, and established a big dynasty of five capitals, fourteen prefectures, and one hundred and seventy-nine counties. Horseback riding and shooting were the living habits of the Jurchens, who specialized in them. Jurchen nationality originally had the custom of willow-shooting, which required good shooting skills and horsemanship. In the volume of *Chronicles of Emperor Taizu* in the *History of the Jin Dynasty*, there are the following records:

> "On May 5 in the first year of the state (AD 1115), the emperor held the activity of shooting willow. In accordance with past customs, the emperor would worship the heaven and shoot willow on May 5, July 15, and September 9; year after year, this custom followed as a matter of routine."[145]

However, there is no record of playing polo at this time. Until the reign of Emperor Shizong, Wanyan Yong in the Jin Dynasty, the records are:

> "On May 5 in the third year of Dading (AD 1163), it happened to be the Double Ninth Festival; the emperor came to the garden and shoot willows. He ordered the princes and all the officials to follow suit. Those winners were rewarded by the majesty in different kinds. The emperor then also visited the Changwu Palace, where he gave banquets and played ball games; year after year, this custom followed as a matter of routine."[146]

Playing polo is not exclusively a traditional activity of Jurchen nationality, but a foreign culture learned from other nationalities. In the volume of *Rites* in the *History of the Jin Dynasty*, after worshiping the heaven, "(All the officials) changed clothes to shoot willow and play polo, typical of the custom in the Liao state. Jin also upheld this custom."[147] This shows that willow-shooting was a common custom of the Liao and Jin Dynasties, while the Jurchen learned polo from the Khitan. Anyway, playing polo is not an inherent traditional activity of the Khitans, who must have learned it from the Central Plains and Balhae area. It is recorded in the *Chronicles of Emperor Muzong* in the *History of the Liao Dynasty*, "(in the lunar March of the third year in the Yingli Period), (the emperor) stroke the ball in Yingzhou, when northern Han sent an emissary to present polo costumes and horses as tribute."[148] Northern Han was at the time (in Shanxi Province today) a subsidiary of the ministate of Han, who presented to the Liao state fine horses and clothes as tribute. It was a nation living on nomads, which had a large number of horses, cattle, and sheep, but relied on a vassal state that was not a livestock area to present polo horses as tribute. It can be seen that most of the polo activities of the Khitan, Jurchen, and Mongols living in northeast China were transmitted from the Central Plains.

For nomadic people who lived on horseback and specialized in riding and shooting, no matter whether the horses had been specially trained for playing polo or not, they could ride them to the court to play. Wanyan Heng, from the imperial family of the Jin Dynasty, was "the best polo player in the world; at many times, he could play against a team and ride a horse well no matter whether the horse was better or worse." This is the very value of polo in military training, namely, by putting riding skills and horse-training skills into practice. However, riding a specially trained horse on a polo court can give full play of playing skills and thus manifest a panorama of polo development. In the late Jin Dynasty, there were already special institutions established for training the horses used for polo game, and the emperor often rewarded his ministers for their best performances in playing polo. Once, Emperor Xizong, Wanyan Mi's wife's brother Wulin Dahui did a great job in fulfilling his duty, "Xizong rewarded him with much money and a chance to play polo in the court."[149] In order to win the support of Wulin Dahui's sister and brother-in-law, Emperor Shizong Wanyan Yong "granted them one hundred gold coins, twenty pieces of excellent brocade, and two polo horses."[150] The emperor has already had trained polo horses in his stables, which fully showed his love for polo along with the high-degree development of polo skills in the Jin Dynasty.

Among the many separatist states established by the northern minorities, the Jin Dynasty attached the greatest importance to polo sports in terms of popularity. The reason why Jurchen people adopted polo culture is mainly for the need to train soldiers. When their forefathers lived in the mountains and forests, they totally relied on hunting to practice their skills of riding and shooting. When the Jurchens led their armies to fight against the Liao and Song Dynasties, they came to realize that polo was the best way to train their horsemanship and bayonet skills. Jin moved its capital to Yanjing and built there "Changwu Palace, Guangwu Palace (for polo)," followed by Linwu Palace (also for polo). Later emperors all went to these three places to play polo, and "ordered people to watch." It is clear that polo and martial arts were closely related. Among the emperors of the Jin Dynasty, Emperor Shizong Wanyan Yong was the most capable of upholding this principle. When his son Wanyan Zhen got ready to attend his mother's funeral, he ordered him to play polo. Then the teacher of the Crown Prince, Wanyan Shou, argued, "(When) in mourning, it is not acceptable." The emperor responded, "This is for the training of martial arts. You certainly can't do it alone, but now I ordered you to do it. What are you afraid of?"[151] Wanyan Yong not only advocated polo games, but also insisted on martial training by means of polo, which caused wide opposition from the ministers. Imperial Astronome Ma Guizhong then presented a petition to the emperor in which he begged the emperor to stop the practice of polo games. However, the answer was: "My forefathers pacified the country by force. How can I soon forget to exercise because of peace? During the reign of Emperor Xizong of Jin (AD 1141–1149), polo was ever forbidden. At that time, people all thought it was wrong. I saw the scene with my own eyes, so I ordered the country to play polo again to practice martial arts."[152] Wanyan Yong insisted on practicing polo for the purpose of training martial arts, which was the reason to account for the prosperity of polo in the Jin Dynasty.

In addition to the historical records, we can still study the development of polo at that time through some cultural images. A brick craving of Jin Tome unearthed in Houma, Shanxi Province, was named *A Picture of Playing Polo*, in which there are four playing postures on the brick. Besides, the player was in good health and spirit, and the horse was vivid and eager. There is a picture in particular in which the player's left hand is holding the reins, while the right is holding the stick; the horse turned after a sudden stop. This picture best displays the vigorous posture of the player and horse. In the Yuan Dynasty, there was once a painting named *The Polo of Jin People*, which has been lost, but the magnificent scene of the Jin people's *Jiju* can still be seen in the poem titled *Jiju of Jin People*, written by Fu Ruojin. "Since ancient times, the people in the north have been good at horse riding and shooting, and everyone could be labeled an expert in this respect. When I looked at the picture of *Jiju of Jin People*, in which everyone was full of spirit, I could see and sense the vigor of the paper. The yellow flags on the court almost covered up the sunshine, and the damask clothes on the players and the facilities on the court were even redder than the sun. When the race started, the athletes were galloping up horses, running on the court, and turning around like a whirlwind. The ball flew back and forth like a meteor, occasionally ruffling the players' clothes. The horse's mane fluttered in the wind as they played, and the scene was so beautiful."[153] The vivid scene was just before the eye. But because the Jin Dynasty was destroyed by the Mongols, Fu's last comment was, "later, the emperor failed to cherish the stability of the country enough, and he indulged so much in martial arts and military training that the country was eventually destroyed."[154] Nothing can be perfect. The martial spirit cultivated by polo can only play a certain role in the country's civil administration and military defense, but can never make the feudal society stable and steady in the long run.

In the Yuan Dynasty, polo developed so well in both productions of the ball and the playing style. Xiong Mengxiang, in the Yuan Dynasty, wrote in the *Xi Jin Zhi*:

"Playing polo is a tradition of the Jin Dynasty, and our dynasty attaches importance to the practice of martial arts. On May 5 and September 9 each year, the emperor ordered all the princes and his brothers to gather in a broad place in Xihua Gate to watch polo games. The emperor also called all the ministers to show up at the same time, as long as he played polo. The players all rode fine horses decorated with golden pheasant feathers, tassels, bells, and wolf tail hair. Two pieces of cloth called 'Zhangni' were tied with two ropes on either side of the horse's belly to keep out the dust. One player rode at first and threw a big leather ball on the ground, and then other riders scrambled to hit it with a long rod. Suddenly someone's rod hit the ball, which may not fall because the horse was too fast to run. Some skilled players took advantage of the rod by lifting the ball into the air without leaving the rod. The horses ran as if they were flying, and all the players struggled to shoot into the goal. The winner finally went to the team that hit the ball most into the goal. When the players were playing polo, their rods rotated in the air like a meteor. The people watching the match on the spot were so thrilled, as if they could feel the vigor of the players. Even if polo was used to show force, the players tried their best to race each other for speed. Rewards and punishments varied depending on their performances. Just as in the days of Zhennan King in Yangzhou, a polo match and a feast were held in front of the palace. The princes and the concubines of the emperor sat on the left and right sides respectively, watching the game. Polo players mounted their horses for polo and competed with each other to their best. And at last, the winner received great rewards, while those who lost were given a little encouragement. This was the royal polo match, as was the custom in the Yuan Dynasty."[155]

At this point, the ball was made of soft leather instead of wood, which was actually closer to modern polo. The rod was lengthened in order to serve and strike the ball easily.

Mongols also played polo at the start of the Mongolian Dynasty. However, its development was far behind that of the Khitan and Jurchen. By the time the Manchus established the Qing Dynasty, there was no record of polo in Mongolia. According to the present documents, the Mongolians, on the one hand, did not develop polo actively and extensively, and on the other hand, the Qing government suppressed polo in many ways. Therefore, we can rarely read related historical records about Mongolian polo.

Polo's development in the exchanges among nationalities in the Western Regions
The towns in the Western Regions, as the platform of communication between Central Plains and its neighboring nationalities, have always been the battleground between them. The ancient Dunhuang area was an important place where the nomadic tribes lived and the soldiers guarded. In the long-term breeding and training of the horses, the local ethnic groups not only developed some fine horse species, but also mastered the superb equestrian. The soldiers who guarded the border took the practice of riding and shooting as an important means to improve their fighting ability. Tang Dynasty rulers were originally descended from the northern minorities, and they later established the Tang Dynasty in times of war and chaos. At that time, the northern Turkic peoples and other ethnic groups also posed a great threat to Central Plains. The government of the Tang Dynasty, knowing the nature of the northern peoples as well as their important role in maintaining the rule of Tang, adopted a policy of ethnic tenderness. Therefore, Tang Dynasty made full use of the relations between the northern groups and Western Regions to develop the national economy and then consolidate its rule. It was due to the trust and appointment of the northern and western nationalities that a large number of people from the Western Regions came to the Central Plains, either as merchants or officials, so there were quite a few minority officials of various ranks spread

all over. People from the north and the Western Regions not only brought about their culture, but also brought back the culture of the Central Plains to their homeland. As a result, polo has been widely developed among the multi-ethnic groups in the Western Regions. Here are some proofs: in 1979, a fur ball made in the middle of the Western Han Dynasty was unearthed at the site of the Han beacon tunnel at Majiajuan in Dunhuang; an underground Tang polo court was discovered in Tashkurgan Tajik Contea Autonoma in Xinjiang; in the Ashtana tomb in Turpan, a clay terracotta figurine who is riding a horse and playing ball in the seventh century was found; a quantity of polo terms are recorded in *Divan lgat at-Turk*, manifesting the prosperity of polo in the Western Regions. From the documents and archaeological discoveries, it appears that in the northern part of the Silk Road, from Yumen Pass to Turpan, from Kucha to Wusun, and in the southern section of Silk Road, from Yangguan Pass to Loulan and Hotan, passing through the Pamir Mountains via the Tashkurgan, existed a road for the spread of polo in the Tang Dynasty.

First, let's take a look at the polo in the Western Regions in Dunhuang literature. There are many unearthed documents in Dunhuang that reflect the polo activities in the Dunhuang area at that time. Dunhuang remaining document S. 2049, and the section of *Flying Rod · Polo* on p. 2544 notes:

> "In the middle of spring, the grass and trees are new, fine horses are often seen in the woods, and beauties are there within our sight. People talk to their friends and visit the polo courts whenever they are bored. The officials are holding white jade whips, riding, and playing. There are a team of men in blue and a team in red who play with each other for fun. Only one match does not have the final say. If you lose the first, you have to play again later. When the game begins, players take off the purple robe and put on the brocade suit. The saddles of gold and silver are gleaming in the sun. In a polo court, the dust flies where the horses run, and the rods fly in the air, too. Polo was dancing like stars, the rods waving like the moon, and horses galloping like the wind to run to the hole ... After the match, the suits are wet, and the horses are sweaty. Players ask each other to stop and rest, probably because both the horses and they are running out of energy, yet the result awaits to count overnight."[156]

The above poem describes the time of the polo match, namely, in the middle of spring. After raining, the air is clean, the flowers and trees are fresh, and the players are in a good mood. The venue is the court in the woods, and the spectators are from all walks of life; fine horses are equipped with gold stirrups and silver saddles. Players are divided into two teams, holding the rod like the moon, and wearing blue and red brocade suits. The poem also depicts the wonderful scene when the players are shooting the goal, as is cited, "the suits are wet, and the horses are sweaty," which indicated the intensity of such sports. "Take off the purple robe and put on the brocade suit ..." is to reveal that when playing polo, people must take off the purple robe and prepare to wear a brocade jacket which has a round collar and narrow sleeves decorated with embroidered flowers. This kind of brocade jacket is assumed to be the polo suit at that time.[157] What's more, it is recorded in the literature that in polo matches, players of the same team should dress in the same color, and different teams should wear different colors. The shoes they wear are usually long leather boots, and the hat they wear is made of tung wood. "Polo was dancing like stars, the rods waving like the moon, and horses galloping like the wind to run to the hole" is a visual confirmation of the polo rule at the time, i.e., whoever gets the ball to shoot into the hole wins. The "hole" refers to either the goal or the net. There are 24 embroidered flags on both sides of the goal during the competition. At that time, the way the judges kept score was called "chang-chou," which means scoring a point is called "one chou." The one-score winner will have a flag added to his side, and one score loser will have a flag removed at the end of the game. The outcome will be decided by the number of flags each side has.

Dunhuang Literature S. 617L *Gong Ci · Shuiguzi* describes the scene of the people living in the palace in the Qingming festival watching the game. The article described: "People were getting dressed for the polo game ... Instead of sitting down in the order as they came, they sat down in accordance with the emperor's favor. A banquet in the court was held to greet the guests for tributes. The players all mounted fine horses, and the spectators urged them to play."[158] Volume 1 of *Jibu Bianwen* in S. 5439, together with S. 5441 and p. 3697, describes Jibu's superb skills in playing polo in front of Zhu Jie. "Jibu showed off his riding techniques on a horse while holding a rod, and suddenly he hit the ball in the air. He demonstrated well his polo skills with a blade and sword on horseback. Suddenly he reined the horse and invited others to play polo with him, and there he was, riding like a god. He waved a horsewhip to show his handsome appearance and rode a horse to show his upright posture. The horses galloped about like lightning. Zhu Jie, relaxingly watching Jibu play, was stunned at the end."[159] And in p. 3618 of *A Book of Qiu Yin* is recorded as follows: "Some people wrote wonderful things with a brush pen ... The horses had carved saddles, and the riders wore brocade."[160] To summarize, Dunhuang Literature vividly depicts the actual situation of the polo games in Chang'an and Dunhuang, as well as the scene of people watching the matches. The book recorded the time, place, and mood of people present watching the game. These polo matches showed the splendor of the decorations on the horse, the excellent riding skills of players, and their cooperation in playing polo, thereby exhibiting a gripping game scene.

Locating at the edge of the Pamir Plateau, Tashkurgan Tajik Contea Autonoma is an important road on the south section of the ancient Silk Road. Polo was popular in Dunhuang, a very important military town located in the border area of the Tang Dynasty. In order to improve the physical fitness of soldiers and strengthen their combat ability, the local government always took polo as an essential means to conduct military training, and thus built polo courts in many large counties. It is a fact that there were many large-scale polo courts in the Dunhuang area, although those courts do not exist now. Even so, we can still find many records in the Dunhuang stone chamber. For example, p. 3239 of Dunhuang Literature records that in the Jiawu Year of AD 914, Deng Hongsi claimed, "the soldiers were already on the pitch, lining up to play polo. But this is a better place to conduct military training for your country than to play polo."[161] *Erlang Wei* records that when the war in the Shazhou ended, in the celebration feast, "The northern side finally settled down, and the officials of the Shazhou greeted the envoys. On the fifteenth day of the first lunar month, the court was filled with music"[162] In order to meet the envoys, the Shazhou civil and military officials met the imperial envoys on the polo court. The scene was grand and spectacular, with a large audience and great excitement. p. 001 and p. 2629 in AD 964? collected in the Dunhuang Research

Institute, recorded: "On the 19th, a feast was held on the Cold Food Festival in the court."[163] This poem depicts the scene when the army defeated Tubo and reigned Hexi. The army was having a feast in the polo court of Dunhuang County. Also, Dunhuang literature, such as p. 3945 and p. 3773, reflected that in addition to training soldiers and batting, the polo court was also used for announcing the edicts and holding banquets of various kinds to entertain guests. *Biography of Zhang Yanshou* is cited as follows: "… determined to seize Changping; he was good at polo, and no one in Binzhou can compete with him. In Huichang, Governor Zhang's skills enabled him to compete with the emperor's polo team."[164] This historical data indicated that Zhang Yanjiao was best at polo, whose skills enabled him to compete for any, even with the players of the Imperial Palace or the emperor. Plus, p. 3451 of *Zhang Huaishen Bianwen* recorded, "There are many envoys, carrying imperial edicts from the emperor, who traveled west to the desert and granted the local officials some rewards, including gold and silver vessels, brocade, silks and satin of all kinds. All those items were placed on the polo court, and people came all over to extend congratulations." "When it was the time, the envoys read the emperor's edicts on the polo court, mainly praising the contribution of local officials." "After the emissary mission was completed, the local people would set up a banquet and arrange song and dance performances.[165] These lines show that when the imperial envoys arrived, all the officials came to the polo court to welcome them. Then the envoys were invited to read the imperial edict, followed by the rewarding ceremony. After that, the locals would offer a big banquet in which everyone, including the imperial envoys, officials, soldiers, and others, would drink together. In order to have fun, they ordered many entertainers to sing and dance to their content. What a lively scene! In general, when the emperor appointed a new military governor, envoys would send the military governor to the border, and the officials in that area would go out and greet the newly appointed military governor. Then the whole group would be escorted into the town to receive the handover of the documents. After a series of procedures, envoys went to the courtside pavilion (stand) to watch a polo match, military training, and other performances.

Dunhuang Literature S. 1196 quotes as follows: "(The player) tried to ride a horse with a rod, while suddenly another raised the rod and hit the ball." This is a tense and vivid scene of a polo match in which the players pass skillfully, swinging the club and hitting the ball. S. 2947 also describes: "When I was in my teens, the spring breeze was thousands of miles away, and the lotus blossomed. My brother and I, with excellent talents, were always praised by our parents. We used to play polo together from dawn and refused to go home until dusk." This poem just depicted the popularity of polo activities, specifically the prevalence of folk polo activities in the Tang Dynasty. To summarize, we can tell that in the Tang Dynasty, from the emperor down to the aristocracy, officials, generals as well as commoners, everyone is all fond of polo games.

In addition, there are also records of polo in the Western Regions from the works *Divan lgat at-Turk*.[166] Mahmud Kasgari was born in the early 11th century in the royal family of Kara-khanid Khanate. This place is now Upal and attached to Azik Village of Shufu County in the Kashgar Region.[167] *Divan lgat at-Turk* was written by Mahmud Kasgari in the Islamic calendar of 464–466 (AD 1072–1074).[168] Mahmud Kasgari left Kasgari in the Islamic calendar (AD 450) and spent 15 years on an academic expedition across the vast Central Asian region. As Mahmud Kasgari said:

I have traveled to every corner of the towns and villages where Turkic people lived, recorded the vocabulary and phonology of different tribes, such as Turkish, Turkmenistan, Uguz, Chigier, Yagma, and Qïrqïz people. And I took great advantage of them. Therefore, every language of these tribes was well arranged in my mind.[169] That is to say, this great work is done on the basis of a thorough investigation by the author, in which the information is authentic and the material is reliable.

In the dictionary, the author mentioned the information that the Turkic-speaking tribes and ethnic groups in Central Asia played polo in the 11th century, indicating that polo was carried out in this region. Such as "he bent the club for me,"[170] "he had a polo club bent,"[171] "he played polo with someone else at stakes of pants,"[172] "a rope was pulled from the side of the court during horse racing and polo,"[173] "a ball hit with a hockey stick,"[174] "polo,"[175] "People hit the ball with a fork." It's a game peculiar to the Turks. If one of the participants wants to lead, he hits the ball with the pitchfork. Whoever can hit the ball forcibly is the kicker.[176] It is not difficult to see from these records that the Turks did indeed carry out polo, and that there was something rare in our Chinese literature. For example, as for the making of the ball club, Chinese literature only described its shape and never discussed how it was made. But here, we can clearly see that it is artificially bent. Polo was sometimes regarded more as a gambling game than a kind of sport. For example, in Central Plains, the emperors of the Tang Dynasty bet on official titles with balls. The polo game in Central Asia did not prevent this from happening either. People there also bet on polo with their livelihoods, from which we can infer that there were regular and frequent polo matches in the region. In a polo game, players pulled the ropes to the side of the court to mark out the area and keep the crowd in line, as if it were not a formal game. In this view, there were not only officially organized matches, but also voluntary matches held by the commoners. Truly the courts for the folk games were obviously not as good as the official ones. Generally speaking, polo was fairly popular in Central Asia.

The Uyghur word for polo is "Qiaogan." In 1970, a 7th-century clay polo player was unearthed in an ancient tomb in Astana, Turpan. The figure was riding a white horse, wearing a small flat hat, a round-collared coat, and high-waisted riding boots, holding the club in his right hand, pretending to be riding a horse, swinging a cue, and playing ball with his eyes forward. The shape of the man and horse is life-like, which vividly reflects the intense scene of a polo competition. There were many accounts of polo in the times of Kara-khanid Khanate. For example, Yousufu Hasi Hajifu, a great scholar of the Uyghur nationality, in his long poem *Happiness and Wisdom* discussed with the king about who should be appointed as an envoy: "He also must know chess so well that he is able to beat all rivals." "He should be able to play Qiaogan (polo ball) and good at shooting, farming, and hunting."[177] In the *Encyclopedia of the Western Regions*, compiled in AD 1003, it wrote: "Don't rush into the game when playing Qiaogan. There should be no more than eight players on the court, with one playing the side, one guarding the end line, and six hitting the ball." In the 1980s, an ancient polo court which was 150 m long and 50–60 m wide with walls and mounds was discovered in the north of Tashkurgan County, which confirms the historical records of the polo court "a thousand steps long as flat as a pancake, and smooth as a mirror."

The above-mentioned historical documents and cultural relics show that polo was a sport with a long history among the ethnic minorities in Xinjiang, especially the Uyghurs. The ethnic minorities who live in the northwest of China have long been engaged in hunting, husbandry, and farming. They know how to ride horses well, which paves the foundation to develop polo games. Due to some historical reasons, the Uyghur people changed from animal husbandry to farming and then settled in cities and towns, with their living environment and living style dramatically changed. During this period, polo also altered gradually from prosperity to decline. To sum up, although the Western Regions are far away from the Central Plains, the military and civilians are still keen on polo activities, which have a direct relationship with the progress of polo in Central Plains.

Decline of polo in the Qing Dynasty

During the Qing Dynasty, the rulers adopted the policy of national oppression to stifle the development of polo. Yet before that, polo was once widely practiced by the Manchu ancestor during the Jin Dynasty. Ball-playing and shooting used to be Jin's two martial arts training methods. In the Qing Dynasty, shooting was still highly valued. At least once a year in the autumn, a large-scale hunting activity was held in Mulan paddock, and "the garrisons of all provinces hunted every year and followed as the routine." It is a pity that polo is not recorded much in the literature. Only during the time of Emperor Kangxi was there once a traditional polo performance held in Baiyun Guan in Beijing. But by the Mid-Qing Dynasty, even this remain also disappeared. Jurchen people governed the Central Plains twice, within which they took the opposite views of polo culture. Here are some reasons: the first is the change in the traditional culture atmosphere in the Qing Dynasty. Yan Fu, a reformist thinker in modern times, wrote in his translated work *The Spirit of the Laws*:

> "If we compare the folk customs after the Song Dynasty with those before the Tang Dynasty, we will find that they are completely different. In terms of country-to-country comparisons, while other countries are becoming more open-minded, China is becoming more conservative. The most obvious one is that people like to practice martial arts. The ancients liked to hunt, and they chose those remote mountainous areas for hunting. Nowadays, people do not hunt in remote mountainous areas, but take hunting as their career instead. Other sports, such as ball play, tug-of-war, and sword dancing, are cases in point. These kinds of sports, appreciated by the ancients, were done mostly on their own, because they were very helpful for improving their spirit and body; by contrast, most people do sports right now mainly for fun. And they always asked others to play sports for them so that they could watch their performances by sitting on a high platform. What a pity they looked down on all forms of athletic skill and looked down on the efforts to improve their health."[178]

After the Song Dynasty, China's feudal society entered a time of autocratic centralization and adopted a policy that strengthened the central forces and weakened the local ones. And other policies were like putting mental pursuits above material arts, valuing agriculture over commerce, putting more emphasis on reading than practice, and valuing eunuchs over other professions. All the above policies caused a social fad of "nothing is lofty except reading books." So the late Ming official Gu Yanwu lamented the destruction of the Ming Dynasty was due to the empty talk of Confucius and Mencius thoughts. The rulers of the Qing Dynasty accepted the government experience of the Song and Ming Dynasties and created a much gentler social atmosphere. As a result, many martial arts activities gradually faded, including the decline of polo under this atmosphere. The second is the Manchu government's distortion of national traditional sports culture. The Jurchen people ruled over other peoples a hundred times more than their own, and thus pursued a policy of ethnic oppression in all aspects, in particular by restricting the martial training of other ethnic groups. In the early years of the Qing Dynasty, the Han people were forbidden to keep horses and hide bows and arrows by themselves. Later on, although the ban was lifted, folk martial training was still strictly prevented to some extent. The martial arts of the Qing Dynasty were called "Yecangxing" because they were developed under the organization of secret societies. Back in the late Jin Dynasty, Jurchen's ruler had already realized that polo was the best way to train soldiers as well as to develop rebels. Therefore, Emperor Xuanzong of Jin ever decreed that "the punishment for playing polo must be strictly enforced." Afterwards, when the Jurchens established the Qing Dynasty, they set up the hunting ceremony instead of polo sports, and suppressed the traditional sports of the Han and other nationalities while developing their own traditional sports. For example, to promote their own national wrestling but boycott the thousand-year-old Sumo wrestling; to advocate skating and ice sports but change the ancient football, which has been popular for thousands of years, into ice *Cuju*; to encourage the dragon boats for the sake of performance nature rather speed nature, and so on. All these have helped in some way to stifle Central Plains' traditional sports culture. Of course, Jin Dynasty, founded by the Jurchens, once adopted the traditional sports culture of Central Plains by making polo a military salute. When it came to the Qing Dynasty, they stopped to promote polo and even forbade private horse breeding for a long time, which has contained the development of polo to a large extent.[179]

Of course, there were other factors that contributed to the decline of polo in China's feudal society, such as the gradual replacement of cold weapons with hot weapons under the influence of modern Western civilization, and the economic decline in the middle and late Qing Dynasty. All the above led to a shortage of horses in the first place, followed by a drop in demand for horsemanship. All in all, from this, we can see that the development of sports and social and cultural atmosphere are closely linked. The prosperity of any sports will be affected more or less by political, economic, military, and other factors.

6.3.3 Evolution of the Ancient Polo

Reasons and characteristics of the polo's evolution
All things in the world are always in a dynamic state of constant development and change. Change always moves with the environment or time. And polo, as a product of social development, is no exception. It is known that polo played an important role in military training in the Tang Dynasty. The Tang government attached great importance to military training, particularly in cavalry, because of the conditions in surrounding nations and its own social economy. First, at the beginning of the Tang Dynasty, the country was confronted with strong military pressure from the neighboring ethnic groups, especially the cavalry forces of the nations on horseback, such as

Tuyuhun and Turkic people, which forced the Tang to develop its cavalry troops. The other reason is that the Tang Dynasty carried out an open and compatible cultural policy, so that the multi-ethnic cultures of variety could coexist, thus providing a space for the development and prosperity of polo. Third, the flourishing economy and stable social environment have provided a guarantee for polo sports. Polo is noted to be an expensive sport in which the court, the ball, the club, the costume, the horse, and so on were all required. In other words, in order to develop polo, one must have a solid economic foundation. The flourishing progress of polo in the Tang Dynasty happened to be the outcome of the high-speed development of the economy.

Polo evolved in the Tang Dynasty. The evolution of everything has its reasons, then what is the reason for the evolution of polo? The author believes that there are the following points: First, polo developed vigorously in the Tang Dynasty, which not only became the favorite sport of officials and nobles, but also continuously infiltrated into the middle and lower classes. However, this part of the population did not have the high level of financial resources of polo; thus, some similar sports, such as donkey ball (Lüju), have developed. Second, polo was so appealing that many women even joined in. Although there have always been women heroes, not all women can do this. Especially for the ladies of the lords, whether they could ride a big, fast horse was uncertain, so they chose the donkey instead horse. Third, polo has got two disadvantages: one is to hurt the horse, and the other is to hurt people. In this sense, people had to choose other safer games, and then Budaqiu (foot play) and Chuiwan (similar to golf) took their shapes. Emperor Xuanzong of Tang used to play in the palace. At that time, Prince Rong fell from his horse and died. So Huang Fanchuo said to the emperor: "Your Majesty is senior and a little bit overweight. If the horse's strength reached its limit and fell down on the road, what hope would there be for all the people in the country? Why not just watch your son-in-law play polo with others? Just like a person looking at a plate full of food, it is pleasing to feast his eyes and satisfy his appetite at the same time. Similarly, don't you enjoy watching others play polo?" The emperor answered: "You are quite right. I won't do it again."[180] It can be seen that the emperor's thinking had changed. Fourth, polo sports require excellent horses and demand higher consumption. As a consequence, some people had to be realistic and consider the actual economic conditions to play somewhat similar sports instead of polo, such as Budaqiu and Chuiwan, which are wiser choices.

From the evolution of polo, such as Lüju, Budaqiu, and Chuiwan, we can obviously see that there are the following characteristics: First, the intensity of the sport is reduced; second, the requirements of sports conditions are not strict; third, it's more secure; and fourth, it is easier to promote and popularize.

Variations of polo

The first is Lüju (donkey ball). *A Collection of New and Old Book of the Tang Dynasty · Biography of Guo Yingyi* said: "Guo Yingyi is the fourth son of Guo Zhiyun, the general of the royal army, who inherited his father's martial skills and learned martial arts when he was young. He was knighted by the emperor during the period when he committed in Gansu ... Just in time with the death of Yan Wu, Jiannan provincial commander, the emperor ordered Yingyi to replace him as Chengdu governor and Jiannan provincial commander. When Yingyi arrived in Chengdu, he did a lot of unscrupulous deeds ... They (Yingyi and his officials) gathered women to play ball on donkeys, make donkey saddles and various tools with silver, and wear luxurious clothes. They spent tens of thousands of coins every day for fun."[181] Dunhuang Literature S. 5637 *A Elegy to Donkeys* records: "You were not born in a general's home, yet you played the full part in ball play till worn out."[182] This text describes the owner's sadness after his donkey died due to the fact that he often struck a ball on this donkey. It reflected the scene of riding a donkey and hitting a ball from another side. It is worth mentioning that in the Tang Dynasty, Lüju has become a feature of women's sports in the Western Regions. In the Song Dynasty, Lüju also developed very well. In *Reminiscences of the Eastern Capital* written by Meng Yuanlao, there is such a record: "The band began to play again, setting up a bristling ball gate. Then came out more than a hundred men dressed in colorful clothes. They were all wrapped in flower scarves, half of them wearing red, half of them blue, and all wore silk shoes on their feet. They rode donkeys with carved saddles and elaborate cushions. They were divided into two teams, each led by an excellent leader, who held a club with colorful patterns, the game of which was called 'Little Da.' One of the leaders struck the ball with his club as if the ball was attached. Once the ball fell to the ground, the two teams scrambled for it and passed it to the leader. The team on the left hit the ball into the goal, and they won. The team on the right then continued to struggle for the ball till the goal. The two teams chased each other and finally received the reward based on the scores they got. Then they thanked the emperor for his kindness and left the court. When the civil servants introduced more than a hundred eunuchs and maids to play the game, it was plainly 'Little Da.' But when they were decorated with pearls and jewels, a jade belt around their waist, and red boots on their feet, each riding a pony, it was turned into 'Big Da.' Everyone rode so well, fast, gracefully, and beautifully that it seemed picturesque."[183] This literature helps to understand that Lüju has already lost its effectiveness in military training, but mainly for entertainment.

The other is Budaqiu (foot play). Emperor Xizong liked to play balls and ducks fighting. He thought he was really good at Budaqiu, so he told the comedian Shi Yezhu: "If I step into the palace examination of Budaqiu, I will definitely get first." Shi Yezhu answered: "If you happen to encounter Yao, Shun, Yu, and Tang as the examiners, you will inevitably have to fall into disgrace." The emperor laughed.[184] In addition, Wang Jian's *One Hundred Palace Poems* and Lady Huarui's *Palace Poems* both mention: "During the Cold Food Festival, people in the palace all played Budaqiu." This shows that Budaqiu has become a common sport. Also, in the Japanese literature, we found that there are Budaqiu pictures,[185] signifying that just like polo, Budaqiu has also spread to other countries. In the *Rites* of *History of the Song Dynasty*, it is recorded: "After the greeting ceremony, the emperor's courtiers went to the palace to drink. There were also people playing Budaqiu, and people riding donkeys and mules to play."[186] It shows that in the palace of the Song Dynasty, there were tributes of Lüju and Budaqiu, which were different from polo in the way that they were mainly used for viewing and entertainment.

The third is Chuiwan. Chuiwan is a kind of sport in ancient China. In the game, a series of holes are dug in the ground. Each player hit the ball into the hole with a rod. The winner would be the player hitting with fewer sticks and scoring more goals. Chuiwan and the Budaqiu are both horseless but hit with a rod. The difference lies in that Budaqiu is to hit the ball into the goal while

Chuiwan is to hit into the hole. In addition, Budaqiu also has a direct confrontation between the two teams, and Chuiwan requires its players to hit their own ball, in which there is no fight for the ball between the two teams. Wei Tai in the Song Dynasty wrote in his book *Hand Written Records on the Eastern Corridor* that when he was a child, he once heard his grandmother, Lady Chen, the wife of the official of Jiqing County, tell a story:

> "During the Southern Tang Dynasty, a county magistrate named Zhong Li expected her daughter to marry the son of a magistrate of the neighboring county surnamed Xu. When Zhong Li's daughter was about to get married, he bought a maid to take care of his daughter. One day, when the maid was sweeping the door of the house, she suddenly felt very sad and cried while looking at the low-lying place on the ground. Seeing this, Zhongli felt very strange and asked her why she cried. The maid wept: "When I was young, my father used to dig a trench here as a ball hole, and I played around. After so many years, the ball hole is still there." Surprised, Zhong asked, "Who is your father?" The maid replied, "My father was once the county magistrate here. After he died, there was none in my family, so I was left on the streets and sold as a servant girl." Zhong Li then called the maid-seller to ask about the situation and repeatedly checked, only to know if it were true."[187]

In this article, "trench (before the court) here as a ball hole" is the target of both sides in the game, similar to the goal. The Southern Tang Dynasty does not use the goal but instead the hole, which proves that Budaqiu is one step forward Chuiwan.[188] There are a few documents and pictures about Chuiwan. At present, there are following pictures that have been discovered: *A Picture of Children Playing Ball in the Tang Dynasty* (see Fig. 6-10), *A Picture of a Child Playing Chuiwan in the Song Dynasty* (see Fig. 6-11), *A Picture of Children Playing Chuiwan for Fun in the Song Dynasty* (see Fig. 6-12), *People in the Song Dynasty Playing Ball Games under Musaceae Trees* (see Fig. 6-13), *A Mural of Children Playing Chuiwan in the Yuan Dynasty* (see Fig. 6-14), *Portrait of a Lady* drawn by Du Jin in the Ming Dynasty (see Fig. 6-15)

Fig. 6-10 Part of the Pabric in Which a Children Were Striking Ball

and so on. At present, the most precious material for studying Chuiwan is the book of *Wan Jing*,[189] written by Yuan Ningzhi in 1282.[190] At the end of the Yuan and the beginning of the Ming Dynasty, Tao Zongyi compiled *Wan Jing* into his book series *Shuo Fu*.[191] According to *Wan Jing*, Chuiwan was formed in the Northern Song Dynasty and was still prosperous in the Yuan and Ming Dynasties. It is a game that all the officials and civilians are very fond of in the Northern Song, Yuan, and Ming Dynasties.

Origin and Evolution of Polo in China

Fig. 6-11 A Pottery Pillow with the Picture of a Child Playing Chuiwan

Fig. 6-12 A Pottery Pillow with the Picture of a Child Playing Chuiwan for Fun

Fig. 6-13 A Volume Page of *People Playing Ball Games under Musaceae Trees*

Fig. 6-14 A Mural of Children Playing Chuiwan in the Yuan Dynasty

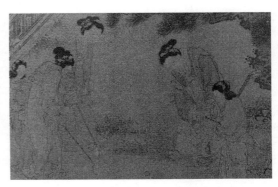

Fig. 6-15 Part of the Portrait of a Lady

6.4 Summary

Ancient polo is one of the most discussed subjects in the field of history and sports in China. After several generations and decades of research, great achievements have been made. However, due to the fact that different researchers have a different grasp of materials, different understanding of the same materials, or different research perspectives, there exist different views on the origin of polo and many other issues. For example, when discussing the origin of polo, there are three main viewpoints: "Persian theory," "Tubo theory," and "Native theory." Moreover, those who hold various origin theories generally believe that polo originated from these three places. This is the biggest problem in discussing the origin theories of polo. Based on the achievements of each theory, combined with the collection of relevant information, the author argues that the origin of polo is pluralistic; namely, polo does not originate from one place. Ancient China, Central Plains, Turk, Tubo, and Persia all had polo games. Polo of Tibet and Persia was not passed from Central Plains, nor was polo of Central Plains passed from Tubo or Persia. There were some differences in the form of polo in these places, which gradually became consistent through communication and integration in the Tang Dynasty.

This chapter also discussed the methods and rules of ancient polo, from the technical characteristics of polo, venue equipment, competition rules, and other aspects.[192] The author combed the knowledge of ancient polo as a whole. On this basis, it also studied the exchange and evolution of ancient polo and discussed the development of ancient polo culture among the northern nationalities at a deep level. And this content confirmed the related theories of this book to a certain extent. On the other hand, this chapter further clarified the important role and position of the ancient northern ethnic sports culture in the communication and integration of various ethnic groups, from the factors that affect the development of sports, and the cultural characteristics of sports, to the organizational system of northern national sports, which includes the training, management, and competition rules of polo, as well as the inheritance and integration of polo culture between the Central Plains and its surrounding ethnic groups as well the northern minorities.

NOTES

1. Xiang Da, *Examination of Polo in Chang'an, Chang'an in Tang Dynasty and Western Civilization*, 1st ed. (Hebei Education Press, November 2001), 79; Luo Xianglin, *Examination of Polo in Tang Dynasty, Research on the Cultural History of Tang Dynasty* (The Commercial Press, 1944).
2. Hao Gengsheng, *An Introduction to Chinese Sports* (The Commercial Press), 1926.
3. Yin Falu, "Introduction of Tibetan Polo into Chang'an in Tang Dynasty," *Historical Research*, no. 6 (1959): 41–43.
4. Lu Shuilin, *Polo in the Northern Areas of Pakistan*, translated by Wang Yao and Wang Qilong (Tibet People's Publishing House, 1983).
5. To better understand this, let us look at the background to *Jing Xing Ji*. Du Huan, the son of Du You (735–812), was captured in the army of Gao Xianzhi in 751, and returned from Guangzhou in 762, the first year of Emperor Daizong's reign. Du You wrote in the *Tung-tien* that his clan son Huan accompanied Gao Xianzhi, the governor of Zhenxi, on his western expedition and arrived at Xihai in the tenth year of Tianbao. At the beginning of the Baoying Period, he returned from Guangzhou on a merchant ship and wrote a book entitled *Jing Xing Ji*; [Tang]

Du You, *Tung-tien*, proofread by Wang Wenjin et al., vol. 191 (Zhonghua Book Company, 1988, reprinted in 1996.)
6. [Tang] Du You, *Tung-tien*, proofread by Wang Wenjin et al., vol. 192 (Zhonghua Book Company, 1988, reprinted in 1996), 1034.
7. [Qing] Dong Gao, *Du Huan · Jing Xing Ji* of *Tazi*, vol. 956 of *The Complete Collection of Tang Literature* (Zhonghua Book Company, 1983), 9924.
8. Diamir County includes Tangir, Gilas, Astor, and Bunji, known as a part of ancient Darada.
9. Lu Shuilin, *Polo in the Northern Areas of Pakistan*, translated by Wang Yao and Wang Qilong, serials 16, 1st ed. (Tibet People's Publishing House, January 2002), 209.
10. Ibid., 194–199.
11. Mahmud Kasgari, *Divan lgat at-Turk*, vol. 2 (The Ethnic Publishing House, February 2002), 22–23.
12. Lu Shuilin, *Polo in the Northern Areas of Pakistan*, translated by Wang Yao and Wang Qilong, serials 16, 1st ed. (Tibet People's Publishing House, January 2002), 196.
13. Ibid., 194–199.
14. [Jin] Ge Hong, *Miscellanies of the Western Capital*, proofread by [Ming] Cheng Yi (Zhonghua Book Company, January 1985), 14.
15. [Song] Shen Kuo, *Annotations to Mengxi Bitan*, proofread by Hu Daojing (Shanghai Ancient Books Publishing House, September 1987), 591–593.
16. [Song] Li Fang et al., *Musical Department · Youchang*, vol. 754 of *Imperial Digest of the Reign of Great Tranquility* (Zhonghua Publishing House, 1960 (photocopy)), 3348–3349.
17. [Han] Sima Qian, *Biography of Weiqing and Huo Qubing*, vol. 111 of *Historical Records* (Zhonghua Book Company, September 1959), 2939.
18. [Qing] Han Yu, vol. 388 of *The Complete Collection of Tang Poetry*, proofread by Peng Dingqiu et al. (Zhonghua Book Company, 1960), 3791.
19. [Qing] Cai Fu, vol. 75 of *The Complete Collection of Tang Poetry*, proofread by Peng Dingqiu et al. (Zhonghua Book Company, 1960), 817.
20. This view is mainly held by Cui Lequan, Li Chongsheng and Li Jinmei. Please refer Cui Lequan, *A Historical Review of the Origin and Development of Ancient Polo*; Li Chongshen and Han Zuosheng, "An Overview of Dunhuang Sports Relics," *Sports Culture Guide*, no. 1 (1992).
21. Tang Hao, "Polo in Ancient China · Polo from Eastern Han to Six Dynasties," in *Reference Materials of Chinese Sports History*, vol. 7 and 8 (People's Sports Press, Mar 1959), 64. Actually, "qiu (毬)" was explained in [Han] Xu Shen, *Shuowen Jiezi*, 1st ed. (Zhonghua Book Company, December 1963). That "qiu (毬)," is a ball for kicking, which was made of fur.
22. Tang Hao, "Polo in Ancient China," *Reference Materials of Chinese Sports History*, vol. 7 and 8 (Peoples Sports Press, Mar 1959), 71.
23. [Qing] Yan Kejun, *Lu Ji*, vol. 98 of *A Collection of Jin Literature* (The Commercial Press, 1999), 1035.
24. [Liang] Xiao Tong, *Cao Zijian*, vol. 27 of *Selected Works*, annotated by [Tang] Li Shan (Zhonghua Book Company, November 1977), 392–393.
25. Yang Mingzhao, *Continuation Notes on Baopuzi*, vol. 35, 1st ed. (Zhonghua Book Company, October 1997), 176–178.
26. [Qing] Yan Kejun, *Zuo Si*, vol. 74 of *A Collection of Jin Literature* (The Commercial Press, 1999), 774.
27. [Tang] Fang Xuanling et al., *Biography of Zhang Zai*, vol. 55 of *Book of the Jin Dynasty*, 1st ed. (Zhonghua Book Company, 1974), 1520.
28. [Tang] Ouyang Xun, *Ministry of Rites II*, vol. 40 of *A Categorized Collection of Literary Writing*, proofread by Wang Shaoying (Zhonghua Book Company, November 1965), 724.
29. This image was excavated from the No. 1 mural tomb of the Liao Dynasty in Pijianggou, Baoguotu Township, Aohan Banner, Inner Mongolia Autonomous Region.
30. Huang Cong, "Doubts about the Introduction of Chinese Central Plains Polo from Persia," *Journal of Chengdu Sport University*, no. 2 (2009): 1–5.
31. Huang Cong, "Feng Shi First-Hand Accounts · Playing Polo," *Journal of Chengdu Sport University*, no. 2 (2008): 42–45, 60.

32. Wang Yao, "A New Proof of Polo," in *A Collection of Tibetan Literature and History Studies* (China Tibetology Press, December 1994).
33. *Ministry of Foreign Affairs*, vol. 999 of *Ce Fu Yuan Gui* (Zhonghua Book Company, 1960), 11692.
34. Westerners sometimes refer to themselves as "Fan." [Northern Song] Wang Qinruo, *Ministry of Foreign Affairs · Requests*, vol. 999 of *Ce Fu Yuan Gui* (Zhonghua Book Company, 1960), 11722.
35. [Later Jin] Liu Xu et al., *Biography of Tubo*, vol. 196 (I) of *Old Book of the Tang Dynasty* (Zhonghua Book Company, May 1975), 5226. The Opera Troupe was originally an important venue for entertainment in the palace in Tang Dynasty, the records of which can be found in Zhou Weizhou, "A New Examination of the Opera Troupe in the Tang Dynasty," in *History Series of Northwest University*, series 1 (San Qin Publishing House, 1998).
36. [Qing] Shen Bingzhen, *Biography of Xirong II*, vol. 258 of *A Collection of New and Old Book of the Tang Dynasty*, published in the 10th year of Tongzhi reign.
37. [Song] Ouyang Xiu and Song Qi, *Western Regions II*, vol. 221 of *New Book of the Tang Dynasty*, 1st ed. (Zhonghua Book Company February 1975), 6245.
38. Persia sent ambassadors to China in the fifth century AD. [Song] Wang Pu, *Persia*, vol. 100 of *Tang Hui Yao*, 1st ed. (Shanghai Ancient Books Publishing House, 1991), 1734; [Britain] H. Yu'er, *Records of the Eastern Regions*, revised by [France] H. Cordier, translated by Zhang Xushan, 1st ed. (Yunnan People's Publishing House, May 2002), 65; [Later Jin] Liu Xu et al., *Biography of Persia*, vol. 148 of *Old Book of the Tang Dynasty*, 1st ed. (Zhonghua Book Company, 1975), 5312–5313.
39. [Tang] Du Huan, *Notes on Jing Xing Ji*, noted by Zhang Yichun, 1st ed. (Zhonghua Book Company, April 2000).
40. [Song] Sima Guang, *Chronicles of the Tang Dynasty*, vol. 232 of *Tzu-chih t'ung chien (A Comprehensive Mirror for Aid in Government)*, annotated by [Yuan] Hu Sansheng, 1st ed. (Zhonghua Book Company, June 1956), 7493.
41. [Tang] Du Huan, *Notes on Jing Xing Ji*, noted by Zhang Yichun, 1st ed. (Zhonghua Book Company, April 2000).
42. Kimberley, ed., *Polo* (R. R. Clark, Limited, Edinburgh, 1936), 17.
43. Zhang Guangda, "The Persians and Sogdians in Chang'an of Tang Dynasty: Their Activities in all Aspects," *Research on Tang Dynasty History*, no. 6: 3–16.
44. Wang Yao, "A New Proof of Polo," in *A Collection of Tibetan Literature and History Studies* (China Tibetology Press, December 1994).
45. [Tang] Du Huan, *Notes on Jing Xing Ji*, noted by Zhang Yichun, 1st ed. (Zhonghua Book Company, April 2000), 4.
46. Hard polo was also used by the end of the Tang Dynasty.
47. Zhang Hongnian, *History of Persian Literature*, 1st ed. (Peking University Press, May 1993), 44.
48. [Qing] *Zhang Jianfeng*, vol. 275 of *The Complete Collection of Tang Poetry*, proofread by Peng Dingqiu et al. (Zhonghua Book Company, 1960), 3117.
49. [Tang] Duan Chengshi, *Tricks*, vol. 5 of *Miscellaneous Notes of Youyang*, 1st ed. (Zhonghua Book Company, December 1980), 53.
50. *Buyi · Zhanghu · Watching Li Changshi Playing Polo*, vol. 883 of *The Complete Collection of Tang Poetry*, proofread by [Qing] Peng Dingqiu et al. (Zhonghua Book Company, 1960), 9985.
51. *Zhang Jianfeng*, vol. 275 of *The Complete Collection of Tang Poetry*, proofread by [Qing] Peng Dingqiu et al. (Zhonghua Book Company, 1960), 3117.
52. [Song] Wang Dang, *Buyi*, vol. 5 of *Annotations of Tangyulin*, proofread by Zhou Xunchu, 1st ed. (Zhonghua Book Company, July 1987), 472.
53. *Wangjian · Chaotian Ci*, vol. 310 of *The Complete Collection of Tang Poetry*, proofread by [Qing] Peng Dingqiu et al. (Zhonghua Book Company, 1960), 3424.
54. Li Jinmei, "An Analysis of Ancient Polo Equipment," in *Research on the History of Chinese Polo* (Gansu People's Publishing House, January 2005).
55. [Yuan] Tuitui et al., *Rites XXIV*, vol. 121 of *History of the Song Dynasty*, 1st ed. (Zhonghua Book Company, November 1977), 2841–2842.
56. [Yuan] Tuitui et al., *Rites VIII · Worshiping Heaven*, vol. 35 of *History of the Jin Dynasty*, 1st ed. (Zhonghua Book Company, July 1975), 826–827.
57. Li Jinmei, "An Analysis of Ancient Polo Equipment," in *Research on the History of Chinese Polo* (Gansu People's Publishing House, January 2005).

58. [Former Shu] Du Guangting, *The Collection of Legendary Stories*, quoted from "Qiu (Polo Play)," in *Kangxi Dictionary (Chen Collection II)*.
59. Yang Juyuan · *Watching Polo Playing*, vol. 3333 of *The Complete Collection of Tang Poetry*, proofread by [Qing] Peng Dingqiu et al. (Zhonghua Book Company, 1960), 3726.
60. [Song] Wang Dang, *Virtue*, vol. 5 of *Annotations to Tangyulin*, proofread by Zhou Xunchu, 1st ed. (Zhonghua Book Company, July 1987), 46.
61. [Song] Sima Guang, *Chronicles of the Tang Dynasty*, vol. 252 of *Tzu-chih t'ung chien (A Comprehensive Mirror for Aid in Government)*, annotated by [Yuan] Hu Sansheng (Zhonghua Book Company, June 1956), 8178.
62. [Northern Song] Wang Qinruo, *Ce Fu Yuan Gui*, vol. 495 (Zhonghua Book Company), 1960.
63. He'ning · *Palace Lyrics*, vol. 735 of *The Complete Collection of Tang Poetry*, proofread by [Qing] Peng Dingqiu et al. (Zhonghua Book Company, 1960), 8396.
64. Zhu Tianshu, *Gold and Silver Wares of Liao Dynasty* (Cultural Relics Publishing House, August 1998), 67.
65. [Song] Sima Guang, *Chronicles of the Tang Dynasty*, vol. 253 of *Tzu-chih t'ung chien (A Comprehensive Mirror for Aid in Government)*, annotated by [Yuan] Hu Sansheng (Zhonghua Book Company, June 1956), 8222.
66. *The Story of the Five Kingdoms* quote from *The Complete Collection of Si Ku Quan Shu* of *Wenyuan Pavilion*, vol. 464 (Shanghai Ancient Books Publishing House, 1987), 207.
67. [Song] Yuan Shu, *Xushi Cuan Wu*, vol. 39 of *Notes of Tong Jian* (Zhonghua Book Company, January 1964), 3696–3697.
68. [Qing] Jiang Tingxi et al., *Art Dictionary · Cuju*, bk. 48 of *Encyclopedia of Books Through Ages* (Zhonghua Book Company, June 1986), 59594.
69. [Tang] Li Zhao, *Supplement to the History of Tang Dynasty*, vol. 2; *Division · Novelists*, vol. 1035 of *The Complete Collection of Si Ku Quan Shu of Wenyuan Pavilion* (Shanghai Ancient Books Publishing House, 1987), 42.
70. [Ming] Mao Jin, *San Jia Gong Ci* (Taipei Xin Wenfeng Publishing Company), 1984.
71. [Tang] Mo Xiufu, *Records of the Natural Scenery and Folk Traditions of Guilin; The Complete Collection of Si Ku Quan Shu of Wenyuan Pavilion*, vol. 589 (Shanghai Ancient Books Publishing House, 1987), 12.
72. [Song] Ouyang Xiu, *New History of the Five Dynasties*, 1st ed. (Zhonghua Book Company, December 1974), 48.
73. [Later Jin] Liu Xu et al., *Biography of Lishen*, vol. 173 of *Old Book of the Tang History* (Zhonghua Book Company, May 1975), 4499.
74. [Song] Yuan Shu, *Huangchang Rebellion*, vol. 37 of *The Whole Story of Tongjian Chronicles* (Zhonghua Book Company, 1964, reprinted in November 1979), 3416.
75. [Tang] Han Yu, *Petition of Polo Play*, vol. 17 of *Works of Han Changli* (China Bookstore, June 1991), 251.
76. [Qing] Shen Bingzhen, *Biography of Liuwu*, vol. 212 of *A Collection of New and Old Book of the Tang Dynasty*, published in the 10th year of Tongzhi reign of Wu's Qinghe Hall.
77. [Song] Ouyang Xiu and Song Qi, *Biography of Li Baochen*, vol. 211 of *New Book of the Tang Dynasty*, 1st ed. (Zhonghua Book Company, February 1975), 5945–5946.
78. [Song] Sima Guang, *Chronicles of the Tang Dynasty*, vol. 218 of *Tzu-chih t'ung chien (A Comprehensive Mirror for Aid in Government)*, annotated by [Yuan] Hu Sansheng (Zhonghua Book Company, June 1956), 6989.
79. [Tang] Duan Chengshi, *Tricks*, vol. 5 of *Miscellaneous Notes of Youyang*, 1st ed. (Zhonghua Book Company, December 1980), 53.
80. [Chao] Zheng Linzhi, *Biography of Yin Guan*, vol. 96 of *History of Koryo* (Kuijangge, Seoul University, Korea, 1957), 12.
81. [Chao] Zheng Linzhi, *History of Koryo*, vol. 49 (Seoul University, Korea, 1957).
82. [Chao] Zheng Linzhi, *Family of Emperor Yizong*, vol. 17 of *History of Koryo* (Kuijangge, Seoul University, Korea, 1957).
83. [Chao] Zheng Linzhi, *Family of King Zhonglie*, vol. 29 of *History of Koryo* (Kuijangge, Seoul University, Korea, 1957).
84. [Chao] Zheng Linzhi, *Biography of Cui Yi*, vol. 129 of *History of Koryo* (Kuijangge, Seoul University, Korea, 1957).
85. [Chao] Zheng Linzhi, *Biography of Xinwu*, vol. 136 of *History of Koryo* (Kuijangge, Seoul University, Korea, 1957).
86. [Chao] Zheng Linzhi, *Biography of Zhongxian*, vol. 129 of *History of Koryo* (Kuijangge, Seoul University, Korea, 1957).

87. [Chao] Zheng Linzhi, *Family of King Zhonglie*, vol. 28 of *History of Koryo* (Kuijangge, Seoul University, Korea, 1957).
88. [Chao] Zheng Linzhi, *Family of Emperor Xianzong*, vol. 5 of *History of Koryo* (Kuijangge, Seoul University, Korea, 1957).
89. [Yuan] Tuitui et al., *Biography of Xiao Xiaozhong*, vol. 81 of *History of the Liao Dynasty*, 1st ed. (Zhonghua Book Company, October 1974), 1285.
90. [Yuan] Tuitui et al., *History of the Liao Dynasty*, vol. 6 and 10, 1st ed. (Zhonghua Book Company, October 1974), 71, 111.
91. Kong Pingzhong, "Tan Yuan," in *Historical Records of the Liao Dynasty*, edited by Li Youtang, vol. 29 (Zhonghua Book Company, 1983), 561.
92. [Song] Li Tao, *Emperor Renzong*, vol. 125 of *Continuation of the Extended Version of Tzu-chih t'ung chien (A Comprehensive Mirror for Aid in Government)* (Zhonghua Book Company, November 1985), 2940.
93. [Yuan] Tuitui et al., *Chronicles of Emperor Tiaozuo VI*, vol. 30 of *History of the Liao Dynasty*, 1st ed. (Zhonghua Book Company, October 1974), 354.
94. [Yuan] Tuitui et al., *Biography of Sa Ba*, vol. 87 of *History of the Liao Dynasty*, 1st ed. (Zhonghua Book Company, October 1974), 1333.
95. [Yuan] Tuitui et al., *Biography of Xiaole Yinnu*, vol. 96 of *History of the Liao Dynasty*, 1st ed. (Zhonghua Book Company, October 1974), 1402.
96. [Yuan] Tuitui et al., *Biography of Yelü Tabuye*, vol. 111 of *History of the Liao Dynasty*, 1st ed. (Zhonghua Book Company, October 1974), 1494.
97. [Yuan] Tuitui et al., *Biography of Gu Die*, vol. 114 of *History of the Liao Dynasty*, 1st ed. (Zhonghua Book Company, October 1974), 1515.
98. [Yuan] Tuitui et al., *Chronicles of Emperor Shengzong*, vol. 12 of *History of the Liao Dynasty*, 1st ed. (Zhonghua Book Company, October 1974), 134–135.
99. [Yuan] Tuitui et al., *Geographia VI · Nanjing Road*, vol. 40 of *History of the Liao Dynasty*, 1st ed. (Zhonghua Book Company, October 1974), 494.
100. Xu Qinjiu, "On Chen Jizhi's Scrolls of Bian Qiao Alliance," *Art Magazine*, no. 12 (1955): 14.
101. "Another Discovery of Mural Tombs of Qidan Family in the Liao Dynasty at Xuanhua," *China Cultural Relics Daily*, September 11, 1998.
102. Museum of Aohan Banner, Chifeng City, Inner Mongolia, "Liao Tombs No. 1 and No. 2 at Pidjianggou, Aohan Banner, Inner Mongolia," *Cultural Relics*, no. 9 (1998): 47–52, 63.
103. [Yuan] Tuitui et al., *Chronicles IV*, vol. 73 of *History of the Jin Dynasty*, 1st ed. (Zhonghua Book Company, July 1975), 543.
104. [Yuan] Tuitui et al., *Biography of Andahai*, vol. 73 of *History of the Jin Dynasty*, 1st ed. (Zhonghua Book Company, July 1975), 1683.
105. [Song] Yuwen Maozhao, *Annotations to National Records of the Great Jin Dynasty*, proofread by Cui Wenyin (Zhonghua Book Company, 1986), 27.
106. [Yuan] Tuitui et al., *Chronicles of Hailing King*, vol. 5 of *History of the Jin Dynasty*, 1st ed. (Zhonghua Book Company, July 1975), 102.
107. [Yuan] Tuitui et al., *Chronicles of Emperor Shizong II*, vol. 8 of *History of the Jin Dynasty*, 1st ed. (Zhonghua Book Company, July 1975), 188.
108. [Yuan] Tuitui et al., *Chronicles of Emperor Zhangzong I*, vol. 9 of *History of the Jin Dynasty*, 1st ed. (Zhonghua Book Company, July 1975), 214.
109. Ibid.
110. [Yuan] Tuitui et al., *Chronicles of Emperor Shizong I*, vol. 6 of *History of the Jin Dynasty*, 1st ed. (Zhonghua Book Company, July 1975), 131.
111. [Yuan] Tuitui et al., *Chronicles of Emperor Xuanzong II*, vol. 16 of *History of the Jin Dynasty*, 1st ed. (Zhonghua Book Company, July 1975), 352.
112. [Yuan] Tuitui et al., *Biography of Eliye*, vol. 120 of *History of the Jin Dynasty*, 1st ed. (Zhonghua Book Company, July 1975), 2625.
113. [Yuan] Tuitui et al., *Biography of Ma Guizhong*, vol. 131 of *History of the Jin Dynasty*, 1st ed. (Zhonghua Book Company, July 1975), 2813–2814.

114. [Song] Yuwen Maozhao, *Chronicles of Emperor Taizong Wenlie*, vol. 5 of *Annotations to National Records of the Great Jin Dynasty*, proofread by Cui Wenyin, 1st ed. (Zhonghua Book Company, July 1986), 75.
115. [Yuan] Tuitui et al., *Biography of Atuhan*, vol. 81 of *History of the Jin Dynasty*, 1st ed. (Zhonghua Book Company, July 1975), 1817.
116. [Yuan] Tuitui et al., *Biography of Empress Zhaosheng*, vol. 64 of *History of the Jin Dynasty*, 1st ed. (Zhonghua Book Company, July 1975), 1526.
117. [Yuan] Tuitui et al., *Biography of Gao Huaizhen*, vol. 129 of *History of the Jin Dynasty*, 1st ed. (Zhonghua Book Company, July 1975), 2789.
118. [Yuan] Tuitui et al., *Biography of Zongben*, vol. 76 of *History of the Jin Dynasty*, 1st ed. (Zhonghua Book Company, July 1975), 1732.
119. [Yuan] Tuitui et al., *Chronicles of Emperor Shizong I*, vol. 6 of *History of the Jin Dynasty*, 1st ed. (Zhonghua Book Company, July 1975).
120. [Yuan] Tuitui et al., *Biography of Liu Wei*, vol. 95 of *History of the Jin Dynasty*, 1st ed. (Zhonghua Book Company, July 1975), 2111–2112.
121. [Yuan] Tuitui et al., *Biography of Mouyan*, vol. 72 of *History of the Jin Dynasty*, 1st ed. (Zhonghua Book Company, July 1975), 1656.
122. [Yuan] Tuitui et al., *Biography of Tushan Zhen*, vol. 132 of *History of the Jin Dynasty*, 1st ed. (Zhonghua Book Company, July 1975), 2826–2827.
123. [Yuan] Tuitui et al., *Chronicles of Emperor Zhangzong VI*, vol. 12 of *History of the Jin Dynasty*, 1st ed. (Zhonghua Book Company, July 1975), 282.
124. [Yuan] Tuitui et al., *Chronicles of Emperor Xuanzong II*, vol. 15 of *History of the Jin Dynasty*, 1st ed. (Zhonghua Book Company, July 1975), 346.
125. [Song] Yuwen Maozhao, *Chronicles of Emperor Taizong Wenlie I*, vol. 3 of *Annotations to National Records of the Great Jin Dynasty*, proofread by Cui Wenyin (Zhonghua Book Company, July 1986), 40.
126. [Yuan] Tuitui et al., *Musical Records · Imperial Music Workshop*, vol. 142 of *History of the Song Dynasty*, 1st ed. (Zhonghua Book Company, November 1977), 3350.
127. [Yuan] Tuitui et al., *Chronicles of Emperor Shizong I*, vol. 6 of *History of the Jin Dynasty*, 1st ed. (Zhonghua Book Company, July 1975), 134.
128. [Yuan] Tuitui et al., *Biography of Guo Yongan*, vol. 6 of *History of the Jin Dynasty*, 1st ed. (Zhonghua Book Company, July 1975), 2564.
129. [Yuan] Tuitui et al., *Chronicles of Official Costume*, vol. 43 of *History of the Jin Dynasty*, 1st ed. (Zhonghua Book Company, July 1975), 974.
130. Tao Fuhai and Xie Xigong, "A Brief Report on the Cleaning Up of Jinyuan Tomb in Quli Village, Xiangfen County, Shanxi Province," *Culture Relics*, no. 12 (1986): 47–52.
131. [Qing] Lu Changchun et al., "Palace Poems of Liao, Jin, and Yuan Dynasties," in *Collection of Parallel Prose of Menghuating* (Cultural Relics Publishing House, 1992).
132. Ibid.
133. [Yuan] Guan Hanqing, "Anonymous · Musical Dance and Willow-Shooting (4th scene)," in *A Collection of Yuan Poetic Drama* (Times Literature and Art Publishing House, 2000).
134. [Qing] Gu Sili, "Mr. Tieya Yang Weizhen · Nine Music Ballads in the Army," in *Selected Poems of the Yuan Dynasty*, 1st ed. (Zhonghua Book Company, 1987).
135. [Qing] Gu Sili, "Sadula · Jungle Trip," in *Selected Poems of Yuan Dynasty I*, 1st ed. (Zhonghua Book Company), 1987.
136. [Qing] Gu Sili, "Dailiang from Jiuling Mountain · Inscription on Picture of Playing Polo," in *Selected Poems of the Yuan Dynasty II*, 1st ed. (Zhonghua Book Company, 1987).
137. He Shaomin, *Biography of Dadalil*, vol. 129 of *New History of the Yuan Dynasty* (China Bookstore, August 1988), 563.
138. [Song] Ouyang Xiu and Song Qi, *Biography of Li Zhengji*, vol. 213 of *New Book of the Tang Dynasty*, 1st ed. (Zhonghua Book Company, February 1975), 5989–5900.
139. Yang Hong, "Cavalry and Heavily-Armored Cavalry with Armored Horses," in *A Collection of Ancient Chinese Weapons (Revised)* (Cultural Relics Publishing House, 1985).

140. Yang Hong, "One of the Research on Military Equipment in Dunhuang Mogao Grottoes Murals: Armed and Armor," in *Proceedings of the National Dunhuang Symposium 1983 · Cave Art I* (Gansu People's Publishing House, 1985); Wang Jian, "Cavalry in the Early Tang Dynasty," in *Wang Jian's Manuscript on the History of Sui and Tang Dynasties* (China Social Science Press, 1981).
141. [Song] Ouyang Xiu, Song Qi, *Military Records*, vol. 50 of *New Book of the Tang Dynasty*, 1st ed. (Zhonghua Book Company, February 1975), 1337.
142. Ibid., 1328.
143. [Later Jin] Liu Xu et al., *Biography of Liuwu*, vol. 161 of *Old Book of the Tang History*, 1st ed. (Zhonghua Book Company, February 1975), 5415.
144. [Song] Ouyang Xiu, Song Qi, *Biography of Tubo*, vol. 216 of *New Book of the Tang Dynasty*, 1st ed. (Zhonghua Book Company, February 1975), 6108.
145. [Yuan] Tuitui et al., *Chronicles of Emperor Taizu*, vol. 2 of *History of the Jin Dynasty*, 1st ed. (Zhonghua Book Company, July 1975), 27.
146. [Yuan] Tuitui et al., *Chronicles of Emperor Shizong I*, vol. 6 of *History of the Jin Dynasty*, 1st ed. (Zhonghua Book Company, July 1975), 131.
147. [Yuan] Tuitui et al., *Rites VIII*, vol. 35 of *History of the Jin Dynasty*, 1st ed. (Zhonghua Book Company, July 1975), 826.
148. [Yuan] Tuitui et al., *Chronicles of Emperor Muzong I*, vol. 6 of *History of the Liao Dynasty*, 1st ed. (Zhonghua Book Company, October 1974), 971.
149. [Yuan] Tuitui et al., *Biography of Wulin Dahui*, vol. 120 of *History of the Jin Dynasty*, 1st ed. (Zhonghua Book Company, July 1975), 2620.
150. [Yuan] Tuitui et al., *Biography of Tushan Zhen*, vol. 132 of *History of the Jin Dynasty*, 1st ed. (Zhonghua Book Company, July 1975), 2827.
151. [Yuan] Tuitui et al., *Biography of Wanyan Shoudao*, vol. 88 of *History of the Jin Dynasty*, 1st ed. (Zhonghua Book Company, July 1975), 1958.
152. [Yuan] Tuitui et al., *Biography of Ma Guizhong*, vol. 131 of *History of the Jin Dynasty*, 1st ed. (Zhonghua Book Company, July 1975), 2813–2814.
153. [Qing] Gu Sili, *Fu Ruojin · Jiju of Jin People*, vol. 5 of *Selected Poems of the Yuan Dynasty II*, 1st ed. (Zhonghua Book Company, 1987), 1185.
154. Ibid.
155. [Yuan] Xiong Mengxiang, *Analysis of Xi Jin Zhi* (Beijing Ancient Books Publishing House, 1983), 203–204. In "Emperor Shizu X" from Volume 13 of the *History of the Yuan Dynasty*, in the June of 21th year of the Yuan Dynasty (1284), Emperor Shizu, Kublai Khan granted his son Tuohuan as the King of Zhennan, awarded him a seal decorated with gold and silver. He arranged him to station at Erhou.
156. Ren Bantang, *A Comprehensive Collection of Dunhuang Songs*, vol. 2 (Shanghai Ancient Books Publishing House, 1987), 727.
157. Ji Yuanzhi, "On Playing Polo in the Tang Dynasty: Research of Zhang Yi's Travel Map (III)," *Dunhuang Research*, no. 2 (1993): 26–36.
158. Ren Bantang, *A Comprehensive Collection of Dunhuang Songs*, vol. 2 (Shanghai Ancient Books Publishing House, 1987), 720.
159. Wang Chongmin, *Collected Works of Dunhuang Bianwen* (People's Literature Publishing House, 1984), 63.
160. Ren Bantang, *A Comprehensive Collection of Dunhuang Songs*, vol. 3 (Shanghai Ancient Books Publishing House, 1987), 812.
161. Tang Geng'ou and Lu Hongji, *Interpretation and Records of Dunhuang Social and Economic Documents* (Catalogs and Documentations Publishing House, 1990), 293.
162. Huang Zheng, "A Textual Research on the Original Dunhuang Manuscripts," *Jiuzhou Academic Journal*, no. 4 (1993): 60; Dunhuang Literature, p. 3702.
163. Dunhuang Literature, p. 1.
164. Dunhuang Literature, p. 2568.
165. Wang Chongmin, *Collected Works of Dunhuang Bianwen* (People's Literature Publishing House, 1984), 125; Dunhuang Literature, p. 3451.

166. Mahmud Kasgari, *Divan lgat at-Turk*, translated by Xiao Zhongyi et al. (The Ethnic Publishing House, February 2002).
167. Ibulayin Mutiyi, "*Divan lgat at-Turk* and Its Related Issues," *Journal of Northwestern Ethnic Studies*, no. 2 (1996): 222.
168. Mahmud Kasgari, *Divan lgat at-Turk*, translated by Xiao Zhongyi et al., bk. 3 (The Ethnic Publishing House, February 2002), 439.
169. Mahmud Kasgari, *Divan lgat at-Turk*, translated by Xiao Zhongyi et al., bk. 1 (The Ethnic Publishing House, February 2002), 6.
170. Ibid., 202.
171. Ibid., 242.
172. Ibid., 262.
173. Ibid., 384.
174. Ibid., 398.
175. Ibid., 424.
176. Mahmud Kasgari, *Divan lgat at-Turk*, translated by Xiao Zhongyi et al., bk. 2 (The Ethnic Publishing House, February 2002), 22–23.
177. Yousufu · Hasi · Hajifu, Chapter 33 of "The Wise Discussing Who are to Be Sent as Envoys," in *Happiness and Wisdom*, translated by Hao Guanzhong, Zhang Hongchao, and Liu Bin, 2nd ed. (Nationalities Publishing House, April 2004), 343.
178. Montesquieu, Article 95 of *The Spirit of Laws*, bk. of *Yanfu Collections*, translated by Yan Fu (Zhonghua Book Company), 1986.
179. Yuan He and Yuan Xuejun, "On the Rise and Fall of Polo in Jin and Qing Dynasties," in *Study on the History of Polo in China* (Gansu People's Publishing House, February 2002), 200–201.
180. [Song] Wang Dang, *Supplement*, vol. 5 of *Annotations to Tangyulin*, proofread by Zhou Xunchu, 1st ed. (Zhonghua Book Company, July 1987), 470.
181. [Qing] Shen Bingzhen, *Records of Guo Yinyi*, vol. 168 of *A Collection of New and Old Books of the Tang Dynasty*, published in the 10th year of Tongzhi reign of Wu's Qing He Tang.
182. Tan Chanxue, "*Tablet Iinscription, Biography and Funeral Oration in Dunhuang Literature*." Edited by Zaiyan Tingliang," in *Introduction to Dunhuang Literature*, edited by Yan Tingliang (Gansu People's Publishing House), 1993.
183. [Song] Meng Yuanlao, *Notes on Reminiscences of the Eastern Capital*, annotated by Deng Zhicheng, vol. 7 (Zhonghua Book Company, 1982, reprinted in 2004).
184. [Song] Wang Dang, *Supplement*, vol. 7 of *Annotations to Tangyulin*, proofread by Zhou Xunchu, 1st ed. (Zhonghua Book Company, July 1987), 670.
185. *National Sports Commission: Reference Materials of Chinese Sports History* (People's Sports Press, December 1957), 12.
186. [Yuan] Tuitui et al., *Rites*, vol. 121 of *History of the Song Dynasty* (Zhonghua Book Company, November 1977), 2842.
187. [Song] Wei Tai, *Hand Written Records on the Eastern Corridor*, vol. 12, 1st ed. (Zhonghua Book Company, October 1983), 138.
188. Liu Bingguo and Zhang Shengping, *Chuiwan, the Golf in Ancient China*, 1st ed. (Shanghai Ancient Books Publishing House, December 2005), 7.
189. *Integrated Preliminary Edition of Series of Books*, vol. 54 (Taipei Xin Wen Feng Publishing Company).
190. Liu Bingguo and Zhang Shengping, Chuiwan, *the Golf in Ancient China*, 1st ed. (Shanghai Ancient Books Publishing House, December 2005), 140.
191. [Qing] Tao Zongyi, *Three Kinds of Shuo Fu*, vol. 110, 1st ed. (Shanghai Ancient Books Publishing House, October 1988).
192. In the process of argumentation, the author referred to the previous research results from, such as Xiang Da, Luo Xianglin, Yin Falu, Wang Yao, Lin Sitong, Wang Saishi, Li Chongshen, Cui Lequan, Li Jinmei, etc. In the article, the author tried to note the source of quotations as clear as possible. Any omission or negligence is expected to be excused.

Acknowledgments

Since the 18th national congress of CPC, President Xi Jinping has issued a series of important instructions on the development of sports undertakings, emphasizing that a strong sports country and a healthy China are the main components of comprehensively building a socialist modern country, and an inevitable requirement for realizing the Chinese Dream of the great rejuvenation of the Chinese nation. Against this backdrop, the newly revised *Sports Law of the People's Republic of China* in 2022 highlighted the importance of actively promoting traditional ethnic sports, due to the fact that only when it is national it is the world. *Textual Research on the National Sports in Northern China* is a translated copy of the Chinese academic book of the same title written by Professor Huang Cong of Shaanxi Normal University, China, which is noted exclusively as the most comprehensive study about the sports of northern ethnic groups in ancient China. In the monograph, the development of ancient northern ethnic sports is divided into four main stages, i.e., origin and sprout, initial development, all-round development, and rise and decline. Besides, wrestling and polo are particularly selected as the cases to introduce northern national sports in terms of origin and evolution. Thus, spreading this ancient northern sports culture to the world and bringing the world closer to access to this heritage has become a must of culture transmission.

First of all, I would like to extend my deepest gratitude to my university, Shaanxi Normal University (SNNU), which granted me the rare opportunity and favorable policy to be involved in this translation project. Without the policy and financial support from my School of International Studies, this volume could never have taken this present shape. I am also grateful to Professor Liu Quanguo, the dean of the School of International Studies at SNNU, who has inspired me with his boundless wisdom and enlightening guidance along the way. Besides, my thanks also go to other leaders and professors in my school, such as Professor Lv Minhong, Professor Cao Ting, Professor Bai Jingyu, Professor Xue Jinqiang, Mr. Dong Zengyun, and Ms. Lu Yan. Without their support and encouragement, this volume could not have been accomplished.

This book is also dedicated to Professor Huang Cong, the author of this academic monograph, who offered me the golden opportunity to work with him and translate this masterpiece of his. I am inexpressibly grateful for his longstanding trust and confidence. With his visionary input and personal instruction, I could have succeeded in completing this translation. Professor Huang has much perseverance and a high level of knowledge, and he has expounded to me some of the literature and events in the book when I encounter some difficulties. This profound study, *Textual*

Research on the National Sports in Northern China, is the crystallization of his hard work and proof of his academic stature. And I have benefited immensely from his infinite learning and rigorous academic attitude, whose help was unmatched.

Truly this book could not have been possible without all the work of many who have contributed greatly to the accomplishment of this volume. Professor Deng Qiufeng has spent quite a considerable time collecting the materials, consulting the literature, and translating the Introduction and Chapter 1; Dr. Ding Liming has conducted the meticulous translation for Chapter 2, and his accurate understanding and clear interpretation have added color to this book; Professor Wang Xinjian (Chapter 3) impressed me most with his relentless efforts and exquisite expertise, who have brought forward a great number of insightful suggestions in the process of translation. Ms. Li Chunfeng has also devoted herself to the precise and authentic translation of some sections of Chapter 6 in terms of sports cultural communication. All their initial translations have paved the way for the further stage of a more specific revision and organization. These above people have not only been instrumental in introducing and promoting the sports culture, but have for such long time they have worked tirelessly for a long time to get the work done.

Above all, I owe millions of thanks to all my graduate students in the last three years for their all-out contribution, who are He Qing, Rong Linfang, Wang Chenjing, He Qianni, Guo Manman, Wang Lin, Yang Fan, He Xianglin, Qin Tong, Wang Yixiang, Zhang Kexin, Li Peipei, Zhao Yuqi, Han Mingli, Hu Jilan, Cui Mengxue, Ren Xinjing, and Li Yihong. They either helped me in looking up the information and collating the literature or collecting the glossary and proofreading the script all the way through the translation. My appreciation goes to them for their hard work and unremitting efforts.

For this book, I also cannot thank enough the following people: Professor Wang Qilong, the President of Xi'an International Studies University (XISU), Professor Wang Shunyu, the dean of Graduate School of XISU, Professor Hu Zongfeng, the president of Shaanxi Translators Association, Professor Yuan Xiaolu, the dean of School of Translation Studies and School of English Language and Literature of Xi'an Fanyi University, Professor Cao Ruonan, the dean of School of Foreign Languages of Northwest University, Professor Li Qingming, the ex-dean of School of Foreign Studies of Shaanxi University of Technology, Professor Li Wenmin, the associate dean of School of Arts and Sciences of SUST and Professor Zhao Yihui, the associate dean of School of Translation Studies. I am immensely thankful to them for their consistent encouragement and brilliant ideas.

I owe thanks beyond measure to my nuclear family, i.e., my husband and daughter, who contributed to this volume in every way and whose all-inclusive love, support, advice, and encouragement inspire and sustain me. A big thank you also goes to my parents for their unconditional love and selfless backing. I dedicated this book to them with all my heart and soul. The harmonious relations in my family have guaranteed that the whole translation and publication moved in a gratifying direction.

Finally, I wish to thank ROYAL COLLINS for its efforts in publishing this book, and especially Ms. Zhang Yanan, who has dedicated much effort to the various stages of the publication. Her timely communication and effective responses have quickened the pace of this project and promoted the final success of this volume.

Bibliography

[Qing] A, Gui, et al. *The Strategy for the Founding of the Qing Dynasty*. Wenhai Publishing House, 1966.
"Another Discovery of Mural Tombs of Qidan Family in Liao Dynasty in Xuanhua." *China Cultural Relics Daily*, 1998.
Aohan Cultural Center. "Liao Tomb of Baitazi in Aohan Banner." *Archaeology*, 1978.
Bai, Shouyi, ed. *General Chinese History*. Shanghai People's Publishing House, 1995.
Bamboo Slips Sorting Group of Yinqueshan Han Tombs. *Bamboo Slips from Yinqueshan Han Tombs*. Cultural Relics Publishing House, 1985.
[Han] Ban, Gu. *Book of the Former Han Dynasty*. Zhonghua Book Company, 1962.
[Sweden] Bergman. *Archaeology in Xinjiang*. Translated by Wang Anhong. Xinjiang People's Publishing House, 1997.
[Song] Cai, Xiang. *Duan Ming Collection*. Vol. 373 of *Complete Collection of the Si Ku Quan Shu of the Imperial Palace*. World Book Company, 1986.
Cao, Erqin. "Distribution of Houses in Chang'an, Tang Dynasty." *Chinese Historical Geography*, 1999.
[Qing] Cao Yin, *Collection of Jian Pavillion · Three Poems on Ice Ball*, vol. 2 (Shanghai Ancient Books Publishing House. 1978), 432.
Cen, Zhongmian. *Collected History of the Turks*. Zhonghua Book Company, 1958.
[France] Chavanne. *Historical Materials of Western Turks*. Translated by Feng Chengjun. Zhonghua Book Company, 2004.
Chen, Bingying. *Research on Xixia Cultural Relics*. Ningxia People's Publishing House, 1985.
Chen, Gaohua, and Xu Jijun, eds. *General History of Chinese Customs*. Shanghai Literature and Art Publishing House, 2001.
[Qing] Chen, Kangqi. *Records of Lang Qian II*. Zhonghua Book Company, 1984.
[Qing] Chen, Li. *Notes on Bai Hu Tong*. Proofread by Wu Zeyu. Zhonghua Book Company, 1994.
[Jin] Chen, Shou. *The History of the Three Kingdoms*. Zhonghua Book Company, 1959.
Chen, Shu, ed. *Collection of Liao and Jin History*. Vol. 1. Shanghai Ancient Books Publishing House, 1987.
Chen, Shu, ed. *Collection of Liao and Jin History*. Vol. 3. Bibliography and Literature Publishing House, 1987.
Chen, Yuan. *An Interpretation of Annotations and Supplements to Yuan Dian Zhang*. China Bookstore, 1980.
Chen, Zhaofu. *Ancient Chinese Minority Art*. People's Fine Arts Publishing House, 1991.

China Sports Museum, and Culture and History Committee of the State Sports Commission. *Records of Traditional Chinese Sports*. Guangxi Nationalities Press, 1990.

[Spain] Claviejo, Ro Gonzalez. *Timur Devrinde Kadistan Semer-Kand's SeyahatRuy*. Translated by Yang Zhaojun. The Commercial Press, 1944.

[Sweden] Constantin Mouradgea d'Ohsson. *Histoire des Mongols*. Translated by Feng Chengjun. Zhonghua Book Company, 1962.

Cui, Lequan. *Catalogue of Chinese Ancient Sports Relics*. Zhonghua Book Company, 2000.

Cui, Lequan. "A Historical Review of the Origin and Development of Ancient Polo," in *Research on the History of Chinese Polo*. Gansu People's Publishing House, 2002.

Cultural Relics Team of Hubei Provincial Bureau of Culture. "Important Cultural Relics Unearthed from Three Chu Tombs in Jiangling, Hubei Province." *Cultural Relics*, no. 5 (1966).

Da Jin Diao Fa Lu. Vol. 408 of *The Complete Collection of Si Ku Quan Shu of Wenyuan Pavilion*. Shanghai Ancient Books Publishing House, 1987.

[Qing] Dai, Xizhang. *Records of Xixia*. Proofread by Luo Maokun. Ningxia People's Publishing House, 1998.

[Song] Diao, Luzi. *Annotations to the Notes of Jiao Li*. Proofread and annotated by Weng Shixun. People's Sports Publishing House, 1990.

Ding, Linghui. *Tibetan Traditional Health Preserving Sports Culture*. Tibet People's Publishing House, 2001.

Ding, Qian. Grand Ceremony of the Yuan Dynasty. *Zhejiang Library Journal*, 1915.

[Qing] Dong Gao. *The Complete Collection of Tang Literature*. Zhonghua Book Company, 1983.

Dong, Meikan. *A Brief History of Chinese Drama*. The Commercial Press, 1950.

Dong, Wanlun. *Outline of Northeast History*. Heilongjiang People's Publishing House, 1987.

[Tang] Du, Huan. *Notes on Jing Xing Ji*. Annotated by Zhang Yichun. Zhonghua Book Company, 2000.

[Tang] Du, You. *Tung-tien*. Proofread by Wang Wenjin et al. Zhonghua Book Company, 1988.

[Tang] Duan, Chengshi. *Miscellaneous Notes of Youyang*. Zhonghua Book Company, 1980.

Encyclopedia of China. China Encyclopedia Press, 1986.

Excavation Team of Xi'an Tang City, Institute of Archaeology, Chinese Academy of Sciences. "A Brief Account of the Archaeology of Chang'an City in the Tang Dynasty." *Archaeology*, no. 11 (1964).

[Tang] Fan, Chuo. *Annotations to Manshu*. Proofread and annotated by Xiang Da. Zhonghua Book Company, 1962.

[Song] Fan, Ye. *Book of the Later Han Dynasty*. Zhonghua Book Company, 1965.

[Song] Fan, Zhongyan. *A Collection of Fan Wenzheng's Essays*. A block printed ed. in the 10th year of Daoguang reign of the Qing Dynasty.

Fang, Xiebang, and Li Finland. "Connotation and Characteristics of Sports Culture in Qinghai Section of the South Silk Road." *Journal of Qinghai Normal University* (Social Science Edition), no. 2 (1999).

[Tang] Fang, Xuanling, et al. *Book of the Jin Dynasty*. Zhonghua Book Company, 1974.

[Tang] Feng, Yan. *Annotations to the Records of Feng's Hearing and Seeing*. Proofread and annotated by Zhao Zhenxin. Zhonghua Book Company, 2005.

Feng, Yongqian, and Deng Baoxue. "Important Findings of Cultural Relics Census in Jianchang County." *Liaoning Cultural Relics*, no. 1 (1980).

Feng, Yongqian. "Main Archaeological Discoveries of Liao Dynasty Since the Founding of the People's Republic of China." In *Collection of Liao and Jin History*. Vol. 1. Shanghai Ancient Books Publishing House, 1987.

[German] Feuerbach, Ludwig. *Selected Works of Feuerbach Philosophy*. Translated by Rong Zhenhua. The Commercial Press, 1984.

[Persia] Fildorsi. *Anthology of Kings*. Translated by Zhang Hongnian. People's Literature Publishing House, 1991.

Fu, Lehuan. *A Study of Liao History*. Zhonghua Book Company, 1984.

Fu, Rongga, et al. *A Chronicle of Wuzhumuqin Customs*. Inner Mongolia People's Publishing House, 1992.

[Qing] Fucha, Dunchong. *Notes on the Age of Yanjing*. Beijing Ancient Books Publishing House, 1981.

Gai, Shanlin. *Yinshan Rock Paintings*. Cultural Relics Publishing House, 1988.

Gan, Zhigeng, and Sun Xiuren. *Outline of the Ancient Ethnic History of Heilongjiang*. Heilongjiang People's Publishing House, 1987.

Gansu Institute of Cultural Relics and Archaeology. "Ten Years of Cultural Relics and Archaeology in Gansu Province," in *Ten Years of Cultural Relics and Archaeology*. Cultural Relics Publishing House, 1991.

Gansu Provincial Museum. "Ancient Rock Paintings in Black Mountain, Jiayuguan, Gansu Province." *Archaeology*, no. 4 (1990).

[Song] Gao, Cheng. *Shi Wu Ji Yuan*. Zhonghua Book Company, 1989.

[Qing] Gao Zongchi *All-Encompassing Library.* Compiled by Wang Yunwu. The Commercial Press, 1935.

[Jin] Ge, Hong. *Miscellanies of the Western Capital*. Proofread by [Ming] Cheng Yi. Zhonghua Book Company, 1985.

A Grand View of the Unofficial History of the Qing Dynasty. Shanghai Bookstore, 1981.

Gu, Shiquan. *History of Chinese Sports*. Beijing Sport University Press, 2003.

[Qing] Gu, Sili. *Selected Poems of Yuan Dynasty*. Zhonghua Book Company, 1987.

[Yuan] Guan, Hanqing, et al. *A Collection of Yuan Poetic Drama*. Times Literature and Art Publishing House, 2000.

Hajifu, Hasi, Yousufu. *Happiness and Wisdom*. Translated by Hao Guanzhong, Zhang Hongchao, and Liu Bin. The Ethnic Publishing House, 2004.

Han, Shiming. *A Glimpse of Life in Liao and Jin Dynasties*. Shenyang Press, 2002.

Han, Xiang. "The Settlement and Sinicization of Central Asian people in Chang'an in Tang Dynasty." *Ethnic Studies*, no. 3 (2000).

Han, Xiang. "The Central Asians Living in Chang'an in a Compact Community during the Tang Dynasty and Their being Assimilated by the Han People." *Ethno-National Studies*, no. 3 (2000).

[Tang] Han, Yu. *Works of Han Changli*. China Bookstore, 1991.

Hao, Gengsheng. *An Introduction to Chinese Sports*. The Commercial Press, 1926.

[Qing] He, Changling. *A Collection of Essays on National Affairs during the Ming Dynasty*. Wen Hai Publishing House, 1966.

He, Jianzhang. *Notes on the Warring States Policy*. Zhonghua Book Company, 1987.

[Qing] He, Ning. *A Brief Account of the Three States*. Cheng Wen Publishing House, 1968.

He, Ning. *A Collection of Notes on Huainanzi*. Zhonghua Book Company, 1998.

He, Shen, and Liang Guozhi. *Chronicles of Rehe*. Tianjin Ancient Books Publishing House, 2002.

Hebei Provincial Institute of Cultural Relics. *Murals of Liao Tombs in Xuanhua*. Cultural Relics Publishing House, 2001.

Heilongjiang Provincial Museum. "Clearance of Neolithic Sites in Niuchang, Ning'an, Heilongjiang Province." *Archaeology*, no. 4 (1960).

Heilongjiang Provincial Museum. "Excavation Report of Dongkang Primitive Society Site." *Archaeology*, no. 3 (1975).

Hu, Bangzhu. "Rock Paintings in Kuluke Mountain." *Xinjiang Art*, no. 1 (1984).

[Ming] Hu, Guang, et al., eds. *Analects of the Ming Dynasty*. Shanghai Bookstore, 1984.

Hua, Yan, and Jie Yong. "Several Bronze Seals Unearthed in Ji'an, Jilin Province." *Northern Cultural Relics*, no. 4 (1985).

[Ming] Huang, Wei, et al. *Memorials Submitted to the Throne by Important Officials for Successive Dynasties*. Taiwan Students' Publishing House, 1964.

Huang, Yisu, and Shi Shaorong. *Chinese Traditional Sports*. Central South University of Technology Press, 2000.

Huang, Zheng. "A Textual Research on the Original Dunhuang Manuscripts." *Jiuzhou Academic Journal*, no. 4 (1993).

[Qing] Huang, Zunxian. *Annals of Japan*. Shanghai Ancient Books Publishing House, 2001.

[Liang] Hui, Jiao, et al. *Collected Biographies of Gao Seng*. Shanghai Ancient Books Publishing House, 1991.

Institute of Archaeology, Chinese Academy of Social Sciences. *Baoji Beishouling*. Cultural Relics Publishing House, 1983.

Institute of Archaeology, Chinese Academy of Social Sciences. *Excavation Report of Lingwu Kiln in Ningxia*. China Encyclopedia Press, 1995.

Institute of History and Literature of Taiwan Academia Sinica, *Chronicles of Ming Emperor Shenzong Xian*. 1962.

Integrated Preliminary Edition of Series of Books. Taipei Xin Wen Feng Publishing Company.

[Mongolia] Ji, Damuding. *Mongolian Wrestling*. Transcribed by Brintegus and Gao Cai. Inner Mongolia Culture Press, 1983.

[Qing] Ji, Huang, et al. *A General Survey of Imperial Documents*. Vol. 632–638 of *The Complete Collection of Si Ku Quan Shu of Wenyuan Pavilion*. Shanghai Ancient Books Publishing House, 1987.

[Qing] Ji, Huang and Cao Renhu, et al. *A General Survey of the Literature of Dynasties*. Vol. 626–631 of *The Complete Collection of Si Ku Quan Shu of Wenyuan Pavilion*. Shanghai Ancient Books Publishing House, 1987.

[Qing] Ji, Huang, et al. *Chronicles of the Qing Dynasty*. Shanghai Ancient Books Publishing House, 1988.

Ji, Yuanzhi. "On Playing Polo in the Tang Dynasty—The Study of Zhang Yi's Travel Map (III)." *Dunhuang Research*, no. 2 (1993).

[Qing] Jiang, Liangqi. *Donghua Lu*. Proofread by Lin Shuhui and Fu Guijiu. Zhonghua Book Company, 1980.

[Qing] Jiang, Tingxi, et al., collect. *Encyclopedia of Books Through Ages*. Zhonghua Book Company, 1986.

[Chao] Jin, Fushi. *Historical Records of the Three Kingdoms*. Kuijangge, Seoul University, Korea.

Jin, Liang, et al., eds. and trans. *The Secret Records of Manchu Old Archives*. 1929.

Jin, Qicong. "The Origin of Chinese Wrestling from Khitan and Mongolia." *Journal of Inner Mongolia University* (Philosophy and Social Sciences), 1979.

Jin, Yufu. *A Long Chapter of Bohai National Records*. Stereotype ed. Jin's Qianhuashan Museum, 1934.

[Qing] Jin, Zhijie. *Annals of Koubei Three Tings*. Cheng Wen Publishing House, 1968.

[Iran] Juvayni. *History of World Conquerors*. Translated by He Gaoji. Revised by Weng Dujian. Inner Mongolia People's Publishing House, 1980.

[Song] Kang, Yuzhi. *Yesterday's Dream*. The Commercial Press, 1930.

Kashgari, Mahmud. *Divan lgat at-Turk* (A Dictionary of Turkic Language). Translated by Xiao Zhongyi, et al. The Ethnic Publishing House, 2002.

Ke, Shaomin. *New History of the Yuan Dynasty*. China Bookstore, 1988.

[Su] Kechanov, E. H., trans. in Russian. *Xixia Code: Records of the Change from Old to New Decrees in the Year of Tiansheng*. Translated by Li Zhongsan. Ningxia People's Publishing House, 1988.

[Su] Kliyashtorne, C. F. *Ancient Turkic Runi Inscriptions—The Original Documents of the History of Central Asia*. Translated by Li Peijuan. Heilongjiang Education Press, 1991.

Kuang, Wennan. "The Development of Martial Arts in Liao, Jin, Xixia, and Yuan Dynasties." *Journal of Chengdu Sport University*, no. 1 (1994).

[Qing] Kun, Gang, et al. *Examples of Qing Huidian*. Zhonghua Book Company, 1994.

Lang, Ying. *On Manas*. Inner Mongolia University Press, 1999.

[Song] Le, Shi. *Annals of Taiping Huanyu Ji*. Song ed. Zhonghua Publishing House, 1999.

[Tang] Li, Baiyao. *Book of the Northern Qi Dynasty*. Zhonghua Book Company, 1972.

Li, Chongshen, and Han Zuosheng. "An Overview of Dunhuang Sports Relics." *Sports Culture Guide*, no. 1 (1992).

[Late Wei] Li, Daoyuan. *The Notes and Commentaries of Shuijingzhu*. Edited by [Qing] Yang Shoujing and Xiong Huizhen. Jiangsu Ancient Books Publishing House, 1989.

[Qing] Li, E. *A Collection of Liao History*. Vol. 289 of *The Complete Collection of Si Ku Quan Shu of Wenyuan Pavilion*. Shanghai Ancient Books Publishing House, 1987.

[Song] Li, Fang, et al. *Imperial Digest of the Reign of Great Tranquility*. Zhonghua Publishing House, 1960.

[Song] Li, Fang, et al. *Taiping Collections*. Zhonghua Book Company, 1961.

[Song] Li, Fang, et al. *A Collection of Chinese Literature*. Zhonghua Book Company, 1966.

Li, Fanwen. *Homonymy Research*. Ningxia People's Publishing House, 1986.

[Qing] Li, Guilin, ed. *General Annals of Jilin*. Amended by Chang Shun. Jilin Literature and History Publishing House, 1986.

Li, Guohua. "*Mingdu* Is not about Polo." *Sports Culture Guide*, no. 3 (1983).

Li, Jifang. "From Gradual Recovery to Unprecedented Development of Wrestling in Ming and Qing Dynasties: A Brief History of Chinese Ancient Wrestling." *Journal of Chengdu Sport University*, no. 2 (1984).

Li, Jifang. "A New Discussion on the Origin of Chinese Polo." *Sports Culture Guide*, no. 5 (1994).

[Song] Li, Jingde, ed. *Quotations from Zhu Zi*. Proofread by Wang Xingxian. Zhonghua Book Company, 1986.

Li, Jinmei. "An Analysis of Ancient Polo Equipment," in *A study of the history of Chinese Polo*. Gansu People's Publishing Pouse, 2002.

Li, Jun. "A Study of 'Deceiving Horses.'" *Historical Research*, no. 5 (2005).

Li, Lianyou. "The Warrior Characteristics of Korean Traditional Sports and Its Causes." *Journal of Chengdu Sport University*, no. 3 (1993).

[Tang] Li, Rong. *Du Yi Zhi*. Proofread by Zhang Yongqin and Hou Zhiming. Zhonghua Book Company, 1983.

[Song] Li, Tao. *Continuation of the Extended Version of the Mirror for Aiding Government*. Zhonghua Book Company, 1985.

Li, Xiangfeng, and Liang Yunhua. *A Collection and Annotations to Guanzi*. Zhonghua Book Company, 2004.

Li, Xiangshi. "Rock Paintings of Helan Mountain in Ningxia." *Cultural Relics*, no. 2 (1987).

Li, Xiangshi, and Zhu Cunshi. *Helan Mountain and Beishan Rock Paintings*. Ningxia People's Publishing House, 1993.

[Song] Li, Xinchuan. *Chronological Records since Jianyan*. Zhonghua Book Company, 1956.

Li, Xiusheng, ed. *A Collection of Yuan Wen*. Phoenix Publishing House (former Jiangsu Ancient Books Publishing House), 2004.

Li, Xueqin, ed. *Rectified Interpretation of Mao's Poems · Notes to the Thirteen Classics*. Peking University Press, 1999.

Li, Xueqin, ed. *Rectified Interpretation of the "Book of History" · Notes to the Thirteen Classics*. Peking University Press, 1999.

[Tang] Li, Yanshou. *History of the Northern Dynasties in the Era of the North-South Division*. Zhonghua Book Company, 1974.

[Tang] Li, Yanshou. *History of the Southern Dynasties in the Era of the North-South Division*. Zhonghua Book Company, 1975.

[Qing] Li, Youtang. *Historical Records of the Liao Dynasty*. Zhonghua Book Company, 1983.

[Tang] Li, Zhao. *Supplement to the History of the Tang Dynasty*. Vol. 1035 of *The Complete Collection of Si Ku Quan Shu of Wenyuan Pavilion*. Shanghai Ancient Books Publishing House, 1987.

Li, Zuoguang. *Zhi Feng Lei Shuo*. Collected by Cai Zhenchu's *Yu Wai*. Beijing Library Press, 2006.

[Qing] Liang, Zhangju. *Notes on Returning to the Fields*. Zhonghua Book Company, 1981.

Liaoning Provincial Museum, and Liaoning Tieling Cultural Relics Group. "Summary of Liao Tomb at Yemaotai in Faku." *Cultural Relics*, no. 12 (1975).

Lin, Guan. *History of Xiongnu*. Rev. Ed. Inner Mongolia People's Publishing House, 1979.

Lin, Guan. *General Theory of the Northern Nationalities in Ancient China*. Inner Mongolia People's Publishing House, 1998.

Lin, Sitong. *An Exploration of Polo in Tang Dynasty*. Gansu People's Publishing House, 1982.

Lin, Yongkuang, and Yuan Lize. *General History of Chinese Customs · Qing Dynasty*. Shanghai Literature and Art Publishing House, 2001.

[Tang] Linghu, Defen, et al. *Book of the Zhou Dynasty*. Zhonghua Book Company, 1971.

Liu, Bingguo, and Zhang Shengping. *Chuiwan: The Golf Ball in Ancient China*. Shanghai Ancient Books Publishing House, 2005.

Liu, Chuncheng, and Cheng Qijun. "The Splendid Life of Tuyuhun People: A Study on the Coffin Paintings Unearthed in Guolimu Township, Delingha City." *China's Tu Nationality*, 2004.

Liu, Ping. "Pu Jiao Xing." *Sports Culture Guide*, no. 4 (1985).

[Jin] Liu, Qi. *Memoirs from Retirement*. Zhonghua Book Company, 1980.

[Qing] Liu, Xianting. *Guangyang Miscellany*. Proofread by Wang Beiping and Xia Zhihe. Zhonghua Book Company, 1957.

[Later Jin Dynasty] Liu, Xu, et al. *Old Book of the Tang Dynasty*. Zhonghua Book Company, 1975.

[Han] Liu, Zhen, et al. *Eastern View of the Han Dynasty*. Proofread and annotated by Wu Shuping. Zhongzhou Ancient Books Publishing House, 1987.

Lu, Bing. *Introduction to Chinese Traditional Sports Culture*. Ethnic Publishing House, 2005.

[Qing] Lu, Changchun, et al. *Palace Poems of Liao, Jin, and Yuan Dynasties*, in the *Collection of Parallel Prose of Menghuating*. Cultural Relics Publishing House, 1992.

Lu, Pingsheng, and Yang Lansheng. *Research on National Traditional Sports*. Gansu Education Press, 2002.

[Song] Lu, You. *Notes of Lao Xue An*. Zhonghua Book Company, 1979.

Luo, Maokun. *Translation and Annotation of Xixia Text Sheng Li Yi Hai*. Ningxia People's Publishing House, 1995.

Luo, Xianglin. *Research on the Cultural History of the Tang Dynasty*. The Commercial Press, 1944.

[Qing] Luobusang, Quedan. *A Guide to Mongolian Customs*. Translated by Zhao Jingyang. Liaoning Ethnic Publishing House, 1988.

[Zhou] Lü, Wang. *Six Arts of War · 1st Edition of Four Series*. Shanghai Bookstore, 1989.

Lü's Spring and Autumn Annals. Collated and annotated by Chen Qiyou. Xue Lin Publishing House, 1984.

Ma, Changshou. *Turks and Turkic Khanate*. Guangxi Normal University Press, 2006.

Ma, Changshou. *Wuhuan and Xianbei*. Guangxi Normal University Press, 2006.

[Yuan] Ma, Duanlin. *Journal of Chinese Literature*. Zhonghua Book Company, 1986.

[Later Tang] Ma, Gao, collect. *Notes on the Knowledge of Ancient and Modern China*. The Commercial Press, 1956.

[Song] Ma, Yongqing. *Nen Zhen Zi*. Vol. 863 of *The Complete Collection of Si Ku Quan Shu of Wenyuan Pavilion*. Shanghai Ancient Books Publishing House, 1987.

[Ming] Mao, Jin, collect. *San Jia Gong Ci*. Vol. 57 of *New Edition of Series Collection*. Taipei Xin Wen Feng Publishing Company, 1985.

Marx, Engels, and Compilation Bureau of Marx and Engels. *Selected Works of Marx and Engels*. People's Publishing House, 1972.

[Song] Meng, Yuanlao. *Notes on Reminiscences of the Eastern Capital*. Annotated by Deng Zhicheng. Zhonghua Book Company, 1982.

[Tang] Mo, Xiufu. *Records of the Natural Scenery and Folk Traditions of Guilin*. Vol. 589 of *The Complete Collection of Si Ku Quan Shu of Wenyuan Pavilion*. Shanghai Ancient Books Publishing House, 1987.

Montesquieu. *The Spirit of Laws*. Translated by Yan Fu. Zhonghua Book Company, 1986.

Mu, Le. "An Overview of Tuyuhun Culture." Translated by Rong Zhen and Guo Xiangdong. *Journal of Northwestern Ethnic Studies*, no. 2 (1989).

Museum of Aohan Banner, Chifeng City, Inner Mongolia. "Liao Tombs No. 1 and No. 2 at Pidjianggou, Aohan Banner, Inner Mongolia." *Cultural Relics*, no. 9 (1998).

Museum of Wuwei District, Gansu Province, Ning Duxue, and Zhong Changfa. "A Brief Report on the Cleaning up of Xixia Tombs in the Forest Farm in the Western Suburbs of Wuwei, Gansu Province." *Archaeology and Cultural Relics*, no. 3 (1980).

Mutiyi, Ibulayin. "*Turkic Dictionary* and Related Issues." *Journal of Northwestern Ethnic Studies*, no. 2 (1996).

National Sports Commission. *Reference Materials of Chinese Sports History*. People's Sports Press, 1956.

Ningxia Hui Autonomous Region Museum. "A Brief Report on the Excavation of Xixia No. 8 Mausoleum." *Cultural Relics*, no. 8 (1978).

[Song] Ouyang, Xiu. *New History of the Five Dynasties*. Zhonghua Book Company, 1974.

[Song] Ouyang, Xiu, and Song Qi. *New Book of the Tang Dynasty*. Zhonghua Book Company, 1975.

[Tang] Ouyang, Xun. *A Categorized Collection of Literary Writing*. Proofread by Wang Shaoying. Zhonghua Book Company, 1965.

[German] Pallas, P. S. *Historical Materials of the Inland Asia of Erlut*. Translated by Shao Jiandong and Liu Yingsheng. Yunnan People's Publishing House, 2002.

[Qing] Peng, Dingqiu, et al., proofreads. *The Complete Collection of Tang Poetry*. Zhonghua Book Company, 1960.

[Russia] Plekhanov. *Anthologies of Plekhanov's Aesthetics*. Translated by Cao Baohua. People's Publishing House, 1983.

[Italy] Polo, Marco. *Marco Polo's Travels*. Translated by Feng Chengjun. Shanghai Bookstore Press, 2000.

[Ming] Qi, Jiguang. *New Version of Ji Xiao*. Zhonghua Book Company, 2001.

Qing Shi Lu. Zhonghua Book Company, 1985.

[Song] Qu, An, and Nai An, eds. *A History of Jingkang*. Annotated by Cui Wenyin. Zhonghua Book Company, 1988.

[Mongolia] Re, Galindibu, and Re Wusuhubayaer. *Three Kind of Arts on the Prairie*. Inner Mongolia Education Press, 1984.

Ren, Bantang. *A Comprehensive Collection of Dunhuang Songs*. Shanghai Ancient Books Publishing House, 1987.

Rong, Suhe, Zhao Yongxian, and Zalaga, et al. *History of Mongolian Literature*. Inner Mongolia People's Publishing House, 2002.

[Qing] Sa, Ying'e. *An Extra Introduction of Ji Lin*. Wen Hai Publishing House, 1974.

Shaanxi Provincial Institute of Archaeology. "A Brief Report on the Excavation of Fengxi, Chang'an, Shaanxi Province, 1955–1957." *Archaeology*, no. 10 (1959).

Shanxi Team, Institute of Archaeology, Chinese Academy of Social Sciences, Shanxi Provincial Institute of Archaeology, and Linfen Municipal Bureau of Cultural Relics. "Excavation Report of Large-scale Building Foundation Site of Sacrifice Community in Taosi City Site, Xiangfen County, Shanxi Province." *Archaeology*, no. 7 (2004).

Shao, Ying. "Archaeological Research on the Forms of Ancient Chinese Inscriptions." Shaanxi Normal University, 2006.

[Qing] Shen, Bingzhen. *A Collection of New and Old Books of the Tang Dynasty*. Published in the 10th year of Tongzhi reign of Wu's Qing He Tang.

[Song] Shen, Kuo. *Annotations to Mengxi Bitan*. Proofread by Hu Daojing. Shanghai Ancient Books Publishing House, 1987.

[Liang] Shen, Yue. *Book of the Song Dynasty*. Zhonghua Book Company, 1974.

Shi, Jinbo, Bai Bin, and Huang Zhenhua. *Wenhai Research*. China Social Sciences Press, 1983.

Shi, Jinbo, Bai Bin, and Wu Fengyun. *Cultural Relics of Xixia*. Cultural Relics Publishing House, 1988.

Shi, Jinbo, Nie Hongyin, and Bai Bin, trans. and annotate. *The New Decrees of Tiansheng*. The Law Press, 2000.

[Ming] Shi, Naian. *Water Margin*. People's Literature Publishing House, 1985.

[Song] Si Shui Qian Fu, collect. *Old Story of Wulin*. Zhejiang People's Publishing House, 1984.

[Song] Sima, Guang. *Tzu-chih t'ung chien* (A Comprehensive Mirror for Aid in Government). Annotated by [Yuan] Hu Sansheng. Zhonghua Book Company, 1956.

[Han] Sima, Qian. *Historical Records*. Zhonghua Book Company, 1959.

[Ming] Song, Lian, et al. *History of the Yuan Dynasty*. Zhonghua Book Company, 1976.

Song, Rubu, and Si Qinbilige. *A Chronicle of Alashan Customs*. Inner Mongolia People's Publishing House, 1989.

[Han] Song, Zhong, annotate. *Eight Kinds of World Books*. Collected by [Qing] Qin Jiamo, et al. The Commercial press, 1957.

Sports History Compilation Group. *Sports History*. Higher Education Press, 1987.

Sports Teaching and Research Section of Central Academy of National Minorities. *Traditional Chinese Ethnic Sports*. Research Office of the Central Institute for Nationalities (internal issue), 1984.

Su, Beihai. *Xinjiang Rock Paintings*. Xinjiang Fine Arts Photography Press, 1994.

[Song] Su, Shunqing. *Collected Works of Su*. Shanghai Bookstore, 1989.

Sun, Jingchen. *History of Chinese Dance*. Culture and Art Press, 1983.

[Qing] Sun, Xidan. *Collection and Interpretation of the Book of Rites*. Proofread by Shen Xiaohuan and Wang Xingxian. Zhonghua Book Company, 1989.

[Qing] Sun, Yirang. *Interpretation of Rites of the Zhou Dynasty*. Proofread by Wang Wenjin and Chen Yuxia. Zhonghua Book Company, 1987.

[Qing] Tai, Long'a. *A Brief Introduction of Xiuyan*. Liaohai series compiled by Jin Yubo, Liao Shen Publishing House, 1985.

Tan, Chanxue. "Tablet Iinscription, Biography and Funeral Oration in Dunhuang Literature." Edited by Zaiyan Tingliang, in *Introduction to Dunhuang Literature*. Gansu People's Publishing House, 1993.

Tang, Geng'ou, and Lu Hongji. *Interpretation and Records of Dunhuang Social and Economic Documents*. National Library Document Microfilm Reproduction Center, 1990.

Tang, Hao. "Historical Materials of Ancient and Modern Sports of Brother Nationalities in China." In *Reference Materials of Chinese Sports History*. Vol. 4. People's Sports Press, 1958.

Tang, Hao. "Polo in Ancient China." In *Reference Materials of Chinese Sports History*. Vol. 7 and 8. People's Sports Press, 1959.

Tang, Huisheng, and Zhang Wenhua. *Rock Paintings in Qinghai-A Study of Binary Opposition Thinking and Its Concept in Prehistoric Art*. Science Press, 2001.

Tao, Fuhai, and Xie Xigong. "A Brief Report on the Cleaning Up of Jinyuan Tomb in Quli Village, Xiangfen County, Shanxi Province." *Cultural Relics*, no. 12 (1986).

[Qing] Tao, Zongyi. *Shuo Fu*. Shanghai Ancient Books Publishing House, 1988.

The Collation Group of Ancient Books of Shanghai Normal University. *Discourses of the States*. Shanghai Ancient Books Publishing House, 1978.

The Compilation Committee of *Baarin Right Banner*. *Annuals of Baarin Right Banner*. Inner Mongolia People's Publishing House, 1990.

Tian, Guangjin, and Guo Suxin. "Xiongnu Relics Found in Aluchaideng, Inner Mongolia." *Archaeology*, no. 4 (1980).

Tian, Zhaolin, et al. *Military History of China*. PLA Publishing Press, 1990.

Tong, Zhuchen. "Distribution and Stages of Primitive Culture in Northeast China." *Archaeology*, no. 10 (1961).

[Japan] Torii, Ryuzo. "The Wrestling of Khitan." *Journal of Yanjing*, 1941.

Tu, Shaosheng, and Xiang Mingkun. *Tujia Folk Sports*. Central University for Nationalities Press, 2000.

[Yuan] Tuitui, et al. *History of Liao*. Zhonghua Book Company, 1974.

[Yuan] Tuitui, et al. *History of the Jin Dynasty*. Zhonghua Book Company, 1975.

[Yuan] Tuitui, et al. *History of the Song Dynasty*. Zhonghua Book Company, 1977.

[Japan] Uchida, Ginfuu, et al. *A Collection of Translations of the History of Northern Ethnic Groups and Mongolian History*. Translated by Yu Dajun. Yunnan People's Publishing House, 2003.

Wang, Chongmin. *Collected Works of Dunhuang Bianwen*. People's Literature Publishing House, 1984.

Wang, Chongmin, collect. *Supplement of Tang Poetry*. Vol. 3 of *Literature in Chinese Dunhuang Studies Centennial Library*. Collated by Liu Xiuye. Gansu Culture Press, 1999.

[Song] Wang, Dang. *Annotations to Tangyulin*. Proofread by Zhou Xunchu. Zhonghua Book Company, 1987.

Wang, Jian. "Cavalry in the Early Tang Dynasty." In *Wang Jian's Manuscript on the History of Sui and Tang Dynasties*. China Social Science Press, 1981.

Wang, Jinglian, and Zhao Chongzhen. "On the Historical Evolution of Sports Concept." *Journal of Anhui University* (Philosophy and Social Sciences Edition), 1995.

Wang, Liqi. *Interpretations of Yan's Family Admonitions* (Supplement). Zhonghua Book Company, 1993.

[Song] Wang, Pu. *Tang Hui Yao*. Shanghai Ancient Books Publishing House, 1991.

Wang, Qihui, and Liu Shaoping. "Zhao Oubei's *Xiangpu Poems*." *Sports Culture Guide*, no. 3 (1985).

[Song] Wang, Qinruo. *Ce Fu Yuan Gui*. Zhonghua Book Company, 1960.

[Five Dynasties] Wang, Renyu. *Ten Bygones in the Kaiyuan and Tianbao Periods*. Shanghai Ancient Books Publishing House, 1985.

Wang, Saishi. "A Comprehensive Examination of Polo in Tang Dynasty." In *Collection of Papers of Chinese Tang History Society*. San Qin Publishing House, 1993.

Wang, Shunan, et al. *Feng Tian Tong Zhi*. Proofread by the Northeast Literature and History Series Editorial Committee. The Northeast Literature and History Series Editorial Committee, 1983.

[Qing] Wang, Shuzhan. *Records of Rites and Customs in Xinjiang*. Cheng Wen Publishing Company, 1958.

[Qing] Wang, Xianshen. *Interpretation of Han Feizi's Collection*. Proofread by Zhong Zhe. Zhonghua Book Company, 1998.

[Ming] Wang, Xin, and Wang Siyi, eds. *Assembled Pictures of the Three Realms-Heaven, Earth and Man*. Shanghai Ancient Books Publishing House, 1988.

[Song] Wang, Yande. *Journey to Gocho*. Shanghai Ancient Books Publishing House, 1988.

Wang, Yao. "A New Proof of Polo," in *A Collection of Tibetan Literature and History Studies*. China Tibetology Press, 1994.

Wang, Yao, and Wang Qilong, eds. *Translated Versions of Foreign Tibetan Studies*. Vol. 16. Tibet People's Publishing House, 2002.

Wang, Zhonghan. *Chinese National History*. Rev. ed. China Social Sciences Press, 1994.

Wei, Cuncheng. *Archaeology of Goguryeo*. Jilin University Press, 1994.

[Beiqi] Wei, Shou. *Book of the Wei Dynasty*. Zhonghua Book Company, 1974.

[Song] Wei, Tai. *Hand Written Records on the Eastern Corridor*. Zhonghua Book Company, 1983.

Wei, Xiaokang. *Research on Zhuang Traditional Sports Culture*. Central University for Nationalities Press, 2004.

[Tang] Wei, Zheng, et al. *Book of the Sui Dynasty*. Zhonghua Book Company, 1973.

Weng, Dujian. *Outline of the History of Chinese Ethnic Relations*. China Social Sciences Press, 2001.

Weng, Shixun. "The Story of 'Lian Pian Ji Ju Rang' is about Polo." *Sports Culture Guide*, no. 3 (1986).

Wu, Aichen, select and collect. *Poems of the Western Regions in Different Dynasties*. Xinjiang People's Publishing House, 1982.

[Qing] Wu, Guangcheng. *Records of Xixia* (Xixia Shushi). Wenkuitang, 1935.

[Qing] Wu, Shijian, et al. *Qing Gong Ci*. Beijing Ancient Books Publishing House, 1986.

Wu Ti Qing Wen Jian. Nationalities Publishing House, 1957.

[Qing] Wu, Zhenchen. *A Brief Account of Ningguta*. Zhaodai series compiled by Zhang Chao. Shikai Tang, the 13th year of Daoguang in Qing Dynasty.

Wu Zi · 1st edition of Four Series. Shanghai Bookstore, 1989.

[Song] Wu, Zimu. *Meng Liang Lu*. Sanqin Publishing House, 2005.

Xiang, Da. *Chang'an in Tang Dynasty and Western Civilization*. Hebei Education Press, 2001.

Xiao, Ping, and Yu Jun. "The Discussion of Xixia National Sports: Centered on the Xixia Cultural and Sports Events Reflected in Wenhai and Tongxin." Selected and edited by the Cultural Propaganda Department of the State, and People's Commission and the Mass Sports Department of the State General Administration of Sports, in *National Sports Thesis Collection*. The Ethnic Publishing House, 2003.

[Liang] Xiao, Tong, ed. *Selected Works*. Annotated by [Tang] Li Shan. Zhonghua Book Company, 1977.

[Qing] Xiao, Xiong. *Zhi Bu Zu Zhai · Playfulness*. Typeset ed. 1934.

[Liang] Xiao, Zixian. *Book of the Southern Qi Dynasty*. Zhonghua Book Company, 1972.

Xinjiang Institute of Cultural Relics and Archaeology, and Xinjiang Uygur Autonomous Region Museum. *New findings of Xinjiang Cultural Relics and Archaeology (1990–1996)*. Xinjiang Fine Arts Photography Press, 1997.

Xinjiang Institute of Cultural Relics and Archaeology. *New findings of Xinjiang Cultural Relics and Archaeology (1979–1989)*. Xinjiang People's Publishing House, 1995.

[Yuan] Xiong, Mengxiang. *Analysis of Xi Jin Zhi*. Beijing Ancient Books Publishing House, 1983.

Xu, Bingkun. "Hengcu Arrow and Willow-shooting Ceremony." *Journal of Social Science*, no. 4 (1980).

Xu, Ke. *Classified Anthology of Anecdotes of the Qing Dynasty*. Vol. 2. Zhonghua Book Company, 1981.

Xu, Ke. *Classified Anthology of Anecdotes of the Qing Dynasty*. Vol. 5. Zhonghua Book Company, 1984.

Xu, Ke. *Classified Anthology of Anecdotes of the Qing Dynasty*. Vol. 6. Zhonghua Book Company, 1986.

Xu, Qinjiu. "On Chen Jizhi's *Bian Qiao Hui Meng Tu Juan* (The Village Bridge Scene Scroll)." *Art Magazine*, no. 12 (1955).

[Han] Xu, Shen. *Shuo Wen Jie Zi* (Origin of Chinese Characters). Zhonghua Book Company, 1963.

Xu, Yuliang. *History of Chinese Minority Sports*. Central University for Nationalities Press, 2005.

[Song] Xue, Juzheng, et al. *Old History of the Five Dynasties*. Zhonghua Book Company, 1976.

Xue, Zongzheng, collect and annotate. *Compilation of Rare Turkic Historical Materials—A Collection of Turkic Documents Outside the Official History*. Xinjiang People's Publishing House, 2005.

[Qing] Yan, Kejun, collect. *A Collection of Late Han Literature*. The Commercial Press, 1999.

[Qing] Yan, Kejun, collect. *A Collection of Jin Literature*. The Commercial Press, 1999.

Yang, Baolong. *About Sushen and Yilou*. China Social Sciences Press, 1989.

Yang, Bojun. *Collected Annotations on Liezi*. Zhonghua Book Company, 1979.

Yang, Hong. "Research on Military Equipment in Dunhuang Mogao Grottoes Murals (I)—Armed and Armor in Northern Dynasty Murals." In *Proceedings of the 1983 National Dunhuang Symposiumin*. Gansu People's Publishing House, 1985.

Yang, Hong. "Cavalry and Heavily-Armored Cavalry with Armored Horses." In *A Collection of Ancient Chinese Weapons*. Rev. Ed. Cultural Relics Publishing House, 1985.

Yang, Hong. "Research on Military Equipment in Dunhuang Mogao Grottoes Murals (II): Tang Dynasty Cavalry Influenced by Xianbei Cavalry and Turks." In *Proceedings of the 1990 National Dunhuang Symposium*. Gansu People's Publishing House, 1990.

Yang, Jinxiang. "Several Messages from Xinjiang Rock Paintings." *Xinjiang art*, no. 1 (1987).
Yang, Mingzhao. *Continuation Notes on Baopuzi*. Zhonghua Book Company, 1997.
[Yuan] Yang, Weizhen. *Collected Works of Yang Tieya*. Late Ming pressed.
Yang, Wenxuan, and Chen Qi. "The Logical Problems of Sports Concepts." *Journal of Physical Education*, no. 1 (1995).
Yang, Xiangdong. *History of Chinese Ancient Sports Culture*. People's Sports Press, 2004.
[Yuan] Yang, Yunfu. *Luan Jing Za Yong*. [Qing] Bao Tingbo's Zhi Bu Zu Zhai Cong Shu ed., 1921.
Yao, Chongjun. *Research on Traditional Sports Culture of Ethnic Minorities*. Ethnic Publishing House, 2004.
[Tang] Yao, Silian. *Book of the Liang Dynasty*. Zhonghua Book Company, 1973.
[Yuan] Yao, Sui. *A Collection of Mu'an*. Shanghai Bookstore, 1989.
[Qing] Yao, Yuanzhi. *Miscellaneous Records of Zhuye Pavilian*. Proofread by Li Jiemin. Zhonghua Book Company, 1982.
[Song] Ye, Longli. *Chronicles of Khitan*. Proofread by Jia Jingyan and Lin Ronggui. Shanghai Ancient Books Publishing House, 1985.
[Qing] Ye, Mingli. *Miscellaneous Records of Qiaoxi*. Zhonghua Book Company, 1985.
Yiduhesige, ed. *General History of Mongolian Nationality*. Inner Mongolia University Press, 2002.
[Su] Yilin, M., and [Su] E. Shegal. *How Man Becomes a Giant*. Translated by Shizhi. San Lian Publishing House, 1950.
Yin, Falu. "Introduction of Tibetan Polo into Chang'an in the Tang Dynasty." *Historical Research*, no. 6 (1959).
[Ming] Yin, Geng. *Translated Words*. Vol. 56 of Shen Jiefu's *Collection of Records*. 1938.
Yu, Chonggan, and Li Zhiqing. "Review and Analysis on the Research of Minority Sports in China in Recent Ten Years." *Sports Science*, no. 10 (2004).
[Yuan]Yu, Que. *Collected Works of Mr. Qingyang*. Shanghai Bookstore, 1985.
Yu, Xingwu. "The Means of Transportation and the System of Post Transmission in the Yin Dynasty." *Jilin University Journal* (Social Sciences Edition), no. 2 (1955).
[Qing] Yuan, Dahua, et al. *Xinjiang Atlas*. Shanghai Ancient Books Publishing House, 1992.
Yuan, He, and Yuan Xuejun. "On the Rise and Fall of Polo in Jin and Qing Dynasties." *Study on the History of Polo in China*. Gansu People's Publishing House, February 2002.
[Song] Yuan, Shu. *The Whole Story of Tongjian Chronicles*. Zhonghua Book Company, 1964.
[Tang] Yuan, Zhen. *The Collection of Yuan Zhen*. Proofread by Ji Qin. Zhonghua Book Company, 1982.
[Britain] Yu'er, H. *Records of the Eastern Regions*. Revised by [France] H. Cordier. Translated by Zhang Xushan. Yunnan People's Publishing House, 2002.
[Song] Yuwen, Maozhao. *Annotations to National Records of the Great Jin Dynasty*. Proofread by Cui Wenyin. Zhonghua Book Company, 1986.
Zeng, Yujiu, and Liu Xingliang. *Introduction to Traditional National Sports*. People's Sports Press, 2000.
Zeng, Zhaomin, et al., eds. *Poems of the Whole Tang Dynasty and Five Dynasties*. Zhonghua Book Company, 1999.
Zhang, Bibo, and Dong Guoyao. *The Cultural History of Ancient Northern China*. Heilongjiang People's Publishing House, 2001.
Zhang, Guangda. "The Persians and Sogdians in Chang'an of Tang Dynasty: Their Activities in all Aspects." *Research on the History of Tang Dynasty*, no. 6.
Zhang, Hongnian. *A History of Persian Literature*. Peking University Press, 1993.

Zhang, Songbai, and Liu Zhiyi. "Investigation Report of Rock Paintings in Baichahe Valley, Inner Mongolia." *Cultural Relics*, no. 2 (1984).

[Qing] Zhang, Tingyu, et al. *History of the Ming Dynasty*. Zhonghua Book Company, 1974.

Zhang, Ying, Ren Wanju, and Luo Xianqing. *Ancient Official Seals Unearthed in Jilin*. Cultural Relics Publishing House, 1992.

Zhang, Zhiyong. "On the Absorption of Confucianism in the Liao Dynasty." *Research on the History of Khitan Jurchen in Liao and Jin Dynasties*, no. 1 (1989).

Zhang, Ziying. *Porcelain Pillow of Cizhou Kiln*. People's Fine Arts Publishing House, 2000.

[Song] Zhao, Buzhi. *Collection of Ji Bei Chao's Ji Lei*. Shanghai Bookstore, 1989.

Zhao, Erxun, et al. *Manuscripts of the Qing History*. Zhonghua Book Company, 1977.

[Qing] Zhao, Lian. *A Continuation of Xiao Ting*. Proofread by He Yingfang. Zhonghua Book Company, 1980.

[Qing] Zhao, Lian. *Miscellaneous Records of Xiao Ting*. Proofread by He Yingfang. Zhonghua Book Company, 1980.

[Qing] Zhao, Yi. *Oubei Poetry*. Vol. 2 of *Wan You Wen Ku*. The Commercial Press, 1935.

[Qing] Zhao, Yi. *Miscellany of Yanpu*. Zhonghua Book Company, 1982.

[Qing] Zhen, Jun. *Tian Zhi Ou Wen* (A Miscellany of Stories of Beijing). Beijing Ancient Books Publishing House, 1982.

[Chao] Zheng, Linzhi. *History of Koryo*. Collected by Kuijangge, Seoul University, Korea.

[Han] Zheng, Xuan, annotate. *Collection and Interpretation of the Book of Rites*. Peking University Press, 2000.

Zhong, Xingqi, Wang Hao, and Han Hui, proofread and annotate. *Collation and Annotation of Western Region Atlas*. Xinjiang People's Publishing House, 2002.

[Qing] Zhou, Chun. *Book of Xixia*. Vol. 334 of *Continuing Collection of Si Ku Quan Shu*. Shanghai Ancient Books Publishing House, 1995.

Zhou, Weizhou. *A Study of the History of Northwest Nationalities*. Zhongzhou Ancient Books Publishing House, 1994.

Zhou, Weizhou. "A New Examination of the Opera Troupe in Tang Dynasty." In *History Series of Northwest University*. Vol. 1. San Qin Publishing House, 1998.

Zhou, Weizhou. *Chile and Rouran*. Guangxi Normal University Press, 2006.

Zhou, Weizhou. *Tangut of the Tang Dynasty*. Guangxi Normal University Press, 2006.

Zhou, Weizhou. *History of Tuyuhun*. Guangxi Normal University Press, 2006.

Zhu, Dawei, Liu Chi, and Liang Mancang, et al. *History of Life of Wei, Jin, Southern and Northern Dynasties*. China Social Sciences Press, 2005.

Zhu, Guochen, and Wei Guozhong. *Bohai History Manuscript*. Heilongjiang Provincial Cultural Relics Publishing and Editing Office, 1984.

Zhu, Tianshu. *Gold and Silver Wares of Liao Dynasty*. Cultural Relics Publishing House, 1998.

[Song] Zhuang, Chuo. *Ji Lei Bian*. Zhonghua Book Company, 1983.

[Liang] Zong, Lin. *Record of Jinchu District*. *A New Edition of Series Collection*. Taipei Xin Wen Feng Publishing Company, 1985.

Index

A

acrobatics, xv, 54, 92, 96, 97, 98, 156, 167, 177, 202, 203, 217, 245, 248, 294
Aguda, 128, 132, 134, 180, 199, 312, 320
Akula (king of the Tazi), 283
Alexander the Great, 282
al-Firdawsi, 293, 294
Altai mountain, 7, 9, 11, 28, 35, 87, 88, 168
Altai Mountain rock paintings, 7
ancient China, ix, x, xiv, xv, xvi, 1, 2, 21, 59, 61, 67, 70, 123, 166, 197, 208, 225, 272, 285, 300, 331
Anguo State, 291
Annotations to Mengxi Bitan, 115
Annotations to National Records of the Great Jin Dynasty, 130, 134
An-Shi Rebellion, 103, 307, 319
Anxi Wuan, 54, 55
arslan (male lion), 255
Ashtana tomb, 324
Azik Village, 326

B

backgammon, 129, 130, 135
Badain Jaran Desert rock paintings, 7
Baixi (Variety Plays), xv, 39, 52, 92, 93, 98, 177, 217, 229
Balhae Kingdom, 307, 309
Balisu, 243, 246
ball hitting, xv, 99
Baltistan, 283
Baoge chess, 170
Beijing, xvi, 81, 162, 165, 174, 176, 182, 186, 189, 191, 196, 197, 202, 208, 256, 274, 310, 311, 328

Beile (a rank of the Manchu nobility below that of the prince), 179, 180, 181, 191, 194, 195, 197, 255, 261, 262, 273
Beizhu, 198
Beizi (a rank of the Manchu nobility below that of the Beile), 179, 194, 195, 197, 261, 273
Bentho Polo, 283
Bohai, xiii, 79, 82, 83, 132, 139
bo luo, 292
Book of the Former Han Dynasty, 23, 30, 32, 34, 36, 54, 56, 69, 70, 109, 216, 217, 218, 219, 221, 285
Book of the Later Han Dynasty, 23, 24, 29, 33, 35, 36, 58, 69, 109, 232
Book of the Sui Dynasty, 39, 79, 82, 84, 93, 230, 234, 235
Book of the Wei Dynasty, 27, 39, 45, 84, 124, 232
Budaqiu, xv, 83, 134, 330, 331, 332
Buku, 175, 178, 195, 253, 255, 256, 260, 261, 263, 266, 270, 272, 274
bulu throwing, 170–72
Bu Mu Ge, 168

C

camel racing, 17, 33, 166
Cao Cao, 36, 37, 228
Cao Wei (Dynasty), 26, 228, 230
Ce Fu Yuan Gui, 91, 290
Central Asia, 35, 69, 86, 100, 254, 283, 284, 292, 327
Central Plains, xi, xiii, 7, 15, 16, 23, 24, 26, 27, 29, 33, 34, 36, 37, 38, 43, 45, 47, 49, 52, 53, 54, 55, 57–63, 65–70, 80, 83, 85, 89, 92, 93, 94, 97, 99, 101, 102, 104, 109, 115, 117, 121, 122, 123, 128, 129, 130, 133, 134, 142, 143, 158, 165, 177, 178, 197, 224,

226, 229, 230, 231, 232, 235, 236, 239, 240, 249, 250, 251, 253, 261, 271, 272, 273, 281, 282, 284, 286, 289–94, 303, 309, 314, 321, 323, 324, 327–29, 334
Chang'an, 37, 49, 55, 71, 84, 104, 112, 188, 218, 219, 222, 223, 224, 226, 291, 300, 302, 311, 317, 318, 325
Chang Hui, 221–22
Chengdu, 196, 300, 302, 305, 330
chess, 39, 48, 81, 96, 111, 118, 119, 124, 126, 129, 130, 131, 134, 135, 157, 169, 170, 176, 308, 327
Chinese chess, 118, 119, 124, 169
Chuiwan, xv, 330–33
Chungcheong, 82
Chupu, 49, 50
Confucianism, 45, 49, 71, 82, 125, 247, 259
Cuju, 4, 80, 100, 111, 118, 124, 178, 197, 201, 248, 250, 284, 285, 286, 287, 293, 295, 297, 318, 319, 329
Cuqiu, 179, 197

D

dance, xiii, 2, 4, 5, 6, 8, 9, 10, 11, 12, 13, 14, 25, 39, 58, 92, 97, 101, 102, 103, 104, 111, 195, 216, 232, 233, 251, 258, 273, 318, 326
dance horse song, 101, 102
Dangxiang Qiang, 109, 110, 121
Datong County, 3, 6, 226
Dawaz, 94, 96, 97, 98, 156
Dayuan, 55, 56, 57, 221, 223
Dayue (grand music), 245
Da Yuezhi, 10, 56, 221, 223
deer chess, 170
Department of Royal Court Affairs, 183, 198, 201
Dingling, 29, 38, 84, 95, 222, 225
Divan lgat at-Turk, 31, 95, 96, 97, 98, 99, 156, 157, 284, 294, 324, 326
Donghu, xvi, 7, 8, 29, 35, 36, 37, 61, 62, 69, 125, 225
Dongyi, 58
Dongzhu, 198
Dragon Boat Festival, 80, 81, 163, 188, 205, 302, 308
Duke Huan of Qi, 59, 61
Dulu, 53, 54, 102, 220
Dulu Xuntong, 53, 54
Dunhuang, 56, 58, 91, 221, 222, 233, 234, 285, 286, 300, 301, 302, 319, 323, 324, 325, 326, 331
Duwei (title of the military officer under general), 141, 222, 226, 317

E

Eastern Han Dynasty, 35, 36, 37, 54, 223, 225, 226, 227, 286, 288
Eight Banners, 180, 184, 186, 187, 189, 193, 201, 203, 204, 205, 263, 265
Ejinaqi, 111
Emperor Akbar, 282
Emperor Kangxi, 166, 175, 191, 192, 256, 260, 328
Emperor Taizong of Jin, 180
Emperor Taizong of Qing, 181, 191
Emperor Taizong of the Liao Dynasty, 132, 244
Emperor Taizong of the Tang Dynasty, 84, 230, 291, 311
Emperor Taizu of Jin, 180, 199
Emperor Wu of the Han Dynasty, 71, 97, 217, 218, 219, 220, 221, 226, 228
Emperor Xuan of the Han Dynasty, 221, 222, 223, 226
equestrian culture, 17, 55, 60, 61, 142
ethnic groups, xi, xii, xiii, xiv, xvi, 1, 5, 8, 13, 15, 16, 17, 21, 22, 24, 27, 28, 29, 30, 31, 33, 34, 35, 36, 37, 38, 39, 47, 52, 53, 54, 56, 57, 58, 59, 60, 61, 63, 65, 66, 67, 68, 69, 70, 81, 85, 89, 94, 99, 100, 101, 102, 104, 106–11, 116, 121, 123, 125, 131, 134, 136, 138, 141, 142, 143, 155, 156, 159, 166, 170, 172, 177, 208, 209, 218, 221, 225, 227, 231, 232, 236, 239, 240, 247, 250, 259, 261, 269, 271–74, 317, 323, 324, 327, 329, 334

F

Fan Zhou, 119
fast race, xv, 51, 111
Fengle Hall, 309
Ferghana, 281, 282, 293
"Five Barbarians," 69
Five Dynasties, 100, 109, 122, 219, 239, 318
Fuchen, xvi
Fuhe Culture, 7

G

Gansu Province, 7, 8, 9, 10, 99, 100, 109, 114, 233, 285
Gaza, 88
Genghis Khan, 113, 116, 158–62, 168, 169, 173, 174, 251, 252
Gerais Valley, 284
Gesi (leather armor), 30
Gilgit, 283, 284

Index

Giselle Mountains, 284
Goddess of the White Turban, The, 96
Goguryeo, xiii, 21–24, 27, 47, 59, 68, 69, 81, 82, 230, 231, 232, 248, 249
governance of Emperor Wen and Emperor Jing, 218
Great Khingan Mountains, 69, 191
Guangxu Period, 188, 197, 205
Guannu family, 81
Guilou family, 81
"Gui You Chi" (Mongolian long-distance race), 165, 166, 178
Gu Yanwu, 328

H
Haixi rock paintings, 7
Han culture, xii, 24, 43, 52, 67, 68, 141, 179, 234, 235, 248, 261, 291
Han Dynasty, 8, 10, 21, 22, 23, 24, 25, 27, 29–38, 40, 48, 52, 53, 54, 56, 57, 58, 65, 66, 68, 69, 70, 71, 93, 97, 109, 114, 115, 216–30, 232, 235, 248, 272, 274, 284, 285, 286, 288, 289, 313, 314, 316–19, 324
Hanguang Palace, 300, 301
Han nationality, xi, 39, 61, 67, 68, 69, 70, 71, 91, 102, 108, 123, 125, 133, 143, 221, 225, 227, 231, 259, 271, 274. *See also* Han people
Han people, 38, 60, 67, 68, 93, 98, 100, 109, 125, 126, 143, 179, 180, 225, 227, 228, 232, 245, 247, 249, 329. *See also* Han nationality
Happiness and Wisdom, 95, 96, 327
Hebei Province, 29, 36, 42, 165, 191, 256, 306, 307, 311
Heilongjiang Province, 24, 27
Heishanmao rock paintings, 9
Helan Mountain, 7–9, 118
Helan Mountain rock paintings, 7, 9
hemp rope, 156
Heqin, 70, 218
Hexi Corridor, 7, 100, 106, 319
Hezhe, 6
Hindu Kush Mountains, 283
Historical Records, 8, 15, 23, 24, 28, 30, 31, 32, 34, 47, 64, 67, 68, 69, 79, 82, 126, 217, 285
Historical Records of the Three Kingdoms, 23, 68, 79
History of Koryo, 81, 82, 308
History of Liao, 83, 110, 126, 127, 128, 129
History of the Jin Dynasty, 94, 127, 132, 134, 135, 140, 141, 247, 248, 249, 297, 298, 301, 314, 315, 320

History of the Song Dynasty, 112, 113, 115, 117, 120, 244, 297, 314, 331
History of the Yuan Dynasty, 116, 158, 172, 253, 254, 316
Homonymy Research, 111, 118
Hongshan Culture, 7
horse dance, 101, 102, 103, 104
horse racing, 32, 39, 42, 51, 94, 95, 96, 155, 159, 163–65, 172, 174, 176, 240, 254, 256, 327
horse-riding invaders, 61
Hotan, 31, 324
Huangtaiji, 175, 177, 180–82, 191, 197
Huihu, xiii, 79, 88, 93–99, 155, 156, 158, 168
huiju, 304
Huns, 31, 33, 34, 68, 84, 85, 88, 95, 110, 218–29, 231, 232, 234, 239, 247, 250, 251, 274, 318
hunting, xiii, 1, 2, 4–17, 22–28, 31, 32, 33, 35, 37, 39, 43, 47, 52, 60, 62, 67, 68, 82, 83, 85, 87, 90, 91, 92, 94, 96, 104, 105, 106, 108, 112, 114, 124, 125, 126, 128, 134, 137, 140, 159, 160, 162, 167, 168, 170, 172, 174, 176, 178, 179, 189, 190, 191–97, 215, 238, 248, 256, 259, 260, 271, 286, 313, 314, 321, 327, 328, 329
Hu people, 62, 86, 109, 122, 236, 291

I
ice skating, 199, 204
Illig-qayan Khan, 84, 86
Imperial College, 23, 50, 68, 69
Imperial Palace, 101, 165, 167, 186, 187, 188, 302, 314, 326
India, x, 54, 90, 97, 293
Inner Mongolia, xvi, 7, 8, 9, 27, 29, 30, 35, 37, 62, 63, 66, 99, 111, 166, 170, 195, 196, 226, 227, 238, 251, 309, 311
Iran, 282

J
Jamah, 166–68, 178, 195
Japanese Mikado, 309
Ĵayan, 255
Jeolla, 82
Jiangsu Province, 196, 306
Jiao-Di mural, 231
Jiao-Di (wrestling), xv, 33, 39, 52, 54, 70, 103, 158, 159, 215–19, 221–26, 228–42, 244, 245, 247–50, 260, 270–72, 274, 313, 314

Jiao-Li, xv, 120, 215, 216, 217, 238, 239, 242, 248, 250, 252
Jiao Wozi (wrestling nests), 274
Jiaqing Period, 184, 190, 191, 196
Jiju (horseback polo), xv, 226, 249, 282, 284, 322
Jilin Province, 21, 22, 27, 230, 231
Jin Qicong, xii, 245–47, 249
Jirang, xv, 39, 48, 49, 197
Joseon Dynasty, 82
Jurchen, xiii, 16, 28, 67, 69, 79, 85, 90, 121, 131–42, 163, 177–79, 189, 199, 243, 247, 248, 250, 260, 261, 266, 303, 307, 312–16, 320, 321, 323, 328, 329
Juyong Pass, 312
Juzhang, 298

K

Kang Polo, 283
Kangxi Period, 182, 183, 187, 191, 192, 196, 265
Kara-khanid Khanate, 93, 94, 96, 326, 327
Karakoram Mountains, 283
Kashgar Region, 326
Ke Zao, 269
Khan, 43, 84, 85, 86, 87, 90, 91, 93, 101, 106, 113, 116, 157–62, 168, 169, 173, 174, 175, 251–53, 282–84, 311
Khitan, xiii, 16, 28, 67, 69, 79, 85, 88, 93, 95, 100, 113, 117, 121–34, 136, 137, 139, 142, 163, 168, 189, 243, 245–47, 249, 250, 266, 290, 303, 309, 310, 311, 313, 314, 316, 320, 321, 323
Khosrau Paiwis, 281, 291
King Wuling of Zhao, 61, 62, 70, 286
Ko Polo, 283
Korean Peninsula, 79, 81, 82
Koryo, xiii, 38, 57, 79–83, 121, 308, 312, 317
Kublai Khan, 158, 160, 175, 253
Kucha, 93, 324
Kundi, 222
Kunlun Mountain rock paintings, 7

L

Liao Dynasty, 67, 71, 100, 121, 125–30, 132, 137, 174, 192, 198, 243–47, 249, 288, 309, 310, 311, 321
Liaojiao (kicking feet), 260, 274
Liaoning Province, 21, 22, 36, 83, 99, 129, 130, 245, 306, 317
Linhu, 7, 34, 61, 62, 63
long-distance race, 165–66

Lotus Xiao, 49
Loufan, 7, 34, 61–64, 225
Loulan, 29, 225, 324
Lüju (donkey ball), xv, 330, 331
Luo Xianglin, xii, 281, 290, 291
Lü's Spring and Autumn Annals, 2, 6, 11

M

Magesong, 32
Mahmud Kasgari, 294, 326
Manas, 98, 157
Manchu(s), xiii, xiv, 22, 26, 28, 69, 155, 158, 167, 168, 175, 177–84, 186, 188–99, 201, 204, 205, 208, 209, 255, 256, 260–63, 266, 269–74, 323, 328, 329
Manchu wrestling, 269, 270, 271, 272, 273
martial arts, 4, 6, 10, 15, 17, 31, 39–45, 54, 55, 56, 80, 81, 82, 89, 90, 94, 98, 106, 111, 113, 120, 121, 123, 124, 126, 127, 133, 134, 135, 139, 159, 163, 167, 168, 171, 174, 175, 181–84, 186, 187, 190, 191, 192, 203, 205, 206, 207, 216, 236, 249, 256, 263, 264, 271, 273, 307, 308, 309, 312–14, 318, 321, 322, 328–30
martialism, 109
martial spirit, 80, 109, 110, 121, 123, 322
Meng'an Mouke, 28, 132, 133, 140, 141
Mingdi, 31. *See also* whistling arrow
Ming Dynasty, 125, 158, 165, 177, 200, 201, 259, 260, 261, 262, 270, 298, 302, 315, 316, 328, 332
Miscellaneous Records of Xiao Ting, 183, 186, 192, 262, 263
Miscellanies of the Western Capital, 3, 6, 284, 286
Modu Chanyu, 29, 30, 85, 95, 225
Mogao Grottoes, 233, 234
Mohe, xiii, 24, 26, 27, 79, 82, 83, 131, 230
Mongol, xiii, xiv, 6, 8, 10, 16, 31, 34, 85, 109, 158, 159, 166, 168, 173, 174, 177, 178, 195
Mongolian army, 30, 136, 161, 168, 173
Mongolian Boke, 251, 254, 255
Mongolian cavalrymen, 160
Mongolian chess, 169, 176
Mongolian Plateau, 7
Mongolian swinging, 172
Mongolian wrestling, 159, 167, 175, 231, 251, 253, 254, 256–59, 262, 263, 266
Mongols, 87, 90, 136, 159–64, 167–70, 172, 174, 175, 178, 251, 252, 254, 255, 256, 260, 315, 316, 321, 322, 323

mounted archery, xiii, 10, 17, 24, 29, 30, 32, 33, 35, 37, 40, 42–45, 47, 52, 54, 56, 57, 59–63, 65, 66, 67, 84, 94, 95, 100, 106, 112, 114, 117, 122, 126, 140, 142, 155, 156, 162, 174, 179, 182, 183, 184, 186–89, 191, 196, 197, 206, 208, 238, 320
Mughal Dynasty, 282
Muhammad Akram Khan, 282–84
Mujian (wooden shield), 30
Mulan Hunting Ground, 191–96
Mulan Qiuxian, 189, 255
murals, 97, 131, 231–33, 291, 293
Murong Bao, 49
Murong clan, 38, 99, 230
Murong Huang, 230
Murong Ke, 46

N

Neolithic age, 3, 5, 7
New Book of the Tang Dynasty, 80, 82, 83, 86, 237, 290, 291, 292, 300, 307, 317, 319
Ningxia, xvi, 7, 8, 9, 111, 118, 196, 224
Northeast China, 59, 68, 122
Northern Qi Dynasty, 39, 46, 49, 50, 51, 131, 234
Northern Silk Road, xi, 106, 294
Northern Song Dynasty, 109, 113, 114, 332
Northern Wei Dynasty, 32, 38, 39, 42, 44, 48, 49, 50, 52, 93, 177, 233, 234
Northern Xiongnu, 31, 35, 38, 95, 227
Northwest China, 8, 17, 99, 109, 289
Nurhachi (Emperor Taizu of the Qing Dynasty), 179, 190, 199, 201, 260

O

Old *Book of the Tang Dynasty*, 80, 82, 97, 237, 239, 290, 291, 302, 330
Oroqen (Ewenki), 4, 7, 177

P

Paekje, xiii, 27, 79, 80, 82
Pair Skating, 204–5
Pakistan, 283, 284, 293, 294
Palace Museum, 199, 223, 256, 264, 265, 266, 311
Pamir Mountains, 294, 324, 325
pearl, 137, 198
pearl ball, 198
Persia, 84, 85, 252, 281–83, 288–94, 334
Persian horses, 100, 101, 291
Persians, 252, 283, 291, 294
Pian Ma (horse skills performance), 263
Pian Tuo (camel skills performance), 263
Pingle Hall, 219, 222–24
pitchfork, 5, 327
pitch pot, 48, 49
Playing Polo in Huaqing Hot Spring, 296, 299, 300, 304, 318
polo, xii, xiv, xv, 18, 69, 70, 83, 94, 96, 134, 176, 238, 281–97, 298, 299, 300, 301–30, 331, 334
polo courts, 299, 300, 301, 304, 305, 306, 308, 310, 312, 313, 319, 321, 324, 325, 326, 327
polo mallet (polo club), 284, 298, 299, 304, 315, 327
polon, 282, 292
po luo, 292
Pre-Qin period, 37, 49, 53, 58, 59, 63, 66, 69, 83, 117, 131, 266, 292
Princess Changning, 300

Q

Qiang people, 8, 10, 29, 38, 56, 69, 100, 105, 109, 110, 111, 115, 117, 120, 121, 123, 221, 225, 240
Qianlong Period, 184, 187, 188, 192, 196, 201, 202, 205, 265
Qiaogan, 327
Qin Dynasty, 9, 48, 68, 108, 143, 216, 217, 225, 269, 286
Qing Dynasty, xvii, 49, 155–58, 164–69, 175, 177, 178, 179, 182, 183, 184, 186–92, 194, 195, 196, 197, 198, 199, 200–209, 254, 255, 256, 258, 260, 261, 262, 263, 264, 265, 266, 269, 270, 271, 272, 273, 274, 293, 323, 328, 329
Qinghai Province, 3, 6, 7, 8, 99, 104, 105, 166, 226
Qinghai-Tibet Plateau, 102, 109
qu qiu (woolen ball), 291

R

Records of Rites and Customs in Xinjiang, 155, 256
riding and shooting, xv, 23, 28, 29, 32, 40, 44, 52, 56, 59, 60, 61, 62, 82, 89, 90, 94, 95, 105, 106, 109, 110, 111, 112, 113, 115, 117, 126, 128, 134, 135, 137, 139–42, 158–60, 162, 163, 172, 174, 178–84, 186–91, 208, 286, 308, 316, 320–23
rolling dice, 81
rope acrobatics, 96, 97, 98, 156
rope skipping, 39, 51, 52, 126, 131
Rouran, 84, 85, 88, 158, 240

S

Saga Tennō, 309
Sahardi, 157
Sanyue, xv, 93, 245
Sassanian Dynasty, 281
Sese Ceremony, 126–28
Shaanxi Province, 5, 29, 50, 112, 196, 224, 226, 233, 249, 250
Shamanism, 15, 96, 136
Shang Dynasty, 8, 24, 58, 60
Shanglin Garden, 219, 222, 224
Shanhai Pass, xiii, 178, 182, 186, 188, 255, 261, 262
Shanpu Camp, 256, 263, 264, 266, 269, 270, 274
Shanrong, 8, 24, 34, 59
Shanxi Province, 2, 5, 6, 100, 135, 309, 315, 321, 322
Sharvosh, 293
Shatar, 169
Shen Kuo, 115, 284
shooting and hunting, 82, 90, 91, 126
"shooting on the horse in Hu dress," 61–64, 70
Shoupai Dao, 82
Shu Bo, 82
Shufu County, 326
Shunzhi Period of the Qing Dynasty, 178, 187, 194
Silk Road, xi, 106, 108, 294, 324, 325
Silla, xiii, 79, 80, 82, 132, 230
Sima Qian, 8
Six Arts of War, 63, 65
Sixteen Kingdoms, 34, 37, 46, 122, 230
Soghdians, 86, 100
Song Dynasty, 48, 49, 95, 98, 101, 102, 108, 109, 111–15, 117, 118, 120, 121, 133, 134, 137, 141–43, 158, 162, 174, 175, 207, 216, 219, 239, 240, 243, 244, 247, 249, 250, 253, 263, 284, 297, 298, 303, 304, 314, 320, 328, 331, 332
Songhua River, 22, 198, 199, 230
South China Sea, 83
Southern and Northern Dynasties, xiii, 21, 24, 35, 38, 45, 49, 50, 59, 101, 106, 108, 120, 129, 143, 230, 247, 251, 289, 318
Southern Song Dynasty, 48, 109, 113, 114, 119, 121, 158, 174, 175, 207
Southern Tang Dynasty, 305, 332
Southern Xiongnu, 32, 33, 38, 227, 228
Soviet Union, xv, 257
Spring and Autumn Period, 7, 8, 24, 54, 59, 60, 61, 67, 129, 216

stone throwing, 79, 80
Sui Dynasty, 39, 79, 82, 83, 84, 91, 92, 93, 105, 109, 230, 234, 235, 236, 239, 293, 317, 318
Sumo, 82, 83, 120, 124, 158, 215, 217, 219, 229, 232, 233, 234, 235, 236, 238–41, 244–46, 249–51, 253, 261, 265, 266, 272–74, 329
Sumo sheds, 158, 238, 253
Sumo wrestling, 124, 219, 229, 232, 233, 234, 236, 239, 240, 241, 244, 250, 274, 329
Sushen clan, xiii, xvi, 21, 24, 25, 26, 58, 131, 142, 177
swinging, xv, 7, 81, 98, 100, 114, 131, 156, 157, 172, 208, 258, 283, 311, 326, 327
"Sword Xiao," 49

T

Taibai Mountain, 83
Taipu Temple, 319
Talas, 282
Tang Dynasty, xiii, 8, 10, 68, 70, 80, 82, 83, 86, 90, 93, 94, 97, 101–4, 108, 109, 112, 114, 117, 121, 142, 157, 158, 188, 230, 236, 237, 238, 239, 241, 253, 272, 281, 282, 283, 285, 287, 288–94, 295, 296–302, 304, 305, 306, 307, 309, 311, 317, 318, 319, 320, 323, 324, 325, 326, 327, 328, 329, 330, 331, 332, 334
Tangut (Dangxiang), xiii, 16, 67, 79, 109, 111–14, 117, 120, 121, 123, 178, 243, 251
Taosi City Site, 5
Tashkurgan Tajik Contea Autonoma, 324–25
Tasuo, 53, 54, 96, 97, 98
Tatar, 59, 88, 155, 158, 168
Taximi, 263
Tazi, 283, 291
Thop, 284
Three Kingdoms, 23, 37, 68, 69, 79, 81, 230, 318
Three Sacrificial Ceremonies, 32–33
Tiakoo Polo, 283
Tianbao era of the Tang Dynasty, 103, 188, 236, 237, 282, 291, 318
Tianshan rock paintings, 7
Tibet, 101, 102, 109, 202, 281, 283, 290, 293, 300, 334
Tiele, 83, 84, 85, 91, 105, 317
Tieyaozi, 117, 120, 123
Tongzhi Period, 197
Torii Ryuzo, 245, 246
Touman Chanyu, 27
Touman City, 27

Tubo, 10, 67, 93, 100, 114, 281, 282, 288, 289, 290, 292, 293, 294, 300, 318, 319, 326, 334
Tung-tien, 85, 91
Tuoba family, 109
Tuoba Hun, 43–45
Tuoba Tao, 45, 47, 48
Tuojie, 86
Turkestan, 281
Turkic Khanate, 83–86, 88
Turkic people, 84, 87, 89, 327, 330
Turk(s), xiii, xvi, 8, 16, 28, 31, 59, 70, 79, 80, 83–93, 95, 97, 98, 99, 105, 156, 157, 158, 168, 230, 251, 282, 284, 290, 293, 294, 324, 326, 327, 334
Turpan, 98, 300, 324, 327
Tuyuhun, xiii, 38, 47, 79, 99–102, 104–8, 122, 290, 317, 330
Tzu-chih t'ung chien (A Comprehensive Mirror for Aid in Government), 299, 300, 304, 307, 310

U
Ulanqab rock paintings, 7–8
upper-class society, 163
Uyghur, xiv, 9, 54, 109, 155–58, 168, 317, 327, 328

W
Wang Yao, xii, 289
Wanyan Dan, 180, 181
Warring States Period, 7, 48, 61, 62, 63, 64, 66, 67, 70, 129, 216, 217, 225, 285, 289, 318
Weiqi (game of Go), 48, 118, 119, 124, 129
Wenhai Research, 111–13, 118, 119, 120, 250
Western Han Dynasty, 10, 22, 25, 35, 36, 37, 40, 48, 54, 218, 225, 226, 324
Western Regions, xiii, 10, 21, 38, 39, 50, 53–58, 70, 71, 84, 85, 93, 96, 97, 98, 99, 100, 106, 155, 157, 158, 218, 221, 223, 229, 236, 240, 251, 281, 290, 291, 292, 294, 317, 318, 323, 324, 326, 327, 328, 331
whistling arrow, 29, 31, 88, 95
willow-shooting, 127, 128, 134, 136, 142, 163, 189, 205, 259, 312, 316, 320, 321
Woshuo, 49, 50
wrestling, xii, xiv, xv, 17, 24, 33, 54, 70, 83, 96, 100, 111, 120, 124, 126, 134, 157, 158, 159, 164, 167, 168, 172, 174–76, 178, 195, 208, 215, 216, 217, 219, 224, 225, 228–34, 236, 237, 239, 240–74, 313, 329
Wuhuan, xiii, 8, 21, 35, 36, 37, 38, 221–23
Wuji, xiii, 21, 24, 26, 27, 82, 131

Wusun, 10, 29, 35, 56, 70, 122, 219, 221–25, 324
Wusun Kunmi, 221–22

X
Xia Dynasty, 58, 59
Xiajiadian, 7, 8
Xianbei people, xiii, 8, 21, 35–40, 42, 43, 45–47, 49–52, 68, 69, 99, 100, 101, 108, 125–27, 131, 143, 158, 168, 227, 228, 230, 232, 247, 250, 318
Xiang Da, xii, 281
Xiangpu, 120
Xifan, 236, 289, 290
Xifang Buge, 258
Xinjiang, xvi, 7, 9, 11, 12, 31, 69, 93, 97, 98, 100, 106, 155–57, 166, 208, 256, 324, 327
Xiongnu, xiii, xvi, 7, 8, 10, 15, 16, 21, 27–36, 38, 39, 56, 62, 63, 66, 68–71, 85, 88, 89, 95, 99, 100, 122, 126, 127, 142, 158, 218, 219, 224–28
Xixia Dynasty, xiii, 39, 70, 79, 109–21, 123, 124, 142, 158, 243, 249, 250
Xubugu Duhou Chanyu, 32

Y
Yaghistan, 284
Yan Fu, 328
Yangtze River, 47, 113, 231, 305
Yellow River, 22, 32, 99, 100, 119, 216, 220
Yelü Yanxi, 198
Yeniugou rock paintings, 10, 105
Yilou clan, xiii, 21, 24, 25, 26, 131
Yilou Mink, 25
Yinggu, 21–22
Yinshan rock paintings, 7, 8, 9
Yong She (courage Shooting), 263
Yongxiao Office, 158, 175, 253, 263
Yuan Dynasty, 100, 109, 113, 116, 118, 158, 160, 162–65, 172, 174, 175, 177, 197, 249, 252–54, 259, 260, 261, 263, 315, 316, 322, 323, 332, 333
Yuezhi, 10, 29, 55, 56, 69, 221, 225

Z
Zhang Qian, 10, 53, 55, 56, 218, 219, 221, 226
Zhejiang Province, 113, 196
Zhou Dynasty, 7, 24, 40, 48, 58, 59, 60, 62, 84, 86, 88, 90, 92, 106, 120, 216, 233
"Zhuoduoge," 246
"Zhuru Fulu," 54

ABOUT THE AUTHOR

HUANG Cong is currently a full professor and doctoral supervisor at Shaanxi Normal University. He once conducted his postdoctoral research at Shanghai University of Sport, and visited Western Kentucky University in the United States in 2010 and Beijing Sport University in 2013 as an academic scholar.

Prof. Huang Cong is mainly engaged in research on sports culture and social development. He has led and completed two projects sponsored by the National Social Science Fund of China and the other two by the Postdoctoral Science Foundation of China. He has published more than 30 academic papers and four academic monographs over the last decades. And his research achievements have ever been awarded the 6th Outstanding Achievement Award for Scientific Research (Humanities and Social Sciences) by the Ministry of Education of the People's Republic of China and Excellent Achievement Award in Philosophy and Social Sciences of Shaanxi Province.

ABOUT THE TRANSLATOR

GAO Fen is an associate professor and has been working in the School of International Studies at Shaanxi Normal University China since 1999. She also serves as the executive director of Shaanxi Translators Association. Prof. Gao teaches a series of interpreting courses at the undergraduate and graduate levels and *comprehensive English* for PhD candidates. During 2009–2010 and 2015–2016, she stayed at the University of Massachusetts in the US and Nottingham University in the UK respectively as a visiting scholar.

Prof. Gao is specialized in the teaching and practice of translation and interpreting, as well as EFL for years. She has published more than 20 papers in a number of Chinese and foreign academic journals over the last decade. Her publications cover a wide range of areas, including translation, interpreting, teacher education, English language teaching, and teaching assessment. She has also published 11 translated works and hosted or participated in a dozen of national and provincial-level projects on translation and language teaching, including *Silk Road: The Study of Dram Culture*, a National Academic Translation project funded by Chinese Fund for the Humanities and Social Sciences in 2015.